ROTHMANS
RUGBY LEAGU
YEARBOOK 1984-85

Rothmans

Editors
Raymond Fletcher
David Howes

Queen Anne Press

A *Queen Anne Press* BOOK

First published in Great Britain in 1984 by
Queen Anne Press
Macdonald & Co (Publishers) Ltd
Maxwell House
74 Worship Street
London EC2A 2EN

A BPCC plc Company

Front Cover:
Ian Wilkinson, of Leeds, gets out his pass despite being tackled in the Slalom Lager Championship match against Hull Kingston Rovers. Close at hand are colleagues David Ward (left) and Kevin Dick.

Back Cover:
Mark Murray, Queensland's Test half back, slips past Hull Kingston Rovers forwards David Watkinson and Roy Holdstock (8) in the opening match of the Australian State's historic three-match tour.

ACKNOWLEDGEMENTS
The compilers would like to acknowledge the assistance of the Rugby League Record Keepers' Club, club secretaries and individuals in providing material as a further source of reference for accuracy.

PHOTOGRAPHS
Modern day photographs in this Rothmans Rugby League Yearbook are from the files of the *Rugby Leaguer,* the only weekly newspaper dedicated solely to the 13-a-side code. The compilers acknowledge the co-operation of Chief Photographer Gerald Webster and his staff.
The colour photographs on the front and back covers are by freelance photographer Andrew Varley.

Rothmans Rugby League Yearbook — 1984-85
1. Rugby football — Great Britain —
Periodicals
796.33.3.0941 GV945.9.G7

ISBN 0 356 10449 4 (cased)
0 356 10450 8 (limp)

Photoset by New Rush Filmsetters, London

Reproduced, printed and bound in Great Britain by
Hazell Watson & Viney Limited,
Member of the BPCC Group,
Aylesbury, Bucks

Rothmans Rugby League Yearbook 1984-85

CONTENTS

EDITORIAL PREFACE

As *Rothmans Rugby League Yearbook* enters its fourth year of publication as the game's best seller, we have again strived to introduce a host of new material.

When deciding on the compilation of the 416-page annual, we tend to view the pages from two angles: as media men and as Rugby League fans.

After three editions, we have taken the opportunity to introduce new subject matter, such as disciplinary records, rule changes and sponsorship.

Still, the bulk of the new material inevitably reflects the past season, the *Rothmans Rugby League Yearbook* framework housing all the relevant statistics from an eventful nine-month 1983-84 campaign.

Due to public demand, Rothmans and publishers Queen Anne Press set strict deadlines to make the Yearbook available nearer the start of the new season. The earlier completion date meant that the M.M.P. tour Down Under was still in progress when printing began.

We would like to pay thanks, in particular, to Gerald Webster and his *Rugby Leaguer* colleagues for their excellent photographs which make a valuable contribution to the Yearbook, and to the media in general for their widespread and constructive reviews.

Finally, we would like to pay tribute to our families for their patience and understanding; to house editor Celia Kent for her professionalism and enthusiasm; to the game of Rugby League for providing such a rich source of material; and to the Rugby League public for finding a place on their bookshelves for this new volume.

● Facts and figures in this Yearbook as at June 1, 1984.

RAYMOND FLETCHER, of the *Yorkshire Post*
DAVID HOWES, Rugby League Public Relations Officer

FOREWORD

It seems a lifetime ago that Rothmans Publications launched *Rothmans Rugby League Yearbook.* Yet this is still only the fourth edition.

The fact that we feel so much a part of the established scene in rugby league reflects great credit on the joint authors of the book, Raymond Fletcher and David Howes. Their extensive knowledge and love of the game are reflected admirably in the pages that follow.

If you are a lover of rugby league this book is essential reading. If you are not yet committed then a glance through these pages will give a fascinating insight into why the game has such a wide and growing following.

1983-84 HEADLINES

Behind the facts and figures of the 1983-84 season were a selection of stories which made the headlines in another incident-packed campaign:

NEW RULES BRING HIGH SCORES

Several new rules introduced at the start of the 1983-84 season meant a further change in the pattern of play and a massive increase in the number of high-scoring matches.

The value of a try was increased from three to four points; a team tackled for a sixth successive time handed over the ball to the opposition instead of a scrum being formed; and the non-offending side had head and ball scrum advantage. There were other less revolutionary rule changes.

The extra point for a try obviously boosted the points totals, but it was the hand-over rule which had the most significant effect. It meant another reduction in the number of scrums and the increased continuity of play was probably the real reason for a record number of tries being scored. In effect, the handing over of the ball rarely occurred more than two or three times per match as teams preferred a variety of kicks. The new scrum rules assured the pack with head and ball advantage of almost certain possession.

The overall effect of the many changes can be assessed from the following scoring statistics: there were 69 matches in which both teams scored 20 points or more, compared with 16 matches in the previous season, and 50 points were scored by one team on 31 occasions, compared with only 11 in 1982-83.

OVERSEAS STARS SHINE

The lifting of restrictions on the Anglo-Aussie signing of players saw an influx of Australian players joining the many New Zealanders already established with English clubs. Several came over as unknowns but soon made a big impact. The most astonishing coup was made by struggling Wakefield Trinity who signed up Australia's Test stand off Wally Lewis for a three-month mid-season spell. He played just 10 matches for £1,000 a game paid for by sponsors. Hull also brought over Peter Sterling, Australia's Test scrum half for eight matches.

TRIAL BY TV GETS GO-AHEAD

'This decision seems to firmly establish the principle of trial by television', said an RL spokesman in September. He was speaking after ACAS upheld the League's six-match ban, suspended for six months, on Roy Holdstock, the Hull K.R. prop. The sentence was imposed after the League's Disciplinary Committee had studied BBC TV film evidence and found Holdstock guilty of an off-the-ball foul against Andy Gregory, the Widnes scrum half, in a Slalom Lager Premiership semi-final on April 30, 1983. Holdstock appealed against the decision, pointing out that the referee, Stan Wall, had not sent him off although he was sent to the sin bin for another offence that arose from the incident. The suspended sentence was due to end on December 31, but on November 20 Holdstock was sent off again soon after going on as a substitute in a match at Leeds. Holdstock was found guilty of illegal use of the elbow and banned for two matches, plus the six-match ban which had to be served.

YEAR OF THE YOUNG ONES

The 1983-84 season saw the emergence of a rich crop of young players as clubs wasted no time in giving teenage talent its first team chance. Almost overnight the English image of the game being full of tired, old players was changed. The success of the Great Britain BARLA youth squad in New Zealand during the summer resulted in several of the youngsters turning professional on their return. Most of them were immediate successes — notably Garry Schofield and Gary Divorty (Hull), David Creasser (Leeds) and Deryck Fox (Featherstone Rovers). Schofield earned a senior Test place after only 16 full first team games and at 18 became Britain's youngest-ever tourist as well as the youngest top tryscorer in a season with 38. Fox was elected by the Players' Association as their Player of the Year, while 20-year-old Joe Lydon, of Widnes, picked up a bagful of awards as the outstanding personality of the season. Shaun Edwards, at 17 years, 6 months and 19 days, became the youngest-ever Wembley finalist when he played for Wigan against Widnes. The young revolution was reflected in Great Britain's tour squad Down Under with more than half of the 30-man squad under 23.

RECORD FEE FOR WONDER BOY

Wigan made the most publicised junior signing of all time when they captured schoolboy star Shaun Edwards seconds after midnight heralded his 17th birthday on October 17, 1983. The signing, which involved a record £35,000 contract, was shown on BBC TV's nationwide Breakfast Time a few hours later. A former England RL and RU schoolboy international half back, Edwards broke another record when he became the youngest-ever player at Wembley the following May. He was then just 17 years, 6 months and 19 days. He was a key member of the first-ever BUSCARLA party to tour Australia during the summer.

LIFE BAN COMMUTED

John Dalgreen, Fulham's Test hooker, was suspended *sine die* by the Disciplinary Committee after being found guilty of pushing referee Gerry Kershaw as he was sent off in a match at Hull K.R. on November 13. His dismissal was for allegedly stamping on Gary Prohm of Hull K.R. Two weeks after the ban was imposed it was quashed by the Appeals Committee. They decided that although the Disciplinary Committee acted correctly on the basis of information available on the day, certain irregularities of procedure had occurred. The Appeals Committee, therefore, had no choice but to quash the *sine die* suspension imposed for allegedly pushing the referee. For the offence of stamping on a player, Dalgreen was suspended for eight matches. Dalgreen decided to retire, however, and did not play again last season.

BRAMLEY REBORN

After 87 years as members of the Rugby Football League, Bramley came close to extinction at the end of 1983. At the start of October, club chairman Ken Watson publicly declared a financial crisis and called in legal and financial advisers who started proceedings for the McLaren Field club to be put in the hands of a liquidator. The Second Division club suspended their fixtures after the home league game with Kent Invicta on October 16 while talks went on with prospective new owners and the local council. A meeting of shareholders and creditors was held at the Griffin Hotel in Leeds on November 10, four days after the club had failed to fulfil a John Player Special Trophy first round tie at Hull K.R., who were given a bye. The meeting decided to allow a further month for talks to continue and on December 8 a resumed gathering at the Griffin Hotel voted in favour of a new board taking over at Bramley, headed by former Hunslet chairman Ronnie Teeman. The 'new' Bramley club, with Peter Jarvis as coach, resumed playing with a league match at Kent Invicta on December 18.

BRAWL MATCH ABANDONED

Leyland referee John Mean caused a sensation when he abandoned the Oldham v. Leigh Slalom Lager Championship match on January 8 after 56 minutes because of a brawl between the teams. The events leading up to the brawl followed a first half of brilliant rugby. In the 52nd minute Leigh forward Tony Cottrell was sent to the sin bin for an offence on Oldham substitute Tom Naidole. Four minutes later Naidole retaliated after Leigh's New Zealand scrum half Shane Varley threw a punch. Both players were dismissed to the sin bin. The resulting scrum broke up into a brawl with a police officer going on to intervene. It was then that the referee abandoned the game and walked off with Leigh leading 26-14. The League's Management Committee later fined both clubs £1,000 each and declared the match void, adding that it was felt the referee had alternative actions at his disposal before taking the ultimate step of abandonment.

CASEY GETS SIX-MONTH BAN

Len Casey, the Hull Kingston Rovers captain, was banned for six months for pushing a touch judge while walking off following his dismissal in the Good Friday league match against Hull at Craven Park. The ban meant the Test forward had to withdraw from the Great Britain tour squad. Casey was sent off by Widnes referee Ron Campbell and the touch judge involved was Keith Worrall, of Leeds. Casey was dismissed for the alleged kicking of Hull forward Neil Puckering, for which he was found not guilty, and then punching opposition scrum half Fred Ah Kuoi, which earned him a six-match ban. At the same meeting he was also suspended for two matches for being sent off at Wakefield Trinity on April 1. The Disciplinary Committee ruled that the six-month ban should follow the other suspensions but, on appeal, it was decided the eight-match ban should be incorporated in the heavier sentence. Casey then appealed to the High Court but, at an interim hearing in Leeds, it was ruled that the Committee had acted lawfully and the ban was not excessive. The six-month ban meant he could resume playing on November 1, 1984.

TWO MORE NEW CLUBS

On April 18 a special meeting of clubs voted in Mansfield and Sheffield as new members, bringing the total to 36. This equalled the record club membership since a major restructure of the League in 1902-03, the first era of two division football. The vote in favour was not as overwhelming as in the case of the previous four candidates, both clubs just gaining the necessary two-thirds majority. The new clubs were both using the ground sharing principle, Mansfield at the Field Mill soccer base of Mansfield FC, and Sheffield at the Owlerton greyhound stadium. For the first time, the League put conditions on their acceptance: 1. That each club show a funding of £50,000; 2. That there was a 10-year lease on the ground; 3. That for the first season neither club shared in the League distribution of TV fees, the levy fund or any League profits. An application for the formation of a new club based at Runcorn FC's Canal Street ground was withdrawn when Huyton opened talks to move the club to Runcorn from its much-vandalised Alt Park ground in Huyton.

NEW SECOND DIVISION FIXTURE FORMAT

Following the acceptance of new clubs Mansfield and Sheffield, the Rugby League Council studied the possible restructure of the league set-up. At the meeting of April 18 the principle of a return to one division was rejected. Two weeks later, on May 2, it was decided to abandon plans for any type of three division structure. On May 9, a proposal formulated by Hull chairman Roy Waudby was accepted by a massive majority. The plan called for the retention of a 16-club Slalom Lager Championship with the remaining clubs competing in the Second Division, but on a restricted fixture format. For the 1984-85 season, it was agreed that the 20 clubs should each play only 28 games, instead of a full 38-match programme. Purely for the purposes of compiling the fixture list, the clubs were divided into two groups, on a geographical basis, with the rankings based on the 1983-84 League placings.

Group One: 1 Wakefield Trinity, 2 York, 3 Bramley, 4 Kent Invicta, 5 Huddersfield, 6 Batley, 7 Dewsbury, 8 Keighley, 9 Doncaster, 10 Mansfield.

Group Two: 11 Fulham, 12 Salford, 13 Whitehaven, 14 Blackpool Borough, 15 Swinton, 16 Cardiff City, 17 Rochdale Hornets, 18 Carlisle, 19 Huyton, 20 Sheffield.

The formula operated as follows:

- Clubs 1-10 play each other home and away
- Clubs 11-20 play each other home and away
- Clubs 1-5 play clubs 11-15 home and away
- Clubs 6-10 play clubs 16-20 home and away.

The clubs were divided into two groups for the fixture compilation only, thereafter the fixture list and League table appeared under the one heading of Second Division, with the four-up promotion structure remaining unchanged.

MEMORIES

Ban puts Casey out of tour

Lydon's the prize guy . . .

Donlan the shock in tour party

ALL OFF!

SHEFFIELD & MANSFIELD ACCEPTED

MEMORIES

JUNE

Summer sale mounted at St. Helens with utility man Roy Haggerty the top priced offer at £65,000 at his own request, Welsh international Roy Mathias listed at £3,000. Also price reductions on Peter Glynn, Steve Peters, Clive Griffiths, Roger Owen and Brian Parkes .... Leeds join Oldham in the chase for New Zealand centre Dean Bell .... Tommy Bishop appointed coach of Leigh .... Whitehaven recruit former Barrow coach Frank Foster .... Leigh sign Tony Manfredi from amateurs Leigh Miners Welfare .... Widnes appoint Vince Karalius as team manager, eight years after his departure from Naughton Park .... Hull K.R. prop Roy Holdstock to appeal St Helens propose swapping Peter Glynn for Salford's Keith Fielding .... Salford sign Fulham forward John Wood in exchange for £35,000-rated centre Trevor Stockley plus £10,000 .... Featherstone Rovers list quartet of Craig Wright (£4,000), Steve Reed (£2,000), Paul Hayden (£1,500) and Vernon Francis (£1,000) .... Newcomers Kent Invicta recruit ex-Rugby Union duo Tony Cooper, from Swinton, and Oldham's Bob Mordell .... Prop forward Gary Van Bellen rocks Bradford Northern with transfer request .... Philips Video announce sponsorship of the Yorkshire Cup in a new three-year £17,500 deal .... Winger Jim Hornby among eight Wigan players given free transfers .... 1982-83 dismissals down by 50 per cent to 105 in 630 matches .... Widnes referee Robin Whitfield invited by Australians to take charge of the second Test with New Zealand in Brisbane .... Leeds list Les Dyl at £35,000 ... Kent Invicta sign Neil Tuffs on a free transfer from Fulham .... Roy Holdstock loses his appeal .... Kiwi centre Dean Bell joins Leeds on a two-year contract .... Hull K.R. back Roy Holdstock in move for arbitration by A.C.A.S. .... Rochdale Hornets players accept 50 per cent reduction in playing terms .... Bramley chairman Doug Alton resigns after 20 years with the club .... Rugby League Council decides by 23-9 to appoint a nine-man management committee to run the day-to-day affairs of the League .... Swinton's Jack Bateman elected chairman with Blackpool Borough's Reg Parker as deputy .... Oldham offer terms to Kiwi Test full back Nick Wright .... Wigan offer Steve Nicholson and Gary Stephens in exchange for Bradford Northern back row man Alan Rathbone .... Kent Invicta beat Oldham for the signature of New Zealander Mark Elia .... Former player Tom Smith appointed chairman of Widnes .... Bradford Northern list five players for a total of £155,000 .... Gary Van Bellen at £55,000, Alan Rathbone for £45,000, Dean Carroll at £25,000, Les Gant and Alan Parker for £15,000 each .... Wigan win the race for scrum half Keith Holden, signed on his 17th birthday.

JULY

Hunslet line up New Zealand stand off Glen Townsend for a September return .... Threatened with retirement through an eye injury, Salford scrum half Steve Nash declares: 'I'll play again' .... Kent Invicta sign Whitehaven stand off Steve Lane for £10,000 .... Oldham reject Salford offer of Keith Fielding and another player for second row man Alan Platt .... Coach Ray Batten quits Wakefield Trinity for the second time in two years .... Long-serving Featherstone Rovers winger Ken Kellett retires .... Keighley list winger David Moll at £55,000 and second row man Mick Hawksworth at £50,000 .... Carlisle announce plans to continue at Brunton Park .... Bill Ashurst bids to make playing comeback with Wakefield Trinity .... Fulham put four on the transfer list — Dave Allen (£40,000), Joe Doherty (£20,000), David Eckersley and Carl Radbone (£15,000 each) .... Roy Lester replaces David Eckersley as Fulham's assistant coach .... Salford beat off competition for the signature of Rugby Union centre Dave Ruddy .... Takeover moves made at Huddersfield .... Great Britain hooker John Dalgreen returns to Fulham after quitting in March .... Wakefield Trinity hooker David Heslop forced to retire because of a neck injury .... Dewsbury forward Alistair Brannan agrees to join Kent Invicta .... Hull K.R. capture Kiwi prop Mark Broadhurst on a two-year contract .... Wakefield Trinity persuade Derek Turner to take up the post of coach after a 10-year absence from the game .... Outline approval given for a first-ever three-week tour of Britain by Queensland .... Local council give Wakefield Trinity a five-year interest free £150,000 loan .... Nick Wright agrees to join Oldham .... Hull K.R. insist on a fee from York for the playing services of coach Phil Lowe.

AUGUST

Historic signing by Bradford Northern of prop Phillip Ralda, captain of the Papua New Guinea Test side .... Hull sign BARLA Youth tour stars Garry Schofield and Gary Divorty .... Quintet on offer at Swinton — Alan Derbyshire (£5,000), Denis Ashcroft (£7,000), Steve Breheny (£6,000), Kevin O'Loughlin (£3,000) and Les Bolton (£2,000) .... Castleford loose forward Jimmy Crampton comes out of retirement .... Leeds snap up BARLA Youth tour centre David Creasser .... Castleford list wing duo Steve Fenton and Terry Richardson .... Hooker Tony Duke retires at the age of 37 after 15 years with Hull .... Hull K.R. express interest in signing Australian Test forward Les Boyd, suspended Down Under for 12 months .... Rochdale Hornets pay £2,000 for York scrum half Brian Hughes .... Featherstone Rovers sign scrum half Deryck Fox, BARLA's Young Player of the Year, despite late competition from neighbours Wakefield Trinity .... Wigan recruit BARLA tour colleague Mike Ford .... Warrington list prop Tony Cooke at £3,500 .... Steve Martin, Balmain captain and former Kangaroo, is lined up by Leeds .... Injury mars Hull's plans to sign Kiwi Test captain Mark Graham .... Featherstone Rovers hooker Ray Handscome retires after breaking an ankle — Long-serving Castleford number nine Bob Spurr signed as a replacement .... Oldham scrum half Gary Bishop moves to Kent Invicta for £8,000 .... Carlisle transfer utility back Joe Bardgett to Featherstone Rovers in £10,000 deal .... Leeds recruit back row forward Terry Webb from Brisbane club Redcliffe .... Consortium of businessmen sound out the possibility of Rugby League in Belfast .... Kent Invicta sign Hull K.R. prop John Millington for £5,000 .... Doncaster angry at David Noble playing in France without permission .... Clear out planned by Hull with prop Charlie Stone first on offer .... Medical advice forces Widnes centre Eddie Cunningham to quit .... Australia decide to vote for the retention of the transfer veto with Britain .... 'Entertain' is the rally call as the new international laws are brought in .... Clampdown on off-the-ball tackles is called for by Castleford after skipper Barry Johnson is ruled out with a broken jaw .... Dave Allen and David Eckersley patch up their differences with Fulham .... Kent Invicta make their Rugby League debut against Cardiff City at Maidstone in front of fewer than 2,000 .... Oldham show interest in Hull back Terry Day, on offer at £25,000 .... Hull offer Charlie Stone at £20,000, Keith Bridges for £15,000 and goalkicking Sammy Lloyd for £10,000 .... Warrington launch new jersey sponsorship with car radio company Sparkomatic .... Bradford Northern prop Gary Van Bellen rejects a move to Kent Invicta .... Jeff Clare casts aside chances of Olympic glory as an athlete by signing for Wigan .... Coach Dave Mortimer walks out at Huddersfield ....

Bramley list Alan Clarkson, Steve Lund and Jack Austin .... Former Test winger John Atkinson hangs up his boots after an illustrious 18-year career.

SEPTEMBER

Wakefield Trinity's Bill Ashurst calls it a day because of recurring knee problems .... Wigan line up Kiwi duo Howie Tamati and Shane Varley .... Warrington sign Salford prop Mal Yates for £14,000 .... The League restage transfer payments by Kent Invicta to Workington Town, Oldham, Whitehaven and Swinton as the new club hits cash flow problems .... A.C.A.S. endorse the six-match ban on Roy Holdstock .... David Noble returns to Doncaster .... Wigan anger as Kiwi Shane Varley flies in to sign for Leigh who battle with the New Zealand authorities for clearance .... Wigan and A-team coach Geoff Lyon part company after his son David, a product of Wigan Colts, signs for Widnes .... Salford list hooker Paul O'Neill at £65,000 .... Specialist tells Whitehaven scrum half Arnold Walker to quit .... Wigan referee John McDonald suspended for comments made in an after dinner speech .... John Pendlebury put on offer by Wigan for £35,000 .... Hull K.R., Wigan and Leeds selected to play Queensland .... Hull K.R. list centre Paul Proctor at £8,000 at his own request .... Former Hull centre Chris Harrison offered at £12,000 by Wakefield Trinity .... Arrival of Kiwi Howie Tamati prompts Wigan hooker Nicky Kiss to seek a move .... Wigan price him at £40,000 .... Featherstone Rovers sign Bradford Northern winger David Barends for a small fee .... Young forwards Brian Dunn, of Wigan, and Hull's Wayne Proctor called up in the 21-strong Under-24 squad .... Salford wingman Keith Fielding retires .... Hull launch 'rent a player' scheme and centre Terry Day joins Warrington for a £5,000 season's rental .... Bramley declare a cash crisis .... Hull sign Parramatta scrum half Peter Sterling, but Kangaroo's arrival put off because of injury .... Fulham managing director Harold Genders quits .... Salford sign Denis Boyd for £6,000 .... Workington Town turn down £12,000 Salford bid for £25,000-rated forward Bill Pattinson .... Featherstone Rovers put scrum half Neil Pickerill up for sale .... Warrington list Bob Eccles at £80,000 and Phil Ford for £65,000 as disciplinary measure .... Bans totalling 100 matches imposed on 25 players as League's Disciplinary Committee mounts a clampdown on foul play .... Six-year ban on transfers between Britain and Australia lifted .... International Board ruling that disciplinary rulings are effective worldwide rules out Hull K.R. bid to sign Manly Test forward Les Boyd.

OCTOBER

Cash crisis Bramley bid to persuade Leeds City Council to purchase McLaren Field .... Kiwi Fred Ah Kuoi makes his debut for Hull in the derby clash with Hull K.R. .... Channel 4 shows highlights of the Sydney Grand Final .... Second Division underdogs Barrow lift the Burtonwood Brewery Lancashire Cup for the first time in 29 years .... Leeds swap Tony Burke for St. Helens packman Gary Moorby .... Lada Cars launch the first-ever £1,000 Team of the Year award .... Oldham's Kiwi back Ashley McEwen retires because of job promotion .... Castleford scrum half Bob Beardmore sets First Division record with a 34-point haul against Leeds .... Jeff Grayshon, the Bradford Northern prop, goes into hospital for a cartilage operation .... Kiwi hooker Howie Tamati and Balmain prop Kerry Helmsley fly in to join Wigan .... Australians Steve Martin and Terry Webb sign for Leeds .... Robin Dewhurst resigns as coach of Leeds in his third season and only days after losing 54-4 at

Castleford .... Captain David Ward and winger Alan Smith act as caretaker coaches .... Fulham sign Alan Dearden, who retired at Widnes through injury .... Paul Faires resigns as chairman of Kent Invicta after only seven weeks and six matches .... Hull K.R. put Andy Kelly, the world's most expensive forward, on the list at £60,000 at his own request .... Leeds seek Frank Stanton as a coaching consultant .... St. Helens offer Gary Bottell at £12,000 .... Brewers Greenall Whitley take over the Trumanns Man of Steel awards with a 50 per cent increase in prize money .... Illawara captain John Dorahy leaves Sydney to join Hull K.R. .... Mal Aspey sacked as coach of Salford after winning only one match in seven after leading the Red Devils to promotion .... The League offer to finance Bramley's next five away matches to ease cash crisis .... Warrington fined £1,000 and St. Helens £500, suspended until the end of 1984-85 season, for brawling .... Salford appoint veteran forward Mick Coulman as coach, their eighth in six seasons .... Wigan transfer list full back Barry Williams at £12,000 .... Hull K.R. recall John Millington from Kent Invicta because of non-payment of the £5,000 fee .... Shock defeat for Queensland in the first of three tour matches, falling 8-6 to Hull K.R. in an explosive match .... Prodigy Shaun Edwards signs for Wigan for a reputed £35,000 on his 17th birthday .... Hull list winger Paul Prendiville at £15,000 .... While Charlie Stone returns to Featherstone Rovers on Hull's rental scheme .... Referee Fred Lindop sends off Bradford Northern coach Peter Fox in the opening minutes of the match at Leigh .... Bramley call in the Receiver .... Workington Town re-sign full back Lynn Hopkins from Kent Invicta .... Then immediately loan him to the Maidstone-based club .... Queensland hammer Wigan 40-2 .... Leeds make an official approach to ace Sydney coach Jack Gibson and sign Paul Prendiville from Hull for the rest of the season in a £3,000 rental scheme .... Keighley dismiss coach Lee Greenwood after fifth successive defeat .... The League clear Peter Fox of verbal abuse charge .... Hull's French winger Patrick Solal out for three months with broken hand .... Former Welsh international Frank Wilson appointed assistant coach at Salford .... £60,000-rated Steve Hartley decides to settle down at Hull K.R. .... Jack Milton quits as chairman of Keighley in support of sacked coach Lee Greenwood .... Wigan sign full back Steve Hampson for Vulcan RU club in Newton-le-Willows .... Queensland wind up their tour with a 58-4 thrashing of Leeds.

NOVEMBER

Centres Garry Schofield and Des Foy drafted into the Great Britain Under-24 squad .... Bramley players reject offer of £200 winning and £100 losing pay in John Player Special tie at Hull K.R. .... Swinton seek their 11th coach in 12 years with the resignation of Tom Grainey .... Wakefield Trinity and Leeds declare interest in Queensland skipper Wally Lewis .... Wigan forward Brian Dunn has two-match ban reduced to one and on the same day is called up for his Under-24 debut, one of five new caps .... Salford offer second row man Ron Smith at £40,000 at his own request .... Arthur Bunting takes a month's rest at Hull, assistant Ken Foulkes taking temporary command .... Swinton appoint former Workington Town, Oldham and Rochdale Hornets centre Jim Crellin as coach .... Acting chairman Jim Thompson declares 'we carry on' at Kent Invicta .... Steve Norton shocks Hull by announcing his retirement .... Under-24s rocked by withdrawal of Ellery Hanley, Lee Crooks and Brian Noble on the eve of French trip .... Wakefield Trinity's Colin Maskill called up for his international debut .... Wigan offer captain Jimmy

Fairhurst at £15,000 .... Businessman sponsors £1,000 towards purchase of Kiwi full back Nick Wright with public asked to raise another £1,500 .... Wigan coach Alex Murphy and Whitehaven's Frank Foster each fined £100, which is suspended to the end of the season, for verbal abuse of a referee .... Castleford express interest in signing Steve Norton or David Topliss from Hull .... Oldham offer £10,000 for Castleford's Ian Birkby, two-thirds of the asking price .... Shareholders give Bramley another 28 days to find a buyer .... Kent Invicta complete a financial restructure .... Leigh reduce the fee for Ian Potter from £55,000 to £35,000 .... Leeds sign Maori hooker Trevor Clark and Parramatta forward Mark Laurie .... Oldham complete the signing of Nick Wright .... Huddersfield appoint former England captain Brian Lockwood as coach .... Under-par Under-24s scrape home by 28-23 in Villeneuve with scrum half Ray Ashton notching a hat-trick .... Dominion Insurance continue their sponsorship of Great Britain with £5,000 backing of the Tests with France, bringing their total two-year investment to £50,000 .... Wakefield Trinity winger Lindsay Rotherforth ruled out for the rest of the season with a shoulder injury .... Swinton sign Wigan prop Geoff Cunliffe .... French complain to the International Board about Britain's misuse of substitutes in their Under-24 match .... Phil Alton, son of former club chairman Doug, heads a consortium bidding for Bramley .... Kent Invicta call off the fixture at York having only nine fit men available .... Wakefield Trinity recruit Australian star Wally Lewis for a reported £1,000 a match .... Leeds appoint Maurice Bamford as coach .... Coach Bill Goodwin leaves Kent Invicta .... ITV plan to screen Friday night League matches .... Wakefield Trinity sign Brad Waugh from Penrith .... Hull prop Keith Tindall set to make his comeback after 14-month absence with broken leg .... BARLA launch campaign for the reinstatement of amateur clubs into the RL Challenge Cup and John Player Special Trophy .... Trevor Skerrett threatens to boycott Great Britain because of imposition of one-match ban .... Fulham hooker John Dalgreen is banned *sine die* for hitting referee Gerry Kershaw in the match at Hull K.R. .... Peter Sterling, Parramatta and Kangaroo scrum-half, joins Hull .... Warrington complete the signing of 17½st. Maori prop Pat Poasa .... Scrum half Andy Gregory walks out on Widnes hours before the John Player Special tie with Wigan .... Hull bid £40,000-plus for Oldham's international forward Andy Goodway .... Widnes winger John Basnett, the League's top try scorer, ruled out for two months with hand injury .... J.P.R. Williams' agent contacts Kent Invicta to talk terms, but the Welsh full back denies desire to turn professional .... John Dalgreen lodges appeal against his *sine die* ban .... Leigh object to Huddersfield being the venue for the John Player Special Trophy semi-final with Leeds.

DECEMBER

Bramley prospects look bleak as the Alton consortium pull out .... Bradford Northern list New Zealander Tom Murray at £3,500 .... Oldham demand £70,000 for Andy Goodway .... Keighley appoint Geoff Peggs as coach and elect local businessman Colin Farrar to the chair .... Hull K.R. put scrum half Paul Harkin on offer at £20,000 and take prop John Millington off the transfer list .... Danny Wilson no longer on offer at Swinton .... Featherstone Rovers full back Nigel Barker out for a month with a broken jaw sustained in a clash with the post at St. Helens .... Salford make an offer to England and Sale RU centre Tony Bond .... Bramley crisis takes a new turn with solicitor Ronnie

Teeman revealing a bid by a six-man consortium .... Warrington prop Tony Cooke joins Workington Town on loan .... Utility back John Butler leaves St. Helens on loan to Leigh, who list hooker Ray Tabern at £25,000 .... More than 8,000 watch Australians Wally Lewis and Peter Sterling make their debuts at Belle Vue in the Wakefield Trinity-Hull encounter .... Oldham ask Goodway to decide whether he wants to move to Hull .... League Appeals Committee replaces John Dalgreen's *sine die* ban with an eight-match sentence .... Oldham announce that Andy Goodway will not be leaving Watersheddings .... Hull K.R. take £40,000 David Hall off the list .... Bradford Northern make a formal complaint to the New Zealand League after Tom Murray returns home in mid-contract .... Carnegie College chief Rod McKenzie appointed as Great Britain's first-ever conditioner for the M.M.P. tour Down Under .... League decide to take 30 players on the round-the-world trip .... Bradford Northern forward Dick Jasiewicz surprise call up in 21-man squad to prepare for the Dominion Insurance Tests against France .... Featherstone Rovers recruit Australian back Allan McMahon .... Hull winger Patrick Solal returns to France to train for the Tests with Great Britain .... Scrum half Kevin Harkin walks out at Hull in protest to the signing of Aussie Peter Sterling .... League decide not to encourage the introduction of a professional club on the Isle of Man, but plan a study visit to Mansfield .... Hull forward Trevor Skerrett appointed captain of Great Britain for the forthcoming French Tests and the tour Down Under .... Hull reject a cash offer from Castleford for skipper David Topliss .... Bramley, out of action since October 16, re-formed by the Teeman consortium .... League launch a 'coaches must qualify' edict .... The M.M.P. tour itinerary has 25 games Down Under, 15 in Australia, eight in New Zealand and two in Papua New Guinea .... Wakefield Trinity list former captain Harold Box at £10,000 .... Salford sign former Test winger Keith Bentley from Barrow for a cut price £5,000 .... Leigh recruit 31-year-old Tony Cotterell, capped 12 times by Great Britain at amateur level .... Leeds turn down three approaches for ball handling forward John Carroll .... Oldham demote Mick Morgan to substitute forward for walking straight to the dressing rooms at Wakefield Trinity after being substituted .... Bramley confirm Peter Jarvis as coach .... Ellery Hanley stays away from Bradford Northern after a pay row .... Winger Tony Garritty signs for Widnes after a loan period, fellow winger Chris Camilleri moving in exchange to Cardiff City .... Ellery Hanley says sorry for the dispute .... Oldham take the captaincy off hooker Alan McCurrie and give it back to Terry Flanagan.

JANUARY

Castleford skipper Barry Johnson considers retirement after breaking his jaw for the second time in the season .... Specialist rules out Widnes wingman John Basnett from the John Player Special Trophy final and his Great Britain debut .... New Great Britain captain Trevor Skerrett out for six weeks with knee ligament trouble .... Featherstone Rovers back row forward Peter Smith makes A-team comeback for first game of the season after back injury .... Wakefield Trinity sign Leeds prop Steve Pitchford on loan .... Second wing blow for Widnes as Tony Garritty breaks his ankle .... Paul Rose stays away from Hull only 18 months after signing for £30,000 .... Bradford Northern borrow £30,000 from the city council to ease cash flow problems .... Full back Lynn Hopkins returns to Workington Town from Kent Invicta .... Dewsbury supporters pay for full back Adrian Plummer's cartilage operation .... Leigh full back Mick Hogan quits after being displaced by on-loan signing John Butler from St.

Helens .... Widnes complain at three Sunday games being switched to Friday night for ITV screening .... Wakefield Trinity list Andrew Fletcher (£20,000), and Clive Pickerill (£12,000) and reduce the fees asked for Billy Harris, Colin Forsyth and Graham Walters .... Hunslet's Danny Rowe joins Huddersfield in loan swap deal for Tony Johnson .... Referee John Mean abandons the Oldham—Leigh league match after 58 minutes for brawling .... Widnes clinch £47,500 three-and-a-half year club sponsorship deal with Stanley Leisure .... Swinton offer stay away skipper Denis Ashcroft at £8,000 and loose forward Tony Peters at £3,000 .... Salford sign veteran prop Tony Cooke on loan .... Castleford coach Malcolm Reilly warns of fines for back chatting to referees .... Oldham scrum half Ray Ashton ordered to rest for a month .... Fulham list Chris Ganley at £35,000 .... Leeds beat Widnes to lift the John Player Special Trophy and a cheque for £10,000 .... Stand off Tony Myler pulls out of the Great Britain squad for the French Test as John Joyner, David Hall and Joe Lydon are called in .... Widnes prop forward Steve O'Neill to appear before the Disciplinary Committee for making an obscene gesture on his way to the sin bin in the John Player Special final .... Wakefield Trinity sign back row forward Lindsay Gill to bring their Australian contingent to seven .... Hull line up New Zealand captain Mark Graham for the 1984-85 season .... Warrington put John Fieldhouse on offer at a club record £85,000 .... Half back Alan Fairhurst settles his differences with Swinton .... Record £1,000 fines imposed on Oldham and Leigh, with their abandoned league match declared null and void .... Great Britain pick eight new caps for Avignon Test .... Castleford recruit Australians Steve Robinson and Brett Atkins .... Fulham swap Chris Ganley for St. Helens' John Butler in loan deal .... Wakefield Trinity players in dispute .... Only four games played as the league programme is hit by weather for second successive weekend .... Bradford Northern's Keith Mumby called up to replace the injured George Fairbairn for French Test .... RL Challenge Cup deadline passed as arctic conditions prevent Oldham registering Gary Bishop and Kevin James, Warrington's Neil Courtney joining Wigan, Kent Invicta recruiting Rochdale Hornets' Sammy Gilmore and Blackpool Borough full back Gary Laird moving to Leigh .... Clubs advised to appeal to the Rugby League Council for a deadline extension .... Paul Rose returns to the Boulevard .... Widnes sign John Wood for the second time, Eric Prescott and John Taylor moving to Salford in part exchange plus £30,000 .... Huddersfield coach Brian Lockwood signs as a player on loan .... Ellery Hanley and David Cairns lead the halfway stage voting for Greenalls Man of Steel divisional awards .... Bradford Northern hooker Brian Noble ruled out of the Avignon Test by two match ban and team-mate Keith Mumby takes over as skipper .... Hull K.R.'s David Watkinson breaks his leg after only 150 seconds of the Test which Britain win 12-0, Keith Rayne taking the Man of the Match award .... Under-24 international Brian Dunn seeks a move from Wigan .... Prop forward Steve Crooks asks for a transfer from Hull K.R., who double the fee on full back John Lydiat to £20,000 .... Steve O'Neill banned for two matches for obscene gesture .... France raise objection to Sydney referee John Gocher taking charge of the second Dominion Insurance Test at Leeds.

FEBRUARY

Wigan list David Stephenson at £45,000 .... Widnes scrum half Andy Gregory withdraws transfer request after talks with coach Harry Dawson .... Despite broken leg, Hull K.R.'s David Watkinson included in 41-man Great Britain training squad; Called up also is Hull's 18-year-old Andy Dannatt after only three full first team games .... Steve Norton returns to Hull after three-month 'retirement' .... Peter Smethurst quits as coach of Oldham .... The Rugby League Council rules that the Challenge Cup deadline stands .... State Express withdrawal from manufacturing in Britain ends Rugby League sponsorship deal after six-year association .... Back row forward Andy Timson listed by Castleford at third request at £35,000 .... Halifax sign Leeds forward John Carroll for £8,000 .... Hull's Steve Evans withdraws from Great Britain training squad and rules himself out of the summer tour .... Former forward Tommy Smales resigns as coach of Dewsbury .... Kent Invicta acting chairman Jim Thompson under pressure from the Maidstone F.C. board of directors .... All 10 Widnes players ordered by the club to boycott Great Britain training; Winger John Basnett attends and is the only Widnes player considered for selection for Great Britain to meet France at Leeds .... Three new caps named for Britain, including centre Garry Schofield after only 16 full games for Hull .... Fulham hooker John Dalgreen quits less than three months after the reprieve of a *sine die* ban .... Bradford Northern coach Peter Fox protests at losing five of his squad to Great Britain in Test week .... Oldham ban Andy Goodway for two weeks as club disciplinary measure .... Castleford forward Kevin Ward called up for Great Britain debut to replace injured Len Casey .... Leigh captain John Woods withdraws from the British Test side and asks not to be considered for the forthcoming tour because of family and business ties .... Great Britain add Ian Wilkinson, of Leeds, and Castleford hooker Kevin Beardmore to the training squad .... Oldham sound out Featherstone Rovers' Allan Agar before upgrading Frank Barrow to the coaching post .... Oldham list hooker and former captain Alan McCurrie at £25,000 .... Warrington duo John Fieldhouse and Phil Ford ask to come off the transfer list .... Five goals from David Hobbs give Britain a 10-0 victory over France at Leeds .... Wigan sign cut price Ian Potter from Leigh for £22,000 .... Great Britain offered £5,000 bonus per Test win over Australia, plus £5,000 for the first Aussie success from sponsors Modern Maintenance Products .... Frank Barrow quits as Oldham coach after only six days and a 42-8 thrashing at Whitehaven, the Cumbrians' first win of the season .... Former player Jack Addy appointed coach of Dewsbury .... Wally Lewis given two-match ban to be served if he returns to British club football .... Test forward Lee Crooks undergoes cartilage operation and bids to regain fitness for tour selection .... Oldham announce appointment of Dave Cox as coach, having held the post in 1971 and 1978 .... Leeds recruit West Yorkshire junior star Richard Gunn on his 17th birthday .... Bradford Northern warned that players' absence from Great Britain training could jeopardise their tour claims .... Great Britain add St. Helens scrum half Neil Holding to the squad .... Northern decide to release their quintet of Great Britain squad players.

MARCH

Derek Turner quits as coach of Wakefield Trinity and complains of lack of dedication, Laurie Gant takes over for the remainder of the season .... Whitehaven skipper Gordon Cottier listed at £7,500 after private row with a club director .... St. Helens clinch a five-year £75,000 sponsorship deal with McEwan-Younger .... Hull cancel remaining two years of three-year contract with French Test winger Patrick Solal .... Halifax sign amateur international hooker Seamus McCallion, previously on trial with Kent Invicta .... Dave Cox decides to stay in Australia and not take up Oldham coaching post .... John Dorahy signs up for another season with Hull K.R. .... Leigh's Tommy Martyn ruled out for the rest of the season with a broken hand ....

League's leading goal scorer Eric Fitzsimons out for the season with a broken leg .... League's Management Committee rules out Great Britain versus New Zealand trial match .... Brian Gartland appointed coach of Oldham .... Leigh reject on-loan Chris Ganley who returns to Fulham .... Bradford Northern put Great Britain star Ellery Hanley on the list at £75,000 after injury and cash rows .... York coach Phil Lowe breaks his pelvis in car crash only hours after shock Challenge Cup win over Castleford .... Leeds blast League decision to stage York versus Wigan Cup semi-final tie at Elland Road, but League point out that Hunslet directly benefit from using the Leeds United F.C. ground .... Widnes coach Harry Dawson walks out after row with manager Vince Karalius over Chemics players being released for Great Britain squad training .... Resigned to Second Division football next season, Wakefield Trinity drop six senior players to bring in youngsters .... Harry Dawson officially quits Widnes .... Mansfield and Sheffield apply for membership of the League, and Runcorn indicate that they are to join the queue .... Hull stop Leeds from equalling the club record of 19 matches without defeat .... Peace talks bring Ellery Hanley off the Bradford Northern transfer list .... Widnes fail in bid to make Harry Dawson return .... Great Britain captain Trevor Skerrett further hindered by knee trouble .... Hull K.R.'s David Hall becomes third player to make himself unavailable for the Great Britain tour because of personal reasons .... Wembley fever hits Wigan, who meet Widnes, in the final for the seventh time in 10 years .... Fulham threaten to turn up at Post Office Road after Featherstone Rovers postpone their Championship fixture .... Leigh's international winger Des Drummond given five-match ban, including three for alleged biting .... Trevor Skerrett rules himself out of the summer tour, but exploratory operation puts him back in the reckoning .... Torn knee cartilage puts Tony Myler's Wembley and tour hopes in jeopardy .... League deputation visits Mansfield on a feasibility study.

APRIL

Huddersfield referee Billy Thompson appointed for the Challenge Cup final as last match of an illustrious 18-year career .... Slalom Lager Championship extended by 24 hours and Second Division by two weeks because of fixture congestion .... Wigan full back Steve Hampson breaks his leg and is ruled out of Wembley .... Widnes forward John Wood pulls out of Great Britain training squad for personal reasons only one week before selection of touring squad .... Hull K.R. winger David Laws, scorer of 12 in last 10 games, out for the rest of the season with a broken bone in the hand .... Former Widnes coach Harry Dawson shelves Oldham job offer until the end of the season .... Workington Town sign Whitehaven forward Gordon Cottier on loan .... Featherstone Rovers fined £100 for 'poor communication' in fixture row with Fulham .... Oldham list stand off Chris Willis and forward Mick Coombes at £5,000 each .... Australian forward Terry Webb signs a three-year contract with Leeds .... Leigh halve the asking price for centre Terry Bilsbury to £10,000 .... The French celebrate their 50th anniversary with a Europe v Oceania match in Paris, the star-studded Australasian outfit winning 54-4 .... Hull K.R. clinch the Slalom Lager Championship title with a convincing 44-16 victory at Leigh .... Leigh back Steve Donlan is the surprise choice as the only non-training squad member in the 30-strong M.M.P. touring squad .... Hull's 18-year-old centre Garry Schofield is chosen as the youngest-ever tourist .... Barrow promoted as Second Division champions .... Sheffield and Mansfield admitted to the League for the biggest-ever membership since 1902 .... The meeting of

Prop forward Trevor Hooper, hero of York's valiant semi-final battle in the State Express Challenge Cup at Elland Road, Leeds, in March.

clubs put three conditions on the new entries with assurances sought regarding ground leasing, capital investment and share of League monies .... St. Helens lead the chase for star Australian tourist Mal Meninga .... Runcorn withdraw their application to join the League as Huyton plan a move from Alt Park to the Runcorn soccer ground in Canal Street .... Hull K.R. captain Len Casey sent off in the derby clash at Craven Park and pushes touch judge Keith Worrall on the way to the tunnel .... Hull K.R. join arch rivals Hull in pursuit of New Zealand captain Mark Graham .... Hooker Nicky Kiss walks out at Wigan .... Newcomers Sheffield appoint Alan Rhodes as coach .... Wigan fly back Balmain prop Kerry Hemsley a week before the Challenge Cup final .... Len Casey receives eight match ban for two sendings off, plus six month suspension for manhandling a touch judge .... Casey appeals against the findings which rule him out of the M.M.P. tour .... Wigan scrum half Gary Stephens given sending off sufficient to clear him for Wembley debut .... Featherstone Rovers scrum half Deryck Fox chosen as Player of the Year by the Players' Association.

MAY

Bradford Northern announce the close season demolition of their main stand as part of the modernisation programme at Odsal .... Wakefield Trinity, with Bob Haigh at the coaching helm since the departure of Derek Turner, launch the search for a new coach .... League's Appeals Committee decides that Len Casey's six-month ban should run concurrent with his eight-match suspension, instead of consecutive .... Balmain prop Kerry Hemsley flies in from Australia to claim a Wigan Wembley place .... Banned Len Casey and injured Trevor Skerrett replaced in Great Britain's tour party by Hull's Wayne Proctor and St. Helens' Chris Arkwright .... Clubs reject a three division structure .... Warrington and coach Kevin Ashcroft part company with two years of his contract to run .... Widnes lift the State Express Challenge Cup .... Tony Myler cleared to tour, but League's specialist pulls out Chris Arkwright because of knee trouble and Oldham loose forward Terry Flanagan called up as a replacement .... Widnes utility star Joe Lydon collects a hat-trick of awards at the Greenalls Man of Steel ceremony, including Man of Steel 1984 .... Clubs vote in favour of a new Second Division structure of 20 clubs playing 28 fixtures .... League sign new three-year contract with John Player Special worth £240,000 .... High Court judge rules that the League's ban on Len Casey was lawful and not excessive .... Hull K.R. lift the Slalom Lager Premiership Trophy .... Arthur Bunting signs a new three-year contract as coach of Hull .... Featherstone Rovers offer eight for sale, utility back Joe Bardgett topping the list at £8,000 .... Cardiff City's Paul Woods suspended for 12 matches .... Great Britain open their M.M.P. tour Down Under with a 40-13 victory over Northern Territory at Darwin .... Warrington centre Ronnie Duane carried off after only nine minutes of the opening match and is ruled out of the rest of the tour with knee trouble, Widnes winger John Basnett called in as the replacement .... Neil Holding comes on as substitute to score the winning try in a 22-18 struggle by Great Britain at Riverina .... Great Britain return to form to hammer North Coast Division 56-6 .... Salford sack coach Mike Coulman and appoint former coach Kevin Ashcroft, with Tommy Grainey as assistant .... Wakefield Trinity appoint former full back Geoff Wraith as coach .... Great Britain record 36-30 success over Western Division .... Kent Invicta coach Steve Lane resigns .... Great Britain maintain unbeaten record with 14-8 defeat of North Sydney.

Leigh's kiwi scrum half Shane Varley.

CLUBS

St. Helens utility man Chris Arkwright, scorer of eight tries in 17 appearances in 1983-84 and dramatically withdrawn from the Great Britain touring squad a week after selection.

CLUBS

The following is a focus on the 36 professional Rugby League clubs competing in the Slalom Lager Championship and the Second Division in 1984-85. The section provides each club with a profile and an analysis of their 1983-84 campaign on a match by match basis with a summary for each first team player.

KEY

In the individual club profiles the following headings are featured:

First season refers to when the club gained senior league status. In some instances clubs have disbanded and re-formed, sometimes under different titles. For record purposes these changes are ignored except where there has been a break of more than one full season.

Honours. Until they were scrapped in 1970, the Yorkshire and Lancashire Leagues were one of the honours in the professional game. Before 1903 they operated under the title of the Yorkshire and Lancashire Senior Competitions. Winners of these senior competitions are listed under Yorkshire and Lancashire League Champions. The pre-1903 Yorkshire Senior Competition should not be confused with the league operating for A-teams in Yorkshire which has the same title.

Coaches. Changes in the appointment of a club's coach during 1983-84 are shown in brackets.

Attendances. Crowds in brackets are at neutral venue.

Appearances. Players' totals are based on official teamsheets submitted to the League after each first team match. + indicates playing substitute appearance.

In the match by match review for each club the following abbreviations are used:

YC	—	Yorkshire Cup	H	—	Home
LC	—	Lancashire Cup	A	—	Away
SLC	—	Slalom Lager Championship	W	—	Won
SD	—	Second Division	L	—	Lost
JPS	—	John Player Special	D	—	Drew
CC	—	Challenge Cup	dg	—	Drop goal
PT	—	Premiership Trophy	Fr	—	France
P	—	Preliminary Round	A	—	Australia
			Pr	—	Probationer

BARROW

Ground: Craven Park
Colours: Royal blue jerseys, blue shorts
First Season: 1900-01
Nickname: Shipbuilders
Chairman: Bob Brady
Secretary: John Elliott
Coach: Tommy Dawes (May 1983-)
Honours: **Challenge Cup** Winners, 1954-55
Beaten finalists, 1937-38, 1950-51, 1956-57, 1966-67
John Player Trophy Beaten finalists 1980-81
Lancashire Cup Winners, 1954-55, 1983-84
Beaten finalists, 1937-38
Division Two Champions, 1975-76, 1983-84
Records: Attendance: 21,651 v. Salford (League) 15 April, 1938
Season
Goals: 135 by J. Ball, 1956-57
Tries: 50 by J. Lewthwaite, 1956-57
Points: 305 by I. Ball, 1979-80
Match
Goals: 12 by F. French v. Maryport, 19 Feb, 1938; W. Horne v. Cardiff, 8 Sep, 1951; S. Tickle v. Kent Invicta, 8 Apr 1984
Tries: 6 by V. Cumberbatch v. Batley, 21 Nov, 1936; J. Thornburrow v. Maryport, 19 Feb, 1938; F. Castle v. York, 29 Sep, 1951
Points: 28 by K. Jarrett v. Doncaster, 25 Aug, 1970; S. Tickle v. Kent Invicta, 8 Apr 1984
Highest score: 83-3 v. Maryport, 1937-38
Highest against: 71-15 v. St. Helens, 1958-59

1983-84 PLAYERS' SUMMARY

	App.	Tries	Goals	D/Gls	Pts
Ball, Ian	25	14	99	5	259
Cairns, David	38 + 1	16	—	5	69
Carter, Dane	8	2	—	—	8
Clough, David	7 + 2	3	—	—	12
Elliott, David	19 + 13	19	—	—	76
Fitzgerald, Mark	1	—	—	—	—
Flynn, Malcolm	12 + 1	1	—	—	4
Garside, Brett	2	—	—	—	—
Gee, Peter	2 + 1	—	—	—	—
Graham, David	2 + 3	2	—	—	8
Hadley, Derek	2 + 7	—	—	—	—
Herbert, Steve	36 + 3	25	2	—	104
Hodkinson, Alan	30 + 3	1	—	—	4
Hughes, Alan	5 + 8	3	—	—	12
Irving, Paul	1 + 1	—	—	—	—
James, Mick	12 + 1	4	—	—	16
Johnson, Robert	1	—	—	—	—
Knowles, Peter	0 + 1	—	1	—	2
Mason, Mel	2 + 1	—	—	—	—
McConnell, Ralph	31 + 1	19	—	—	76
McJennet, Mark	33 + 5	7	—	—	28
Milby, David	21 + 4	11	5	—	54
Moore, Terry	41	22	—	—	88
Mossop, Steve	41	1	—	1	5
Quirk, Les	20	11	—	—	44
Rea, Steve	5 + 6	6	—	—	24
Szymala, Eddie	17 + 2	5	—	—	20
Tickle, Steve	39	8	78	13	201
Tyson, David	7 + 3	—	—	—	—
Wall, Les	40	6	—	—	24
Whittle, Andy	33 + 1	23	—	—	92
TOTALS					
31 players		209	185	24	1,230

1983-84 MATCH ANALYSIS

Date	Competition	H/A	Opponent	Rlt	Score	Tries	Goals	Attendance	Referee
21.8.83	SD	H	Huddersfield	W	40-8	Wall (2), Whittle, McConnell, Elliott, Moore	Tickle (8)	2366	Mean
28.8.83	SD	A	Workington T.	L	8-15	Whittle	Tickle (2)	—	—
4.9.83	LC(1)	H	Whitehaven	W	13-6	Moore, Wall	Ball (2), Tickle (dg)	2707	Spencer
11.9.83	SD	H	Dewsbury	W	42-4	Elliott (3), Milby (2), Ball, McJennett, Whittle, Cairns	Ball (3)	1985	Allatt
14.9.83	LC(2)	A	Salford	W	13-2	Cairns (2)	Ball (2), Cairns (dg)	—	—
18.9.83	SD	A	Swinton	W	30-10	Moore, Elliott, Ball, Milby, Cairns	Ball (4), Knowles	—	—
21.9.83	LC(SF)	A	Warrington	W	19-18	Ball, Cairns	Ball (4, 1dg), Cairns (dg), Mossop (dg)	—	—
25.9.83	SD	H	Bramley	W	36-19	Tickle, Moore, Herbert, Szymala, Ball, McConnell	Ball (6)	2890	Volante
1.10.83	LC(F)	Wigan	Widnes	W	12-8	McConnell	Ball (3, 1dg), Tickle (dg)	(7007)	Allatt
5.10.83	SD	H	Hunslet	W	28-12	Milby, Szymala, Whittle, Ball	Ball (5, 1dg), Tickle (dg)	4696	Hodgson

1983-84 MATCH ANALYSIS (continued)

Date	Com-petition	H/A	Opponent	Rlt	Score	Tries	Goals	Atten-dance	Referee
9.10.83	SD	H	Doncaster	W	30-0	Cairns (2), Whittle (2), Milby, Bail	Ball (3)	3118	Haigh
16.10.83	SD	A	Blackpool B.	W	12-8	Whittle (2)	Ball (2)	—	—
23.10.83	SD	H	Huyton	W	48-8	Moore (2), Ball (2), Graham, Milby, Herbert, Hughes, Whittle	Ball (6)	2802	Thompson
30.10.83	SD	A	Dewsbury	W	26-6	Milby (2), Graham, Herbert, McConnell	Ball (3)	—	—
6.11.83	JPS(1)	A	Halifax	W	29-12	McConnell (3), Whittle	Ball (5, 1dg),Cairns (dg), Tickle (dg)	—	—
13.11.83	SD	H	Halifax	W	28-21	Elliott, Herbert, Moore, McConnell, Ball	Ball (3), tickle	4007	Lindop
20.11.83	JPS(2)	A	Widnes	L	6-18	—	Herbert (2), Tickle	—	—
4.12.83	SD	H	Keighley	W	35-10	Moore (2), James, Cairns, Szymala, Whittle, Ball	Ball (3, 1dg)	3171	Holdsworth
18.12.83	SD	H	York	W	42-18	McConnell (3), Herbert (2), Ball, Moore	Ball (7)	3156	McDonald
26.12.83	SD	A	Huyton	W	24-6	McConnell (2), Herbert, Szymala	Ball (4)	—	—
2.1.84	SD	H	Blackpool B.	W	22-2	James (2), Ball, Herbert	Ball (3)	3143	Beaumont
8.1.84	SD	A	Cardiff C.	W	26-14	McConnell, Whittle, Szymala, Herbert	Ball (5)	—	—
15.1.84	SD	H	Rochdale H.	W	30-6	James, Quirk, McJennett, Tickle, Herbert	Ball (5)	2891	Robinson
29.1.84	SD	H	Kent Invicta	W	34-16	McJennett, McConnell, Elliott, Herbert, Moore	Ball (7)	3911	Mean
5.2.84	SD	A	Batley	W	36-16	Wall (2), Tickle, Ball, Quirk, Herbert, Cairns	Ball (4)	—	—
12.2.84	CC(1)	H	Workington T.	L	12-14	McConnell, Ball	Ball, Tickle(dg), Cairns(dg)	5132	Allatt
19.2.84	SD	H	Cardiff C.	W	36-7	Moore, Tickle, Quirk, Cairns, McConnell, Clough	Ball (6)	3109	Berry
26.2.84	SD	A	Rochdale H.	W	14-6	Whittle, McConnell	Ball (3)	—	—
4.3.84	SD	A	Halifax	W	30-0	Elliott (2), Herbert, Moore, Cairns	Tickle (4, 2dg)	—	—
11.3.84	SD	A	Keighley	W	24-2	Whittle (2), Carter, Moore, Herbert	Tickle (2)	—	—
18.3.84	SD	H	Carlisle	W	58-18	Elliott (2), Whittle (2), Tickle (2) Flynn, Moore, Carter, McConnell	(2, 1dg)	3161	Volante
25.3.84	SD	A	Hunslet	L	21-24	Moore, Whittle, McJennett, Elliott	Tickle (2, 1dg)	—	—
28.3.84	SD	A	Carlisle	W	43-8	Moore (3), Milby, Whittle, Quirk, Herbert	Tickle (7, 1dg)	—	—
1.4.84	SD	H	Batley	W	64-2	Rea (2), Moore (2), Herbert (2), Milby, Tickle, Elliott, Whittle, McJennett, Mossop	Milby (5), Tickle (3)	2635	Whitfield
8.4.84	SD	A	Kent Invicta	W	80-8	Quirk (3), Elliott (3), Whittle (3), Hughes (2), Herbert, Clough, Tickle	Tickle (12)	—	—
11.4.84	SD	A	Bramley	W	19-6	Herbert, Elliott	Tickle (5, 1dg)	—	—
15.4.84	SD	A	Huddersfield	W	27-20	Herbert (2), Clough, Milby, Tickle	Tickle (3, 1dg)	—	—
20.4.84	SD	H	Workington T.	W	26-14	Cairns (2), Quirk, Hodkinson	Tickle (4, 1dg), Cairns (dg)	4845	Smith
22.4.84	SD	A	Doncaster	W	66-0	Rea (3), Herbert (2), Cairns (2), Wall, McJennett, Elliott, Moore, Tickle	Tickle (9)	—	—
25.4.84	SD	A	York	W	27-11	Elliott, Herbert, Cairns, Quirk, Rea	Tickle (3, 1dg)	—	—
29.4.84	SD	H	Swinton	W	14-7	Herbert, McJennett	Tickle (3)	3537	Robinson

BATLEY

Ground: Mount Pleasant
Colours: Cerise and fawn jerseys, cerise shorts
First Season: 1895-96
Nickname: Gallant Youths
Chairman: Michael Lumb
Secretary: Les Hardy
Coach: Terry Crook (June 1982-)
Honours: **Championship** Winners, 1923-24
Challenge Cup Winners, 1896-97, 1897-98, 1900-01
Yorkshire League Winners, 1898-99, 1923-24
Yorkshire Cup Winners, 1912-13
Beaten finalists, 1909-10, 1922-23, 1924-25, 1952-53
Records: Attendance: 23,989 v. Leeds (RL Cup) 14 March, 1925
Season
Goals: 120 by S. Thompson, 1958-59
Tries: 29 by J. Tindall, 1912-13
Points: 281 by J. Perry, 1950-51
Match
Goals: 9 by W. Davies v. Widnes, 27 Mar, 1909; S. Thompson v. Keighley, 20 Sep, 1958
Tries: 5 by J. Oakland v. Bramley, 19 Dec, 1908; Brannan v. Swinton, 17 Jan, 1920; J. Wale v. Bramley, 4 Dec, 1926 and v. Cottingham, 12 Feb, 1927
Points: 26 by J. Perry v. Liverpool C, 16 Sep, 1951
Highest score: 52-0 v. Widnes, 1908-09
Highest against: 78-9 v. Wakefield T., 1967-68

1983-84 PLAYERS' SUMMARY

	App.	Tries	Goals	D/Gls	Pts
Barraclough, Neil	6 + 3	—	—	—	—
Bell, Michael	2	—	—	—	—
Clark, Phil	0 + 1	—	—	—	—
Cousins, Kevin	33 + 2	2	—	—	8
Cummins, Brendan	25 + 1	6	—	—	24
Crook, Terry	3 + 2	—	1	1	3
Dobek, Andrew	5	—	—	1	1
Douglas, Ian	16	—	—	—	—
Finn, Brendan	13 + 9	—	5	1	11
Gibson, Carl	37	26	—	—	104
Harrington, Michael	12	1	—	—	4
Harwood, Mark	0 + 1	—	—	—	—
Hemingway, Neil	4 + 1	1	—	—	4
Hodgson, Chris	0 + 2	—	—	—	—
Hudson, Roger	0 + 1	—	—	—	—
Jennings, Alan	4 + 1	1	—	—	4
Jones, John	19 + 3	7	8	—	44
Madden, Shaun	23 + 3	2	—	—	8
McCleary, Jack	2	1	—	—	4
Mullaney, Steve	7	—	—	—	—
Oulton, Henry	30	4	71	4	162
Presley, Steve	20 + 5	2	—	—	8
Ratcliffe, Paul	2 + 2	—	—	—	—
Reed, Steve	22 + 1	6	—	—	24
Render, Ian	8	—	—	—	—
Robbins, Garry	16	—	—	—	—
Savage, Martin	20	4	—	—	16
Snee, Steve	0 + 1	—	—	—	—
Speight, Mark	2 + 2	—	—	—	—
Stainburn, John	3 + 4	—	—	3	3
Storey, Paul	37	5	—	—	20
Swale, Graham	16	3	—	1	13
Watson, Bernard	8	—	—	1	1
West, Brian	2 + 1	—	—	—	—
Wilson, Mike	34	8	—	—	32
Winterbottom, Ricky	27 + 1	3	—	—	12
Woodall, Derek	23 + 2	—	—	—	—
TOTALS 37 players		82	85	12	510

Graham Swale . . . 13 points in 16 appearances.

1983-84 MATCH ANALYSIS

Date	Com-petition	H/A	Opponent	Rlt	Score	Tries	Goals	Atten-dance	Referee
21.8.83	SD	H	Keighley	W	15-13	Gibson, Oulton	Oulton (3, 1dg)	670	Smith
24.8.83	SD	H	Rochdale H.	W	20-14	Gibson, Cousins, Oulton	Oulton (4)	596	Robinson
28.8.83	SD	A	Swinton	L	10-14	Cummins, Storey	Oulton	—	—
4.9.83	YC(1)	H	Leeds	L	14-30	Winterbottom, Wilson	Oulton (3)	2111	Beaumont
7.9.83	SD	A	Bramley	W	17-14	Gibson, Wilson, Cummins	Oulton (2, 1dg)	—	—
11.9.83	SD	H	Kent Invicta	L	8-18	Cummins	Oulton (2)	964	Holdsworth
18.9.83	SD	A	Carlisle	L	14-21	Presley, Cousins	Oulton (3)	—	—
25.9.83	SD	H	Doncaster	W	34-12	Gibson (3), Madden, Storey	Oulton (7)	790	Campbell
2.10.83	SD	A	Blackpool B.	L	6-20	Oulton	Oulton	—	—
9.10.83	SD	H	Huyton	W	19-5	Gibson (2), Winterbottom, Presley	Oulton, Crook (dg)	776	Allatt
16.10.83	SD	A	Huddersfield	W	18-16	Gibson, Cummings, Jennings	Oulton (3)	—	—
23.10.83	JPS(P)	H	Doncaster	L	11-12	Gibson	Oulton (3, 1dg)	782	Fox
30.10.83	SD	A	Doncaster	L	10-21	Winterbottom, Storey	Oulton	—	—
13.11.83	SD	H	Cardiff C.	W	21-15	Gibson, Oulton, Savage	Oulton (4), Watson (dg)	754	Wall
20.11.83	SD	H	Halifax	L	11-23	Gibson (2)	Oulton, Stainburn (dg)	1540	Spencer
27.11.83	SD	A	Keighley	L	1-25	—	Stainburn (dg)	—	—
4.12.83	SD	H	Carlisle	W	22-15	Jones (2), Cummins, Gibson	Oulton (3)	690	McDonald
18.12.83	SD	H	Swinton	W	9-7	Swales	Oulton (2, 1dg)	878	Kendrew
26.12.83	SD	A	Dewsbury	W	16-10	Gibson	Oulton (5), Finn (dg), Dobek (dg)	—	—
1.1.84	SD	H	Dewsbury	L	4-6	—	Oulton (2)	1553	Lindop
8.1.84	SD	A	Halifax	L	10-28	Savage, Jones	Finn	—	—
5.2.84	SD	H	Barrow	L	16-36	Gibson (2), Reed	Oulton (2)	891	Kershaw
12.2.84	CC(1)	A	Doncaster	L	8-11	Wilson	Oulton (2)	—	—
19.2.84	SD	A	Kent Invicta	L	8-30	Jones, Gibson	—	—	—
4.3.84	SD	H	Huddersfield	L	1-15	—	Swale (dg)	843	Fox
11.3.84	SD	A	Rochdale H.	W	30-14	Savage (2), Wilson, Jones, Reed, Gibson	Oulton (3)	—	—
16.3.84	SD	A (at Work'n AFC)	Workington T.	L	8-36	Jones	Oulton (2)	—	—
18.3.84	SD	H	Hunslet	L	12-42	Jones, Storey	Oulton (2)	1138	Allatt
25.3.84	SD	H	Workington T.	W	36-10	Cummins, Storey, Reed, Harrington, Swale, Gibson	Oulton (6)	503	Holdsworth
27.3.84	SD	A (at Bramley)	Hunslet	L	18-38	Reed (2), Wilson	Oulton (3)	—	—
1.4.84	SD	A	Barrow	L	2-64	—	Jones	—	—
8.4.84	SD	A	Cardiff C.	L	16-40	Wilson, Gibson, McCleary	Finn (2)	—	—
11.4.84	SD	A	York	L	8-36	Gibson	Finn (2)	—	—
15.4.84	SD	H	Blackpool B.	L	0-10	—	—	678	Smith
20.4.84	SD	H	York	W	22-14	Wilson, Swale, Hemingway	Jones (5)	713	Massey
23.4.84	SD	A	Huyton	L	14-30	Gibson, Reed, Wilson	Crook	—	—
29.4.84	SD	H	Bramley	L	21-26	Gibson (3), Madden	Jones (2), Stainburn	703	Beaumont

BLACKPOOL BOROUGH

Ground: Borough Park
Colours: Tangerine jerseys with black and white broad bands, white shorts
First Season: 1954-55
Nickname: Seasiders
Chairman: Jack Hart
Secretary: Deryk Brown
Coach: Tommy Dickens (March 1982-)
Honours: **John Player Trophy** Beaten finalists, 1976-77
Records: Attendance: 7,614 v. Castleford (RL Cup) March 14, 1964. There was an attendance of 21,000 in an RL Cup-tie against Leigh on Blackpool FC ground on March 9, 1957.

Season
Goals: 89 by J. Maughan, 1958-59
Tries: 22 by J. Johnson, 1970-71
Points: 201 by P. Fearis, 1957-58

Match
Goals: 11 by N. Turley v. Carlisle, 26 Apr, 1984
Tries: 4 by T. Wilkshire v. Bradford N, 14 Jan, 1961; J. Stockley v. Doncaster, 1 Apr, 1984
Points: 27 by N. Turley v. Carlisle, 26 Apr, 1984
Highest score: 48-8 v. Thames Board, 1963-64
Highest against: 77-8 v. Wigan, 1963-64

1983-84 PLAYERS' SUMMARY

	App.	Tries	Goals	D/Gls	Pts
Briscoe, Carl	27 + 3	7	—	—	28
Cole, Peter	3 + 1	—	—	—	—
Cowburn, Martin	4 + 1	1	—	—	4
Coyle, Bernard	22 + 4	7	—	—	28
Davies, Steve	35	5	—	—	20
Dickinson, Gerald	23 + 4	2	—	—	8
Gamble, Paul	22 + 5	4	—	—	16
Gaynor, Bruce	18	3	—	—	12
Glover, John	11	—	—	—	—
Green, Jimmy	20	4	—	—	16
Greenall, Alan	29 + 2	10	—	—	40
Grimshaw, Steve	15 + 1	3	—	1	13
Grundy, Tracey	11 + 5	—	—	—	—
Johns, Graeme	25	5	18	—	56
Kelly, Paul	4 + 6	—	—	—	—
Laird, Gary	7	—	17	—	34
McLoughlan, Brendan	8 + 2	—	—	—	—
Ogden, Ian	2 + 4	—	—	—	—
O'Hara, Michael	8	—	—	—	—
Parry, Don	10	1	—	—	4
Price, Billy	22 + 2	5	—	—	20
Runciman, Andrew	0 + 1	—	—	—	—
Sivori, Martin	7	6	—	—	24
Stockley, John	29	19	3	—	82
Turley, Norman	32	8	65	15	177
Waddell, Hugh	31	5	—	—	20
Webb, Andrew	5 + 2	—	—	—	—
Wills, Steve	23 + 9	3	—	—	12
Wilson, Steve	27 + 2	6	—	—	24
Trialist	1	—	—	—	—
TOTALS					
30 players		104	103	16	638

John Glover ... 11 appearances on loan.

1983-84 MATCH ANALYSIS

Date	Competition	H/A	Opponent	Rlt	Score	Tries	Goals	Attendance	Referee
21.8.83	SD	H	Swinton	W	16-4	Briscoe (2), Greenall	Laird (2)	939	Wall
24.8.83	SD	A	Huyton	W	18-8	Cowburn, Greenall, Coyle	Stockley (3)	—	—
28.8.83	SD	A	York	D	14-14	Coyle (2)	Laird (3)	—	—
4.9.83	LC(1)	H	Warrington	L	4-30	—	Laird (2)	1756	Wall
11.9.83	SD	H	Huddersfield	L	10-14	Briscoe	Johns (3)	720	Campbell
18.9.83	SD	A	Dewsbury	W	20-18	Turley, Green, Stockley	Laird (4)	—	—
25.9.83	SD	H	Kent Invicta	L	13-14	Gamble, Wilson	Laird (2), Turley (dg)	692	Smith
2.10.83	SD	H	Batley	W	20-6	Wilson (2), Davies	Laird (4)	635	Walker
9.10.83	SD	A	Halifax	L	8-10	Wilson, Davies	—	—	—
16.10.83	SD	H	Barrow	L	8-12	Waddell	Johns (2)	987	McDonald
23.10.83	SD	A	Rochdale H.	L	4-13	Davies	—	—	—
30.10.83	SD	H	Hunslet	W	24-18	Parry, Wilson, Green, Briscoe	Johns (4)	815	Allatt
6.11.83	JPS(1)	H	Leeds	L	9-12	Waddell	Johns (2), Turley (dg)	1351	Haigh
13.11.83	SD	A	Workington T.	D	19-19	Greenall, Stockley, Waddell	Johns (3), Turley (dg)	—	—
27.11.83	SD	H	York	L	8-12	Stockley	Turley (2)	322	Kendrew
4.12.83	SD	A	Hunslet	W	31-30	Green, Price, Wilson, Johns, Gamble	Johns (4), Turley (3dg)	—	—
11.12.83	SD	H	Rochdale H.	L	8-10	Turley	Turley (2)	580	Volante
18.12.83	SD	A	Huddersfield	W	20-14	Greenall, Gamble, Turley	Turley (4)	—	—
26.12.83	SD	H	Keighley	W	16-10	Green, Price	Turley (4)	662	Fox
2.1.84	SD	A	Barrow	L	2-22	—	Turley	—	—
8.1.84	SD	H	Workington T.	W	8-2	Greenall	Turley (2)	505	Lindop
22.1.84	SD	H	Bramley	D	2-2	—	Turley	403	Massey
5.2.84	SD	H	Dewsbury	W	24-6	Stockley (3), Gaynor, Greenall	Turley (2)	523	Thompson
12.2.84	CC(1)	H	Hull K.R.	L	10-27	Waddell	Turley (3)	2758	Walker
19.2.84	SD	A	Keighley	W	16-11	Greenall (2), Sivori	Turley (2)	—	—
26.2.84	SD	H	Cardiff C.	W	32-25	Sivori (2), Coyle, Stockley, Davies	Turley (5,2dg)	484	Kendrew
4.3.84	SD	A	Cardiff C.	L	18-19	Stockley, Sivori, Johns	Turley (2,2dg)	—	—
11.3.84	SD	H	Halifax	W	18-17	Wills, Turley, Sivori	Turley (3)	815	Holdsworth
18.3.84	SD	A	Kent Invicta	W	36-24	Johns, Gamble, Turley, Greenall, Sivori, Briscoe	Turley (6)	—	—
23.3.84	SD	A	Carlisle	L	14-16	Greenall, Grimshaw, Price	Turley	—	—
25.3.84	SD	A	Bramley	W	22-12	Grimshaw, Stockley, Coyle	Turley (4, 1dg), Grimshaw (dg)	—	—
1.4.84	SD	H	Doncaster	W	36-12	Stockley (4), Davies, Grimshaw, Briscoe	Turley (4)	456	Berry
8.4.84	SD	A	Swinton	L	3-22	—	Turley (1, 1dg)	—	—
15.4.84	SD	A	Batley	W	10-0	Dickinson, Gaynor	Turley	—	—
20.4.84	SD	H	Huyton	W	26-16	Gaynor, Stockley, Turley, Johns, Price	Turley (3)	580	Spencer
23.4.84	SD	A	Doncaster	W	44-16	Stockley (2), Coyle (2), Briscoe, Johns, Dickinson, Wills, Price	Turley (4)	—	—
26.4.84	SD	H	Carlisle	W	47-18	Stockley (3), Turley (2), Wills, Waddell	Turley (8, 3dg)	511	Volante

BRADFORD NORTHERN

Ground: Odsal Stadium
Colours: White jerseys with red, amber and black hoops, white shorts
First Season: 1895-96 as "Bradford". Disbanded and became Bradford Northern in 1907-08. Disbanded during 1963-64 and re-formed for start of 1964-65
Nickname: Northern
Chairman: Jack Bates
Secretary: Mrs. Bessie Higgins
Coach: Peter Fox (April 1977-)
Honours: **Challenge Cup** Winners, 1905-06, 1943-44, 1946-47, 1948-49
Beaten finalists, 1897-98, 1944-45, 1947-48, 1972-73
Championship Beaten finalists, 1947-48, 1951-52
Division One Champions, 1903-04, 1979-80, 1980-81
Division Two Champions, 1973-74
War-time Emergency League Championship winners, 1939-40, 1940-41, 1944-45
Beaten finalists, 1941-42
Yorkshire League Winners, 1899-00, 1900-01, 1939-40, 1940-41, 1947-48
Yorkshire Cup Winners, 1906-07, 1940-41, 1941-42, 1943-44, 1945-46, 1948-49, 1949-50, 1953-54, 1965-66, 1978-79
Beaten finalists, 1913-14, 1981-82, 1982-83
Premiership Winners, 1977-78
Beaten finalists, 1978-79, 1979-80
John Player Trophy Winners, 1974-75, 1979-80
Records: Attendance: 102,569 Warrington v. Halifax (RL Cup Final replay) 5 May, 1954.
Home: 69,429 v. Huddersfield (RL Cup) 14 March, 1953

Season
Goals: 173 by E. Tees, 1971-72
Tries: 63 by J. McLean, 1951-52
Points: 364 by E. Tees, 1971-72
Match
Goals: 14 by J. Phillips v. Batley, 6 Sep, 1952
Tries: 7 by J. Dechan v. Bramley, 13 Oct, 1906
Points: 34 by E. Ward v. Liverpool S., 20 Oct, 1945
Highest score: 72-9 v. Doncaster, 1973-74
Highest against: 75-18 v. Leeds, 1931-32

1983-84 PLAYERS' SUMMARY

	App.	Tries	Goals	D/Gls	Pts
Atherton, Michael	10 + 1	2	—	—	8
Barends, David	1	—	—	—	—
Carroll, Dean	20 + 11	9	14	9	73
Davies Richard	32	6	—	—	24
Fennell, Dale	8	1	—	2	6
Fleming, Mark	15 + 10	6	—	—	24
Francis, Richard	2	1	—	—	4
Gill, Tony	2 + 1	—	—	—	—
Grayshon, Jeff	19	6	—	—	24
Green, John	3	1	—	—	4
Hale, Gary	16 + 2	—	—	—	—
Hanley, Ellery	22	12	2	1	53
Idle, Graham	18 + 3	—	—	—	—
Jackson, Robert	3	—	—	—	—
Jasiewicz, Dick	33 + 2	10	—	—	40
Mallender, Paul	5	1	—	—	4
McGowan, Steve	5 + 1	1	—	—	4
Mumby, Keith	32	8	5	—	42
Murray, Tom	1 + 1	—	—	—	—
Noble, Brian	29	5	—	—	20
Parrish, Steve	34	9	75	—	186
Parrott, Chris	1 + 3	—	—	—	—
Pennant, Audley	23 + 1	1	—	—	4
Preece, Chris	8	1	—	—	4
Ralda, Philip	1 + 1	—	—	—	—
Rathbone, Alan	16 + 3	4	—	—	16
Redfearn, Alan	7 + 5	—	—	4	4
Robinson Andy	21	2	—	1	9
Sheldon, Ian	26 + 6	2	—	—	8
Sherratt, Ian	2 + 4	1	—	—	4
Sidebottom, Gary	3 + 1	—	6	—	12
Smith, David	23	3	—	—	12
Van Bellen, Gary	35 + 1	4	—	—	16
Whiteman, Keith	18 + 6	5	—	—	20
TOTALS					
34 players		101	102	17	625

1983-84 MATCH ANALYSIS

Date	Competition	H/A	Opponent	Rlt	Score	Tries	Goals	Attendance	Referee
21.8.83	SLC	A	Whitehaven	W	45-4	Noble (2), Fennell, Atherton, Whiteman, Grayshon, Hanley	Mumby (5), Hanley (2, 1dg), Parrish	—	—
28.8.83	SLC	H	Oldham	W	14-8	Hanley, Parrish	Parrish (3)	5607	Robinson
4.9.83	YC(1)	H	Hull K. R.	W	25-22	Smith, Parrish, Hanley, Mumby, Whiteman	Parrish (2), Redfearn (dg)	4356	Holdsworth
11.9.83	SLC	A	Wigan	W	24-16	Atherton, Rathbone, Jasiewicz, Smith	Parrish (4)	—	—
14.9.83	YC(2)	H	Castleford	L	8-12	—	Parrish (4)	4684	Fox
18.9.83	SLC	H	St. Helens	W	14-10	Robinson, Fleming	Parrish (2), Redfearn (2 dg)	4701	Kershaw
25.9.83	SLC	A	Leigh	W	24-0	Parrish, Hanley, Rathbone, Fleming	Parrish (3), Carroll	—	—
2.10.83	SLC	H	Salford	W	38-14	Fleming (2), Hanley (2), Mumby, Davies, Carroll	Parrish (5)	4853	Campbell
9.10.83	SLC	A	Hull K. R.	L	14-16	Hanley, Davies	Parrish (3)	—	—
16.10.83	SLC	H	Featherstone R.	W	30-10	Sheldon, Parrish, Jasiewicz, Davies, Hanley, Carroll	Parrish (3)	4380	Smith
23.10.83	SLC	A	St. Helens	L	14-29	Parrish, Green	Parrish (3)	—	—
30.10.83	SLC	H	Fulham	W	21-2	Carroll, Mallender	Parrish (5), Carroll (3 dg)	4377	Whitfield
6.11.83	JPS(1)	A	Widnes	L	1-2	—	Carroll (dg)	—	—
11.11.83	SLC	A	Salford	W	14-12	Carroll, Hanley	Parrish (3)	—	—
27.11.83	SLC	H	Wakefield T.	W	20-15	Jasiewicz (2), Pennant, Parrish	Parrish (2)	5339	Walker
4.12.83	SLC	A	Warrington	W	13-11	Whiteman, Jasiewicz	Parrish (2), Redfearn (dg)	—	—
18.12.83	SLC	A	Fulham	W	16-6	Carroll (2)	Parrish (3), Carroll (2 dg)	—	—
26.12.83	SLC	H	Widnes	L	14-24	Smith, Davies, Fleming	Parrish	7827	Wall
1.1.84	SLC	H	Castleford	D	2-2	—	Parrish	7167	Berry
8.1.84	SLC	A	Hull	L	8-16	Mumby	Parrish (2)	—	—
3.2.84	SLC	H	Hull K.R.	W	20-0	Grayshon (2), Mumby, Hanley	Parrish (2)	5314	Smith
12.2.84	CC(1)	H	Featherstone R.	W	20-4	Whiteman, Davies, Jasiewicz	Parrish (4)	7542	Haigh
19.2.84	SLC	A	Castleford	L	6-29	Fleming	Carroll	—	—
26.2.84	CC(2)	A	Hunslet	W	17-7	Grayshon, Noble	Parrish (4), Robinson (dg)	—	—
1.3.84	SLC	H	Wigan	L	6-15	Grayshon	Parrish	4944	Haigh
4.3.84	SLC	A	Oldham	L	4-10	—	Parrish (2)	—	—
11.3.84	CC(3)	A	Leeds	D	13-13	Rathbone	Parrish (4), Carroll (dg)	—	—
15.3.84	CC(3) Replay	H	Leeds	L	10-12	Noble, Carroll	Parrish	18424	Whitfield
18.3.84	SLC	A	Wakefield T.	W	12-0	Sheldon, Whiteman, Rathbone	—	—	—
23.3.84	SLC	H	Whitehaven	W	22-8	Parrish (2), Noble, Sherratt, Van Bellen	Parrish	3417	Volante
27.3.84	SLfC	H	Leigh	W	23-18	Mumby, Jasiewicz, Van Bellen	Carroll (5, 1dg)	4053	Allatt
1.4.84	SLC	H	Warrington	L	16-19	Carroll, Parrish, Mumby	Carroll (2)	4770	Thompson
4.4.84	SLC	A	Widnes	L	23-32	Robinson, Mumby, Carroll	Carroll (5, 1dg)	—	—
8.4.84	SLC	A	Featherstone R.	L	8-10	Van Bellen	Sidebottom (2)	—	—
15.4.84	SLC	H	Hull	L	10-29	Grayshon, Jasiewicz	Sidebottom	7065	Lindop
20.4.84	SLC	A	Leeds	D	10-10	Van Bellen	Parrish (2), Fennell (2dg)	—	—
24.4.84	SLC	H	Leeds	W	34-4	Hanley (2), Jasiewicz (2), McGowan, Mumby, Francis	Sidebottom (3)	5920	Campbell
29.4.84	PT(1)	A	Hull	L	12-42	Davies, Preece	Parrish (2)	—	—

BRAMLEY

Ground: McLaren Field
Colours: Amber jerseys with black collar, cuffs and V, black shorts
First Season: 1896-97
Nickname: Villagers
Chairman: Ron Teeman
Secretary: Don Senior
Coach: Maurice Bamford (May 1982-Oct. 1983)
Peter Jarvis (Oct. 1983-)
Honours: **BBC2 Floodlit Trophy** Winners, 1973-74
Records: Attendance: 12,600 v. Leeds (League) 7 May, 1947
Season
Goals: 130 by J. Wilson, 1961-62
Tries: 20 by W. Rushton, 1958-59; A. Smith, 1972-73
Points: 276 by G. Langfield, 1956-57
Match
Goals: 11 by B. Ward v. Doncaster, 1 Sep, 1974
Tries: 7 by J. Sedgewick v. Normanton, 16 Apr, 1906
Points: 28 by B. Ward v. Doncaster, 1 Sep, 1974
Highest score: 52-17 v. Doncaster, 1974-75
Highest against: 92-7 v. Australia, 1921-22

1983-84 PLAYERS' SUMMARY

	App.	Tries	Goals	D/Gls	Pts
Austin, Jack	1 + 1	—	—	—	—
Bibb, Trevor	29 + 1	4	13	1	43
Bowman, Chris	12 + 9	3	—	—	12
Branch, Malcolm	1	—	—	—	—
Brannan, Alistair	2 + 1	—	—	—	—
Bullough, David	15 + 1	2	—	—	8
Carroll, Steve	33 + 2	4	—	9	25
Carter, John	0 + 3	—	—	—	—
Clarkson, Allan	25 + 1	3	—	—	12
Clayton, Peter	2 + 2	—	—	—	—
Cook, William	14 + 12	2	—	—	8
Dyas, David	35	14	—	—	56
Edginton, David	15 + 1	4	—	—	16
Fletcher, Paul	27	5	—	2	22
Fox, Mark	0 + 1	—	—	—	—
Garforth, Tony	31	2	—	—	8
Gascoigne, Andy	25	10	—	—	40
Green, Karl	19 + 4	1	—	—	4
Harrison, Karl	28 + 1	3	—	—	12
Hickinson, Paul	2 + 1	—	—	—	—
Hindley, Alan	28 + 1	3	—	—	12
Hindley, Steve	9 + 4	4	—	—	16
Jarvis, Peter	0 + 1	—	—	—	—
Kelly, Hayden	14 + 5	3	—	—	12
Kilner, Shaun	34	4	85	1	187
Lister, Peter	20 + 1	13	—	—	52
Lund, Steve	2 + 2	1	—	—	4
Nelson, David	1 + 2	1	—	—	4
Nicholson, Steve	1	1	—	—	4
O'Beirne, Mark	2	1	—	—	4
O'Hara, Paul	2	—	—	—	—
Okulicz, Eddie	4	—	—	—	—
Parrott, Chris	7	—	—	—	—
Paterson, John	3 + 1	—	—	—	—
Pickerill, Neil	12	7	—	—	28
Piwinski, Ziggy	4	—	—	1	1
Roach, Steve	1 + 1	—	—	—	—
Rose, Steve	12 + 1	2	—	—	8
Walker, Steve	8 + 1	3	—	—	12
Trialists (2)	1 + 3	—	—	—	—
TOTALS					
41 players		100	98	14	610

Jack Austin . . . restricted to two appearances.

1983-84 MATCH ANALYSIS

Date	Competition	H/A	Opponent	Rlt	Score	Tries	Goals	Attendance	Referee
21.8.83	SD	H	Dewsbury	W	28-18	Gascoigne, Fletcher, Harrison, Dyas, Rose	Kilner (4)	700	Massey
24.8.83	SD	H	Hunslet	L	10-25	Rose, S. Hindley	Kilner	1480	Berry
27.8.83	SD	A	Cardiff C.	L	10-27	Fletcher, A. Hindley	Kilner	—	—
4.9.83	YC(1)	A	Doncaster	L	12-16	Fletcher, S. Hindley	Kilner (2)	—	—
7.9.83	SD	H	Batley	L	14-17	Gascoigne, Dyas	Kilner (3)	750	Kendrew
11.9.83	SD	A	Halifax	L	12-18	Gascoigne (2)	Kilner (2)	—	—
18.9.83	SD	H	Huyton	W	34-6	Gascoigne (2), Nicholson, S. Hindley, A. Hindley	Kilner (7)	500	Wall
25.9.83	SD	A	Barrow	L	19-36	Carroll (3)	Kilner (3), Carroll (dg)	—	—
2.10.83	SD	H	Rochdale H.	D	21-21	Kelly, Lister, Harrison, Walker	Kilner (2), Carroll (dg)	655	Lindop
9.10.83	SD	A	Carlisle	W	22-6	Lister (2), Dyas, Walker	Kilner (3)	—	—
16.10.83	SD	H	Kent Invicta	W	12-6	Lister, Kilner	Kilner (2)	510	Allatt
18.12.83	SD	A	Kent Invicta	L	11-15	Lister	Kilner (3), Carroll (dg)	—	—
26.12.83	SD	H	Doncaster	W	32-0	Lister (2), Dyas (2), Kelly, Green	Kilner (4)	960	Kershaw
1.1.84	SD	A	Doncaster	W	34-7	Bibb (2), Clarkson, Harrison, Gascoigne, Kelly	Kilner (5)	—	—
8.1.84	SD	H	Swinton	L	10-12	Lister, Dyas	Kilner	1280	Smith
22.1.84	SD	A	Blackpool B.	D	2-2	—	Kilner	—	—
5.2.84	SD	A	Huyton	W	21-8	Dyas (2), Lund	Kilner (4), Fletcher (dg)	—	—
12.2.84	CC(1)	H	Wigan	D	10-10	Lister	Kilner (2, 1dg), Carroll (dg)	3968	Spencer
15.2.84	CC(1) replay	A	Wigan	L	4-34	Lister	—	—	—
19.2.84	SD	H	York	L	12-18	A. Hindley, Cook	Kilner (2)	650	Thompson
26.2.84	SD	A	Keighley	W	32-4	Bowman, Pickerill, Edgington, Clarkson, Fletcher	Kilner (6)	—	—
4.3.84	SD	H	Keighley	W	14-10	Dyas (2), Pickerill	Kilner	700	Haig
9.3.84	SD	A (at Work'n AFC)	Workington T.	W	16-10	Pickerill, Edgington	Kilner (3), Piwinski (dg) Carroll (dg)	—	—
11.3.84	SD	A	Dewsbury	W	20-7	Dyas (3)	Kilner (3), Carroll (2dg)	—	—
15.3.84	SD	A	Rochdale H.	W	9-7	—	Kilner (4), Carroll (dg)	—	—
18.3.84	SD	A	Swinton	L	8-15	Bullough, Dyas	—	—	—
21.3.84	SD	H	Halifax	L	14-17	Pickerill, Bibb	Kilner (3)	1150	Wall
25.3.84	SD	H	Blackpool B.	L	12-22	Kilner, O'Beirne	Kilner (2)	600	Allatt
1.4.84	SD	A	Huddersfield	L	10-25	Kilner, Garforth	Kilner	—	—
4.4.84	SD	H	Huddersfield	L	6-28	Bowman	Kilner	700	Whitfield
8.4.84	SD	H	Workington T.	W	26-16	Pickerill, Bullough, Kilner, Fletcher	Kilner (4), Fletcher (dg), Carroll (dg)	700	Kendrew
11.4.84	SD	H	Barrow	L	6-19	Pickerill	Kilner	610	Campbell
18.4.84	SD	A	Hunslet	L	12-36	Pickerill, Gascoigne	Kilner (2)	—	—
20.4.84	SD	H	Carlisle	W	22-18	Edgington (2), Lister, Cook	Kilner (2), Bibb	477	McDonald
23.4.84	SD	A	York	L	22-28	Lister (2), Bibb, Bowman	Bibb (3)	—	—
29.4.84	SD	A	Batley	W	26-21	Gascoigne (2), Carroll, Walker	Bibb (5)	—	—
2.5.84	SD	H	Cardiff C.	W	25-20	Clarkson, Garforth, S. Hindley, Nelson	Bibb (4, 1dg)	480	Walker

CARDIFF CITY

Ground: Ninian Park
Colours: Blue jerseys with yellow V, blue shorts
First Season: 1981-82. A Cardiff team competed in the 1951-52 campaign
Nickname: Blue Dragons
Chairman: Jack Leonard
Managing Director: David Watkins
Secretary: Ron Jones
Coach: David Watkins (Dec. 1981-)
Records: Attendance: 9,247 v. Salford (Div. 2) 30 August, 1981

Season
Goals: 140 by L. Hallett, 1983-84
Tries: 26 by T. David, 1982-83
Points: 279 by L. Hallett, 1983-84

Match
Goals: 9 by L. Hallett v. Rochdale H., 6 Nov, 1983; v. Workington T., 23 Apr, 1984
Tries: 4 by T. David v. Swinton, 20 Feb, 1983; v. Batley, 8 Apr, 1984
Points: 18 by L. Hallett, 23 Apr, 1984; v. Huyton, 29 Apr, 1984
Highest score: 41-6 v. Rochdale H. 1983-84
Highest against: 50-16 v. York, 1983-84

1983-84 PLAYERS' SUMMARY

	App.	Tries	Goals	D/Gls	Pts
Barwood, Adrian	30	8	—	—	32
Barwood, David	28 + 4	4	—	—	16
Camilleri, Chris	17	6	—	—	24
Chinnock, Mike	10 + 4	3	—	—	12
Daley, Arthur	28 + 6	2	—	—	8
David, Tom	25 + 1	22	—	—	88
Davies, Geoff	32 + 1	9	—	—	36
Evans, Alan	12	1	—	—	4
Fenwick, Steve	20 + 1	6	15	1	55
Fleay, Bob	12 + 1	4	—	—	16
Gwilliam, Ken	26 + 6	2	—	—	8
Hallett, Lyn	38	7	111	29	279
Harris, Bob	4 + 12	—	—	—	—
Marshall, Mike	19	5	—	—	20
Morgan, Peter	20	—	—	—	—
Nanson, Terry	25 + 6	1	—	—	4
O'Brien, Chris	32 + 2	16	—	—	64
Pritchard, Gordon	19 + 2	7	—	—	28
Ringer, Paul	9 + 1	3	—	—	12
Seldon, Chris	8 + 6	—	—	—	—
Walters, Graham	4	2	—	—	8
Williams, Brynmor	6 + 2	3	—	—	12
Woods, Paul	34	7	—	1	29
Trialists (5)	36 + 10	12	—	—	48
TOTALS					
28 players		130	126	31	803

Adrian Barwood ... eight tries in 30 appearances.

1983-84 MATCH ANALYSIS

Date	Competition	H/A	Opponent	Rlt	Score	Tries	Goals	Attendance	Referee
21.8.83	SD	A	Kent Invicta	W	31-12	Davies, Fleay, Hallett, Woods	Fenwick (7), Hallett (dg)	—	—
27.8.83	SD	H	Bramley	W	27-10	A. Barwood, Camilleri, Gwilliam, David, Davies	Fenwick (3), Hallett (dg)	566	Beaumont
10.9.83	SD	H	Carlisle	W	21-16	Camilleri, O'Brien, Ringer, Woods	Hallett (2, 1 dg)	462	Smith
18.9.83	SD	A	Hunslet	L	18-40	Pritchard, O'Brien	Hallett (5)	—	—
24.9.83	SD	H	Huddersfield	D	26-26	David (2), Hallett, O'Brien, Walters	Hallett (3)	502	Kershaw
2.10.83	SD	A	Doncaster	W	36-8	Davies (2), O'Brien (2), Pritchard, D. Barwood	Hallett (6)	—	—
9.10.83	SD	H	Dewsbury	W	26-14	Pritchard, Camilleri, Hallett, Gwilliam, David	Hallett (3)	580	Holdsworth
16.10.83	SD	A	Huyton	W	23-18	David (2), O'Brien, Camilleri	Hallett (3, 1 dg)	—	—
23.10.83	SD	A	York	L	16-50	O'Brien, David	Hallett (4)	—	—
30.10.83	SD	H	Keighley	L	6-11	—	Hallett (3)	526	Mean
6.11.83	JPS(1)	H	Rochdale H.	W	41-6	David (2), Woods, Evans, O'Brien, Ringer	Hallett (8, 1 dg)	645	Fox
13.11.83	SD	A	Batley	L	15-21	Woods, Williams	Hallett (2, 2 dg), Woods (dg)	—	—
20.11.83	JPS(2)	H	Huyton	W	38-12	Williams (2), Woods, Ringer, O'Brien, Camilleri	Hallett (6, 2 dg)	1085	Campbell
27.11.83	JPS(3)	A	Leigh	L	8-12	Davies	Hallett, Fenwick	—	—
4.12.83	SD	H	Swinton	L	12-25	Camilleri, Daley	Hallett (2)	705	Massey
18.12.83	SD	H	Halifax	W	26-18	D. Barwood, Woods, O'Brien, Pritchard	Hallett (4, 2 dg)	579	Holdsworth
1.1.84	SD	A	Rochdale H.	L	4-7	A. Barwood	—	—	—
8.1.84	SD	H	Barrow	L	14-26	Fenwick (2), A. Barwood	Fenwick	697	Whitfield
15.1.84	SD	A	Huddersfield	L	10-14	Pritchard, A. Barwood	Hallett	—	—
22.1.84	SD	H	Hunslet	L	6-34	Walters	Hallett	575	Haigh
12.2.84	CC(1)	H	Hull	L	6-34	—	Hallett (3)	2735	Lindop
19.2.84	SD	A	Barrow	L	7-36	David	Hallett (1, 1 dg)	—	—
26.2.84	SD	A	Blackpool B.	L	25-32	David, Daley, Trialist	Hallett (6, 1dg)	—	—
4.3.84	SD	H	Blackpool B.	W	19-18	David (3), A.N. Other	Hallett (1, 1dg)	449	Hodgson
11.3.84	SD	H	Workington T	L	20-22	David, Davies, O'Brien	Hallett (3, 1dg), Fenwick (dg)	457	Robinson
18.3.84	SD	A	Halifax	L	20-22	Davies, Chinnock, David	Fenwick (3), Hallett	—	—
25.3.84	SD	A	Dewsbury	W	16-12	David, Fenwick, Chinnock	Hallett (1, 2dg)	—	—
6.4.84	SD	H	Rochdale H.	W	27-5	A. Barwood (2), D. Barwood, Fenwick, Hallett	Hallett (3, 1dg)	365	Wall
8.4.84	SD	H	Batley	W	40-16	David (4), O'Brien, Pritchard, Chinnock	Hallett (4, 4dg)	478	Thompson
11.4.84	SD	H	Kent Invicta	W	21-12	Fenwick (2), Marshall (2), Fleay	Hallett (dg)	538	Spencer
15.4.84	SD	A	Carlisle	L	10-14	Fleay	Hallett (2, 2dg)	—	—
20.4.84	SD	H	Doncaster	W	32-21	A. Barwood (2), Marshall, Pritchard, Davies, Fleay	Hallett (4)	545	Robinson
23.4.84	SD	A	Workington T.	L	30-38	A.N. Other (2), O'Brien	Hallett (9)	—	—
24.4.84	SD	A	Keighley	W	30-6	A.N. Other (2), Marshall, Nanson, O'Brien	Hallett (4, 2dg)	—	—
29.4.84	SD	H (at Ebbw Vale)	Huyton	W	34-16	Hallett (2), Trialist (2), O'Brien, A.N. Other	Hallett (5)	1400	Berry
2.5.84	SD	A	Bramley	L	20-25	O'Brien, David, Trialist	Hallett (4)	—	—
7.5.84	SD	A	Swinton	L	16-44	Woods, Davies, Trialist	Hallett (2)	—	—
13.5.84	SD	H	York	L	26-28	Marshall, Hallett, D. Barwood, Trialist	Hallett (4, 2dg)	446	Walker

CARLISLE

Ground: Brunton Park
Colours: Blue jerseys with red and white band, white shorts
First Season: 1981-82. A Carlisle City team entered the League in 1928-29 but withdrew after 10 matches, winning one
Chairman: Geoff Holmes
Coach: John Atkinson (Feb. 1983-)
Records: Attendance: 5,903 v. Workington T. (Div 2) 6 Sept, 1981

Season
Goals: 113 by S. Ferres, 1981-82
Tries: 25 by M. Morgan, 1981-82
Points: 242 by S. Ferres, 1981-82

Match
Goals: No player has scored more than 6
Tries: No player has scored more than 3
Points: No player has scored more than 15
Highest score:
38-16 v. Doncaster, 1983-84
Highest against: 68-17 v. Leigh, 1983-84

1983-84 PLAYERS' SUMMARY

	App.	Tries	Goals	D/Gls	Pts
Armitage, Des	6 + 5	1	—	—	4
Atkinson, John	2	1	—	—	4
Bell, Ian	4	—	—	—	—
Binder, Tony	33	7	—	—	28
Birts, Jimmy	14 + 1	2	—	—	8
Brierley, Steve	12 + 5	—	—	—	—
Crowther, Ian	30	2	—	—	8
Evans, Graham	9 + 4	3	—	—	12
Ferres, Steve	13	1	21	2	48
Friend, Clayton	2 + 1	1	—	—	4
Gaitley, Bob	18 + 2	2	25	1	59
Hardy, Alan	13	—	—	4	4
Hobson, Ian	11 + 6	8	—	—	32
Langton, Steve	20 + 1	7	—	—	28
Limb, Barry	4 + 1	—	—	—	—
Lucas, Maurice	5	1	—	—	4
McDonald, Ian	11	6	—	—	24
Miller, Sean	23 + 3	1	—	—	4
Newton, Andy	15 + 1	2	27	—	62
Peacham, Gary	36	20	—	—	80
Pearson, Alan	1 + 2	—	3	—	6
Portz, Karl	32 + 4	2	—	—	8
Risman, John	19 + 4	3	—	—	12
Robinson, Brian	3 + 6	1	—	—	4
Robinson, Graeme	32 + 2	1	7	2	20
Robinson, Kevan	33	5	—	—	20
Sanderson, John	9 + 2	3	—	—	12
Scott, Tony	0 + 1	—	—	—	—
Smith, David	4	—	4	—	8
Starbuck, Paul	0 + 2	—	—	—	—
Sutton, Mick	32 + 1	3	—	1	13
Tissiman, Les	9 + 9	1	—	—	4
Todd, Alan	0 + 1	—	—	—	—
Ward, Martyn	7 + 4	3	—	—	12
Youngman, Wally	32	14	—	—	56
TOTALS 35 players		101	87	10	588

John Risman . . . three tries in 23 appearances.

1983-84 MATCH ANALYSIS

Date	Competition	H/A	Opponent	Rlt	Score	Tries	Goals	Attendance	Referee
21.8.83	SD	H	Workington T.	L	10-36	Youngman, Atkinson	Ferres	2613	Beaumont
28.8.83	SD	A	Keighley	L	14-18	Youngman	Ferres (5)	—	—
4.9.83	LC(1)	A	Leigh	L	10-52	Peacham, Newton	Ferres	—	—
10.9.83	SD	A	Cardiff C.	L	16-21	Peacham, Binder, Robinson	Ferres (2)	—	—
18.9.83	SD	H	Batley	W	21-14	Youngman, Ferres, Risman	Newton (4), Ferres (dg)	931	Mean
25.9.83	SD	A	Halifax	L	16-25	Youngman, Newton, Binder	Newton (2)	—	—
5.10.83	SD	A	Dewsbury	L	30-39	Hobson, Miller, Gaitley, Evans, Binder	Newton (5)	—	—
9.10.83	SD	H	Bramley	L	6-22	Tissiman	Newton	912	Walker
16.10.83	SD	A	Swinton	L	4-22	Youngman	—	—	—
23.10.83	SD	A	Hunslet	L	13-28	Peacham, Lucas	Ferres (2, 1 dg)	—	—
30.10.83	SD	H	Rochdale H.	L	22-24	Peacham, G. Robinson, Sanderson	Ferres (5)	725	Wall
6.11.83	JPS(1)	H	Workington T.	W	10-5	Youngman, Risman	Ferres	1297	Kershaw
13.11.83	SD	A	Kent Invicta	L	12-28	Youngman, Hobson	Ferres (2)	—	—
20.11.83	JPS(2)	H	Leigh	L	17-68	Risman, Youngman, Langton	Ferres (2), Sutton (dg)	2152	Whitfield
27.11.83	SD	H	Huddersfield	W	15-6	Sutton, Langton	Newton (3), Robinson (dg)	687	Haigh
4.12.83	SD	A	Batley	L	15-22	Birts, Langton, Hobson	G. Robinson (1, 1 dg)	—	—
18.12.83	SD	A	Rochdale H.	W	14-10	Friend, Langton	Newton (3)	—	—
26.12.83	SD	A	Workington T.	L	4-11	—	Newton (2)	—	—
5.2.84	CC(P)	H	Widnes	L	12-20	Portz, Sutton	Newton (2)	1271	Fox
19.2.84	SD	A	Huddersfield	W	14-10	Hobson, Peacham	Newton (3)	—	—
26.2.84	SD	H	Halifax	L	10-12	Ward, Youngman	Newton	883	Massey
4.3.84	SD	H	Swinton	L	4-26	Binder	—	804	Berry
11.3.84	SD	H	Doncaster	W	14-5	Gaitley, B. Robinson, Evans	Gaitley	524	Walker
18.3.84	SD	A	Barrow	L	18-58	Youngman, Peacham, Sanderson	Gaitley (3)	—	—
23.3.84	SD	H	Blackpool B.	W	16-14	Armitage, Evans	Gaitley (4)	452	Robinson
25.3.84	SD	H	Huyton	W	27-26	McDonald (2), Crowther, Peacham, Langton	Pearson (3), Hardy (dg)	447	Campbell
28.3.84	SD	H	Barrow	L	8-43	McDonald, Peacham	—	599	Berry
1.4.84	SD	H	York	L	24-26	Peacham (2), Birts, McDonald	Gaitley (3), Newton	350	Beaumont
4.4.84	SD	A	York	L	6-50	Sutton	G. Robinson	—	—
8.4.84	SD	A	Doncaster	W	38-16	Bind r (2), Peacham (2), Youngman, Sanderson, Hobson	Gaitley (5)	—	—
10.4.84	SD	A	Huyton	L	10-17	McDonald, Langton	Gaitley	—	—
13.4.84	SD	H	Keighley	W	29-19	Peacham (2) K. Robinson (2), Portz	Gaitley (4, 1dg)	437	Campbell
15.4.84	SD	H	Cardiff C.	W	14-10	Hobson (2)	G. Robinson (2), Hardy (2 dg)	649	Hodgson
20.4.84	SD	A	Bramley	L	18-22	Peacham, Langton, K. Robinson	G. Robinson (3)	—	—
22.4.84	SD	H	Kent Invicta	W	34-12	Peacham (3), Youngman (2), K. Robinson, Hobson	Smith (3)	870	Mean
26.4.84	SD	A	Blackpool B.	L	18-47	McDonald, Binder, Youngman, Peacham	Gaitley	—	—
29.4.84	SD	H	Dewsbury	L	0-19	—	—	500	Lindop
2.5.84	SD	H	Hunslet	W	25-22	Ward (2), Crowther, Peacham	Gaitley (3), Smith, Hardy (dg)	400	Fox

CASTLEFORD

Ground: Wheldon Road
Colours: Yellow jerseys with black panels, black shorts
First Season: 1926-27. There was also a Castleford team from 1896-97 to 1905-06, inclusive
Nickname: Glassblowers
Chairman: Gordon Appleyard
Secretary: Mrs Denise Cackett
Coach: Mal Reilly (Dec. 1974-)
Honours: **Championship** Beaten finalists, 1938-39, 1968-69
Challenge Cup Winners, 1934-35, 1968-69, 1969-70
Yorkshire League Winners, 1932-33, 1938-39, 1964-65
Yorkshire Cup Winners, 1977-78, 1981-82
Beaten finalists, 1948-49, 1950-51, 1968-69, 1971-72, 1983-84
Eastern Division Championship Beaten finalists, 1963-64
BBC2 Floodlit Trophy Winners, 1965-66, 1966-67, 1967-68, 1976-77
John Player Trophy Winners, 1976-77
Premiership Beaten finalists, 1983-84
Records: Attendance: 25,449 v. Hunslet (RL Cup) 3 March, 1935
Season
Goals: 158 by S. Lloyd, 1976-77
Tries: 36 by K. Howe, 1963-64
Points: 334 by R. Beardmore, 1983-84
Match
Goals: 17 by S. Lloyd v. Millom, 16 Sep, 1973
Tries: 5 by D. Foster v. Hunslet, 10 Nov, 1972; J. Joyner v. Millom, 16 Sep, 1973; S. Fenton v. Dewsbury, 27 Jan, 1978
Points: 43 by S. Lloyd v. Millom, 16 Sep, 1973
Highest score: 88-5 v. Millom, 1973-74
Highest against: 58-8 v. Workington T., 1953-54

1983-84 PLAYERS' SUMMARY

	App.	Tries	Goals	D/Gls	Pts
Anderson, Kevin	2 + 3	—	1	—	2
Atkins, Brett	14 + 2	12	—	—	48
Battye, Neil	1 + 5	—	—	—	—
Beardmore, Bob	34 + 2	13	140	2	334
Beardmore, Kevin	25	2	—	—	8
Coen, Darren	30 + 2	5	—	—	20
Connell, Gary	29	5	—	—	20
Crampton, Jimmy	16 + 1	5	—	—	20
England, Keith	30	6	—	—	24
Fenton, Steve	24	5	—	—	20
Freeman, Gary	15 + 2	4	—	—	16
Gill, Steve	16	3	—	—	12
Hardy, Alan	14	—	—	—	—
Higgins, Barry	12 + 2	4	—	—	16
Horton, Stuart	15	1	—	—	4
Hyde, Gary	34 + 2	17	26	—	120
James, Neil	19 + 11	5	—	—	20
Johnson, Barry	4	1	—	—	4
Jones, Kevin	5 + 3	2	—	—	8
Joyner, John	39 + 1	14	—	—	56
Kear, John	27 + 4	9	—	—	36
Marchant, Tony	36	16	—	—	64
Mountain, Dean	0 + 2	—	—	—	—
Orum, Ian	5 + 12	—	—	—	—
Reilly, Malcolm	6 + 3	1	—	—	4
Robinson, Steve	15	5	—	—	20
Roockley, David	19 + 3	1	3	1	11
Spedding, Paul	5 + 3	—	—	—	—
Timson, Andrew	12 + 2	2	—	—	8
Ward, Kevin	30	6	—	—	24
TOTALS 30 players		144	170	3	919

1983-84 MATCH ANALYSIS

Date	Competition	H/A	Opponent	Rlt	Score	Tries	Goals	Attendance	Referee
21.8.83	SLC	A	Featherstone R.	W	46-22	Hyde (2), R. Beardmore, K. Beardmore, Marchant, Higgins, Connell, Joyner	R. Beardmore (7)	—	—
24.8.83	SLC	A	Hull K. R.	W	26-14	R. Beardmore (2), Higgins, Joyner	R. Beardmore (5)	—	—
28.8.83	SLC	H	Hull	L	18-40	Jones, Connell, James	R. Beardmore (3)	6258	Whitfield

1983-84 MATCH ANALYSIS (continued)

Date	Competition	H/A	Opponent	Rlt	Score	Tries	Goals	Attendance	Referee
4.9.83	YC(1)	H	Huddersfield	W	36-20	Higgins (2), Fenton, England, Coen, Reilly	R. Beardmore (6)	2499	Berry
11.9.83	SLC	A	St. Helens	W	22-10	Hyde, James, Marchant, Connell	R. Beardmore (3)	—	—
14.9.83	YC(2)	A	Bradford N.	W	12-8	Connell	R. Beardmore (4)	—	—
18.9.83	SLC	H	Leigh	W	28-18	Ward, K. Beardmore, Hyde, Joyner	R. Beardmore (6)	4033	Court
23.9.83	YC(SF)	A	Wakefield T.	W	34-12	Fenton, Marchant, Coen, Hyde, Connell, Kear	R. Beardmore (4), Hyde	—	—
25.9.83	SLC	A	Salford	W	34-14	Crampton, Ward, Kear, England, R. Beardmore, Marchant	R. Beardmore (5)	—	—
2.10.83	SLC	H	Leeds	W	54-4	R. Beardmore (3), James (2), Kear, Fenton, Marchant	R. Beardmore (11)	5372	Allatt
9.10.83	SLC	A	Whitehaven	W	26-2	Marchant (2), Gill, Kear, R. Beardmore	R. Beardmore (2), Rookley	—	—
15.10.83	YC(F)	Leeds U FC	Hull	L	2-13	—	R. Beardmore	(14049)	Thompson
19.10.83	SLC	H	Oldham	L	16-18	Marchant (2), Fenton	R. Beardmore (2)	3880	Kershaw
30.10.83	SLC	H	Hull K. R.	L	8-18	—	R. Beardmore (4)	5706	Lindop
6.11.83	JPS(1)	H	Hull	L	4-8	—	R. Beardmore (2)	7979	Campbell
13.11.83	SLC	A	Leeds	W	28-10	Joyner, Hyde, R. Beardmore, Marchant	R. Beardmore (6)	—	—
20.11.83	SLC	H	Whitehaven	W	50-2	Timson (2), Kear (2), Hyde, Joyner, Coen, Ward	R. Beardmore (9)	2775	Smith
27.11.83	SLC	A	Warrington	L	14-16	England	R. Beardmore (5)	—	—
4.12.83	SLC	A	Fulham	D	6-6	—	R. Beardmore (3)	—	—
11.12.83	SLC	H	Salford	W	40-12	Joyner (4), England, Hyde, Crampton	Hyde (6)	2998	Beaumont
26.12.83	SLC	H	Wakefield T.	W	24-8	Freeman (2), Hyde, Johnson, Marchant	Hyde (2)	8329	Thompson
1.1.84	SLC	A	Bradford N.	D	2-2	—	R. Beardmore	—	—
8.1.84	SLC	A	Wigan	L	6-32	Crampton	R. Beardmore	—	—
1.2.84	SLC	A	Widnes	L	8-14	England	R. Beardmore (2)	—	—
5.2.84	SLC	H	Fulham	W	26-7	Freeman, Robinson, Joyner, Roockley, Hyde	R. Beardmore (3)	3132	Gocher (A)
11.2.84	CC(1)	A	Kent Invicta	W	42-20	Atkins (2), Ward (2), England, Hyde	R. Beardmore (9)	—	—
19.2.84	SLC	H	Bradford N.	W	29-6	Joyner (2), Gill, Hyde, R. Beardmore	R. Beardmore (4, 1dg)	5168	Whitfield
26.2.84	CC(2)	H	Warrington	W	23-16	Robinson (2), Hyde	R. Beardmore (5, 1dg)	8029	McDonald
4.3.84	SLC	H	Warrington	L	10-21	Horton	Hyde (3)	3799	Allatt
11.3.84	CC(3)	A	York	L	12-14	Robinson, Marchant, R. Beardmore (2)	—	—	
18.3.84	SLC	H	Featherstone R.	D	8-8	James	R. Beardmore (2)	4323	Spencer
25.3.84	SLC	H	St. Helens	W	26-22	Atkins (3), Jones	Hyde (3), R. Beardmore (2)	2560	Lindop
28.3.84	SLC	H	Wigan	W	38-10	Atkins (2), Fenton, Gill, Kear, Freeman	Hyde (7)	2825	Mean
1.4.84	SLC	A	Leigh	L	4-30	Hyde	—	—	—
8.4.84	SLC	A	Hull	L	10-40	Joyner, Hyde	Anderson	—	—
11.4.84	SLC	A	Oldham	W	13-2	Hyde	Hyde (4), Coen (dg)	—	—
15.4.84	SLC	H	Widnes	W	24-18	Coen, Robinson, Crampton, Kear, Atkins	Roockley (2)	3163	Thompson
23.4.84	SLC	A	Wakefield T.	W	42-12	R. Beardmore (2), Atkins (2), Marchant (2), Coen	R. Beardmore (7)	—	—
29.4.84	PT(1)	H	Widnes	W	36-4	Marchant (2), R. Beardmore, Atkins, Joyner	R. Beardmore (8)	3283	Smith
7.5.84	PT(SF)	A	Hull	W	22-12	Hyde, Atkins, Ward, Crampton	R. Beardmore (3)	—	—
12.5.84	PT(F)	Leeds	Hull K.R.	L	10-18	Kear	R. Beardmore (3)	(12515)	Campbell

DEWSBURY

Ground: Crown Flatt
Colours: Red, amber and black jerseys, white shorts
First Season: 1901-02
Chairman: John Senior
Secretary: Bernard Shooman
Player-Coach: Tommy Smales (May 1983 — Feb. 1984)
Jack Addy (Feb. 1984-)

Honours: **Championship** Winners, 1972-73
Beaten finalists, 1946-47
Division Two Champions, 1904-05
Challenge Cup Winners, 1911-12, 1942-43
Beaten finalists, 1928-29
Yorkshire League Winners, 1946-47
Yorkshire Cup Winners, 1925-26, 1927-28, 1942-43
Beaten finalists, 1918-19, 1921-22, 1940-41, 1972-73
BBC2 Floodlit Trophy Beaten finalists, 1975-76
War League Championship Winners, 1941-42. (1942-43 won final but championship declared null and void because Dewsbury played an ineligible player).
Beaten finalists, 1943-44

Records: Attendance: 26,584 v. Halifax (Yorkshire Cup) 30 October, 1920

Season
Goals: 145 by N. Stephenson, 1972-73
Tries: 40 by D. Thomas, 1906-07
Points: 368 by N. Stephenson, 1972-73

Match
Goals: 10 by J. Ledgard v. Yorkshire Amateurs, 13 Sep, 1947; N. Stephenson v. Blackpool B, 28 Aug, 1972
Tries: 8 by D. Thomas v. Liverpool C, 13 Apr, 1907
Points: 29 by J. Lyman v. Hull, 22 Apr, 1919
Highest score: 64-0 v. Liverpool C., 1906-07
Highest against:
62-5 v. Hull, 1957-58
62-2 v. Halifax, 1957-58

1983-84 PLAYERS' SUMMARY

	App.	Tries	Goals	D/Gls	Pts
Barron, Steve	5	1	—	—	4
Briggs, David	2	—	—	—	—
Brunt, Allan	5	—	—	—	—
Buckton, John	0 + 3	—	—	—	—
Catling, Geoff	13	1	—	2	6
Cockx, Richard	8 + 7	—	—	—	—
Collins, Mike	35	12	—	—	48
Dickinson, Allan	7	—	—	—	—
Diskin, Tony	12 + 2	—	—	—	—
Dufton, Steve	19	1	—	—	4
Dunford, Shaun	35	5	87	1	195
Fox, Phil	1	—	—	—	—
Jennings, Paul	16 + 6	2	—	—	8
Kelly, Neil	31 + 1	7	—	1	29
Keyworth, Mark	34 + 1	17	—	2	70
King, Gerald	17 + 2	—	—	—	—
Lowe, Ernest	0 + 1	—	—	—	—
Marsden, Graham	11 + 1	1	—	—	4
Mason, Keith	29 + 1	—	—	—	—
Mitchell, Gary	6	—	—	—	—
Mook, Graham	33 + 1	9	—	—	36
Moore, John	9	1	—	—	4
Paterson, John	0 + 1	—	—	—	—
Pickerill, Neil	3 + 2	2	—	—	8
Plummer, Adrian	3 + 3	—	—	—	—
Ramsden, Andrew	29 + 1	7	—	—	28
Richardson, Don	12 + 1	1	—	—	4
Snee, Mick	6 + 2	1	—	—	4
Squires, Chris	29 + 2	12	—	1	49
Talbot, Gordon	1 + 3	1	—	1	5
Vasey, Chris	34	8	3	—	38
Walker, Chris	3 + 3	—	1	—	2
Westbury, Mark	4 + 2	1	—	—	4
Wood, David	21 + 3	1	—	—	4
Womersley, Shaun	8	1	—	—	4
TOTALS					
35 players		92	91	8	558

1983-84 MATCH ANALYSIS

Date	Competition	H/A	Opponent	Rlt	Score	Tries	Goals	Attendance	Referee
21.8.83	SD	A	Bramley	L	18-28	Collins, Squires, Catling	S. Dunford (3)	—	—
24.8.83	SD	A	York	W	12-10	Keyworth	S. Dunford (4)	—	—
28.8.83	SD	H	Halifax	L	14-24	Keyworth, Vasey	S. Dunford (3)	918	Wall
4.9.83	YC(1)	H	Keighley	L	8-18	Squires	S. Dunford (2)	518	Thompson
11.9.83	SD	A	Barrow	L	4-42	—	S. Dunford (2)	—	—
18.9.83	SD	H	Blackpool B.	L	18-20	Squires, Vasey, Barron	S. Dunford (3)	478	Spencer
25.9.83	SD	A	Huyton	L	10-12	S. Dunford, Richardson	S. Dunford	—	—
2.10.83	SD	H	Keighley	W	28-18	Squires, S. Dunford, Moore, Ramsden, Vasey	S. Dunford (4)	596	Kershaw
5.10.83	SD	H	Carlisle	W	39-30	Keyworth (2), Collins, Westbury, Vasey, Marsden, Ramsden, Squires	S. Dunford (2), Walker, Keyworth (dg)	520	Beaumont
9.10.83	SD	A	Cardiff C.	L	14-26	Vasey, Keyworth	S. Dunford (3)	—	—
16.10.83	SD	H	York	L	10-12	Kelly, Mook	S. Dunford	550	Mean
23.10.83	SD	A	Kent Invicta	L	16-28	Dufton, Collins	S. Dunford (4)	—	—
30.10.83	SD	H	Barrow	L	6-26	Mook	S. Dunford	602	Fox
6.11.83	JPS(1)	H	Keighley	L	14-17	Wood, Ramsden	S. Dunford (3)	814	Thompson
13.11.83	SD	A	Keighley	W	23-19	Kelly (2), Vasey	S. Dunford (5), Squires (dg)	—	—
20.11.83	SD	A	Hunslet	W	32-28	Squires (2), Keyworth, Pickerill, Kelly	S. Dunford (6)	—	—
27.11.83	SD	H	Workington T.	L	22-28	Keyworth (2), Squires, Collins	S. Dunford (3)	655	Robinson
4.12.83	SD	A	Huddersfield	L	12-26	Mook, Ramsden	S. Dunford (2)	—	—
18.12.83	SD	A	Workington T.	L	6-32	Keyworth	S. Dunford	—	—
26.12.83	SD	H	Batley	L	10-16	Pickerill	S. Dunford (3)	1535	Hodgson
1.1.84	SD	A	Batley	W	6-4	Kelly	S. Dunford	—	—
8.1.84	SD	H	Doncaster	W	20-0	Squires, Kelly, Jennings, Collins	S. Dunford (2)	596	Holdsworth
15.1.84	SD	A	Swinton	L	2-42	—	S. Dunford	—	—
5.2.84	SD	A	Blackpool B.	L	6-24	Jennings	S. Dunford	—	—
12.2.84	CC(1)	A	Widnes	L	10-54	Mook, Keyworth	S. Dunford	—	—
26.2.84	SD	H	Kent Invicta	W	15-2	Keyworth, Collins	S. Dunford (3), Catlin (dg)	550	Walker
4.3.84	SD	A	Doncaster	W	24-15	Collins (2), S. Dunford, Mook	S. Dunford (4)	—	—
11.3.84	SD	H	Bramley	L	7-20	Keyworth	S. Dunford, Catlin (dg)	768	Mean
18.3.84	SD	A	Rochdale H.	L	21-38	S. Dunford (2), Ramsden	S. Dunford (4, 1dg)	—	—
25.3.84	SD	H	Cardiff C.	L	12-16	Squires, Mook	S. Dunford (2)	450	Smith
1.4.84	SD	H	Rochdale H.	W	42-15	Collins (2), Squires, Mook, Ramsden, Kelly, Vasey	S. Dunford (7)	561	Allatt
4.4.84	SD	H	Huyton	L	9-15	Talbot, Squires	Talbot (dg)	454	Kershaw
8.4.84	SD	A	Halifax	L	0-19	—	—	—	—
15.4.84	SD	H	Swinton	W	22-13	Mook, Keyworth, Ramsden, Collins	S. Dunford (3)	839	Fox
18.4.84	SD	H	Huddersfield	L	13-22	Keyworth, Collins	S. Dunford, Vasey, Keyworth (dg)	742	Mean
23.4.84	SD	H	Hunslet	L	14-28	Keyworth (2), Vasey	Vasey	1184	Robinson
29.4.84	SD	A	Carlisle	W	19-0	Womersley, Mook, Snee, Keyworth	Vasey, Kelly (dg)	—	—

DONCASTER

Ground: Tatters Field
Colours: White jerseys with blue and gold bands, white shorts
First Season: 1951-52
Nickname: Dons
Chairman: John Barron
General Manager: Tom Morton
Coach: Clive Sullivan MBE (Mar. 1983-May 1984)
John Sheridan (June 1984-)
Records: Attendance: 4,793 v. Wakefield T. (League) 7 April, 1962. There was an attendance of 10,000 for a Challenge Cup tie against Bradford N. at York Road Stadium on 16 Feb, 1952

Season
Goals: 91 by D. Noble, 1981-82
Tries: 18 by J. Buckton, 1981-82, 1982-83
Points: 188 by D. Noble, 1982-83

Match
Goals: 9 by D. Towle v. York, 9 Sep, 1967
Tries: 4 by V. Grace v. Rochdale H, 4 Oct, 1952; B. Tasker v. Leeds, 26 Oct, 1963; J. Buckton v. Rochdale H, 30 Aug, 1981
Points: 18 by D. Towle v. York, 9 Sep, 1967; I. Fortis v. Blackpool B, 5 Sep, 1970
Highest score: 43-5 v. Batley, 1964-65
Highest against: 75-3 v. Leigh, 1975-76

1983-84 PLAYERS' SUMMARY

	App.	Tries	Goals	D/Gls	Pts
Atherton, Clive	4 + 9	—	—	—	—
Briggs, Andy	1 + 1	1	—	—	4
Buckton, John	31 + 1	9	—	—	36
Chester, Robin	19	8	—	—	32
Deighton, Kevin	1 + 2	1	—	—	4
Douglas, Graham	19 + 1	1	—	—	4
Ellis, Graham	12 + 4	—	—	—	—
Ellis, Ken	35	—	—	—	—
Harrison, Neil	1	—	—	—	—
Jeff, Tony	26 + 4	3	—	—	12
Knapp, Conrad	7 + 1	—	—	—	—
Knott, Kevin	39 + 1	6	—	—	24
Leighton, Steve	2 + 1	1	—	—	4
Marshall, Alf	28 + 3	3	—	—	12
Masson, James	31 + 3	4	—	—	16
McHugh, Gary	8	1	—	—	4
Mears, Brian	13	—	12	—	24
Noble, David	30 + 1	1	54	19	131
Pearson, Ian	6	—	—	—	—
Peat, John	8 + 5	1	—	—	4
Pennant, Milton	10 + 1	1	—	—	4
Perigo, Graham	5 + 7	—	—	—	—
Pflange, David	14 + 1	2	—	—	8
Portz, Jimmy	20	—	—	—	—
Russell, John	32 + 6	8	—	—	32
Salmon, Tony	14	3	—	—	12
Smith, Ray	26 + 1	7	—	—	28
Straw, Peter	5 + 2	1	—	—	4
Sullivan, Clive	1 + 3	—	—	—	—
Tyers, Andy	16	—	10	—	20
Wileman, Roy	3 + 1	—	—	—	—
Wilkes, Calvin	24 + 3	7	—	—	28
Wilkinson, Terry	1	—	—	—	—
Williams, Chappie	24 + 3	1	—	—	4
Wilson, Ray	4 + 1	1	—	—	4
TOTALS					
35 players		71	76	19	455

Clive Sullivan ... resigned as coach in May 1984.

1983-84 MATCH ANALYSIS

Date	Com-petition	H/A	Opponent	Rlt	Score	Tries	Goals	Atten-dance	Referee
21.8.83	SD	A	Hunslet	L	18-50	Buckton (2), Russell	Tyas (3)	—	—
24.8.83	SD	H	Keighley	W	30-0	Marshall, Williams, Wilkes, Russell, Buckton	Tyas (5)	218	Kendrew
28.8.83	SD	A	Kent Invicta	L	12-22	Wilkes, Marshall	Tyas (2)	—	—
4.9.83	YC(1)	H	Bramley	W	16-12	Salmon (2), Wilson, Buckton	—	357	Kershaw
11.9.83	SD	A	Rochdale H.	L	20-40	Leighton, Buckton, Wilkes	Noble (4)	—	—
14.9.83	YC(2)	A	Wakefield T.	L	14-32	Knott, Deighton	Noble (3)	—	—
18.9.83	SD	H	York	L	10-44	McHugh	Noble (3)	478	Berry
25.9.83	SD	A	Batley	L	12-34	Peat, Buckton	Noble (2)	—	—
2.10.83	SD	H	Cardiff C.	L	8-36	Russell	Noble (2)	198	Spencer
9.10.83	SD	A	Barrow	L	0-30	—	—	—	—
16.10.83	SD	H	Halifax	L	12-37	Salmon, Russell	Noble (2)	471	Beaumont
23.10.83	JPS(P)	A	Batley	W	12-11	Buckton	Noble (4)	—	—
30.10.83	SD	H	Batley	W	21-10	Smith, Knott	Noble (5, 3 dg)	323	Thompson
6.11.83	JPS(1)	H	Salford	L	11-22	Russell	Noble (3, 1 dg)	458	Mean
13.11.83	SD	A	York	L	9-40	Knott	Noble (2, 1 dg)	—	—
20.11.83	SD	A	Huddersfield	L	11-19	Smith (2)	Noble (1, 1 dg)	—	—
27.11.83	SD	H	Rochdale H.	L	12-36	Smith (2)	Noble (2)	251	Allatt
4.12.83	SD	A	Workington T.	L	4-44	Jeff	—	—	—
18.12.83	SD	A	Keighley	L	12-30	Briggs, Smith	Noble (2)	—	—
26.12.83	SD	A	Bramley	L	0-32	—	—	—	—
1.1.84	SD	H	Bramley	L	7-34	Chester	Noble (1, 1 dg)	254	Fox
8.1.84	SD	A	Dewsbury	L	0-20	—	—	—	—
5.2.84	SD	H	Hunslet	L	12-14	Smith, Jeff	Noble (2)	376	Lindop
12.2.84	CC(1)	H	Batley	W	11-8	Masson	Noble (2, 3dg)	634	Mean
19.2.84	SD	A	Swinton	L	0-42	—	—	—	—
26.2.84	CC(2)	A	Hull K.R.	L	7-40	Noble	Noble (1, 1dg)	—	—
4.3.84	SD	H	Dewsbury	L	15-24	Pflange, Douglas, Chester	Noble (1, 1dg)	301	Wall
11.3.84	SD	A	Carlisle	L	5-14	Jeff	Noble (dg)	—	—
18.3.84	SD	H	Huddersfield	L	0-36	—	—	284	Smith
25.3.84	SD	H	Swinton	L	2-28	—	Noble (2 dg)	250	Haigh
1.4.84	SD	A	Blackpool B.	L	12-36	Knott, Marshall	Mears (2)	—	—
4.4.84	SD	A	Halifax	L	6-43	Buckton	Mears	—	—
8.4.84	SD	H	Carlisle	L	16-38	Chester (2), Masson	Mears (2)	154	Fox
15.4.84	SD	A	Huyton	L	22-44	Russell, Straw, Pflange, Buckton	Mears (3)	—	—
20.4.84	SD	A	Cardiff C.	L	21-32	Wilkes, Chester, Russell	Noble (4, 1dg)	—	—
22.4.84	SD	H	Barrow	L	0-66	—	—	228	Massey
23.4.84	SD	H	Blackpool B.	L	16-44	Wilkes (2), Chester	Noble (2)	130	Thompson
27.4.84	SD	H	Workington T.	L	23-24	Chester (2), Knott, Pennant	Noble (3, 1dg)	105	Campbell
29.4.84	SD	H	Kent Invicta	L	20-24	Masson, Knott, Russell	Noble (3, 2dg)	170	Walker
2.5.84	SD	H	Huyton	D	16-16	Wilkes, Masson	Mears (4)	137	Hodgson

FEATHERSTONE ROVERS

Ground: Post Office Road
Colours: Blue and white hooped jerseys, blue shorts
First Season: 1921-22
Nickname: Colliers
Chairman: Bob Ashby
Secretary: Terry Jones
Coach: Allan Agar (Dec. 1982-)
Honours: **Challenge Cup** Winners, 1966-67, 1972-73, 1982-83
Runners-up, 1951-52, 1973-74
Championship Beaten finalists, 1927-28
Division One Champions, 1976-77
Division Two Champions, 1979-80
Yorkshire Cup Winners, 1939-40, 1959-60
Beaten finalists, 1928-29, 1963-64, 1966-67, 1969-70, 1970-71, 1976-77, 1977-78
Captain Morgan Trophy Beaten finalists, 1973-74
Records: Attendance: 17,531 v. St. Helens (RL Cup) 21 March, 1959
Season
Goals: 163 by S. Quinn, 1979-80
Tries: 31 by C. Woolford, 1958-59
Points: 375 by S. Quinn, 1979-80
Match
Goals: 12 by D. Fox v. Stanningley, 8 Feb, 1964
Tries: 6 by M. Smith v. Doncaster, 13 Apr, 1968
Points: 29 by S. Quinn v. Doncaster, 4 Nov, 1979
Highest score: 65-5 v. Whitehaven, 1970-71
Highest against: 70-2 v. Halifax, 1940-41

1983-84 PLAYERS' SUMMARY

	App.	Tries	Goals	D/Gls	Pts
Banks, Alan	32 + 1	6	—	—	24
Bardgett, Joe	26 + 2	3	—	—	12
Barends, David	24 + 1	6	—	—	24
Barker, Nigel	25 + 2	2	—	—	8
Barker, Steve	0 + 1	—	—	—	—
Bell, Keith	2 + 1	—	—	—	—
Chapman, Tony	8 + 3	2	—	—	8
Clarkson, Geoff	11 + 1	—	—	—	—
Clarkson, Peter	4	—	—	—	—
Dakin, Alan	1 + 4	1	—	—	4
Fox, Deryck	30 + 2	6	19	7	69
Gibbins, Mick	13 + 5	—	—	—	—
Gilbert, John	8	1	—	—	4
Hankins, Steve	24	2	—	—	8
Hobbs, David	25 + 2	9	4	8	52
Hopkins, Calvin	0 + 3	1	—	—	4
Hudson, Terry	25 + 4	1	—	—	4
Johnson, Phil	4 + 1	—	—	—	—
Lund, Steve	7	1	—	—	4
Lyman, Paul	10 + 6	3	—	—	12
Marsden, John	0 + 2	—	—	—	—
Marsh, Richard	27 + 3	10	—	—	40
McMahon, Allan	9	—	—	—	—
Mortimer, Andrew	1	—	—	—	—
Nicholson, Tony	2	—	—	—	—
Pickerill, Neil	4	1	—	—	4
Quinn, Steve	30	4	74	3	167
Robinson, Tim	1	—	—	—	—
Saddington, Malcolm	1	—	—	—	—
Siddall, Gary	30 + 1	4	—	—	16
Slater, Ian	7	3	—	—	12
Slatter, Tim	10 + 4	2	—	—	8
Smith, Peter	1 + 1	—	—	—	—
Spurr, Bob	35	8	—	—	32
Stone, Charlie	14	1	—	—	4
Tonks, Kevin	0 + 1	—	—	—	—
Tuffs, Neil	1	—	—	—	—
Ward, Garry	2 + 2	—	—	—	—
Welburn, Chris	1	—	—	—	—
TOTALS					
39 players		77	97	18	520

David Hobbs ... Great Britain tourist.

1983-84 MATCH ANALYSIS

Date	Competition	H/A	Opponent	Rlt	Score	Tries	Goals	Attendance	Referee
21.8.83	SLC	H	Castleford	L	22-46	Banks, Marsh, Pickerill	Quinn (5)	4737	Haigh
28.8.83	SLC	A	Fulham	L	11-21	Hobbs	Quinn (3), Hobbs (dg)	—	—
4.9.83	YC(1)	A	Hull	L	8-24	Slatter	Quinn (2)	—	—
11.9.83	SLC	H	Oldham	L	16-24	Hobbs, Spurr, Siddall	Quinn (2)	2711	Thompson
18.9.83	SLC	A	Whitehaven	W	18-14	Spurr, Hobbs, Hudson	Quinn (3)	—	—
25.9.83	SLC	H	Warrington	W	32-16	Hobbs (3), Spurr, Siddall	Fox (5), Hobbs	2309	Berry
7.10.83	SLC	H	Wakefield T.	L	8-12	Quinn	Quinn (2)	3458	Campbell
16.10.83	SLC	A	Bradford N.	L	10-30	Fox, Gilbert	Quinn	—	—
19.10.83	SLC	A	Widnes	L	4-40	Marsh	—	—	—
30.10.83	SLC	A	St. Helens	L	13-19	Spurr, Marsh	Quinn (2), Fox (dg)	—	—
6.11.83	JPS(1)	H	Fulham	W	12-10	Barends	Fox (2, 2 dg), Hobbs (2 dg)	2011	Spencer
13.11.83	SLC	H	Whitehaven	W	52-10	Fox (2), Chapman (2), Bardgett (2), Banks, Marsh, Barends	Fox (8)	1890	Kendrew
20.11.83	JPS(2)	H	Hull	W	20-14	Barends, N. Barker, Fox	Fox (4)	7833	Holdsworth
27.11.83	JPS(3)	A	St. Helens	L	12-16	Hankins, Marsh	Quinn (2)	—	—
4.12.83	SLC	H	Widnes	W	21-6	Quinn, Hobbs	Quinn (6), Hobbs (dg)	2877	Lindop
18.12.83	SLC	H	Leeds	D	12-12	Marsh	Quinn (4)	4156	Kershaw
27.12.83	SLC	A	Hull	L	4-37	—	Quinn (2)	—	—
2.1.84	SLC	H	Hull	L	12-22	Banks, Barends	Quinn (2)	5479	Allatt
8.1.84	SLC	H	Salford	W	30-18	Hobbs, Hankins, Bardgett, Banks, Spurr	Quinn (5)	2269	McDonald
11.1.84	SLC	H	Wigan	W	15-6	Banks, Marsh	Quinn (2, 2 dg), Hobbs (dg)	3023	Robinson
15.1.84	SLC	A	Hull K.R.	L	0-34	—	—	—	—
29.1.84	SLC	A	Leigh	W	18-16	Quinn, Siddall, Stone	Quinn (3)	—	—
1.2.84	SLC	A	Oldham	W	19-4	Fox (2), Marsh	Quinn (2), Hobbs (2dg) Fox (dg)	—	—
5.2.84	SLC	A	Wakefield T.	L	1-8	—	Fox (dg)	—	—
12.2.84	CC(1)	A	Bradford N.	L	4-20	—	Quinn (2)	—	—
19.2.84	SLC	A	Salford	W	10-6	Quinn	Quinn (3)	—	—
24.2.84	SLC	H	Leigh	L	5-21	Barends	Fox (dg)	2081	Volante
4.3.84	SLC	H	St. Helens	L	13-21	Marsh, Spurr	Quinn (2), Fox (dg)	2111	Smith
9.3.84	SLC	A	Warrington	L	22-23	Spurr (2), Siddall	Hobbs (3), Quinn (2)	—	—
18.3.84	SLC	A	Castleford	D	8-8	—	Quinn (3, 1dg), Hobbs (dg)	—	—
25.3.84	SLC	H	Hull K.R.	L	18-24	Banks, Slater, N. Barker	Quinn (3)	3406	Fox
1.4.84	SLC	A	Wigan	L	12-26	Slater, Lyman	Quinn (2)	—	—
8.4.84	SLC	H	Bradford N.	W	10-8	Barends	Quinn (3)	3009	Walker
13.4.84	SLC	A	Leeds	L	10-12	Marsh, Slater	Quinn	—	—
22.4.84	SLC	H	Fulham	W	38-18	Lyman (2), Hobbs, Lund, Dakin, Slatter, Hopkins	Quinn (5)	1961	Volante

FULHAM

Ground: Craven Cottage
Colours: Black jerseys with red and white chevron, black shorts
First Season: 1980-81
Nickname: Londoners
Chairman: Ernie Clay
Secretary: Mrs Y. Haines
Player-Coach: Reg Bowden (July 1980-June 1984)
Honours: **Division Two** Champions, 1982-83
Records: Attendance: 15,013 v. Wakefield T. (RL Cup) 15 February, 1981

Season
Goals: 136 by S. Diamond, 1982-83
Tries: 27 by J. Crossley, 1982-83
Points: 308 by S. Diamond, 1982-83

Match
Goals: 8 by I. MacCorquodale v. Huddersfield, 12 Oct, 1980
Tries: No player has scored more than 3
Points: 18 by I. MacCorquodale v. Huddersfield, 12 Oct, 1980
Highest score: 50-5 v. Huyton, 1982-83
Highest against: 58-32 v. Warrington, 1983-84

1983-84 PLAYERS' SUMMARY

	App.	Tries	Goals	D/Gls	Pts
Allen, David	21 + 3	5	—	—	20
Bayliss, Steve	25	8	—	—	32
Beverley, Harry	27 + 1	—	—	—	—
Bowden, Reg	31 + 1	—	—	—	—
Butler, John	1 + 2	—	—	—	—
Cambriani, Adrian	6 + 1	2	—	—	8
Crossley, John	24 + 1	6	—	—	24
Dalgreen, John	7	—	—	—	—
Dearden, Alan	21+ 1	1	—	—	4
Diamond, Steve	35	5	77	3	177
Doherty, Joe	24 + 3	2	—	—	8
Eckersley, David	14 + 2	1	—	1	5
Ganley, Chris	9 + 1	1	—	—	4
Gourley, Tony	25 + 1	—	—	—	—
Herdman, Martin	12 + 1	2	—	—	8
Hoare, Sean	4 + 9	—	—	—	—
Hodson, Mark	1	—	—	—	—
Hull, David	24	4	—	—	16
Jackson, Robert	8	1	—	—	4
Jones, Charlie	14 + 5	1	—	—	4
Kinsey, Tony	29 + 3	3	—	9	21
Lester, Roy	1 + 1	—	—	—	—
M'Barki, Hussein	32	17	—	—	68
Mills, Steve	9 + 6	3	—	—	12
Souto, Peter	12	1	—	—	4
Stockley, Trevor	31 + 1	10	—	—	40
Tabern, Ray	7	1	—	—	4
Ward, Jimmy	1 + 2	1	—	—	4
TOTALS					
28 players		75	77	13	467

David Hull . . . four tries in 24 appearances.

1983-84 MATCH ANALYSIS

Date	Competition	H/A	Opponent	Rlt	Score	Tries	Goals	Attendance	Referee
21.8.83	SLC	A	Wakefield T.	L	14-18	Stockley, M'Barki, Bayliss	Diamond	—	—
24.8.83	SLC	A	Leigh	L	8-22	Bayliss	Diamond (2)	—	—
28.8.83	SLC	H	Featherstone R.	W	21-11	M'Barki (2), Bayliss, Ganley	Diamond (2), Kinsey (dg)	2401	Walker
4.9.83	LC(1)	A	Salford	L	15-16	M'Barki, Stockley	Diamond (3), Kinsey (dg)	—	—
11.9.83	SLC	H	Whitehaven	W	24-6	Bayliss, Diamond, M'Barki, Hull	Diamond (4)	2010	Berry
18.9.83	SLC	A	Oldham	L	12-30	Doherty (2)	Diamond (2)	—	—
25.9.83	SLC	H	Hull	W	29-24	Allen (2), Bayliss, M'Barki, Crossley	Diamond (4), Kinsey (dg)	3838	Robinson
2.10.83	SLC	A	Warrington	L	9-29	Kinsey	Diamond (2, 1 dg)	—	—
9.10.83	SLC	A	St. Helens	L	14-18	M'Barki, Diamond	Diamond (3)	—	—
16.10.83	SLC	H	Leeds	L	10-44	Crossley, Bayliss	Diamond	2994	Wall
22.10.83	SLC	H	Wakefield T.	W	16-14	M'Barki, Crossley, Stockley	Diamond (2)	1546	Beaumont
30.10.83	SLC	A	Bradford N.	L	2-21	—	Diamond	—	—
6.11.83	JPS(1)	A	Featherstone R.	L	10-12	Hull	Diamond, Kinsey (4 dg)	—	—
13.11.83	SLC	A	Hull K. R.	L	10-42	M'Barki, Stockley	Diamond	—	—
20.11.83	SLC	H	Oldham	W	21-4	Cambriani, Dearden, Kinsey	Diamond (4), Eckersley (dg)	2437	Massey
4.12.83	SLC	H	Castleford	D	6-6	M'Barki	Diamond	2515	Spencer
11.12.83	SLC	A	Hull	L	11-36	Cambriani, M'Barki	Diamond, Kinsey (dg)	—	—
18.12.83	SLC	H	Bradford N.	L	6-16	Herdman	Diamond	2482	Thompson
26.12.83	SLC	A	Leeds	L	6-30	Hull	Diamond	—	—
2.1.84	SLC	A	Salford	W	6-4	Eckersley	Diamond	—	—
8.1.84	SLC	H	Hull K. R.	L	18-38	Mills (2), Jackson	Diamond (3)	3037	Haigh
22.1.84	SLC	H	St. Helens	L	0-30	—	—	2067	McDonald
29.1.84	CC(P)	H	Swinton	W	14-4	Allen, Jones, Bayliss	Diamond	1680	Holdsworth
5.2.84	SLC	A	Castleford	L	7-26	—	Diamond (3), Kinsey (dg)	—	—
12.2.84	CC(1)	A	Whitehaven	W	17-10	Allen, Stockley	Diamond (4, 1dg)	—	—
19.2.84	SLC	H	Wigan	W	22-10	Diamond (2), M'Barki, Crossley	Diamond (3)	2293	Kendrew
26.2.84	CC(2)	H	Widnes	L	10-12	M'Barki, Herdman	Diamond	3591	Smith
4.3.84	SLC	A	Whitehaven	L	0-18	—	—	—	—
18.3.84	SLC	A	Wigan	L	18-38	Crossley, M'Barki, Hull	Diamond (3)	—	—
21.3.84	SLC	A	Widnes	W	16-14	M'Barki, Allen, Stockley	Diamond (2)	—	—
25.3.84	SLC	H	Leigh	L	12-24	Stockley, Bayliss	Diamond (2)	1464	Massey
8.4.84	SLC	H	Salford	L	10-12	Crossley	Diamond (3)	1622	Lindop
15.4.84	SLC	H	Warrington	L	32-58	Souto, Tabern, Stockley, Mills, M'Barki	Diamond (6)	1719	Whitfield
22.4.84	SLC	A	Featherstone R.	L	18-38	Kinsey, Diamond, Stockley	Diamond (3)	—	—
25.4.84	SLC	H	Widnes	W	23-13	Stockley, M'Barki, Ward	Diamond (5, 1dg)	1146	Fox

HALIFAX

Ground: Thrum Hall
Colours: Blue and white hooped jerseys, white shorts
First Season: 1895-96
Nickname: Thrum Hallers
Chairman: Stan Ackroyd
Secretary: Bernard Kearns
Coach: Colin Dixon (Oct. 1982-)
Honours: **Championship** Winners, 1906-07, 1964-65
Beaten finalists, 1952-53, 1953-54, 1955-56, 1965-66
Division One Champions, 1902-03
War League Beaten finalists, 1942-43, 1944-45
Challenge Cup Winners, 1902-03, 1903-04, 1930-31, 1938-39
Beaten finalists, 1920-21, 1940-41, 1941-42, 1948-49, 1953-54, 1955-56
Yorkshire League Winners, 1908-09, 1920-21, 1952-53, 1953-54, 1955-56, 1957-58
Eastern Division Championship Winners, 1963-64
Yorkshire Cup Winners, 1908-09, 1944-45, 1954-55, 1955-56, 1963-64
Beaten finalists, 1905-06, 1907-08, 1941-42, 1979-80
John Player Trophy Winners, 1971-72
Records: Attendance: 29,153 v. Wigan (RL Cup) 21 March, 1959
Season
Goals: 147 by T. Griffiths, 1955-56
Tries: 48 by J. Freeman, 1956-57
Points: 297 by T. Griffiths, 1955-56
Match
Goals: 14 by B. Burton v. Hunslet, 27 Aug, 1972
Tries: 8 by K. Williams v. Dewsbury, 9 Nov, 1957
Points: 31 by B. Burton v. Hunslet, 27 Aug, 1972
Highest score: 76-8 v. Hunslet, 1972-73
Highest against: 64-0 v. Wigan, 1922-23

1983-84 PLAYERS' SUMMARY

	App.	Tries	Goals	D/Gls	Pts
Agar, Malcolm	29 + 5	13	88	6	234
Beevers, Graham	11 + 2	1	—	—	4
Bentley, Lindsay	1	—	—	—	—
Bond, Steve	29 + 1	6	—	1	25
Brennan, Peter	1 + 1	—	—	—	—
Carroll, John	12	—	—	1	1
Cawood, Gary	30	7	—	2	30
Cerchione, Mario	1 + 2	1	—	—	4
Dickinson, Andy	24 + 1	15	—	—	60
Garrod, Graham	27	9	—	—	36
Goodall, Adrian	1 + 1	—	—	—	—
Goodwin, Neil	15	—	—	—	—
Greenwood, Brett	4 + 4	1	—	—	4
Hall, Steve	1	—	—	—	—
Humphreys, Lee	0 + 6	1	—	—	4
Langton, Terry	31 + 2	7	—	3	31
Laws, Steve	3	—	—	—	—
Marshall, Nigel	10 + 3	1	—	1	5
Martin, Paul	11 + 5	3	—	—	12
McCallion, Seamus	9	2	—	—	8
Moses, Paul	27 + 2	4	—	9	25
O'Byrne, Mick	37	17	—	—	68
Pritchard, Neil	5 + 2	—	—	—	—
Roberts, Ken	0 + 1	—	—	—	—
Sharp, Greg	28 + 2	2	—	—	8
Shillito, Alan	24 + 4	9	—	—	36
Smith, Steve	31	7	26	—	80
Waites, Keith	31 + 2	17	—	—	68
Walton, David	20 + 8	2	—	—	8
Whitehouse, Nigel	28	—	—	—	—
Wilson, Scott	0 + 2	—	—	—	—
TOTALS					
31 players		125	114	23	751

Bruce Burton ... record goals in a match scorer.

1983-84 MATCH ANALYSIS

Date	Competition	H/A	Opponent	Rlt	Score	Tries	Goals	Attendance	Referee
21.8.83	SD	H	Huyton	D	20-20	Moses, Langton, Waites	Agar (4)	918	Robinson
28.8.83	SD	A	Dewsbury	W	24-14	Agar, Smith, Waites	Agar (5), Cawood (dg), Moses (dg)	—	—
4.9.83	YC(1)	A	Wakefield T.	L	10-18	Cerchione, O'Byrne	Agar	—	—
11.9.83	SD	H	Bramley	W	18-12	Waites (3), O'Byrne	Moses (2 dg)	912	Volante
18.9.83	SD	A	Rochdale H.	W	18-6	Agar (3)	Agar (3)	—	—
25.9.83	SD	H	Carlisle	W	25-16	O'Byrne, Smith, Cawood, Garrod	Agar (4), Moses (dg)	1304	Allatt
2.10.83	SD	A	Swinton	W	35-22	O'Byrne (2), Moses, Bond, Waites, Shillito	Agar (5), Moses (dg)	—	—
9.10.83	SD	H	Blackpool B.	W	10-8	Garrod, Shillito	Agar	1518	Thompson
16.10.83	SD	A	Doncaster	W	37-12	Shillito (2), Martin (2), Garrod, Cawood	Agar (6), Moses (dg)	—	—
30.10.83	SD	H	York	W	17-4	O'Byrne, Sharp	Agar (4, 1 dg)	1472	Tickle (Pr)
6.11.83	JPS(1)	H	Barrow	L	12-29	O'Byrne	Agar (4)	2699	Kendrew
13.11.83	SD	A	Barrow	L	21-28	O'Byrne, Sharp, Moses	Agar (4, 1 dg)	—	—
20.11.83	SD	A	Batley	W	23-11	Bond, Walton, Shillito, Agar	Agar (3), Bond (dg)	—	—
27.11.83	SD	H	Hunslet	L	15-48	Cawood, Walton	Agar (3, 1 dg)	1889	Kershaw
4.12.83	SD	A	Kent Invicta	W	19-16	Waites (2), Agar	Agar (2, 1 dg), Moses (dg), Langton (dg)	—	—
18.12.83	SD	A	Cardiff C.	L	18-26	Moses, Bond, Langton	Agar (3)	—	—
26.12.83	SD	A	Huddersfield	W	28-4	Shillito, Dickinson, Bond, Cawood, Garrod	Smith (4)	—	—
1.1.84	SD	H	Huddersfield	W	19-14	Shillito, Dickinson	Smith (5), Moses (dg)	1525	Hodgson
8.1.84	SD	H	Batley	W	28-10	Bond, Dickinson, Garrod, Waites	Smith (6)	1493	Campbell
5.2.84	SD	H	Swinton	W	14-13	Cawood, Waites	Smith (3)	1470	Walker
12.2.84	CC(1)	H	Wakefield T.	L	7-19	Langton	Smith, Cawood (dg)	4402	Volante
19.2.84	SD	A	Hunslet	L	12-21	Agar, Garrod	Agar (2)	—	—
26.2.84	SD	A	Carlisle	W	12-10	Agar (2)	Agar (2)	—	—
4.3.84	SD	H	Barrow	L	0-30	—	—	1743	Lindop
11.3.84	SD	A	Blackpool B.	L	17-18	Dickinson (2), Cawood	Agar (2), Langton (dg)	—	—
14.3.84	SD	H	Kent Invicta	W	21-16	Martin, Garrod, Cawood Dickinson	Agar (2), Carroll (dg)	1017	Kendrew
18.3.84	SD	H	Cardiff C.	W	22-20	Agar, Garrod, Dickinson, O'Byrne	Agar (3)	1179	McDonald
21.3.84	SD	A	Bramley	W	17-14	Shillito, Agar, Marshall	Agar (2), Moses (dg)	—	—
28.3.84	SD	H	Workington T.	W	24-0	Dickinson (3), Beevers, O'Byrne	Agar (2)	921	Fox
1.4.84	SD	A	Huyton	L	12-19	Dickinson, Agar	Agar (2)	—	—
4.4.84	SD	H	Doncaster	W	43-6	Langton (3), O'Byrne (2) Shillito, Agar	Agar (7), Langton (dg)	820	Haigh
8.4.84	SD	H	Dewsbury	W	19-0	Waites, Langton, Garrod	Agar (3), Marshall (dg)	1132	Hodgson
13.4.84	SD	A	Workington T.	L	10-28	Dickinson, O'Byrne	Agar	—	—
15.4.84	SD	A	York	L	21-27	Humphreys, McCallion, O'Byrne	Agar (4, 1dg)	—	—
20.4.84	SD	A	Keighley	W	34-18	Waites (3), Smith (3), McCallion,	Agar (3)	—	—
22.4.84	SD	H	Keighley	D	19-19	Greenwood, Bond, Dickinson, Waites	Agar (1, 1dg)	1087	Lindop
29.4.84	SD	H	Rochdale H.	W	50-9	O'Byrne (3), Dickinson (2), Smith (2), Waites (2)	Smith (7)	916	Spencer

HUDDERSFIELD

Ground: Arena 84, Fartown
Colours: Claret and gold hooped jerseys, white shorts
First Season: 1895-96
Nickname: Barracudas
Chairman: John Bailey
Coach: Dave Mortimer (Nov. 1982 - Aug. 1983)
Mel Bedford (Aug.-Nov. 1983)
Brian Lockwood (Nov. 1983-)
Honours: **Championship** Winners, 1911-12, 1912-13, 1914-15, 1928-29, 1929-30, 1948-49, 1961-62
Beaten finalists, 1913-14, 1919-20, 1922-23, 1931-32, 1945-46, 1949-50
Division Two Champions, 1974-75
Challenge Cup Winners, 1912-13, 1914-15, 1919-20, 1932-33, 1944-45, 1952-53
Beaten finalists, 1934-35, 1961-62
Yorkshire League Winners, 1911-12, 1912-13, 1913-14, 1914-15, 1919-20, 1921-22, 1928-29, 1929-30, 1948-49, 1949-50, 1951-52
Eastern Division Beaten finalists, 1962-63
Yorkshire Cup Winners, 1909-10, 1911-12, 1913-14, 1914-15, 1918-19, 1919-20, 1926-27, 1931-32, 1938-39, 1950-51, 1952-53, 1957-58
Beaten finalists, 1910-11, 1923-24, 1925-26, 1930-31, 1937-38, 1942-43, 1949-50, 1960-61
Records: Attendance: 35,136 Leeds v. Wakefield T. (RL Cup SF) 19 April, 1947. Home: 32,912 v. Wigan (League) 4 March, 1950
Season
Goals: 147 by B. Gronow, 1919-20
Tries: 80 by A. Rosenfeld, 1913-14
Points: 330 by B. Gronow, 1919-20
Match
Goals: 18 by M. Holland v. Swinton Park, 28 Feb, 1914
Tries: 10 by L. Cooper v. Keighley, 17 Nov, 1951
Points: 39 by M. Holland v. Swinton Park, 28 Feb, 1914
Highest score: 119-2 v. Swinton Park, 1913-14
Highest against: 64-17 v. Leeds, 1958-59

1983-84 PLAYERS' SUMMARY

	App.	Tries	Goals	D/Gls	Pts
Barton, Edward	20	1	—	—	4
Blacker, Brian	28 + 2	12	—	—	48
Bostock, Mick	1 + 3	—	—	—	—
Cramp, Peter	28 + 1	9	25	—	86
Davies, Tom	29 + 5	—	—	—	—
Dixon, Paul	26 + 7	14	—	—	56
Doughty, Greg	0 + 1	—	—	—	—
Fitzpatrick, Dennis	27 + 8	1	—	—	4
Gerard, Greg	2	—	—	—	—
George, Wilf	23	12	—	—	48
Greenwood, Alan	16 + 2	3	—	—	12
Hirst, Bob	17 + 1	1	46	5	101
Johnson, Jimmy	31	9	—	—	36
Johnson, Phil	11 + 1	3	—	—	12
Knight, Glenn	19 + 7	8	—	2	34
Leathley, Trevor	17 + 7	7	—	—	28
McHugh, Gordon	5 + 3	—	—	—	—
Morris, Roger	0 + 1	—	—	—	—
Murray, Nigel	10 + 4	4	—	—	16
Paterson, John	14	2	—	—	8
Price, Ray	22 + 1	1	—	3	7
Punter, Michael	2	—	—	—	—
Rose, Tony	14 +1	—	—	—	—
Rowe, Danny	16 + 1	1	—	—	4
Senior, Gary	35	14	5	—	66
Slater, Ian	13 + 3	4	1	—	18
Thomas, Ian	11	4	7	—	30
Thornton, Graham	4	—	—	—	—
Wilson, Andy	8 + 1	2	3	—	14
Wood Allan	18 + 1	1	—	—	4
Wroe, Derek	14 + 3	2	—	—	8
TOTALS					
31 players		115	87	10	644

1983-84 MATCH ANALYSIS

Date	Competition	H/A	Opponent	Rlt	Score	Tries	Goals	Attendance	Referee
21.8.83	SD	A	Barrow	L	8-40	Dixon, Leathley	—	—	—
28.8.83	SD	H	Rochdale H.	D	24-24	Murray (2), Thomas, Blacker, Leathley	Wilson, Senior	629	Massey
4.9.83	YC(1)	A	Castleford	L	20-36	J. Johnson, Leathley, Senior	Thomas (4)	—	—
7.9.83	SD	H	York	W	30-14	J. Johnson (3), Knight, Cramp, Leathley	Senior (3)	490	Spencer
11.9.83	SD	A	Blackpool B.	W	14-10	Leathley (2), Greenwood	Senior	—	—
18.9.83	SD	H	Keighley	L	12-14	Wilson (2)	Cramp (2)	832	Lindop
24.9.83	SD	A	Cardiff C.	D	26-26	Slater, Blacker, Knight, Murray, Dixon	Cramp (2), Slater	—	—
2.10.83	SD	H	Workington T.	L	18-22	Wroe, Dixon, Slater	Cramp (3)	596	Croft (Pr)
9.10.83	SD	A	Kent Invicta	L	10-32	Dixon (2)	Cramp	—	
16.10.83	SD	H	Batley	L	16-18	Thomas, J. Johnson, Barton	Thomas (2)	677	Hodgson
6.11.83	JPS(1)	H	Huyton	L	8-21	Blacker, Cramp	—	582	Volante
13.11.83	SD	H	Swinton	L	11-14	Knight	Wilson (2), Cramp, Knight (dg)	823	Holdsworth
20.11.83	SD	H	Doncaster	W	19-11	Blacker (2), George	Cramp (3), Knight (dg)	587	Kendrew
27.11.83	SD	A	Carlisle	L	6-15	Cramp	Cramp	—	—
4.12.83	SD	H	Dewsbury	W	26-12	Greenwood (2), Slater, J. Johnson	Cramp (5)	788	Whitfield
18.12.83	SD	H	Blackpool B.	L	14-20	Senior (2), Slater	Cramp	516	Campbell
26.12.83	SD	H	Halifax	L	4-28	George	—	1634	Massey
1.1.84	SD	A	Halifax	L	14-19	Cramp, Wroe	Cramp (3)	—	—
8.1.84	SD	A	York	L	6-10	Cramp	Hirst	—	—
15.1.84	SD	H	Cardiff C.	W	14-10	Senior, George	Hirst (3)	354	Volante
5.2.84	SD	A	Workington T.	L	6-16	Senior	Hirst	—	—
12.2.84	CC(1)	A	Warrington	L	16-34	Murray, Price	Hirst (4)	—	—
19.2.84	SD	H	Carlisle	L	10-14	P. Johnson	Hirst (3)	536	Haigh
26.2.84	SD	A	Huyton	W	18-4	Senior, Paterson, George	Hirst (3)	—	—
4.3.84	SD	A	Batley	W	15-1	George, Rowe	Hirst (3), Price (dg)	—	—
11.3.84	SD	H	Hunslet	W	18-14	Senior, P. Johnson, Cramp	Hirst (3)	834	Berry
18.3.84	SD	A	Doncaster	W	36-0	Blacker (2), Dixon (2), J. Johnson, George, Knight	Hirst (4)	—	—
21.3.84	SD	H	Huyton	W	33-8	George (2), Cramp, Senior, Knight, Dixon, J. Johnson	Cramp (2), Price (dg)	427	Campbell
25.3.84	SD	A	Keighley	D	15-15	Senior (2), J. Johnson	Cramp, Price (dg)	—	—
1.4.84	SD	H	Bramley	W	25-10	Dixon, Senior, Cramp, Blacker	Hirst (4, 1dg)	644	Volante
4.4.84	SD	A	Bramley	W	28-6	Cramp, Paterson, Wood, Fitzpatrick	Hirst (5, 2dg)	—	—
8.4.84	SD	A	Rochdale H.	L	0-3	—	—	—	—
15.4.84	SD	H	Barrow	L	20-27	Knight, Dixon, Senior, Blacker	Hirst (2)	964	Holdsworth
18.4.84	SD	A	Dewsbury	W	22-13	Gregory (2), Knight (2), Dixon	Hirst	—	—
21.4.84	SD	H	Kent Invicta	W	31-1	George (2), Thomas, Dixon, Blacker, P. Johnson	Hirst (3, 1 dg)	548	Hodgson
23.4.84	SD	A	Swinton	L	22-58	Senior (2), Blacker, Leathley	Hirst	—	—
29.4.84	SD	A	Hunslet	W	29-16	Dixon (2), Thomas, Blacker, Hirst	Hirst (3, 1dg), Thomas	—	—

HULL

Ground: The Boulevard
Colours: Irregular black and white hooped jerseys, white shorts
First Season: 1895-96
Nickname: Airlie Birds
Chairman: Roy Waudby
General Manager: Mike Dooley
Team Manager: Arthur Bunting (Jan. 1978-)
Honours: **Championship** Winners, 1919-20, 1920-21, 1935-36, 1955-56, 1957-58
Beaten finalists, 1956-57
Division One Champions, 1982-83
Division Two Champions, 1976-77, 1978-79
Challenge Cup Winners, 1913-14, 1981-82
Beaten finalists, 1907-08, 1908-09, 1909-10, 1921-22, 1922-23, 1958-59, 1959-60, 1979-80, 1982-83
Yorkshire League Winners, 1918-19, 1922-23, 1926-27, 1935-36
Yorkshire Cup Winners, 1923-24, 1969-70, 1982-83, 1983-84
Beaten finalists, 1912-13, 1914-15, 1920-21, 1927-28, 1938-39, 1946-47, 1953-54, 1954-55, 1955-56, 1959-60, 1967-68
John Player Trophy Winners 1981-82
Beaten finalists, 1975-76
BBC2 Floodlit Trophy Winners, 1979-80
Premiership Beaten finalists, 1980-81, 1981-82, 1982-83
Records: Attendance: 28,798 v. Leeds (RL Cup) 7 March, 1936

Season
Goals: 170 by S. Lloyd, 1978-79
Tries: 52 by J. Harrison, 1914-15
Points: 369 by S. Lloyd, 1978-79

Match
Goals: 14 by J. Kennedy v. Rochdale H, 7 April, 1921; S. Lloyd v. Oldham, 10 Sep, 1978
Tries: 7 by C. Sullivan v. Doncaster, 15 April, 1968
Points: 36 by J. Kennedy v. Keighley, 29 Jan, 1921
Highest score: 86-0 v. Elland, 1898-99
Highest against:
56-8 v. Wigan, 1957-58
56-0 v. Dewsbury, 1918-19

1983-84 PLAYERS' SUMMARY

	App.	Tries	Goals	D/Gls	Pts
Ah Kuoi, Fred	21	7	—	—	28
Banks, Barry	9 + 4	5	—	—	20
Crane, Mick	18 + 3	3	—	1	13
Crooks, Lee	19 + 1	6	36	—	96
Dannatt, Andy	11 + 6	3	—	—	12
Dean, Tony	4	1	—	—	4
Divorty, Gary	26 + 5	5	16	3	55
Edmonds, Phil	28	10	—	—	40
Evans, Steve	34 + 1	22	3	—	94
Harkin, Kevin	12 + 1	3	—	—	12
Kemble, Gary	29	6	—	—	24
Leuluai, James	40	23	—	—	92
Madley, Ian	0 + 1	—	—	—	—
Norton, Steve	19 + 2	3	—	—	12
O'Hara, Dane	36	13	—	—	52
Patrick, Shaun	26	3	—	—	12
Prendiville, Paul	9	2	33	—	74
Proctor, Wayne	19 + 11	5	—	—	20
Puckering, Neil	5 + 4	—	—	—	—
Rose, Paul	21 + 1	3	—	—	12
Schofield, Garry	30 + 3	37	57	—	262
Skerrett, Trevor	20	2	—	—	8
Solal, Patrick	17 + 5	7	—	—	28
Sterling, Peter	8	1	—	—	4
Stone, Charlie	5 + 1	—	—	—	—
Tindall, Keith	16 + 4	—	—	—	—
Tomlinson, Alan	0 + 1	—	—	—	—
Topliss, David	29	15	—	—	60
Wileman, Ronnie	8	1	—	—	4
Trialist	1	1	—	—	4
TOTALS: 30 players		187	145	4	1,042

1983-84 MATCH ANALYSIS

Date	Comp.	H/A	Opponent	Rlt	Score	Tries	Goals	Att.	Referee
21.8.83	SLC	H	Warrington	D	22-22	Topliss, Leuluai, Solal	Prendiville (5)	10101	Fox
28.8.83	SLC	A	Castleford	W	40-18	Solal, Edmonds, Topliss, Leuluai, Skerrett, Harkin	Prendiville (8)	—	—
4.9.83	YC(1)	H	Featherstone R.	W	24-8	Prendiville (2), Leuluai, Banks, Harkin	Prendiville (2)	10168	Lindop
11.9.83	SLC	A	Leigh	W	20-12	Leuluai, Harkin, O'Hara, Proctor	Prendiville (2)	—	—
14.9.83	YC(2)	A	Keighley	W	30-8	Solal (2), Topliss, Leuluai, Schofield	Prendiville (5)	—	—

1983-84 MATCH ANALYSIS (continued)

Date	Comp.	H/A	Opponent	Rlt	Score	Tries	Goals	Att.	Referee
18.9.83	SLC	H	Wigan	W	24-8	Banks (2), Evans, Leuluai	Prendiville (4)	11585	Haigh
25.9.83	SLC	A	Fulham	L	24-29	Leuluai, O'Hara, Topliss, Wileman	Prendiville (2), Evans (2)	—	—
28.9.83	YC(SF)	A	Leeds	W	20-16	Evans, Leuluai, Crane	Prendiville (3), Crooks	—	—
2.10.83	SLC	H	Hull K. R.	L	8-23	Crooks	Prendiville (2)	18185	Thompson
9.10.83	SLC	A	Leeds	W	40-12	Schofield (3), O'Hara, Topliss, Solal	Crooks (7), Divorty	—	—
15.10.83	YC(F)	Lds U	Castleford	W	13-2	O'Hara, Crane, Proctor	Crane (dg)	(14049)	Thompson
23.10.83	SLC	A	Oldham	L	12-18	Leuluai, Schofield	Crooks, Schofield	—	—
30.10.83	SLC	H	Salford	W	58-6	Ah Kuoi (2), Schofield (2), Crooks (2), Kemble, O'Hara, Skerrett, Evans, Leuluai, Divorty	Crooks (3), Divorty (2)	8589	Kendrew
6.11.83	JPS(1)	A	Castleford	W	8-4	Evans	Crooks (2)	—	—
13.11.83	SLC	A	Widnes	L	0-30	—	—	—	—
20.11.83	JPS(2)	A	Featherstone R.	L	14-20	Dean, Schofield, Evans	Crooks	—	—
4.12.83	SLC	A	Wakefield T.	W	32-16	Evans (2), Edmonds, Dannatt, Banks, Trialist	Divorty (4)	—	—
11.12.83	SLC	H	Fulham	W	36-11	Schofield (2), Topliss, Banks, Evans, Crooks	Divorty (3), Crooks (3)	10045	Smith
18.12.83	SLC	A	Wigan	L	12-14	Schofield (2), Evans	—	—	—
27.12.83	SLC	H	Featherstone R.	W	37-4	Leuluai (4), Sterling, Schofield, Evans	Crooks (4), Divorty (dg)	11093	Whitfield
2.1.84	SLC	A	Featherstone R.	W	22-12	Evans, Kemble, Topliss, Schofield	Crooks (3)	—	—
8.1.84	SLC	H	Bradford N.	W	16-8	Schofield (2), Evans	Crooks (2)	11222	Beaumont
11.1.84	SLC	H	St. Helens	W	30-24	Schofield (2), Evans, Patrick, Crane, Edmonds	Crooks (2), Divorty	10143	Massey
19.1.84	SLC	H	Leigh	W	14-0	Solal, Patrick	Divorty (3)	8821	Beaumont
5.2.84	SLC	H	Oldham	W	20-8	Divorty, Schofield, O'Hara	Crooks (4)	10482	Berry
12.2.84	CC(1)	A	Cardiff C.	W	34-6	Kemble (2), Schofield (2), Topliss, Patrick	Crooks (3), Schofield (2)	—	—
19.2.84	SLC	A	Warrington	L	6-18	Rose	Evans	—	—
25.2.84	CC(2)	A	St. Helens	L	14-24	Schofield (2), Dannatt	Divorty	—	—
4.3.84	SLC	H	Widnes	W	30-12	Schofield (3), Edmonds, Dannatt, Ah Kuoi	Schofield (3)	10836	Robinson
11.3.84	SLC	A	Salford	W	42-6	Leuluai (3), Topliss (2), Edmonds, Evans, Schofield	Schofield (5)	—	—
16.3.84	SLC	A	St. Helens	L	10-22	Schofield	Schofield (3)	—	—
21.3.84	SLC	H	Leeds	W	23-10	Leuluai (2), Schofield, Divorty	Schofield (3), Divorty (dg)	10842	Beaumont
25.3.84	SLC	H	Wakefield T.	W	66-12	Evans (3), O'Hara (2), Leuluai, Proctor, Edmonds, Ah Kuoi, Topliss, Schofield, Norton	Schofield (9)	8549	Whitfield
1.4.84	SLC	A	Whitehaven	W	28-10	O'Hara (2), Leuluai, Evans, Topliss	Schofield (4)	—	—
8.4.84	SLC	H	Castleford	W	40-10	Schofield (2), Edmonds, Leuluai, Topliss, Solal, Rose Norton	Schofield (4)	10629	Wall
15.4.84	SLC	A	Bradford N.	W	29-10	Rose, Ah Kuoi, Proctor, Schofield, O'Hara	Schofield (4), Divorty (dg)	—	—
20.4.84	SLC	A	Hull K.R.	W	36-16	Ah Kuoi (2), Topliss, Leuluai, Crooks	Schofield (8)	—	—
23.4.84	SLC	H	Whitehaven	W	54-0	Evans (3), Divorty (2), Edmonds, Proctor, Schofield, Crooks, O'Hara	Schofield (7)	9061	Fox
29.4.84	PT(1)	H	Bradford N.	W	42-12	Edmonds (2), Schofield (2), Kemble (2), O'Hara, Norton, Evans	Schofield (2), Divorty	10986	Holdsworth
7.5.84	PT(SF)	H	Castleford	L	12-22	Schofield, Topliss	Schofield (2)	12571	Allatt

HULL KINGSTON ROVERS

Ground: Craven Park
Colours: White jerseys with red band, white shorts (1983-84 club centenary colours: red jerseys with blue band)
First Season: 1899-1900
Nickname: Robins
Chairman: Colin Hutton
Secretary: Ron Turner
Coach: Roger Millward MBE (Mar. 1977-)
Honours: **Championship** Winners, 1922-23, 1924-25
Beaten finalists, 1920-21, 1967-68
First Division Champions, 1978-79, 1983-84
Challenge Cup Winners, 1979-80
Beaten finalists, 1904-05, 1924-25, 1963-64, 1980-81
John Player Trophy Beaten finalists, 1981-82
Premiership Winners, 1980-81, 1983-84
Yorkshire League Winners, 1924-25, 1925-26
Yorkshire Cup Winners, 1920-21, 1929-30, 1966-67, 1967-68, 1971-72, 1974-75
Beaten finalists, 1906-07, 1911-12, 1933-34, 1962-63, 1975-76, 1980-81
BBC2 Floodlit Trophy Winners, 1977-78
Beaten finalists, 1979-80
Eastern Division Championship Winners, 1962-63
Records: Attendance: 22,282 v. Hull, 7 October, 1922. There was a crowd of 27,670 for a League match v. Hull at Hull City FC's Boothferry Park on 3 April, 1953

Season
Goals: 166 by G. Fairbairn, 1981-82
Tries: 42 by G. Dunn, 1974-75
Points: 366 by S. Hubbard, 1979-80
Match
Goals: 14 by A. Carmichael v. Merthyr Tydfil, 8 Oct, 1910
Tries: 11 by G. West v. Brookland R, 4 Mar, 1905
Points: 53 by G. West v. Brookland R, 4 Mar, 1905
Highest score: 73-5 v. Brookland R., 1904-05
Highest against: 68-0 v. Halifax, 1955-56

1983-84 PLAYERS' SUMMARY

	App.	Tries	Goals	D/Gls	Pts
Broadhurst, Mark	31	10	—	—	40
Burton, Chris	28 + 4	5	—	—	20
Casey, Len	26 + 2	3	—	—	12
Clark, Garry	37	24	—	—	96
Crooks, Steve	1 + 1	1	—	—	4
Dobson, Steve	1	—	—	—	—
Dorahy, John	26 + 1	18	74	2	222
Ema, Asuquo	0 + 2	—	—	—	—
Fairbairn, George	30 + 2	—	58	1	117
Hall, David	33	9	—	—	36
Harkin, Paul	9 + 2	—	—	1	1
Hartley, Steve	20 + 8	16	—	—	64
Hogan, Phil	20 + 3	3	2	—	16
Holdstock, Roy	11 + 3	—	—	—	—
Kelly, Andy	15 + 13	7	—	—	28
Laws, David	29 + 2	18	—	—	72
Lazenby, Tracey	6 + 5	1	—	—	4
Lydiat, John	8 + 5	5	7	—	34
Millington, John	16 + 4	1	—	—	4
Parker, Frank	4	2	—	—	8
Proctor, Paul	4 + 3	—	—	—	—
Prohm, Gary	36	25	—	—	100
Robinson, Ian	6 + 1	4	—	—	16
Rudd, Chris	23	6	—	—	24
Simpson, Mark	0 + 1	—	—	—	—
Smith, Gordon	30 + 1	5	—	2	22
Smith, Mike	34	13	—	—	52
Walsh, Mike	1	—	—	1	1
Watkinson, David	16	1	—	—	4
Watson, Kevin	6 + 2	1	—	—	4
TOTALS 30 players		178	141	7	1,001

1983-84 MATCH ANALYSIS

Date	Competition	H/A	Opponent	Rlt	Score	Tries	Goals	Attendance	Referee
21.8.83	SLC	A	St. Helens	L	11-30	Prohm, Hall	Fairbairn, Walsh (dg)	—	—
24.8.83	SLC	H	Castleford	L	14-26	Robinson, Watson	Hogan (2), Lydiat	6115	Fox
28.8.83	SLC	H	Wakefield T.	W	38-0	Robinson (2), Parker (2), Hartley (2), Clark, Hall	Fairbairn (3)	5224	Smith

1983-84 MATCH ANALYSIS (continued)

Date	Competition	H/A	Opponent	Rlt	Score	Tries	Goals	Attendance	Referee
4.9.83	YC(1)	A	Bradford N.	L	22-25	Hartley (2), Casey, Clark	Fairbairn (3)	—	—
11.9.83	SLC	H	Widnes	W	10-4	M. Smith	Lydiat (3)	5371	Beaumont
18.9.83	SLC	A	Warrington	L	10-26	Hartley	Lydiat (3)	—	—
25.9.83	SLC	H	Oldham	D	18-18	Clark, Hogan	Fairbairn (5)	6541	Haigh
2.10.83	SLC	A	Hull	W	23-8	Clark (2), Laws, M. Smith	Fairbairn (3), G. Smith (dg)	—	—
9.10.83	SLC	H	Bradford N.	W	16-14	Broadhurst (2), M. Smith	Fairbairn (2)	7080	Beaumont
16.10.83	Tour	H	Queensland	W	8-6	M. Smith	Fairbairn (2)	6383	Whitfield
23.10.83	SLC	H	Warrington	W	34-19	G. Smith (2), Burton (2), Prohm, Dorahy	Fairbairn (5)	6653	Berry
30.10.83	SLC	A	Castleford	W	18-8	M. Smith, Dorahy, Hogan	Fairbairn (3)	—	—
6.11.83	SLC	H	Whitehaven	W	56-6	Prohm (3), Clark (2), Hall (2), Laws, Burton, Hogan	Fairbairn (8)	5381	Wall
13.11.83	SLC	H	Fulham	W	42-10	Hall (2), Watkinson, Prohm, G. Smith, Laws, Lazenby, Clark	Fairbairn (5)	6200	Kershaw
20.11.83	JPS(2)	A	Leeds	L	6-12	Clark	Fairbairn	—	—
27.11.83	SLC	A	Oldham	W	18-10	Kelly (2), Broadhurst	Fairbairn (3)	—	—
4.12.83	SLC	H	St. Helens	W	32-7	Hall (2), Lydiat (2), Kelly, Prohm	Fairbairn (4)	6531	Kendrew
2.1.84	SLC	A	Whitehaven	W	22-10	Clark (2), Dorahy (2)	Fairbairn (3)	—	—
8.1.84	SLC	A	Fulham	W	38-18	Laws (2), Prohm (2), Burton, Hartley, Dorahy	Dorahy (5)	—	—
15.1.84	SLC	H	Featherstone R.	W	34-0	Dorahy (2), Kelly, Prohm, M. Smith, Clark	Dorahy (5)	6003	Campbell
29.1.84	SLC	H	Wigan	W	24-10	Hartley, Dorahy, Kelly, Crooks	Dorahy (4)	7017	Allatt
3.2.84	SLC	A	Bradford N.	L	0-20	—	—	—	—
12.2.84	CC(1)	A	Blackpool B.	W	27-10	Prohm (2), Laws (2), Clark, Broadhurst	Fairbairn (1, 1dg)	—	—
19.2.84	SLC	H	Leigh	W	47-8	Rudd (2), Laws (2), Broadhurst (2), Kelly, Clark	Dorahy (7), G. Smith (dg)	6471	Spencer
26.2.84	CC(2)	H	Doncaster	W	40-7	Laws (2), Clark (2), Prohm, Millington, Broadhurst, Dorahy	Dorahy (4)	6959	Holdsworth
4.3.84	SLC	A	Leeds	D	14-14	Prohm, Laws	Dorahy (3)	—	—
10.3.84	CC(3)	A	Widnes	L	10-21	Clark	Dorahy (3)	—	—
14.3.84	SLC	A	Widnes	W	17-8	Laws (2), Clark	Dorahy (2, 1dg)	—	—
18.3.84	SLC	H	Salford	W	51-32	Prohm (3), Laws (2), Clark, Dorahy, M. Smith, Rudd	Fairbairn (4), Dorahy (3, 1dg)	6139	Wall
25.3.84	SLC	A	Featherstone R.	W	24-18	Dorahy (2), Casey, Hartley, M. Smith	Fairbairn (2)	—	—
1.4.84	SLC	A	Wakefield T.	W	46-11	Hartley (4), G. Smith, Laws, Prohm, M. Smith	Dorahy (7)	—	—
8.4.84	SLC	A	Wigan	W	30-14	Clark, Broahurst, Prohm, Hall, Casey	Dorahy (5)	—	—
10.4.84	SLC	A	Salford	W	32-0	Hartley (2), Rudd, Broadhurst, Dorahy, Lydiat	Dorahy (4)	—	—
15.4.84	SLC	A	Leigh	W	44-16	Hartley (2), Prohm (2), M. Smith, Clark, Broadhurst, Dorahy	Dorahy (6)	—	—
20.4.84	SLC	H	Hull	L	16-36	G. Smith, Dorahy, Clark	Dorahy (2)	16081	Campbell
22.4.84	SLC	H	Leeds	L	16-20	Kelly, Prohm, Clark	Dorahy (2)	7683	Haigh
29.4.84	PT(1)	H	Leeds	W	54-0	Dorahy (2), Lydiat (2), Prohm (2), Robinson, Burton, Clark, Rudd	Dorahy (7)	5910	Whitfield
7.5.84	PT(SF)	H	St. Helens	W	21-16	M. Smith (2), Rudd	Dorahy (4), Harkin (dg)	7733	Lindop
12.5.84	PT(F)	Leeds	Castleford	W	18-10	Dorahy, Laws, Prohm, M. Smith	Dorahy	(12515)	Campbell

HUNSLET

Ground: Leeds U. FC, Elland Road
Colours: Myrtle, flame and white jerseys, white shorts
First Season: 1895-96. Disbanded at end of 1972-73. Re-formed as New Hunslet in 1973-74. Retitled Hunslet from start of 1979-80
Chairman: Jerry Mason
Secretary: Derek Preece
Coach: Paul Daley (April 1981-)
Honours: **Challenge Cup** Winners, 1907-08, 1933-34
Beaten finalists, 1898-99, 1964-65
Championship Winners, 1907-08, 1937-38
Beaten finalists, 1958-59
Division Two Champions, 1962-63
Yorkshire Cup Winners, 1905-06, 1907-08, 1962-63
Beaten finalists, 1908-09, 1929-30, 1931-32, 1944-45, 1956-57, 1965-66
Yorkshire League Winners, 1897-98, 1907-08, 1931-32
Records: Attendance: 54,112 v. Leeds (Championship final), 30 April, 1938
Season
Goals: 181 by W. Langton, 1958-59
Tries: 34 by A. Snowden, 1956-57
Points: 380 by W. Langton, 1958-59
Match
Goals: 12 by W. Langton v. Keighley, 18 Aug, 1959
Tries: 7 by G. Dennis v. Bradford N, 20 Jan, 1934
Points: 27 by W. Langton v. Keighley, 18 Aug, 1959
Highest score: 75-5 v. Broughton Rec., 1896-97
Highest against: 76-8 v. Halifax, 1972-73

1983-84 PLAYERS' SUMMARY

	App.	Tries	Goals	D/Gls	Pts
Bateman, Andy	1 + 3	—	—	—	—
Booth, Dean	14 + 1	3	—	—	12
Bowden, Billy	4 + 3	1	—	—	4
Briers, Paul	31	—	—	—	—
Brown, Peter	15 + 1	1	4	—	12
Burgess, Mark	4 + 5	—	—	—	—
Coombes, Mick	4	—	—	—	—
Farrar, Andrew	1 + 4	1	—	—	4
Fitzsimons, Eric	26	4	117	14	264
Foley, Bill	4	2	—	—	8
Gibson, Phil	16	—	—	—	—
Gray, Neil	15	3	2	—	16
Hullock, Steve	20	13	—	—	52
Hunt, Ian	11	1	—	—	4
Johnson, Tony	7 + 3	2	—	—	8
Kay, Andrew	9	2	29	—	66
King, Graham	34	28	—	—	112
Lean, Neil	16 + 5	4	—	—	16
Mitchell, Keith	3 + 1	1	—	—	4
Murrell, Bryan	33 + 1	15	—	—	60
Nicholson, Ian	2	1	—	—	4
Nicholson, Martin	1	—	—	—	—
Olbison, Kevin	5 + 2	3	—	—	12
Payne, Andy	6	—	—	—	—
Roe, Peter	28	10	—	—	40
Rudd, Neil	11 + 9	7	—	—	28
Sampson, Ian	22 + 3	8	—	—	32
Sampson, Roy	6 + 6	1	—	—	4
Sanderson, Phil	9 + 7	1	—	—	4
Smith, Stewart	23 + 3	12	—	—	48
Tate, Phil	32	19	—	—	76
Tosney, Andrew	4	—	—	—	—
Townsend, Glen	10 + 3	1	—	—	4
White, Brendan	6 + 2	2	—	—	8
Wolford, John	35	4	—	1	17
Wood, Mark	1	1	—	—	4
Wright, Geoff	23 + 13	4	—	—	16
Trialist	2	—	8	—	16
TOTALS					
38 players		155	160	15	955

1983-84 MATCH ANALYSIS

Date	Competition	H/A	Opponent	Rlt	Score	Tries	Goals	Attendance	Referee
21.8.83	SD	H	Doncaster	W	50-18	King (2), Tate (2), Smith, Foley, Wolford, Fitzsimons, Murrell	Fitzsimons (7)	1250	Hodgson
24.8.83	SD	A	Bramley	W	25-10	Sanderson, King, Booth	Fitzsimons (6, 1 dg)	—	—
28.8.83	SD	A	Huyton	W	14-10	Foley, Tate, Smith	Fitzsimons	—	—
4.9.83	PVYC(1)	H	York	L	11-21	Murrell	Fitzsimons (3, 1 dg)	1061	Fox
11.9.83	SD	A	Workington T.	W	16-14	King, Tate	Fitzsimons (3, 2 dg)	—	—
18.9.83	SD	H	Cardiff C.	W	40-18	King (2), Murrell, Booth, Wolford, Smith	Fitzsimons (8)	1079	Volante
25.9.83	SD	A	Keighley	W	18-14	Booth, Lean, Tate	Fitzsimons (3)	—	—
2.10.83	SD	H	Kent Invicta	W	48-10	Wolford, Rudd, Murrell, Wright, Smith, Roe, R. Sampson, Hunt	Fitzsimons (8)	1420	Haigh
5.10.83	SD	A	Barrow	L	12-28	Murrell (2)	Fitzsimons (2)	—	—
9.10.83	SD	H	Swinton	W	26-18	Murrell (2), Roe, Tate	Fitzsimons (5)	1500	Kershaw
16.10.83	SD	A	Rochdale H.	W	13-10	King	Fitzsimons (4, 1 dg)	—	—
23.10.83	SD	H	Carlisle	W	28-13	King, Murrell, Olbison, Smith	Fitzsimons (6)	1650	Lindop
30.10.83	SD	A	Blackpool B.	L	18-24	Murrell, Fitzsimons	Fitzsimons (5)	—	—
6.11.83	JPS(1)	A	Swinton	L	16-17	Wright, Murrell, Tate	Fitzsimons (2)	—	—
20.11.83	SD	H	Dewsbury	L	28-32	Smith, King, Wright, Gray, Hullock	Fitzsimons (4)	1600	McDonald
27.11.83	SD	A	Halifax	W	48-15	King (3), Tate (2), Smith, Murrell, Hullock	Fitzsimons (7, 2 dg)	—	—
4.12.83	SD	H	Blackpool B.	L	30-31	Hullock (2), Tate, Wolford, R. Sampson	Fitzsimons (5)	1425	Berry
18.12.83	SD	H	Huyton	W	52-0	Hullock (2), Smith (2), Lean, Fitzsimons, Roe, Murrell, Tate	Fitzsimons (8)	1020	Allatt
26.12.83	SD	A	York	W	37-20	Hullock (2), King (2), Roe, R. Sampson	Fitzsimons (6, 1 dg)	—	—
1.1.84	SD	H	York	W	13-9	King, Smith	Fitzsimons (2, 1 dg)	1740	Haigh
22.1.84	SD	A	Cardiff C.	W	34-6	Hullock, King, R. Sampson, Wright, Lean, Tate	Fitzsimons (5)	—	—
5.2.84	SD	A	Doncaster	W	14-12	Tate, Hullock	Fitzsimons (3)	—	—
12.2.84	CC(1)	H	Keighley	W	21-10	Roe, King, I. Sampson	Fitzsimons (3, 3dg)	1466	Smith
19.2.84	SD	H	Halifax	W	21-12	King, Fitzsimons	Fitzsimons (6, 1dg)	1650	Beaumont
26.2.84	CC(2)	H	Bradford N.	L	7-17	Rudd	Fitzsimons (1, 1dg)	6956	Campbell
4.3.84	SD	H	Rochdale H.	W	30-20	Smith (2), Lean, Bowden, Rudd	Fitzsimons (4), Brown	1330	Whitfield
7.3.84	SD	A	Swinton	L	10-28	Townsend, Nicholson	Brown	—	—
11.3.84	SD	A	Huddersfield	L	14-18	Murrell, Kay	Kay (3)	—	—
18.3.84	SD	A	Batley	W	42-12	I. Sampson (3), King (2), Tate, Rudd, White	Kay (4), Brown	—	—
25.3.84	SD	H	Barrow	W	24-21	Gray (2), Hullock (2)	Kay (4)	1159	Hodgson
27.3.84	SD	H (at Bramley)	Batley	W	38-18	Roe (2), Tate (2), White, Olbison, Brown, Hullock	Gray (2), Brown	1047	Spencer
4.4.84	SD	H	Workington T.	L	10-28	Tate, Rudd	Kay	1419	Wall
8.4.84	SD	H	Keighley	W	29-24	Roe (2), Tate, Murrell, Kay	Kay (4), Wolford (dg)	1239	Volante
15.4.84	SD	A	Kent Invicta	L	16-24	King (2)	Kay (4)	—	—
18.4.84	SD	H	Bramley	W	36-12	King (4), Rudd, Tate, I. Sampson	Kay (4)	997	Massey
23.4.84	SD	A	Dewsbury	W	28-14	Roe, King, Johnson, Olbison	Trialist (6)	—	—
29.4.84	SD	H	Huddersfield	L	16-29	King, Johnson, Rudd	Trialist (2)	1213	McDonald
2.5.84	SD	A	Carlisle	L	22-25	Mitchell, Farrar, Wood	Kay (5)	—	—

HUYTON

Ground: Alt Park

Colours: Black jerseys with white collar, white shorts

First Season: 1922-23 as Wigan Highfield. Became London Highfield in 1933-34. Became Liverpool Stanley in 1934-35 and changed to Liverpool City in 1951-52. Huyton began at the start of 1968-69. There was also a Liverpool City in 1906-07

Chairman: Terry Hughes

Secretary: Tony Almond

Coach: Geoff Fletcher (Aug 1977-)

Honours: **Lancashire League** Winners, 1935-36

Records: Attendance: 14,000 v. Widnes (Championship semi-final) 2 May, 1936 (at Prescott Road)

Season

Goals: 97 by S. Oakley, 1933-34

Tries: 28 by J. Maloney, 1930-31

Points: 211 by J. Wood, 1954-55

Match

Goals: 10 by S. Oakley v. Bramley, 4 May, 1934

Tries: 5 by J. Maloney v. Bramley, 25 April, 1931

Points: 20 by Barnes v. Featherstone Jnrs, 7 Feb, 1931; S. Oakley v. Bramley, 4 May, 1934; P. Twiss v. Warrington, 20 Aug, 1958

Highest score: 59-11 v. Bramley, 1933-34

Highest against: 73-0 v. Warrington, 1950-51

● From the 1984-85 season Huyton moved to Runcorn AFC's ground in Canal Street, Runcorn, changing their club name to Runcorn Highfield and their colours to green and yellow

1983-84 PLAYERS' SUMMARY

	App.	Tries	Goals	D/Gls	Pts
Andrews, James	31 + 1	3	—	1	13
Bailey, Graham	6	—	—	—	—
Bishop, Alan	16 + 2	3	—	—	12
Blackburn, Ian	30	—	—	—	—
Bruen, Bob	6	—	—	—	—
Coop, John	24 + 4	3	—	—	12
Cooper, Tony	28 + 2	—	—	—	—
Corwell, Chris	17 + 2	—	—	—	—
Crehan, Glen	17 + 8	4	1	1	19
Crompton, David	11	8	—	—	32
Fletcher, Geoff	5 + 4	2	—	—	8
Garvey, John	12 + 5	3	—	—	12
Grady, Mike	13 + 1	—	—	—	—
Glover, Peter	9	—	6	—	12
Hartley, Gerard	0 + 3	—	—	—	—
Ingle, Derek	18	1	—	—	4
Jackson, Mark	31 + 1	6	—	—	24
Jackson, Tony	15	4	—	—	16
McCabe, John	28	1	—	—	4
Middlehurst, Peter	22 + 2	1	—	—	4
Morris, David	1	—	—	—	—
O'Toole, Stuart	6 + 2	2	—	—	8
Peters, Tony	3 + 1	1	—	—	4
Prescott, David	1	—	—	—	—
Seacombe, Tony	9 + 2	—	—	—	—
Shaw, Mark	20	5	4	—	28
Simms, Steve	9 + 2	1	—	—	4
Smith, Ian	35	18	—	—	72
Spence, Paul	1	—	—	—	—
Tabern, John	29 + 1	3	23	7	65
Trundle, John	0 + 1	—	—	—	—
Walker, Frank	1 + 1	—	—	—	—
Whelan, Tom	0 + 3	—	—	—	—
Williams, David	2	1	—	—	4
Williams, Ken	7 + 1	1	—	—	4
Wood, Peter	19	—	42	13	97
Wragg, Chris	12 + 1	7	—	—	28
TOTALS 37 players		78	76	22	486

Glen Crehan ... scorer of 19 points.

1983-84 MATCH ANALYSIS

Date	Competition	H/A	Opponent	Rlt	Score	Tries	Goals	Attendance	Referee
21.8.83	SD	A	Halifax	D	20-20	Ingle, Smith, Crehan	Tabern (4)	—	—
24.8.83	SD	H	Blackpool B.	L	8-18	Smith	Tabern (2)	210	Walker
28.8.83	SD	H	Hunslet	L	10-14	Smith, Shaw	Shaw	180	Mean
4.9.83	LC(1)	H	Swinton	L	12-13	Smith, Coop	Shaw, Tabern	306	McDonald
11.9.83	SD	A	Keighley	L	6-10	Bishop	Tabern	—	—
18.9.83	SD	A	Bramley	L	6-34	Tabern	Tabern	—	—
25.9.83	SD	H	Dewsbury	W	12-10	Shaw, Smith	Tabern (1, 2 dg)	135	Whitfield
2.10.83	SD	H	York	L	11-21	Jackson, Smith	Shaw, Tabern (dg)	151	McDonald
9.10.83	SD	A	Batley	L	5-19	—	Tabern (2, 1 dg)	—	—
16.10.83	SD	H	Cardiff C.	L	18-23	Smith (2), Coop	Tabern (3)	226	Lindop
23.10.83	SD	A	Barrow	L	8-48	M. Jackson, A. Jackson	—	—	—
30.10.83	SD	H	Workington T.	W	15-10	Andrews, Bishop	Wood (3), Andrews (dg)	200	Holdsworth
6.11.83	JPS(1)	A	Huddersfield	W	21-8	Garvey, Crehan	Wood (5, 2 dg), Crehan (dg)	—	—
13.11.83	SD	A	Rochdale H.	L	5-10	A. Jackson	Wood (dg)	—	—
20.11.83	JPS(2)	A	Cardiff C.	L	12-38	Smith, Shaw	Wood (2)	—	—
27.11.83	SD	H	Kent Invicta	L	20-35	Jackson (2), Bishop	Wood (4)	137	Thompson
4.12.83	SD	A	York	L	6-54	Smith	Wood	—	—
18.12.83	SD	A	Hunslet	L	0-52	—	—	—	—
26.12.83	SD	H	Barrow	L	6-24	Smith	Shaw	180	Berry
1.1.84	SD	A	Swinton	L	4-36	Smith	—	—	—
8.1.84	SD	H	Keighley	L	8-12	Wragg	Glover, Crehan	145	Kendrew
5.2.84	SD	H	Bramley	L	8-21	Peters	Glover (2)	115	Volante
12.2.84	CC(1)	A	Oldham	L	10-28	Shaw, Smith	Glover	—	—
26.2.84	SD	H	Huddersfield	L	4-18	—	Glover (2)	155	Spencer
4.3.84	SD	A	Kent Invicta	W	12-10	Williams, M. Jackson	Tabern (2)	—	—
11.3.84	SD	H	Swinton	L	6-22	McCabe	Tabern	245	Haigh
18.3.84	SD	A	Workington T.	L	12-24	P. Jackson, Fletcher	Wood (1, 2dg)	—	—
21.3.84	SD	A	Huddersfield	L	8-33	Simms	Wood (2)	—	—
25.3.84	SD	A	Carlisle	L	26-27	M. Jackson (2), Crompton, Andrews, Coop	Wood (3)	—	—
1.4.84	SD	H	Halifax	W	19-12	Wragg, Smith, Crompton	Wood (3, 1dg)	190	McDonald
4.4.84	SD	A	Dewsbury	W	15-9	Garvey (2), Wragg	Wood (1, 1dg)	—	—
10.4.84	SD	H	Carlisle	W	17-10	Smith, Wragg	Wood (3, 2dg), Tabern (dg)	105	Wall
15.4.84	SD	H	Doncaster	W	44-22	Crompton (3), Middlehurst, Andrews, Fletcher, Smith, Tabern	Wood (6)	175	Mean
20.4.84	SD	A	Blackpool B.	L	16-26	O'Toole, Williams, Smith	Wood (2)	—	—
23.4.84	SD	H	Batley	W	30-14	Smith, Crompton, Tabern, O'Toole, Crehan	Wood (4, 2dg)	180	Hodgson
26.4.84	SD	H	Rochdale H.	W	14-12	Shaw, Wragg	Wood (2, 2dg)	200	Allatt
29.4.84	SD (at Ebbw Vale)	A	Cardiff C.	L	16-34	Wragg, Crompton	Tabern (3, 2dg)	—	—
2.5.84	SD	A	Doncaster	D	16-16	Crompton, Wragg, Crehan	Tabern (2)	—	—

KEIGHLEY

Ground: Lawkholme Lane
Colours: White jerseys with scarlet and emerald green V, white shorts
First Season: 1901-02
Nickname: Lawkholmers
Chairman: Colin Farrar
Secretary: Mrs Betty Spencer
Coach: Lee Greenwood (Sept. 1982-Oct. 1983)
Geoff Peggs (Nov. 1983-)
Honours: **Division Two** Champions, 1902-03
Challenge Cup Beaten finalists, 1936-37
Yorkshire Cup Beaten finalists, 1943-44, 1951-52
Records: Attendance: 14,500 v. Halifax (RL Cup) 3 March, 1951
Season
Goals: 155 by B. Jefferson, 1973-74
Tries: 30 by J. Sherburn, 1934-35
Points: 331 by B. Jefferson, 1973-74
Match
Goals: 11 by R. Walker v. Castleford, 13 Jan, 1906; H. Cook v. Hull KR, 31 Oct, 1953
Tries: 5 by I. Jagger v. Castleford, 13 Jan, 1906; S. Stacey v. Liverpool C, 9 Mar, 1907
Points: 24 by J. Phillips v. Halifax, 5 Oct, 1957
Highest score: 67-0 v. Castleford, 1905-06
Highest against: 80-7 v. Hull, 1920-21

1983-84 PLAYERS' SUMMARY

	App.	Tries	Goals	D/Gls	Pts
Allan, Mick	5 + 1	—	—	—	—
Alred, David	1	—	3	—	6
Arnold, Derek	21 + 1	3	—	—	12
Atkins, Ken	0 + 3	—	—	—	—
Bailey, Andrew	1	—	—	—	—
Beale, Graham	7	—	4	1	9
Brearley, Graham	12 + 2	—	—	—	—
Brearley, Terry	23	4	—	—	16
Briggs, Trevor	9 + 1	—	—	1	1
Butterfield, Geoff	1	—	—	—	—
Cholmondeley, David	33 + 2	—	52	2	106
Ellis, David	11	2	—	—	8
Ellis, Kevin	11 + 1	2	—	—	8
Fairhurst, Ian	25 + 5	4	7	—	30
Farrell, Kevin	13 + 1	2	—	—	8
Ferres, Steve	13	3	—	3	15
Gaitley, Bob	1	—	—	—	—
Greenwood, Lee	8 + 1	2	—	—	8
Hawksworth, Mick	36 + 1	14	—	1	57
Hinchley, Keith	1	—	—	—	—
Hodgson, Gary	22 + 2	—	—	—	—
Illingworth, Sam	2 + 1	—	—	—	—
Kalinowski, Alex	8 + 3	1	—	—	4
Kirk, Steve	6 + 2	1	—	—	4
Kitchingman, Phil	1	—	—	—	—
Lenaghan, Carl	5	—	—	—	—
Lunn, Martyn	5	—	—	—	—
Mitchell, Gary	3 + 1	2	—	—	8
Moll, David	31	15	—	—	60
Morgan, Kevin	4	—	—	—	—
Nicholson, Steve	22	10	—	—	40
North, Colin	5 + 1	1	—	3	7
Palmer, Glen	0 + 2	—	—	—	—
Palmer, Neil	1	—	—	—	—
Parker, Andrew	0 + 1	—	—	—	—
Parsons, John	1	—	6	—	12
Pickerill, Neil	2 + 1	—	—	—	—
Priestley, Ray	2	—	—	—	—
Proctor, Rob	19 + 1	1	—	—	4
Pullen, Steve	3	—	—	—	—
Raistrick, Dean	8 + 3	1	—	5	9
Robinson, Colin	32 + 1	4	—	—	16
Rowse, Gary	12	—	9	—	18
Scanlon, Andy	18	—	—	—	—
Sellers, Les	28 + 1	1	—	—	4
Spencer, John	0 + 1	—	—	—	—
Starbuck, Paul	5	—	—	—	—
Watts, Gary	7 + 1	—	—	—	—
Whitehead, Bob	4	—	—	—	—
Winter, Martin	1	—	—	—	—
Wood, Neil	15 + 7	3	—	—	12
Trialists (3)	3	1	—	—	4
TOTALS					
54 players		77	81	16	486

1983-84 MATCH ANALYSIS

Date	Com-petition	H/A	Opponent	Rlt	Score	Tries	Goals	Atten-dance	Referee
21.8.83	SD	A	Batley	L	13-15	Greenwood, Fairhurst	Fairhurst (2), Briggs (dg)	—	—
24.8.83	SD	A	Doncaster	L	0-30	—	—	—	—
28.8.83	SD	H	Carlisle	W	18-14	Brearley, Kirk	Cholmondeley (5)	680	Volante
4.9.83	YC(1)	A	Dewsbury	W	18-8	Arnold (2), North	Cholmondeley (3)	—	—
11.9.83	SD	H	Huyton	W	10-6	Moll	Cholmondeley (3)	595	Haigh
14.9.83	YC(2)	H	Hull	L	8-30	Hawksworth, Moll	—	2503	Kershaw
18.9.83	SD	A	Huddersfield	W	14-12	Greenwood	Cholmondeley (5)	—	—
25.9.83	SD	H	Hunslet	L	14-18	Moll, Robinson	Cholmondeley (3)	1086	Holdsworth
2.10.83	SD	A	Dewsbury	L	18-28	Nicholson (2), Arnold	Fairhurst (2), Cholmondeley	—	—
9.10.83	SD	H	Rochdale H.	L	10-28	Hawksworth	Cholmondeley (3)	743	Spencer
16.10.83	SD	A	Workington T.	L	6-14	—	Cholmondeley (3)	—	—
23.10.83	SD	H	Swinton	L	14-23	Hawksworth, Robinson	Cholmondeley (3)	973	Whitfield
30.10.83	SD	A	Cardiff C.	W	11-6	Nicholson, Hawksworth	Cholmondeley (1, 1 dg)	—	—
6.11.83	JPS(1)	A	Dewsbury	W	17-14	Hawksworth, Nicholson	Cholmondeley (4), Raistrick	—	—
13.11.83	SD	H	Dewsbury	L	19-23	Hawksworth, Farrell, Fairhurst	Cholmondeley (3), North (dg)	904	Walker
20.11.83	JPS(2)	H	Swinton	L	8-23	Hawksworth	Cholmondeley, North (2 dg)	1577	Allatt
27.11.83	SD	H	Batley	W	25-1	Nicholson (2), Hawksworth, Ferres	Cholmondeley (3), Ferres (2 dg), Hawksworth (dg)	739	Massey
4.12.83	SD	A	Barrow	L	10-35	Moll, Nicholson	Cholmondeley	—	—
18.12.83	SD	H	Doncaster	W	30-12	Hawksworth, Sellers, Ferres, Moll, Fairhurst	Cholmondeley (5)	726	Robinson
26.12.83	SD	A	Blackpool B.	L	10-16	Wood, Nicholson	Cholmondeley	—	—
1.1.84	SD	H	Kent Invicta	L	14-20	Hawksworth, Wood	Cholmondeley (3)	821	Volante
8.1.84	SD	A	Huyton	W	12-8	Robinson, Nicholson, Moll	—	—	—
5.2.84	SD	A	Kent Invicta	L	16-26	Moll (2), Wood	Beale (2)	—	—
12.2.84	CC(1)	A	Hunslet	L	10-21	Moll, Proctor	Rowse	—	—
19.2.84	SD	H	Blackpool B.	L	11-16	Moll (2)	Beale, Ferres (dg)	634	Campbell
26.2.84	SD	H	Bramley	L	4-32	Fairhurst	—	670	Hodgson
29.2.84	SD	H	York	L	1-18	—	Beale (dg)	430	Berry
4.3.84	SD	A	Bramley	L	10-14	Raistrick, Ferres	Rowse	—	—
11.3.84	SD	H	Barrow	L	2-24	—	Beale	758	Kendrew
18.3.84	SD	A	York	D	11-11	Nicholson, Moll	Rowse, Raistrick (dg)	—	—
25.3.84	SD	H	Huddersfield	D	15-15	Moll, Ellis	Rowse (2), Cholmondeley, Raistrick (dg)	646	Kershaw
1.4.84	SD	A	Swinton	L	1-66	—	Raistrick (dg)	—	—
8.4.84	SD	A	Hunslet	L	24-29	Kalinowski, Brearley, Moll	Parsons (6)	—	—
11.4.84	SD	A	Rochdale H.	L	6-18	Moll	Rowse	—	—
13.4.84	SD	A	Carlisle	L	19-29	Priestley, Robinson, Hawksworth	Rowse (3), Cholmondeley (dg)	—	—
20.4.84	SD	H	Halifax	L	18-34	Farrell, Hawksworth, Ellis	Aldred (3)	1136	Walker
22.4.84	SD	A	Halifax	D	19-19	Hawksworth, T. Brearley, Ellis	Fairhurst (3), Raistrick (dg)	—	—
24.4.84	SD	H	Cardiff C.	L	6-30	Ellis	Mitchell	478	Whitfield
29.4.84	SD	H	Workington T.	L	14-38	T. Brearley, Hawksworth, Trialist	Mitchell	465	Kendrew

KENT INVICTA

Ground: London Road Stadium, Maidstone
Colours: White jerseys with blue V, white shorts
First Season: 1983-84
Nickname: Invicta
Chairman: Len Pearce
Secretary: Bob Fox
Coach: Bill Goodwin (Apr.-Nov. 1983)
Steve Lane (Nov. 1983-May 1984)
Records: Attendance: 2,107 v. St. Helens (JPS Trophy) 6 Nov, 1983

Season

Goals: 51 by L. Hopkins, 1983-84
Tries: 19 by M. Elia, 1983-84
Points: 130 by L. Hopkins, 1983-84

Match

Goals: 7 by L. Hopkins v. Huyton, 17 Nov, 1983
Tries: No player has scored more than 3
Points: 18 by L. Hopkins v. Huyton, 27 Nov, 1983; T. O'Shea v. Batley, 19 Feb, 1984
Highest score: 35-20 v. Huyton, 1983-84
Highest against: 80-8 v. Barrow, 1983-84

● From the 1984-85 season, Kent Invicta moved to Southend FC ground, being retitled Southend Invicta.

1983-84 PLAYERS' SUMMARY

	App.	Tries	Goals	D/Gls	Pts
Alexander, Adrian	2 + 5	—	—	—	—
Bishop, Gary	16	2	—	8	16
Bishop, Neil	18 + 1	3	—	—	12
Brannan, Alistair	19	4	—	—	16
Briscoe, Phil	16 + 6	—	8	—	16
Bruen, Bob	4	1	—	—	4
Clarkson, Peter	5 + 1	—	—	—	—
Cooper, Neil	1 + 1	—	—	—	—
Cooper, Tony	18 + 1	2	—	—	8
Elia, Mark	32 + 1	19	—	—	76
Feighan, Frank	34	6	—	—	24
Ferres, Steve	7	—	3	3	9
Freeman, Gary	3 + 5	2	—	—	8
French, Nigel	14	2	4	1	17
Gilmore, John	1 + 2	1	—	—	4
Harding, Dave	19	3	—	—	12
Heron, Wayne	5 + 1	—	—	—	—
Hetherington, Gary	17 + 1	1	—	—	4
Highley, Frank	1	—	—	—	—
Hopkins, Lynn	16	7	51	—	130
James, Kevin	1	—	—	—	—
Kellett, Neil	15 + 1	5	—	—	20
Lane, Steve	29 + 1	18	—	—	72
Law, David	1 + 1	1	—	—	4
Mattison, Neil	0 + 1	—	—	—	—
McCallion, Seamus	3 + 1	—	—	—	—
Meehan, Gary	7 + 3	—	—	—	—
Millington, John	6	—	—	—	—
Millington, Wayne	23 + 1	2	—	—	8
Mordell, Bob	23 + 2	1	—	—	4
Noel, Tony	4 + 3	1	—	—	4
Norton, Graeme	6 + 9	2	—	—	8
O'Shea, Terry	23 + 1	8	31	—	94
Page, Steve	3 + 2	1	—	—	4
Penola, Colin	29 + 1	5	—	—	20
Richardson, Terry	8	2	—	—	8
Rose, Steve	2 + 2	—	—	—	—
Spencer, Paul	0 + 1	—	—	—	—
Telea, Andrew	0 + 1	—	—	—	—
Thaler, Peter	4	—	—	—	—
Tuffs, Neil	3 + 1	1	—	—	4
Tuffs, Phil	0 + 1	—	—	—	—
Van Bellen, Ian	19 + 5	2	—	—	8
Wainwright, Graham	1	—	—	—	—
Webb, Andy	6 + 1	1	—	—	4
Trialists (2)	4	1	—	—	4
TOTALS					
47 players		104	97	12	622

1983-84 MATCH ANALYSIS

Date	Competition	H/A	Opponent	Rlt	Score	Tries	Goals	Attendance	Referee
21.8.83	SD	H	Cardiff C.	L	12-31	Lane	Hopkins (4)	1815	Whitfield
28.8.83	SD	H	Doncaster	W	22-12	Elia (2), French, Cooper	Hopkins (3)	511	Fox
11.9.83	SD	A	Batley	W	18-8	Brannan, Lane, Penola	Hopkins (3)	—	—
18.9.83	SD	H	Workington T.	L	11-12	Hopkins	Hopkins (3), G. Bishop (dg)	826	Thompson
25.9.83	SD	A	Blackpool B.	W	14-13	Penola, Hopkins	Hopkins (3)	—	—
2.10.83	SD	A	Hunslet	L	10-48	O'Shea, Hopkins	Hopkins	—	—
9.10.83	SD	H	Huddersfield	W	32-10	O'Shea, French, G. Bishop, Brannan, Lane	Hopkins (4), G. Bishop (4 dg)	835	Wall
16.10.83	SD	A	Bramley	L	6-12	N. Tuffs	Hopkins	—	—
23.10.83	SD	H	Dewsbury	W	28-16	Lane, O'Shea, G. Bishop, Hopkins	Hopkins (6)	745	Kendrew
30.10.83	SD	A	Swinton	W	13-10	Feighan, Freeman, Elia	French (dg)	—	—
6.11.83	JPS(1)	H	St. Helens	L	7-40	—	Hopkins (3), G. Bishop (dg)	2107	Berry
13.11.83	SD	H	Carlisle	W	28-12	Freeman, Hopkins, Elia, O'Shea, Norton	Hopkins (4)	892	Smith
27.11.83	SD	A	Huyton	W	35-20	Lane (2), Harding, Elia, Hopkins	Hopkins (7), G. Bishop (dg)	—	—
4.12.83	SD	H	Halifax	L	16-19	Brannan, Van Bellen, Hopkins	Hopkins (2)	846	Labadie (Fr)
18.12.83	SD	H	Bramley	W	15-11	Brannan, Hetherington	Hopkins (3), G. Bishop (dg)	523	Lindop
1.1.84	SD	A	Keighley	W	20-14	Lane, Noel, Kellett	Hopkins (4)	—	—
8.1.84	SD	A	Rochdale H.	L	10-29	Elia	O'Shea (3)	—	—
15.1.84	SD	H	York	W	22-18	Lane (2), Elia	O'Shea (5)	649	Massey
22.1.84	SD	H	Swinton	W	14-6	Elia, Feighan, Cooper	O'Shea	633	Lindop
29.1.84	SD	A	Barrow	L	16-34	N. Bishop, Norton, Elia	O'Shea (2)	—	—
5.2.84	SD	H	Keighley	W	26-16	Richardson (2), Harding (2), Lane	O'Shea (3)	684	Holdsworth
11.2.84	CC(1)	H	Castleford	L	20-42	Feighan (2), Elia	O'Shea (4)	1643	Campbell
19.2.84	SD	H	Batley	W	30-8	O'Shea (3), Elia (3)	O'Shea (3)	608	McDonald
26.2.84	SD	A	Dewsbury	L	2-15	—	O'Shea	—	—
4.3.84	SD	H	Huyton	L	10-12	Elia, Kellett	O'Shea	686	Beaumont
14.3.84	SD	A	Halifax	L	16-21	N. Bishop, Gilmour, Trialist	O'Shea (2)	—	—
18.3.84	SD	H	Blackpool B.	L	24-36	Lane (2), O'Shea, Feighan	O'Shea (4)	615	Kershaw
1.4.84	SD	A	Workington T.	L	12-21	Lane (2)	O'Shea (2)	—	—
8.4.84	SD	H	Barrow	L	8-80	Kellett, Lane	—	629	Allatt
11.4.84	SD	A	Cardiff C.	L	12-21	Webb, Penola	French (2)	—	—
15.4.84	SD	H	Hunslet	W	24-16	N. Bishop, Feighan, Page, W. Millington	French (2), Ferres (1, 2dg)	518	Haigh
21.4.84	SD	A	Huddersfield	L	1-31	—	Ferres (dg)	—	—
22.4.84	SD	A	Carlisle	L	12-34	Penola, Lane	Ferres (2)	—	—
28.4.84	SD	A	York	L	20-22	Elia (2), Bruen, Mordell	Briscoe (2)	—	—
29.4.84	SD	A	Doncaster	W	24-20	Elia, Penola, Kellett, Law, Van Bellen	Briscoe (2)	—	—
12.5.84	SD	H	Rochdale H.	W	32-12	Lane (2), Elia (2), Kellett, W. Millington	Briscoe (4)	416	Robinson

LEEDS

Ground: Headingley
Colours: Blue and amber jerseys, white shorts
First Season: 1895-96
Nickname: Loiners
Chairman: Harry Jepson
General Manager: Joe Warham
Coach: Robin Dewhurst (June 1981-Oct. 1983)
Maurice Bamford (Nov. 1983-)
Honours: **Championship** Winners, 1960-61, 1968-69, 1971-72
Beaten finalists, 1914-15, 1928-29, 1929-30, 1930-31, 1937-38, 1969-70, 1972-73
League Leaders Trophy Winners, 1966-67, 1967-68, 1968-69, 1969-70, 1971-72
Challenge Cup Winners, 1909-10, 1922-23, 1931-32, 1935-36, 1940-41, 1941-42, 1956-57, 1967-68, 1976-77, 1977-78
Beaten finalists, 1942-43, 1946-47, 1970-71, 1971-72
Yorkshire League Winners, 1901-02, 1927-28, 1930-31, 1933-34, 1934-35, 1936-37, 1937-38, 1950-51, 1954-55, 1956-57, 1960-61, 1966-67, 1967-68, 1968-69, 1969-70
Yorkshire Cup Winners, 1921-22, 1928-29, 1930-31, 1932-33, 1934-35, 1935-36, 1937-38, 1958-59, 1968-69, 1970-71, 1972-73, 1973-74, 1975-76, 1976-77, 1979-80, 1980-81
Beaten finalists, 1919-20, 1947-48, 1961-62, 1964-65
BBC2 Floodlit Trophy Winners, 1970-71
John Player Trophy Winners, 1972-73, 1983-84
Beaten finalists, 1982-83
Premiership Winners, 1974-75, 1978-79
Records: Attendance: 40,175 v. Bradford N. (League) 21 May, 1947

Season
Goals: 166 by L. Jones, 1956-57
Tries: 63 by E. Harris, 1935-36
Points: 431 by L. Jones, 1956-57
Match
Goals: 13 by B.L. Jones v. Blackpool B, 19 Aug, 1957
Tries: 8 by F. Webster v. Coventry, 12 Apr, 1913; E. Harris v. Bradford N, 14 Sep, 1931
Points: 31 by B.L. Jones v. Bradford N, 22 Aug, 1956
Highest score: 102-0 v. Coventry, 1912-13
Highest against: 71-0 v. Wakefield T., 1945-46

1983-84 PLAYERS' SUMMARY

	App.	Tries	Goals	D/Gls	Pts
Bell, Dean	22	4	—	—	16
Burke, Tony	6	1	—	—	4
Campbell, Mark	1 + 1	—	—	—	—
Carroll, John	3	—	—	—	—
Clark, Trevor	14 + 3	5	—	—	20
Conway, Mark	16 + 1	3	38	—	88
Cooper, Colin	3 + 4	—	—	—	—
Creasser, David	33 + 2	16	76	—	216
Dick, Kevin	22 + 6	3	8	—	28
Dickinson, Roy	23 + 2	1	—	—	4
Gill, Paul	5	—	—	—	—
Gunn, Richard	0 + 2	—	—	—	—
Hague, Neil	25 + 3	2	—	1	9
Healy, David	3 + 1	—	—	—	—
Heron, David	22 + 3	4	—	—	16
Heron, Wayne	2 + 4	—	—	—	—
Heselwood, David	14 + 9	5	—	—	20
Holmes, John	36	12	—	—	48
Ingham, Gareth	2 + 1	—	—	—	—
James, Kevin	0 + 1	—	—	—	—
Laurie, Mark	16 + 1	2	—	—	8
Lulham, Richard	1 + 1	—	—	—	—
Mackintosh, Andrew	5	—	—	—	—
Martin, Steve	21 + 4	4	—	—	16
Massa, Mark	8 + 1	3	—	—	12
Mitchell, Patrick	11	5	1	—	22
Moorby, Gary	26 + 4	4	—	—	16
Pitchford, Steve	2	—	—	—	—
Powell, Roy	0 + 1	—	—	—	—
Prendiville, Paul	25 + 1	5	4	—	28
Rayne, Keith	37 + 1	11	—	—	44
Rayne, Kevin	35 + 5	3	—	—	12
Smith, Andy	35	5	—	—	20
Sowden, Russell	7	—	—	—	—
Squire, Kevin	17 + 11	7	—	1	29
Sykes, Andy	5 + 1	—	—	—	—
Ward, David	21 + 1	2	—	—	8
Webb, Terry	23 + 1	10	—	—	40
Whitehead, Paul	3	—	1	—	2
Wilkinson, Ian	34	10	—	—	40
Wilson, Mark	1 + 2	—	—	—	—
TOTALS					
41 players		127	128	2	766

1983-84 MATCH ANALYSIS

Date	Competition	H/A	Opponent	Rlt	Score	Tries	Goals	Attendance	Referee
21.8.83	SLC	A	Oldham	L	16-25	Kevin Rayne, Dick	Conway (3), Dick	—	—
28.8.83	SLC	H	Salford	W	40-10	Wilkinson (3), Holmes (2), Heselwood	Conway (8)	4253	Campbell
4.9.83	YC(1)	A	Batley	W	30-14	Mitchell (2), Squire, Burke, Conway	Conway (5)	—	—
11.9.83	SLC	H	Warrington	L	12-14	Massa, D. Heron	Conway (2)	4861	Kershaw
14.9.83	YC(2)	A	York	W	24-16	Keith Rayne, Kevin Rayne, Mitchell, Holmes	Conway (4)	—	—
18.9.83	SLC	A	Wakefield T.	W	20-19	Creasser (3), Hague	Conway (2)	—	—
25.9.83	SLC	H	Whitehaven	W	48-8	Creasser (2), Massa (2), Mitchell, Kevin Rayne, Heselwood, Holmes, Ward	Conway (5), Mitchell	4500	Fox
28.9.83	YC(SF)	H	Hull	L	16-20	Creasser (2), Squire	Creasser (2)	10094	Fox
2.10.83	SLC	A	Castleford	L	4-54	D. Heron	—	—	—
9.10.83	SLC	H	Hull	L	12-40	Martin, Mitchell	Creasser (2)	8541	Whitfield
16.10.83	SLC	A	Fulham	W	44-10	Squire (2), Kevin Rayne (2), Smith, Creasser, Holmes, Webb	Creasser (6)	—	—
19.10.83	SLC	A	Wigan	L	6-20	—	Creasser (3)	—	—
26.10.83	SLC	H	Widnes	W	20-14	Martin, Creasser	Creasser (6)	5662	Mean
29.10.83	Tour	H	Queensland	L	2-58	—	Creasser	5651	Thompson
6.11.83	JPS(1)	A	Blackpool B.	W	12-9	Prendiville, Holmes	Dick (2)	—	—
13.11.83	SLC	H	Castleford	L	10-28	Holmes, Ward	Creasser	6424	Thompson
20.11.83	JPS(2)	H	Hull K. R.	W	12-6	Wilkinson, Bell	Creasser (2)	8623	Fox
27.11.83	JPS(3)	A	Swinton	W	16-12	Creasser, Wilkinson, Bell	Creasser (2)	—	—
4.12.83	SLC	A	Salford	W	24-10	Squire (2), Wilkinson, Moorby, Keith Rayne	Dick (2)	—	—
10.12.83	JPS(SF)	Hudd	Leigh	W	18-11	Keith Rayne (2), Prendiville	Creasser (3)	(5740)	Lindop
18.12.83	SLC	A	Featherstone R.	D	12-12	Webb, Holmes	Prendiville (2)	—	—
26.12.83	SLC	H	Fulham	W	30-6	Smith (2), Creasser, Moorby, Clark, Keith Rayne	Creasser (3)	6465	Allatt
2.1.84	SLC	H	Oldham	W	16-12	Dick, Prendiville, Keith Payne	Creasser (2)	7864	Walker
8.1.84	SLC	A	Widnes	W	17-8	Conway, Webb	Creasser (4), Squire (dg)	—	—
14.1.84	JPS(F)	Wigan	Widnes	W	18-10	Holmes, Dick	Creasser (5)	(9536)	Thompson
29.1.84	SLC	H	Wakefield T.	W	26-16	Webb(2), Holmes, Hague	Dick (3), Prendiville (2)	9291	Massey
5.2.84	SLC	A	Leigh	W	30-6	Creasser, Wilkinson, Smith, Clark, Keith Rayne	Creasser (5)	—	—
12.2.84	CC(1)	A	Salford	W	24-16	Creasser, Clark, Prendiville, Wilkinson	Creasser (4)	—	—
19.2.84	SLC	H	St. Helens	W	18-7	Webb, Keith Rayne, Laurie	Creasser (2), Conway	6652	Fox
26.2.84	CC(2)	A	Workington T.	W	12-3	Webb, Creasser	Creasser (2)	—	—
4.3.84	SLC	H	Hull K.R.	D	14-14	Laurie, Webb	Creasser (3)	9908	McDonald
11.3.84	CC(3)	H	Bradford N.	D	13-13	Martin, Holmes	Creasser (2), Hague (dg)	17494	Whitfield
15.3.84	CC(3) Replay	A	Bradford N.	W	12-10	Prendiville, Squire	Creasser (2)	—	—
18.3.84	SLC	A	Whitehaven	W	28-2	Moorby (2), Holmes, Bell	Creasser (6)	—	—
21.3.84	SLC	A	Hull	L	10-23	Clark, Wilkinson	Creasser	—	—
31.3.84	CC(SF)	Swinton	Widnes	L	4-15	Martin	—	(14046)	Thompson
3.4.84	SLC	H	Leigh	L	18-24	Dickinson, Bell, Creasser	Creasser (3)	5219	Lindop
8.4.84	SLC	A	Warrington	L	12-28	Conway, Heselwood	Conway (2)	—	—
10.4.84	SLC	A	St. Helens	L	10-20	Smith, Heselwood	Conway	—	—
13.4.84	SLC	H	Featherstone R.	W	12-10	Webb, Wilkinson	Conway (2)	5351	Kershaw
17.4.84	SLC	H	Wigan	L	10-14	Clark, Webb	Creasser	5914	Wall
20.4.84	SLC	H	Bradford N.	D	10-10	D. Heron	Creasser (3)	7230	Whitfield
22.4.84	SLC	A	Hull K.R.	W	20-16	D. Heron, Heselwood, Kevin Rayne	Conway (3), Whitehead	—	—
24.4.84	SLC	A	Bradford N.	L	4-34	Creasser	—	—	—
29.4.84	PT(1)	A	Hull K.R.	L	0-54	—	—	—	—

LEIGH

Ground: Hilton Park
Colours: Cherry and white jerseys, white shorts
First Season: 1895-96
Chairman: Basil Lowe
Secretary: John Stringer
Coach: Tommy Bishop (June 1983-June 1984)
John Woods (June 1984-)
Honours: **Championship** Winners, 1905-06
Division One Champions, 1981-82
Division Two Champions, 1977-78
Challenge Cup Winners, 1920-21, 1970-71
Lancashire Cup Winners, 1952-53, 1955-56, 1970-71, 1981-82
Beaten finalists, 1905-06, 1909-10, 1920-21, 1922-23, 1949-50, 1951-52, 1963-64, 1969-70
BBC2 Trophy Winners, 1969-70, 1972-73
Beaten finalists, 1967-68, 1976-77
Records: Attendance: 31,324 v. St. Helens (RL Cup) 14 March, 1953
Season
Goals: 166 by S. Ferguson, 1970-71
Tries: 36 by W. Kindon, 1956-57
Points: 356 by S. Ferguson, 1970-71
Match
Goals: 15 by M. Stacey v. Doncaster, 28 Mar, 1976
Tries: 6 by J. Wood v. York, 4 Oct, 1947
Points: 38 by J. Woods v. Blackpool B, 11 Sep, 1977
Highest score: 75-3 v. Doncaster, 1975-76
Highest against: 52-9 v. Wigan, 1924-25

1983-84 PLAYERS' SUMMARY

	App.	Tries	Goals	D/Gls	Pts
Ainsworth, Gary	13 + 12	6	—	—	24
Alexander, Adrian	8 + 4	3	—	—	12
Atherton, Wayne	7 + 4	1	6	—	16
Beazant, Darren	1 + 1	—	—	—	—
Bilsbury, Terry	1	—	—	—	—
Bishop, Neil	1	—	—	—	—
Boyd, Denis	3	—	—	—	—
Butler, John	3	—	—	—	—
Clarke, Jeff	23	3	—	—	12
Clarkson, Geoff	5 + 1	—	—	—	—
Cottrell, Tony	17 + 1	3	—	—	12
Donlan, Steve	38	16	6	3	79
Drummond, Des	32	17	—	—	68
Fairhurst, Shaun	0 + 1	—	—	—	—
Fitzmartin, Steve	6 + 3	—	—	—	—
Fox, Phil	31	19	—	—	76
Green, Ken	7 + 1	1	—	—	4
Griffiths, Steve	3	—	—	—	—
Henderson, John	30 + 2	7	1	—	30
Herdman, Martin	2	—	—	—	—
Hogan, Mike	17	2	—	—	8
Howarth, Roy	7 + 1	1	—	—	4
Hughes, Gary	11 + 2	3	—	—	12
Hunter, Edwin	5 + 1	1	—	—	4
Johnson, Chris	10 + 1	3	—	—	12
Johnson, Phil	10	1	—	—	4
Manfredi, Tony	1	—	—	—	—
Martyn, Tom	13 + 3	1	—	—	4
Potter, Ian	19	2	—	—	8
Pyke, Derek	33	6	—	—	24
Stradins, Gary	13 + 4	1	—	—	4
Tabern, Ray	14 + 6	4	—	—	16
Tomlinson, Steve	0 + 2	—	—	—	—
Varley, Shane	22	3	—	—	12
Waller, Tony	1	—	—	—	—
Westhead, John	32	6	—	—	24
Wilkinson, Alf	19 + 4	1	—	—	4
Woods, John	35	27	123	1	355
Worgan, Graham	1 + 3	1	—	—	4
TOTALS					
39 players		139	136	4	832

MANSFIELD MARKSMAN

Ground: Field Mill
Colours: Light and dark blue jerseys with gold trim
First Season: 1984-85
Chairman: Paul Tomlinson
General Manager: David Parker
Coach: Mick Blacker (May 1984-)

1983-84 MATCH ANALYSIS

Date	Competition	H/A	Opponent	Rlt	Score	Tries	Goals	Attendance	Referee
21.8.83	SLC	H	Widnes	L	12-19	Fox, Hunter	Woods (2)	5340	Spencer
24.8.83	SLC	H	Fulham	W	22-8	Donlan, Drummond, Westhead, Woods	Woods (3)	3638	McDonald
28.8.83	SLC	A	Wigan	W	26-12	Henderson (2), Tabern, Hogan	Donlan (4), Henderson	—	—
4.9.83	BBLC(1)	H	Carlisle	W	52-10	Westhead (2), Pyke (2), Hogan, Green, Drummond, Potter, Atherton, Martyn	Atherton (4), Donlan (2)	4000	Massey
7.9.83	SLC	A	Salford	W	38-6	Drummond, Henderson, Pyke, Donlan, Ainsworth	Woods (9)	—	—
11.9.83	SLC	H	Hull	L	12-20	Woods	Woods (4)	5951	Mean
14.9.83	BBLC(2)	H	Widnes	L	10-27	Woods, Fox	Woods	6500	Hodgson
18.9.83	SLC	A	Castleford	L	18-28	Fox (2), Woods	Woods (3)	—	—
25.9.83	SLC	H	Bradford N.	L	0-24	—	—	5064	Lindop
2.10.83	SLC	A	Wakefield T.	L	18-20	Donlan, Stradins	Woods (5)	—	—
9.10.83	SLC	H	Wigan	W	24-18	Drummond, Fox, Woods	Woods (6)	7742	Fox
16.10.83	SLC	A	Widnes	L	20-28	Varley, Pyke	Woods (6)	—	—
30.10.83	SLC	A	Whitehaven	W	38-16	Henderson (2), Donlan, Woods, Wilkinson, Varley, Ainsworth	Woods (5)	—	—
6.11.83	JPS(1)	A	Oldham	W	20-12	Woods (2), Donlan, Fox	Woods (2)	—	—
13.11.83	SLC	H	St. Helens	W	20-12	Ainsworth (2), Woods	Woods (4)	5487	Campbell
20.11.83	JPS(2)	A	Carlisle	W	68-17	Drummond (5), Tabern (2), Ainsworth, Alexander, Woods, Fox, Worgan	Woods (10)	—	—
27.11.83	JPS(3)	H	Cardiff C.	W	12-8	Fox, Alexander	Woods (2)	4134	Beaumont
10.12.83	JPS(SF)	Hudd	Leeds	L	11-18	Clarke, Drummond	Woods, Donlan (dg)	(5740)	Lindop
18.12.83	SLC	H	Whitehaven	W	68-14	Donlan (3), Drummond (2), Fox (2), Varley, Ainsworth, Pyke, Tabern, Clarke, Woods	Woods (8)	2753	Berry
27.12.83	SLC	A	Warrington	L	18-34	Woods (3)	Woods (3)	—	—
1.1.84	SLC	H	Wakefield T.	W	14-12	Fox (2), Donlan	Woods	4629	Kendrew
8.1.84	SLC	A	Oldham	Ab.*	26-14	Fox (2), Pyke, Drummond	Woods (5)	—	—
19.1.84	SLC	A	Hull	L	0-14	—	—	—	—
29.1.84	SLC	H	Featherstone R.	L	16-18	Potter, Woods	Woods (4)	2987	Hodgson
5.2.84	SLC	H	Leeds	L	6-30	Cottrell	Woods	4168	Whitfield
12.2.84	CC(1)	A	St. Helens	L	10-16	Drummond, Westhead	Woods	—	—
19.2.84	SLC	A	Hull K. R.	L	8-47	Cottrell	Woods (2)	—	—
24.2.84	SLC	A	Featherstone R.	W	21-5	Fox (2), Woods, Westhead	Woods (2), Donlan (dg)	—	—
4.3.84	SLC	H	Salford	W	31-22	Donlan (2), Clarke, Hughes, Alexander	Woods (5), Donlan (dg)	3297	Kershaw
11.3.84	SLC	A	Oldham	L	10-13	Drummond	Woods (3)	—	—
21.3.84	SLC	H	Oldham	L	15-21	Woods, Donlan, Fox	Woods (1, 1 dg)	3261	Thompson
25.3.84	SLC	A	Fulham	W	24-12	Woods (2), Fox, Hughes, Drummond	Woods (2)	—	—
27.3.84	SLC	A	Bradford N.	L	18-23	Woods, Hughes, Donlan	Woods (3)	—	—
1.4.84	SLC	H	Castleford	W	30-4	Woods, Henderson, Westhead, Cottrell, Donlan	Woods (5)	3053	Robinson
3.4.84	SLC	A	Leeds	W	24-18	Woods (3)	Woods (6)	—	—
6.4.84	SLC	A	St. Helens	L	12-37	Henderson, Fox	Atherton (2)	—	—
15.4.84	SLC	H	Hull K. R.	L	16-44	Woods, Howarth, C. Johnson	Woods (2)	5115	Spencer
23.4.84	SLC	H	Warrington	W	44-20	Woods (2), Donlan (2), C. Johnson (2), P. Johnson, Drummond	Woods (6)	4020	Holdsworth

*Abandoned after 56 minutes because of brawling. Match replayed.

OLDHAM

Ground: Watersheddings

Colours: Red and white hooped jerseys, red sleeves, white shorts

First Season: 1895-96

Nickname: Roughyeds

Chairman: Harvey Ashworth

Coach: Peter Smethurst (Apr. 1983-Feb. 1984)
Frank Barrow (Feb.-Feb. 1984)
Brian Gartland (Mar.-June 1984)
Frank Myler (June 1984-)

Honours: **Championship** Winners, 1909-10, 1910-11,1956-57
Beaten finalists, 1906-07, 1907-08, 1908-09, 1921-22, 1954-55
Division One Champions, 1904-05
Division Two Champions, 1963-64, 1981-82
Challenge Cup Winners, 1898-99, 1924-25, 1926-27
Beaten finalists, 1906-07, 1911-12, 1923-24, 1925-26
Lancashire League Winners, 1897-98, 1900-01, 1907-08, 1909-10, 1921-22, 1956-57, 1957-58
Lancashire Cup Winners, 1907-08, 1910-11, 1913-14, 1919-20, 1924-25, 1933-34, 1956-57, 1957-58, 1958-59
Beaten finalists, 1908-09, 1911-12, 1918-19, 1921-22, 1954-55, 1966-67, 1968-69

Records: Attendance: 28,000 v. Huddersfield (League) 24 February, 1912
Season
Goals: 200 by B. Ganley, 1957-58
Tries: 49 by R. Farrar, 1921-22
Points: 412 by B. Ganley, 1957-58
Match
Goals: 14 by B. Ganley v. Liverpool C, 4 Apr, 1959
Tries: 7 by Miller v. Barry, 31 Oct, 1908
Points: 30 by A. Johnson v. Widnes, 9 Apr, 1928
Highest score: 67-6 v. Liverpool C., 1958-59
Highest against: 67-11 v. Hull K.R., 1978-79

1983-84 PLAYERS' SUMMARY

	App.	Tries	Goals	D/Gls	Pts
Ashton, Ray	27 + 1	13	—	3	55
Bardgett, Joe	4	4	—	—	16
Birkby, Ian	17 + 7	3	—	1	13
Bishop, Gary	1 + 2	1	—	—	4
Chadwick, Les	1 + 1	—	—	—	—
Coombes, Michael	1 + 1	—	—	—	—
Coyle, Craig	2 + 4	1	—	—	4
Flanagan, Terry	31 + 1	3	—	—	12
Foy, Des	34	13	—	—	52
Goodway, Andy	23 + 1	10	—	—	40
Hawkyard, Colin	14 + 2	3	—	—	12
Hornby, Jimmy	30 + 1	5	—	—	20
Jones, Wally	30	1	—	—	4
Kirwan, Paddy	14 + 3	1	—	—	4
Littler, Steve	18	—	—	—	—
Lowndes, Paul	7	2	—	—	8
McCurrie, Alan	31 + 1	3	—	4	16
Meadows, Kevin	4	6	—	—	24
Morgan, Mick	29 + 5	3	—	—	12
Munro, Geoff	1	—	—	—	—
Naidole, Tom	9 + 9	—	—	—	—
Parrish, Mick	33	5	101	—	222
Platt, Alan	5	1	4	—	12
Sanderson, Ian	3	1	—	—	4
Sherman, Paul	2 + 1	1	—	—	4
Sinclair, Alan	17 + 3	2	—	—	8
Taylor, Michael	20 + 1	8	—	—	32
Vigo, Green	8	3	—	—	12
Willis, Chris	14 + 1	—	—	—	—
Worrall, Mick	30	9	2	—	40
Wright, Nick	8	—	3	—	6
TOTALS					
31 players		102	110	8	636

Ray Ashton . . . Great Britain tourist.

1983-84 MATCH ANALYSIS

Date	Competition	H/A	Opponent	Rlt	Score	Tries	Goals	Attendance	Referee
21.8.83	SLC	H	Leeds	W	25-16	Taylor (2), Worrall, Ashton	Parrish (4), Ashton (dg)	3549	Lindop
28.8.83	SLC	A	Bradford N.	L	8-14	Ashton	Parrish (2)	—	—
4.9.83	LC(1)	H	Workington T.	W	26-20	Worrall (2), Goodway, Ashton, Parrish, Foy	Parrish	2567	Mean
11.9.83	SLC	A	Featherstone R.	W	24-16	Goodway (2), Lowndes, Flanagan	Platt (4)	—	—
14.9.83	LC(2)	A	Swinton	L	6-8	Vigo	Parrish	—	—
18.9.83	SLC	H	Fulham	W	30-12	Ashton (3), Morgan, Goodway	Parrish (5)	3222	Allatt
25.9.83	SLC	A	Hull K. R.	D	18-18	Platt, Flanagan, Ashton	Parrish (3)	—	—
2.10.83	SLC	H	St. Helens	W	32-6	Foy (2), Ashton (2), Vigo (2)	Parrish (4)	3877	Smith
9.10.83	SLC	H	Widnes	L	10-20	Ashton	Parrish (3)	4541	Berry
19.10.83	SLC	A	Castleford	W	18-16	Foy (2)	Parrish (5)	—	—
23.10.83	SLC	H	Hull	W	18-12	Ashton, Worrall, Hawkyard	Parrish (3)	5935	Spencer
30.10.83	SLC	A	Warrington	D	22-22	Hornby (2), Lowndes	Parrish (4), Birkby (dg), Ashton (dg)	—	—
6.11.83	JPS(1)	H	Leigh	L	12-20	Hornby, Worrall	Parrish (2)	6264	Holdsworth
13.11.83	SLC	H	Wigan	W	8-4	Foy	Parrish (2)	6493	Beaumont
20.11.83	SLC	A	Fulham	L	4-21	—	Parrish (2)	—	—
27.11.83	SLC	H	Hull K. R.	L	10-18	Ashton	Wright (3)	4619	Hodgson
18.12.83	SLC	A	Wakefield T.	L	22-28	Foy (2), Ashton, Worrall, Hornby	Worrall	—	—
26.12.83	SLC	H	Salford	W	18-6	Sanderson, Foy, Taylor	Parrish (2), Worrall	3975	Volante
2.1.84	SLC	A	Leeds	L	12-16	Birkby, Worrall	Parrish (2)	—	—
8.1.84	SLC	H	Leigh	Ab.*	14-26	Sinclair, Taylor	Parrish (3)	4455	Mean
1.2.84	SLC	H	Featherstone R.	L	4-19	Sinclair	—	2423	Wall
5.2.84	SLC	A	Hull	L	8-20	Bishop	Parrish (2)	—	—
12.2.84	CC(1)	H	Huyton	W	28-10	Foy (2), Sherman, Parrish	Parrish (6)	2552	Whitfield
19.2.84	SLC	A	Whitehaven	L	8-42	Coyle	Parrish (2)	—	—
26.2.84	CC(2)	A	Wigan	L	6-30	McCurrie	Parrish	—	—
4.3.84	SLC	H	Bradford N.	W	10-4	—	Parrish (5)	3510	Massey
11.3.84	SLC	H	Leigh	W	13-10	Hornby, Birkby	Parrish (2), McCurrie (dg)	3918	Smith
14.3.84	SLC	A	Wigan	L	6-12	Goodway	Parrish	—	—
18.3.84	SLC	H	Warrington	L	11-14	Taylor (2)	Parrish, McCurrie (dg)	4081	Haigh
21.3.84	SLC	A	Leigh	W	21-15	Taylor, Parrish, Goodway	Parrish (4), McCurrie	—	—
25.3.84	SLC	H	Whitehaven	W	24-13	Hawkyard (2), Birkby, Goodway	Parrish (4)	2340	Beaumont
1.4.84	SLC	A	St. Helens	L	20-31	Parrish, Goodway, Foy	Parrish (4)	—	—
8.4.84	SLC	A	Widnes	W	34-28	Bardgett (2), Morgan, Worrall, Kirwan	Parrish (6), McCurrie (dg), Ashton (dg)	—	—
11.4.84	SLC	H	Castleford	L	2-13	—	Parrish	2616	Walker
15.4.84	SLC	H	Wakefield T.	W	54-4	Jones, Goodway, Taylor, Flanagan, Morgan, McCurrie, Parrish, Meadows, Bardgett	Parrish (9)	2523	Kendrew
20.4.84	SLC	A	Salford	W	50-10	Meadows (5), McCurrie, Goodway, Worrall, Bardgett, Foy	Parrish (5)	—	—

*Abandoned after 56 minutes because of brawling. Match replayed.

ROCHDALE HORNETS

Ground: Athletic Ground
Colours: White jerseys with blue and red band, white shorts
First season: 1895-96
Nickname: Hornets
Chairman: David Ratcliffe
Secretary: Keith Mort
Coach: Bill Kirkbride (June 1982-)
Honours: **Challenge Cup** Winners, 1921-22
Lancashire League Winners, 1918-19
Lancashire Cup Winners, 1911-12, 1914-15, 1918-19
Beaten finalists, 1912-13, 1919-20, 1965-66
John Player Trophy Beaten finalists 1973-74
BBC2 Floodlit Trophy Beaten finalists 1971-72
Records: Attendance: 41,831 Wigan v. Oldham (RL Cup Final) 12 Apr 1924
Home: 26,664 v. Oldham (RL Cup) 25 March, 1922
Season
Goals: 107 by W. Holliday, 1973-74
Tries: 30 by J. Williams, 1934-35
Points: 235 by G. Starkey, 1966-67
Match
Goals: 10 by H. Lees v. Glasshoughton, 19 Feb, 1938
Tries: 5 by J. Corsi v. Barrow, 31 Dec, 1921 and v. Broughton Moor, 25 Feb, 1922; J. Williams v. St. Helens, 4 Apr, 1933; N. Brelsford v. Whitehaven, 3 Sep, 1972
Points: 27 by F. Blincow v. Normanton, 17 Oct, 1903
Highest score: 75-15 v. Broughton M., 1914-15
Highest against: 79-2 v. Hull, 1920-21

1983-84 PLAYERS' SUMMARY

	App.	Tries	Goals	D/Gls	Pts
Allan, Tony	2	—	—	—	—
Birdsall, Charlie	28	3	1	3	17
Brierley, Mark	1	—	—	—	—
Brown, Dave	0 + 1	—	—	—	—
Brown, Graham	4	—	—	—	—
Buckley, Denis	18	3	—	—	12
Claughton, George	1	—	—	—	—
Davies, Garry	15 + 1	5	—	—	20
Deakin, Chris	29	4	—	—	16
Duffy, Andy	17 + 6	2	—	—	8
Ellis, Ian	1 + 2	—	—	—	—
Glover, John	0 + 1	—	—	—	—
Grattan, Martin	7	—	—	—	—
Hartley, Neil	1	—	—	—	—
Haslam, Rod	16 + 5	—	3	—	6
Hughes, Brian	37	1	—	6	10
Keaveney, Alan	1	—	—	—	—
Langan, Terry	13	1	—	—	4
Lowe, Kevin	30	—	—	—	—
McGiffen, Steve	33	6	—	—	24
Molyneux, Jim	13 + 1	1	—	—	4
Morris, Geoff	20 + 8	4	—	—	16
Munro, Geoff	17	7	—	—	28
Platt, Billy	33 + 2	6	14	16	68
Sanderson, Mark	5 + 4	—	—	—	—
Simpkin, Kevin	34	3	—	—	12
Standidge, George	16 + 5	1	—	—	4
Stapleton, John	17 + 6	21	—	1	85
Turner, Steve	31 + 2	3	85	—	182
Ubermanowicz, Tony	7	2	—	—	8
Wainwright, Tony	19 + 1	10	—	1	41
Whitehead, Craig	1	—	—	—	—
Wiltshire, Roy	14	1		—	4
TOTALS 33 players		84	103	27	569

George Standidge ... one try in 21 appearances.

1983-84 MATCH ANALYSIS

Date	Competition	H/A	Opponent	Rlt	Score	Tries	Goals	Attendance	Referee
21.8.83	SD	H	York	L	14-26	Morris, Davies	Haslam (3)	365	Volante
24.8.83	SD	A	Batley	L	14-20	Wainwright, Platt	Platt (3)	—	—
28.8.83	SD	A	Huddersfield	D	24-24	Stapleton, Wainwright, McGiffen	Platt (6)	—	—
3.9.83	LC(1)	H	St. Helens	L	4-28	Davies	—	720	Campbell
11.9.83	SD	H	Doncaster	W	40-20	Stapleton (2), Duffy, Morris, Buckley, Platt, Davies	Turner (6)	409	Whitfield
18.9.83	SD	H	Halifax	L	6-18	—	Platt (3)	902	Campbell
25.9.83	SD	A	York	L	15-28	Stapleton, Birdsall	Turner (3), Platt (dg)	—	—
2.10.83	SD	A	Bramley	D	21-21	Stapleton (3), Buckley	Turner, Hughes (2 dg), Platt (dg)	—	—
9.10.83	SD	A	Keighley	W	28-10	Stapleton (2), Buckley, Deakin, Morris	Turner (4)	—	—
16.10.83	SD	H	Hunslet	L	10-13	—	Turner (4), Birdsall	694	Kendrew
23.10.83	SD	H	Blackpool B.	W	13-4	Stapleton (2), Ubermanowicz	Birdsall (dg)	551	Holdsworth
30.10.83	SD	A	Carlisle	W	24-22	Wainwright (2), Ubermanowicz, Stapleton	Turner (4)	—	—
6.11.83	JPS(1)	A	Cardiff C.	L	6-41	Wainwright	Turner	—	—
13.11.83	SD	H	Huyton	W	10-5	Stapleton	Turner (2), Platt (2 dg)	371	Carter (Pr)
27.11.83	SD	A	Doncaster	W	36-12	McGiffen (2), Wainwright, Simpson, Munro, Haslam	Turner (6)	—	—
11.12.83	SD	A	Blackpool B.	W	10-8	Platt	Turner (2), Wainwright (dg), Platt (dg)	—	—
18.12.83	SD	H	Carlisle	L	10-14	Munro	Turner (3)	473	Mean
26.12.83	SD	A	Swinton	L	10-30	Simpkin	Turner (3)	—	—
1.1.84	SD	H	Cardiff C.	W	7-4	Munro	Platt (2 dg), Hughes (dg)	446	Smith
8.1.84	SD	H	Kent Invicta	W	29-10	Standidge, Deakin, McGiffen, Wainwright	Turner (6), Platt (dg)	532	Hodgson
15.1.84	SD	A	Barrow	L	6-30	Hughes	Turner	—	—
12.2.84	CC(1)	H	York	L	8-17	Birdsall	Turner, Platt (dg) Hughes (dg)	756	McDonald
26.2.84	SD	H	Barrow	L	6-14	Wainwright	Platt (2dg)	641	Fox
4.3.84	SD	A	Hunslet	L	20-30	Munro, Stapleton	Turner (5), Platt	—	—
11.3.84	SD	H	Batley	L	14-30	Duffy, Wainwright	Turner (3)	509	Lindop
15.3.84	SD	H	Bramley	L	7-9	Deakin	Turner, Platt (dg)	275	Berry
18.3.84	SD	H	Dewsbury	W	38-21	Stapleton (2), Davies, McGiffen, Birdsall Platt, Wainwright	Turner (5)	541	Campbell
22.3.84	SD	H	Workington T.	D	8-8	—	Turner (4)	373	Volante
1.4.84	SD	A	Dewsbury	L	15-42	Wiltshire, Turner Munro	Turner, Hughes (dg)	—	—
6.4.84	SD	A	Cardiff C.	L	5-27	McGiffen	Birdsall (dg)	—	—
8.4.84	SD	H	Huddersfield	W	3-0	—	Turner, Platt (dg)	746	Massey
11.4.84	SD	H	Keighley	W	18-6	Deakin, Turner	Turner (5)	273	Beaumont
15.4.84	SD	A	Workington T.	L	26-38	Stapleton (3), Munro,	Turner (5)	—	—
20.4.84	SD	H	Swinton	W	31-27	Simpkin, Turner, Stapleton, Platt, Munro	Turner (4), Birdsall (dg) Platt (dg), Stapleton (dg)	1044	Haigh
26.4.84	SD	A	Huyton	L	12-14	Stapleteon, Morris	Turner (2)	—	—
29.4.84	SD	A	Halifax	L	9-50	Molyneux	Turner (2), Platt (dg)	—	—
12.5.84	SD	A	Kent Invicta	L	12-32	Platt, Davies	Platt (1, 1dg), Hughes (dg)	—	—

ST. HELENS

Ground: Knowsley Road
Colours: Red and white jerseys, white shorts
First Season: 1895-96
Nickname: Saints
Chairman: John Clegg
Secretary: Geoff Sutcliffe
Coach: Billy Benyon (May 1982-)
Honours: **Championship** Winners, 1931-32, 1952-53, 1958-59, 1965-66, 1969-70, 1970-71
Beaten finalists, 1964-65, 1966-67, 1971-72
Division One Champions, 1974-75
League Leaders Trophy Winners, 1964-65, 1965-66
Club Championship (Merit Table) Beaten finalists, 1973-74
Challenge Cup Winners, 1955-56, 1960-61, 1965-66, 1971-72, 1975-76
Beaten finalists, 1896-97, 1914-15, 1929-30, 1952-53, 1977-78
Lancashire Cup Winners, 1926-27, 1953-54, 1960-61, 1961-62, 1962-63, 1963-64, 1964-65, 1967-68, 1968-69
Beaten finalists, 1932-33, 1952-53, 1956-57, 1958-59, 1959-60, 1970-71, 1982-83
Lancashire League Winners, 1929-30, 1931-32, 1952-53, 1959-60, 1964-65, 1965-66, 1966-67, 1968-69
Premiership Winners, 1975-76, 1976-77
Beaten finalists, 1974-75
Western Division Championship Winners, 1963-64
BBC2 Trophy Winners, 1971-72, 1975-76
Beaten finalists, 1965-66, 1968-69, 1970-71, 1977-78, 1978-79
Records: Attendance: 35,695 v. Wigan (League) 26 December, 1949
Season
Goals: 214 by K. Coslett, 1971-72
Tries: 62 by T. Van Vollenhoven, 1958-59
Points: 452 by K. Coslett, 1971-72
Match
Goals: 13 by G. Lewis v. Wardley, 16 Feb, 1924; P. Fearis v. Barrow, 14 Feb, 1959; G. Pimblett v. Bramley, 5 Mar, 1978
Tries: 6 by A. Ellaby v. Barrow, 5 Mar, 1932; S. Llewellyn v. Castleford, 3 Mar, 1956 and v. Liverpool C, 20 Aug, 1956; T. Vollenhoven v. Wakefield T, 21 Dec, 1957 and v. Blackpool B, 23 Apr, 1962; F. Myler v. Maryport, 1 Sep, 1969
Points: 29 by P. Fearis v. Barrow, 14 Feb, 1959
Highest score: 73-0 v. Wardley, 1923-24
Highest against: 78-3 v. Warrington, 1908-09

1983-84 PLAYERS' SUMMARY

	App.	Tries	Goals	D/Gls	Pts
Allen, Shaun	20 + 7	4	—	—	16
Arkwright, Chris	17	8	—	—	32
Bottell, Gary	5 + 8	—	—	—	—
Bowes, Mick	1	—	—	—	—
Burke, Tony	32	3	—	—	12
Butler, John	1	—	—	—	—
Fairclough, David	0 + 1	—	—	—	—
Forber, Paul	4 + 2	—	—	—	—
Gelling, Brian	1 + 2	1	—	—	4
Glover, Mick	4	—	—	—	—
Gorley, Peter	37	4	—	—	16
Griffiths, Clive	23	5	77	5	179
Grimes, Paul	23	4	—	—	16
Haggerty, Roy	32	17	—	1	69
Holding, Neil	34	19	2	8	88
James, Mel	5 + 2	—	—	—	—
Ledger, Barry	37	17	12	2	94
Liptrot, Graham	34	4	—	—	16
Litherland, Dennis	16 + 4	7	—	—	28
Loughlin, Paul	1 + 2	—	2	—	4
McIntyre, Colin	13	4	—	—	16
Meadows, Kevin	7	2	—	—	8
Moorby, Gary	6	1	—	—	4
Parkes, Brian	11 + 2	6	—	—	24
Peters, Steve	23	5	—	—	20
Pinner, Harry	34	4	—	14	30
Platt, Andy	31 + 1	10	—	1	41
Round, Paul	28	5	—	—	20
Rule, Steve	36 + 1	5	49	—	118
Seabrook, Derek	6 + 3	1	—	—	4
Smith, John	10 + 11	1	—	—	4
Wellens, Kevin	0 + 4	—	—	—	—
TOTALS					
32 players		137	142	31	863

1983-84 MATCH ANALYSIS

Date	Comp.	H/A	Opponent	Rlt	Score	Tries	Goals	Att.	Referee
21.8.83	SLC	H	Hull K. R.	W	30-11	Parkes, Grimes, Haggerty, Platt, Ledger	Rule (5)	4724	McDonald
28.8.83	SLC	A	Warrington	W	12-8	Platt (2)	Rule (2)	—	—
3.9.83	LC(1)	A	Rochdale H.	W	28-4	Holding (2), Ledger, Meadows, Peters	Rule (4)	—	—
11.9.83	SLC	H	Castleford	L	10-22	Holding	Rule (3)	4470	Wall
14.9.83	LC(2)	H	Warrington	L	26-30	Ledger (2), Holding, Platt, Grimes	Rule (3)	5047	Wall
18.9.83	SLC	A	Bradford N.	L	10-14	Gelling, Meadows	Rule	—	—
25.9.83	SLC	H	Wakefield T.	W	50-12	Peters (3), Haggerty (2), Smith, Moorby, Griffiths, Rule	Griffiths (7)	3390	Spencer
2.10.83	SLC	A	Oldham	L	6-32	Gorley	Griffiths	—	—
9.10.83	SLC	H	Fulham	W	18-14	Holding, Parkes	Rule (5)	3158	Mean
23.10.83	SLC	H	Bradford N.	W	29-14	Litherland (2), Ledger, Grimes, Griffiths	Rule (4), Platt (dg)	4913	Hodgson
30.10.83	SLC	H	Featherstone R.	W	19-13	Parkes, Holding, Gorley	Rule (3), Pinner (dg)	3770	Beaumont
6.11.83	JPS(1)	A	Kent Invicta	W	40-7	McIntyre (2), Platt, Griffiths, Ledger, Parkes, Grimes	Griffiths (5), Rule	—	—
13.11.83	SLC	A	Leigh	L	12-20	Ledger, Round	Rule (2)	—	—
19.11.83	JPS(2)	A	Warrington	W	18-10	Holding, Peters	Griffiths (3), Pinner (2 dg), Holding (dg), Ledger (dg)	—	—
27.11.83	JPS(3)	H	Featherstone R.	W	16-12	Holding, Liptrot	Griffiths (3, 1 dg), Ledger (dg)	5196	Whitfield
4.12.83	SLC	A	Hull K. R.	L	7-32	Liptrot	Griffiths (1, 1 dg)	—	—
17.12.83	JPS(SF)	War'n	Widnes	L	4-18	—	Griffiths, Rule	(5729)	Fox
20.12.83	SLC	A	Salford	W	18-16	Round, Litherland, Ledger	Rule (3)	—	—
26.12.83	SLC	A	Wigan	L	8-12	Gorley	Rule (2)	—	—
1.1.84	SLC	H	Widnes	L	12-20	Platt, Haggerty	Ledger (2)	7184	Holdsworth
8.1.84	SLC	A	Wakefield T.	L	22-31	Haggerty, Allan, Ledger, Platt	Rule (3)	—	—
11.1.84	SLC	A	Hull	L	24-30	Holding, Arkwright, Litherland, Burke	Rule (3), Holding	—	—
15.1.84	SLC	H	Whitehaven	W	40-10	Haggerty (2), McIntyre, Arkwright, Rule, Holding, Litherland, Burke	Rule (4)	1222	Spencer
22.1.84	SLC	A	Fulham	W	30-0	Haggerty, Rule, Litherland, Griffiths	Griffiths (7)	—	—
5.2.84	SLC	H	Salford	W	20-0	Haggerty (2), Round	Griffiths (4)	3431	Campbell
12.2.84	CC(1)	H	Leigh	W	16-10	Platt, Holding	Griffiths (3, 1dg), Holding (dg)	6556	Gocher (A)
19.2.84	SLC	A	Leeds	L	7-18	—	Griffiths (3, 1dg)	—	—
25.2.84	CC(2)	H	Hull	W	24-14	Haggerty, Pinner, Holding	Griffiths (4), Pinner (4dg)	5815	Thompson
4.3.84	SLC	A	Featherstone R.	W	21-13	Ledger (2), Holding	Griffiths (4), Holding (dg)	—	—
11.3.84	CC(3)	H	Wigan	L	7-16	Ledger	Griffiths, Holding (dg)	20007	Fox
16.3.84	SLC	H	Hull	W	22-10	Holding (2), Haggerty	Griffiths (4, 1dg), Pinner (dg)	3375	Massey
20.3.84	SLC	H	Warrington	W	37-25	Ledger (3), Round, Parkes, Arkwright	Ledger (5), Holding, Pinner (dg)	5216	Kershaw
25.3.84	SLC	A	Castleford	L	22-26	Arkwright, Allen, Holding, Haggerty	Griffiths (3)	—	—
1.4.84	SLC	H	Oldham	W	31-20	Arkwright (2), Allen (2), Holding, Ledger	Ledger (2), Loughlin, Holding (dg)	4737	Spencer
6.4.84	SLC	H	Leigh	W	37-12	Holding (2), Rule (2), Liptrot, Gorley	Griffiths (6), Pinner (dg)	4410	Campbell
10.4.84	SLC	H	Leeds	W	20-10	Haggerty, Ledger, Griffiths	Griffiths (3), Pinner (dg), Haggerty (dg)	3953	Whitfield
15.4.84	SLC	A	Whitehaven	W	27-21	Platt (2), Pinner (2)	Griffiths (5), Holding (dg)	—	—
20.4.84	SLC	H	Wigan	W	20-13	Arkwright, Haggerty, Seabrook, Pinner	Griffiths (2)	11894	Fox
23.4.84	SLC	A	Widnes	D	28-28	Burke, Liptrot, Litherland, Parkes, McIntyne	Ledger (3), Loughlin	—	—
29.4.84	PT(1)	A	Warrington	W	19-13	Round, Haggerty	Griffiths (4), Pinner (3dg)	—	—
9.5.84	PT(SF)	A	Hull K. R.	L	16-21	Arkwright, Haggerty	Griffiths (3), Holding (2dg)	—	—

SALFORD

Ground: The Willows
Colours: Red jerseys, white shorts
First Season: 1896-97
Nickname: Red Devils
Chairman: John Wilkinson
Secretary: Graham Morris
Coach: Mal Aspey (May 1982-Oct. 1983)
Mike Coulman (Oct. 1983-May 1984)
Kevin Ashcroft (May 1984-)
Honours: **Championship** Winners, 1913-14, 1932-33, 1936-37, 1938-39
Beaten finalists, 1933-34
Division One Champions, 1973-74, 1975-76
Challenge Cup Winners, 1937-38
Beaten finalists, 1899-00, 1901-02, 1902-03, 1905-06, 1938-39, 1968-69
Lancashire League Winners, 1932-33, 1933-34, 1934-35, 1936-37, 1938-39
Lancashire Cup Winners, 1931-32, 1934-35, 1935-36, 1936-37, 1972-73
Beaten finalists, 1929-30, 1938-39, 1973-74, 1974-75, 1975-76
Premiership Beaten finalists, 1975-76
John Player Trophy Beaten finalists 1972-73
BBC2 Trophy Winners, 1974-75
Records: Attendance: 26,470 v. Warrington (RL Cup) 13 February, 1937
Season
Goals: 221 by D. Watkins, 1972-73
Tries: 46 by K. Fielding, 1973-74
Points: 493 by D. Watkins, 1972-73
Match
Goals: 13 by A. Risman v. Bramley, 5 Apr, 1933 and v. Broughton R, 18 May, 1940; D. Watkins v. Keighley, 7 Jan, 1972; S. Rule v. Doncaster, 4 Sep, 1981
Tries: 6 by F. Miles v. Lees, 5 Mar, 1898; E. Bone v. Goole, 29 Mar, 1902; J. Hilton v. Leigh, 7 Oct, 1939
Points: 39 by J. Lomas v. Liverpool C, 2 Feb, 1907
Highest score: 78-0 v. Liverpool C., 1906-07
Highest against: 60-5 v. Workington T., 1962-63

1983-84 PLAYERS' SUMMARY

	App.	Tries	Goals	D/Gls	Pts
Aspey, Mal	1	—	—	—	—
Beckett, Adrian	0 + 2	—	—	—	—
Bentley, Keith	21	3	—	—	12
Blackwood, Bob	2 + 2	—	—	—	—
Bloor, Darren	17 + 7	5	—	—	20
Boyd, Denis	15	—	—	—	—
Brownbill, Paul	6	—	—	—	—
Byrne, Gerard	31	18	—	—	72
Dickens, Steve	11 + 1	—	—	—	—
Driver, David	12	3	—	—	12
Fletcher, Paul	30 + 2	1	16	—	36
Gee, Peter	5	—	—	—	—
Gill, Mick	5 + 4	—	—	—	—
Glynn, Peter	30 + 1	4	—	—	16
Griffiths, David	0 + 2	—	—	—	—
Groves, Paul	31	3	—	—	12
Henney, Harold	8 + 6	1	—	—	4
Hunter, Brian	0 + 1	—	—	—	—
Jamieson, Ged	1 + 2	—	—	—	—
Lamb, Nigel	2 + 2	—	—	—	—
Maggs, Keith	11	2	—	—	8
Major, David	13 + 9	—	—	—	—
McTigue, Mick	30	4	—	—	16
Meachin, Colin	1 + 1	—	—	—	—
Nash, Steve	22	1	—	1	5
Nicholls, George	7	—	—	—	—
O'Neill, Paul	4	1	—	—	4
Prescott, Eric	7	1	—	—	4
Richards, Maurice	1	1	—	—	4
Rogers, Jon	4	1	—	—	4
Ruddy, David	6 + 1	1	—	—	4
Shuttleworth, Paul	24 + 1	5	18	2	58
Smith, Ron	20 + 3	1	23	—	50
Taylor, John	5 + 3	—	—	—	—
Turnbull, Sam	11 + 2	—	—	—	—
Twist, David	5	—	9	—	18
Williams, Stewart	35	12	—	—	48
Wood, John	18	4	—	—	16
Yates, Malcolm	2	—	—	—	—
Trialist	1	—	—	—	—
TOTALS					
40 players		72	66	3	423

SHEFFIELD EAGLES

Ground: Owlerton Stadium
Colours: Black, red and yellow jerseys
First Season: 1984-85
Chairman: David Betts
General Manager: Gary Hetherington
Coach: Alan Rhodes (May 1984-)

1983-84 MATCH ANALYSIS

Date	Com-petition	H/A	Opponent	Rlt	Score	Tries	Goals	Atten-dance	Referee
21.8.83	SLC	H	Wigan	L	14-16	Richards, McTigue	Smith (3)	3858	Allatt
28.8.83	SLC	A	Leeds	L	10-40	Driver, Glynn	Smith	—	—
4.9.83	LC(1)	H	Fulham	W	16-15	Driver, Fletcher, Williams	Smith (2)	1986	Whitfield
7.9.83	SLC	H	Leigh	L	6-38	Groves	Smith	3723	Robinson
11.9.83	SLC	H	Wakefield T.	W	27-26	Bloor, Byrne, Henney, Williams	Smith (5), Nash (dg)	1900	Hodgson
14.9.83	LC(2)	H	Barrow	L	2-13	—	Smith	—	—
18.9.83	SLC	A	Widnes	L	4-28	Williams	—	—	—
25.9.83	SLC	H	Castleford	L	14-34	Williams (2)	Twist (3)	2249	Walker
2.10.83	SLC	A	Bradford N.	L	14-38	Shuttleworth, Driver	Twist (3)	—	—
9.10.83	SLC	H	Warrington	L	8-12	Shuttleworth, Williams	—	2733	Lindop
16.10.83	SLC	A	Wakefield T.	W	16-5	Byrne (2), Williams	Twist (2)	—	—
30.10.83	SLC	A	Hull	L	6-58	Byrne	Twist	—	—
6.11.83	JPS(1)	A	Doncaster	W	22-11	Shuttleworth (2), Williams, Wood	Smith (3)	—	—
11.11.83	SLC	H	Bradford N.	L	12-14	Maggs, Byrne	Smith (2)	2730	Spencer
20.11.83	JPS(2)	A	Wigan	L	15-24	Wood, Byrne	Smith (2), Shuttleworth (1 g, 1 dg)	—	—
27.11.83	SLC	A	Whitehaven	W	13-10	Byrne (3)	Shuttleworth (dg)	—	—
4.12.83	SLC	H	Leeds	L	10-24	Bentley, Byrne	Shuttleworth	2748	Smith
11.12.83	SLC	A	Castleford	L	12-40	Nash, Byrne	Shuttleworth (2)	—	—
20.12.83	SLC	H	St. Helens	L	16-18	Wood (2), Byrne	Shuttleworth (2)	1833	Wall
26.12.83	SLC	A	Oldham	L	6-18	Bloor	Shuttleworth	—	—
2.1.84	SLC	H	Fulham	L	4-6	Williams	—	1847	McDonald
8.1.84	SLC	A	Featherstone R.	L	18-30	McTigue (2), Smith	Smith (3)	—	—
27.1.84	SLC	A	Warrington	L	8-14	O'Neill	Shuttleworth (2)	—	—
5.2.84	SLC	A	St. Helens	L	0-20	—	—	—	—
12.2.84	CC(1)	H	Leeds	L	16-24	Groves, Ruddy, Bloor	Shuttleworth (2)	4299	Kendrew
19.2.84	SLC	H	Featherstone R.	L	6-10	Bentley	Shuttleworth	1865	Mean
26.2.84	SLC	H	Whitehaven	W	26-16	Byrne (2), Bloor, Williams	Shuttleworth (5)	1472	Whitfield
4.3.84	SLC	A	Leigh	L	22-31	Byrne (2), Groves	Fletcher (5)	—	—
11.3.84	SLC	H	Hull	L	6-42	Byrne	Fletcher	2692	Spencer
18.3.84	SLC	A	Hull K.R.	L	32-51	Glynn (2), Byrne, Bloor, Bentley	Fletcher (6)	—	—
23.3.84	SLC	H	Widnes	L	12-22	Williams, Shuttleworth	Fletcher (2)	1825	McDonald
8.4.84	SLC	A	Fulham	W	12-10	Williams, Prescott	Fletcher (2)	—	—
10.4.84	SLC	H	Hull K.R.	L	0-32	—	—	1816	Holdsworth
15.4.84	SLC	A	Wigan	L	8-34	Glynn, Rogers	—	—	—
20.4.84	SLC	H	Oldham	L	10-50	McTigue, Maggs	Shuttleworth	2700	Allatt

SWINTON

Ground: Station Road
Colours: Blue jerseys with white V, white shorts
First Season: 1896-97
Nickname: Lions
Chairman: Ian Clift
Secretary: Ken Heley
Coach: Tom Grainey (May 1981-Oct. 1983)
Jim Crellin (Nov. 1983-)
Honours: **Championship** Winners, 1926-27, 1927-28, 1930-31, 1934-35
Beaten finalists, 1924-25, 1932-33
War League Beaten finalists, 1939-40
Division One Champions, 1962-63, 1963-64
Challenge Cup Winners, 1899-00, 1925-26, 1927-28
Beaten finalists, 1926-27, 1931-32
Lancashire League Winners, 1924-25, 1927-28, 1928-29, 1930-31, 1960-61
Lancashire War League Winners, 1939-40
Lancashire Cup Winners, 1925-26, 1927-28, 1939-40, 1969-70
Beaten finalists, 1910-11, 1923-24, 1931-32, 1960-61, 1961-62, 1962-63, 1964-65, 1972-73
BBC Trophy Beaten finalists, 1966-67
Western Division Championship Beaten finalists, 1963-64
Records: Attendance: 44,621 Wigan v. Warrington (RL Cup SF) 7 Apr, 1951
Season
Goals: 128 by A. Blan, 1960-61
Tries: 42 by J. Stopford, 1963-64
Points: 283 by A. Blan, 1960-61
Match
Goals: 12 by K. Gowers v. Liverpool C, 3 Oct, 1959
Tries: 5 by T. Bevan v. Morecambe, 10 Sep, 1898; W. Wallwork v. Widnes, 15 Dec, 1900; J. Evans v. Bradford N, 30 Sep, 1922; H. Halsall v. St. Helens, 24 Jan, 1925; R. Cracknell v. Whitehaven Rec, 11 Feb, 1928; R. Lewis v. Keighley, 12 Jan, 1946; J. Stopford v. Bramley, 22 Dec, 1962; A. Buckley v. Salford, Apr 8, 1964
Points: 29 by B. McMahon v. Dewsbury, 15 Aug, 1959
Highest score: 76-4 v. Pontefract, 1906-07
Highest against: 76-3 v. Huddersfield, 1945-46

1983-84 PLAYERS' SUMMARY

	App.	Tries	Goals	D/Gls	Pts
Allen, John	5 + 1	—	—	—	—
Armitage, Paul	18 + 2	—	—	—	—
Arrowsmith, Gary	18 + 4	1	—	—	4
Ashcroft, Dennis	7	—	—	—	—
Bate, Derek	26	13	—	—	52
Bolton, Les	10	2	—	—	8
Brown, Jeff	19	1	—	—	4
Clark, Terry	6	1	—	—	4
Coates, Mike	0 + 1	—	—	—	—
Connor, Sean	19 + 1	3	2	—	16
Derbyshire, Alan	17 + 4	3	—	1	13
Fairhurst, Alan	11 + 1	1	1	2	8
Gittins, Tommy	3 + 2	—	—	—	—
Gorton, John	1	—	—	—	—
Higgins, Brian	17	1	—	—	4
Hitchin, Gary	2	—	—	—	—
Holliday, Les	35 + 2	9	2	5	45
Hunter, Clive	35	10	—	—	40
Johnson, Bill	7 + 4	1	—	—	4
Jones, Ken	29 + 3	14	80	—	216
Lee, Martin	30 + 3	16	—	1	65
Lomax, Bill	25 + 1	1	—	—	4
Maloney, David	4 + 1	1	—	—	4
Melling, Alex	21	1	—	—	4
Mellor, Paul	22 + 2	2	7	—	22
O'Loughlin, Kevin	14 + 2	2	—	1	9
Peers, Mike	2 + 1	1	—	—	4
Pierce, Daryl	11 + 3	2	—	—	8
Ratcliffe, Alan	31 + 1	11	—	—	44
Rowbottom, Mark	19 + 2	7	—	—	28
Rowley, Alan	6 + 2	—	—	—	—
Snape, Steve	15	8	—	—	32
Sutton, David	2 + 2	2	—	—	8
Tomlinson, Steve	1	1	4	—	12
Twist, Bob	1 + 1	—	—	—	—
Viller, Mark	4 + 2	2	22	—	52
Walsh, Steve	12 + 2	1	—	—	4
Whittle, Steve	0 + 1	1	—	—	4
Wilson, Danny	28 + 2	22	10	19	127
TOTALS					
39 players		141	128	29	849

1983-84 MATCH ANALYSIS

Date	Competition	H/A	Opponent	Rlt	Score	Tries	Goals	Attendance	Referee
21.8.83	SD	A	Blackpool B.	L	4-16	—	Jones (2)	—	—
28.8.83	SD	H	Batley	W	14-10	Sutton, Ratcliffe, Bate	Connor	968	Lindop
31.8.83	SD	H	Workington T.	L	6-18	Derbyshire	Connor	946	Volante
4.9.83	LC(1)	A	Huyton	W	13-12	Peers, Sutton	Jones (2), O'Loughlin (dg)	—	—
11.9.83	SD	A	York	W	9-4	Lee (2)	Holliday (dg)	—	—
14.9.83	LC(2)	H	Oldham	W	8-6	Jones	Jones (2)	1881	McDonald
18.9.83	SD	H	Barrow	L	10-30	Jones, Ratcliffe	Jones	1158	Whitfield
21.9.83	LC(SF)	H	Widnes	L	8-22	Bate	Jones (2)	2614	Wall
25.9.83	SD	A	Workington T.	L	18-22	Pierce (2), Lee	Jones (3)	—	—
2.10.83	SD	H	Halifax	L	22-35	Clark, Hunter, Bolton	Jones (5)	1454	Hodgson
9.10.83	SD	A	Hunslet	L	18-26	Ratcliffe, Lee, Bolton	Jones (3)	—	—
16.10.83	SD	H	Carlisle	W	22-4	Wilson (2), Jones (2), Holliday	Jones	860	Fox
23.10.83	SD	A	Keighley	W	23-14	Wilson, Ratcliffe, Jones	Jones (5), Wilson (dg)	—	—
30.10.83	SD	H	Kent Invicta	L	10-13	Jones, Ratcliffe	Jones	1076	Walker
6.11.83	JPS(1)	H	Hunslet	W	17-16	Wilson	Jones (4), Wilson 5 dg)	1243	Beaumont
13.11.83	SD	A	Huddersfield	W	14-11	Jones, Lee	Jones, Wilson (3 dg), Holliday (dg)	—	—
20.11.83	JPS(2)	A	Keighley	W	23-8	Connor (2), Holliday, Hunter, Jones	Jones, Holliday (dg)	—	—
27.11.83	JPS(3)	H	Leeds	L	12-16	Wilson (2)	Jones, Wilson (dg), Lee (dg)	3438	Campbell
4.12.83	SD	A	Cardiff C.	W	25-12	O'Loughlin (2), Lee	Jones (6), Wilson (dg)	—	—
18.12.83	SD	A	Batley	L	7-9	Ratcliffe	Jones, Wilson (dg)	—	—
26.12.83	SD	H	Rochdale H.	W	30-10	Wilson (3), Higgins, Bate	Jones (4), P. Mellor	1331	Haigh
1.1.84	SD	H	Huyton	W	36-4	Hunter (2), Rowbottom, Wilson, Bate, Ratcliffe	Wilson (6)	971	Robinson
8.1.84	SD	A	Bramley	W	12-10	Wilson	Wilson (3, 1 dg), Holliday (dg)	—	—
15.1.84	SD	H	Dewsbury	W	42-2	Lee (3), Ratcliffe, P. Mellor, Connor, Wilson, Brown, Holliday	Holliday (2), Wilson	964	Kershaw
22.1.84	SD	A	Kent Invicta	L	6-14	—	P. Mellor (3)	—	—
29.1.84	CC(P)	A	Fulham	L	4-14	Jones	—	—	—
5.2.84	SD	A	Halifax	L	13-14	Hunter, Ratcliffe	P. Mellor (2), Fairhurst (dg)	—	—
15.2.84	SD	H	York	W	25-20	Snape (2), Holliday	Jones (6), Fairhurst (dg)	763	Campbell
19.2.84	SD	H	Doncaster	W	42-0	Holliday (3), Rowbottom (2), Jones, Lomax, Hunter	Jones (3), Fairhurst, P. Mellor	830	Allatt
4.3.84	SD	A	Carlisle	W	26-4	Wilson (2), Hunter, Lee, Viller	Jones (3)	—	—
7.3.84	SD	H	Hunslet	W	28-10	Derbyshire, Snape, Hunter, Ratcliffe	Jones (6)	1018	Thompson
11.3.84	SD	A	Huyton	W	22-6	Ratcliffe, Snape, P. Mellor, Jones	Jones (3)	—	—
18.3.84	SD	H	Bramley	W	15-8	Fairhurst, Rowbottom	Jones (3), Wilson (dg)	1214	Whitfield
25.3.84	SD	A	Doncaster	W	28-2	Wilson (2), Jones, Arrowsmith, Derbyshire	Jones (4)	—	—
1.4.84	SD	H	Keighley	W	66-1	Lee (4), Bate (3), Wilson (2), Jones, Hunter, Rowbottom, Johnson	Jones (7)	1040	Mean
8.4.84	SD	H	Blackpool B.	W	22-3	Lee, Wilson, Bate	Viller (4), Holliday (dg) Derbyshire (dg)	1405	McDonald
15.4.84	SD	A	Dewsbury	L	13-22	Wilson, Jones, Viller	Wilson (dg)	—	—
20.4.84	SD	A	Rochdale H.	L	27-31	Tomlinson, Bate, Snape, Lee	Tomlinson (4), Wilson (3dg)	—	—
23.4.84	SD	H	Huddersfield	W	58-22	Bate (3), Rowbottom (2), Snape, Wilson, Melling, Hunter	Viller (11)	1191	Wall
29.4.84	SD	A	Barrow	L	7-14	Snape	Viller, Wilson (dg)	—	—
7.5.84	SD	H	Cardiff C.	W	44-16	Holliday (2), Snape, Bate, Walsh, Maloney, Whittle, Wilson	Viller (6)	1114	Holdsworth

WAKEFIELD TRINITY

Ground: Belle Vue
Colours: White jerseys with red and blue hoops, white shorts
First Season: 1895-96
Nickname: Dreadnoughts
Chairman: Eric Ingham
Secretary: Alan Pearman
Coach: Derek Turner (July 1983-Mar. 1984)
Bob Haigh (Mar-May 1984)
Geoff Wraith (May 1984-)
Honours: **Championship** Winners, 1966-67, 1967-68
Beaten finalists, 1959-60, 1961-62
Division Two Champions, 1903-04
Challenge Cup Winners, 1908-09, 1945-46, 1959-60, 1961-62, 1962-63
Beaten finalists, 1913-14, 1967-68, 1978-79
Yorkshire League Winners, 1909-10, 1910-11, 1945-46, 1958-59, 1959-60, 1961-62, 1965-66
Yorkshire Cup Winners, 1910-11, 1924-25, 1946-47, 1947-48, 1951-52, 1956-57, 1960-61, 1961-62, 1964-65
Beaten finalists, 1926-27, 1932-33, 1934-35, 1936-37, 1939-40, 1945-46, 1958-59, 1973-74, 1974-75
John Player Trophy Beaten finalists, 1971-72
Records: Attendance: 37,906 Leeds v. Huddersfield (RL Cup SF) 21 March, 1936. Home: 28,254 v. Wigan (RL Cup) March 24, 1962
Season
Goals: 163 by N. Fox, 1961-62
Tries: 38 by F. Smith, 1959-60, D. Smith, 1973-74
Points: 407 by N. Fox, 1961-62
Match
Goals: 12 by N. Fox v. Workington T, 19 Sep, 1970 and v. Batley, 26 Aug, 1967; B. Ward v. Hunslet, 6 Feb, 1971
Tries: 7 by F. Smith v. Keighley, 25 Apr, 1959; K. Slater v. Hunslet, 6 Feb, 1971
Points: 33 by N. Fox v. Batley, 26 Aug, 1967
Highest score: 78-9 v. Batley, 1967-68
Highest against:
69-11 v. Hull, 1920-21
69-17 v. St. Helens, 1952-53

1983-84 PLAYERS' SUMMARY

	App.	Tries	Goals	D/Gls	Pts
Adams, Bryan	6 + 5	2	—	—	8
Ashurst, Bill	1	—	—	1	1
Bell, Nigel	13	5	—	—	20
Box, Harold	24 + 4	1	1	—	6
Bratt, Roy	20	—	—	—	—
Burns, Alan	9	5	—	—	20
Cocks, Gary	5 + 4	2	—	—	8
Coventry, Paul	28	3	—	—	12
Eden, Philip	16 + 1	1	—	—	4
Fletcher, Andrew	20	8	—	—	32
Gearey, Paul	29 + 2	6	—	—	24
Gill, Lindsay	4 + 1	—	—	—	—
Hampsol, Paul	4	—	—	—	—
Harris, Billy	19 + 1	1	—	—	4
Harrison, Chris	9	2	—	—	8
Hendry, Paul	7	2	3	—	14
Hopkinson, Ian	12	2	—	—	8
Hughes, Ian	19 + 2	3	—	—	12
Jones, David	33	7	—	—	28
Kelly, Richard	9	1	—	—	4
Lewis, Scott	6	6	—	—	24
Lewis, Wally	10	6	—	—	24
Lyons, John	3 + 1	—	—	—	—
Maskill, Colin	27	3	75	2	164
McDermott, Paul	5	1	—	1	5
Moore, Gary	1	—	—	—	—
Muscroft, Peter	1	—	—	—	—
Norton, Michael	7 + 2	3	2	1	17
Oglethorpe, George	1 + 3	—	—	—	—
Pickerill, Clive	17	1	—	2	6
Rollin, Steve	5	—	—	—	—
Ross, Andrew	0 + 1	—	—	—	—
Rotherforth, Lindsay	3	—	—	—	—
Stephenson, Nigel	29 + 1	9	1	7	45
Stringer, Chris	9 + 2	—	—	—	—
Sutcliffe, John	1	—	1	—	2
Swann, Malcolm	12 + 3	—	—	—	—
Thompson, John	15 + 3	—	—	—	—
Waugh, Bradley	8	—	—	—	—
Wilkinson, Andrew	2 + 4	—	—	—	—
Williams, Dean	8 + 6	2	—	—	8
Worne, Glenn	7 + 4	2	1	—	10
Trialists (4)	4 + 2	1	2	—	8
TOTALS					
46 players		85	86	14	526

1983-84 MATCH ANALYSIS

Date	Competition	H/A	Opponent	Rlt	Score	Tries	Goals	Attendance	Referee
21.8.83	SLC	H	Fulham	W	18-14	Harrison, Coventry	Maskill (5)	2347	Court
24.8.83	SLC	H	Wigan	L	11-18	Coventry, Jones	Maskill, Ashurst (dg)	3044	Holdsworth
28.8.83	SLC	A	Hull K. R.	L	0-38	—	—	—	—
4.9.83	YC(1)	H	Halifax	W	18-10	Hughes, Hopkinson, Stephenson	Maskill (3)	2195	Court
11.9.83	SLC	A	Salford	L	26-27	Jones (2), Hopkinson, Box	Maskill (5)	—	—
14.9.83	YC(2)	H	Doncaster	W	32-14	Jones (2), Pickerill, Stephenson, Fletcher	Maskill (6)	1587	Holdsworth
18.9.83	SLC	H	Leeds	L	19-20	Williams (2), Harrison	Maskill (3), Pickerill (dg)	4162	McDonald
23.9.83	YC(SF)	H	Castleford	L	12-34	Fletcher, Maskill	Maskill (2)	5592	Kershaw
25.9.83	SLC	A	St. Helens	L	12-50	Norton (2)	Norton (2)	—	—
2.10.83	SLC	H	Leigh	W	20-18	Fletcher (2), Norton Stephenson	Maskill (2)	2426	Whitfield
7.10.83	SLC	A	Featherstone R.	W	12-8	Cocks, Stephenson	Maskill (2)	—	—
16.10.83	SLC	H	Salford	L	5-16	Cocks	Stephenson (dg)	2135	Thompson
22.10.83	SLC	A	Fulham	L	14-16	Fletcher (2), Harris	Sutcliffe	—	—
30.10.83	SLC	H	Widnes	L	20-23	Stephenson, Fletcher, Burns	Maskill (3, 1 dg), Norton (dg)	2350	Smith
6.11.83	JPS(1)	H	Warrington	L	18-32	Burns (2), Hughes	Maskill (3)	2935	Allatt
13.11.83	SLC	H	Warrington	L	9-17	Warne, Stephenson	Pickerill (dg)	2542	McDonald
27.11.83	SLC	A	Bradford N.	L	15-20	Maskill, Burns	Maskill (3), Stephenson (dg)	—	—
4.12.83	SLC	H	Hull	L	16-32	S. Lewis, Gearey	Maskill (4)	8179	Wall
11.12.83	SLC	A	Whitehaven	W	38-10	Burns, Stephenson, Kelly, Maskill, Geary, S. Lewis	Maskill (6), Stephenson (2dg)	—	—
18.12.83	SLC	H	Oldham	W	28-22	S. Lewis (2), Fletcher, Stephenson	Maskill (6)	4837	Spencer
26.12.83	SLC	A	Castleford	L	8-24	W. Lewis	Maskill (2)	—	—
1.1.84	SLC	A	Leigh	L	12-14	S. Lewis (2)	Maskill (2)	—	—
8.1.84	SLC	H	St. Helens	W	31-22	W. Lewis (3), Bell (2)	Maskill (5, 1 dg)	3957	Pourret (Fr)
15.1.84	SLC	A	Warrington	L	12-16	Stephenson	Maskill (4)	—	—
29.1.84	SLC	A	Leeds	L	16-26	Adams	Maskill (6)	—	—
5.2.84	SLC	H	Featherstone R.	W	8-1	Gearey	Maskill, Stephenson (2 dg)	5736	Robinson
12.2.84	CC(1)	A	Halifax	W	19-7	W. Lewis (2), Adams, Jones	Maskill, Stephenson (dg)	—	—
19.2.84	SLC	A	Widnes	L	14-42	Bell (2), Worne	Worne	—	—
26.2.84	CC(2)	H	York	L	12-20	Hendry, Bell	Stephenson, Box	3222	Allatt
4.3.84	SLC	A	Wigan	L	0-34	—	—	—	—
11.3.84	SLC	H	Whitehaven	L	12-32	Hughes, Coventry, Eden	—	1466	Campbell
18.3.84	SLC	H	Bradford N.	L	0-12	—	—	2997	Holdsworth
25.3.84	SLC	A	Hull	L	12-66	Gearey (2)	Hendry (2)	—	—
1.4.84	SLC	H	Hull K. R.	L	11-46	McDermott, Hendry	Hendry, McDermott (dg)	3236	Kershaw
15.4.84	SLC	A	Oldham	L	4-54	Gearey	—	—	—
23.4.84	SLC	H	Castleford	L	12-42	Trialist, Jones	Trialist (2)	2825	Beaumont

WARRINGTON

Ground: Wilderspool
Colours: White jerseys with primrose and blue hoop, white shorts
First Season: 1895-96
Nickname: Wire
Chairman: Peter Higham
General Manager: Graham McCarty
Coach: Kevin Ashcroft (March 1982-May 1984)
Reg Bowden (June 1984-)
Honours: **Championship** Winners, 1947-48, 1953-54, 1954-55
Beaten finalists, 1925-26, 1934-35, 1936-37, 1948-49, 1950-51, 1960-61
League Leaders Trophy Winners, 1972-73
Club Championship (Merit Table) Winners, 1973-74
Premiership Beaten finalists, 1976-77
Challenge Cup Winners, 1904-05, 1906-07, 1949-50, 1953-54, 1973-74
Beaten finalists, 1900-01, 1903-04, 1912-13, 1927-28, 1932-33, 1935-36, 1974-75
Lancashire League Winners, 1937-38, 1947-48, 1948-49, 1950-51, 1953-54, 1954-55, 1955-56, 1967-68
Lancashire Cup Winners, 1921-22, 1929-30, 1932-33, 1937-38, 1959-60, 1965-66, 1980-81, 1982-83
Beaten finalists, 1906-07, 1948-49, 1950-51, 1967-68
John Player Trophy Winners, 1973-74, 1977-78, 1980-81
Beaten finalists, 1978-79
Captain Morgan Trophy Winners, 1973-74
BBC2 Trophy Beaten finalists, 1974-75
Records: Attendance: 35,000 Wigan v. Leigh (Lancs Cup Final) 29 Oct., 1949.
Home: 34,304 v. Wigan (League) 22 January, 1949

Season
Goals: 170 by S. Hesford, 1978-79
Tries: 66 by B. Bevan, 1952-53
Points: 363 by H. Bath, 1952-53
Match
Goals: 14 by H. Palin v. Liverpool C, 13 Sep, 1950
Tries: 7 by B. Bevan v. Leigh, 29 Mar, 1948 and v. Bramley, 22 Apr, 1953
Points: 33 by G. Thomas v. St. Helens, 12 Apr, 1909
Highest score: 78-3 v. St. Helens, 1908-09
Highest against: 68-14 v. Hunslet, 1927-28

1983-84 PLAYERS' SUMMARY

	App.	Tries	Goals	D/Gls	Pts
Bevan, John	19	10	—	—	40
Blacker, Mick	24 + 4	4	—	—	16
Campbell, Roy	4 + 1	—	—	—	—
Carbert, Brian	13	7	2	—	32
Chisnall, David	11 + 4	—	—	—	—
Courtney, Neil	2	—	—	—	—
Cullen, Paul	8	1	—	—	4
Day, Terry	12	1	—	—	4
Duane, Ronnie	36	16	3	—	70
Eccles, Bob	34	19	—	1	77
Fellows, Paul	3 + 1	1	—	—	4
Fieldhouse, John	26	4	—	—	16
Finnegan, Derek	5 + 2	—	—	—	—
Ford, Paul	4 + 1	1	4	1	13
Ford, Phil	29	20	—	—	80
Forster, Mark	21	7	—	—	28
Gleave, Mark	2 + 2	—	—	—	—
Gregory, Mike	29 + 4	9	—	—	36
Hesford, Steve	35	7	135	7	305
Kelly, Ken	36	6	—	4	28
Kelly, Mike	1	1	—	—	4
Kerr, John	5 + 1	3	—	—	12
McGinty, Bill	0 + 2	—	—	—	—
Morris, Steve	0 + 2	—	—	—	—
Moylan, Steve	1 + 2	—	—	—	—
Muller, Rob	12 + 2	3	—	—	12
O'Mahoney, Steve	37	1	—	—	4
Peters, Barry	6 + 1	2	—	—	8
Poasa, Pat	5 + 1	1	—	—	4
Rawlinson, Tom	1	—	—	—	—
Roberts, Mark	0 + 1	1	—	—	4
Scott, Alan	6 + 9	—	—	—	—
Webb, Carl	19 + 4	—	—	—	—
Worrall, Tony	26 + 1	—	—	—	—
Yates, Mal	22 + 2	1	—	—	4
TOTALS					
35 players		126	144	13	805

1983-84 MATCH ANALYSIS

Date	Com-petition	H/A	Opponent	Rlt	Score	Tries	Goals	Atten-dance	Referee
21.8.83	SLC	A	Hull	D	22-22	Fellows, Cullen, Eccles	Hesford (5)	—	—
24.8.83	SLC	A	Widnes	L	4-12	R. Duane	—	—	—
28.8.83	SLC	H	St. Helens	L	8-12	Bevan	R. Duane (2)	5001	Thompson
4.9.83	LC(1)	A	Blackpool B.	W	30-4	Eccles (2), R. Duane, Forster, Bevan	Hesford (5)	—	—
11.9.83	SLC	A	Leeds	W	14-12	K. Kelly, Bevan	Hesford (2), R. Duane	—	—
14.9.83	LC(2)	A	St. Helens	W	30-26	Blacker (2), Eccles, Hesford, Fieldhouse	Hesford (5)	—	—
18.9.83	SLC	H	Hull K. R.	W	26-10	Forster (2), Phil Ford, Gregory	Hesford (5)	4362	Hodgson
21.9.83	LC(SF)	H	Barrow	L	18-19	Phil Ford, Forster	Hesford (5)	3349	Whitfield
25.9.83	SLC	A	Featherstone R.	L	16-32	K. Kelly, Hesford, Eccles	Hesford (2)	—	—
2.10.83	SLC	H	Fulham	W	29-9	Bevan (2), Carbert (2)	Hesford (6, 1 dg)	3039	Holdsworth
9.10.83	SLC	A	Salford	W	12-8	Blacker, Bevan	Hesford (2)	—	—
16.10.83	SLC	H	Whitehaven	W	50-16	Muller (2), R. Duane (2), Hesford, Eccles, Gregory, Fieldhouse, O'Mahoney	Hesford (7)	2520	Haigh
23.10.83	SLC	A	Hull K. R.	L	19-34	R. Duane, M. Kelly, Carbert	Hesford (3, 1 dg)	—	—
30.10.83	SLC	H	Oldham	D	22-22	Day, Fieldhouse	Hesford (7)	4956	Campbell
6.11.83	JPS(1)	A	Wakefield T.	W	32-18	Eccles, Blacker, Fieldhouse, Bevan, Hesford	Hesford (6)	—	—
13.11.83	SLC	A	Wakefield T.	W	17-9	R. Duane, K. Kelly, Carbert	Hesford (2), K. Kelly (dg)	—	—
19.11.83	JPS(2)	H	St. Helens	L	10-18	R. Duane	Hesford (3)	4171	Lindop
27.11.83	SLC	H	Castleford	W	16-14	Phil Ford (2), Eccles	Hesford (2)	2843	Volante
4.12.83	SLC	H	Bradford N.	L	11-13	Bevan, Gregory	Hesford, K. Kelly (dg)	4030	Fox
27.12.83	SLC	H	Leigh	W	34-18	Phil Ford (2), R. Duane (2), Hesford, Eccles	Hesford (5)	6119	Smith
8.1.84	SLC	A	Whitehaven	W	20-0	Phil Ford (2), Eccles, K. Kelly	Hesford (2)	—	—
15.1.84	SLC	H	Wakefield T.	W	16-12	Phil Ford, R. Duane	Hesford (4)	3135	Berry
27.1.84	SLC	H	Salford	W	14-8	Bevan, Forster	Hesford (3)	2474	Fox
5.2.84	SLC	A	Wigan	W	24-6	Phil Ford (2), Eccles, Gregory	Hesford (4)	—	—
12.2.84	CC(1)	H	Huddersfield	W	34-16	Eccles (2), Gregory, K. Kelly, Bevan, R. Duane	Hesford (5)	3064	Wall
19.2.84	SLC	H	Hull	W	18-6	Gregory, Hesford, Phil Ford	Hesford (3)	5073	Holdsworth
26.2.84	CC(2)	A	Castleford	L	16-23	Gregory, R. Duane, Eccles	Hesford (2)	—	—
4.3.83	SLC	A	Castleford	W	21-10	Muller, Paul Ford, Poasa	Paul Ford (4, 1 dg)	—	—
9.3.84	SLC	H	Featherstone R.	W	23-22	R. Duane, Hesford	Hesford (6, 1 dg), Eccles (dg), K. Kelly (dg)	2929	Beaumont
18.3.84	SLC	A	Oldham	W	14-11	R. Duane, Phil Ford	Hesford (3)	—	—
20.3.84	SLC	A	St. Helens	L	25-37	Eccles, Roberts, Phil Ford	Hesford (6), K. Kelly (dg)	—	—
1.4.84	SLC	A	Bradford N.	W	19-16	Forster, Eccles	Hesford (4, 3 dg)	—	—
4.4.84	SLC	H	Wigan	L	6-34	Phil Ford	Hesford	5086	Massey
8.4.84	SLC	H	Leeds	W	28-12	Carbert (2), Yates, Peters, Phil Ford	Hesford (4)	3525	Smith
15.4.84	SLC	A	Fulham	W	58-32	Phil Ford (3), Gregory (2), Eccles (2), Carbert, Kerr, R. Duane	Hesford (9)	—	—
20.4.84	SLC	H	Widnes	L	16-35	Eccles, K. Kelly, Peters	Hesford (2)	5798	Wall
23.4.84	SLC	A	Leigh	L	20-44	Kerr (2), Forster, R. Duane	Carbert (2)	—	—
29.4.84	PT(1)	H	St. Helens	L	13-19	Phil Ford	Hesford (4, 1 dg)	5032	Campbell

WHITEHAVEN

Ground: Recreation Ground
Colours: White jerseys with chocolate, blue and gold bands, white shorts
First Season: 1948-49
Nickname: Haven
Chairman: David Wigham
Secretary: Eric Robinson
Coach: Frank Foster (June 1983-)
Records: Attendance: 18,500 v. Wakefield T. (RL Cup) 19 Mar, 1960

Season

Goals: 141 by J. McKeown, 1956-57
Tries: 29 by W. Smith, 1956-57
Points: 291 by J. McKeown, 1956-57

Match

Goals: 11 by W. Holliday v. Hunslet, 31 Mar, 1962
Tries: 5 by F. Colloby v. Liverpool C, 10 Mar, 1962; L. Lowther v. Bradford N, 23 Feb, 1963
Points: 25 by W. Holliday v. Hunslet, 31 Mar, 1962
Highest score: 61-0 v. Hunslet, 1961-62
Highest against: 68-14 v. Leigh, 1983-84

1983-84 PLAYERS' SUMMARY

	App.	Tries	Goals	D/Gls	Pts
Banks, Alan	29	2	—	—	8
Barnes, David	6 + 7	—	—	—	—
Barwise, Michael	2 + 1	—	—	—	—
Cameron, Graeme	12 + 2	—	—	—	—
Cottier, Gordon	19 + 1	4	—	—	16
Dalton, James	21	7	—	—	28
D'Leny, Anthony	27 + 1	1	—	—	4
Fidler, Raymond	2	—	—	—	—
Fisher, William	22 + 2	4	—	—	16
Frazer, Neil	17 + 1	1	—	—	4
Gee, Peter	8	2	—	—	8
Graham, David	5	—	—	—	—
Gribbin, Vince	29	8	48	—	128
Hall, Colin	20 + 3	4	—	1	17
Hartley, John	15 + 5	—	—	—	—
Hoare, Sean	2	—	—	—	—
Huddart, Milton	23 + 1	8	—	—	32
Kirkby, Steve	19 + 1	2	—	—	8
Litt, Ian	1 + 1	—	—	—	—
Mackie, Bob	23	7	2	—	32
Mason, Mel	15	2	—	—	8
McArthur, Peter	5	—	—	1	1
McCarron, Alf	6	—	—	—	—
Pattinson, Steve	2	1	—	—	4
Phythian, Steve	30	1	—	—	4
Ratcliffe, Norman	6 + 9	—	—	—	—
Simpson, Jeff	13 + 1	—	—	—	—
Stewart, Joe	4 + 2	1	—	—	4
Stoddart, Peter	13 + 3	—	—	1	1
Taylor, Michael	0 + 1	—	—	—	—
Thompson, Ian	8	1	2	—	8
Tomlinson, Brian	9 + 1	—	—	—	—
Walker, Arnold	2	—	1	—	2
Weir, Brian	1 + 1	1	—	—	4
Wilkinson, Ken	0 + 1	—	—	—	—
Wright, David	9	1	—	—	4
Trialists (2)	4	—	—	—	—
TOTALS					
38 players		58	53	3	341

Gordon Cottier . . . 20 appearances before an on-loan move to Workington Town.

1983-84 MATCH ANALYSIS

Date	Competition	H/A	Opponent	Rlt	Score	Tries	Goals	Attendance	Referee
21.8.83	SLC	H	Bradford N.	L	4-45	Fisher	—	2416	Thompson
28.8.83	SLC	A	Widnes	L	10-44	Cottier	Gribbin (2), Walker	—	—
4.9.83	LC(1)	A	Barrow	L	6-13	Huddart	Gribbin	—	—
11.9.83	SLC	A	Fulham	L	6-24	Mackie	Gribbin	—	—
18.9.83	SLC	H	Featherstone R.	L	14-18	Gribbin, Cottier, Mackie	Gribbin	1620	Massey
25.9.83	SLC	A	Leeds	L	8-48	Kirkby	Gribbin (2)	—	—
2.10.83	SLC	H	Wigan	L	0-24	—	—	2060	Wall
9.10.83	SLC	H	Castleford	L	2-26	—	Gribbin	1735	McDonald
16.10.83	SLC	A	Warrington	L	16-50	Huddart, Mackie, Gribbin	Gribbin	—	—
23.10.83	JPS(P)	H	Widnes	L	0-36	—	—	1655	Kershaw
30.10.83	SLC	H	Leigh	L	16-38	Huddart, Thompson, Gribbin	Gribbin, Mackie	1695	Volante
6.11.83	SLC	A	Hull K. R.	L	6-56	Weir	Gribbin	—	—
13.11.83	SLC	A	Featherstone R.	L	10-52	Stewart, Gee	Thompson	—	—
20.11.83	SLC	A	Castleford	L	2-50	—	Thompson	—	—
27.11.83	SLC	H	Salford	L	10-13	Pattinson, Fraser	Mackie	1383	Cattaneo (Fr)
4.12.83	SLC	A	Wigan	L	11-33	Huddart, Gee	Gribbin, McArthur (dg)	—	—
11.12.83	SLC	H	Wakefield T.	L	10-38	Mackie (2)	Gribbin	1537	Holdsworth
18.12.83	SLC	A	Leigh	L	14-68	Dalton (2), Mackie	Gribbin	—	—
2.1.84	SLC	H	Hull K. R.	L	10-22	Dalton, Cottier	Gribbin	1350	Whitfield
8.1.84	SLC	H	Warrington	L	0-20	—	—	1373	Thompson
15.1.84	SLC	A	St. Helens	L	10-40	D'Leny, Wright	Gribbin	—	—
29.1.84	SLC	H	Widnes	L	4-18	—	Gribbin (2)	1209	Haigh
12.2.84	CC(1)	H	Fulham	L	10-17	Gribbin, Fisher	Gribbin	1683	Fox
19.2.84	SLC	H	Oldham	W	42-8	Huddart (3), Cottier, Gribbin, Hall, Dalton	Gribbin (7)	1267	Robinson
26.2.84	SLC	A	Salford	L	16-26	Gribbin, Banks	Gribbin (4)	—	—
4.3.84	SLC	H	Fulham	W	18-0	Banks, Gribbin, Mackie	Gribbin (3)	1116	Campbell
11.3.84	SLC	A	Wakefield T.	W	32-12	Hall (2), Phythian, Gribbin, Mason	Gribbin (6)	—	—
18.3.84	SLC	H	Leeds	L	2-28	—	Gribbin	2120	Berry
23.3.84	SLC	A	Bradford N.	L	8-22	Kirby	Gribbin (2)	—	—
25.3.84	SLC	A	Oldham	L	13-24	Hall, Fisher	Gribbin (2), Stoddart (dg)	—	—
1.4.84	SLC	H	Hull	L	10-28	Dalton (2)	Gribbin	2001	Smith
15.4.84	SLC	H	St. Helens	L	21-27	Mason, Huddart, Dalton, Fisher	Gribbin (2), Hall (dg)	1705	Allatt
23.4.84	SLC	A	Hull	L	0-54	—	—	—	—

WIDNES

Ground:	Naughton Park
Colours:	White jerseys, black shorts
First Season:	1895-96
Nickname:	Chemics
Chairman:	Tom Smith
Secretary:	Ron Close
Coach:	Vince Karalius (May 1983-) *Harry Dawson quit as coach in Mar. 1984, but Karalius continued as team manager*
Honours:	**Division One** Champions, 1977-78
	Championship Beaten finalists, 1935-36
	Challenge Cup Winners, 1929-30, 1936-37, 1963-64, 1974-75, 1978-79, 1980-81, 1983-84
	Beaten finalists, 1933-34, 1949-50, 1975-76, 1976-77, 1981-82
	Lancashire League Winners, 1919-20
	Lancashire Cup Winners 1945-46, 1974-75, 1975-76, 1976-77, 1978-79, 1979-80
	Beaten finalists, 1928-29, 1939-40, 1955-56, 1971-72, 1981-82, 1983-84
	John Player Trophy Winners, 1975-76, 1978-79
	Beaten finalists, 1974-75, 1977-78, 1979-80, 1983-84
	Premiership Winners, 1979-80, 1981-82, 1982-83
	Beaten finalists, 1977-78
	BBC2 Floodlit Trophy Winners, 1978-79
	Beaten finalists, 1972-73, 1973-74
	Western Division Championship Beaten finalists, 1962-63
Records:	Attendance: 24,205 v. St. Helens (RL Cup) 16 February, 1961

Season
Goals: 140 by M. Burke, 1978-79
Tries: 34 by F. Myler, 1958-59
Points: 316 by M. Burke, 1978-79
Match
Goals: 11 by R. Whitfield v. Oldham, 28 Oct, 1965
Tries: 5 by E. Cunningham v. Doncaster, 15 Feb, 1981; J. Basnett v. Hunslet, 17 Oct, 1981
Points: 27 by H. Dawson v. Liverpool C, 22 Apr, 1957
Highest score: 59-0 v. Bramley, 1952-53
Highest against: 60-5 v. Oldham, 1927-28

1983-84 PLAYERS' SUMMARY

	App.	Tries	Goals	D/Gls	Pts
Adams, Mick	38	1	1	3	9
Basnett, John	37	26	—	—	104
Blackwood, Bob	2	—	—	—	—
Burke, Mick	40	14	74	—	204
Currier, Andrew	2 + 5	2	—	—	8
Dowd, Barry	3 + 3	3	—	—	12
Elwell, Keith	46	5	—	2	22
Finnigan, Paul	0 + 1	—	—	—	—
Garritty, Tony	14 + 1	5	—	—	20
Gladwin, Michael	1 + 1	—	—	—	—
Gorley, Les	25 + 4	1	—	—	4
Gormley, Ian	2	—	—	—	—
Gregory, Andrew	36 + 2	7	4	4	40
Houghton, Paul	0 + 1	—	—	—	—
Hughes, Eric	44	9	—	—	36
Hulme, David	19 + 9	15	—	—	60
Hulme, Paul	2	—	—	—	—
Lamb, David	1 + 1	—	—	—	—
Linton, Ralph	20 + 7	12	—	—	48
Lydon, David	5 + 3	1	—	—	4
Lydon, Joe	37	27	54	—	216
Myler, Anthony	22 + 1	9	—	—	36
Myler, John	17 + 2	3	3	—	18
Newton, Keith	7 + 2	1	—	—	4
O'Loughlin, Keiron	31	14	—	—	56
O'Neill, Mike	14 + 2	1	—	—	4
O'Neill, Steve	36	2	—	5	13
Quinn, Kevin	0 + 1	—	—	—	—
Prescott, Eric	12 + 3	5	—	—	20
Ruane, Andrew	3 + 6	—	—	—	—
Smith, Martyn	0 + 1	—	—	—	—
Tamati, Kevin	40	5	—	—	20
Whitfield, Fred	28 + 8	5	—	—	20
Wood, John	14	1	—	—	4
Wright, Stuart	13	4	—	—	16
TOTALS					
35 players		178	136	14	998

1983-84 MATCH ANALYSIS

Date	Comp.	H/A	Opponent	Rlt	Score	Tries	Goals	Att.	Referee
21.8.83	SLC	A	Leigh	W	19-12	Burke (2), Tamati	Lydon (3), Gregory (dg)	—	—
24.8.83	SLC	H	Warrington	W	12-4	Basnett, Burke	Lydon (2)	5691	Wall
28.8.83	SLC	H	Whitehaven	W	44-10	Hughes (2), Basnett (2), D. Hulme (2), Lydon, Prescott, O'Loughlin	Burke (4)	3352	Allatt

1983-84 MATCH ANALYSIS (continued)

Date	Comp.	H/A	Opponent	Rlt	Score	Tries	Goals	Att.	Referee
4.9.83	LC(1)	H	Wigan	W	36-20	Basnett (2), Newton, O'Loughlin, Lydon, Elwell	Lydon (6)	7016	Allatt
11.9.83	SLC	A	Hull K. R.	L	4-10	—	Lydon (2)	—	—
14.9.83	LC(2)	A	Leigh	W	27-10	Burke, Basnett, Lydon, Elwell, O'Loughlin	Lydon (2), Burke, Gregory (dg)	—	—
18.9.83	SLC	H	Salford	W	28-4	Lydon (2), O'Loughlin, Gregory, S. O'Neill, Currier	Lydon (2)	4231	Holdsworth
21.9.83	LC(SF)	A	Swinton	W	22-8	Lydon, O'Loughlin, Hughes, Basnett, A. Myler	Burke	—	—
25.9.83	SLC	A	Wigan	W	31-16	S. O'Neill, Basnett, Adams, Linton, Hughes	Lydon (4), J. Myler, Elwell (dg)	—	—
1.10.83	LC(F)	Wigan	Barrow	L	8-12	Lydon	Lydon (2)	(7007)	Allatt
9.10.83	SLC	A	Oldham	W	20-10	Prescott (2), Basnett	Lydon (4)	—	—
16.10.83	SLC	H	Leigh	W	28-20	Lydon (2), Gregory, Basnett, Dowd, Prescott	Lydon, Gregory	5150	Walker
19.10.83	SLC	H	Featherstone R.	W	40-4	Basnett (2), A. Myler (2), Linton (2), Gregory, Garritty	Burke (2), Gregory (2)	3325	Fox
23.10.83	JPS(P)	A	Whitehaven	W	36-0	A. Myler (2), Gregory (2), Lydon, Garritty	Burke (6)	—	—
26.10.83	SLC	A	Leeds	L	14-20	Prescott, Lydon	Lydon (3)	—	—
30.10.83	SLC	A	Wakefield T.	W	23-20	Basnett (3), Garritty	Burke (3), S. O'Neill (dg)	—	—
6.11.83	JPS(1)	H	Bradford N.	W	2-1	—	S. O'Neill (dg), Gregory (dg)	5640	McDonald
13.11.83	SLC	H	Hull	W	30-0	Basnett (3), Hughes (2), Dowd	Burke, J. Myler (2)	6297	Haigh
20.11.83	JPS(2)	H	Barrow	W	18-6	Garrity, Lydon, Burke, D. Hulme	Burke	7030	Thompson
26.11.83	JPS(3)	H	Wigan	W	20-15	A. Myler (2), Lydon	Burke (4)	6492	Holdsworth
4.12.83	SLC	A	Featherstone R.	L	6-21	D. Hulme	Burke	—	—
17.12.83	JPS(SF)	War'n	St. Helens	W	18-4	Garritty, Linton	Burke (5)	(5729)	Fox
26.12.83	SLC	A	Bradford N.	W	24-14	Lydon (3), Lyon	Lydon (4)	—	—
1.1.84	SLC	A	St. Helens	W	20-12	J. Myler, Dowd, Currier, Linton	Lydon (2)	—	—
8.1.84	SLC	H	Leeds	L	8-17	A. Myler	Burke (2)	5119	Spencer
14.1.84	JPS(F)	Wigan	Leeds	L	10-18	Linton, Lydon	Burke	(9536)	Thompson
29.1.84	SLC	A	Whitehaven	W	18-4	Linton (2), D. Hulme, J. Myler	Adams	—	—
1.2.84	SLC	H	Castleford	W	14-8	Wright, Hughes, Gregory	Gregory	3911	Hodgson
5.2.84	CC(P)	A	Carlisle	W	20-12	Basnett (2), Wright, Whitfield	Burke (2)	—	—
12.2.84	CC(1)	H	Dewsbury	W	54-10	Tamati (2), D. Hulme (2), Basnett (2), Linton (2), Wood, Lydon, O'Loughlin	Lydon (5)	4005	Massey
19.2.84	SLC	H	Wakefield T.	W	42-14	Elwell (2), Tamati, Whitfield, Hughes, D. Hulme, J. Myler	Burke (4), Lydon (3)	4267	Hodgson
26.2.84	CC(2)	A	Fulham	W	12-10	O'Loughlin (2)	Burke (2)	—	—
4.3.84	SLC	A	Hull	L	12-30	A. Myler, Basnett	Burke, Lydon	—	—
10.3.84	CC(3)	H	Hull K. R.	W	21-10	Lydon, Gregory, D. Hulme	Burke (3), Gregory (dg), Adams (dg), S. O'Neill (dg)	8017	Kershaw
14.3.84	SLC	H	Hull K. R.	L	8-17	Whitfield	Burke (2)	4909	Mean
21.3.84	SLC	H	Fulham	L	14-16	Burke (2)	Burke (3)	3417	Holdsworth
23.3.83	SLC	A	Salford	W	22-12	Gorley, Linton, Burke, Lydon	Burke (3)	—	—
31.3.84	CC(SF)	Swin- ton	Leeds	W	15-4	Burke, Lydon	Burke (3), S. O'Neill (dg)	(14046)	Thompson
4.4.84	SLC	H	Bradford N.	W	32-23	Burke (3), Lydon, D. Hulme, Whitfield	Burke (2), Lydon (2)	4003	Kendrew
8.4.84	SLC	H	Oldham	L	28-34	Tamati, Hughes, Wright, Burke, O'Loughlin	Burke (4)	4888	Berry
11.4.84	SLC	H	Wigan	W	21-14	O'Loughlin (2), Lydon, Basnett	Lydon (2), Adams (dg)	—	Smith
15.4.84	SLC	A	Castleford	L	18-24	Basnett, Whitfield, D. Hulme	Burke (3)	—	—
20.4.84	SLC	A	Warrington	W	35-16	D. Hulme (2), Burke, Wright, Linton, M. O'Neill	Burke (5), Elwell (dg)	—	—
23.4.84	SLC	H	St. Helens	D	28-28	D. Hulme (2), O'Loughlin (2), Lydon	Lydon (4)	4860	Haigh
25.4.84	SLC	A	Widnes	L	13-23	Lydon, Elwell	Burke (2), Adams (dg)	—	—
29.4.84	PT(1)	A	Castleford	L	4-36	Basnett	—	—	—
5.5.84	CC(F)	Wem- bley	Wigan	W	19-6	Lydon (2), O'Loughlin	Burke (3), S. O'Neill (1 dg)	(80116)	Thompson

WIGAN

Ground: Central Park
Colours: Cherry and white hooped jerseys, white shorts
First Season: 1895-96
Nickname: Riversiders
Chairman: Jack Hilton
Coach: Alex Murphy (June 1982-)
Honours: **Championship** Winners, 1908-09, 1921-22, 1925-26, 1933-34, 1945-46, 1946-47, 1949-50, 1951-52, 1959-60
Beaten finalists, 1909-10, 1910-11, 1911-12, 1912-13, 1923-24, 1970-71
League Leaders Trophy Winners, 1970-71
Challenge Cup Winners, 1923-24, 1928-29, 1947-48, 1950-51, 1957-58, 1958-59, 1964-65
Beaten finalists, 1910-11, 1919-20, 1943-44, 1945-46, 1960-61, 1962-63, 1965-66, 1969-70, 1983-84
Lancashire League Winners, 1901-02, 1908-09, 1910-11, 1911-12, 1912-13, 1913-14, 1914-15, 1920-21, 1922-23, 1923-24, 1925-26, 1945-46, 1946-47, 1949-50, 1951-52, 1958-59, 1961-62, 1969-70
Lancashire War League Winners, 1940-41
Lancashire Cup Winners, 1905-06, 1908-09, 1909-10, 1912-13, 1922-23, 1928-29, 1938-39, 1946-47, 1947-48, 1948-49, 1949-50, 1950-51, 1951-52, 1966-67, 1971-72, 1973-74
Beaten finalists, 1913-14, 1914-15, 1925-26, 1927-28, 1930-31, 1934-35, 1935-36, 1936-37, 1945-46, 1953-54, 1957-58, 1977-78, 1980-81
John Player Trophy Winners 1982-83
BBC2 Floodlit Trophy Winners, 1968-69
Beaten finalists, 1969-70
War League Championship Winners, 1943-44
Beaten finalists, 1940-41
Records: Attendance: 47,747 v. St. Helens (League) 27 March, 1959

Season
Goals: 176 by F. Griffiths, 1958-59
Tries: 62 by J. Ring, 1925-26
Points: 394 by F. Griffiths, 1958-59
Match
Goals: 22 by J. Sullivan v. Flimby & Fothergill, 14 Feb, 1925
Tries: 7 by J. Ring v. Flimby & Fothergill, 14 Feb, 1925; v. Salford, 13 April, 1925 and V. Pemberton R, 12 Feb, 1927; W. Boston v. Dewsbury, 20 Aug, 1955 and v. Salford, 30 Apr, 1962; G. Vigo v. St. Helens, 21 Aug, 1976
Points: 44 by J. Sullivan v. Flimby & Fothergill, 14 Feb, 1925
Highest score: 116-0 v. Flimby & Fothergill, 1924-25
Highest against: 58-3 v. Leeds, 1972-73

1983-84 PLAYERS' SUMMARY

	App.	Tries	Goals	D/Gls	Pts
Bamber, Lee	0 + 1	—	—	—	—
Braithwaite, Ron	9	1	—	—	4
Campbell, Danny	12 + 2	2	—	—	8
Cannon, Mark	18	10	—	—	40
Case, Brian	30 + 1	5	—	—	20
Clare, Jeff	9 + 4	3	11	—	34
Courtney, Neil	4 + 1	—	—	—	—
Dunn, Brian	12 + 6	3	—	—	12
Edwards, Shaun	24	6	1	—	26
Elvin, Wayne	19 + 3	2	—	—	8
Fairhurst, Jimmy	6 + 5	—	—	—	—
Ford, Michael	4 + 2	—	—	—	—
Foy, Martin	5	1	—	—	4
Gill, Henderson	30	16	—	—	64
Hampson, Steve	22	1	6	—	16
Hemsley, Kerry	12 + 1	2	—	—	8
Holden, Keith	12	1	—	—	4
Juliff, Brian	13 + 5	1	—	—	4
Kiss, Nicky	9	—	—	—	—
Nanyn, Mick	2 + 1	—	—	—	—
Owen, Gary	1	—	—	—	—
Pendlebury, John	17 + 5	4	—	—	16
Potter, Ian	10 + 2	2	—	—	8
Ramsdale, Dennis	30 + 2	5	—	—	20
Scott, Mick	20 + 10	2	—	—	8
Shaw, Glyn	13	—	—	—	—
Stephens, Gary	23	3	—	—	12
Stephenson, David	31	10	—	1	41
Tamati, Howie	29	3	—	—	12
Wane, Shaun	13 + 4	3	—	—	12
West, Graeme	36	13	—	—	52
Whitfield, Colin	37	13	119	3	293
Wilby, Tim	3	1	—	—	4
Williams, Barry	8	—	—	—	—
Wood, David	9 + 3	—	2	—	4
Trialist	1	—	—	—	—
TOTALS					
36 players		113	139	4	734

1983-84 MATCH ANALYSIS

Date	Competition	H/A	Opponent	Rlt	Score	Tries	Goals	Attendance	Referee
21.8.83	SLC	A	Salford	W	16-14	Clare, Ramsdale	Whitfield (4)	—	—
24.8.83	SLC	A	Wakefield T.	W	18-11	Case, Gill, Foy	Whitfield (3)	—	—
28.8.83	SLC	H	Leigh	L	12-26	Whitfield	Whitfield (4)	9243	Hodgson
4.9.83	LC(1)	A	Widnes	L	20-36	Gill (2), Whitfield	Whitfield (4)	—	—
11.9.83	SLC	H	Bradford N.	L	16-24	Dunn, Clare, West	Whitfield, Wood	5828	Massey
18.9.83	SLC	A	Hull	L	8-24	Holden	Whitfield (2)	—	—
25.9.83	SLC	H	Widnes	L	16-31	West, Campbell, Clare	Whitfield, Clare	7215	Thompson
2.10.83	SLC	A	Whitehaven	W	24-0	Stephenson (2), West, Wane	Clare (4)	—	—
9.10.83	SLC	A	Leigh	L	18-24	Whitfield, Campbell, Gill	Whitfield (3)	—	—
19.10.83	SLC	H	Leeds	W	20-6	West (2), Wilby	Whitfield (4)	7394	Berry
23.10.83	Tour	H	Queensland	L	2-40	—	Whitfield	9749	Campbell
6.11.83	JPS(1)	H	York	W	30-13	Whitfield (2), Gill, Stephenson	Whitfield (7)	6388	Hodgson
13.11.83	SLC	A	Oldham	L	4-8	—	Whitfield (2)	—	—
20.11.83	JPS(2)	H	Salford	W	24-15	Gill (3), Dunn	Whitfield (4)	7290	Kershaw
26.11.83	JPS(3)	A	Widnes	L	15-20	West, Case	Whitfield (3, 1 dg)	—	—
4.12.83	SLC	H	Whitehaven	W	33-11	Hemsley, Whitfield, Tamati, Stephenson, Juliff	Whitfield (6, 1 dg)	5114	Allatt
18.12.83	SLC	H	Hull	W	14-12	Hampson	Whitfield (5)	7102	Walker
26.12.83	SLC	H	St. Helens	W	12-8	Whitfield	Whitfield (4)	12719	Lindop
8.1.84	SLC	H	Castleford	W	32-6	West (2), Case, Edwards	Whitfield (8)	7439	Wall
11.1.84	SLC	A	Featherstone R.	L	6-15	—	Whitfield (3)	—	—
29.1.84	SLC	A	Hull K. R.	L	10-24	Cannon, West	Whitfield	—	—
5.2.84	SLC	H	Warrington	L	6-24	—	Clare (3)	7666	Beaumont
11.2.84	CC(1)	A	Bramley	D	10-10	Gill, West	Whitfield	—	—
15.2.84	CC(1) Replay	H	Bramley	W	34-4	Cannon (2), Elvin, Dunn, Whitfield, West	Whitfield (5)	5815	Spencer
19.2.84	SLC	A	Fulham	L	10-22	Stephens	Whitfield (2), Wood	—	—
26.2.84	CC(2)	H	Oldham	W	30-6	Cannon (2), Gill (2), Edwards, Stephenson	Whitfield (3)	9515	Lindop
1.3.84	SLC	A	Bradford N.	W	15-6	Cannon, Gill, Case	Whitfield (1, 1 dg)	—	—
4.3.84	SLC	H	Wakefield T.	W	34-0	Edwards (3), Gill (2), Case, Stephenson	Whitfield (2), Hampson	6455	Thompson
11.3.84	CC(3)	A	St. Helens	W	16-7	Pendlebury, Cannon	Whitfield (4)	—	—
14.3.84	SLC	H	Oldham	W	12-6	Whitfield, Cannon	Whitfield (2)	6457	Fox
18.3.84	SLC	H	Fulham	W	38-18	Stephenson (2), Whitfield, Potter, Cannon	Hampson (5), Whitfield (4)	6761	Hodgson
24.3.84	CC(SF)	Leeds U. FC	York	W	14-8	Whitfield, Scott	Whitfield (3)	(17156)	Campbell
28.3.84	SLC	A	Castleford	L	10-38	Braithwaite, Elvin	Edwards	—	—
1.4.84	SLC	H	Featherstone R.	W	26-12	Whitfield (2), West, Gill, Scott	Whitfield (3)	6163	Campbell
4.4.84	SLC	A	Warrington	W	34-6	Pendlebury (2), Cannon, Stephens, Tamati	Whitfield (7)	—	—
8.4.84	SLC	H	Hull K. R.	L	14-30	Tamati, Edwards, Ramsdale	Whitfield	10130	Campbell
11.4.84	SLC	A	Widnes	L	14-21	Pendlebury, Wane	Clare (3)	—	—
15.4.84	SLC	H	Salford	W	34-8	Ramsdale (2), West, Potter, Gill, Stephenson	Whitfield (5)	6653	Berry
17.4.84	SLC	A	Leeds	W	14-10	Stephenson, Stephens	Whitfield (3)	—	—
20.4.84	SLC	A	St. Helens	L	13-20	Wane, Ramsdale	Whitfield (2), Stephenson (dg)	—	—
5.5.84	CC(F)	Wembley	Widnes	L	6-19	Hemsley	Whitfield	(80116)	Thompson

WORKINGTON TOWN

Ground: Derwent Park
Colours: White jerseys with blue band, white shorts
First Season: 1945-46
Nickname: Town
Chairman: John Bell
Secretary: John Bell
Coach: Harry Archer and Bill Smith (May 1983-)
Honours: **Championship** Winners, 1950-51
Beaten finalists, 1957-58
Challenge Cup Winners, 1951-52
Beaten finalists, 1954-55, 1957-58
Lancashire Cup Winners, 1977-78
Beaten finalists, 1976-77, 1978-79, 1979-80
Western Division Championship Winners, 1962-63
Records: Attendance: 17,741 v. Wigan (RL Cup) 3 March, 1965. There was a crowd of 20,403 at Borough Park for a RL Cup-tie v. St. Helens on 8 March, 1952.
Season
Goals: 186 by L. Hopkins, 1981-82
Tries: 49 by J. Lawrenson, 1951-52
Points: 438 by L. Hopkins, 1981-82
Match
Goals: 11 by I. MacCorquodale v. Blackpool B, 6 Jan, 1973
Tries: 7 by I. Southward v. Blackpool B, 17 Sep, 1955
Points: 33 by I. Southward v. Blackpool B, 17 Sep, 1955
Highest score: 62-15 v. Hunslet, 1963-64
Highest against: 59-5 v. Leeds, 1971-72

1983-84 PLAYERS' SUMMARY

	App.	Tries	Goals	D/Gls	Pts
Banks, John	10 + 5	3	—	—	12
Beattie, John	28 + 1	6	4	—	32
Beck, David	28 + 1	14	—	—	56
Burns, Howard	31 + 2	22	2	—	92
Collister, David	3 + 1	1	—	—	4
Cooke, Tony	3	—	—	—	—
Cottier, Gordon	6	—	—	—	—
Denny, Ian	5	—	2	—	4
Dobie, John	26 + 1	3	—	—	12
Falcon, Colin	6 + 5	1	—	—	4
Gartland, Kevin	2 + 5	—	—	—	—
Hartley, Ian	23 + 2	3	—	—	12
Henney, Harold	12	2	—	—	8
Hopkins, Lyn	10 + 1	6	36	1	97
Hutchinson, Brian	8	—	—	—	—
Jones, John	7	2	—	—	8
Lewis, Ray	8 + 5	—	—	—	—
Lightfoot, John	28 + 1	4	—	—	16
Maguire, Steve	18 + 3	4	35	6	92
Maughan, Kevin	14 + 1	6	3	—	30
Nixon, Garry	29 + 3	8	—	—	32
O'Neill, Kevin	1	—	—	—	—
Pattinson, Bill	38	10	—	—	40
Pattinson, Bob	23 + 2	4	—	—	16
Roper, Tony	32	8	—	—	32
Rudd, Ian	17	1	1	—	6
Skillen, Mark	6 + 2	2	—	—	8
Smith, David	19 + 5	3	27	3	69
Taylor, Michael	1	—	—	—	—
Thompson, Ian	26 + 1	9	1	—	38
Todd, Colin	18 + 6	3	—	—	12
Wallbanks, Garry	1	—	—	—	—
Trialists (5)	7 + 3	5	2	—	24
TOTALS					
37 players		130	113	10	756

Lynn Hopkins ... record goals and points scorer.

1983-84 MATCH ANALYSIS

Date	Com-petition	H/A	Opponent	Rlt	Score	Tries	Goals	Atten-dance	Referee
21.8.83	SD	A	Carlisle	W	36-10	Burns (3), Beck (2), W. Pattinson	Smith (6)	—	—
28.8.83	SD	H	Barrow	W	15-8	Beattie, Todd	Smith (3, 1 dg)	1723	Spencer
31.8.83	SD	A	Swinton	W	18-6	R. Pattinson, Burns, Roper, Lightfoot	Smith	—	—
4.9.83	LC(1)	A	Oldham	L	20-26	Hartley, Beck, Burns	Maguire (3), Smith	—	—
11.9.83	SD	H	Hunslet	L	14-16	Skillen, Nixon	Smith (3)	1308	Walker
18.9.83	SD	A	Kent Invicta	W	12-11	R. Pattinson, Maguire	Maguire (1, 2 dg)	—	—
25.9.83	SD	H	Swinton	W	22-18	Beattie, Maguire, Smith	Maguire (5)	1151	Mean
2.10.83	SD	A	Huddersfield	W	22-18	Collister, Burns, Smith, W. Pattinson	Smith (3)	—	—
9.10.83	SD	A	York	W	18-17	Jones (2), Falcon	Denny (2), Burns	—	—
16.10.83	SD	H	Keighley	W	14-6	Roper (2), Burns	Burns	828	Berry
30.10.83	SD	A	Huyton	L	10-15	Todd, Rudd	Rudd	—	—
6.11.83	JPS(1)	A	Carlisle	L	5-10	Beck	Maguire (dg)	—	—
13.11.83	SD	H	Blackpool B.	D	19-19	Beattie, Lightfoot, W. Pattinson	Maguire (3, 1 dg)	732	Whitfield
27.11.83	SD	A	Dewsbury	W	28-22	Burns (2), Beck, Maughan, ?. Pattinson	Beattie (4)	—	—
4.12.83	SD	H	Doncaster	W	44-4	Burns (3), Beck (2), Dobie (2), Lightfoot	Smith (4), Maughan (2)	655	Campbell
18.12.83	SD	H	Dewsbury	W	32-6	Maughan (2), R. Pattinson, Banks, Smith	Smith (6)	705	Beaumont
26.12.83	SD	H	Carlisle	W	11-4	Burns, Maughan	Maughan, Smith (dg)	1592	Spencer
8.1.84	SD	A	Blackpool B.	L	2-8	—	Thompson	—	—
5.2.84	SD	H	Huddersfield	W	16-6	Burns, Lightfoot, Hopkins	Maguire, Hopkins	620	Kendrew
12.2.84	CC(1)	A	Barrow	W	14-12	Burns, Hartley, Roper	Hopkins	—	—
26.2.84	CC(2)	H	Leeds	L	3-12	—	Hopkins (1, 1 dg)	4110	Wall
4.3.84	SD	H	York	W	26-9	Nixon (2), Beattie, W. Pattinson	Hopkins (5)	851	Mean
9.3.84	SD	H (at Work'n AFC)	Bramley	L	10-16	Thompson (2)	Hopkins	1092	Volante
11.3.84	SD	A	Cardiff C.	W	22-20	Nixon (2), Beattie, Hopkins	Hopkins (3)	—	—
16.3.84	SD	H (at Work'n AFC)	Batley	W	36-8	Hopkins (2), Burns, Nixon, Hartley, W. Pattinson, Beattie	Hopkins (4)	804	Walker
18.3.84	SD	H	Huyton	W	24-12	Roper (2), Maughan, Todd, Thompson	Maguire (2)	701	Thompson
22.3.84	SD	A	Rochdale H.	D	8-8	Roper	Maguire (2)	—	—
25.3.84	SD	A	Batley	L	10-36	Burns (2)	Maguire	—	—
28.3.85	SD	A	Halifax	L	0-24	—	—	—	—
1.4.84	SD	H	Kent Invicta	W	21-12	Beck, Burns, Nixon	Hopkins (4), Smith (dg)	629	Lindop
4.4.84	SD	A	Hunslet	W	28-10	Henney (2), Thompson, Beck	Hopkins (5), Maguire (2 dg)	—	—
8.4.84	SD	A	Bramley	L	16-26	Beck, Skilling, Burns	Maguire (2)	—	—
13.4.84	SD	H	Halifax	W	28-10	Thompson (2), Nixon, Hopkins, W. Pattinson	Hopkins (4)	819	Spencer
15.4.84	SD	H	Rochdale H.	W	38-26	Thompson, Beck, W. Pattinson, Burns, Banks, Hopkins	Hopkins (7)	796	Beaumont
20.4.84	SD	A	Barrow	L	14-26	Maughan, Burns, Thompson	Maguire	—	—
23.4.84	SD	H	Cardiff C.	W	38-30	Beck (2), Roper, Thompson, Dobie, Maguire	Maguire (7)	873	Allatt
27.4.84	SD	A	Doncaster	W	24-23	Trialists (4)	Maguire (4)	—	—
29.4.84	SD	A	Keighley	W	38-14	W. Pattinson (2), Beck, Banks, Maguire, R. Pattinson, Trialist	Maguire (3), Trialist (2)	—	—

YORK

Ground: Wiggington Road
Colours: Amber and black jerseys, black shorts
First Season: 1901-02
Nickname: Wasps
Chairman: Charles Magson
Secretary: Ian Clough
Coach: Phil Lowe (Mar. 1983-)
Honours: **Division Two** Champions, 1980-81
Challenge Cup Beaten finalists, 1930-31
Yorkshire Cup Winners, 1922-23, 1933-34, 1936-37
Beaten finalists, 1935-36, 1957-58, 1978-79
Records: Attendance: 14,689 v. Swinton (RL Cup) 10 February, 1934
Season
Goals: 146 by V. Yorke, 1957-58
Tries: 35 by J. Crossley, 1980-81
Points: 301 by V. Yorke, 1957-58
Match
Goals: 11 by V. Yorke v. Whitehaven, 6 Sep, 1958; C. Gibson v. Dewsbury, 28 Sep, 1980
Tries: 6 by R. Hardgrave v. Bramley, 5 Jan, 1935
Points: 24 by G. Steadman v. Carlisle, 4 Apr, 1984; v. Batley, 11 Apr, 1984
Highest score: 60-0 v. Barrow, 1971-72
Highest against: 75-3 v. Warrington, 1950-51

1983-84 PLAYERS' SUMMARY

	App.	Tries	Goals	D/Gls	Pts
Blackburn, Steve	20 + 6	3	11	—	34
Brettell, Kevin	5 + 1	—	—	—	—
Carr, Alan	2 + 1	—	—	—	—
Clancey, Bob	12 + 8	1	—	—	4
Colley, Michael	15 + 8	3	—	—	12
Dunkerley, David	3	—	—	—	—
Ford, Chris	4 + 5	1	1	—	6
Gibson, Chris	2	—	6	—	12
Hagan, Michael	2	1	—	—	4
Hambly, Gary	4	—	—	—	—
Harrison, Chris	23	15	1	—	62
Hooper, Terry	28 + 4	4	—	—	16
Hughes, Brian	31 + 3	1	—	—	4
Hughes, Mick	26 + 3	3	—	—	12
Kain, John	10	2	—	—	8
Midgley, Trevor	40	5	—	—	20
Morgan, Terry	14	6	40	—	104
Morrell, Wayne	37 + 1	19	—	—	76
Nuttall, Steve	7	—	—	—	—
Orr, Paul	10 + 9	3	1	1	15
Phillippo, Peter	26 + 1	—	—	—	—
Pitts, Graham	0 + 1	—	—	—	—
Price, Gary	31 + 1	7	—	—	28
Pryce, Dennis	1 + 1	—	—	—	—
Pryce, Geoff	38	16	—	—	64
Rhodes, Chris	1 + 5	1	—	—	4
Smith, Gary	40	5	—	—	20
Smith, Peter	6	1	—	—	4
Spedding, Steve	1	—	—	—	—
Steadman, Graham	28	25	71	7	249
Tansley, Ian	30 + 1	8	—	—	32
Townend, Jeff	1	—	—	—	—
Wilson, Ian	32	9	12	2	62
Trialist	3	—	—	—	—
TOTALS					
34 players		139	143	10	852

Mick Hughes ... three tries in 29 appearances.

1983-84 MATCH ANALYSIS

Date	Comp.	H/A	Opponent	Rlt	Score	Tries	Goals	Att.	Referee
21.8.83	SD	A	Rochdale H.	W	26-14	P. Smith, Morrell, M. Hughes, Price	Gibson (5)	—	—
24.8.83	SD	H	Dewsbury	L	10-12	Morrell	Wilson (2), Gibson	1288	Lindop
28.8.83	SD	H	Blackpool B.	D	14-14	Morrell, Pryce	Blackburn (2), Wilson	925	Kendrew
4.9.83	YC(1)	A	Hunslet	W	21-11	Wilson (2)	Wilson (6, 1 dg)	—	—
7.9.83	SD	A	Huddersfield	L	14-30	Price, Steadman	Steadman (3)	—	—
11.9.83	SD	H	Swinton	L	4-9	—	Steadman (2)	767	Robinson
14.9.83	YC(2)	H	Leeds	L	16-24	Hooper (2), Steadman	Steadman (2)	1296	Lindop
18.9.83	SD	A	Doncaster	W	44-10	Wilson (2), Steadman, Midgley, B. Hughes, Pryce, Morrell, Orr	Steadman (5), Orr	—	—
25.9.83	SD	H	Rochdale H.	W	28-15	Hooper (2), Tansley	Morgan (8)	1009	Beaumont
2.10.83	SD	A	Huyton	W	21-11	Steadman, Pryce, Morrell	Morgan (4), Steadman (dg)	—	—
9.10.83	SD	H	Workington T.	L	17-18	Colley (2), Price	Morgan (2), Orr (dg)	1036	Smith
16.10.83	SD	A	Dewsbury	W	12-10	Orr, Clancy	Morgan (2)	—	—
23.10.83	SD	H	Cardiff C.	W	50-16	Morrell (2), Pryce (2), Steadman, Tansley, Morgan, Colley	Morgan (9)	1030	Allatt
30.10.83	SD	A	Halifax	L	4-17	Smith	—	—	—
6.11.83	JPS(1)	A	Wigan	L	13-30	Pryce, Midgley	Morgan (2), Steadman (dg)	—	—
13.11.83	SD	H	Doncaster	W	40-9	Morrell (2), Harrison (2), Morgan (2), Steadman, Wilson	Morgan (4)	1413	Volante
27.11.83	SD	A	Blackpool B.	W	12-8	Morgan (2)	Morgan (2)	—	—
4.12.83	SD	H	Huyton	W	54-6	Smith (3), Midgley (2), Tansley, Morrell, Steadman, Price, Orr, Morgan	Morgan (5)	1056	Haigh
18.12.83	SD	A	Barrow	L	18-42	Price (2), Harrison	Morgan (2), Ford	—	—
26.12.83	SD	H	Hunslet	L	20-37	Harrison (2), Steadman	Steadman (4)	2003	Mean
1.1.84	SD	A	Hunslet	L	9-13	Pryce	Steadman (2, 1 dg)	—	—
8.1.84	SD	H	Huddersfield	W	10-6	Morrell, Wilson	Wilson	984	Walker
15.1.84	SD	A	Kent Invicta	L	18-22	Morrell, Steadman, Kain	Steadman (3)	—	—
12.2.84	CC(1)	A	Rochdale H.	W	17-8	Steadman, Tansley, Price	Steadman (2, 1dg)	—	—
15.2.84	SD	A	Swinton	L	20-25	Steadman, Harrison, Tansley	Steadman (3), Blackburn	—	—
19.2.84	SD	A	Bramley	W	18-12	Harrison (2), Kain	Blackburn (3)	—	—
26.2.84	CC(2)	A	Wakefield T.	W	20-12	Price, Morrell, Blackburn	Steadman (4)	—	—
29.2.84	SD	A	Keighley	W	18-1	Steadman (2), Morrell	Steadman (2), Blackburn	—	—
4.3.84	SD	A	Workington T.	L	9-26	Hagan	Wilson (2, 1dg)	—	—
11.3.84	CC(3)	H	Castleford	W	14-12	Steadman (2)	Steadman (3)	8529	Wall
18.3.84	SD	H	Keighley	D	11-11	Blackburn, Morrell	Steadman (1, 1dg)	1486	Fox
24.3.84	CC(SF)	Leeds U.FC	Wigan	L	8-14	Harrison	Steadman (2)	(17156)	Campbell
1.4.84	SD	A	Carlisle	W	26-24	Harrison (2), Morrell, Midgley, M. Hughes	Blackburn (2), Harrison	—	—
4.4.84	SD	H	Carlisle	W	50-6	Harrison (3), Steadman (3), Blackburn, Morrell, Wilson	Steadman (6), Blackburn	1024	Hodgson
11.4.84	SD	H	Batley	W	36-8	Steadman (3), Wilson, Pryce, Morrell	Steadman (6)	1118	McDonald
15.4.84	SD	H	Halifax	W	27-21	Steadman, G. Smith, Pryce, Harrison	Steadman (5, 1dg)	2010	Robinson
20.4.84	SD	A	Batley	L	14-22	Rhodes, Pryce	Steadman (2), Blackburn	—	—
23.4.84	SD	H	Bramley	W	28-22	Steadman (2), Pryce (2), Morrell	Steadman (4)	1105	Smith
25.4.84	SD	H	Barrow	L	11-27	Tansley	Steadman (3, 1dg)	1356	Spencer
28.4.84	SD	H	Kent Invicta	W	22-20	Steadman, M. Hughes, Pryce, Ford	Steadman (3)	1048	Wall
13.5.84	SD	A	Cardiff C.	W	28-26	Tansley (2), Price (2), Wilson	Steadman (4)	—	—

LEADING SCORERS FOR 1983-84

TOP TEN TRIES:

1.	Garry Schofield (Hull)	38
2.	Joe Lydon (Widnes)	28
	Graham King (Hunslet)	28
4.	John Woods (Leigh)	27
5.	John Basnett (Widnes)	26
	Carl Gibson (Batley)	26
7.	Steve Herbert (Barrow)	25
	Graham Steadman (York)	25
	Gary Prohm (Hull K.R.)	25
10.	Garry Clark (Hull K.R.)	24

● Others with 20 or more: James Leuluai (Hull), Andy Whittle (Barrow) 23; Terry Moore (Barrow), Howard Burns (Workington T.), Steve Evans (Hull), Tommy David (Cardiff C.), Danny Wilson (Swinton) 22; John Stapleton (Rochdale H.) 21; Gary Peacham (Carlisle), Phil Ford (Warrington) 20.

TOP TEN GOALS:
(Including drop goals)

1.	Steve Hesford (Warrington)	142
	Bob Beardmore (Castleford)	142
3.	Lyn Hallett (Cardiff C.)	140
4.	Eric Fitzsimons (Hunslet)	131
5.	John Woods (Leigh)	124
6.	Colin Whitfield (Wigan)	122
7.	Ian Ball (Barrow)	104
8.	Mick Parrish (Oldham)	101
9.	Malcolm Agar (Halifax)	94
10.	Steve Tickle (Barrow)	91

TOP FIVE POINTS

	T	G	DG	Pts
1. John Woods (Leigh)	27	123	1	355
2. Bob Beardmore (Castleford)	13	140	2	334
3. Steve Hesford (Warrington)	7	135	7	305
4. Colin Whitfield (Wigan)	13	119	3	293
5. Lyn Hallett (Cardiff C.)	7	111	29	279

TOP FIVE DROP GOALS

1.	Lyn Hallett (Cardiff C.)	29
2.	David Noble (Doncaster)	19
	Danny Wilson (Swinton)	19
4.	Billy Platt (Rochdale H.)	16
5.	Norman Turley (Blackpool B.)	15

OUTSTANDING SCORING FEATS IN 1983-84

INDIVIDUAL

Most tries in a match:

5 by Des Drummond (Leigh) at Carlisle .... JPS (2)
Kevin Meadows (Oldham) at Salford .. Division One

Most goals in a match:

12 by Steve Tickle (Barrow) at Kent Invicta. Division Two
11 by Mark Viller (Swinton) v. Huddersfield Division Two
Norman Turley (Blackpool B.) v. Carlisle .... Division Two
Bob Beardmore (Castleford) v. Leeds.. Division One
10 by John Woods (Leigh) at Carlisle .... JPS (2)

Most points in a match:

34 by Bob Beardmore (Castleford) v. Leeds.. Division One
28 by Steve Tickle (Barrow) at Kent Invicta. Division Two
27 by Norman Turley (Blackpool B.) v. Carlisle .... Division Two

Most drop goals in a match:

5 by Danny Wilson (Swinton) v. Hunslet......... JPS (1)

TEAM

Highest score and widest margin, home or away:

Kent Invicta 8 v. Barrow 80.............. Division Two

There was a total of 31 matches in which one team scored 50 points or more. Other 60-plus scores were:

Home:

Leigh 68 v. Whitehaven 14	Division One
Hull 66 v. Wakefield T. 12	Division One
Swinton 66 v. Keighley 1	Division Two
Barrow 64 v. Batley 2	Division Two

Away:

Carlisle 17 v. Leigh 68	JPS (2)
Doncaster 0 v. Barrow 66	Division Two

Highest score by losing team:

Hull K.R. 51 v. Salford 32	Division One
Fulham 32 v. Warrington 58	Division One

There was a total of 62 matches in which a team scored 20 points or more and lost.

High-scoring draws:

Widnes 28 v. St. Helens 28	Division One
Cardiff C. 26 v. Huddersfield 26	Division Two
Huddersfield 24 v. Rochdale H. 24	Division Two
Warrington 22 v. Oldham 22	Division One
Hull 22 v. Warrington 22	Division One
Bramley 21 v. Rochdale H. 21	Division Two
Halifax 20 v. Huyton 20	Division Two

Castleford captain Bob Beardmore, breaker of club and First Division points records.

RECORDS

RECORDS

• From the start of the 1983-84 season, the value of a try was raised from three points to four points. It was officially decided that records for most points in a match, season or career would subsequently include the four-point try and that no attempt would be made to adjust existing records featuring the three-point try.

RECORD-BREAKING FEATS IN 1983-84

NEW RECORDS AT A GLANCE . . .

LYN HALLETT broke a succession of Cardiff City records. He scored most goals (9) and most points (18) in a match twice, while scoring most goals (140) and points (279) in a season. He also kicked a record 29 drop goals.

JOHN WOODS of Leigh totalled a Division One record 295 points in a season.

STEVE HESFORD finished the season with a Warrington career record 2,396 points.

JOHN BUCKTON ended the campaign with a Doncaster career record 66 tries.

BOB BEARDMORE of Castleford scored a Division One record 34 points in a match and finished the season with a club record 334 points.

KEVIN MEADOWS of Oldham equalled the Division One record of five tries in a match.

DANNY WILSON of Swinton kicked a record five one-point drop goals in a match.

DES DRUMMOND of Leigh equalled the John Player record of five tries in a match.

JOHN DORAHY of Hull Kingston Rovers scored a Premiership match record of 22 points.

JOE LYDON broke two Great Britain Under-24 records with eight goals and 20 points in a match.

TONY MYLER equalled the Great Britain Under-24 record of three tries in a match.

TOMMY DAVID equalled the Cardiff City tries in a match record with four.

JOHN STOCKLEY equalled the Blackpool Borough tries in a match record with four.

GRAHAM STEADMAN broke the York points in a match record with 24 and equalled the new figure a week later.

NORMAN TURLEY broke two Blackpool Borough match records with 11 goals and 27 points.

STEVE TICKLE equalled two Barrow match records with 12 goals and 28 points.

HULL Kingtson Rovers ran up a Premiership record score of 54-0.

BARROW totalled a record 1,230 points in all matches, including Division Two records of 80 in a match and 1,126 in a season.

HULL broke two Division One records with 147 tries and 831 points.

WIDNES and ST. HELENS produced a Division One record high-scoring draw of 28-28.

SALFORD and FULHAM both had Division One record losing scores of 32.

CARLISLE, HUNSLET and CARDIFF CITY all had Division Two record losing scores of 30.

WHITEHAVEN suffered a Division One record losing sequence of 20 matches, including a club record defeat of 68-14.

CARLISLE gained a club record 38-16 victory but also suffered their worst defeat of 68-17.

CARDIFF CITY had a club record defeat of 50-16 followed by a record 41-6 victory.

FULHAM went down to a club record 58-32 defeat.

GREAT BRITAIN Under-24s had a record 48-1 victory.

NEW RECORDS IN DETAIL . . .

LYN HALLETT collected several Cardiff City records during the season and also kicked the most one-point drop goals by any player.

He began by beating the Cardiff goals in a match record with nine against Rochdale Hornets in a John Player Special Trophy tie on November 6. They included one drop goal to give him a record-equalling 17 points. Steve Fenwick had held the goals record with eight against Swinton in 1983 and the points record with 17 against Hunslet in 1981.

Hallett then equalled the match goals record and extended the points tally. He scored nine goals and 18 points in a Division Two match at Workington Town on April 23 and six days later scored another 18 points from five goals and two tries against Huyton.

The full back or stand off also finished the season with a club record 140 goals and 279 points. Steve Fenwick had held the goals record with 110 in 1982-83. Hallett passed that figure with the third of his nine goals at Workington in April.

Fenwick's points record of 256, made up of 108 goals, 1 drop and 13 tries, held since the club's inaugural season of 1981-82, went at Bramley on May 2 where Hallett kicked four goals.

Included in Hallett's records were 29 drop goals, the most by any player since they were reduced to one point in 1974. Arnold Walker, the former Whitehaven and Workington Town Test scrum half, had held the record with 22 drops in 1980-81. Hallett took his total to 23 with one against Kent Invicta on April 11.

Hallett was Cardiff's only ever-present during the season with 38 appearances and his match-by-match scoring figures were as follows:

Welsh international Lyn Hallett.

		T	G	DG	Pts
Kent Invicta	(A)	1	0	1	5
Bramley	(A)	0	0	1	1
Carlisle	(H)	0	2	1	5
Hunslet	(A)	0	5	0	10
Huddersfield	(H)	1	3	0	10
Doncaster	(A)	0	6	0	12
Dewsbury	(H)	1	3	0	10
Huyton	(A)	0	3	1	7
York	(A)	0	4	0	8
Keighley	(H)	0	3	0	6
Rochdale H (John Player)	(H)	0	8	1	17
Batley	(A)	0	2	2	6
Huyton (John Player)	(H)	0	6	2	14
Leigh (John Player)	(A)	0	1	0	2
Swinton	(H)	0	2	0	4
Halifax	(H)	0	4	2	10
Rochdale H.	(A)	0	0	0	0
Barrow	(H)	0	0	0	0
Huddersfield	(A)	0	1	0	2
Hunslet	(H)	0	1	0	2
Hull (Challenge Cup)	(H)	0	3	0	6
Barrow	(A)	0	1	1	3
Blackpool B	(A)	0	6	1	13
Blackpool B	(H)	0	1	1	3
Workington T	(H)	0	3	1	7
Halifax	(A)	0	1	0	2
Dewsbury	(A)	0	1	2	4
Rochdale H	(H)	1	3	1	11
Batley	(H)	0	4	4	12
Kent Invicta	(H)	0	0	1	1
Carlisle	(A)	0	2	2	6
Doncaster	(H)	0	4	0	8
Workington T	(A)	0	9	0	18
Keighley	(A)	0	4	2	10
Huyton	(H)	2	5	0	18
Bramley	(A)	0	4	0	8
Swinton	(A)	0	2	0	4
York	(H)	1	4	2	14
Totals					
Division Two		7	93	26	240
John Player		0	15	3	33
Challenge Cup		0	3	0	6
GRAND TOTALS		7	111	29	279

JOHN WOODS of Leigh scored 295 league points last season — a record Division One total since the reintroduction of two divisions in 1973.

Playing at stand off or centre, Woods scored 23 tries and kicked 102 goals including one drop. The old record was set by David Watkins with 288 points for Salford from 126 goals and 12 tries in 1973-74.

Woods broke the record with 20 points in Leigh's last match of the season, at home to Warrington on April 23.

His match-by-match Division One scoring figures were as follows (not including five goals scored in an abandoned match at Oldham which was expunged from the Division One table):

		T	G	DG	Pts
Widnes	(H)	0	2	0	4
Fulham	(H)	1	3	0	10
Wigan	(A)	Did not play			
Salford	(A)	0	9	0	18
Hull	(H)	1	4	0	12
Castleford	(A)	1	3	0	10
Bradford N.	(H)	0	0	0	0
Wakefield T	(A)	0	5	0	10
Wigan	(H)	1	6	0	16
Widnes	(A)	0	6	0	12
Whitehaven	(A)	1	5	0	14
St. Helens	(H)	1	4	0	12
Whitehaven	(H)	1	8	0	20
Warrington	(A)	3	3	0	18
Wakefield T	(H)	0	1	0	2
Hull	(A)	0	0	0	0
Featherstone R.	(H)	1	4	0	12
Leeds	(H)	0	1	0	2
Hull K.R.	(A)	0	2	0	4
Featherstone R	(A)	1	2	0	8
Salford	(H)	0	5	0	10
Oldham	(A)	0	3	0	6
Oldham	(H)	1	1	1	7
Fulham	(A)	2	2	0	12
Bradford N	(A)	1	3	0	10
Castleford	(H)	1	5	0	14
Leeds	(A)	3	6	0	24
St. Helens	(A)	Did not play			
Hull K.R.	(H)	1	2	0	8
Warrington	(H)	2	6	0	20
Totals		23	101	1	295

JOHN BUCKTON collected another Doncaster record during the season, finishing with a club career best of 66 tries. The previous record was 63 by winger Graham Arrand between 1965 and 1980.

Buckton broke the record in dramatic fashion in the preliminary round of the John Player Special Trophy at Batley on October 23. After going on as a substitute in the second half, Buckton scored Doncaster's only try in the last minute for David Noble to kick the goal from in front of the posts for a 12-11 victory.

Doncaster signed Buckton from Hunslet in 1979-80 and he opened his tryscoring account with two against Swinton on March 16, 1980. He finished with only four tries that season but each successive season has been a record one for him.

The stand off or centre equalled the Doncaster record for tries in a season with 17 in 1980-81, broke it the following season with 18 and equalled it in 1982-83 despite a brief spell on loan to Wakefield Trinity.

He managed only nine tries last season after missing many matches, but they were sufficient to give him a Doncaster career record of 66 tries.

Buckton is also joint holder of the Doncaster tries in a match record with four against Rochdale Hornets on August 30, 1981.

His season-by-season figures are as follows:

1979-80	4
1980-81	17
1981-82	18
1982-83	18
1983-84	9
Total	66

STEVE HESFORD finished the season as Warrington's most prolific points scorer of all time with a grand total of 2,396. The previous record of 2,288 was held by Brian Bevan, the legendary Australian winger whose total was made up of a record 740 tries and 34 goals between 1945 and 1962.

Hesford's total is made up of 46 tries and a club record 1,149 goals, including 47 drop goals, and has been achieved in a much shorter spell than Bevan's. He made his debut with two goals at Wakefield Trinity on November 2, 1975 and broke the record with the second of his five goals against Huddersfield on February 12, 1984.

After playing much of his early career in the threequarter line Hesford has now settled at full back. His 170 goals in 1978-79 is another club record.

Hesford's season-by-season totals for Warrington are as follows.

	T	G	DG	Pts
1975-76	4	46	0	104
1976-77	10	122	7	281
1977-78	7	155	3	334
1978-79	5	157	13	342
1979-80	3	122	6	259
1980-81	7	142	5	310
1981-82	2	110	6	232
1982-83	1	113	0	229
1983-84	7	135	7	305
Totals	46	1,102	47	2,396

BOB BEARDMORE broke the Division One points in a match record with 34 in Castleford's 54-4 defeat of Leeds on October 2. The scrum half's total was made up of 11 goals and three tries.

John Woods had set the record with 29 points, from 10 goals and three tries, for Leigh against York in 1981-82.

Beardmore went on to finish with a club record 334 points from 142 goals, including two drops, and 13 tries. The previous record holder was Sammy Lloyd with 331 from 158 goals and five tries in 1976-77.

Beardmore broke the record in Castleford's last match of the season, the Slalom Lager Premiership final against Hull K.R. at Headingley on May 12.

KEVIN MEADOWS equalled the Division One record of five tries in a match while on loan to Oldham from St. Helens. The winger's feat came in Oldham's last match of the season, a 50-10 victory at Salford on Good Friday, April 20.

Others to score five tries in a Division One match were: Roy Mathias (St. Helens) v. Rochdale Hornets in 1973-74 and v. Workington Town in 1979-80; Parry Gordon (Warrington) v. Dewsbury in 1973-74; Peter Glynn (St. Helens) v. Hull in 1977-78; Steve Fenton (Castleford) v. Dewsbury in 1977-78; Steve Hartley (Hull K.R.) v. Huddersfield in 1978-79.

DES DRUMMOND of Leigh equalled the John Player record of five tries in a match in the 68-17 second round victory at Carlisle on November 20.

Others to score five tries in a John Player tie were: John Joyner (Castleford) v. Millom amateurs in 1973-74; John Basnett (Widnes) away to Hunslet in 1981-82; Bob Eccles (Warrington) v. Blackpool Borough in 1982-83.

DANNY WILSON of Swinton kicked a record five one-point drop goals in a 17-16 John Player Special Trophy first round victory over Hunslet on November 6.

Earlier in the season the old record of four one-point drop goals had been equalled by Kent Invicta's Gary Bishop in a Division Two match against Huddersfield on October 9.

Others who had kicked four drop goals in a match since they were reduced to one point in 1974 were: Allan Agar (Hull K.R.) at Leeds in 1979-80, and Johnny Blair (Halifax) v. Wakefield Trinity in 1979-80.

JOHN DORAHY of Hull Kingston Rovers scored a Premiership match record of 22 points in the 54-0 first round defeat of Leeds on April 29. The Australian stand off's tally came from seven goals and two tries to beat the record of 19 points, from five goals and three tries, by Castleford's Sammy Lloyd against Wakefield Trinity in 1974-75.

JOE LYDON and TONY MYLER both achieved records in Great Britain under-24s record 48-1 defeat of France at Oldham on December 4. Full back Lydon's eight goals and 20 points, including a try, were new Under-24 records, while his Widnes colleague, Myler, scored a record-equalling three tries at stand off.

TOMMY DAVID equalled the Cardiff City tries in a match record with four in the 40-16 defeat of Batley on April 8. The prop or second row forward set the record himself with four against Swinton in 1982-83.

JOHN STOCKLEY equalled the Blackpool Borough tries in a match record when the winger scored four in the 36-12 defeat of Doncaster on April 1. The only other Blackpool player to score four tries was Tony Wilkshire against Bradford Northern in 1960-61.

NORMAN TURLEY broke two Blackpool Borough records with 11 goals and 27 points in their last match of the season, a 47-18 defeat of Carlisle on April 26. The forward's total included three drop goals and two tries.

The previous records had been held by Gary Laird with nine goals, adding a try for 21 points against Doncaster in 1982-83. Tex McCarrick also kicked nine goals against Thames Board Mills amateurs in 1963-64.

GRAHAM STEADMAN broke the York points in a match record with 24 . . . and equalled the new figure a week later. The stand off scored six goals and three tries in the 50-6 defeat of Carlisle on April 4 and repeated the feat on April 11 when York beat Batley 36-8.

Earlier in the season winger Terry Morgan equalled the old record of 22 points with nine goals and a try in the 50-16 defeat of Cardiff City on October 23. Other York players who had scored 22 points were: Vic Yorke (11g) v. Whitehaven in 1958-59; Steve Quinn (8g, 2t) v. Hunslet in 1972-73; Chris Gibson (11g) v. Dewsbury in 1980-81.

STEVE TICKLE equalled two Barrow match records with 12 goals and 28 points in the 80-8 victory at Kent Invicta on April 8. The full backs' tally included one try.

Others to score 12 goals were Fred French v. Maryport amateurs in 1937-38 and Willie Horne v. Cardiff in 1951-52. Keith Jarrett scored 28 points from 11 goals and two tries against Doncaster in 1970-71.

HULL KINGSTON ROVERS ran up a Premiership record score with their 54-0 first round victory over Leeds on April 29. The record had stood since the inaugural year of 1975 when St. Helens beat Oldham 42-5 in the first round.

BARROW amassed a record 1,230 points from 41 Cup and Division Two matches in the season. Their total was made up of 209 tries and 209 goals, including 24 drop goals. The previous record was held by Leeds who in 1972-73 played 52 matches in the Cup, League and one tour game. They totalled 1,220 points from 263 tries and 216 goals, including one drop.

Barrow's total included 1,126 points scored in 34 Division Two matches . . . a record under any league system. It was made up of 196 tries and 177 goals, including 12 drops. The only other side to total over 1,000 league points was St. Helens in 1958-59. Under the old one league system St. Helens played 38 matches and scored 1,005 points from 215 tries and 180 goals.

Barrow broke another Division Two record during the season with their 80-8 win at Kent Invicta on April 8. It was the highest score in any league match since the reintroduction of two divisions in 1973. It is also believed to be the highest away in any competitive match in this country other than by a touring side. Barrow's 80 points came from 14 tries and 12 goals. The previous record Division Two win was 75-3 by Leigh against Doncaster in 1975-76 when they scored 15 tries and 15 goals.

HULL, who finished second in the Slalom Lager Championship, broke two Division One records with 147 tries and 831 points. The previous records had been held by St. Helens, who finished third in 1977-78 when they scored 142 tries and 678 points.

WIDNES and ST. HELENS produced a record high-scoring draw for a Division One match with a 28-28 result on April 23. It produced 10 tries compared with the 12 tries when Wakefield Trinity and Workington Town drew 27-27 in 1979-80.

FULHAM and SALFORD both had the consolation of scoring the most points by a losing side in a Division One match. Fulham's 32-58 home defeat against Warrington on April 15 was also the most points they had conceded in their brief history. Salford produced their record losing score in the 51-32 defeat at Hull K.R. on March 18.

The previous league record score by a losing team had stood since the first season of the reintroduction of two divisions in 1973-74 when Leeds beat Rochdale Hornets 30-28.

CARDIFF CITY, CARLISLE and HUNSLET all had Division Two record losing scores as follows: Workington Town 38 v. Cardiff City 30 on April 23; Dewsbury 39 v. Carlisle 30 on October 5; Hunslet 30 v. Blackpool Borough 31 on December 4.

The previous record Division Two losing scores were: Swinton 25 v. Doncaster 32 in 1977-78 and Wakefield Trinity 25 v. Cardiff City 27 in 1982-83.

WHITEHAVEN suffered a Division One record losing sequence of 20 matches, which included the worst opening sequence of defeats and a club record 68-14 defeat at Leigh on December 18. The record loss had stood since 1970-71 when they were beaten 65-5 at Featherstone Rovers.

The Cumbrians were the holders of the previous record run of defeats from the beginning of a season when they lost 12 at the start of 1980-81. They then drew and had two more draws before gaining their first league win in their 24th match . . . a Division One record opening run without a win which still stands.

Last season Whitehaven's losing run extended to 20 matches, passing the worst sequence at any stage of a season by Swinton who lost 17 matches between September and February in 1975-76.

Whitehaven's losing run ended with a 42-8 home victory over Oldham on February 19, the Cumbrians' highest score in three seasons of Division One rugby.

CARLISLE'S 38-16 win at Doncaster on April 8 was the highest score in their brief history, beating three scores of 36 points in their inaugural season of 1981-82.

Earlier in the season, Carlisle went down to a record defeat of 68-17 at home to Leigh in the second round of the John Player Special Trophy on November 20. In 1982-83 they lost 66-8 in a 'home' match against Castleford, played at Wakefield Trinity.

CARDIFF CITY'S 41-6 home defeat of Rochdale Hornets in the first round of the John Player Special Trophy on November 6 was the Welsh club's record score. It beat the 40-12 win over Swinton in 1982-83.

Only two weeks before their record score, Cardiff crashed to their biggest defeat when they lost 50-16 at York on October 23. Previously, they had twice conceded 36 points in their inaugural season of 1981-82.

FULHAM twice conceded record scores during the season. The previous record was set in 1981-82, losing 36-17 at home to Featherstone Rovers. Last season the Riversiders went down 44-10 at home to Leeds on October 16, then on April 15 they lost 58-32 to Warrington, again at home.

MILESTONES . . .

JOHN WOODS of Leigh passed three notable milestones during the season. He scored his 100th try in all matches for Leigh and his 1,000th Division One point, including 500 league goals.

Woods signed for Leigh in December 1975 and scored his first try for them at Widnes on October 10, 1976. He has twice scored four tries in a match, plus two other hat-tricks.

His 100th try for Leigh came in the home victory over Wigan on October 9, 1983. At the end of the season the Test back's total stood at 122 made up as follows:

1976-77	3
1977-78	16
1978-79	10
1979-80	22
1980-81	14
1981-82	18
1982-83	12
1983-84	27
Total	122

Woods scored the 1,000th Division One point of his career at home to Fulham on August 24, 1983. His 500th Division One goal came with the last of six goals when he scored all Leigh's points in a 24-18 win at Leeds on April 3, 1984. He was the top Division One kicker in 1981-82 with 110 goals and last season broke the Division One record with 295 points.

Woods' Division One totals are as follows:

	T	G	DG	Pts
1976-77	3	60	2	131
1977-78	Leigh in Division Two			
1978-79	7	71	2	165
1979-80	18	53	2	162
1980-81	10	61	1	153
1981-82	14	109	1	261
1982-83	10	43	1	117
1983-84	23	101	1	295
Totals	85	498	10	1,284

(Not including scores in abandoned matches that were replayed)

Record breaker John Woods, currently the youngest coach in the game.

IAN BALL scored the 1,000th point of his professional career early last season. He reached the milestone with 13 points in Barrow's 19-18 Lancashire Cup semi-final victory at Warrington on September 21, 1983. His total includes 29 points for Cumbria.

The former Wasps and Waterloo RU player signed for Barrow after scoring a try as an unnamed trialist in a 21-12 home defeat against Leeds on October 29, 1978.

He broke the Barrow points record with 305 in 1979-80 and was well on the way to improving it and breaking the goals record held by his late father, Joe, when injury cut short last season in February.

Ball's career totals are made up as follows:

For Barrow	T	G	Pts
1978-79	14	53(1)	147
1979-80	26	119(11)	305 + 1t for Cumbria
1980-81	18	92(6)	232 + 1t, 12(1)g, 26 pts for Cumbria
1981-82	7	80(7)	174
1982-83	4	37(4)	82
1983-84	14	104(5)	259
Totals			
Barrow	83	485(34)	1,199
Cumbria	2	12(1)	29
GRAND TOTALS	85	497(35)	1,228

() Drop goals included in total

STEVE DIAMOND kicked the 500th goal of his career with the one that helped Fulham to a 6-6 home draw against Castleford on December 4, 1983.

A former Welsh RU club player with Newbridge, gaining county honours with Gwent, Diamond turned professional with Wakefield Trinity after making a tryscoring debut for them as a trialist at home to Castleford on September 3, 1978. He kicked eight goals, including a drop, in that first season and became Wakefield's regular goal kicker the following campaign.

Diamond had three seasons at Wakefield — mainly as a centre — and scored a total of 234 goals, including two drops.

He joined Fulham for the start of the 1981-82 season and marked his debut with seven goals in a Lanchashire Cup first round victory at home to Swinton on August 16, 1981. The Welshman finished the season with a Fulham best of 93 goals and increased the record to 136 the following season, when he pushed the points record to 308.

Diamond has settled at full back and played in every Fulham match since his debut — a total of 113 matches — and failed to score in only four. He has totalled 309 goals, including four drops.

He was the game's top goalscorer in 1982-83 with 136 and has finished in the top ten on two other occasions.

His career total of 541 goals includes two for Wales against France in 1980. His season-by-season totals are as follows:

Wakefield Trinity		
1978-79	8(1)	
1979-80	114	+2 for Wales
1980-81	112(1)	
Fulham		
1981-82	93(1)	
1982-83	136	
1983-84	80(3)	
Totals		
Wakefield T	234(2)	
Fulham	309(4)	
Wales	2	
GRAND TOTAL	545(6)	

() Drops goals included in total

MICK PARRISH, the Oldham and former Hunslet centre, took his career total of goals past the 500-mark during the season.

He reached the milestone with the first of his three goals in Oldham's home victory over Hull on October 23 and finished the season with 572, including three for Yorkshire.

The former Morley RU player signed for Hunslet in November 1978 and made a tryscoring debut at home on the old Greyhound Stadium ground on November 26 that year. He opened his goalscoring account with two at Doncaster on December 10, 1978.

The following season Parrish played and scored in every match for Hunslet but failed to kick a goal in one of them when he scored a try.

He moved to Oldham in September 1980 for £20,000 and kicked four goals on his debut in a defeat at Hull on September 21. In 1981-82 Parrish kicked a goal in every match for Oldham to become the only player to have scored points in every match throughout a season for two clubs.

All Parrish's goals have come from placed kicks, being one of the few regular kickers not to have landed a drop goal. His season-by-season totals are as follows:

Hunslet		
1978-79	24	
1979-80	95	+ 3 for Yorkshire
1980-81	23	
Oldham		
1980-81	72	
1981-82	164	
1982-83	90	
1983-84	101	
TOTALS		
Hunslet	142	
Oldham	427	
Yorkshire	3	
GRAND TOTAL	572	

DES DRUMMOND scored his 100th try for Leigh in the Burtonwood Brewery Lancashire Cup first round victory at home to Carlisle on September 4. At the end of the season the Test winger's total for Leigh stood at 115.

Drummond made his debut for Leigh on December 27, 1976 at Hull Kingston Rovers. Scoring only one try that season, he has finished in the top ten twice, being seventh in 1980-81 and second in 1981-82.

He has scored eight hat-tricks for Leigh, including a John Player record equalling five at Carlisle on November 20, 1983. His season-by-season totals for Leigh are as follows:

1976-77	1
1977-78	19
1978-79	13
1979-80	13
1980-81	17
1981-82	16
1982-83	19
1983-84	17
Total	115

JOHN JOYNER scored his 100th Division One try with the first of two touchdowns fo. Castleford in the home defeat of Bradford Northern on February 19. At the end of the season he had edged his total to 102.

Most of Joyner's career has been spent in the centre but he played several games at stand off last season before moving to loose forward. He was at stand off when he had his best match feat of four tries, against Salford on December 11, 1983.

His Division One total does not include two tries scored in a league match at Salford in 1974-75, which had to be replayed because fans invaded the pitch and prevented Castleford scoring. The tries do not count towards Division One records because they were expunged from the league table.

Joyner's Division One tryscoring record is as follows:

1973-74	5
1974-75	11
1975-76	11
1976-77	6
1977-78	11
1978-79	13
1979-80	11
1980-81	8
1981-82	4
1982-83	9
1983-84	13
Total	102

STEVE EVANS, the Hull and former Featherstone Rovers utility player, at 25 became the youngest player to total a century of Division One tries and the first to do so after making his debut following the reintroduction of two divisions in 1973.

Evans reached his century with the first of three tries in Hull's last Division One match of the season, at home to Whitehaven on April 23. It was his third league hat-trick for Hull, including his best feat of four tries at York in 1981-82.

He scored four Division One hat-tricks for Featherstone for whom he signed in June, 1976, making his debut the following season. His first two tries for Rovers clinched a 7-5 victory at Barrow and the 1976-77 Division One Championship.

His best league season was 1982-83 when he finished as joint top Division One scorer with 20 tries.

Evans' Division One total of tries was built up as follows:

Featherstone R

1976-77	2
1977-78	18
1978-79	14
1979-80	Division Two
1980-81	13
1981-82	7

Hull

1981-82	10
1982-83	20
1983-84	18

Totals

Featherstone R	54
Hull	48
GRAND TOTAL	**102**

NORMAN TURLEY kicked the 50th one-point drop goal of his career with the first of three in Blackpool Borough's 31-30 win at Hunslet on December 4. The back row forward landed his sixth hat-trick of drop goals in Borough's last match of the season to give him a career total of 61.

Turley began his first team career with Warrington in 1974-75, the season the drop goal was reduced to one point, but it was not until he moved to Blackpool in January 1978 that he scored his first drop goal.

The following season he popped over a then record of 18 in one season. His season-by-season drop goal tally since leaving Warrington is as follows:

Blackpool B

1977-78	4
1978-79	18

Oldham

1979-80	0

Rochdale H

1979-80	4
1980-81	14
1981-82	3

Swinton

1981-82	0

Rochdale H

1982-83	3

Blackpool B

1983-84	15

Blackpool Borough drop kick ace Norman Turley.

FIFTY TRIES IN A SEASON

FOR the second successive year the Greenall Whitley-Sunday People scoring award scheme offered a £5,000 prize to the first player to score 50 tries in a season, but again no one went near to collecting the money.

It is now 22 years since the half-century barrier was reached.

The sponsors were hoping the £5,000 offer would encourage wing play but, although more tries were scored last season than in any other two-division era, only two regular wingers finished in the top ten.

Last season's top tryscorer was Hull centre Garry Schofield with 38 in his first season. At 18 he was also the youngest-ever leader.

It was the fifth time in the last six seasons that a non-winger had headed the list. The others were Steve Hartley (Hull K.R. centre or stand off), John Crossley (York stand off), John Jones (Workington Town centre) and Bob Eccles (Warrington forward).

The last wingers to head the list were Salford's Keith Fielding and Hull K.R.'s Steve Hubbard with 30 in 1979-80.

Last season's top tryscoring winger was John Basnett of Widnes with 26.

For 60 years — until 1967-68 — a winger always headed the tryscoring list. Then Hull K.R. stand off Roger Millward led with 38 in 1967-68. Bob Haigh of Leeds became the first forward to finish on top with 40 in 1970-71 followed by Warrington's Bob Eccles with 37 in 1982-83.

The last player to crash the 50-try barrier was Wigan's great winger Billy Boston in 1961-62 with 51, including two for Britain.

It was the end of an era in which the 50-try feat had been achieved 42 times — all by wingers. Since then the nearest approach was by Keith Fielding who scored 49 in 1973-74, his first season in Rugby League, and including a Salford record of 46 tries.

Other facts about the 50-try feat are as follows:

* It was first achieved in 1911-12 by both the Huddersfield wingers — Albert Rosenfeld (78) and Stan Moorhouse (55).
* Two seasons later Rosenfeld scored a record 80 tries.
* The most to score 50 in one season is four in 1951-52: Lionel Cooper (Huddersfield) 71, Jack McLean (Bradford N.) 63, Frank Castle (Barrow) 52, Brian Bevan (Warrington) 51.
* Brian Bevan achieved the feat a record nine times, including six seasons in succession from 1950-51.

LEADING SCORERS 1895-1970

	TRIES	GOALS	POINTS
1895-96	Hurst (Oldham)...........28	Lorimer (Manningham) 35	Cooper (Bradford)........106
			Lorimer (Manningham) ...106
1896-97	Hannah (Hunslet).........19	Goldthorpe (Hunslet)......26	Rigg (Halifax)...........112
		Sharpe (Liversedge).......26	
1897-98	Hoskins (Salford).........30	Goldthorpe (Hunslet)......66	Goldthorpe (Hunslet).....135
1898-99	Williams (Oldham)........39	Goldthorpe (Hunslet)......67	Jaques (Hull)............169
1899-00	Williams (Oldham)........36	Cooper (Bradford).........39	Williams (Oldham).......108
1900-01	Williams (Oldham)........47	Goldthorpe (Hunslet)......44	Williams (Oldham).......141
1901-02	Wilson (Broughton R.).....38	James (Broughton R.)......75	Lomas (Salford)..........172
1902-03	Evans (Leeds)............27	Goldthorpe (Hunslet)......48	Davies (Batley)..........136
1903-04	Hogg (Broughton R.)......34	Lomas (Salford)...........66	Lomas (Salford)..........222
1904-05	Dechan (Bradford)........31	Ferguson (Oldham)........50	Lomas (Salford)..........146
1905-06	Leytham (Wigan).........40	Ferguson (Oldham)........49	Leytham (Wigan)........160
1906-07	Eccles (Halifax)...........41	Lomas (Salford)...........86	Lomas (Salford)..........280
1907-08	Leytham (Wigan).........44	Goldthorpe (Hunslet).....101	Goldthorpe (Hunslet).....217
1908-09	Miller (Wigan)...........49	Lomas (Salford)...........88	Lomas (Salford)..........272
	Williams (Halifax).........49		
1909-10	Leytham (Wigan).........48	Carmichael (Hull K.R.) 78	Leytham (Wigan)........232
1910-11	Kitchen (Huddersfield) 40	Carmichael (Hull K.R.) ...129	Carmichael (Hull K.R.) ...261
	Rosenfeld (Huddersfield)...40		
	Miller (Wigan)...........40		
1911-12	Rosenfeld (Huddersfield)...78	Carmichael (Hull K.R.) ...127	Carmichael (Hull K.R.) ...254
1912-13	Rosenfeld (Huddersfield)...56	Carmichael (Hull K.R.) 93	Thomas (Wigan).........198
1913-14	Rosenfeld (Huddersfield)...80	Holland (Huddersfield) ...131	Holland (Huddersfield) ...268
1914-15	Rosenfeld (Huddersfield)...56	Gronow (Huddersfield) ...136	Gronow (Huddersfield) ...284
●	Competitive matches suspended during war years		
1918-19	Francis (Hull)............25	Kennedy (Hull)...........54	Kennedy (Hull)..........135
1919-20	Moorhouse (Huddersfield)..39	Gronow (Huddersfield) ...148	Gronow (Huddersfield) ...332
1920-21	Stone (Hull)..............41	Kennedy (Hull)..........108	Kennedy (Hull)..........264
1921-22	Farrar (Oldham)..........49	Sullivan (Wigan).........100	Farrar (Oldham).........213
1922-23	Ring (Wigan).............44	Sullivan (Wigan).........161	Sullivan (Wigan).........349
1923-24	Ring (Wigan).............49	Sullivan (Wigan).........158	Sullivan (Wigan).........319
1924-25	Ring (Wigan).............54	Sullivan (Wigan).........138	Sullivan (Wigan).........282
1925-26	Ring (Wigan).............63	Sullivan (Wigan).........131	Sullivan (Wigan).........274
1926-27	Ellaby (St. Helens)........55	Sullivan (Wigan).........149	Sullivan (Wigan).........322
1927-28	Ellaby (St. Helens)........37	Thompson (Leeds).......106	Thompson (Leeds).......233
1928-29	Brown (Wigan)...........44	Sullivan (Wigan).........107	Sullivan (Wigan).........226
	Mills (Huddersfield).......44		
1929-30	Ellaby (St. Helens)........39	Thompson (Leeds).......111	Thompson (Leeds).......243
1930-31	Harris, E. (Leeds).........58	Sullivan (Wigan).........133	Sullivan (Wigan).........278
1931-32	Mills (Huddersfield).......50	Sullivan (Wigan).........117	Sullivan (Wigan).........249
1932-33	Harris, E. (Leeds).........57	Sullivan (Wigan).........146	Sullivan (Wigan).........307
1933-34	Brown (Salford)...........45	Sullivan (Wigan).........193	Sullivan (Wigan).........404
1934-35	Harris, E. (Leeds).........47	Sullivan (Wigan).........165	Sullivan (Wigan).........348
1935-36	Harris, E. (Leeds).........63	Sullivan (Wigan).........117	Sullivan (Wigan).........246

	TRIES	GOALS	POINTS
1936-37	Harris, E. (Leeds) 40	Sullivan (Wigan) 117	Winnard (Bradford N.) 257
1937-38	Harris, E. (Leeds) 45	Sullivan (Wigan) 128	Sullivan (Wigan) 271
1938-39	Markham (Huddersfield) . . . 39	Sullivan (Wigan) 124	Risman (Salford) 267
●	For the next six seasons emergency war-time competitions resulted in a reduction of matches and players were allowed to 'guest' for other clubs		
1939-40	Batten (Hunslet) 34	Hodgson (Swinton) 96	Hodgson (Swinton) 207
1940-41	Walters (Bradford N.) 32	Lockwood (Halifax) 70	Belshaw (Warrington) 174
1941-42	Francis (Barrow) 29	Lockwood (Halifax) 91	Lockwood (Halifax) 185
1942-43	Batten (Hunslet) 24	Lockwood (Halifax) 65	Lockwood (Halifax) 136
1943-44	Lawrenson (Wigan) 21	Horne (Barrow) 57	Horne (Barrow) 144
1944-45	Batten (Bradford N.) 41	Stott (Wakefield T.) 51	Stott (Wakefield T.) 129
●	Normal peace-time rugby resumed		
1945-46	Batten (Bradford N.) 35	Ledgard (Dewsbury) 88	Bawden (Huddersfield) 239
1946-47	Bevan (Warrington) 48	Miller (Hull) 103	Bawden (Huddersfield) 243
1947-48	Bevan (Warrington) 57	Ward (Wigan) 139	Ward (Wigan) 302
1948-49	Cooper (Huddersfield) 60	Ward (Wigan) 155	Ward (Wigan) 361
1949-50	Nordgren (Wigan) 57	Gee (Wigan) . . . . 133 Palin (Warrington) 133	Palin (Warrington) 290
1950-51	Bevan (Warrington) 68	Cook (Leeds) 155	Cook (Leeds) 332
1951-52	Cooper (Huddersfield) 71	Ledgard (Leigh) 142	Horne (Barrow) 313
1952-53	Bevan (Warrington) 72	Bath (Warrington) 170	Bath (Warrington) 379
1953-54	Bevan (Warrington) 67	Metcalfe (St. Helens) . . . . . 153 Bath (Warrington) 153	Metcalfe (St. Helens) 369
1954-55	Cooper (Huddersfield) 66	Ledgard (Leigh) 178	Ledgard (Leigh) 374
1955-56	McLean (Bradford N.) 61	Ledgard (Leigh) 155	Bath (Warrington) 344
1956-57	Boston (Wigan) 60	Jones (Leeds) 194	Jones (Leeds) 496
1957-58	Sullivan (Wigan) 50	Ganley (Oldham) 219	Ganley (Oldham) 453
1958-59	Vollenhoven (St. Helens) . . . 62	Ganley (Oldham) 190	Griffiths (Wigan) 394
1959-60	Vollenhoven (St. Helens) . . . 54	Rhodes (St. Helens) . . . . . . 171 Fox (Wakefield T.) 171	Fox (Wakefield T.) 453
1960-61	Vollenhoven (St. Helens) . . . 61	Rhodes (St. Helens) 145	Rhodes (St. Helens) 338
1961-62	Boston (Wigan) 51	Fox (Wakefield T. 183	Fox (Wakefield T.) 456
1962-63	Glastonbury (Work'ton T.) . 41	Coslett (St. Helens) 156	Coslett (St. Helens) 324
1963-64	Stopford (Swinton) 45	Coslett (St. Helens) 138	Fox (Wakefield T.) 313
1964-65	Lake (Wigan) 40	Kellett (Hull K.R.) 150	Killeen (St. Helens) 360
1965-66	Killeen (St. Helens) . . . . 32 Lake (Wigan) 32	Killeen (St. Helens) 120	Killeen (St. Helens) 336
1966-67	Young (Hull K.R.) . . . . 34 Howe (Castleford) 34	Risman (Leeds) 163	Killeen (St. Helens) 353
1967-68	Millward (Hull K.R.) 38	Risman (Leeds) 154	Risman (Leeds) 332
1968-69	Francis (Wigan) 40	Risman (Leeds) 165	Risman (Leeds) 345
1969-70	Atkinson (Leeds) 38	Tyrer (Wigan) 167	Tyrer (Wigan) 385

LEADING SCORERS 1970-83

TRIES

1970-71
Haigh (Leeds)........40
Jones (St. Helens)........38
Atkinson (Leeds)........36
Sullivan (Hull)........33
Slater (Wakefield T.)........33
Wright (Wigan)........33
Wilson (St. Helens)........27
Hynes (Leeds)........25
A. Smith (Leeds)........23
Topliss (Wakefield T.)........23
Richards (Salford)........23
Benyon (St. Helens)........23

1971-72
Atkinson (Leeds)........36
Lamb (Bradford N.)........36
Richards (Salford)........35
D. Redfearn (Bradford N.)........35
Sullivan (Hull)........33
Watkins (Salford)........29
Hardisty (Leeds)........27
Brown (Widnes)........27
O'Neill (Widnes)........25
Topliss (Wakefield T.)........24

1972-73
Atkinson (Leeds)........39
Richards (Salford)........38
Charlton (Salford)........33
Topliss (Wakefield T.)........30
Lowe (Hull K.R.)........29
Hardisty (Leeds)........28
A. Smith (Leeds)........28
Dunn (Hull K.R.)........27
D. Redfearn (Bradford N.)........27
N. Stephenson (Dewsbury)........26
Mathias (St. Helens)........26

1973-74
Fielding (Salford)........49
Mathias (St. Helens)........40
D. Smith (Wakefield T.)........38
Eckersley (St. Helens)........26
Fleay (Swinton)........26
Jones (St. Helens)........25
Wilson (St. Helens)........25
Watkins (Salford)........24
Atkinson (Leeds)........23
Lamb (Bradford N.)........22
A. Smith (Leeds)........22
Bevan (Warrington)........22
Ayres (Wigan)........22

1974-75
Dunn (Hull K.R.)........42
Fielding (Salford)........35
Bevan (Warrington)........31
A. Smith (Leeds)........30
Millward (Hull K.R.)........30
Atkinson (Leeds)........29
Richards (Salford)........28
Sullivan (Hull K.R.)........28
Mathias (St. Helens)........27
Dyl (Leeds)........26

1975-76
Richards (Salford)........37
Fielding (Salford)........33
Jones (St. Helens)........31
Briggs (Leigh)........27
D. Smith (Wakefield T.)........26
Burton (Castleford)........25
Clark (Hull)........23
Wright (Workington T.)........22
Barends (York)........21
Boxall (Hull)........21
Holmes (Leeds)........21
Mathias (St. Helens)........21
Butler (Salford)........21

1976-77
Wright (Widnes)........31
Burton (Castleford)........29
D. Smith (Leeds)........28
Fielding (Salford)........27
Dunn (Hull K.R.)........26
Cunningham (St. Helens)........26
Topliss (Wakefield T.)........24
Richards (Salford)........23
Mathias (St. Helens)........23
Barends (York)........22

1977-78
Wright (Widnes)........33
Fielding (Salford)........31
Cunningham (St. Helens)........30
Bevan (Warrington)........30
Fenton (Castleford)........30
Vigo (Wigan)........29
Glynn (St. Helens)........28
D. Smith (Leeds)........28
T. Morgan (York)........27
Burton (Castleford)........27

1978-79

Hartley (Hull K.R.)	35
Wright (Widnes)	28
Barends (Bradford N.)	25
Lowe (Hull K.R.)	25
Prendiville (Hull)	25
Fielding (Salford)	24
D. Redfearn (Bradford N.)	23
Mathias (St. Helens)	22
Bray (Hull)	21
O'Loughlin (Wigan)	21
Sullivan (Hull K.R.)	21

1979-80

Fielding (Salford)	30
Hubbard (Hull K.R.)	30
Munro (Oldham)	29
Ball (Barrow)	27
Bentley (Widnes)	27
Glynn (St. Helens)	27
Mathias (St. Helens)	27
Bevan (Warrington)	26
D. Redfearn (Bradford N.)	26
D. Smith (Leeds)	24

1980-81

Crossley (York)	35
Richardson (Castleford)	28
Hubbard (Hull K.R.)	25
Hartley (Hull K.R.)	23
McDermott (York)	23
Slater (Huddersfield)	23
Drummond (Leigh)	20
Ball (Barrow)	19
Bevan (Warrington)	19
Cramp (Huddersfield)	19
Hyde (Castleford)	19
Ramsdale (Wigan)	19

1981-82

Jones (Workington T.)	31
Drummond (Leigh)	26
Basnett (Widnes)	26
Ashton (Oldham)	26
Morgan (Carlisle)	25
Hartley (Hull K.R.)	23
Hopkins (Workington T.)	23
Day (Hull)	23
Evans (Hull)	22
D. Hobbs (Featherstone R.)	21
Moll (Keighley)	21

1982-83

Eccles (Warrington)	37
Evans (Hull)	28
Crossley (Fulham)	27
David (Cardiff City)	26
Topliss (Hull	24
M'Barki (Fulham)	23
Hyde (Castleford)	22
McDermott (York)	22
Leuluai (Hull)	21
Phil Ford (Warrington)	20
Clark (Hull K.R.)	20

GOALS
(including drop goals)

1970-71

Coslett (St. Helens)	183
Ferguson (Leigh)	166
Holmes (Leeds)	159
Watkins (Salford)	155
Tyrer (Wigan)	141
Stephenson (Dewsbury)	134
Clawson (Hull K.R.)	114
Fox (Wakefield T.)	110
Davies (Huddersfield)	99
Jefferson (Keighley)	98

1971-72

Coslett (St. Helens)	214
Watkins (Salford)	193
Tees (Bradford N.)	173
Dutton (Widnes)	120
Clawson (Hull K.R.—Leeds)	120
Gowers (Swinton)	119
Tyrer (Wigan)	117
Larder (Oldham)	114
Whitehead (Warrington)	108
Maloney (York—Hull)	108

1972-73

Watkins (Salford)	221
Coslett (St. Helens)	162
Tees (Bradford N.)	160
Stephenson (Dewsbury)	149
C. Kellett (Featherstone R.)	139
Fox (Wakefield T.)	138
Whitehead (Warrington)	136
Larder (Oldham)	127
Jefferson (Keighley)	120
Quinn (York)	107

1973-74
Watkins (Salford)....183
Whitehead (Warrington)....168
Jefferson (Keighley)....165
Coslett (St. Helens)....134
Mumby (Bradford N.)....131
Dutton (Widnes)....129
Lloyd (Castleford)....121
Quinn (York)....112
Fiddler (Leigh)....111
Holliday (Rochdale H.)....107

1974-75
Fox (Hull K.R.)....146
Coslett (St. Helens)....129
Dutton (Widnes)....122
Lloyd (Castleford)....112
Quinn (York)....112
Hartley (Huddersfield)....110
MacCorquodale (Workington T.)....107
Marshall (Leeds)....107
Mumby (Bradford N.)....96
Fiddler (Salford—Leigh)....85

1975-76
Watkins (Salford)....175
Pimblett (St. Helens)....149
Lloyd (Castleford)....149
Dutton (Widnes)....148
Fairbairn (Wigan)....146
Stacey (Leigh)....137
MacCorquodale (Workington T.)....130
Fox (Hull K.R.—York)....102
Marshall (Leeds)....101
Gaitley (New Hunslet)....100

1976-77
Lloyd (Castleford)....163
Quinn (Featherstone R)....152
Pimblett (St. Helens)....152
Hesford (Warrington)....132
MacCorquodale (Workington T.)....128
Watkins (Salford)....125
Stephenson (Dewsbury)....106
Fairbairn (Wigan)....105
Dutton (Widnes)....97
Woods (Leigh)....90

1977-78
Pimblett (St. Helens)....178
Hesford (Warrington)....158
Woods (Leigh)....149
MacCorquodale (Workington T.)....138
Woods (Widnes)....122
Watkins (Salford)....110
Mumby (Bradford N.)....107
Lloyd (Castleford)....104
Fox (Bradford N.)....95
Oulton (Leeds)....80

1978-79
Lloyd (Hull)....172
Hesford (Warrington)....170
Burke (Widnes)....140
MacCorquodale (Workington T.)....114
Pimblett (St. Helens)....105
Beale (Keighley)....96
Woods (Leigh)....96
Birts (Halifax)....86
Fairbairn (Wigan)....86
Norton (Castleford)....82

1979-80
Quinn (Featherstone R.)....163
Hubbard (Hull K.R.)....138
Rule (Salford)....134
Hesford (Warrington)....128
Burke (Widnes)....127
Ball (Barrow)....119
Diamond (Wakefield T.)....116
Fitzsimons (Oldham)....108
Parrish (Hunslet)....98
Birts (Halifax)....97

1980-81
Hesford (Warrington)....147
Quinn (Featherstone R.)....123
Diamond (Wakefield T.)....112
Burke (Widnes)....110
Hubbard (Hull K.R.)....109
Ball (Barrow)....104
Birts (Halifax)....100
Beale (Keighley)....97
Parrish (Oldham)....95
Fairbairn (Wigan)....94

1981-82
Hopkins (Workington T.)....190
Fairbairn (Hull K.R.)....168
Parrish (Oldham)....164
Woods (Leigh)....158
Rule (Salford)....130
Dick (Leeds)....125
Quinn (Featherstone R.)....120
Agar (Halifax)....119
Crooks (Hull)....118
Hesford (Warrington)....116

1982-83
Diamond (Fulham)....136
Fitzsimons (Hunslet)....121
Crooks (Hull)....120
R. Beardmore (Castleford)....117
Hesford (Warrington....113
Fenwick (Cardiff C.)....111
Jones (Swinton)....110
Whitfield (Wigan)....104
Kilner (Bramley)....104
Quinn (Featherstone R.)....98

POINTS

1970-71	Coslett (St. Helens)	375
1971-72	Watkins (Salford)	473
1972-73	Watkins (Salford)	493
1973-74	Watkins (Salford)	438
1974-75	Fox (Hull K.R.)	333
1975-76	Watkins (Salford)	385
1976-77	Lloyd (Castleford)	341
1977-78	Pimblett (St. Helens)	381
1978-79	Lloyd (Hull)	373
1979-80	Quinn (Featherstone R.)	375
1980-81	Hesford (Warrington)	310
1981-82	Hopkins (Workington T.)	446
1982-83	Diamond (Fulham)	308

DROP GOALS

1974-75	Seabourne (Bradford N.)	10
1975-76	Hancock (Hull)	10
1976-77	N. Stephenson (Dewsbury)	16
1977-78	Fiddler (Bramley, Leigh)	10
1978-79	Turley (Blackpool B.)	18
1979-80	Dean (Hunslet)	18
1980-81	Walker (Whitehaven)	22
1981-82	Agar (Halifax)	17
	Donlan (Leigh)	17
1982-83	Pinner (St. Helens)	13
1983-84	Hallett (Cardiff C.)	29

ALL TIME RECORDS

Most goals in a match:
22 by Jim Sullivan (Wigan) v. Flimby & Fothergill (Challenge Cup), February 14, 1925

Most goals in a season:
DAVID WATKINS holds the record for most goals in a season with 221 — all for Salford — in 1972-73. Watkins played and scored a goal in every match that season as follows:

1972				
Aug	19	Leeds	(H)	5
	23	Featherstone R.	(A)	3
	26	Whitehaven	(A)	4
	28	Swinton	(H)	1
Sep	1	Oldham	(LC) (H)	10
	9	Leeds	(A)	2
	15	Rochdale H.	(LC) (H)	11
	17	Leigh	(A)	6
	24	Barrow	(JP) (A)	4
	29	Huyton	(H)	10
Oct	3	Oldham	(FT) (A)	4
	6	Wigan	(LC) (A)	4
	8	Blackpool B.	(A)	5
	13	Blackpool B.	(H)	8
	21	Swinton	(LCF)	5
Nov	5	Huyton	(A)	8
	10	Rochdale H.	(H)	6
	17	Warrington	(A)	4
	19	New Zealand	(H)	10
	24	Dewsbury	(JP) (H)	4
	26	Workington T.	(H)	6
Dec	1	Barrow	(H)	9
	9	Bradford N.	(JP) (H)	9
	13	Oldham	(A)	4
	15	Leigh	(H)	3
	24	Bradford N.	(A)	5
	26	Workington T.	(A)	3
	30	Hull K.R.	(JP) (A)	5

1973			
Jan	3	Bradford N.	(H) 6
	7	Rochdale H.	(A) 2
	12	Featherstone R.	(H) 4
	28	Featherstone R. (RL Cup)	(A) 4
Feb	2	Whitehaven	(H) 4
	11	Barrow	(A) 5
	23	St. Helens	(H) 3
Mar	7	Widnes	(A) 3
	9	Dewsbury	(H) 3
	16	St. Helens	(A) 2
	24	Leeds	(JP Final) 2
	30	Warrington	(H) 1
Apl	6	Widnes	(H) 4
	13	Oldham	(H) 3
	15	Dewsbury	(A) 2
	17	Wigan	(A) 3
	20	Swinton	(A) 7
	23	Wigan	(H) 3
	29	Rochdale H. (top 16)	(H) 2

	App	Gls
League	34	147
Lancs Cup	4	30
John Player	5	24
Tour match	1	10
RL Cup	1	4
Floodlit Cup	1	4
Top 16	1	2
Totals	47	221

Fastest century:
Three players share the record of scoring the fastest 100 goals from the start of a season in terms of number of matches played. They are Bernard Ganley, David Watkins and Steve Quinn, who achieved the century in 18 matches.

Ganley reached 100 goals on November 16, 1957, after playing 17 matches for Oldham and one for Great Britain.

Watkins scored his 100th goal on November 17, 1972, all for Salford.

Quinn scored his 100th goal on December 16, 1979, all for Featherstone Rovers.

Most goals in a career:
JIM SULLIVAN holds the record for most goals in a career with 2,859 between 1921-22 and 1945-46. He scored a century of goals in every season after leaving Welsh Rugby Union for Wigan until the War interrupted the 1939-40 campaign.

The Test full-back played all of his club rugby for Wigan apart from War-time appearances with Bradford Northern, Dewsbury and Keighley.

Sullivan's total includes 441 in representative matches, including three tours of Australasia. These figures are accepted by the Record Keepers' Club following research by James Carter and Malcolm Bentley.

Most one-point drop goals in a match:
5 by Danny Wilson (Swinton) v. Hunslet (John Player Special) Nov. 6, 1983

Most one-point drop goals in a season:
29 by Lyn Hallett — (Cardiff C.) 1983-84

Most one-point drop goals in a career:
71 by Arnold Walker (Workington T, Whitehaven)

Most tries in a match:
11 by George West (Hull K.R.) v. Brookland Rovers (Challenge Cup). . . . . March 4, 1905

Most tries in a career:
BRIAN BEVAN holds the record for most tries in a career with 796 between 1946 and 1964. His season-by-season record is:

1946-47	48
1947-48	57
1948-49	56
1949-50	33
1950-51	68
1951-52	51
1952-53	72
1953-54	67
1954-55	63
1955-56	57
1956-57	17
1957-58	46
1958-59	54
1959-60	40
1960-61	35
1961-62	15
1962-63	10
1963-64	7

Totals

Warrington	740
Blackpool Borough	17
Other Nationalities	26
Other representative matches	13
Grand Total	796

The Australian winger played his first game for Warrington on November 11, 1945 and his last on April 23, 1962 before having two seasons at Blackpool Borough.

Most tries in a season:
ALBERT ROSENFELD holds the record for most tries in a season with 80 in 1913-14 — all for Huddersfield — as follows:

1913			
Sep	6	York (A)	4
	8	Warrington (H)	2
	13	Leeds (H)	5
	20	Halifax (A)	2
	27	Batley (A)	0
Oct	4	Oldham (H)	2
	11	Rochdale H. (A)	0
	18	Bramley (YC) (H)	2
	25	Dewsbury (A)	4
Nov	1	Halifax (YC) (A)	2
	8	Wigan (A)	1
	15	Dewsbury (YC) (H)	3
	19	Bradford N. (H)	3
	22	Leeds (A)	3
	29	Bradford N. (Halifax, YCF)	1
Dec	3	Halifax (H)	3
	6	Hunslet (A)	2
	13	Rochdale H. (H)	3
	20	Hull K.R. (A)	2
	25	Hull (A)	0
	26	Wakefield T. (H)	3
	27	Hunslet (H)	0
1914			
Jan	1	St. Helens (A)	0
	3	Warrington (A)	0
	10	York (H)	3
	17	Keighley (A)	2
	24	Dewsbury (H)	1
	31	Batley (H)	0
Feb	7	Oldham (A)	0
	14	Bramley (H)	5
	21	Wigan (H)	3
	28	Swinton Park R. (RL Cup) (H)	7
Mar	7	Wakefield T. (A)	2
	14	Hull K.R. (RL Cup) (A)	2
	18	Bramley (A)	3
	21	Widnes (RL Cup) (H)	0
	25	Keighley (H)	3
	28	Hull K.R. (H)	1
	30	Bradford N. (A)	1
Apl	4	Hull (Leeds, RL Cup SF)	0
	11	Hull (H)	did not play
	13	St. Helens (H)	0
	20	Hull (Play-off) (H)	did not play
	25	Salford (Leeds, Championship final)	0

	App	Tries
League	33	63
Yorks Cup	4	8
RL Cup	4	9
Play Off	1	0
Totals	42	80

Most points in a season:
LEWIS JONES holds the record for most points in a season with 496 for Leeds and representative teams in 1956-57 as follows:

For Leeds

			Gls	Tries	Pts
1956					
Aug	17	Halifax (H)	3	0	6
	22	Bradford N. (A)	11	3	31
	25	Wigan (A)	4	0	8
	27	Featherstone R. (H)	4	1	11
Sep	1	Wakefield T. (YC) (A)	3	1	9
	8	Dewsbury (A)	6	0	12
	15	Warrington (H)	7	0	14
	22	Huddersfield (A)	3	0	6
	29	York (H)	6	0	12
Oct	6	Batley (A)	4	2	14
	13	Australia (H)	Did not play		
	20	Hull K.R.	Did not play		
	27	Wigan (H)	2	0	4
Nov	3	Hunslet (A)	1	0	2
	10	Barrow (H)	3	2	12
	17	Halifax (A)	4	0	8
	24	Keighley (H)	3	3	15
Dec	1	Barrow (A)	4	0	8
	8	Bramley (A)	5	0	10
	15	Doncaster (H)	1	2	8
	22	Bradford N. (abandoned) (H)	1	1	5
	25	Batley (H)	8	1	19
	29	Keighley (A)	3	0	6
1957					
Jan	5	Hull (H)	5	2	16
	12	Warrington (A)	0	3	9
	19	St. Helens (H)	5	1	13
	26	Doncaster (A)	Did not play		
Feb	2	Huddersfield (H)	6	0	12
	9	Wigan (RL Cup) (H)	2	1	7
	16	York (A)	7	1	17
	23	Workington T. (RL Cup) (H)	5	1	13
	27	Castleford (H)	4	1	11
Mar	9	Halifax (RL Cup) (A)	5	0	10
	16	Wakefield T. (H)	5	1	13
	20	Bradford N. (H)	5	1	13
	23	Hull (A)	2	0	4
	30	Whitehaven (Odsal, RL Cup SF)	1	0	2
Apl	3	Wakefield T. (A)	3	0	6
	6	St. Helens (A)	0	0	0
	12	Hull K.R. (H)	Did not play		
	13	Dewsbury (H)	6	2	18
	19	Hunslet (H)	5	2	16
	20	Featherstone R. (H)	2	0	4
	22	Castleford (A)	2	0	4
	23	Bramley (H)	7	1	17
May	4	Oldham (Play-off) (A)	3	0	6
	11	Barrow (Wembley, RL Cup final)	0	0	0

Representative matches
For Great Britain:

Jan 26	France.....................(at Leeds)	9	1	21
Mar 3	France...............(at Toulouse)	5	1	13
Apl 10	France.............(at St. Helens)	7	1	17

For The Rest:

Oct 3	Great Britain XIII....(at Odsal)	4	0	8

For RL XIII:

Oct 29	Australia..................(at Leigh)	3	0	6

	App	Gls	Tries	Pts
League	36	147	30	384
RL Cup	5	13	2	32
Yorks Cup	1	3	1	9
Play-off	1	3	0	6
Representative	5	28	3	65
Totals	48	194	36	496

Most points in a match:
53 (11t, 10g) by George West (Hull K.R.) v. Brookland Rovers (RL Cup)..March 4, 1905

Most points in a career:
NEIL FOX holds the record for most points in a career with 6,220 between 1956 and 1979. This total does not include points scored during a spell of club rugby in New Zealand.

Fox was a month short of his 17th birthday when he made his debut for Wakefield Trinity on April 10, 1956. Apart from a brief time at Bradford Northern Fox had 19 seasons at Wakefield before moving to a succession of clubs in later years.

After a long career as an international centre Fox moved into the forwards and played his last professional match for Bradford in their opening fixture of the 1979-80 season, on August 19. That match enabled him to join the elite few who have played first team rugby at 40 years of age.

Fox's season-by-season tally is as follows:

	Gls	Tries	Pts
1955-56	6	0	12
1956-57	54	10	138
1957-58	124	32	344
1958-59	148	28	380
1959-60	171	37	453
1960-61	94	20	248
1961-62	183	30	456
1962 Tour			
Australasia	85	19	227
South Africa	19	4	50
1962-63	125	14	292
1963-64	125	21	313
1964-65	121	13	281
1965-66	98	11	229
1966-67	144	16	336
1967-68	98	18	250
1968-69	95	9	217
1969-70	17	5	49
1970-71	110	12	256
1971-72	84	6	186
1972-73	138	8	300
1973-74	62	8	148
1974-75	146(1)	14	333
1975-76	102(1)	4	215
1976-77	79(1)	6	175
1977-78	95(1)	9	216
1978-79	50	4	112
1979-80	2	0	4

A breakdown of Fox's club and representative totals is as follows:

	App	Gls	Tries	Pts
Wakefield T.	574	1,836	272	4,488
Bradford N.	70	85(1)	12	205
Hull K.R.	59	212(2)	16	470
York	13	42	2	90
Bramley	23	73	6	164
Huddersfield	21	73(1)	5	160
Club Totals	**760**	**2,321(4)**	**313**	**5,577**
Yorkshire	17	60	9	147
Britain v. Australia	8	26	3	61
New Zealand	4	11	1	25
France	17	56	10	142
Other representative games including tour	22	101	22	268
Representative Totals	**68**	**254**	**45**	**643**
Grand Totals	**828**	**2,575(4)**	**358**	**6,220**

( ) Figures in brackets are one point drop goals included in total.

Score-a-match:
The following players have appeared and scored in all of their club's matches in one season:

Jim Hoey (Widnes)	1932-33
Billy Langton (Hunslet)	1958-59
Stuart Ferguson (Leigh)	1970-71
David Watkins (Salford)	1972-73
David Watkins (Salford)	1973-74
John Woods (Leigh)	1977-78
Steve Quinn (Featherstone R.)	1979-80
Mick Parrish (Hunslet)	1979-80
John Gorton (Swinton)	1980-81
Mick Parrish (Oldham)	1981-82

Longest scoring run:
DAVID WATKINS holds the record for the longest scoring run, playing and scoring in 92 consecutive matches for Salford from August 19, 1972 to April 25, 1974. He totalled 403 goals, 41 tries and 929 points.

Longest run of appearances:
KEITH ELWELL holds the record for the longest run of appearances with one club with a total of 239 for Widnes. The consecutive run started at Wembley in the 1977 Challenge Cup final against Leeds on May 7 and ended after he played in a Lancashire Cup-tie at home to St. Helens on September 5, 1982. He was dropped for the match at Featherstone Rovers a week later. Although he went on as a substitute the record refers to full appearances only.

Highest score:
Huddersfield 119 v. Swinton Park 2 (Challenge Cup)
.... February 28, 1914

Most points in all matches in a season:
1,230 by Barrow from 41 matches in 1983-84 as follows:

34 Division Two matches	1,126
4 Burtonwood Brewery Lancashire Cup	57
2 John Player Trophy	35
1 State Express Challenge Cup	12

1,000 points in a League season:
1,126 by Barrow from 34 Division Two matches in 1983-84
1,005 by St. Helens from 38 matches in one-league system in 1958-59.

Longest unbeaten run:
40 Cup and League matches by Huddersfield in 1914-15, including three draws.

Longest winning run in the League:
31 matches by Wigan. Last 8 matches of 1969-70 and first 23 of 1970-71.
* In 1978-79 Hull won all of their 26 Division Two matches, the only time a club has won all its league matches in one season.

Longest League losing run:
40 Division Two matches by Doncaster between November 1975 and April 1977. This period included a run of 37 Cup and League defeats.
* In 1906-07 Liverpool City lost all 30 of their league matches, the only time a team playing more than 12 league matches has lost them all. Liverpool also lost their two cup ties and dropped out after only one season. Liverpool did manage a home league draw against Bramley but when they were unable to fulfil a return fixture the match was expunged from league records.

An uplifting occasion for Widnes team manager Vince Karalius after their 1984 Wembley victory, riding high on the shoulders of John Basnett (left) and Keiron O'Loughlin.

CUPS

CUPS

RUGBY LEAGUE CHALLENGE CUP

1984 Final

Joe Lydon, of Widnes, collected two long-range spectacular tries and the coveted Lance Todd Trophy to wreck his hometown Wigan's Wembley hopes.

Nine years after starring for Wigan Under-11s against Widnes in the inaugural Wembley schoolboy curtain raiser, Lydon returned to the twin towers to teach Wigan a lesson.

The 20-year-old centre's tries were two memorable moments which lifted the Challenge Cup final out of the ordinary. The touchdowns also earned the design student the Man of the Match award with 19 votes from the adjudicating pressmen, 15 ahead of his nearest rival.

Until his second try in the 71st minute, no player had left an indelible impression on a mediocre game and the destiny of the individual award was still wide open. Lydon's brilliant 85-yard score following his 75-yard sprint for the first, made him an overwhelming winner.

Wigan's near-30,000 army of fans were left standing at ease as the Riversiders failed to hit the form which had earned them a Wembley place for the first time in 14 years. The cherry and whites fielded a Wembley record five Australasians, none of whom shone, including Balmain prop forward Kerry Hemsley who was flown 12,000 miles in the week of the final after a 12-match run of appearances up to the end of January.

Although Lydon stole the individual limelight, the Widnes workmanlike victory was based on team strength and depth. Props Kevin Tamati — Widnes' only import — and Steve O'Neill contributed wholeheartedly on both attack and defence, while veterans Keith Elwell and Les Gorley supported well, Gorley announcing his retirement after the game.

Wigan took the lead after 14 minutes with a penalty goal from centre Colin Whitfield, after which they rarely threatened to pierce the Widnes defence, except for the attacking interventions of full back Shaun Edwards, youngest-ever player at Wembley at 17 years, 6 months, 19 days.

Wigan were to be plagued by native talent in Widnes colours. As well as match winner Lydon, scrum half Andy Gregory was a thorn in their side all afternoon and Keiron O'Loughlin opened the try scoring account. Former Wigan prop Steve O'Neill fed his brother Mike, for winger John Basnett to pound for the line, his pass finding O'Loughlin who managed to grab the ball at the third attempt to touch down. Full back Mick Burke added the goal.

Alex Murphy's men continued to disappoint. Antipodeans Graeme West — the tallest player to appear in a Wembley final at 6ft. 5ins. — Howie Tamati, substitute Wayne Elvin and Hemsley, concentrated on one man rugby. At half back Gary Stephens buzzed around without ever stinging and Australian Mark Cannon failed to fire. Wigan's only real progress was by Mick Scott in the second row.

Cannon's first notable contribution to a lack lustre opening period was an ill-judged kick on the half hour which was deflected to Gorley, who fed Tamati for the ball to be handed to the quicksilver Lydon for a majestic sprint to the line, Burke again adding the goal. The 1984 final was over as a contest at that point.

After the interval Steve O'Neill scooped over his third drop goal of the competition before Lydon's second try, to be ranked among the all-time great touchdowns at Wembley.

In the 71st minute, the Great Britain international swooped on a loose ball, cut between two defenders and swerved round the full back before sprinting clear of the crossfield cover.

With four minutes left, Hemsley, hesitating at first, finally decided to use his power and, despite the attentions of three Widnes defenders, crashed over the line for Wigan's only try.

Burke added a penalty to close the scoring and help rewrite several chapters in the Wembley record book.

Widnes won the Cup for a record seventh time at Wembley, making a record 12th appearance in the stadium, a feat being shared on the day by Wigan.

Captain Eric Hughes, Mick Adams and Elwell collected winners' medals for a record-equalling fourth time after apppearing at Wembley on a record seventh occasion.

The record day was crowned by highest-ever receipts of £686,171.

The 1984 final marked the last game for referee Billy Thompson, the Huddersfield official retiring after 18 years in the middle. Having celebrated his 50th birthday in the previous September, he faced compulsory retirement at the end of the season and hung up his whistle after a typical no-nonsense display.

The game was the sixth and final Wembley tie to be staged under the State Express sponsorship banner, due to the company ceasing to trade in Britain, having invested over £500,000 in the 13-a-side code in sponsorship fees.

STATE EXPRESS CHALLENGE CUP FINAL

5th May **Wembley**

WIDNES 19		**WIGAN 6**
Mick Burke	1.	Shaun Edwards
Stuart Wright	2.	Dennis Ramsdale
Eric Hughes	3.	David Stephenson
Joe Lydon	4.	Colin Whitfield
John Basnett	5.	Henderson Gill
Keiron O'Loughlin	6.	Mark Cannon
Andy Gregory	7.	Gary Stephens
Steve O'Neill	8.	Kerry Hemsley
Keith Elwell	9.	Howie Tamati
Kevin Tamati	10.	Brian Case
Les Gorley	11.	Graeme West, Capt.
Mike O'Neill	12.	Mick Scott
Mick Adams, Capt.	13.	John Pendlebury
David Hulme	14.	Wayne Elvin
Fred Whitfield	15	Brian Juliff
T: Lydon (2), O'Loughlin		T: Hemsley
G: Burke (3), S. O'Neill (dg)		G: Whitfield
Substitutions:		Substitutions:
Hulme for Hughes (72 min.)		Elvin for Whitfield (46 min.)
Whitfield for M. O'Neill (72 min.)		Juliff for Case (67 min.)

Half-time: 12—2
Referee: Billy Thompson (Huddersfield)
Attendance: 80,116
Receipts: £686,171

Challenge Cup celebrations in the Widnes camp, from left to right, Hulme, Elwell, Whitfield, Mike O'Neill, Stuart Wright, Steve O'Neill with the Cup, Basnett, Hughes, O'Loughlin and Tamati.

Grasping the ball at the third attempt, Widnes stand off Keiron O'Loughlin touches down for their opening try.

1984 Round by Round

Rugby League Chairman and Swinton director Jack Bateman drew his own club out of the bag for the long trip to Fulham, who managed one of their rare victories of the season in the preliminary round. In the other tie of the round, Widnes travelled to Carlisle where second row man Fred Whitfield scored a try two minutes from time to clinch victory. Carlisle, playing their first match since Boxing Day, were looking capable of pulling off one of the biggest shocks in Challenge Cup history trailing only 12-14 before the Whitfield touchdown paved the way for a 20-12 success for Widnes.

In the first round, newcomers Kent Invicta made their debut in the Challenge Cup and on BBC Television, entertaining Castleford. After falling behind 14-0, Invicta rallied to draw level at 14-14 before Castleford moved into gear to record a 42-20 victory. Holders Featherstone Rovers held Bradford Northern to 4-4 at half-time at Odsal Stadium before the home side ran in 16 points without reply. Colliers' back row forward Peter Smith came on as substitute for his first appearance since Wembley.

Bottom club Doncaster ended a 10-match losing run by beating Batley for the third time in the season. Steve Hesford passed Brian Bevan's record points total for the club as Warrington disposed of Huddersfield by 34-16. £1,000-a-match Wally Lewis marked his last appearance for Wakefield Trinity by scoring two tries in the 19-7 victory at Halifax. Widnes led 16-0 after only 14 minutes in the home tie with lowly Dewsbury and ran out 54-10 victors, although Dewsbury's persistence was rewarded with two late tries.

Lancashire Cup holders and promotion favourites Barrow had their Wembley hopes dashed by Workington Town, the only team to have beaten them in the Second Division. Town scrum half Howard Burns, a Great Britain training squad reject, outplayed Test rival David Cairns as the visitors scored two tries in the first eight minutes. Centre Peter Roe, a try scorer, starred in Hunslet's victory over his old club Keighley. Whitehaven looked set for their first Challenge Cup victory in 18 years before Fulham rallied to secure a 17-10 success at the Recreation Ground.

Full back Shaun Kilner dropped his first goal of the season to gain a shock 10-10 draw for Bramley at home to Wigan, in only their seventh match since re-formation. Three days later Wigan fired on all cylinders to romp through to the second round. Cup runners-up Hull flew down to Cardiff City to hit the Second Division side for six tries. Hull K.R.'s international loose forward David Hall set up five of the Robins' six tries at Blackpool Borough, while Leeds scored all their 24 points in the first half at Salford, winning 24-16. The only second half scores came from a Darren Bloor try and a Paul Shuttleworth penalty goal. Rochdale Hornets' hopes of Cup progress were killed by a superb Graham Steadman try as York set off on their shock run. St. Helens recovered from a 10-point deficit to clinch the home tie with Leigh, who complained to the League about Australian guest referee John Gocher's handling of the match. Second from bottom of the tables Huyton battled bravely at the Watersheddings before Oldham secured a 28-10 passage into the next round.

In the televised second round tie, St. Helens' captain Harry Pinner took the Man of the Match award with an outstanding performance, highlighted by four drop goals and a try, as Hull crashed 24-14. With Neil Holding also in great form, the success-hungry Saints overwhelmed a Hull side featuring four of their promising teenagers. At Elland Road, Hunslet led 5-4 before two tries from play-the-balls from Jeff Grayshon and Brian Noble put Bradford Northern through. York reached the quarter-finals for the first time in 12 years with victory at First Division Wakefield Trinity.

York became the only Second Division side to reach the third round with a try by reserve scrum half Steve Blackburn, playing on the wing, who touched down in the corner. Graham Steadman added the goal, plus a penalty to seal the victory. Workington Town entertained Leeds and opened the scoring with a drop goal and could have built up a healthy lead, but full back Lynn Hopkins missed three reasonable shots at goal. Australian loose forward Terry Webb opened Leeds' account as the Loiners worked hard for a 12-3 victory.

Warrington built up a 12-0 lead at Castleford before losing captain Ken Kelly for 13 minutes with an arm injury. They also lost the lead as Castleford rallied and when Kelly returned, top scorer Steve Hesford went off with an ankle injury, the Wire going down 23-16. Doncaster travelled to top-of-the-table Hull K.R. as 10,000-1 Cup outsiders and with a 51-point handicap on the pools coupons. The 6,959 crowd gave the Dons a standing ovation after the high-speed Robins had won 40-7.

Australian stand off Mark Cannon scored two tries and made another as Wigan overran Oldham at Central Park. With Gary Stephens and Wayne Elvin outstanding, the Riversiders ran in six tries. Relegation-haunted Fulham gave Cup kings Widnes a scare with the Chemics snatching victory by 12-10. All the scoring in a tense tie came in the first 25 minutes with four tries being shared, Mick Burke adding two goals to Steve Diamond's one.

In a third round which attracted over 50,000 fans, drama was in plentiful supply. The derby clash between Leeds and Bradford Northern attracted more than 17,000 to Headingley who saw Northern build up a seemingly invincible 12-0 lead inside only 20 minutes. An Alan Rathbone try and four Steve Parrish goals received a 28th minute reply from Leeds with a Steve Martin try, created by John Holmes and Keith Rayne, David Creasser adding the goal. A Dean Carroll drop goal gave Northern a 13-6 interval lead, but Leeds refused to give up the challenge and a pin point kick from Martin gave Holmes the touchdown, Creasser again obliging with the kick. With two minutes to go, left winger Neil Hague dropped his first goal of the season to level the scores at 13-13 .... but still the drama had not finished. From the resultant kick off, Dean Bell dropped the ball over the line and from the drop out, Rathbone fed Carroll for the expected drop goal attempt which hung high before finally drifting wide.

In the replay at Odsal, more than 18,000 fans saw even more high drama. In a tense cup tie dominated by Northern, Parrish missed three out of four kicks at goal which would have secured victory. Northern still held a 10-6 lead with two minutes left, when Leeds substitute forward Kevin Squire squeezed over from a play-the-ball and Creasser coolly added the goal to put Leeds unexpectedly ahead by 12-10. With the hooter about to sound, Northern were given a penalty, 25 yards out and towards the touchline. Carroll took over the kicking duties and sent the attempt wide.

In another derby encounter, St. Helens entertained Wigan and looked to have the tie sewn up at 7-4 with 10 minutes to go. Ironically, the try scoring hero was John Pendlebury, who Wigan coach Alex Murphy had been trying to substitute for three minutes. He rounded off a four-man movement to put Wigan ahead, a further try from Australian Mark Cannon and two goals from Colin Whitfield securing a semi-final spot.

York pulled off the shock of the round by defeating fancied Castleford by 14-12 at Wiggington Road. Stand off Graham Steadman scored all the York points with two tries and three goals as the Minster side tackled Castleford out of the competition to secure a semi-final billing for the first time since 1931. Previous joint favourites Widnes and Hull K.R. met at Naughton Park where the home side hit peak form to gain a 21-10 success over the league leaders. Scrum half Andy Gregory produced his international form to score a try and inspire two others against a disappointing Hull K.R. side for whom only David Hall shone.

In the first semi-final, York met Wigan on a waterlogged Elland Road, Leeds, pitch. The atrocious conditions inevitably meant that luck was to be a vital factor and chance favoured Wigan. The Riversiders' two touchdowns were both influenced by the ground conditions while Second Division York produced the try of the match by centre Chris Harrison. Man of the Match was Wigan scrum half Gary Stephens, who nearly joined York earlier in the season! Tries by Colin Whitfield and Mick Scott after the interval helped Wigan build up a 14-2 lead before York's late try brought the final result of 14-8, Wigan reaching Wembley for the first time in 14 years.

A week later at Swinton, Widnes reached their seventh Challenge Cup final in a decade by defeating Leeds 15-4. After seven successive defeats at the hands of the Loiners, Widnes produced one of their typical professional displays highlighted by a solo touchdown from winger Joe Lydon, described by Leeds coach Maurice Bamford as 'a world class try'. The 60-yard kick-and-score came eight minutes into the second half and ended Leeds' hopes of a comeback on a day on which they never looked like fulfilling the potential which had brought them only one defeat in 19 games. Scrum half Andy Gregory took the Man of the Match award, with top class support from Mick Adams and Kevin Tamati, only John Holmes and Ian Wilkinson showing form for Leeds.

1984 Prizes

Round	**Per Round**	**Total**
Preliminary	4 × £ 1,000	£ 4,000
First	16 × £ 1,000	£16,000
Second	8 × £ 1,400	£11,200
Third	4 × £ 2,400	£ 9,600
Semi-Finals	2 × £ 4,325	£ 8,650
Runners-up	1 × £ 8,000	£ 8,000
Winners	1 × £14,555	£14,555
Total		£72,005
Development fund		£48,000
Grand total		£120,005

Australian prop Kerry Hemsley, flown over by Wigan from Sydney specially for the Wembley final.

1984 Results

Preliminary Round: FULHAM 14 SWINTON 4, CARLISLE 12 WIDNES 20

BARROW	12								
WORKINGTON T.	14	WORKINGTON T.	3						
				LEEDS	13				
SALFORD	16	LEEDS	12						
LEEDS	24								
				Replay: 10-12		LEEDS	4		
HUNSLET	21	HUNSLET	7						
KEIGHLEY	10								
				BRADFORD N.	13				
BRADFORD N.	20	BRADFORD N.	17						
FEATHERSTONE R.	4								
								WIDNES	19
WHITEHAVEN	10	FULHAM	10						
FULHAM	17								
				WIDNES	21				
WIDNES	54	WIDNES	12						
DEWSBURY	10								
						WIDNES	15		
BLACKPOOL B.	10	HULL K.R.	40						
HULL K.R.	27								
				HULL K.R.	10				
DONCASTER	11	DONCASTER	7						
BATLEY	8								
HALIFAX	7	WAKEFIELD T.	12						
WAKEFIELD T.	19								
				YORK	14				
ROCHDALE H.	8	YORK	20						
YORK	17								
						YORK	8		
KENT INVICTA	20	CASTLEFORD	23						
CASTLEFORD	42								
				CASTLEFORD	12				
WARRINGTON	34	WARRINGTON	16						
HUDDERSFIELD	16								
								WIGAN	6
ST. HELENS	16	ST. HELENS	24						
LEIGH	10								
				ST. HELENS	7				
CARDIFF C.	6	HULL	14						
HULL	34								
						WIGAN	14		
BRAMLEY	10†	WIGAN	30						
WIGAN	10†								
				WIGAN	16				
OLDHAM	28	OLDHAM	6						
HUYTON	10								

† *Replay:* 34-4

CHALLENGE CUP ROLL OF HONOUR

Year	*Winners*		*Runners-up*		*Venue*	*Attendance*	*Receipts*
1897	Batley	10	St Helens	3	Leeds	13,492	£624.17.7
1898	Batley	7	Bradford	0	Leeds	27,941	£1,586.3.0
1899	Oldham	19	Hunslet	9	Manchester	15,763	£946.16.0
1900	Swinton	16	Salford	8	Manchester	17,864	£1,100.0.0
1901	Batley	6	Warrington	0	Leeds	29,563	£1,644.16.0
1902	Broughton R.	25	Salford	0	Rochdale	15,006	£846.11.0
1903	Halifax	7	Salford	0	Leeds	32,507	£1,834.8.6
1904	Halifax	8	Warrington	3	Salford	17,041	£936.5.6
1905	Warrington	6	Hull K.R.	0	Leeds	19,638	£1,271.18.0
1906	Bradford N.	5	Salford	0	Leeds	16,000	£920.0.0
1907	Warrington	17	Oldham	3	Broughton	18,500	£1,010.0.0
1908	Hunslet	14	Hull	0	Huddersfield	18,000	£903.0.0
1909	Wakefield T.	17	Hull	0	Leeds	30,000	£1,490.0.0
1910	Leeds	7	Hull	7	Huddersfield	19,413	£1,102.0.0
Replay	Leeds	26	Hull	12	Huddersfield	11,608	£657.0.0
1911	Broughton R.	4	Wigan	0	Salford	8,000	£376.0.0
1912	Dewsbury	8	Oldham	5	Leeds	15,271	£853.0.0
1913	Huddersfield	9	Warrington	5	Leeds	22,754	£1,446.9.6
1914	Hull	6	Wakefield T.	0	Halifax	19,000	£1,035.5.0
1915	Huddersfield	37	St Helens	3	Oldham	8,000	£472.0.0
1920	Huddersfield	21	Wigan	10	Leeds	14,000	£1,936.0.0
1921	Leigh	13	Halifax	0	Broughton	25,000	£2,700.0.0
1922	Rochdale H.	10	Hull	9	Leeds	32,596	£2,964.0.0
1923	Leeds	28	Hull	3	Wakefield	29,335	£2,390.0.0
1924	Wigan	21	Oldham	4	Rochdale	41,831	£3,712.0.0
1925	Oldham	16	Hull K.R.	3	Leeds	28,000	£2,879.0.0
1926	Swinton	9	Oldham	3	Rochdale	27,000	£2,551.0.0
1927	Oldham	26	Swinton	7	Wigan	35,000	£3,170.0.0
1928	Swinton	5	Warrington	3	Wigan	33,909	£3,158.1.11
1929	Wigan	13	Dewsbury	2	Wembley	41,500	£5,614.0.0
1930	Widnes	10	St. Helens	3	Wembley	36,544	£3,102.0.0
1931	Halifax	22	York	8	Wembley	40,368	£3,908.0.0
1932	Leeds	11	Swinton	8	Wigan	29,000	£2,479.0.0
1933	Huddersfield	21	Warrington	17	Wembley	41,874	£6,465.0.0
1934	Hunslet	11	Widnes	5	Wembley	41,280	£6,686.0.0
1935	Castleford	11	Huddersfield	8	Wembley	39,000	£6,000.0.0
1936	Leeds	18	Warrington	2	Wembley	51,250	£7,070.0.0
1937	Widnes	18	Keighley	5	Wembley	47,699	£6,704.0.0
1938	Salford	7	Barrow	4	Wembley	51,243	£7,174.0.0
1939	Halifax	20	Salford	3	Wembley	55,453	£7,681.0.0
1940	*No competition*						
1941	Leeds	19	Halifax	2	Bradford	28,500	£1,703.0.0
1942	Leeds	15	Halifax	10	Bradford	15,250	£1,276.0.0
1943	Dewsbury	16	Leeds	9	Dewsbury	10,470	£823.0.0
	Dewsbury	0	Leeds	6	Leeds	16,000	£1,521.0.0
	Dewsbury won on aggregate 16-15						
1944	Bradford	0	Wigan	3	Wigan	22,000	£1,640.0.0
	Bradford	8	Wigan	0	Bradford	30,000	£2,200.0.0
	Bradford won on aggregate 8-3						
1945	Huddersfield	7	Bradford N.	4	Huddersfield	9,041	£1,184.3.7
	Huddersfield	6	Bradford N.	5	Bradford	17,500	£2,050.0.0
	Huddersfield won on aggregate 13-9						

Year	*Winners*		*Runners-up*		*Venue*	*Attendance*	*Receipts*
1946	Wakefield T.	13	Wigan	12	Wembley	54,730	£12,013.13.6
1947	Bradford N.	8	Leeds	4	Wembley	77,605	£17,434.5.0
1948	Wigan	8	Bradford N.	3	Wembley	92,500	£21,121.9.9
1949	Bradford N.	12	Halifax	0	Wembley	95,050	£21,930.5.0
1950	Warrington	19	Widnes	0	Wembley	94,249	£24,782.13.0
1951	Wigan	10	Barrow	0	Wembley	94,262	£24,797.19.0
1952	Workington T.	18	Featherstone R.	10	Wembley	72,093	£22,374.2.0
1953	Huddersfield	15	St Helens	10	Wembley	89,588	£30,865.12.3
1954	Warrington	4	Halifax	4	Wembley	81,841	£29,706.7.3
Replay	Warrington	8	Halifax	4	Bradford	102,569	£18,623.7.0
1955	Barrow	21	Workington T.	12	Wembley	66,513	£27,453.16.0
1956	St Helens	13	Halifax	2	Wembley	79,341	£29,424.7.6
1957	Leeds	9	Barrow	7	Wembley	76,318	£32,671.14.3
1958	Wigan	13	Workington T.	9	Wembley	66,109	£33,175.17.6
1959	Wigan	30	Hull	13	Wembley	79,811	£35,718.19.9
1960	Wakefield T.	38	Hull	5	Wembley	79,773	£35,754.16.0
1961	St Helens	12	Wigan	6	Wembley	94,672	£38,479.11.9
1962	Wakefield T.	12	Huddersfield	6	Wembley	81,263	£33,390.18.4
1963	Wakefield T.	25	Wigan	10	Wembley	84,492	£44,521.17.0
1964	Widnes	13	Hull K.R.	5	Wembley	84,488	£44,840.19.0
1965	Wigan	20	Hunslet	16	Wembley	89,016	£48,080.4.0
1966	St Helens	21	Wigan	2	Wembley	*98,536	£50,409.0.0
1967	Featherstone R.	17	Barrow	12	Wembley	76,290	£53,465.14.0
1968	Leeds	11	Wakefield T.	10	Wembley	87,100	£56,171.16.6
1969	Castleford	11	Salford	6	Wembley	*97,939	£58,848.1.0
1970	Castleford	7	Wigan	2	Wembley	95,255	£89,262.2.0
1971	Leigh	24	Leeds	7	Wembley	85,514	£84,452.15
1972	St Helens	16	Leeds	13	Wembley	89,495	£86,414.30
1973	Featherstone R.	33	Bradford N.	14	Wembley	72,395	£125,826.40
1974	Warrington	24	Featherstone R.	9	Wembley	77,400	£132,021.05
1975	Widnes	14	Warrington	7	Wembley	85,098	£140,684.45
1976	St Helens	20	Widnes	5	Wembley	89,982	£190,129.40
1977	Leeds	16	Widnes	7	Wembley	80,871	£241,488.00
1978	Leeds	14	St Helens	12	Wembley	*96,000	£330,575.00
1979	Widnes	12	Wakefield T.	3	Wembley	94,218	£383,157.00
1980	Hull K.R.	10	Hull	5	Wembley	*95,000	£448,202.90
1981	Widnes	18	Hull K.R.	9	Wembley	92,496	£591,117.00
1982	Hull	14	Widnes	14	Wembley	92,147	£684,500.00
Replay	Hull	18	Widnes	9	Leeds U. FC	41,171	£180,525.00
1983	Featherstone R.	14	Hull	12	Wembley	84,969	£655,510.00
1984	Widnes	19	Wigan	6	Wembley	80,116	£686,171.00

*Indicates a capacity attendance. The upper limit is fixed annually taking into account variable factors.

RUGBY LEAGUE CHALLENGE CUP .... A REVIEW

1961-62

Wakefield T 12 Round; F. Smith, Skene, N. Fox (3g, 1t), Hirst (1t); Poynton, Holliday; Wilkinson, Oakes, Firth, Briggs, Williamson, Turner
Huddersfield 6 Dyson; Breen, Booth, Haywood, Wicks; Deighton, Smales (1t); Slevin, Close, Noble, Clark, Bowman, Ramsden (1t)
Referee: D.T.H. Davies (Manchester)

1962-63

Wakefield T 25 Round; Greenwood, Brooke (1t), N. Fox (5g), Coetzer (2t); Poynton (1t), Holliday; Wilkinson, Kosanovic, M. Sampson (1t), Vines, Turner, Pearman
Wigan 10 Bolton; Boston, Ashton (2g), Davies, Carlton (1t); McLeod, Pitchford (1t); Barton, Sayer, McTigue, Collier, Lyon, Evans
Referee: D.T.H. Davies (Manchester)

1963-64

Widnes 13 Randall (2g); R. Chisnall, Briers (1t), F. Myler (1t), Thompson; Lowe, Owen; Hurtsfield, Kemel, Collier (1t), Measures, A. Hughes, V. Karalius
Hull K.R. 5 Kellett (1g); Paul, Major, Elliott, Blackmore; A. Burwell (1t), Bunting; Tyson, Flanagan, Mennell, Palmer, Clark, Poole
Referee: R.L. Thomas (Oldham)

1964-65

Wigan 20 Ashby; Boston, Ashton (1g), Holden (1t), Lake (2t); C. Hill, Parr; Gardiner, Clarke, McTigue, Evans, A. Stephens, Gilfedder (3g, 1t)
Hunslet 16 Langton (5g); Griffiths (1t), Shelton (1t), Preece, Lee; Gabbitas, Marchant; Hartley, Prior, K. Eyre, Ramsey, Gunney, Ward
Referee: J. Manley (Warrington)

1965-66

St. Helens 21 F. Barrow; Vollenhoven, Murphy (1g), Benyon, Killeen (5g, 1t); Harvey, Bishop (1t); Halsall, Sayer, Watson, French, Warlow, Mantle (1t)
Wigan 2 Ashby; Boston, D. Stephens, Ashton, Lake; C. Hill, Parr; Gardiner, Woosey, McTigue, A. Stephens, Gilfedder (1g), Major
Referee: H.G. Hunt (Prestbury)

1966-67

Featherstone R. 17 Wrigglesworth; Thomas (1t), Cotton, Jordan, Greatorex; M. Smith, Dooler (1g); Tonks, Harris, Dixon, A. Morgan (1t), Thompson (1t), Smales (1t, 3g)
Barrow 12 Tees (1g); Burgess, Challinor, Hughes, Murray; Brophy (1t), G. Smith; Kelland, Redhead, Hopwood, Sanderson, Delooze (2g), Watson (1t)
Referee: E. Clay (Leeds)

1967-68

Leeds 11 Risman (4g); Alan Smith, Hynes, Watson, Atkinson (1t); Shoebottom, Seabourne; Clark, Crosby, K. Eyre, Ramsey, A. Eyre, Batten
Wakefield T 10 Cooper, Hirst (2t), Brooke, Coetzer, Batty; Poynton, Owen; Jeanes, Shepherd, D. Fox (2g), Haigh, McLeod, Hawley
Referee: J.P. Hebblethwaite (York)

1968-69

Castleford 11 Edwards; Briggs, Howe (1t), Thomas, Lowndes; Hardisty (1t), Hepworth (1t); Hartley, C. Dickinson, J. Ward, Redfearn (1g), Lockwood, Reilly
Salford 6 K. Gwilliam; Burgess, Whitehead, Hesketh, Jackson; Watkins, Brennan; Ogden, Dickens, Bott, Coulman, Dixon, Hill (3g)
Referee: D.S. Brown (Preston)

1969-70

Castleford 7 Edwards; Briggs, Thomas, Stenton, Lowndes (1t); Hardisty (Hargrave), Hepworth; Hartley, C. Dickinson, Redfearn (2g), Kirkbride, Lockwood, Reilly
Wigan 2 Tyrer (1g) (C. Hill); Jones, Francis, Rowe, Kevin O'Loughlin; D. Hill, Parr; Ashcroft, Burdell, Hogan, Ashurst, D. Robinson, Laughton
Referee: G.F. Lindop (Wakefield)

1970-71

Leigh 24 Eckersley (1t, 1g); Ferguson (5g), Dorrington (1t), Collins, Walsh; A. Barrow, Murphy (2g) (L. Chisnall); Watts, Ashcroft, Fiddler (1g), Grimes, Clarkson, Smethurst
Leeds 7 Holmes (2g); Langley, Hynes, Cowan (Dyl), Atkinson; Wainwright (1t), Seabourne; J. Burke, Fisher, Barnard, Hick, Haigh, Ramsey
Referee: W.H. Thompson (Huddersfield)

1971-72

St. Helens 16 G. Pimblett; L. Jones (1t), Benyon, Walsh, Wilson; K. Kelly, Heaton; Rees (1t), Greenall, J. Stephens, Mantle, E. Chisnall, Coslett (5g)
Leeds 13 Holmes; Alan Smith, Hynes (Langley), Dyl, Atkinson; Hardisty, Hepworth; Clawson (5g), Fisher, Ramsey, Cookson (1t), Haigh, Batten
Referee: E. Lawrinson (Warrington)

1972-73

Featherstone R. 33 C. Kellett (8g); Coventry, M. Smith (1t) (Hartley) (1t), Newlove (2t), K. Kellett; Mason, Nash (1g); Tonks, Bridges, Farrar (1t), Rhodes (Hollis), Thompson, Stone
Bradford N. 14 Tees (4g); Lamb, Stockwell, Watson, D. Redfearn (1t); Blacker (Treasure), Seabourne; Hogan, Dunn, Earl (Long), Joyce, W. Pattinson, Fearnley (1t)
Referee: M.J. Naughton (Widnes)

1973-74
Warrington 24 Whitehead (7g); M. Philbin, Noonan, Whittle, Bevan; Murphy (2g) (Pickup), Gordon; D. Chisnall, Ashcroft (1t), Brady (Wanbon), Wright, Nicholas (1t), B. Philbin
Featherstone R. 9 Box (3g); Dyas, M. Smith, Hartley, Bray; Newlove (1t), Nash; Tonks, Bridges, Harris, Rhodes (Busfield), Thompson (Stone), Bell
Referee: S. Shepherd (Oldham)
1974-75
Widnes 14 Dutton (5g, 1dg); A. Prescott, George, Aspey, Anderson; Hughes, Bowden; Mills (1t), Elwell, Sheridan, Foran, Adams, Laughton
Warrington 7 Whitehead (2g); M. Philbin, Noonan, Reynolds (W. Briggs), Bevan (1t); Whittle, Gordon; D. Chisnall, Ashcroft, Wanbon, Conroy, Martyn (Nicholas), B. Philbin
Referee: P. Geraghty (York)
1975-76
St. Helens 20 G. Pimblett (3g, 2dg); L. Jones, Cunningham (1t), Noonan, Mathias; Benyon (Glynn 2t), Heaton (1t); Mantle (James), A. Karalius, Coslett, Nicholls, E. Chisnall, Hull
Widnes 5 Dutton (2g); A. Prescott (D. O'Neill), Hughes, George, Jenkins; Eckersley, Bowden; Nelson, Elwell (1dg), Wood, Foran (Sheridan), Adams, Laughton
Referee: R. Moore (Wakefield)
1976-77
Leeds 16 Murrell; Alan Smith (D. Smith), Hague, Dyl (1t), Atkinson (1t); Holmes, Dick (1t, 3g, 1dg); Harrison, Ward, Pitchford, Eccles, Cookson, Fearnley (Dickinson)
Widnes 7 Dutton (2g); Wright (George), Aspey (1t), Eckersley, D. O'Neill; Hughes, Bowden; Ramsey, Elwell, Mills, Dearden (Foran), Adams, Laughton
Referee: V. Moss (Manchester)
1977-78
Leeds 14 Oulton (1g); D. Smith (1t), Hague, Dyl, Atkinson (1t); Holmes (1dg), J. Sanderson (Dick); Harrison (Dickinson), Ward (2dg), Pitchford, Cookson (1t), Eccles, Crane
St. Helens 12 G. Pimblett (3g), L. Jones, Noonan, Glynn, Mathias; Francis (1t), K. Gwilliam; D. Chisnall, Liptrot (1t), James, Nicholls, Cunningham, Pinner
Referee: W.H. Thompson (Huddersfield)
1978-79
Widnes 12 Eckersley (1dg); Wright (1t), Aspey, George (Hull), Burke (2g); Hughes (1t), Bowden; Mills, Elwell (1dg), Shaw, Adams, Dearden (M. O'Neill), Laughton
Wakefield T. 3 Sheard; Fletcher (1t), K. Smith, Diamond, Juliff; Topliss, Lampkowski; Burke, McCurrie, Skerrett, Ashurst, Keith Rayne, Idle
Referee: J.E. Jackson (Pudsey)
1979-80
Hull K.R. 10 Hall; Hubbard (3g, 1t) (Hogan), M. Smith, Hartley, Sullivan; Millward (1dg), Agar; Holdstock, Watkinson, Lockwood, Lowe, Rose (Millington), Casey
Hull 5 Woods; Bray, Walters, Wilby (1t), Prendiville; Newlove (Hancock), Pickerill; Tindall, Wileman, Stone (Farrar), Birdsall, Lloyd (1g), Norton
Referee: G.F. Lindop (Wakefield)
1980-81
Widnes 18 Burke (4g, 1t); Wright, George (1t), Cunningham (J. Myler), Bentley; Hughes, Gregory (1t); M. O'Neill (Shaw), Elwell, Lockwood, L. Gorley, E. Prescott, Adams (1dg)
Hull K.R. 9 Hall; Hubbard (3g), M. Smith, Hogan, Muscroft; Hartley, Harkin; Holdstock (Millington), Watkinson, Crooks (Proctor), Lowe, Burton (1t), Casey
Referee: D.G. Kershaw (Easingwold)
1981-82
Hull 14 Kemble; O'Hara (1t), Day, S. Evans, Prendivillle; Topliss, Harkin; Skerrett, Wileman, Stone, Crane (Crooks), Lloyd (4g), Norton (1t)
Widnes 14 Burke (1g), (A. Myler); Wright (1t), Keiron O'Loughlin, Cunningham (2t), Basnett; Hughes, Gregory (1g); M. O'Neill, Elwell (1dg), Lockwood (S. O'Neill), L. Gorley, E. Prescott, Adams
Referee: G.F. Lindop (Wakefield)
Replay
Hull 18 Kemble (1t); Sullivan, Leuluai, S. Evans, Prendiville; Topliss (2t), Dean; Tindall, Duke, Stone, Skerrett, Crooks (1t, 3g), Norton (Crane)
Widnes 9 Burke (3g); Wright (1t), Keiron O'Loughlin, Cunningham, Basnett; Hughes, Gregory; M. O'Neill, Elwell, Lockwood, L. Gorley, E. Prescott, Adams
Referee: G.F. Lindop (Wakefield)
1982-83
Featherstone R. 14 N. Barker; Marsden, Quinn (4g), Gilbert (Lyman), K. Kellett; A. Banks, Hudson; Gibbins, Handscombe, Hankins, D. Hobbs (2t), Slatter (Siddall), Smith
Hull 12 Kemble; O'Hara, S. Evans, Leuluai (1t), Prendiville; Topliss, Harkin (Day), (Crane); Skerrett, Bridges, Stone, Rose, Crooks (1t, 3g), Norton
Referee: M.R. Whitfield (Widnes)

THE LANCE TODD TROPHY

The Lance Todd Trophy is presented to the Man of the Match in the Rugby League Challenge Cup Final, the decision being reached by a ballot of members of the Rugby League Writers' Association present at the game.

Lance Todd made his name in Britain as a player with Wigan and as manager of Salford. His untimely death in a road accident on the return journey from a game at Oldham was commemorated by the introduction of the Lance Todd Trophy.

The award was instituted by Australian-born Harry Sunderland, Warrington director Bob Anderton and Yorkshire journalist John Bapty.

Around 1950, the Red Devils' Association at Salford, comprising players and officials who had worked with Todd, raised sufficient funds to provide a trophy and replica for each winner.

The trophy is now sponsored by brewers Greenall Whitley, who help to finance the annual dinner and trophy presentation at the Willows, Salford.

Gerry Helme, of Warrington, is the only player to win the trophy twice, Len Killeen, of St. Helens, is the only winger to earn the title, Hull's Tommy Harris the only hooker, and Ray Ashby and Brian Gabbitas the only players to share the honour.

Following the 1954 replay, it was decided by the Red Devils that in future the trophy would be awarded for the Wembley game. In 1954, Gerry Helme had received the trophy for his performance in the Odsal replay.

The 1984 winner was Widnes centre Joe Lydon, the 20-year-old Great Britain international celebrating two long-range spectacular tries by collecting 19 Press votes. A reflection of Widnes' domination of the final, the other candidates were team-mates Kevin Tamati with four votes, try scorer Keiron O'Loughlin (two), and one vote apiece for captain Eric Hughes, Andy Gregory, Steve O'Neill and Mick Adams.

Lance Todd Trophy winner Joe Lydon sprinting for the first of his two Wembley touchdowns.

The Lance Todd Trophy Roll of Honour

Year	*Winner*	*Team*	*Position*
1946	Billy Stott	Wakefield Trinity (v Wigan)	Centre
1947	Willie Davies	Bradford Northern (v Leeds)	Stand off
1948	Frank Whitcombe	Bradford Northern (v Wigan)	Prop
1949	Ernest Ward	Bradford Northern (v Halifax)	Centre
1950	Gerry Helme	Warrington (v Widnes)	Scrum half
1951	Cec Mountford	Wigan (v Barrow)	Stand off
1952	Billy Ivison	Workington Town (v Featherstone Rovers)	Loose forward
1953	Peter Ramsden	Huddersfield (v St. Helens)	Stand off
1954	Gerry Helme	Warrington (v Halifax)	Scrum half
1955	Jack Grundy	Barrow (v Workington Town)	Second row
1956	Alan Prescott	St. Helens (v Halifax)	Prop
1957	Jeff Stevenson	Leeds (v Barrow)	Scrum half
1958	Rees Thomas	Wigan (v Workington Town)	Scrum half
1959	Brian McTigue	Wigan (v Hull)	Second row
1960	Tommy Harris	Hull (v Wakefield Trinity)	Hooker
1961	Dick Huddart	St. Helens (v Wigan)	Second row
1962	Neil Fox	Wakefield Trinity (v Huddersfield)	Centre
1963	Harold Poynton	Wakefield Trinity (v Wigan)	Stand off
1964	Frank Collier	Widnes (v Hull K.R.)	Prop
1965	Ray Ashby	Wigan	Full back
	Brian Gabbitas	Hunslet	Stand off
1966	Len Killeen	St. Helens (v Wigan)	Winger
1967	Carl Dooler	Featherstone Rovers (v Barrow)	Scrum half
1968	Don Fox	Wakefield Trinity (v Leeds)	Prop
1969	Malcolm Reilly	Castleford (v Salford)	Loose forward
1970	Bill Kirkbride	Castleford (v Wigan)	Second row
1971	Alex Murphy	Leigh (v Leeds)	Scrum half
1972	Kel Coslett	St. Helens (v Leeds)	Loose forward
1973	Steve Nash	Featherstone Rovers (v Bradford Northern)	Scrum half
1974	Derek Whitehead	Warrington (v Featherstone Rovers)	Full back
1975	Ray Dutton	Widnes (v Warrington)	Full back
1976	Geoff Pimblett	St. Helens (v Widnes)	Full back
1977	Steve Pitchford	Leeds (v Widnes)	Prop
1978	George Nicholls	St. Helens (v Leeds)	Second row
1979	David Topliss	Wakefield Trinity (v Widnes)	Stand off
1980	Brian Lockwood	Hull K.R. (v Hull)	Prop
1981	Mick Burke	Widnes (v Hull K.R.)	Full back
1982	Eddie Cunningham	Widnes (v Hull)	Centre
1983	David Hobbs	Featherstone Rovers (v Hull)	Second row
1984	Joe Lydon	Widnes (v Wigan)	Centre

CHALLENGE CUP RECORDS

ALL ROUNDS

TEAM
Highest score:
Huddersfield 119 v. *Swinton Park 2 1914

INDIVIDUAL

Most goals in a match:
22 by Jim Sullivan (Wigan) v. *Flimby and Fothergill 1925

Most tries in a match:
11 by George West (Hull K.R.) v. *Brookland Rovers 1905

Most points in a match:
53 (11t,10g) by George West (Hull K.R.) as above.

*Amateur teams

FINAL RECORDS

TEAM

Most wins: 10 by Leeds

Most finals: 16 by Wigan

Highest score:
Wakefield T. 38 v. Hull 5 1960

Widest margin:
Huddersfield 37 v. St. Helens 3.................. 1915

Biggest attendance:
102,569 Warrington v. Halifax (Replay) at Bradford 1954

INDIVIDUAL

Most goals:
8 by Cyril Kellett (Featherstone R.) v. Bradford N. 1973

Most tries:
3 by Bob Wilson (Broughton R.) v. Salford 1902
Stan Moorhouse (Huddersfield) v. Warrington . 1913
Tom Holliday (Oldham) v. Swinton 1927

Most points:
20 (7g,2t) by Neil Fox (Wakefield T.) v. Hull 1960

WEMBLEY FACTS

FIVE players share the record of playing in four Cup-winning sides at Wembley — Alex Murphy, Brian Lockwood, Eric Hughes, Keith Elwell and Mick Adams.

Murphy was in St. Helens' victorious side of 1961 and as captain led St. Helens (1966), Leigh (1971) and Warrington (1974) to victory. He played in three different positions — stand off, centre and scrum half. Murphy was a scorer in each final with a total of five drop goals and a try.

Brian Lockwood was in the winning final teams of Castleford (1969 and 1970), Hull K.R. (1980) and Widnes (1981). He also appeared with Widnes in the drawn final of 1982.

Hughes, Elwell and Adams each played in the Widnes teams that won the Cup in 1975, 1979, 1981 and 1984. They also appeared in the drawn final of 1982.

THE Widnes trio of Eric Hughes, Keith Elwell and Mick Adams also hold the record for most appearances at Wembley . . . seven. In addition to the five finals mentioned above they were on the losing side in 1976 and 1977.

ERIC ASHTON captained a record six teams at Wembley — Wigan in 1958, 1959, 1961, 1963, 1965 and 1966. His record of three wins (in 1958, 1959, 1965) is shared with Derek Turner (Wakefield Trinity 1960, 1962, 1963) and Alex Murphy (St. Helens 1966, Leigh 1971 and Warrington 1974).

THE YOUNGEST player to appear in a Wembley Cup final was Shaun Edwards who was 17 years, 6 months and 19 days when he played full back for Wigan against Widnes in 1984.

THE OLDEST at Wembley was Gus Risman, who at 41 years 29 days led Workington Town to victory over Featherstone Rovers in 1952. He played full back.

IN 1984 Widnes and Wigan met at Wembley with each making a record 12th appearance at the stadium. Whoever won would also claim a record seventh Wembley victory. The honour went to Widnes, with Wigan's six wins followed by St. Helens and Leeds who each have five successes.

OVERSEAS players numbered a record six in the 1984 final. Widnes had New Zealander Kevin Tamati, while Wigan fielded Mark Cannon, Kerry Hemsley and playing substitute Wayne Elvin (Australia) plus Graeme West, Howie Tamati (New Zealand). The Wigan five was the most overseas players to play for one side at Wembley.

SCHOOLBOYS who have appeared in an Under-11 curtain-raiser at Wembley and gone on to play in the major final at the stadium are Joe Lydon and David Hulme. Lydon became the first to achieve the feat with Widnes in the 1984 final against Wigan, followed by Hulme who went on as a 72nd minute substitute. Both had played in the first schoolboys' curtain-raiser in 1975 — Lydon for Wigan, and Hulme for Widnes.

CYRIL KELLETT holds the record for most goals in a Challenge Cup final with his eight for Featherstone Rovers in 1973.

In the most remarkable exhibition of kicking seen at Wembley, the veteran full back was successful with every one of his attempts as Bradford Northern crashed 33-14.

Nine years earlier he scored only one for Hull Kingston Rovers in the 13-5 defeat by Widnes.

NEIL FOX — the record aggregate points scorer of all time — piled up the most points in a Challenge Cup final in 1960. His 20 points helped Wakefield Trinity to a 38-5 defeat of Hull. Fox's points came from two tries and seven goals.

His three drop goals for Trinity in the 12-6 victory over Huddersfield two years later was another extraordinary feat in the days when the drop goal was a rarity.

NO player has scored a hat trick of tries at Wembley, the feat being achieved only three times in the preceding era.

The last to do it was Oldham winger Tom Holliday in the 26-7 defeat of Swinton in 1927.

Bob Wilson, the Broughton Rangers centre and captain, was the first to score three tries, in the 25-0 victory over Salford in 1902.

In between, Stan Moorhouse's three-try feat accounted for all of Huddersfield's points when they beat Warrington 9-5 in 1913. Moorhouse was winger to Harold Wagstaff, recognised as the greatest centre of all time.

MANY great players have gone through an entire career without achieving their ambition of playing at Wembley. Hull's Mike Smith achieved it in his first senior game.

Smith made one of the most remarkable debuts in sporting history when he played in the second row of an injury-hit Boulevard side against Wakefield Trinity in 1960.

In contrast, Freddie Miller signed for Hull in 1932 and did not play at Wembley until 1952 ... two years after joining Featherstone Rovers.

A NOTABLE Wembley captain was Gus Risman who led two clubs to victory ... 14 years apart.

He was captain of Salford when they beat Barrow in 1938. At 41, he led Workington Town to their triumph over Featherstone Rovers in 1952.

PROBABLY the unluckiest Challenge Cup finalist was Dai Davies who appeared in four finals and was on the losing side each time.

Three of those occasions were at Wembley with different clubs. He was a loser with Warrington (1933), Huddersfield (1935) and Keighley (1937).

Before the Wembley era he was also in Warrington's beaten team of 1928.

OF the 15 clubs who have yet to play at Wembley, fate seems to be against Swinton and Oldham.

In the five years preceding the move to Wembley, one or the other appeared in the final, twice meeting each other.

Oldham played in four successive finals in that period. Swinton's run of three finals ended when the first Wembley took place in 1929.

They did get through to the final again three years later ... only for it to be played at Wigan!

THE highest score in a Challenge Cup final was Wakefield Trinity's 38 against Hull's five in 1960. The widest margin was Huddersfield's 37-3 defeat of St. Helens in 1915.

Warrington had the consolation of scoring most points by a beaten finalist when they went down 21-17 to Huddersfield at Wembley in 1933.

Wigan's Shaun Edwards, the youngest-ever player in a Wembley final.

CHALLENGE CUP

Wembley Era Semi-Finals

It is generally felt that it is better to have played at Wembley and lost than never to have played there at all. This makes the semi-final stage of the RL Challenge Cup almost as important as the final with no consolation for the losers.

Of the 13 clubs who have never appeared at Wembley four have been beaten semi-finalists. They are Oldham (three times), Swinton, Rochdale Hornets (twice) and Whitehaven.

Probably the unluckiest are Oldham. They have reached the penultimate stage three times without being able to realise their ambition. Oldham almost made it in 1964. After drawing 5-5 with Hull K.R. they were winning 17-14 in extra time of the replay when bad light stopped play and they were beaten in the third game.

Swinton did win a semi-final in 1932 but the final that year was switched from Wembley to Wigan!

There have been three occasions when Yorkshire has provided all four semi-finalists in one year — in 1962, 1973 and 1983. Only once have all four semi-finalists come from west of the Pennines — in 1930.

Until 1962 the two semi-finals were always played on the same Saturday, but with four Yorkshire clubs competing for the first time it decided to play one mid-week. Both matches were played at Odsal Stadium, Bradford. The first was on a Wednesday evening — without floodlights — when 43,625 saw Wakefield Trinity beat Featherstone Rovers and on the following Saturday there were 31,423 to see Huddersfield beat Hull K.R.

The following year both semi-finals were again played on the same Saturday, but since then they have been staged on different Saturdays.

Some semi-final facts during the Wembley era are:

Biggest attendance: 69,898 Warrington v. Leeds at Bradford in 1950

Biggest aggregate: 104,453 in 1939 (Only other six-figure aggregate was 101,814 in 1951)

Record receipts: £65,498 Hull v. Castleford at Leeds U.F.C. in 1983

Lowest attendance: 7,971 Featherstone R. v. Leigh at Leeds in 1974

Highest score and widest margin:
Huddersfield 30 v. Leeds 8 in 1933

CHALLENGE CUP SEMI-FINALS

Year	*Winners*		*Runners-up*		*Venue*	*Attendance*	*Receipts*
1929	Dewsbury	9	Castleford	3	Huddersfield	25,000	£1,562
	Wigan	7	St. Helens Recs.	7	Swinton	31,000	£2,209
Replay	Wigan	13	St. Helens Recs.	12	Leigh	21,940	£1,437
1930	Widnes	10	Barrow	3	Warrington	25,500	£1,630
	St. Helens	5	Wigan	5	Swinton	37,169	£2,666
Replay	St. Helens	22	Wigan	10	Leigh	24,000	£1,657
1931	Halifax	11	St. Helens	2	Rochdale	21,674	£1,498
	York	15	Warrington	5	Leeds	32,419	£2,329
1932	Leeds	2	Halifax	2	Huddersfield	31,818	£2,456
Replay	Leeds	9	Halifax	2	Wakefield	21,000	£1,417
	Swinton	7	Wakefield T.	4	Rochdale	21,273	£1,369
	(Final was played at Wigan, not Wembley)						
1933	Huddersfield	30	Leeds	8	Wakefield	36,359	£2,299
	Warrington	11	St. Helens	5	Swinton	30,373	£2,055

Year	*Winners*		*Runners-up*		*Venue*	*Attendance*	*Receipts*
1934	Hunslet	12	Huddersfield	7	Wakefield	27,450	£1,797
	Widnes	7	Oldham	4	Swinton	17,577	£1,050
1935	Castleford	11	Barrow	5	Swinton	24,469	£1,534
	Huddersfield	21	Hull	5	Leeds	37,111	£2,753
1936	Leeds	10	Huddersfield	5	Wakefield	37,906	£2,456
	Warrington	7	Salford	2	Wigan	41,538	£2,796
1937	Keighley	0	Wakefield T.	0	Leeds	39,998	£2,793
Replay	Keighley	5	Wakefield T.	3	Huddersfield	14,400	£1,052
	Widnes	13	Wigan	9	Warrington	29,260	£1,972
1938	Barrow	4	Halifax	2	Huddersfield	31,384	£2,431
	Salford	6	Swinton	0	Belle Vue, Manchester	31,664	£2,396
1939	Halifax	10	Leeds	4	Bradford	64,453	£3,645
	Salford	11	Wigan	2	Rochdale	40,000	£2,154
●	During the war the semi-finals were two-legged and the finals were not played at Wembley						
1946	Wakefield T.	7	Hunslet	3	Leeds	33,000	£4,991
	Wigan	12	Widnes	5	Swinton	36,976	£4,746
1947	Bradford N.	11	Warrington	7	Swinton	33,474	£4,946
	Leeds	21	Wakefield T.	0	Huddersfield	35,136	£6,339
1948	Bradford N.	14	Hunslet	7	Leeds	38,125	£7,437
	Wigan	11	Rochdale H.	0	Swinton	26,004	£4,206
1949	Bradford N.	10	Barrow	0	Swinton	26,572	£4,646
	Halifax	11	Huddersfield	10	Bradford	61,875	£8,638
1950	Warrington	16	Leeds	4	Bradford	69,898	£9,861
	Widnes	8	Bradford N.	0	Wigan	25,390	£3,936
1951	Barrow	14	Leeds	14	Bradford	57,459	£8,248
Replay	Barrow	28	Leeds	13	Huddersfield	31,078	£5,098
	Wigan	3	Warrington	2	Swinton	4,621	£7,358
1952	Featherstone R.	6	Leigh	2	Leeds	35,621	£6,494
	Workington T.	5	Barrow	2	Wigan	31,206	£4,782
1953	Huddersfield	7	Wigan	0	Bradford	58,722	£10,519
	St. Helens	9	Warrington	3	Swinton	38,059	£7,768
1954	Halifax	18	Hunslet	3	Bradford	46,961	£8,243
	Warrington	8	Leeds	4	Swinton	36,993	£7,596
1955	Barrow	9	Hunslet	6	Wigan	25,493	£4,671
	Workington T.	13	Featherstone R.	2	Leeds	33,499	£7,305
1956	Halifax	11	Wigan	10	Bradford	51,889	£9,054
	St. Helens	5	Barrow	5	Swinton	38,897	£7,793
Replay	St. Helens	10	Barrow	5	Wigan	44,731	£7,750
1957	Barrow	2	Leigh	2	Wigan	34,628	£6,340
Replay	Barrow	15	Leigh	10	Swinton	28,081	£5,695
	Leeds	10	Whitehaven	9	Bradford	49,094	£8,987
1958	Wigan	5	Rochdale H.	3	Swinton	28,597	£6,354
	Workington T.	8	Featherstone R.	2	Bradford	31,517	£6,325
1959	Wigan	5	Leigh	0	Swinton	27,906	£6,068
	Hull	15	Featherstone R.	5	Bradford	52,131	£9,776
1960	Wakefield T.	11	Featherstone R.	2	Bradford	55,935	£10,390
	Hull	12	Oldham	9	Swinton	27,545	£6,093

Year	*Winners*		*Runners-up*		*Venue*	*Attendance*	*Receipts*
1961	St. Helens	26	Hull	9	Bradford	42,935	£9,231
	Wigan	19	Halifax	10	Swinton	35,118	£7,557
1962	Wakefield T.	9	Featherstone R.	0	Bradford	43,625	£8,496
	Huddersfield	6	Hull K.R.	0	Bradford	31,423	£6,685
1963	Wakefield T.	5	Warrington	2	Swinton	15,565	£3,530
	Wigan	18	Hull K.R.	4	Leeds	21,420	£6,029
1964	Widnes	7	Castleford	7	Swinton	25,603	£5,541
Replay	Widnes	7	Castleford	5	Wakefield	28,739	£5,313
	Hull K.R.	5	Oldham	5	Leeds	28,823	£7,411
Replay	Hull K.R.	14	Oldham	17	Swinton	27,209	£5,929
Score after 80 min was 14-14, then bad light caused match to be abandoned after 12 minutes of extra time							
Second Replay	Hull K.R.	12	Oldham	2	Huddersfield	28,732	£6,183
1965	Wigan	25	Swinton	10	St. Helens	26,658	£6,384
	Hunslet	8	Wakefield T.	0	Leeds	21,262	£6,090
1966	St. Helens	12	Dewsbury	5	Swinton	13,046	£3,102
	Wigan	7	Leeds	2	Huddersfield	22,758	£5,971
1967	Featherstone R.	16	Leeds	8	Huddersfield	20,052	£6,276
	Barrow	14	Dewsbury	9	Swinton	13,744	£4,560
1968	Leeds	25	Wigan	4	Swinton	30,058	£9,845
	Wakefield T.	0	Huddersfield	0	Bradford	21,569	£6,196
Replay	Wakefield T.	15	Huddersfield	10	Leeds	20,983	£6,425
1969	Castleford	16	Wakefield T.	10	Leeds	21,497	£8,477
	Salford	15	Warrington	8	Wigan	20,600	£7,738
1970	Castleford	6	St. Helens	3	Swinton	18,913	£7,171
	Wigan	19	Hull K.R.	8	Leeds	18,495	£7,862
1971	Leeds	19	Castleford	8	Bradford	24,464	£9,120
	Leigh	10	Huddersfield	4	Wigan	14,875	£5,670
1972	St. Helens	10	Warrington	10	Wigan	19,300	£8,250
Replay	St. Helens	10	Warrington	6	Wigan	32,380	£12,604
	Leeds	16	Halifax	3	Bradford	16,680	£6,851
1973	Featherstone R.	17	Castleford	3	Leeds	15,369	£9,454
	Bradford N.	23	Dewsbury	7	Leeds	14,028	£9,221
1974	Warrington	17	Dewsbury	7	Wigan	11,789	£6,821
	Featherstone R.	21	Leigh	14	Leeds	7,971	£4,461
1975	Widnes	13	Wakefield T.	7	Bradford	9,155	£5,856
	Warrington	11	Leeds	4	Wigan	13,168	£9,581
1976	Widnes	15	Featherstone R.	9	Swinton	13,019	£9,078
	St. Helens	5	Keighley	4	Huddersfield	9,829	£6,113
1977	Leeds	7	St. Helens	2	Wigan	12,974	£11,379
	Widnes	14	Hull K.R.	5	Leeds	17,053	£16,068
1978	Leeds	14	Featherstone R.	9	Bradford	12,824	£11,322
	St. Helens	12	Warrington	8	Wigan	16,167	£13,960
1979	Widnes	14	Bradford N.	11	Swinton	14,324	£16,363
	Wakefield T.	9	St. Helens	7	Leeds	12,393	£14,195
1980	Hull K.R.	20	Halifax	7	Leeds	17,910	£31,650
	Hull	10	Widnes	5	Swinton	18,347	£29,415
1981	Widnes	17	Warrington	9	Wigan	12,624	£20,673
	Hull K.R.	22	St. Helens	5	Leeds	17,073	£30,616
1982	Hull	15	Castleford	11	Leeds	21,207	£41,867
	Widnes	11	Leeds	8	Swinton	13,075	£25,796
1983	Featherstone R.	11	Bradford N.	6	Leeds	10,784	£22,579
	Hull	14	Castleford	7	Leeds U. FC	26,031	£65,498
1984	Wigan	14	York	8	Leeds U. FC	17,156	£52,888
	Widnes	15	Leeds	4	Swinton	14,046	£37,183

NON-LEAGUE CLUBS IN THE CHALLENGE CUP

THE tradition of non-league clubs appearing in the first round of the RL Challenge Cup ended in 1982 when the growth of senior clubs to 33 left no place for the amateurs.

Nevertheless, the non-league clubs have an historic part in the progress of the competition and their records remain of interest.

In the early years of the Northern Union Challenge Cup — as it was then called — the line between professional and amateurs was less clearly defined.

A variety of leagues also make it difficult to set non-league clubs apart. Fifty six clubs appeared in the inaugural First Round of 1897 and four others received byes. The complications continued until 1904 when the league format settled down and non-league clubs had to qualify for the First Round.

Not since 1909 when BEVERLEY beat Ebbw Vale 7-2 had a senior team been knocked out by a non-League club although amateur teams twice had victories in the two-leg era of 1946-54.

RECORDS OF NON-LEAGUE CLUBS IN THE RUGBY LEAGUE CHALLENGE CUP SINCE 1904

(Non-league clubs in capitals)

Victories over Senior Clubs:

1905-06
*FEATHERSTONE ROVERS 23 v. Widnes 2 (Round Two)

1907-08
WHITEHAVEN RECREATION 13 v. St. Helens 8 (Lost 33-5 at Merthyr Tydfil in Round Two)

1908-09
BEVERLEY 7 v. Ebbw Vale 2 (Lost 53-2 at Halifax in Round Two)

1945-46
SHARLSTON RED ROSE 12 v. Workington Town 7 (1st leg) (Workington won 2nd leg 16-2)

1947-48
RISEHOW and GILLHEAD 10 v. Keighley (2) (2nd leg) (Keighley won 1st leg 11-0)

*FEATHERSTONE ROVERS are the only non-league club to appear in Round Three when they lost 3-0 at Keighley. In the First Round they beat BROOKLAND ROVERS 16-5.

There have been several other instances of non-league clubs meeting in the First Round. The last occasion was in 1960 when WALNEY CENTRAL beat LOCK LANE 10-5 before losing at Oldham 55-4 in the Round Two.

In 1964 THAMES BOARD MILLS received a bye when Bradford Northern disbanded, but lost 48-8 at Blackpool in Round Two.

Draws against Senior Clubs:

1905-06 VICTORIA RANGES 0 v. Widnes 0
Widnes won replay 8-3

1906-07 WORKINGTON 3 v. Wakefield Trinity 3
Wakefield Trinity won replay 16-5

1907-08 WIGAN HIGHFIELD 3 v. Bramley 3
Bramley won replay 8-6

1911-12
NORMANTON ST. JOHN'S 6 v. Warrington 6
Warrington won replay 75-0

1921-22 Widnes 5 v. WIGAN HIGHFIELD 5
Widnes won replay 9-4

1951-52 RYLAND RECS 9 v. Whitehaven 9 (2nd leg)
Whitehaven won first leg 16-0

Record Scores (Team):

Huddersfield 119 v. SWINTON PARK 2 (1913-14)

This is the highest score in any competitive match in England.

Non-league teams have provided other sides with club records as follows:

Hull K.R.	73 v. BROOKLAND ROVERS 5 (1905)
Rochdale H.	75 v. BROUGHTON MOOR 13 (1915)
Wigan	116 v. FLIMBY & FOTHERGILL 0 (1924-25)
Barrow	83 v. MARYPORT 3 (1938)
Blackpool B.	48 v. THAMES BOARD MILLS 8 (1964)
St. Helens	73 v. WARDLEY 0 (1924 at Swinton)

All told, non-league clubs have conceded 50 points or more on 41 occasions but none after 1973-74 (B.A.R.L.A.'s first season).
The lowest score by a senior club was in the 0-0 draw between VICTORIA RANGERS and Widnes in 1906.

Record Scores (Individual):

Most tries and points:
11 tries (10g) 53 points by George West (Hull K.R.) v. BROOKLAND ROVERS (1905)

Most goals:
22 by Jim Sullivan (Wigan) v. FLIMBY & FOTHERGILL (1925)

All three feats are records for any competitive matches in England.

Highest Non-League Scores

FEATHERSTONE ROVERS 23 v. Widnes 2 (Round Two 1906)

Only other 20 score:

LATCHFORD ALBION 20 v. Wigan 40 (1st Leg 1954)
Wigan won second leg 41-2

PILKINGTON RECS. 22 v. Castleford 23 (1978)

CHALLENGE CUP PROGRESS CHART

Key: W — Winners. F — Beaten finalists. SF — Semi-final. P — Preliminary round.

	1983-84	1982-83	1981-82	1980-81	1979-80	1978-79	1977-78	1976-77	1975-76	1974-75	1973-74	1972-73	1971-72	1970-71	1969-70	1968-69	1967-68	1966-67	1965-66	1964-65	1963-64	1962-63
BARROW	1	2	2	1	2	3	1	2	1	1	1	1	2	1	2	1	1	F	2	1	3	1
BATLEY	1	1	2	1	1	1	1	1	1	1	1	1	1	1	1	1	1	2	1	2	2	1
BLACKPOOL B.	1	1	1	1	1	1	1	1	1	1	1	1	1	1	1	1	1	1	1	3	3	2
BRADFORD N.	3	SF	3	1	3	SF	3	3	2	3	3	F	2	1	1	2	2	1	3	2		1
BRAMLEY	1	1	1	1	1	2	1	1	1	1	2	1	3	3	2	2	2	1	1	2	1	2
CARDIFF C.	1	P	1																			
CARLISLE	P	1	1																			
CASTLEFORD	3	SF	SF	2	2	3	3	3	1	1	1	SF	2	SF	W	W	3	3	1	1	SF	1
DEWSBURY	1	1	1	2	1	2	1	3	1	1	SF	SF	1	2	1	1	1	SF	SF	1	1	1
DONCASTER	2	1	1	1	1	1	1	1	2	1	1	1	1	1	3	1	1	2	1	1	1	1
FEATHERSTONE R.	1	W	P	3	1	1	SF	2	SF	1	F	W	2	2	1	2	3	W	2	2	2	2
FULHAM	2	2	2	1																		
HALIFAX	1	2	3	2	SF	1	1	1	1	1	1	1	SF	1	1	1	2	1	1	2	1	2
HUDDERSFIELD	1	1	1	1	2	3	3	1	1	1	1	1	2	SF	2	2	SF	1	3	1	1	1
HULL	2	F	W	2	F	3	2	2	1	2	1	2	2	3	1	1	1	3	2	1	1	1
HULL K.R.	3	1	2	F	W	2	1	SF	2	3	2	2	1	1	SF	1	1	2	3	1	F	SF
HUNSLET	2	3	1	1	1	1	2	1	2	3	1	2	1	2	1	1	1	1	1	F	3	3
HUYTON	1	2	1	1	1	1	1	1	1	1	2	1	1	1	2	1	1	2	1	1	2	2
KEIGHLEY	1	1	1	2	1	2	1	1	SF	1	1	1	1	2	1	2	3	1	1	1	1	1
KENT INVICTA	1																					
LEEDS	SF	2	SF	1	2	1	W	W	3	SF	3	1	F	F	3	3	W	SF	SF	3	1	2
LEIGH	1	1	3	2	1	2	1	1	3	2	SF	2	2	W	3	1	2	1	2	1	1	1
OLDHAM	2	1	2	3	2	2	2	1	3	3	1	3	1	1	2	2	3	2	1	1	SF	3
ROCHDALE H.	1	1	2	1	2	2	1	2	1	2	2	2	1	1	2	3	1	1	1	1	1	1
ST. HELENS	3	3	1	SF	2	SF	F	SF	W	2	3	2	W	2	SF	3	1	1	W	2	1	1
SALFORD	1	2	1	3	3	1	2	2	2	2	2	1	1	3	3	F	2	3	1	2	2	1
SWINTON	P	2	1	1	1	1	2	2	1	1	2	1	3	3	2	1	1	3	2	SF	3	1
WAKEFIELD T.	2	2	3	3	3	F	2	2	1	SF	1	3	3	1	1	SF	F	2	1	SF	1	W
WARRINGTON	2	3	1	SF	3	1	SF	1	3	F	W	3	SF	2	2	SF	1	1	3	3	1	SF
WHITEHAVEN	1	1	1	1	1	1	1	1	1	1	1	1	1	1	1	1	1	1	2	2	2	2
WIDNES	W	1	F	W	SF	W	3	F	F	W	2	2	1	2	1	3	2	1	2	1	W	3
WIGAN	F	1	2	1	1	2	2	2	2	2	3	3	2	2	F	2	SF	2	F	W	1	F
WORKINGTON T.	2	3	2	2	1	1	2	3	2	2	2	2	1	1	1	2	2	1	2	3	2	2
YORK	SF	1	1	2	2	1	1	1	2	2	1	1	3	1	1	1	2	2	1	1	2	3

JOHN PLAYER SPECIAL TROPHY

1983-84 Final

Only two months after taking the coaching reins at Leeds, Maurice Bamford tasted cup glory for the first time in a professional Rugby League career spanning 30 years.

The Loiners took their unbeaten run under Bamford to nine matches, lifting the John Player Special Trophy and a cheque for £10,000 in the process.

Bamford's first involvement in a trophy-winning side as a player or coach was achieved with a Headingley side containing 10 of the players who had figured in the record 58-2 defeat by Queensland only three months earlier.

On a Central Park pitch swept by icy, gale force winds, Leeds showed all their Bamford-inspired dedication and commitment to send favourites Widnes crashing to their second cup final defeat of the season.

Discipline was one of the main features of the Loiners' second victory over the Chemics in a week. While Widnes lost their composure, conceding seven penalties for fouls and having prop Steve O'Neill sent to the sin bin, Leeds refused to be intimidated and did not concede one penalty for foul play.

The contrast in attitude was best summed up in the battle of scrum halves, where Kevin Dick was mischievous but in total control, while Andy Gregory was niggling and quick tempered.

The John Player Special Man of the Match award went to Leeds second row man Mark Laurie, who proved to be a man for all seasons. Four months earlier the Australian had helped Parramatta win the Grand Final in sunny Sydney, and then produced a high standard back row game in the freezing British winter.

Leeds' character was put to the test when Widnes took a six-point lead after only two minutes. Great Britain full back Mick Burke charged onto Gregory's pass in great style, turning the ball inside to left winger Ralph Linton to touch down, Burke adding the goal for his only success from three shots.

Leeds' teenage centre David Creasser kicked the first of five goals from six attempts in the ninth minute. Laurie and Dick figured prominently as Leeds took the lead for the first time in the 12th minute, stand off John Holmes touching down for Creasser to add the goal.

With Keith Rayne celebrating his Great Britain squad selection with another powerful display at prop forward and David Ward leading by example, Leeds added their second try through Dick. The number seven supported another Laurie break to end a sweeping movement by reaching back to take Keith Rayne's pass one handed and lunge over by the posts. Creasser added the goal to take Leeds into a 14-6 lead after 22 minutes.

On the half hour, Widnes clawed their way back into the game with a now typical piece of Mick Adams kicking. His perfectly placed up and under — reminiscent of the kicking magic which robbed Leeds of a Wembley place in 1981 — dropped over the goal line for Joe Lydon to leap for a touchdown.

The second half scoring was restricted to two further penalties from the boot of young Creasser, the target being hit in the 57th and 74th minutes. A difficulty for both goakickers was that one of the posts had been broken in half by gale force winds the day before.

Only one substitute was used on a strength-sapping afternoon, former Devon Rugby Union forward Kevin Squire coming on for skipper Ward, who retired with rib damage before going up to receive the trophy. Only Ward and Holmes were Headingley survivors from the 1973 side which lifted the John Player Trophy for the only other time.

JOHN PLAYER SPECIAL TROPHY FINAL

14th January **Wigan**

LEEDS 18		**WIDNES 10**
Ian Wilkinson	1.	Mick Burke
Paul Prendiville	2.	Stuart Wright
David Creasser	3.	Keiron O'Loughlin
Dean Bell	4.	Joe Lydon
Andy Smith	5.	Ralph Linton
John Holmes	6.	Eric Hughes, Capt.
Kevin Dick	7.	Andy Gregory
Keith Rayne	8.	Steve O'Neill
David Ward, Capt.	9.	Keith Elwell
Kevin Rayne	10.	Kevin Tamati
Gary Moorby	11.	Les Gorley
Mark Laurie	12.	Fred Whitfield
Terry Webb	13.	Mick Adams
Neil Hague	14.	John Myler
Kevin Squire	15.	Eric Prescott
T: Holmes, Dick		T: Linton, Lydon
G: Creasser (5)		G: Burke
Substitution:		Half-time: 14-10
Squire for Ward (72 min.)		Referee: Billy Thompson (Huddersfield)
		Attendance: 9,510

Only three months after taking over as coach of Leeds, Maurice Bamford holds aloft the 1984 John Player Special Trophy.

1983-84 Round by Round

In the preliminary round, high-flying Widnes travelled to Whitehaven who were still seeking a League win since promotion from the Second Division. True to form, the Chemics handed out a 36-0 defeat to the Cumbrians. A late touchdown by Doncaster try scoring record breaker John Buckton brought Doncaster a rare cup victory, toppling fellow Second Division Batley 12-11 at Mount Pleasant.

In the first round, holders Wigan unveilled new signings Shaun Edwards and Steve Hampson at home to Second Division York. It was winger Henderson Gill who stole the spotlight with a marvellous 50-yard touchdown. Aided by seven goals and two tries from centre Colin Whitfield, the Riversiders romped home 30-13. Widnes overcame the loss of loose forward Mick Adams with a fractured cheekbone to snatch a 2-1 victory over Bradford Northern at Naughton Park. A last-minute drop goal by half back Andy Gregory clinched success after Dean Carroll had given Northern a lead which they held until the 68th minute when Chemics prop Steve O'Neill dropped a rare goal. Ellery Hanley, who was sent to the sin bin after the Adams injury, should have sealed victory for the visitors after a glorious 75-yard run which was spoiled by a forward pass to David Smith with the line wide open.

Wakefield Trinity, leading 6-0 after a minute's play, fell 32-18 to Warrington who ran in three tries to build an 18-8 interval lead. Kent Invicta, in their first-ever John Player tie, attracted a record 2,107 to the London Road Stadium for the visit of St. Helens, but crashed 40-7 after holding the lead twice, 3-0 and 5-4. Joint favourites Hull had front row colleagues Trevor Skerrett and Ron Wileman sent off within a minute of each other after half-an-hour of the tie at Castleford. Hull's 11 men put on a tremendous display to win 8-4, a try in the corner by Evans clinching a passage into the second round. Referee Ronnie Campbell dismissed Castleford prop Gary Connell after the final whistle for verbal abuse. The tie was to have been televised on the Saturday, but was switched to Sunday because of a TV technicians' strike.

A last minute lucky try by John Holmes gave Leeds victory at Blackpool Borough, while Leigh repeated last season's John Player victory over Oldham, this time by 20-12. John Woods touched down twice in the first 20 minutes before Oldham pulled back to trail 14-12, winger Phil Fox sealing victory with a late try. New Swinton coach Jim Crellin got off to a flying start with a 17-16 win over Hunslet, Danny Wilson contributing a record five drop goals and a superb try.

A hat-trick of tries by Ralph McConnell inspired Barrow to their 13th successive victory as they overcame Halifax 29-12, the Thrum Hallers second defeat of the season. Carlisle beat Workington Town for the first time in six meetings, first half tries by Wally Youngman and John Risman providing the base for the shock success. Huddersfield were booed off at Fartown by a crowd of only 582 after defeat by Huyton, while Keighley came back from 14-2 down to record a 17-14 success at Dewsbury. Cardiff City put two successive defeats behind them to beat Rochdale Hornets 41-6, lowly Doncaster making First Divison Salford battle all the way for victory at Tatters Field. Eight drop goals were the main feature of Featherstone Rovers' home win over Fulham, the goals coming from Fulham's Tony Kinsey (4) and two apiece from Rovers David Hobbs and Deryck Fox.

In the second round, Maurice Bamford took charge of Leeds for the first time to inflict a shock defeat on joint favourites Hull K.R. Leeds held a 12-2 lead after first half tries from Ian Wilkinson and Dean Bell. After the sending off of substitute Roy Holdstock — on the field for only 10 minutes — Rovers pounded the Leeds line but could only add a Garry Clark try. Featherstone Rovers repeated their Wembley shock success over Hull with a 20-14 victory at Post Office Road. Teenage scrum half Deryck Fox was their star after Hull had clawed their way back into the game at 14-14 despite having Paul Rose sent off. Fox, with his drop goal route blocked, drove through the Hull cover to score the vital try, then added the goal bringing his personal tally to 12 points.

Widnes gained revenge for the Lancashire Cup final defeat by Barrow with an 18-6 victory at Naughton Park, while Cardiff City loose forward Paul Ringer followed up a 15th minute try with his marching orders four minutes later. His dismissal, for an alleged stiff arm tackle, was the only blackspot of the Dragons' 38-12 victory over Huyton, who chartered two aircraft for the journey South. Holders Wigan had to endure their fourth nerve-wracking finish with Salford in just over a year, a Henderson Gill hat-trick finally clinching a 24-15 victory.

St. Helens reached the quarter-finals for the first time in seven years with a shock 18-10 win at Warrington. Stand off Neil Holding set the pace with a blistering try in the third minute. Welshman Danny Wilson made three tries as Swinton triumphed 23-8 at Keighley but was brought off in the last minute as fighting broke out. Leigh winger Des Drummond equalled the John Player record with a five-try haul at Carlisle, the bottom-of-the-table side receiving a 68-17 hammering.

Holders Wigan staged a second half fightback at Widnes after trailing 20-7. Inspired by substitute Kerry Helmsley, the Riversiders battled to within five points of the Chemics. Over at Leigh, Tommy Bishop's charges were given a fright by Second Division Cardiff City in a controversial tie. A try by Geoff Davies and two goals from Lyn Hallett gave the Welshmen a shock lead before a late try from Adrian Alexander and two John Woods goals secured a semi-final place for Leigh. Second Division Swinton led 11-0 at home to Leeds after a rousing first half display, Danny Wilson touching down twice and Ken Jones adding a goal and a drop goal. Leeds staged a late rally with centre David Creasser adding the goal to his try before full back Ian Wilkinson dived over for Creasser to add two vital points for a 16-12 victory. Persistent rain played a part in a disappointing contest at Knowsley Road where St. Helens beat Featherstone Rovers 16-12 to avenge the previous season's RL Challenge Cup defeat. A Barry Ledger drop goal clinched victory for Saints, although Rovers' poor performance should not have put the result in doubt.

In the first semi-final, Leeds and Leigh met at Fartown after 24 hours of storms had blown off the roof of a stand and waterlogged the pitch. The Yorkshiremen won 18-11 to reach the John Player final for the second successive season, prop forward Keith Rayne celebrating his Great Britain call up with a Man of the Match performance. Leigh's New Zealand forward Jeff Clarke looked set to take the individual award after scoring the opening try to put Leigh into a 7-2 lead. Rayne's first try and a goal by David Creasser put Leeds ahead, but only for three minutes as international winger Des Drummond flew in at the corner for a spectacular try although the TV recording showed he lost the ball diving for the line. Rayne appeared again to link with Creasser for Paul Prendiville to take a high pass for a 73rd minute touchdown. Rayne then added his second try, Creasser adding the goal, to give the Loiners a seven-point margin.

In the second semi-final at Warrington a week later, Widnes extended their record of John Player final appearances to six by beating St. Helens 18-4. Fuelled by a hard working, efficient pack, the young Widnes backs launched long range strikes which clinched the

1983-84 Results

Preliminary Round: BATLEY 11 DONCASTER 12, WHITEHAVEN 0 WIDNES 36

CARLISLE	10	CARLISLE	17						
WORKINGTON T.	5			LEIGH	12				
OLDHAM	12	LEIGH	68						
LEIGH	20					LEIGH	11		
CARDIFF C.	41	CARDIFF C.	38						
ROCHDALE H.	6			CARDIFF C.	8				
HUDDERSFIELD	8	HUYTON	12						
HUYTON	21							LEEDS	18
DEWSBURY	14	KEIGHLEY	8						
SWINTON	23			SWINTON	12				
SWINTON	17	SWINTON	23						
HUNSLET	16					LEEDS	18		
BLACKPOOL B.	9	LEEDS	12						
LEEDS	12			LEEDS	16				
HULL K.R.	BYE	HULL K.R.	6						
BRAMLEY									
WAKEFIELD T.	18	WARRINGTON	10						
WARRINGTON	32			ST. HELENS	16				
KENT INVICTA	7	ST. HELENS	18						
ST. HELENS	40					ST. HELENS	4		
FEATHERSTONE R.	12	FEATHERSTONE R.	20						
FULHAM	10			FEATHERSTONE R.	12				
CASTLEFORD	4	HULL	14						
HULL	8							WIDNES	10
WIDNES	2	WIDNES	18						
BRADFORD N.	1			WIDNES	20				
HALIFAX	12	BARROW	6						
BARROW	29					WIDNES	18		
WIGAN	30	WIGAN	24						
YORK	13			WIGAN	15				
DONCASTER	11	SALFORD	15						
SALFORD	22								

match against a mistake-ridden Saints outfit who paid the price for indifferent finishing. Wingman Ralph Linton finished off a 60-yard move for the first Widnes try, opposite winger Tony Garritty adding the second touchdown, with Mick Burke landing all his five goal kicks. Saints, relying very heavily on skipper Harry Pinner, could only muster penalties from Steve Rule and Clive Griffiths, the Man of the Match award going to Widnes hooker Keith Elwell.

1983-84 Prize Money

Round	Per Team	Total
Preliminary	4 × £ 700	£ 2,800
First	16 × £ 700	£11,200
Second	8 × £ 900	£ 7,200
Third	4 × £ 1,175	£ 4,700
Semi-Finals	2 × £ 2,500	£ 5,000
Runners-up	1 × £ 5,000	£ 5,000
Winners	1 × £10,000	£10,000
	Total Prizes	£45,900
	Capital Development Fund	£14,100
	Grand total	£60,000

JOHN PLAYER SPECIAL TROPHY ROLL OF HONOUR

Season	*Winners*		*Runners-up*		*Venue*	*Attendance*	*Receipts*
1971-72	Halifax	22	Wakefield T.	11	Bradford	7,975	£2,545
1972-73	Leeds	12	Salford	7	Huddersfield	10,102	£4,563
1973-74	Warrington	27	Rochdale H.	16	Wigan	9,347	£4,380
1974-75	Bradford N.	3	Widnes	2	Warrington	5,935	£3,305
1975-76	Widnes	19	Hull	13	Leeds	9,035	£6,275
1976-77	Castleford	25	Blackpool B.	15	Salford	4,512	£2,919
1977-78	Warrington	9	Widnes	4	St. Helens	10,258	£8,429
1978-79	Widnes	16	Warrington	4	St. Helens	10,743	£11,709
1979-80	Bradford N.	6	Widnes	0	Leeds	9,909	£11,560
1980-81	Warrington	12	Barrow	5	Wigan	12,820	£21,020
1981-82	Hull	12	Hull K.R.	4	Leeds	25,245	£42,987
1982-83	Wigan	15	Leeds	4	Leeds U FC	19,553	£49,027
1983-84	Leeds	18	Widnes	10	Wigan	9,510	£19,824

Five-goal hero David Creasser.

Try scorer Kevin Dick.

JOHN PLAYER SPECIAL FINAL .... A REVIEW

1971-72

Halifax 22 Hepworth; Rayner, Davies (1t), Willicombe (1t), Kelly (1t); Burton (5g), Baker (Sanderson); Dewhirst, Hawksley, Callon (1t), (Reeves), Fogerty, J. Martin, Halmshaw

Wakefield T. 11 Wraith (Ward); Slater (1t), Marston, Hegarty, Major; Topliss (1t), Harkin; Jeanes, Morgan, Lyons, Harrison (Spencer), Valentine (1t), N. Fox (1g)

Referee: S. Shepherd (Oldham)

1972-73

Leeds 12 Holmes (1g); Alan Smith, Hynes, Dyl, Atkinson (2t); Hardisty, Hepworth; Clawson (2g) (Ward), Fisher (Pickup), Jeanes, Haigh, Cookson, Eccles

Salford 7 Charlton; Colloby, Watkins (2g), Hesketh, Richards; Gill (P. Ward), Banner; Ramshaw, J. Ward, Mackay, Grice (Davies), Kirkbride, Dixon (1t)

Referee: W.H. Thompson (Huddersfield)

1973-74

Warrington 27 Whitehead (6g, 1t); M. Philbin, Noonan (2t), Reynolds (Pickup), Bevan (1t); Whittle, Gordon; D. Chisnall, (Nicholas 1t), Ashcroft, Brady, Wright, Wanbon, B. Philbin

Rochdale H. 16 Crellin; Brelsford (2t), Brophy (1t), Taylor (1t), Aspinall; Butler (Wood), Gartland; Holliday (2g), Harris, Whitehead, Fogerty, Sheffield, Halmshaw

Referee: D.G. Kershaw (York)

1974-75

Bradford N. 3 Carlton (1t); Francis, Ward, Gant, D. Redfearn; Blacker, Seabourne, Earl, Jarvis, Jackson, Joyce, Trotter, Fearnley

Widnes 2 Dutton (1g); A. Prescott, D. O'Neill, Aspey, Anderson; Hughes, Bowden; Mills, Elwell, Sheridan, Adams, Blackwood, Laughton

Referee: G.F. Lindop (Wakefield)

1975-76

Widnes 19 Dutton (3g); A. Prescott, George, Aspey, Jenkins (2t); Hughes, Bowden (1t, 1dg); Mills, Elwell, Wood, Foran, Sheridan, Adams (1t)

Hull 13 Stephenson; A. Macklin, Clark, Portz, Hunter (1t); Hancock, Foulkes (Davidson); Ramsey, Flanagan, Wardell, Boxall (2g), Walker, Crane (2t)

Referee: J.V. Moss (Manchester)

1976-77

Castleford 25 Wraith (1t); Fenton, Joyner (1t), P. Johnson (1t), Briggs; Burton (1t), Stephens (1t); Khan, Spurr, A. Dickinson, Reilly, Lloyd (5g), S. Norton

Blackpool B 15 Reynolds; Robinson, Heritage, Machen (1t), Pitman; Marsh, Newall; Hamilton, Allen (1t), Egan (3g, 1t), Gamble, Groves (Hurst), M. Pattinson

Referee: M. J. Naughton (Widnes)

1977-78

Warrington 9 Finnegan; Hesford (3g), Benyon, Wilson, Bevan (1t); K. Kelly, Gordon; Lester, Dalgreen, Nicholas, Martyn, B. Philbin, Potter

Widnes 4 Eckersley; Wright, Aspey, George, Woods (2g); Hughes, Bowden; Ramsey, Elwell, Shaw (Dearden), Adams, Hull, Laughton

Referee: W.H. Thompson (Huddersfield)

1978-79

Widnes 16 Eckersley; Wright (1t), Aspey, Hughes, Burke (3g); Moran, Bowden; Mills, Elwell (2dg), Shaw, Dearden, Hull (1t), Adams (2dg)

Warrington 4 Finnegan; M. Kelly, Hesford (2g), Benyon, Sutton; K. Kelly, (Hunter), Gordon; Lester, Waller, Nicholas, Case, Martyn, A. Gwilliam

Referee: G.F. Lindop (Wakefield)

1979-80

Bradford N. 6 Mumby (1g); Barends, D. Redfearn, D. Parker (1t), Gant; Stephenson (1dg), A. Redfearn; Thompson, Bridges, Forsyth (I. Van Bellen), Grayshon, G. Van Bellen (Ferres), Casey

Widnes 0 Eckersley; Wright, Aspey, George, Burke; Hughes, Bowden; Hogan (Mills), Elwell, Shaw, L. Gorley, Hull, Adams

Referee: W.H. Thompson (Huddersfield)

1980-81

Warrington 12 Hesford (2g, 2dg); Thackray, I. Duane, Bevan (2t), M. Kelly; K. Kelly, A. Gwilliam; Courtney, Waller, Case, Martyn, Potter, Hunter (Eccles)

Barrow 5 Elliott; McConnell, French, Ball (1g), Wainwright; Mason (1t), Cairns; D. Chisnall, Allen (Szymala), Flynn, K. James, Kirkby, Hadley

Referee: W.H. Thompson (Huddersfield)

1981-82

Hull 12 Banks; O'Hara, Harrison, Leuluai, Prendiville; Day, Dean (1dg) (K. Harkin); Skerrett, Wileman (1t), Stone, Crane, L. Crooks (4g), Norton

Hull K.R. 4 Fairbairn (2g); Hubbard, M. Smith, Hogan, Muscroft; Hartley, P. Harkin (Burton); Holdstock (Millington), Watkinson, S. Crooks, Lowe, Casey, Hall

Referee: G.F. Lindop (Wakefield)

1982-83

Wigan 15 Williams; Ramsdale, Stephenson, Whitfield (4g, 1dg), Gill (1t) (Juliff 1t); M. Foy, Fairhurst; Shaw, Kiss, Campbell, West (Case), Scott, Pendlebury

Leeds 4 Hague; Campbell, Wilkinson, Dyl, Andy Smith; Holmes, Dick (2g); Dickinson, Ward, Burke, Sykes, W. Heron, D. Heron

Referee: R. Campbell (Widnes)

JOHN PLAYER SPECIAL MAN OF THE MATCH

Season	*Winner*	*Team*	*Position*
1971-72	Bruce Burton	Halifax (v. Wakefield T.)	Stand off
1972-73	Keith Hepworth	Leeds (v. Salford)	Scrum half
1973-74	Kevin Ashcroft	Warrington (v. Rochdale H.)	Hooker
1974-75	Barry Seabourne	Bradford N. (v. Widnes)	Scrum half
1975-76	Reg Bowden	Widnes (v. Hull)	Scrum half
1976-77	Gary Stephens	Castleford	Scrum half
	Howard Allen	Blackpool B.	Hooker
1977-78	Steve Hesford	Warrington (v. Widnes)	Winger
1978-79	David Eckersley	Widnes (v. Warrington)	Full back
1979-80	Len Casey	Bradford N. (v. Widnes)	Loose forward
1980-81	Tommy Martyn	Warrington (v. Barrow)	Second row
1981-82	Trevor Skerrett	Hull (v. Hull K.R.)	Prop
1982-83	Martin Foy	Wigan (v. Leeds)	Stand off
1983-84	Mark Laurie	Leeds (v. Widnes)	Second row

1984 Man of the Match Mark Laurie, Leeds' Australian second row man, is sent flying by Widnes prop Steve O'Neill, Loiners' skipper David Ward in support.

JOHN PLAYER SPECIAL TROPHY RECORDS

ALL ROUNDS

TEAM

*Highest score: Castleford 88 v. Millom 5
Biggest attendance: 25,165 Hull v. Hull K.R. (at Leeds)............. Final 1981-82

INDIVIDUAL

Most goals: 17 by Sammy Lloyd (Castleford)
*Most tries: 5 by John Joyner (Castleford)
Most points: 43 (17g,3t) by Sammy Lloyd (Castleford)
The above records were all achieved in the Castleford v. Millom first round tie in 1973-74.
*John Basnett (Widnes) also scored 5 tries in the first round tie away to Hunslet in 1981-82.
*Bob Eccles (Warrington) also scored 5 tries in the second round tie at home to Blackpool B. in 1982-83.
* Des Drummond (Leigh) also scored 5 tries in the second round tie away to Carlisle in 1983-84.

JOHN PLAYER SPECIAL TROPHY FINAL RECORDS

Most final appearances: 6 by Widnes
Most wins: 3 by Warrington
Most tries: No player has scored 3 or more
Most goals: 6 by Derek Whitehead (Warrington) v. Rochdale H....................... 1973-74
Most points: 15 (6g,1t) by Derek Whitehead (Warrington) v. Rochdale H.................... 1973-74
Highest score: Warrington 27 v. Rochdale H. 16.. 1973-74
Widest margin win: Widnes 16 v. Warrington 4... 1978-79
Biggest attendance: 25,165 Hull v. Hull K.R. (at Leeds)................. 1981-82
Biggest receipts: £49,027 Wigan v. Leeds (at Leeds U FC)............... 1982-83

●*BEFORE 1977-78 the competition was known as the Player's No.6 Trophy, then the John Player Trophy. In 1983-84 it became the John Player Special Trophy. It was not until 1979-80 that semi-finals were played at neutral venues.*

NON-LEAGUE CLUBS IN THE JOHN PLAYER TROPHY

UNTIL the growth of professional clubs to 33 in 1981-82 left no place for non-league clubs, the amateurs added spice to the John Player Trophy.

Two amateur teams went into the first round draw, except for only one in 1980-81 and their fate varied from the record 88-5 hammering Millom received at Castleford, to Cawoods' historic victory over Halifax — the first time a non-league club had knocked out professionals from either the Challenge Cup or John Player Trophy since 1909.

RECORDS OF NON-LEAGUE CLUBS IN THE JOHN PLAYER TROPHY

(Non-League clubs in capitals)

VICTORIES OVER A SENIOR CLUB:

Halifax 8 v. CAWOODS 9 (1977-78)
(Lost 31-7 at Wakefield in round two)

RECORD SCORES (TEAM):

Castleford 88 v. MILLOM 5 (1973-74)
The only other 50-point score was:
Salford 57 v. MAYFIELD 3 (1975-76)
The lowest score by a senior club was Blackpool Borough's 6-3 defeat of WEST HULL in 1979-80.
The highest non-league score was:
Castleford 30 v. PILKINGTON RECS 17 (1980-81)

ATTENDANCE RECORD

The record attendance at a tie involving a non-league team was 6,500 for PILKINGTON RECS. v. Wigan at St. Helens in 1979-80.

Record goals and points scorer Sammy Lloyd.

JOHN PLAYER TROPHY PROGRESS CHART

Key: W — Winners. F — Beaten finalists. SF — Semi-final. P — Preliminary round.

	1983-84	1982-83	1981-82	1980-81	1979-80	1978-79	1977-78	1976-77	1975-76	1974-75	1973-74	1972-73	1971-72
BARROW	2	3	3	F	1	1	1	1	2	1	1	1	3
BATLEY	P	1	1	1	1	1	1	1	2	1	1	2	1
BLACKPOOL B.	1	2	P	2	2	1	1	F	1	1	1	1	3
BRADFORD N.	1	3	2	1	W	SF	SF	2	1	W	1	3	1
BRAMLEY	*	1	1	1	2	1	1	2	1	2	SF	2	2
CARDIFF C.	3	1	1										
CARLISLE	2	2	2										
CASTLEFORD	1	1	2	SF	3	3	2	W	SF	1	2	1	2
DEWSBURY	1	1	1	1	1	2	1	1	1	1	3	2	1
DONCASTER	1	1	1	1	1	1	1	1	1	2	1	1	1
FEATHERSTONE R.	3	1	2	2	2	2	3	2	1	1	1	2	1
FULHAM	1	1	1	2									
HALIFAX	1	1	1	3	1	2	1	2	1	1	2	1	W
HUDDERSFIELD	1	2	2	2	1	1	3	1	3	1	1	2	2
HULL	2	2	W	SF	1	2	1	3	F	1	1	3	3
HULL K.R.	2	3	F	2	1	SF	1	1	3	SF	1	SF	2
HUNSLET	1	1	1	2	1	1	2	1	2	1	1	1	1
HUYTON	2	P	1	1	1	1	1	1	1	2	1	1	1
KEIGHLEY	2	1	2	1	2	3	2	1	1	2	3	1	2
KENT INVICTA	1												
LEEDS	W	F	3	1	2	1	1	3	2	3	3	W	SF
LEIGH	SF	2	1	3	3	3	3	SF	2	1	2	2	1
OLDHAM	1	1	SF	1	1	1	2	2	2	2	1	1	1
ROCHDALE H.	1	2	1	1	1	1	1	1	1	1	F	1	2
ST. HELENS	SF	2	1	1	2	2	2	2	3	1	SF	SF	SF
SALFORD	2	3	3	2	SF	2	2	2	SF	3	2	F	1
SWINTON	3	1	SF	1	1	1	1	1	1	3	1	3	1
WAKEFIELD T.	1	1	1	1	SF	3	SF	1	2	2	3	2	F
WARRINGTON	2	SF	2	W	3	F	W	1	1	3	W	1	1
WHITEHAVEN	P	1	1	3	1	1	1	1	1	SF	2	1	2
WIDNES	F	SF	3	3	F	W	F	SF	W	F	1	3	1
WIGAN	3	W	1	1	2	2	3	2	2	2	2	1	3
WORKINGTON T.	1	1	2	1	3	2	2	3	3	1	2	1	1
YORK	1	2	1	2	2	1	1	3	1	2	2	2	2

*Bramley withdrew from the Trophy while in liquidation, opponents Hull K.R. receiving a bye.

PREMIERSHIP TROPHY

1984 Final

Hull Kingston Rovers played a game of patience to become the first club to complete a Premiership and Championship double.

Rovers' coach Roger Millward fielded three prop forwards in a heavyweight pack in the first half of the Slalom Lager Premiership final in a bid to take the steam out of the mobile Castleford six.

It looked as if the plan had backfired when Castleford turned round at the interval with an 8-0 lead. For the second half of a pulsating contest, Millward sent on substitute centre Ian Robinson and switched Mike Smith to the pack to replace prop John Millington.

Great Britain centre Smith revelled in the role of loose forward in a reshuffled pack as the Robins ran in four scintillating tries to lift the Premiership Trophy for the second time in four years.

Even during Millward's tactical waiting ploy, one man was outstanding, going on to win the coveted Harry Sunderland Trophy with the unanimous vote of the Press. Australian stand off John Dorahy combined direct running with subtle touches and vast experience to outplay completely his opposite number, young fellow countryman Steve Robinson.

It was Castleford who dominated the first half, their only try living up to their nickname of 'high speed Cas'. In the sixth minute Castleford put together a blistering five-man move for one of the tries of the season. Top speed support play between John Joyner, Bob Beardmore, Jimmy Crampton and Steve Robinson, saw the teenage stand off send winger John Kear over by the post, Beardmore adding the goal.

Inspired by open side prop Kevin Ward, the West Yorkshire side continued to dominate an entertaining finale to the season and in the 19th minute scrum half Beardmore struck a penalty goal to create a new club points-in-a-season record of 332 to give Castleford an 8-0 interval lead.

But before the break Castleford began to show signs of a transition which has often driven their loyal fans to despair. The commitment lessened, self-doubt crept in and the losses of concentration became more frequent as the pendulum began to swing back into Rovers' favour.

Even though Millward was looking for a second half improvement, he could not have expected such a dramatic effect. Within a minute of the restart Dorahy spilt the defence to send in Kiwi centre Gary Prohm for a superb try. Dorahy added the goal to reduce the deficit to 8-6 and continued to be the major threat to Castleford with his no-nonsense, rugged approach.

Centre-cum-packman Smith scored the next try in the 54th minute to put Rovers in the

Triumphant Hull K.R. captain David Hall shows off the Slalom Lager Premiership Trophy.

lead for the first time, then Dorahy himself showed a clean pair of heels to add his name to the scoresheet three minutes later. Finally, winger David Laws was sent in by a beautifully judged floating pass from Prohm in the 77th minute.

All Castleford had to offer was a 70th minute penalty goal from Beardmore which took him to the top of the goal scoring chart on 142 along with Warrington's Steve Hesford to share sponsorship prize money of £710 at the rate of £5 per goal.

Rovers' four tries were all scored within a few yards of the same left hand corner flag to leave Dorahy with difficult kicks at goal. As well as failing to add the goal to three of the tries, he also missed the target with three drop goal attempts.

But it was in open play that the strong running Dorahy outshone his team-mates and the opposition to crown a memorable first season with the Robins and become the first overseas player to receive the Harry Sunderland Trophy.

Despite switching around the back row, Hull K.R. captain David Hall was also outstanding, having a hand in all four tries, while prop Roy Holdstock gave a powerful display over the full 80 minutes having graduated back to first team football after a long spell in the A-team, as was the case with eye-catching scrum half Paul Harkin.

Played at a fast and furious pace, the Premiership final once again presented an entertaining finale to the season as a tournament in its own right.

SLALOM LAGER PREMIERSHIP FINAL

12th May	**Leeds**	
Castleford 10		**Hull Kingston Rovers 18**
David Roockley	1.	George Fairbairn
Darren Coen	2.	Garry Clark
Tony Marchant	3.	Mike Smith
Gary Hyde	4.	Gary Prohm
John Kear	5.	David Laws
Steve Robinson	6.	John Dorahy
Bob Beardmore, Capt.	7.	Paul Harkin
Kevin Ward	8.	Roy Holdstock
Stuart Horton	9.	Chris Rudd
Gary Connell	10.	John Millington
Jimmy Crampton	11.	Chris Burton
Brett Atkins	12.	Mark Broadhurst
John Joyner	13.	David Hall, Capt.
Ian Orum	14.	John Lydiat
Dean Mountain	15	Ian Robinson
T: Kear		T: Prohm, Smith, Dorahy, Laws
G: Beardmore (3)		G: Dorahy
Half-time: 8-0		Substitutions:
Referee: Ron Campbell (Widnes)		Robinson for Millington (Half-time)
Attendance: 12,515		Lydiat for Burton (78 min.)

Cheers .... from the jubilant Hull K.R. team after their Slalom Lager Premiership Trophy success.

1984 Round by Round

A week after spoiling Hull K.R.'s Championship party by inflicting a shock defeat on the new title holders, injury-hit Leeds returned to Craven Park to find the Robins in record breaking form. Rovers took their revenge in a 10-try Premiership first round rout, the 54-0 hammering creating a new record score for the 10-year competition, stand off John Dorahy amassing a Premiership record points tally of 22 with seven goals and two tries.

On the other side of the city, Championship runners-up Hull, seeking their fourth consecutive Premiership final, sent Bradford Northern to their heaviest defeat since Peter Fox took over as coach seven years ago. The Airlie Birds ran in three tries in the first 12 minutes, going on to notch a total of nine touchdowns.

Third-placed Warrington led St. Helens 3-2 at half-time before visiting captain Harry Pinner took control with the handling and astute kicking which had earned him a Great Britain tour spot. The loose forward had a hand in both Saints' tries before adding three drop goals to put the sixth-placed Knowsley Road side into the semi-finals. In the other first round tie, Widnes left out four internationals and clearly had Wembley on their minds as Castleford romped home 36-4. Wheldon Road captain Bob Beardmore ran up a personal tally of 20 points with a try and eight goals.

Still in rampant mood, it was Castleford who pulled off the shock result in the semi-finals. They travelled to the Boulevard having lost to Hull in all four previous meetings during the season to meet an Airlie Birds side with eight consecutive wins under their belt, running up more than 300 points in the process. Castleford swept into a 10-0 shock lead which was reduced when teenage centre Garry Schofield scored his 38th try of the season, adding the goal himself. But Castleford added a further 12 points before a late consolation try and goal from skipper David Topliss and Schofield respectively.

Earlier on the Bank Holiday Monday, Hull K.R. left it to the final seven minutes to earn a place in the final over a stubborn St. Helens lacking skipper and main inspiration Harry Pinner. Saints looked to have demoralised the Robins when centre Mike Smith, switched to loose forward, went over for his second try for John Dorahy to add the goal and Man of the Match Paul Harkin to drop a goal.

Castleford prop forward Kevin Ward, a first half inspiration.

The start of Hull K.R.'s revival, a try by Kiwi centre Gary Prohm with Castleford skipper Bob Beardmore chasing in vain.

1983 Results

Figures in brackets denote position in the Slalom Lager Championship table.

HULL (2)	42	HULL	5		
BRADFORD N. (7)	12				
				CASTLEFORD	10
CASTLEFORD (4)	36	CASTLEFORD	22		
WIDNES (5)	4				
HULL K.R. (1)	54	HULL K.R.	21		
LEEDS (8)	0				
				HULL K.R.	18
WARRINGTON (3)	13	ST. HELENS	16		
ST. HELENS (6)	19				

1983 Prize Money: Winners £7,000

PREMIERSHIP ROLL OF HONOUR

Year	*Winners*		*Runners-up*		*Venue*	*Attendance*	*Receipts*
1975	Leeds	26	St. Helens	11	Wigan	14,531	£7,795
1976	St. Helens	15	Salford	2	Swinton	18,082	£13,138
1977	St. Helens	32	Warrington	20	Swinton	11,178	£11,626
1978	Bradford N.	17	Widnes	8	Swinton	16,813	£18,677
1979	Leeds	24	Bradford N.	2	Huddersfield	19,486	£21,291
1980	Widnes	19	Bradford N.	5	Swinton	10,215	£13,665
1981	Hull K.R.	11	Hull	7	Leeds	29,448	£47,529
1982	Widnes	23	Hull	8	Leeds	12,100	£23,749
1983	Widnes	22	Hull	10	Leeds	17,813	£34,145
1984	Hull K.R.	18	Castleford	10	Leeds	12,515	£31,769

● *For history of Premiership see page 205*

PREMIERSHIP FINAL . . . . A REVIEW

1974-75

Leeds 26 Holmes (2g) (Marshall 3g); Alan Smith (1t), Hynes (1t, 1dg) (Eccles), Dyl, Atkinson (2t) Mason (1t), Hepworth; Dickinson, Ward, Pitchford, Cookson, Batten, Haigh

St. Helens 11 G. Pimblett; L. Jones (1t), Wilson, Hull, Mathias (1t); Walsh, Heaton (1t); Warlow (Cunningham), A. Karalius, Mantle (K. Gwilliam), E. Chisnall, Nicholls, Coslett (1g)

Referee: W.H. Thompson (Huddersfield)

1975-76

St. Helens 15 G. Pimblett (3g); L. Jones, Glynn (1t), Noonan, Mathias; Benyon, Heaton (K. Gwilliam); Mantle, A. Karalius (1t), James, Nicholls, E. Chisnall (1t), Coslett

Salford 2 Watkins (2dg); Fielding, Richards, Hesketh, Graham; Butler, Nash; Coulman, Raistrick, Sheffield, Knighton (Turnbull), Dixon, E. Prescott

Referee: M. J. Naughton (Widnes)

1976-77

St. Helens 32 G. Pimblett (7g, 1t); L. Jones, Benyon (1t), Cunningham (1t), Mathias (1t), Glynn (Ashton); K. Gwilliam (1t); D. Chisnall, Liptrot, James (1t), Nicholls (A. Karalius), E. Chisnall, Pinner

Warrington 20 Finnegan; Curling, Bevan (Cunliffe), Hesford (4g), M. Kelly; A. Gwilliam (1t), Gordon (1t); Weavill (1t), Price, Case, Martyn (Peers), Lester, B. Philbin (1t)

Referee: G.F. Lindop (Wakefield)

1977-78

Bradford N. 17 Mumby (2g); Barends (1t), Roe (1t), Austin, D. Redfearn (1t); Wolford (1dg), A. Redfearn; I. Van Bellen (Fox), Raistrick, Thompson, Joyce (Forsyth), Trotter, Haigh (1t)

Widnes 8 Eckersley; Wright, Hughes, Aspey (2t), Woods (1g); Gill, Bowden; Mills, Elwell, Shaw (Ramsey) (George), Adams, Hull, Laughton

Referee: J.E. Jackson (Pudsey)

1978-79

Leeds 24 Hague; Alan Smith (1t), D. Smith (1t), Dyl (Fletcher), Atkinson; Dick (7g, 1dg); J. Sanderson, Harrison, Ward (1t), Pitchford, Joyce, Eccles (Adams), Cookson

Bradford N. 2 Mumby; D. Parker, Okulicz, Gant, Spencer; Ferres (1g), A. Redfearn; Thompson, Bridges, Forsyth (I. Van Bellen), Trotter (Mordue), Grayshon, Casey

Referee: W.H. Thompson (Huddersfield)

1979-80

Widnes 19 Burke (1g); Wright (1t), George, Aspey (1t), Bentley (1t); Eckersley (1dg), Bowden; Shaw, Elwell (1t, 1dg), M. O'Neill, L. Gorley (1t), Hull (Hogan), Adams

Bradford N. 5 Mumby (1g); MacLean (Ferres), D. Redfearn (1t), D. Parker, Gant; Stephenson, A. Redfearn; Thompson, Bridges, Forsyth, Clarkson (G. Van Bellen), Grayshon, Hale

Referee: W.H. Thompson (Huddersfield)

1980-81

Hull K.R. 11 Proctor; Hubbard (1g), M. Smith (1t), Hogan (1t), Muscroft; Hartley (1t), Harkin; Holdstock, Watkinson, Millington, Lowe, Casey, Hall (Burton)

Hull 7 Woods (2g); Peacham, Elliott, Wilby, Prendiville; Banks, Dean; Tindall, Wileman, Stone, Skerrett (Madley), Crane (1t), Norton

Referee: J. Holdsworth (Leeds)

1981-82

Widnes 23 Burke (4g, 1t); Wright (1t), Kieron O'Loughlin, Cunningham (A. Myler), Basnett (1t); Hughes (1t), Gregory; M. O'Neill, Elwell, Lockwood (Whitfield), L. Gorley, E. Prescott, Adams (1t)

Hull 8 Kemble; O'Hara (Day), Leuluai, S. Evans, Prendiville; Topliss, Harkin; Tindall, Wileman (Lloyd), Stone, Skerrett, Crooks (1t, 2g, 1dg), Norton

Referee: S. Wall (Leigh)

1982-83

Widnes 22 Burke; Linton, Hughes, Lydon (5g), Basnett (2t); A. Myler (1t), Gregory (1t) (Hulme); M. O'Neill, Elwell, L. Gorley, Whitfield (S. O'Neill), Prescott, Adams

Hull 10 Kemble; O'Hara (1t), Day (Solal), Leuluai, S. Evans; Topliss (1t), Dean; Skerrett, Bridges, Stone, Rose, Crooks (2g), Norton (Crane)

Referee: F. Lindop (Wakefield)

THE HARRY SUNDERLAND TROPHY

The trophy, in memory of the famous Queenslander, a former Australian Tour Manager, broadcaster and journalist, is presented to the Man of the Match in the end of season Championship or Premiership final.

The award is donated and judged by the Rugby League Writers' Association and is sponsored by Slalom Lager.

In the 1984 Press poll Hull K.R. stand off John Dorahy was the unanimous choice, becoming the first overseas player to win the coveted award.

The Harry Sunderland Trophy Roll of Honour

Year	*Winner*	*Team*	*Position*
1965	Terry Fogerty	Halifax (v. St. Helens)	Second row
1966	Albert Halsall	St. Helens (v. Halifax)	Prop
1967	Ray Owen	Wakefield T. (v. St. Helens)	Scrum half
1968	Gary Cooper	Wakefield T. (v. Hull K.R.)	Full back
1969	Bev Risman	Leeds (v. Castleford)	Full back
1970	Frank Myler	St. Helens (v. Leeds)	Stand off
1971	Bill Ashurst	Wigan (v. St. Helens)	Second row
1972	Terry Clawson	Leeds (v. St. Helens)	Prop
1973	Mick Stephenson	Dewsbury (v. Leeds)	Hooker
1974	Barry Philbin	Warrington (v. St. Helens)	Loose forward
1975	Mel Mason	Leeds (v. St. Helens)	Stand off
1976	George Nicholls	St. Helens (v. Salford)	Second row
1977	Geoff Pimblett	St. Helens (v. Warrington)	Full back
1978	Bob Haigh	Bradford N. (v. Widnes)	Loose forward
1979	Kevin Dick	Leeds (v. Bradford N.)	Stand off
1980	Mal Aspey	Widnes (v. Bradford N.)	Centre
1981	Len Casey	Hull K.R. (v. Hull)	Second row
1982	Mick Burke	Widnes (v. Hull)	Full back
1983	Tony Myler	Widnes (v. Hull)	Stand off
1984	John Dorahy	Hull K.R. (v. Castleford)	Stand off

PREMIERSHIP RECORDS
First staged 1975

ALL ROUNDS
TEAM

Highest score:
Hull K.R. 54 v. Leeds 0 1984
(Also widest margin)
Biggest attendance:
29,448 Hull v. Hull K.R. .... Final at Leeds 1981

INDIVIDUAL

Most goals:
9 by Andy Gregory (Widnes) v. Leeds .... Round 1 1982
Most points:
22 (7g, 2t) by John Dorahy (Hull K.R.) v. Leeds .... Round 1 1984
Most tries:
4 by David Hall (Hull K.R.) v. Castleford .... Round 1 1983

PREMIERSHIP FINAL RECORDS
TEAM

Most final appearances:
4 by Widnes
Most wins:
3 by Widnes
Highest score:
St. Helens 32 v. Warrington 20 1977
Widest margin:
Leeds 24 v. Bradford N.2 1979
Biggest attendance:
29,448 Hull v. Hull K.R. (at Leeds) 1981

INDIVIDUAL

Most tries:
No player has scored 3 or more
Most goals:
8 by Kevin Dick (Leeds) v. Bradford N. 1979
Most points: 17 (7g, 1t) by Geoff Pimblett (St. Helens) v. Warrington 1977

LANCASHIRE CUP

1983 Final

Second Division underdogs Barrow dethroned Cup Kings Widnes to lift the Burtonwood Brewery Lancashire Cup for the first time in 29 years.

Barrow captain Alan Hodkinson received the trophy along with his first medal after more than 15 years as a professional.

In an emotional final at Central Park, Wigan, Widnes — five times winners in the last nine tournaments — were put out of their stride by the Cumbrian side motivated by coach Tommy Dawes asking them to play for their families, fans and town.

Taking charge of a final for the first time, Southport referee Kevin Allatt bid to control tempers by sending Kevin Tamati, Andy Gregory and Eddie Szymala to the sin bin for 10 minutes. Gregory's temporary dismissal came after 22 minutes when he flattened his opposite number David Cairns as the Barrow scrum half laid on a pass for centre Andy Whittle to knock over two men and feed Ralph McConnell for a clear run to the line, Ian Ball adding the goal.

In an all-action encounter, Barrow did not allow the Widnes attack, packed with internationals, a spare inch with Hodkinson and second row man Steve Herbert leading the tackling stint. McConnell and Cairns blunted the Widnes pair of Great Britain half backs, Gregory and Tony Myler, as the Chemics battled to get back into a match for which they had been clear favourites.

Test centre Joe Lydon hit a penalty goal, then struck the upright with a further attempt after the interval. Barrow promptly went further ahead into a 9-2 lead with a drop goal by Tickle and a penalty goal from Ball.

Widnes succeeded in mounting a rare period of sustained pressure and after Lydon, Tamati and Myler had all gone close to scoring, Lydon picked up a rolling ball to beat Cairns and Szymala for a try to which he added the goal.

Most pundits had forecast that Barrow would wilt, but with hooker Les Wall outhooking ex-international Keith Elwell — playing in his 25th final — Barrow doubled their resolve and pulled away to 12-8 with a Ball penalty and drop goal.

Barrow scrum half Cairns topped the Press poll for the Man of the Match award, his dominance of Test number seven Gregory not going unnoticed by the Great Britain management.

1983 Round by Round

In the first round, Wigan held the lead four times before falling to Widnes 36-20 at Naughton Park, while cup holders Warrington were easy 30-4 winners at Second Division Blackpool Borough. Second row man Tommy Martyn scored a try and helped make six others in Leigh's 10-try romp over Carlisle. Despite the dismissal of winger Mike Taylor, Oldham beat Workington Town 26-20, with Salford suffering the loss of new prop Colin Meachin with a broken leg in their thrilling 16-15 victory over Fulham, sealed by a late try from Stewart Williams with Ron Smith adding the goal. Lowly Huyton gave Swinton a scare, leading 12-7 before going down 13-12. In a Cumbrian derby, Barrow put out Whitehaven 13-6, while in a Saturday fixture, Rochdale Hornets fell to the previous year's runners-up St. Helens by 28-4.

In a controversial second round tie, Leigh referee Stan Wall sent off five players as Warrington beat St. Helens. Dismissed for fighting were Saints duo Roy Haggerty and Steve Peters, plus Wire trio Phil Ford, Mal Yates and Mark Forster. In addition, Warrington forwards Bob Eccles and Mike Gregory were sent to the sin bin for 10 minutes. Steve

Hesford's two extra goals made the vital difference as Warrington secured a 30-26 victory. Leigh faced Widnes without four regular forwards and a back, out with injury, and found the drawback too great, while Green Vigo's last second try could not prevent Second Division Swinton eliminating Oldham at Station Road, Jones scoring all the Lions' points in an 8-6 shock win. Second Division title favourites Barrow and Slalom Lager Championship opponents Salford provided a high speed contest despite the heavy rain, the Cumbrians gaining a passage to the last four.

In the semi-finals brave Swinton held mighty Widnes to 8-8 for most of an exciting tie at Station Road, the Chemics leading only 12-8 with 10 minutes to go. Tries in the final minutes by John Basnett and Tony Myler provided Widnes with a comfortable victory margin. Fellow Second Division outfit Barrow pulled off a shock at Wilderspool, knocking out the holders Warrington to reach their first Lancashire Cup final for 29 years. The 19-18 thriller was based on the Wire trailing 12-8 after giving a mistake-ridden first half performance. Hero of the Barrow victory was centre Ian Ball, scorer of a first half try, four goals and a drop goal.

BURTONWOOD BREWERY LANCASHIRE CUP FINAL

1st October	**Wigan**	
BARROW 12		**WIDNES 8**
Steve Tickle	1.	Mick Burke
Terry Moore	2.	Joe Lydon
Andy Whittle	3.	Eric Hughes, Capt.
Ian Ball	4.	Keiron O'Loughlin
David Milby	5.	John Basnett
Ralph McConnell	6.	Tony Myler
David Cairns	7.	Andy Gregory
Alan Hodkinson, Capt.	8.	Steve O'Neill
Les Wall	9.	Keith Elwell
Mark McJennett	10.	Kevin Tamati
Steve Herbert	11.	Fred Whitfield
Eddie Szymala	12.	Eric Prescott
Steve Mossop	13.	Mick Adams
David Elliott	14.	Tony Garritty
Dave Tyson	15.	Paul Houghton
T: McConnell		T: Lydon
G: Ball (3, 1dg), Tickle (1dg)		G: Lydon (2)

Half-time: 6-2
Referee: Kevin Allatt (Southport)
Attendance: 7,007

Barrow celebrate lifting the Lancashire Cup for the first time in 29 years, captain Alan Hodkinson holding the prized trophy.

1983 Results

ROCHDALE H.	4						
ST. HELENS	28	ST. HELENS	26				
				WARRINGTON	18		
BLACKPOOL B.	4						
WARRINGTON	30	WARRINGTON	30				
						BARROW	12
SALFORD	16						
FULHAM	15	SALFORD	2				
				BARROW	19		
BARROW	13						
WHITEHAVEN	6	BARROW	13				
HUYTON	12						
SWINTON	13	SWINTON	8				
				SWINTON	8		
OLDHAM	26						
WORKINGTON T.	20	OLDHAM	6				
						WIDNES	8
LEIGH	52						
CARLISLE	10	LEIGH	10				
				WIDNES	22		
WIDNES	36						
WIGAN	20	WIDNES	27				

LANCASHIRE CUP ROLL OF HONOUR

Season	*Winners*		*Runners-up*		*Venue*	*Attendance*	*Receipts*
1905-06	Wigan	0	Leigh	0	Broughton	16,000	£400
(replay)	Wigan	8	Leigh	0	Broughton	10,000	£200
1906-07	Broughton R.	15	Warrington	6	Wigan	14,048	£392
1907-08	Oldham	16	Broughton R.	9	Rochdale	14,000	£340
1908-09	Wigan	10	Oldham	9	Broughton	20,000	£600
1909-10	Wigan	22	Leigh	5	Broughton	14,000	£296
1910-11	Oldham	4	Swinton	3	Broughton	14,000	£418
1911-12	Rochdale H.	12	Oldham	5	Broughton	20,000	£630
1912-13	Wigan	21	Rochdale H.	5	Salford	6,000	£200
1913-14	Oldham	5	Wigan	0	Broughton	18,000	£610
1914-15	Rochdale H.	3	Wigan	2	Salford	4,000	£475
1915-16 to 1917-18 *Competition suspended*							
1918-19	Rochdale H.	22	Oldham	0	Salford	18,617	£1,365
1919-20	Oldham	7	Rochdale H.	0	Salford	19,000	£1,300
1920-21	Broughton R.	6	Leigh	3	Salford	25,000	£1,800
1921-22	Warrington	7	Oldham	5	Broughton	18,000	£1,200
1922-23	Wigan	20	Leigh	2	Salford	15,000	£1,200
1923-24	St. Helens Recs.	17	Swinton	0	Wigan	25,656	£1,450
1924-25	Oldham	10	St. Helens Recs.	0	Salford	15,000	£1,116
1925-26	Swinton	15	Wigan	11	Broughton	17,000	£1,115
1926-27	St. Helens	10	St. Helens Recs.	2	Warrington	19,439	£1,192
1927-28	Swinton	5	Wigan	2	Oldham	22,000	£1,275
1928-29	Wigan	5	Widnes	4	Warrington	19,000	£1,150
1929-30	Warrington	15	Salford	2	Wigan	21,012	£1,250
1930-31	St. Helens Recs.	18	Wigan	3	Swinton	16,710	£1,030

Season	*Winners*		*Runners-up*		*Venue*	*Attendance*	*Receipts*
1931-32	Salford	10	Swinton	8	Broughton	26,471	£1,654
1932-33	Warrington	10	St. Helens	9	Wigan	28,500	£1,675
1933-34	Oldham	12	St. Helens Recs.	0	Swinton	9,085	£516
1934-35	Salford	21	Wigan	12	Swinton	33,544	£2,191
1935-36	Salford	15	Wigan	7	Warrington	16,500	£950
1936-37	Salford	5	Wigan	2	Warrington	17,500	£1,160
1937-38	Warrington	8	Barrow	4	Wigan	14,000	£800
1938-39	Wigan	10	Salford	7	Swinton	27,940	£1,708
1939-40*	Swinton	5	Widnes	4	Widnes	5,500	£269
	Swinton	16	Widnes	11	Swinton	9,000	£446
	Swinton won on aggregate 21-15						
1940-41 to 1944-45 *Competition suspended*							
1945-46	Widnes	7	Wigan	3	Warrington	28,184	£2,600
1946-47	Wigan	9	Belle Vue R.	3	Swinton	21,618	£2,658
1947-48	Wigan	10	Belle Vue R.	7	Warrington	23,110	£3,043
1948-49	Wigan	14	Warrington	8	Swinton	39,015	£5,518
1949-50	Wigan	20	Leigh	7	Warrington	35,000	£4,751
1950-51	Wigan	28	Warrington	5	Swinton	42,541	£6,222
1951-52	Wigan	14	Leigh	6	Swinton	33,230	£5,432
1952-53	Leigh	22	St. Helens	5	Swinton	34,785	£5,793
1953-54	St. Helens	16	Wigan	8	Swinton	42,793	£6,918
1954-55	Barrow	12	Oldham	2	Swinton	25,204	£4,603
1955-56	Leigh	26	Widnes	9	Wigan	26,507	£4,090
1956-57	Oldham	10	St. Helens	3	Wigan	39,544	£6,274
1957-58	Oldham	13	Wigan	8	Swinton	42,497	£6,918
1958-59	Oldham	12	St. Helens	2	Swinton	38,780	£6,933
1959-60	Warrington	5	St. Helens	4	Wigan	39,237	£6,424
1960-61	St. Helens	15	Swinton	9	Wigan	31,755	£5,337
1961-62	St. Helens	25	Swinton	9	Wigan	30,000	£4,850
1962-63	St. Helens	7	Swinton	4	Wigan	23,523	£4,122
1963-64	St. Helens	15	Leigh	4	Swinton	21,231	£3,857
1964-65	St. Helens	12	Swinton	4	Wigan	17,383	£3,393
1965-66	Warrington	16	Rochdale H.	5	St. Helens	21,360	£3,800
1966-67	Wigan	16	Oldham	13	Swinton	14,193	£3,558
1967-68	St. Helens	2	Warrington	2	Wigan	15,000	£3,886
(replay)	St. Helens	13	Warrington	10	Swinton	7,577	£2,485
1968-69	St. Helens	30	Oldham	2	Wigan	17,008	£4,644
1969-70	Swinton	11	Leigh	2	Wigan	13,532	£3,651
1970-71	Leigh	7	St. Helens	4	Swinton	10,776	£3,136
1971-72	Wigan	15	Widnes	8	St. Helens	6,970	£2,204
1972-73	Salford	25	Swinton	11	Warrington	6,865	£3,321
1973-74	Wigan	19	Salford	9	Warrington	8,012	£2,750
1974-75	Widnes	6	Salford	2	Wigan	7,403	£2,833
1975-76	Widnes	16	Salford	7	Wigan	7,566	£3,880
1976-77	Widnes	16	Workington T.	11	Wigan	8,498	£6,414
1977-78	Workington T.	16	Wigan	13	Warrington	9,548	£5,038
1978-79	Widnes	15	Workington T.	13	Wigan	10,020	£6,261
1979-80	Widnes	11	Workington T.	0	Salford	6,887	£7,100
1980-81	Warrington	26	Wigan	10	St. Helens	6,442	£8,629
1981-82	Leigh	8	Widnes	3	Wigan	9,011	£14,029
1982-83	Warrington	16	St. Helens	0	Wigan	6,462	£11,732
1983-84	Barrow	12	Widnes	8	Wigan	7,007	£13,160

*Emergency Competition

LANCASHIRE CUP FINAL .... A REVIEW

1961-62
St. Helens 25 Rhodes (1t, 5g); Vollenhoven (1t), Large (1t), McGinn, Sullivan (1t); Smith, Murphy (1t); Leyland, Dagnall, Watson, French, Huddart, V. Karalius
Swinton 9 Gowers; McMahon, Fleet, Cummings, Speed; Parkinson, Cartwright; Thompson, T. Roberts, Bretherton (1t), K. Roberts, Norburn, Blan (3g)
Referee: R. Gelder (Wilmslow)
1962-63
St. Helens 7 Coslett (2g); Vollenhoven (1t), Donovan, Smith, Sullivan; Benyon, Heaton; Arkwright, Dagnall, Watson, Tembey, Huddart, Major
Swinton 4 Gowers; McMahon, Halliwell, Buckley, Speed; Parkinson, Cartwright; K. Roberts, T. Roberts, Morgan, Norburn, Bonser, Blan (2g)
Referee: M. Coates (Pudsey)
1963-64
St. Helens 15 Coslett (3g); Killeen (1t), Vollenhoven (1t), Northey, Harvey; Smith (1t), A. Murphy; Tembey, Dagnall, Watson, French, Ashcroft, Major
Leigh 4 Risman; Tyrer (2g), G. Lewis, Collins, Leadbetter; Rhodes, Entwistle; Robinson, J. Lewis, Owen, M. Murphy, M. Martyn, Hurt
Referee: R. Gelder (Wilmslow)
1964-65
St. Helens 12 F. Barrow; T. Pimblett, Northey, Benyon (1t), Killeen; (3g) Harvey, Murphy; Tembey, Dagnall, Warlow, French, Hicks (1t), Laughton
Swinton 4 Gowers (2g); Harries, Fleet, Buckley, Speed; Parkinson, Williams; Bate, D. Clarke, Halliwell, Rees, Simpson, Hurt
Referee: E. Clay (Leeds)
1965-66
Warrington 16 Bootle (2g); Fisher (1t), Pickavance, Melling (2t), Glover (1t); Aspinall, Smith; Payne, Oakes, Winslade, Robinson, Thomas, Hayes
Rochdale H. 5 Pritchard; Pratt, Starkey (1t, 1g), Chamberlain, Unsworth; Garforth, Fishwick; Birchall, Ashcroft, Owen, Parr (Drui), Toga, Baxter
Referee: E. Clay (Leeds)
1966-67
Wigan 16 Ashby; Boston (1t), Ashton (1t), Holden, Lake; C. Hill, Parr; Gardiner, Clarke (1t), J. Stephens, Lyon, Gilfedder (2g, 1t), Major
Oldham 13 McLeod; Dolly, McCormack, Donovan (1t), Simms; Warburton (5g), Canning; Wilson, Taylor, Fletcher, Smethurst, Irving, Mooney
Referee: P. Geraghty (York)
1967-68
St. Helens 2 F. Barrow; Vollenhoven, Whittle, Benyon, A. Barrow; Douglas, Bishop; Warlow, Sayer, Watson, Hogan, Mantle, Coslett (1g)
Warrington 2 Affleck; Coupe, Melling, Harvey (Pickavance), Glover; Aspinall (1g), Gordon; Ashcroft, Harrison, Brady, Parr, Briggs, Clarke
Referee: G.F. Lindop (Wakefield)
Replay
St. Helens 13 F. Barrow; Vollenhoven, Smith, Benyon, Jones (1t); Douglas (Houghton 2g), Bishop; Warlow (1t), Sayer, Watson, E. Chisnall (1t), Mantle, Coslett
Warrington 10 Conroy; Coupe, Melling (1t), Allen (2g), Glover; Scahill, Gordon; Ashcroft, Harrison, Price, Parr, Briggs, Clarke
Referee: G.F. Lindop (Wakefield)
1968-69
St. Helens 30 Rhodes; F. Wilson (2t), Benyon, Myler, Williams (1t); Whittle, Bishop (1t); Warlow, Sayer, Watson, Rees (1t), E. Chisnall (1t) Coslett (6g)
Oldham 2 Murphy; Elliott, Larder, McCormack, Whitehead; Briggs (1g), Canning; K. Wilson, Taylor, Fletcher (Maders), Irving, McCourt, Hughes
Referee: W.H. Thompson (Huddersfield)
1969-70
Swinton 11 Gowers; Gomersall, Fleet, Buckley, Philbin (1t); Davies, Kenny (4g); Bate, D. Clarke, Mackay, Holliday, Smith, Robinson
Leigh 2 Grainey; Tickle, Warburton, Collins, Stringer (Brown); Eckersley, Murphy (1g); D. Chisnall, Ashcroft, Watts, Welding, Fiddler, Lyon
Referee: E. Clay (Leeds)
1970-71
Leigh 7 Ferguson (2g); Tickle (Canning), L. Chisnall, Collins, Walsh; Eckersley (1t), Murphy; D. Chisnall, Ashcroft, Watts, Grimes, Clarkson, Mooney
St. Helens 4 F. Barrow; L. Jones, Benyon, Walsh, Wilson; Myler, Whittle; Halsall, A. Karalius, Rees (Prescott), Mantle, E. Chisnall, Coslett (2g)
Referee: W.H. Thompson (Huddersfield)
1971-72
Wigan 15 Tyrer (3g); Eastham (1t), Francis (1t), Fuller, Wright (Gandy); D. Hill, Ayres (1t); Ashcroft, Clarke, Fletcher, Ashurst, Kevin O'Loughlin, Laughton
Widnes 8 Dutton; Brown, McLoughlin, Aspey (1g), Gaydon (1t); D. O'Neill (1t), Bowden; Warlow, Foran, Doughty, Kirwan, Walsh (Lowe), Nicholls
Referee: W.H. Thompson (Huddersfield)

1972-73
Salford 25 Charlton (1t); Eastham (1t), Watkins (5g, 1t), Hesketh, Richards (1t); Gill, Banner (1t); Mackay, Walker, Ward, Whitehead, Dixon, Prescott
Swinton 11 Jackson; Fleay (1t), Cooke, Buckley, Gomersall; Kenny (1g) (M. Philbin), Gowers (3g); Halsall, Evans, Bate, R. Smith (Holliday), Hoyle, W. Pattinson
Referee: W.H. Thompson (Huddersfield)
1973-74
Wigan 19 Francis; Vigo, D. Hill, Keiron O'Loughlin (2t), Wright (1t); Cassidy, Ayres (1g); Smethurst, Clarke, Gray (4g), Irving, D. Robinson, Cunningham
Salford 9 Charlton; Fielding, Watkins (1t, 3g), Hesketh, Holland; Gill, Banner; Mackay, Walker, Davies (Grice), Dixon, Kear (Knighton), E. Prescott
Referee: W.H. Thompson (Huddersfield)
1974-75
Widnes 6 Dutton (1g); George (1t), D. O'Neill, Aspey, A. Prescott; Hughes (1dg), Bowden; Mills, Elwell, J. Stephens, Adams, Blackwood, Laughton
Salford 2 Charlton; Fielding (1g), Dixon, Graham, Richards; Taylor, Banner; Mackay, Devlin, Grice, Knighton, Coulman, E. Prescott
Referee: G.F. Lindop (Wakefield)
1975-76
Widnes 16 Dutton (3g, 1dg); A. Prescott (1t), George (1t), Aspey (1t), Jenkins; Hughes, Bowden; Mills, Elwell, Nelson, Foran, Fitzpatrick (Sheridan), Adams
Salford 7 Watkins (2g); Fielding, Butler, Hesketh, Richards (1t); Gill, Nash; Fiddler, Hawksley, Dixon (Mackay), Turnbull, Knighton, E. Prescott
Referee: W.H. Thompson (Huddersfield)
1976-77
Widnes 16 Dutton (4g, 1dg); Wright (1t), Aspey, George (1t), A. Prescott; Eckersley, Bowden (1dg); Ramsey, Elwell, Nelson, Dearden, Adams, Laughton
Workington T. 11 Charlton; Collister, Wilkins (1t), Wright, MacCorquodale (4g); Lauder, Walker; Mills, Banks, Calvin, Bowman, L. Gorley, W. Pattinson (P. Gorley)
Referee: W.H. Thompson (Huddersfield)
1977-78
Workington T. 16 Charlton (Atkinson); Collister, Risman, Wright (1t), MacCorquodale (4g); Wilkins (1t), Walker (2dg); Watts, Banks, Bowman, L. Gorley, W. Pattinson, P. Gorley
Wigan 13 Swann; Vigo, Davies (Burke 1g), Willicombe (1t), Hornby; Taylor, Nulty (1t, 1g); Hogan, Aspinall, Irving, Ashurst (1t), Blackwood, Melling (Regan)
Referee: W.H. Thompson (Huddersfield)
1978-79
Widnes 15 Eckersley; Wright (1t), Aspey, George, Burke (3g); Hughes, Bowden; Mills, Elwell, Shaw, Adams, Dearden (Hull), Laughton (2t)
Workington T. 13 Charlton; Collister, Risman, Wilkins (1t), MacCorquodale (1t, 2g), McMillan, Walker; Beverley, Banks, Bowman, Blackwood, P. Gorley, W. Pattinson (L. Gorley 1t)
Referee: W.H. Thompson (Huddersfield)
1979-80
Widnes 11 Eckersley; Wright, Aspey, Hughes (George), Burke (2g); Moran (1t), Bowden; Hogan, Elwell (1dg), Shaw, L. Gorley, Dearden, Adams (1t)
Workington T. 0 Charlton; MacCorquodale; Maughan, Thompson, Beck; Rudd, Walker (Roper); Beverley, Banks, Wellbanks (Varty), W. Pattinson, Lewis, Dobie
Referee: W.H. Thompson (Huddersfield)
1980-81
Warrington 26 Finnegan; Thackray (1t), I. Duane, Bevan (1t), Hesford (7g, 1t); K. Kelly, A. Gwilliam; Courtney, Waller, Case, Martyn (1t), Eccles (Potter), Hunter
Wigan 10 Fairbairn (1t, 2g); Ramsdale (1t), Willicombe, Davies, Hornby; M. Foy, Bolton (Coyle); Breheny, Pendlebury (M. Smith), S. O'Neill, Melling, Clough, Hollingsworth
Referee: D. G. Kershaw (York)
1981-82
Leigh 8 Hogan; Drummond, Bilsbury (1t), Donlan (1dg), Worgan; Woods (2g), Green; Wilkinson, Tabern, Cooke, Martyn (Platt), Clarkson, McTigue
Widnes 3 Burke; George, Hughes, Cunningham, Bentley (1t); Moran, Gregory; M. O'Neill, Elwell, Lockwood, L. Gorley, E. Prescott, Adams
Referee: W.H. Thompson (Huddersfield)
1982-83
Warrington 16 Hesford (2g); Fellows (1t), R. Duane, Bevan, M. Kelly (1t); Cullen, K. Kelly (1t); Courtney, Webb, Cooke (D. Chisnall), Eccles (1t), Fieldhouse, Gregory
St. Helens 0 Parkes (Smith); Ledger, Arkwright, Haggerty, Litherland; Peters, Holding; James, Liptrot, Bottell (Mathias), Moorby, P. Gorley, Pinner
Referee: J. Holdsworth (Leeds)

MAN OF THE MATCH AWARDS

An award for the adjudged man of the match in the Lancashire Cup final was first presented in 1974-75. For four years the award was sponsored by the *Rugby Leaguer* newspaper. From 1978-79 the trophy was presented by Burtonwood Brewery as part of their sponsorship of the Lancashire Cup. Under the auspices of the *Rugby Leaguer*, the choice was made by the Editor, while Burtonwood Brewery invited a panel of the Press to make the decision.

Season	*Winner*	*Team*	*Position*
1974-75	Mike Coulman	Salford (v. Widnes)	Second row
1975-76	Mick George	Widnes (v. Salford)	Centre
1976-77	David Eckersley	Widnes (v. Workington T.)	Stand off
1977-78	Arnold Walker	Workington T. (v. Wigan)	Scrum half
1978-79	Arnold Walker	Workington T. (v. Widnes)	Scrum half
1979-80	Mick Adams	Widnes (v. Workington T.)	Loose forward
1980-81	Tony Waller	Warrington (v. Wigan)	Hooker
1981-82	Ray Tabern	Leigh (v. Widnes)	Hooker
1982-83	Steve Hesford	Warrington (v. St. Helens)	Full back
1983-84	David Cairns	Barrow (v. Widnes)	Scrum half

LANCASHIRE CUP FINAL RECORDS

TEAM

Most appearances: 29 by Wigan
Most wins: 16 by Wigan
Highest score: St. Helens 30 v. Oldham 2 1968
(Also widest margin)
Biggest attendance:
42,793 St. Helens v. Wigan (at Swinton) 1953

INDIVIDUAL

Most tries:
4 by Brian Nordgren (Wigan) v. Leigh 1949
Most goals:
7 by Jim Ledgard (Leigh) v. Widnes 1955
Steve Hesford (Warrington) v. Wigan 1980
Most points:
17 (7g, 1t) by Steve Hesford (Warrington) v. Wigan 1980

Barrow beneficiary Eddie Szymala in the grips of Widnes second row man Fred Whitfield.

YORKSHIRE CUP

1983 Final

Chain-smoking Hull loose forward Mick Crane left Castleford coughing and spluttering as he produced a smokescreen of deception to star in the Airlie Birds' Philips Video Yorkshire Cup final success.

Hull took the county cup for the second successive season with a comfortable 13-2 victory, scoring three tries to none on a rain-sodden Elland Road pitch.

Great Britain packman Crane took the White Rose Trophy as Man of the Match to crown a top class display featuring a try, the making of another touchdown and a late drop goal.

The crowd of 14,049 — the best Yorkshire Cup final gate for 15 years — paid record receipts of £33,522, only to be disappointed by a Castleford display which produced just two highlights, not reflecting their current Championship challenging form.

Wingman Dane O'Hara — aided by fellow Kiwis Gary Kemble and James Leuluai — opened the scoring with an 18th minute try, Castleford responding seven minutes later with a controversial claim for a touchdown under the posts. A shallow cross kick by scrum half Bob Beardmore was caught over the goal line by centre Tony Marchant, only to be ruled offside by referee Billy Thompson.

With both sides making handling errors in the relentless rain, Crane being a particular victim of support players not being able to hold his passes, further first half scoring was restricted to a penalty goal by Bob Beardmore in the 34th minute.

Castleford prop Gary Connell was sent to the sin bin a minute before the break, O'Hara joining him four minutes into the second half. While they were off the field, Crane produced that extra touch of class to score a try in the 47th minute, deciding to go on his own with a deft dummy, a hand off and a spring to the line to give Hull an 8-2 lead.

Crane was also prominent in the build up to the Boulevarders' third try, centre Leuluai controlling the slippery ball to send second row man Wayne Proctor in at the corner. With four minutes left, Crane had the final say with a drop goal skewed over from 30 yards.

Crane collected the Man of the Match award with 12 votes from the Press, hard-working colleague Trevor Skerrett picking up six and rival scrum halves Tony Dean and Beardmore one apiece.

Castleford paid the price for handling errors, their own fact sheet showing a loss of possession on 30 occasions. Former Test loose forward Malcolm Reilly was forced to turn out at prop because of injuries, but his threat of tactical kicking was blotted out by the Hull pack.

A strike by television technicians blacked out the screening of the highlights of the final at the last minute, the tournament being the first of a two-year sponsorship by Philips Video.

1983 Round by Round

In the first round, holders Hull took revenge for their shock defeat at Wembley by disposing of RL Challenge Cup winners Featherstone Rovers 24-8 at the Boulevard. Neighbours Hull K.R. had their cup hopes dented with the dismissal of second row man Chris Burton in the 17th minute of the tie at Bradford Northern. A rally proved to be too late with Northern securing a 25-22 victory. Batley prop forward Garry Robbins spent 10 minutes in the sin bin during the home tie with Leeds to return to find the visitors had scored two vital tries, through Kevin Squire and Tony Burke, the basis of a sound 30-14 success for the Loiners. With Castleford trailing at home to Second Division Huddersfield by 14-8, coach Malcolm Reilly brought himself on as substitute to lead a late scoring charge to victory. In all-Second Division games, lowly Doncaster pulled off a shock 16-12 success over visiting Bramley; Keighley beat Dewsbury; while former Hull half back Ian Wilson scored all York's points in a 21-11 win at Hunslet with two tries, six goals and a drop goal. Veteran Nigel Stephenson celebrated his 500th senior game with a try in Wakefield Trinity's 18-10 victory over Halifax, Mario Cerchione scoring a try on his debut for the Thrum Hallers.

In the second round, John Holmes shone on attack and defence as Leeds disposed of York. The former Test star stopped his opposite number Graham Steadman from scoring in the first half and after the interval scored himself to put the Loiners in front for the first time, finally setting up the clinching touchdown for Kevin Rayne. Doncaster travelled to Wakefield Trinity, who led 14-4 at half-time. Two tries and goals in the opening 10 minutes of the second half ended the game as a contest, Trinity running out 32-14 winners. Injury-hit League leaders Bradford Northern, beaten finalists for the past two years, were knocked out by title rivals Castleford 12-8 after leading 6-2 at the break. Hull ran in 14 points in a 15-minute spell in the first half to build the foundation for a comfortable 30-8 success at Keighley.

In the semi-finals, Castleford opened the scoring at Wakefield Trinity after eight minutes with a 40-yard try by Steve Fenton, going on to outclass the Dreadnoughts by 34-12. Castleford scored 12 points in three minutes just before the interval and it was 10 minutes from time before Trinity broke their duck and crossed the line twice. In a thrilling encounter at Headingley, Hull swept into a 20-6 lead, Kiwi centre James Leuluai scoring a try for the eighth consecutive match to equal the club's post-war record. A Leeds revival with two tries and a goal gave the Airlie Birds a nerve-wracking 20-16 passage into the final.

PHILIPS VIDEO YORKSHIRE CUP FINAL

15th October — **Elland Road, Leeds**

CASTLEFORD 2		**HULL 13**
Darren Coen	1.	Gary Kemble
Steve Fenton	2.	Patrick Solal
Tony Marchant	3.	Garry Schofield
Gary Hyde	4.	James Leuluai
John Kear	5.	Dane O'Hara
John Joyner	6.	David Topliss, Capt.
Robert Beardmore, Capt.	7.	Tony Dean
Gary Connell	8.	Phil Edmonds
Stuart Horton	9.	Ron Wileman
Malcolm Reilly	10.	Trevor Skerrett
Andrew Timson	11.	Wayne Proctor
Neil James	12.	Lee Crooks
Keith England	13.	Mick Crane
Ian Orum	14.	Barry Banks
Alan Hardy	15.	Paul Rose
		T: O'Hara, Crane, Proctor
G: Beardmore		G: Crane (dg)

Substitution: Orum for Hyde (69 min.)
Half-time: 2-4
Referee: Billy Thompson (Huddersfield)
Attendance: 14,049

1983 Results

WAKEFIELD T.	18	WAKEFIELD T.	32				
HALIFAX	10			WAKEFIELD T.	12		
DONCASTER	16	DONCASTER	14				
BRAMLEY	12					CASTLEFORD	2
BRADFORD N.	25	BRADFORD N.	8				
HULL K.R.	22			CASTLEFORD	34		
CASTLEFORD	36	CASTLEFORD	12				
HUDDERSFIELD	20						
HUNSLET	11	YORK	16				
YORK	21			LEEDS	16		
BATLEY	14	LEEDS	24				
LEEDS	30					HULL	13
DEWSBURY	8	KEIGHLEY	8				
KEIGHLEY	18			HULL	20		
HULL	24	HULL	30				
FEATHERSTONE R.	8						

Hull's Kiwi centre James Leuluai attempting to hand off Castleford's Tony Marchant.

Yorkshire Cup victory hoist for Hull captain David Topliss.

YORKSHIRE CUP ROLL OF HONOUR

Year	*Winners*		*Runners-up*		*Venue*	*Attendance*	*Receipts*
1905-06	Hunslet	13	Halifax	3	Bradford P.A.	18,500	£465
1906-07	Bradford	8	Hull K.R.	5	Wakefield	10,500	£286
1907-08	Hunslet	17	Halifax	0	Leeds	15,000	£397
1908-09	Halifax	9	Hunslet	5	Wakefield	13,000	£356
1909-10	Huddersfield	21	Batley	0	Leeds	22,000	£778
1910-11	Wakefield T.	8	Huddersfield	2	Leeds	19,000	£696
1911-12	Huddersfield	22	Hull K.R.	10	Wakefield	20,000	£700
1912-13	Batley	17	Hull	3	Leeds	16,000	£523
1913-14	Huddersfield	19	Bradford N.	3	Halifax	12,000	£430
1914-15	Huddersfield	31	Hull	0	Leeds	12,000	£422
1918-19	Huddersfield	14	Dewsbury	8	Leeds	21,500	£1,309
1919-20	Huddersfield	24	Leeds	5	Halifax	24,935	£2,096
1920-21	Hull K.R.	2	Hull	0	Leeds	20,000	£1,926
1921-22	Leeds	11	Dewsbury	3	Halifax	20,000	£1,650
1922-23	York	5	Batley	0	Leeds	33,719	£2,414
1923-24	Hull	10	Huddersfield	4	Leeds	23,300	£1,728
1924-25	Wakefield T.	9	Batley	8	Leeds	25,546	£1,912
1925-26	Dewsbury	2	Huddersfield	0	Wakefield	12,616	£781
1926-27	Huddersfield	10	Wakefield T.	3	Leeds	11,300	£853
1927-28	Dewsbury	8	Hull	2	Leeds	21,700	£1,466
1928-29	Leeds	5	Featherstone R.	0	Wakefield	13,000	£838
1929-30	Hull K.R.	13	Hunslet	7	Leeds	11,000	£687
1930-31	Leeds	10	Huddersfield	2	Halifax	17,812	£1,405
1931-32	Huddersfield	4	Hunslet	2	Leeds	27,000	£1,764
1932-33	Leeds	8	Wakefield T.	0	Huddersfield	17,685	£1,183
1933-34	York	10	Hull K.R.	4	Leeds	22,000	£1,480
1934-35	Leeds	5	Wakefield T.	5	Dewsbury	22,598	£1,529
Replay	Leeds	2	Wakefield T.	2	Huddersfield	10,300	£745
Replay	Leeds	13	Wakefield T.	0	Hunslet	19,304	£1,327
1935-36	Leeds	3	York	0	Halifax	14,616	£1,113
1936-37	York	9	Wakefield T.	2	Leeds	19,000	£1,294
1937-38	Leeds	14	Huddersfield	8	Wakefield	22,000	£1,508
1938-39	Huddersfield	18	Hull	10	Bradford	28,714	£1,534
1939-40*	Featherstone R.	12	Wakefield T.	9	Bradford	7,077	£403
1940-41*	Bradford N.	15	Dewsbury	5	Huddersfield	13,316	£939
1941-42*	Bradford N.	24	Halifax	0	Huddersfield	5,989	£635
1942-43*	Dewsbury	7	Huddersfield	0	Dewsbury	11,000	£680
	Huddersfield	2	Dewsbury	0	Huddersfield	6,252	£618
	Dewsbury won on aggregate 7-2						
1943-44*	Bradford N.	5	Keighley	2	Bradford	10,251	£757
	Keighley	5	Bradford N.	5	Keighley	8,993	£694
	Bradford N. won on aggregate 10-7						

1937-38	Leeds	14	Huddersfield	8	Wakefield	22,000	£1,508
1938-39	Huddersfield	18	Hull	10	Bradford	28,714	£1,534
1939-40*	Featherstone R.	12	Wakefield T.	9	Bradford	7,077	£403
1940-41*	Bradford N.	15	Dewsbury	5	Huddersfield	13,316	£939
1941-42*	Bradford N.	24	Halifax	0	Huddersfield	5,989	£635
1942-43*	Dewsbury	7	Huddersfield	0	Dewsbury	11,000	£680
	Huddersfield	2	Dewsbury	0	Huddersfield	6,252	£618
	Dewsbury won on aggregate 7-2						
1943-44*	Bradford N.	5	Keighley	2	Bradford	10,251	£757
	Keighley	5	Bradford N.	5	Keighley	8,993	£694
	Bradford N. won on aggregate 10-7						

Year	*Winners*		*Runners-up*		*Venue*	*Attendance*	*Receipts*
1944-45*	Hunslet	3	Halifax	12	Hunslet	11,213	£744
	Halifax	2	Hunslet	0	Halifax	9,800	£745
	Halifax won on aggregate 14-3						
1945-46	Bradford N.	5	Wakefield T.	2	Halifax	24,292	£1,934
1946-47	Wakefield T.	10	Hull	0	Leeds	34,300	£3,718
1947-48	Wakefield T.	7	Leeds	7	Huddersfield	24,344	£3,461
Replay	Wakefield T.	8	Leeds	7	Bradford	32,000	£3,251
1948-49	Bradford N.	18	Castleford	9	Leeds	31,393	£5,053
1949-50	Bradford N.	11	Huddersfield	4	Leeds	36,000	£6,365
1950-51	Huddersfield	16	Castleford	3	Leeds	28,906	£5,152
1951-52	Wakefield T.	17	Keighley	3	Huddersfield	25,495	£3,347
1952-53	Huddersfield	18	Batley	8	Leeds	14,705	£2,471
1953-54	Bradford N.	7	Hull	2	Leeds	22,147	£3,833
1954-55	Halifax	22	Hull	14	Leeds	25,949	£4,638
1955-56	Halifax	10	Hull	10	Leeds	23,520	£4,385
Replay	Halifax	7	Hull	0	Bradford	14,000	£2,439
1956-57	Wakefield T.	23	Hunslet	5	Leeds	30,942	£5,609
1957-58	Huddersfield	15	York	8	Leeds	22,531	£4,123
1958-59	Leeds	24	Wakefield T.	20	Bradford	26,927	£3,833
1959-60	Featherstone R.	15	Hull	14	Leeds	23,983	£4,156
1960-61	Wakefield T.	16	Huddersfield	10	Leeds	17,456	£2,937
1961-62	Wakefield T.	19	Leeds	9	Bradford	16,329	£2,864
1962-63	Hunslet	12	Hull K.R.	2	Leeds	22,742	£4,514
1963-64	Halifax	10	Featherstone R.	0	Wakefield	13,238	£2,471
1964-65	Wakefield T.	18	Leeds	2	Huddersfield	13,527	£2,707
1965-66	Bradford N.	17	Hunslet	8	Leeds	17,522	£4,359
1966-67	Hull K.R.	25	Featherstone R.	12	Leeds	13,241	£3,482
1967-68	Hull K.R.	8	Hull	7	Leeds	16,729	£5,515
1968-69	Leeds	22	Castleford	11	Wakefield	12,573	£3,746
1969-70	Hull	12	Featherstone R.	9	Leeds	11,089	£3,419
1970-71	Leeds	23	Featherstone R.	7	Bradford	6,753	£1,879
1971-72	Hull K.R.	11	Castleford	7	Wakefield	5,536	£1,589
1972-73	Leeds	36	Dewsbury	9	Bradford	7,806	£2,659
1973-74	Leeds	7	Wakefield T.	2	Leeds	7,621	£3,728
1974-75	Hull K.R.	16	Wakefield T.	13	Leeds	5,823	£3,090
1975-76	Leeds	15	Hull K.R.	11	Leeds	5,743	£3,617
1976-77	Leeds	16	Featherstone R.	12	Leeds	7,645	£5,198
1977-78	Castleford	17	Featherstone R.	7	Leeds	6,318	£4,528
1978-79	Bradford N.	18	York	8	Leeds	10,429	£9,188
1979-80	Leeds	15	Halifax	6	Leeds	9,137	£9,999
1980-81	Leeds	8	Hull K.R.	7	Huddersfield	9,751	£15,578
1981-82	Castleford	10	Bradford N.	5	Leeds	5,852	£10,359
1982-83	Hull	18	Bradford N.	7	Leeds	11,755	£21,950
1983-84	Hull	13	Castleford	2	Leeds U. FC	14,049	£33,572

* Emergency competition.

YORKSHIRE CUP FINAL .... A REVIEW

1961-62

Wakefield T. 19 Round; F. Smith (1t), Skene (1t), Fox (5g), Greenwood; Poynton, Holliday; Wilkinson, Kosanovic, Firth, Briggs, Vines, Turner (1t)
Leeds 9 Thornett; Hemingway (1t), Pickup, Goodwin, Ratcliffe; Jones (3g), Evans; Robinson, Simms, Whitehead, Fairbank, Sykes, Tomlinson
Referee: T.W. Watkinson (Manchester)

1962-63

Hunslet 12 Langton (2g); Lee, Shelton (1t), Preece, Render; Gabbitas, Stevenson; Hartley (1g), Prior, K. Eyre, Baldwinson (1t), Lambert, Ward
Hull K.R. 2 Kellett (1g); Paul, Major, Blackmore, Harris; Elliott, Hatch; Grice, Lockwood, J. Drake, Tyson, Taylor, Poole
Referee: R. Gelder (Wilmslow)

1963-64

Halifax 10 James (2g); Jackson (1t), Burnett, C. Dixon, Freeman; Robinson, Marchant; Fox, Shaw, Scroby, Phillips, Fogerty, Renilson (1t)
Featherstone R. 0 Fennell; Greatorex, Hunt, Lynch, Jordan; Lingard, Fox; Terry, Fawley, M. Dixon, Ramshaw, Brown, Clifft
Referee: D.T.H. Davies (Manchester)

1964-65

Wakefield T. 18 Metcalfe; Jones (2t), Thomas, Fox (2t, 3g), Coetzer; Poynton, Owen; Campbell, Shepherd, Vines, Haigh, Plumstead, Holliday
Leeds 2 Dewhurst (1g); Cowan, Broatch, Gemmell, Wrigglesworth; Shoebottom, Seabourne; W. Drake, Lockwood, Chamberlain, Clark, Neumann, J. Sykes
Referee: D.T.H. Davies (Manchester)

1965-66

Bradford N. 17 Scattergood; Williamson (2t), Brooke (1t), Rhodes, Walker; Stockwell, Smales; Tonkinson, Morgan, Hill, Ashton, Clawson (4g), Rae
Hunslet 8 Langton (1g); Lee (1t), Shelton, Render, Thompson (1t); Preece, Marchant; Hartley, Prior, Baldwinson, Ramsey, Gunney, Ward
Referee: W.E. Lawrinson (Warrington)

1966-67

Hull K.R. 25 C. Kellett (5g); Young (1t), A. Burwell (1t), Moore (1t), Blackmore (1t); Millward, Bunting; F. Fox, Flanagan (1t), Tyson, Holliday, Foster, Major
Featherstone R. 12 D. Kellett; Thomas, Greatorex, Wrigglesworth (1t), Westwood; M. Smith, Dooler; Dixon, Kosanovic, Forsyth (1t), A. Morgan, Lyons, Smales (3g)
Referee: B. Baker (Wigan)

1967-68

Hull K.R. 8 Kellett (1g); Young, Moore, Elliott, A. Burwell (1t); Millward (1t), Cooper; Holliday, Flanagan, Mennell, Lowe, Hickson (Foster), Major
Hull 7 Keegan; Oliver, Doyle-Davidson, Maloney (1g), Stocks; Devonshire, Davidson (1t, 1g); Harrison, McGlone, Broom, Edson, J. Macklin, Sykes
Referee: D.T.H. Davies (Manchester)

1968-69

Leeds 22 Risman (5g); Alan Smith (1t), Hynes, Watson (1t), Atkinson (1t); Shoebottom, Seabourne; Clarke, Crosby, K. Eyre, Ramsey (Hick 1t), A. Eyre, Batten
Castleford 11 Edwards; Howe, Hill (1t, 2g), Thomas, Stephens; Hardisty (2g), Hargrave; Hartley, C. Dickinson, Ward, Small, Lockwood (Redfearn), Reilly
Referee: J. Manley (Warrington)

1969-70

Hull 12 Owbridge; Sullivan (1t), Gemmell, Maloney (2g), A. Macklin; Hancock, Davidson; Harrison, McGlone, J. Macklin (1t), Kirchin, Forster, Brown (1g)
Featherstone R. 9 C. Kellett (3g); Newlove, Jordan, M. Smith, Hartley (T. Hudson); D. Kellett, Nash (1t); Tonks, Farrar, Lyons, A. Morgan, Thompson, Smales
Referee: R.L. Thomas (Oldham)

1970-71

Leeds 23 Holmes; Alan Smith (2t), Hynes (4g), Cowan, Atkinson (1t); Wainwright (Langley), Shoebottom; J. Burke, Dunn (1t), Cookson, Ramsey (1t), Haigh, Batten
Featherstone R. 7 C. Kellett (2g); M. Smith, Cotton, Newlove, Hartley (1t); Harding (Coventry), Hudson; Windmill, D. Morgan, Lyons, Rhodes, Thompson, Farrar
Referee: D.S. Brown (Preston)

1971-72

Hull K.R. 11 Markham; Stephenson, Coupland, Kirkpatrick, Longstaff (1t); Millward (4g), Daley; Wiley, Flanagan, Millington, Wallis, Palmer (Cooper), Brown
Castleford 7 Edwards; Foster (1t), S. Norton, Worsley, Lowndes; Hargrave, Stephens; Hartley, Miller, I. Van Bellen (Ackroyd 2g), A. Dickinson, Lockwood, Blakeway
Referee: A. Givvons (Oldham)

1972-73
Leeds 36 Holmes (3t); Alan Smith, Hynes (1g), Dyl (2t), Atkinson (1t); Hardisty (1t), Hepworth (Langley); Clawson (5g) (Fisher), Ward, Ramsey, Cookson, Eccles (1t), Batten
Dewsbury 9 Rushton; Ashcroft (1t), Childe, Day, Yoward; Agar (3g), A. Bates; Bell (Beverley), M. Stephenson, Lowe, Grayshon, J. Bates (Lee), Hankins
Referee: M.J. Naughton (Widnes)
1973-74
Leeds 7 Holmes; Langley (1t) (Marshall 1g), Hynes (1g), Dyl, Atkinson; Hardisty, Hepworth; Jeanes (Ramsey), Ward, Clarkson, Eccles, Cookson, Batten
Wakefield T. 2 Wraith (Sheard); D. Smith, Crook (1g), Hegarty, B. Parker; Topliss, Bonnar; Valentine, Morgan, Bratt, Knowles (Ballantyne), Endersby, Holmes
Referee: M.J. Naughton (Widnes)
1974-75
Hull K.R. 16 Smithies; Sullivan (Dunn lt), Watson (2t), Coupland, Kirkpatrick (1t); Millward, Stephenson; Millington, Heslop, Rose, Wallis, N. Fox (2g) (Madley), Brown
Wakefield T. 13 Sheard; D. Smith (1t), Crook (2g), Hegarty (1t), Archer; Topliss, Bonnar; Ballantyne, Handscombe, Bratt (1t), Skerrett, A. Tonks (Goodwin), (Holmes), Morgan
Referee: M.J. Naughton (Widnes)
1975-76
Leeds 15 Marshall; Alan Smith, Hague, Dyl (1t), Atkinson; Holmes (4g, 1dg), Hynes; Harrison, Payne, Pitchford, (Dickinson), Eccles, Batten, Cookson (1t)
Hull K.R. 11 Wallace; Dunn, A. Burwell, Watson, Sullivan (1t); Turner, Millward (1dg); Millington, Dickinson, Lyons, Rose, N. Fox (2g, 1t), Hughes (Holdstock)
Referee: J.V. Moss (Manchester)
1976-77
Leeds 16 Marshall (2g); Hague, Hynes, Dyl (2t), D. Smith; Holmes, Banner; Dickinson, Ward, Pitchford, Eccles (1t), Burton, Cookson (1t)
Featherstone R. 12 Box; Bray (1t), Coventry, Quinn (3g), K. Kellett; Newlove, Fennell; Gibbins, Bridges, Farrar, Stone, P. Smith (1t), Bell (Spells)
Referee: M.J. Naughton (Widnes)
1977-78
Castleford 17 Wraith; Richardson, Joyner, P. Johnson, Fenton; Burton (2t, 1dg), Pickerill (Stephens); Fisher (Woodall), Spurr, Weston, Huddlestone, Reilly, Lloyd (5g)
Featherstone R. 7 Marsden; Evans, Gilbert, Quinn (1g) (N. Tuffs), K. Kellett; Newlove, Butler; Townend (1g), Bridges, Farrar, Gibbins, Stone (P. Smith 1t), Bell
Referee: M.J. Naughton (Widnes)
1978-79
Bradford N. 18 Mumby; Barends, Gant (1t), D. Parker (1t), D. Redfearn; Slater (Wolford), A. Redfearn (1t); Thompson, Fisher, Forsyth (Joyce), Fox (3g), Trotter, Haigh (1t)
York 8 G. Smith (1t); T. Morgan, Day (Crossley), Foster, Nicholson; Banks (2g), Harkin; Dunkerley, Wileman, Harris, Rhodes, Hollis (1dg) (Ramshaw), Cooper
Referee: M.J. Naughton (Widnes)
1979-80
Leeds 15 Hague; Alan Smith (2t), D. Smith (1t), Dyl, Atkinson; Holmes (J. Sanderson), Dick (3g); Dickinson, Ward, Pitchford, Eccles, D. Heron (Adams), Cookson
Halifax 6 Birts (3g); Howard (Snee), Garrod, Cholmondeley, Waites; Blacker, Langton; Jarvis (Callon), Raistrick, Ward, Scott, Sharp, Busfield
Referee: M.J. Naughton (Widnes)
1980-81
Leeds 8 Hague; Alan Smith (1t), D. Smith, Atkinson, Oulton; Holmes, Dick (2g, 1dg); Harrison, Ward, Pitchford, Eccles, Cookson (Carroll), D. Heron
Hull K.R. 7 Robinson; McHugh (1t), M. Smith, Hogan (2g), Youngman; Hall, Harkin; Holdstock, Price, Crooks (Rose), Lowe, Casey, Crane
Referee: R. Campbell (Widnes)
1981-82
Castleford 10 Claughton; Richardson, Fenton, Hyde (1t), Morris; Joyner (1t), R. Beardmore; Hardy (P. Norton), Spurr, B. Johnson, Finch (2g), Ward, Timson
Bradford N. 5 Mumby; Barends, Hale, A. Parker (1t), Gant; Hanley (1g), A. Redfearn; Grayshon, Noble, Sanderson (D. Redfearn), G. Van Bellen (Jasiewicz), Idle, Rathbone
Referee: M.R. Whitfield (Widnes)
1982-83
Hull 18 Kemble; Evans (1t), Day, Leuluai, Prendiville (1t); Topliss, Harkin; Skerrett, Bridges, Stone, Rose (2t), Crooks (2g, 2dg), Crane (Norton)
Bradford N. 7 Mumby; Barends, Gant, A. Parker, Pullen (Smith); Whiteman (1t), Carroll (1g, 2dg); Grayshon, Noble, G. Van Bellen (Sanderson), Idle, Jasiewicz, Hale
Referee: S. Wall (Leigh)

THE WHITE ROSE TROPHY

First awarded in 1966, the trophy is presented to the adjudged man of the match in the Yorkshire Cup final.

Donated by the late T.E. Smith, of York, the award is organised by the Yorkshire Federation of Rugby League Supporters' Clubs and judged by a panel of the Press.

The Humberside clubs and Leeds have dominated the trophy, their players winning 14 of 18 awards, including the first 11 in succession.

Season	*Winner*	*Team*	*Position*
1966-67	Cyril Kellett	Hull K.R. (v. Featherstone R.)	Full back
1967-68	Chris Davidson	Hull (v. Hull K.R.)	Scrum half
1968-69	Barry Seabourne	Leeds (v. Castleford)	Scrum half
1969-70	Joe Brown	Hull (v. Featherstone R.)	Loose forward
1970-71	Syd Hynes	Leeds (v. Featherstone R.)	Centre
1971-72	Ian Markham	Hull K.R. (v. Castleford)	Full back
1972-73	John Holmes	Leeds (v. Dewsbury)	Full back
1973-74	Keith Hepworth	Leeds (v. Wakefield T.)	Scrum half
1974-75	Roger Millward	Hull K.R. (v. Wakefield T.)	Stand off
1975-76	Neil Fox	Hull K.R. (v. Leeds)	Second row
1976-77	Les Dyl	Leeds (v. Featherstone R.)	Centre
1977-78	Bruce Burton	Castleford (v. Featherstone R.)	Stand off
1978-79	Bob Haigh	Bradford N. (v. York)	Loose forward
1979-80	Alan Smith	Leeds (v. Halifax)	Winger
1980-81	Kevin Dick	Leeds (v. Hull K.R.)	Scrum half
1981-82	Barry Johnson	Castleford (v. Bradford N.)	Prop
1982-83	Keith Mumby	Bradford N. (v. Hull)	Full back
1983-84	Mick Crane	Hull (v. Castleford)	Loose forward

YORKSHIRE CUP FINAL RECORDS

TEAM

Most appearances: 20 Huddersfield, Leeds
Most wins: 16 Leeds
Highest score: Leeds 36 v. Dewsbury 9 1972
Widest margin win: Huddersfield 31 v. Hull 0 1914
Biggest attendance:
36,000 Bradford N. v. Huddersfield (at Leeds) 1949

INDIVIDUAL

Most tries:
4 by George Todd (Huddersfield) v. Bradford N. ... 1913
Stan Moorhouse (Huddersfield) v. Leeds 1919
Most points:
12 by Todd and Moorhouse (as above) plus
(3g,2t) A. Edwards (Bradford N.) v. Castleford 1948
(3g,2t) Neil Fox (Wakefield T.) v. Leeds 1964
Most goals: No player has scored more than 5

BBC-2 FLOODLIT TROPHY

The BBC-2 Floodlit Trophy competition was launched in 1965 for clubs with floodlights. Eight clubs competed in the first year and the total had grown to 22 in 1980 when the competition was abolished as part of the BBC's financial cut-backs.

For 15 years the matches became a regular television feature on Tuesday evenings throughout the early winter months.

Although the format changed slightly over the years, it was basically a knockout competition on the lines of the Challenge Cup.

In 1966 the Floodlit Competition was used to introduce the limited tackle rule, then four tackles, which proved such a great success it was adopted in all other matches before the end of the year.

BBC-2 FLOODLIT TROPHY FINALS

(Only the 1967, at Leeds, and 1972, at Wigan, finals were played on neutral grounds)

Season	*Winners*		*Runners-up*		*Venue*	*Attendance*	*Receipts*
1965-66	Castleford	4	St. Helens	0	St. Helens	11,510	£1,548
1966-67	Castleford	7	Swinton	2	Castleford	8,986	£1,692
1967-68	Castleford	8	Leigh	5	Leeds	9,716	£2,099
1968-69	Wigan	7	St. Helens	4	Wigan	13,479	£3,291
1969-70	Leigh	11	Wigan	6	Wigan	12,312	£2,854
1970-71	Leeds	9	St. Helens	5	Leeds	7,612	£2,189
1971-72	St. Helens	8	Rochdale H.	2	St. Helens	9,300	£2,493
1972-73	Leigh	5	Widnes	0	Wigan	4,691	£1,391
1973-74	Bramley	15	Widnes	7	Widnes	4,422	£1,538
1974-75	Salford	0	Warrington	0	Salford	4,473	£1,913
Replay	Salford	10	Warrington	5	Warrington	5,778	£2,434
1975-76	St. Helens	22	Dewsbury	2	St. Helens	3,858	£1,747
1976-77	Castleford	12	Leigh	4	Leigh	5,402	£2,793
1977-78	Hull K.R.	26	St. Helens	11	Hull K.R.	10,099	£6,586
1978-79	Widnes	13	St. Helens	7	St. Helens	10,250	£7,017
1979-80	Hull	13	Hull K.R.	3	Hull	18,500	£16,605

BBC2 FLOODLIT TROPHY . . . . A REVIEW

1965-66

Castleford 4 Edwards; C. Battye, M. Battye, Willett (2g), Briggs; Hardisty, Millward; Terry, J. Ward, C. Dickinson, Bryant, Taylor, Small

St. Helens 0 F. Barrow; Vollenhoven, Wood, Benyon, Killeen; Murphy, Prosser; French, Dagnall, Watson, Hicks, Mantle, Laughton

Referee: L. Gant (Wakefield)

1966-67

Castleford 7 Edwards; Howe, Stenton, Willett (1g), Austin (1t); Hardisty, Hepworth (1g); Hartley, C. Dickinson, McCartney, Bryant, Small, Walker

Swinton 2 Gowers; Whitehead (1g), Gomersall, Buckley, Davies; Fleet, G. Williams; Halliwell, D. Clarke, Scott (Cummings), Rees, Simpson, Robinson

Referee: J. Manley (Warrington)

1967-68

Castleford 8 Edwards; Harris, Thomas, Stenton, Willett (4g); Hardisty, Hepworth; Hartley, J. Ward, Walton, Bryant (C. Dickinson), Redfearn, Reilly

Leigh 5 Grainey; Tickle (1t), Lewis, Collins, Walsh; Entwistle, A. Murphy; Whitworth, Ashcroft, Major, Welding, M. Murphy, Gilfedder (1g)

Referee: G.F. Lindop (Wakefield)

1968-69

Wigan 7 Tyrer (2g); Francis, Ashton, Ashurst, Rowe; C. Hill (1t), Jackson; J. Stephens, Clarke, Mills, Fogerty (Lyon), Kevin O'Loughlin, Laughton

St. Helens 4 Williams; Wilson, Benyon, Myler, Willis; Whittle, Bishop; Warlow, Sayer, Watson, Mantle, Hogan, Coslett (2g)

Referee: E. Clay (Leeds)

1969-70

Leigh 11 Ferguson (3g) (Lewis); Tickle (1t), Dorrington, Collins, Walsh; Eckersley, Murphy (1g); D. Chisnall, Ashcroft, Watts, Welding, Grimes, Lyon

Wigan 6 C. Hill; Wright, Francis (2g), Rowe, Kevin O'Loughlin; D. Hill (1g), Jackson; J. Stephens, Clarke, Ashcroft, Ashurst, Mills, Laughton

Referee: W.H. Thompson (Huddersfield)

1970-71

Leeds 9 Holmes (2g); Alan Smith, Hynes (1t, 1g), Cowan, Atkinson; Wainwright, Shoebottom; J. Burke, Fisher, Barnard, Haigh, Ramsey, Batten

St. Helens 5 F. Barrow; L. Jones (1t), Benyon, Walsh, Wilson; Whittle, Heaton; Rees, A. Karalius, E. Chisnall, Mantle, E. Prescott, Coslett (1g)

Referee: E. Lawrinson (Warrington)

1971-72

St. Helens 8 G. Pimblett; L. Jones, Benyon, Walsh, Wilson; Kelly, Heaton; Rees, A. Karalius, E. Chisnall, E. Prescott, Mantle, Coslett (4g)

Rochdale H. 2 Chamberlain (1g); Brelsford, Crellin, Taylor, Glover; Myler, Gartland; Birchall, P. Clarke, Brown, Welding, Sheffield (Hodkinson), Delooze

Referee: E. Clay (Leeds)

1972-73

Leigh 5 Hogan; Lawson (1t) (Lester), Atkin, Collins, Stacey; A. Barrow, Sayer (Ryding); Grimes, D. Clarke, Fletcher, Fiddler (1g), F. Barrow; Martyn

Widnes 0 Dutton; A. Prescott, Aspey, Blackwood, McDonnell; Lowe, Ashton; Mills, Elwell, Warlow, Foran, Sheridan, Nicholls

Referee: G.F. Lindop (Wakefield)

1973-74

Bramley 15 Keegan; Goodchild (1t), Bollon, Hughes, Austin (1t); T. Briggs, Ward (1g) (Ashman); D. Briggs, Firth, Cheshire, D. Sampson (1t), Idle, Wolford (2g)

Widnes 7 Dutton (2g); D. O'Neill, Hughes, Aspey, Macko (1t); Warburton, Bowden; Hogan, Elwell, Nelson, Sheridan, Blackwood (Foran) Laughton

Referee: D. G. Kershaw (York)

1974-75

Salford 0 Charlton; Fielding, Hesketh, Graham, Richards; Brophy (Taylor), Banner; Coulman, Devlin, Grice, Knighton, Dixon, E. Prescott

Warrington 0 Whitehead; Sutton, Cunliffe (Lowe), Whittle, Bevan; Briggs, Gordon; D. Chisnall, Ashcroft, Wright, Gaskell, Conroy, B. Philbin (Jewitt)

Referee: W.H. Thompson (Huddersfield)

Replay

Salford 10 Stead; Fielding (1t), Watkins (2g), Hesketh, Richards (1t); Gill, Banner; Grice, Walker, Mackay, Dixon, Knighton, E. Prescott

Warrington 5 Cunliffe; Whitehead (1g), Pickup, Whittle, Bevan (1t); Noonan (Briggs), Gordon; D. Chisnall, Ashcroft, Wanbon, Conroy, Nicholas (Brady), B. Philbin

Referee: W.H. Thompson (Huddersfield)

1975-76

St. Helens 22 G. Pimblett (2g); L. Jones, Benyon (1t), Hull (1t), Mathias (2t); Wilson (1t), Heaton (1dg); Mantle, A. Karalius, James, Nicholls, E. Chisnall, Coslett (1g)

Dewsbury 2 Langley; Hegarty, Chalkley, Simpson, Mitchell; N. Stephenson (1g) (Lee), A. Bates; Beverley, Price, Hankins, Halloran, (Artis), Bell, Grayshon

Referee: W.H. Thompson (Huddersfield)

1976-77
Castleford 12 Wraith; Fenton, Joyner, P. Johnson, Walsh (1t); Burton (1t), Stephens; Khan, Spurr, A. Dickinson, Reilly, Lloyd (3g), S. Norton
Leigh 4 Hogan; A. Prescott, Stacey, Woods, Walsh (1t); Taylor, Sayer; D. Chisnall, Ashcroft (1dg), Fletcher, Macko, Grimes, Boyd
Referee: J.E. Jackson (Pudsey)
1977-78
Hull K.R. 26 Hall (4g); Dunn (2t), M. Smith (1t), Watson, Sullivan (1t); Hartley (1t), Millward; Millington, Watkinson, Cunningham (Hughes), Lowe, Rose (1t), Casey
St. Helens 11 G. Pimblett (Platt); L. Jones (Courtney), Noonan, Cunningham (1t), Glynn (2t, 1g); Francis, K. Gwilliam; D. Chisnall, Liptrot, James, Hope, A. Karalius, Pinner
Referee: M. J. Naughton (Widnes)
1978-79
Widnes 13 Eckersley; Wright (2t), Hughes, Aspey, P. Shaw; Burke (2g, 1t), Bowden; Hogan, Elwell, Mills, Adams, Dearden, Laughton
St. Helens 7 G. Pimblett (2g), L. Jones, Glynn, Cunningham, Mathias; Francis, Holding; D. Chisnall (1t), Liptrot, James, Nicholls, Knighton (E. Chisnall), Pinner
Referee: J. McDonald (Wigan)
1979-80
Hull 13 Woods; Bray, G. Evans (1t), Coupland, Dennison (1t, 2g); Newlove, Hepworth; Tindall, Wileman, Farrar, Stone, Boxall (Birdsall 1t), Norton
Hull K.R. 3 Robinson; Hubbard (1t), M. Smith, Watson, Sullivan; Hall, Agar; Holdstock, Tyreman, Lockwood, Clarkson (Hartley), Lowe, Hogan (Millington)
Referee: W.H. Thompson (Huddersfield)

CAPTAIN MORGAN TROPHY

This sponsored competition, with a winners' prize of £3,000, lasted only one season. Entry was restricted to the 16 clubs who won their Yorkshire and Lancashire Cup first round ties. The Lancashire contingent was made up to eight by including the side which lost their first round county Cup-tie by the narrowest margin. The first round of the Captain Morgan Trophy was zoned with clubs being drawn against those in their own county. The remainder of the competition was integrated. The final was on a neutral ground as follows:

1973-74	Warrington	4	Featherstone R.	0	Salford	5,259	£2,265

1973-74
Warrington 4 Whitehead (2g); M. Philbin, Noonan, Reynolds (Pickup), Bevan; Whittle, Gordon; D. Chisnall, Ashcroft, Brady, Wanbon (Price), Wright, Mather
Featherstone R. 0 Box; Coventry, M. Smith, Hartley, Bray; Mason, Wood; Tonks, Bridges, Harris, Gibbins (Stone), Rhodes, Bell
Referee: G.F. Lindop (Wakefield)

Hull Kingston Rovers captain Len Casey lifts the Slalom Lager Championship Trophy.

LEAGUE

LEAGUE

1983-84 CHAMPIONSHIP

After winning only two of their opening six League matches, Hull Kingston Rovers dropped just three points from a possible 44 to lift the Slalom Lager Championship title.

Rovers clinched their second Championship in five years with a free-flowing 44-16 victory at Leigh in mid-April. Ironically, the Robins opened and closed the 1983-84 campaign with two defeats, overall recording 22 wins and two draws in the 30-match programme.

Boosted by the capture of Kiwi prop forward Mark Broadhurst and Australian stand off John Dorahy, Hull K.R. finished with the second highest scoring and the third best defensive records.

The Robins opened the League season with a 30-11 defeat at St. Helens, followed by a 26-14 home loss to Castleford. Victories at Craven Park over Wakefield Trinity and Widnes came before defeat at Warrington.

Thus it was September 25 before Rovers launched themselves onto the Championship trail with a home 18-18 draw against Oldham. A week later they pulled of a shock 23-8 derby victory at Hull .... the start of a 22-match run which was to bring them 41 points.

Rovers did not drop a point for four months until a 20-0 defeat at Bradford Northern at the start of February ended a winning run of 12 successive victories, just one short of equalling the Division One record sequence of wins by Widnes in 1981-82.

In the next nine matches, Hull K.R. dropped only one point — a superb 14-14 draw at Leeds — to win the title and £12,000 Slalom Lager prize money in their 28th League fixture, running in eight glorious tries at Leigh.

Unfortunately, the celebrations were dampened by a 36-16 home defeat by arch rivals Hull and a shock 20-16 reversal at home to injury-hit Leeds on the day of the trophy presentation.

Four clubs held the leading position in the Slalom Lager Championship during the season. Bradford Northern were table-toppers until the start of October when Castleford took over for a fortnight. Widnes then led for a month from late October, with Northern returning to the top for the whole of December. Rovers climbed into the number one slot on January 8 to maintain command for title success.

Hull clinched second place, having won the title in the previous season and finished second two years earlier.

At the other end of the table, the four clubs promoted 12 months earlier returned to the Second Division in the same order.

For bottom-placed Whitehaven, it was a record-breaking demotion. The Cumbrians did not record a League point until February 19 with a shock 42-8 home victory over Oldham.

The win ended a losing run of League matches at a Division One record of 20 successive defeats. They had also lost three cup ties during the sequence.

Ironically, the Oldham victory was Whitehaven's highest score in three seasons of First Division football, dating back to 1973-74. That first League success of the season started a three-out-of-four winning run, the other victories being at home to Fulham and at Wakefield Trinity .... the Cumbrians' only three League wins.

In the Second Division, Barrow made an immediate return to higher grade football in record fashion. The Shipbuilders were rarely off the top of the table, losing only two of their 34 League fixtures, away at fellow promoted clubs Workington Town and Hunslet.

On 18 occasions they ran up 30 or more points, including 80 at Kent Invicta, 66 at Doncaster, 64 at home to Batley and 58 at home to Carlisle. The final Barrow tally in the Second Division of 1,126 points and 196 tries were League records for either division.

The Second Division fixtures were disrupted

by Bramley being threatened by liquidation. The Villagers' fixtures were not fulfilled between October 16 and December 18 while the McLaren Field club's future was in the balance, a new board of directors eventually taking over. The club squeezed in 16 matches in the last two months of the campaign to finish in a creditable eighth place.

Newcomers Kent Invicta gained a 50 per cent success rate to gain ninth position in their first season, despite an early cash flow problem which saw the demise of their chairman Paul Faires.

Doncaster finished at the bottom of the table for the sixth time since 1975, coach Clive Sullivan quitting at the end of a disappointing season during which signs of improvement had been shown.

Unfashionable Huyton were in the news at both ends of the season. The Alt Park club backed up their pre-season confidence of promotion by putting £200 on special William Hill odds of 500-1 to gain a top four spot hoping to earn themselves a £100,000 promotion bonus.

They opened with a surprise 20-20 draw at Halifax but still had only five points by the start of February! However, the Merseysiders finished with a flourish by building up a sequence of six wins out of seven to amass a total of 20 League points, their highest tally for six years.

Cardiff City, in their third season of League football, broke new territory by staging a Second Division fixture at Ebbw Vale. The April 29 meeting with Huyton attracted 1,400 — double the normal Cardiff City attendance and was said to be a forerunner of more fixtures in the Valleys.

Hull K.R.'s £72,500 full back George Fairbairn outstrips Castleford centre Gary Hyde.

FINAL TABLES 1983-84

SLALOM LAGER CHAMPIONSHIP

					FOR				AGAINST				
	P.	W.	D.	L.	Dr.	Gls.	Trs.	Pts.	Dr.	Gls.	Trs.	Pts.	Pts.
Hull K.R.	30	22	2	6	5	115	140	795	3	77	66	421	46
Hull	30	22	1	7	3	120	147	831	5	70	64	401	45
Warrington	30	19	2	9	12	109	98	622	8	96	82	528	40
Castleford	30	18	3	9	2	122	110	686	4	85	66	438	39
Widnes	30	19	1	10	6	89	118	656	9	82	71	457	39
St. Helens	30	18	1	11	13	108	105	649	9	81	84	507	37
Bradford N.	30	17	2	11	13	83	85	519	9	63	61	379	36
Leeds	30	15	3	12	1	92	92	553	8	97	78	514	33
Wigan	30	16	0	14	3	103	81	533	7	75	77	465	32
Oldham	30	15	2	13	8	96	86	544	8	88	74	480	32
Leigh	30	14	0	16	3	108	101	623	7	94	101	599	28
Featherstone R.	30	11	2	17	14	85	70	464	10	82	97	562	24
Fulham	30	9	1	20	7	67	65	401	8	119	112	694	19
Wakefield T.	30	7	0	23	13	69	66	415	4	110	139	780	14
Salford	30	5	0	25	2	55	60	352	3	120	136	787	10
Whitehaven	30	3	0	27	3	51	55	325	6	133	171	956	6

SECOND DIVISION

					FOR				AGAINST				
	P.	W.	D.	L.	Dr.	Gls.	Trs.	Pts.	Dr.	Gls.	Trs.	Pts.	Pts.
Barrow	34	32	0	2	12	165	196	1126	8	48	57	332	64
Workington T.	34	24	2	8	8	107	123	714	18	89	77	504	50
Hunslet	34	24	0	10	10	151	147	900	15	107	92	597	48
Halifax	34	23	2	9	22	108	121	722	13	91	86	539	48
Blackpool B.	34	20	3	11	15	96	102	615	10	74	77	466	43
Swinton	34	21	0	13	20	116	128	764	11	67	73	437	42
York	34	19	2	13	7	122	123	743	14	100	89	570	40
Bramley	34	16	2	16	12	94	96	584	23	83	89	545	34
Kent Invicta	34	17	0	17	11	90	101	595	18	111	115	700	34
Huddersfield	34	15	3	16	10	79	108	600	17	96	84	545	33
Cardiff C.	34	15	1	18	28	107	117	710	17	118	116	717	31
Rochdale H.	34	13	3	18	25	101	81	551	11	116	106	667	29
Batley	34	13	0	21	11	77	78	477	22	108	125	738	26
Dewsbury	34	12	0	22	8	85	87	526	16	99	121	698	24
Carlisle	34	12	0	22	9	81	92	539	16	116	133	780	24
Huyton	34	9	2	23	19	66	70	431	10	105	135	760	20
Keighley	34	7	3	24	13	74	66	425	12	106	126	728	17
Doncaster	34	2	1	31	14	63	61	384	3	148	196	1083	5

Barrow captain Alan Hodkinson receives the Second Division Trophy and £7,000 prize money from Slalom Lager Sales Director Philip Lee.

TWO DIVISION CHAMPIONSHIP ROLL OF HONOUR

	FIRST DIVISION	SECOND DIVISION
1902-03	Halifax	Keighley
1903-04	Bradford	Wakefield Trinity
1904-05	Oldham	Dewsbury
1962-63	Swinton	Hunslet
1963-64	Swinton	Oldham
1973-74	Salford	Bradford Northern
1974-75	St. Helens	Huddersfield
1975-76	Salford	Barrow
1976-77	Featherstone Rovers	Hull
1977-78	Widnes	Leigh
1978-79	Hull Kingston Rovers	Hull
1979-80	Bradford Northern	Featherstone Rovers
1980-81	Bradford Northern	York
1981-82	Leigh	Oldham
1982-82	Hull	Fulham
1983-84	Hull Kingston Rovers	Barrow

THE UPS AND DOWNS OF TWO DIVISION FOOTBALL

*Figure in brackets indicates position in division.

	RELEGATED	PROMOTED
1902-03	St. Helens (17) Brighouse (18)	Keighley (1) Leeds (2)
1903-04	Keighley (17) Huddersfield (18)	Wakefield Trinity (1) St. Helens (2)
*1904-05	St. Helens (17) Runcorn (18)	Dewsbury (1) Barrow (2)
1962-63	Oldham (15) Bramley (16)	Hunslet (1) Keighley (2)
*1963-64	Keighley (15) Hull (16)	Oldham (1) Leigh (2)
1973-74	Oldham (13) Hull K.R. (14) Leigh (15) Whitehaven (16)	Bradford Northern (1) York (2) Keighley (3) Halifax (4)
1974-75	York (13) Bramley (14) Rochdale Hornets (15) Halifax (16)	Huddersfield (1) Hull K.R. (2) Oldham (3) Swinton (4)

1975-76	Dewsbury (13) Keighley (14) Huddersfield (15) Swinton (16)	Barrow (1) Rochdale Hornets (2) Workington T. (3) Leigh (4)
1976-77	Rochdale Hornets (13) Leigh (14) Barrow (15) Oldham (16)	Hull (1) Dewsbury (2) Bramley (3) New Hunslet (4)
1977-78	Hull (13) New Hunslet (14) Bramley (15) Dewsbury (16)	Leigh (1) Barrow (2) Rochdale Hornets (3) Huddersfield (4)
1978-79	Barrow (13) Featherstone Rovers (14) Rochdale Hornets (15) Huddersfield (16)	Hull (1) New Hunslet (2) York (3) Blackpool Borough (4)
1979-80	Wigan (13) Hunslet (14) York (15) Blackpool Borough (16)	Featherstone Rovers (1) Halifax (2) Oldham (3) Barrow (4)
1980-81	Halifax (13) Salford (14) Workington T. (15) Oldham (16)	York (1) Wigan (2) Fulham (3) Whitehaven (4)
1981-82	Fulham (13) Wakefield T. (14) York (15) Whitehaven (16)	Oldham (1) Carlisle (2) Workington T. (3) Halifax (4)
1982-83	Barrow (13) Workington T. (14) Halifax (15) Carlisle (16)	Fulham (1) Wakefield T. (2) Salford (3) Whitehaven (14)
1983-84	Fulham (13) Wakefield T. (14) Salford (15) Whitehaven (16)	Barrow (1) Workington T. (2) Hunslet (3) Halifax (4)

*Two divisions scrapped following season.

FIRST DIVISION RECORDS

Since reintroduction in 1973

INDIVIDUAL

Match records

Most tries:
5 Roy Mathias (St. Helens) v. Rochdale H. Feb 17, 1974
Roy Mathias (St. Helens) v. Workington T. Dec 23, 1979
Parry Gordon (Warrington) v. Dewsbury Mar 3, 1974
Peter Glynn (St. Helens) v. Hull Oct 16, 1977
Steve Fenton (Castleford) v. Dewsbury Jan 27, 1978
Steve Hartley (Hull K.R.) v. Huddersfield Apr 13, 1979
Kevin Meadows (Oldham) at Salford Apr 20, 1984

Most goals: 13 Geoff Pimblett (St. Helens) v. Bramley Mar 5, 1978

Most points: 34 (11g, 3t) Bob Beardmore (Castleford)) v. Leeds Oct 2, 1983

Season records

Most tries: 36 Keith Fielding (Salford) 1973-74
Most goals: 130 Steve Hesford (Warrington) 1978-79
Most points: 295 (101g, 1dg, 23t) John Woods (Leigh) 1983-84

TEAM

Highest score: St. Helens 71 v. Bramley 7 Mar 5, 1978 (Also widest margin)

Highest away score: Carlisle 8 v. Castleford 66 at Wakefield Apr 7, 1983 (Also widest margin)

In an orthodox away match:
Warrington won 58-32 at Fulham on Apr 15, 1984
Castleford won 47-2 at Halifax on Apr 14, 1983 (widest margin)

Most points by losing team:
Fulham 32 v. Warrington 58 Apr 15, 1984
Hull K.R. 54 v. Salford 32 Mar 18, 1984

Scoreless draw: Wigan 0 v. Castleford 0 Jan 26, 1974

Highest score draw: Widnes 28 v. St. Helens 28 Apr 23, 1984

Best opening sequence: 13 wins then a draw by Widnes 1981-82

Longest winning run: 13 by Widnes 1981-82

Longest unbeaten run: 16 by Widnes (won last 12 of 1973-74, drew first match of 1974-75 and won next three)

Longest losing run: 20 by Whitehaven 1983-84

Longest run without a win: 23, including 3 draws, by Whitehaven 1981-82 (Also worst opening sequence)

Biggest attendance: 20,569 Hull v. Hull K.R. Apr 7, 1983

100 Division One tries

165 Keith Fielding (Salford)
141 David Smith (Wakefield T., Leeds, Bradford N.)
136 Roy Mathias (St. Helens)
132 Stuart Wright (Wigan, Widnes)
129 John Bevan (Warrington)
124 Steve Hartley (Hull K.R.)
122 Maurice Richards (Salford)
115 David Topliss (Wakefield T., Hull)
102 Steve Evans (Featherstone R., Hull)
102 John Joyner (Castleford)
101 David Redfearn (Bradford N.)

500 Division One goals

841 Steve Hesford (Warrington)
625 George Fairbairn (Wigan, Hull K.R.)
625 Steve Quinn (Featherstone R.)
586 Sammy Lloyd (Castleford, Hull)
508 John Woods (Leigh)

1,000 Division points

1,748 Steve Hesford (Warrington)
1,364 Steve Quinn (Featherstone R.)
1,344 George Fairbairn (Wigan, Hull K.R.)
1,284 John Woods (Leigh)
1,264 Sammy Lloyd (Castleford, Hull)

20 Division One tries in a season

1973-74	36	Keith Fielding (Salford)
	29	Roy Mathias (St. Helens)
	21	David Smith (Wakefield T.)
1974-75	21	Maurice Richards (Salford)
	21	Roy Mathias (St. Helens)
1975-76	26	Maurice Richards (Salford)
	20	David Smith (Wakefield T.)
1976-77	22	David Topliss (Wakefield T.)
	21	Keith Fielding (Salford)
	21	Ged Dunn (Hull K.R.)
	20	David Smith (Leeds)
	20	Stuart Wright (Widnes)
1977-78	26	Keith Fielding (Salford)
	25	Steve Fenton (Castleford)
	24	Stuart Wright (Widnes)
	20	David Smith (Leeds)
	20	Bruce Burton (Castleford)
	20	John Bevan (Warrington)
1978-79	28	Steve Hartley (Hull K.R.)
1979-80	24	Keith Fielding (Salford)
	21	Roy Mathias (St. Helens)
	21	Steve Hubbard (Hull K.R.)
	20	David Smith (Leeds)
1980-81	20	Steve Hubbard (Hull K.R.)
1981-82		David Hobbs (Featherstone R.) was top scorer with 19 tries.
1982-83	22	Bob Eccles (Warrington)
	20	Steve Evans (Hull)
1983-84	28	Garry Schofield (Hull)
	23	John Woods (Leigh)
	20	James Leuluai (Hull)

Top Division One goalscorers
1973-74 126 David Watkins (Salford)
1974-75 96 Sammy Lloyd (Castleford)
1975-76 118 Sammy Lloyd (Castleford)
1976-77 113 Steve Quinn (Featherstone R.)
1977-78 116 Steve Hesford (Warrington)
1978-79 130 Steve Hesford (Warrington)
1979-80 104 Steve Hubbard (Hull K.R.)
1980-81 96 Steve Diamond (Wakefield T.)
1981-82 110 Steve Quinn (Featherstone R.)
John Woods (Leigh)
1982-83 105 Bob Beardmore (Castleford)
1983-84 106 Steve Hesford (Warrington)

Top Division One pointscorer 1983-84
295 (101g, 1dg, 23t) John Woods (Leigh)

SECOND DIVISION RECORDS
Since reintroduction in 1973

INDIVIDUAL

Match records
Most tries: 6 Ged Dunn (Hull K.R.) v. New Hunslet Feb 2, 1975
Most goals: 15 Mick Stacey (Leigh) v. Doncaster Mar 28, 1976
Most points: 38 (13g, 4t) John Woods (Leigh) v. Blackpool B. Sep 11, 1977

Season records
Most tries: 34 John Crossley (York) 1980-81
Most goals: 166 Lynn Hopkins (Workington T.) 1981-82
Most points: 395 (163g, 3dg, 22t) Lynn Hopkins (Workington T.) 1981-82

TEAM

Highest score (home and away): Kent Invicta 8 v. Barrow 80 Apr 8, 1984
(Also widest margin win with Leigh 75 v. Doncaster 3 Mar 28, 1976)

Most points by losing team:
Dewsbury 39 v. Carlisle 30 Oct 5, 1983
Hunslet 30 v. Blackpool B. 31 Dec 4, 1983
Workington T. 38 v. Cardiff C. 30 Apr 23, 1984

Highest score draw: Doncaster 30 v. Rochdale H. 30 Apr 6, 1980

Scoreless draw: Dewsbury 0 v. Rochdale H. 0. Jan 30, 1983

Longest winning run: Hull won all 26 matches in 1978-79

Longest losing run: 40 by Doncaster (16 in 1975-76 and 24 in 1976-77)

Biggest attendance: 12,424 Hull v. New Hunslet May 18, 1979

1983-84 Top scorers
Most tries: 27 Graham King (Hunslet)
Most goals: 119 Lyn Hallett (Cardiff C.)
Most points: 241 (108g, 9dg, 4t) Eric Fitzsimons (Hunslet)

NB. Division One and Two records do not include scores in abandoned matches that were replayed.

TWO DIVISION SCORING

A record total of tries for any two division era was scored last season, almost certainly the result of several rule changes. In particular, the hand over of the ball after a sixth successive tackle reduced the number of scrums and provided greater continuity of play. It is unlikely that the increased value of a try from three to four points had a significant effect.

The 1,479 tries scored in Division One last season were almost 100 more than the previous season and beat the record of 1,448 in 1978-79.

It was another indication of how the game has changed since the first two division era of 1902-05 when Division One clubs each played four more matches than they do now and yet scored only half as many tries.

A more interesting comparison is between the present era and that of 1962-63 and 1963-64. The unlimited tackle rule was still in force then but the tryscoring boom of the 1950s under a one league system was over.

The six-tackle rule, followed by a scrum, was in operation when the present two division era was introduced in 1973 and each season since has produced more tries than were scored under the old rule. Last season's change to the hand-over rule gave tryscoring a further boost, 235 more tries being scored in Division One than 20 years ago.

The number of drop goals per season has varied with a succession of rule changes since they were reduced to one point in 1974. Only 48 were scored in Division One during that season of devaluation but they grew to a peak of 147 in 1980-81. There was an unaccountable fall to 64 in 1982-83 before last season's hand-over rule pushed the total up to 108.

The fluctuating number of matches in Division Two make comparisons for the lower league difficult but the increased scoring rate is equally evident.

The tables at the bottom of page 186 show the scoring totals for each two division season.

ELEVEN SEASON TABLE

Widnes have retained their position as the most successful Division One side since the reintroduction of two divisions in 1973. Despite winning the Championship only once they head an 11-season table with 438 points from 330 matches.

The Chemics have remained in Division One throughout the period, a record shared by St. Helens, Leeds, Warrington and Castleford. Only three clubs have spent the entire 11 seasons in Division Two .... Batley, Huyton and Doncaster.

Bradford Northern, Hull and Leigh were all Division Two champions who went on to win the Division One Championship only a few seasons after promotion.

In contrast, Salford and Featherstone Rovers were Division One champions who were relegated after a few seasons, the latter becoming Division Two champions.

The highest place gained by a newly-promoted club is third by Hull in 1979-80 after winning the Division Two Championship with a 100 per cent record the previous season.

The records of the five clubs who have appeared in Division One throughout the 11 seasons are as follows:

	P	W	D	L	F	A	Pts
1. Widnes	330	212	14	104	5,472	3,739	438
2. St. Helens	330	208	14	108	5,979	4,012	430
3. Leeds	329	191	12	126	5,765	4,632	394
4. Warrington	330	183	13	134	5,112	4,386	379
5. Castleford	330	167	21	142	5,814	4,973	355

● Although Bradford Northern and Hull Kingston Rovers have had only 10 seasons in Division One they have earned more points than Castleford, Rovers gaining 377 and Northern 362.

DIVISION ONE

Season	Matches each club played	Goals	1-Point drop goals	Tries	Pts
1902-03	34	541	—	692	3,158
1903-04	34	568	—	796	3,524
1904-05	34	659	—	817	3,769
1962-63	30	1,269	—	1,144	5,970
1963-64	30	1,234	—	1,244	6,200
1973-74	30	1,508	—	1,295	6,901
1974-75	30	1,334	48	1,261	6,499
1975-76	30	1,498	53	1,331	7,042
1976-77	30[1]	1,435	91	1,423	7,230
1977-78	30[2]	1,402	99	1,443	7,232
1978-79	30	1,367	119	1,448	7,197
1979-80	30	1,389	131	1,349	6,956
1980-81	30	1,439	147	1,342	7,051
1981-82	30	1,486	132	1,354	7,166
1982-83	30	1,369	64	1,386	6,960
1983-84	30	1,472	108	1,479	8,968

[1] Salford & Leeds played 29 matches — their final match was abandoned and not replayed. This match was expunged from league records.

[2] Featherstone R. & Bradford N. played 29 matches — their final match was cancelled following Featherstone's strike.

DIVISION TWO

Season	Matches each club played	Goals	1-Point drop goals	Tries	Pts
1902-03	34	542	—	723	3,253
1903-04	32	510	—	786	3,378
1904-05	26[1]	369	—	516	2,286
1962-63	26	907	—	856	4,382
1963-64	24[2]	739	—	701	3,581
1973-74	26	1,054	—	955	4,973
1974-75	26	992	36	919	4,777
1975-76	26	1,034	49	963	5,006
1976-77	26	942	78	1,046	5,100
1977-78	26	976	86	1,020	5,098
1978-79	26	971	114	972	4,972
1979-80	26	1,046	106	1,069	5,405
1980-81	28	1,133	123	1,220	6,049
1981-82	32	1,636	150	1,589	8,189
1982-83	32	1,510	103	1,648	8,067
1983-84	34	1,782	254	1,897	11,406

[1] Birkenhead withdrew after 4 matches. These matches were expunged from league records.

[2] Bradford N. withdrew after 13 matches. These matches were expunged from league records.

TWO DIVISION FINAL TABLES

Three eras
1902-05, 1962-64, 1973-83

1902-03:

FIRST DIVISION

					FOR			AGAINST			
	P.	W.	D.	L.	G.	T.	Pts.	G.	T.	Pts.	Pts.
Halifax	34	23	3	8	32	45	199	17	17	85	49
Salford	34	20	5	9	32	60	244	26	26	130	45
Swinton	34	18	7	9	40	58	254	25	23	119	43
Runcorn	34	19	4	11	34	57	239	26	29	139	42
Broughton R.	34	17	7	10	33	52	222	20	19	97	41
Oldham	34	20	0	14	28	48	200	25	26	128	40
Bradford	34	16	5	13	35	50	220	31	33	161	37
Warrington	34	14	7	13	23	34	148	28	36	164	35
Hunslet	34	16	3	15	52	27	185	32	52	220	35
Hull	34	16	2	16	27	50	204	33	42	192	34
Batley	34	15	4	15	34	36	176	38	46	214	34
Leigh	34	12	5	17	32	24	136	26	42	178	29
Widnes	34	13	2	19	25	27	131	25	39	167	28
Hull K.R.	34	13	2	19	22	37	155	40	45	215	28
Huddersfield	34	13	2	19	13	30	116	32	44	196	28
Wigan	34	10	6	18	28	23	125	30	38	174	26
St. Helens	34	9	2	23	31	21	125	39	77	309	20
Brighouse R.	34	7	4	23	20	13	79	48	58	270	18

SECOND DIVISION

					FOR			AGAINST			
	P.	W.	D.	L.	G.	T.	Pts.	G.	T.	Pts.	Pts.
Keighley	34	27	2	5	51	56	270	16	20	92	56
Leeds	34	26	1	7	41	84	334	19	20	98	53
Millom	34	22	3	9	32	58	238	26	22	118	47
Rochdale H.	34	20	6	8	55	71	323	14	20	88	46
Holbeck	34	20	5	9	39	45	213	13	19	83	45
Barrow	34	22	0	12	31	56	230	31	26	140	44
Wakefield T.	34	18	2	14	43	59	263	32	44	196	38
Bramley	34	16	4	14	28	41	179	26	33	151	36
Birkenhead	34	14	6	14	25	25	125	22	32	140	34
Manningham	34	14	5	15	30	27	141	22	42	170	33
Lancaster	34	13	4	17	21	27	123	41	44	214	30
Normanton	34	12	4	18	38	28	160	30	56	228	28
York	34	11	4	19	21	23	111	29	44	190	26
South Shields	34	10	2	22	22	38	158	39	62	264	22
Castleford	34	9	4	21	21	21	105	47	58	268	22
Dewsbury	34	8	5	21	18	29	123	40	55	245	21
Morecambe	34	9	2	23	17	18	88	41	46	220	20
Stockport	34	5	1	28	9	17	69	54	80	348	11

1903-04:

FIRST DIVISION

					FOR			AGAINST			
	P.	W.	D.	L.	G.	T.	Pts.	G.	T.	Pts.	Pts.
Bradford	34	25	2	7	45	71	303	18	20	96	52
Salford	34	25	2	7	57	84	366	15	26	108	52
Broughton R.	34	21	4	9	33	80	306	29	28	142	46
Hunslet	34	22	1	11	50	50	250	20	39	157	45
Oldham	34	20	3	11	37	47	215	19	24	110	43
Leeds	34	19	5	10	29	51	211	20	35	145	43
Warrington	34	17	3	14	29	52	214	27	33	153	37
Hull K.R.	34	17	2	15	31	43	191	22	41	167	36
Halifax	34	14	3	17	25	25	125	32	28	148	31
Wigan	34	11	6	17	33	37	177	27	40	174	28
Swinton	34	12	4	18	23	31	139	34	49	215	28
Batley	34	12	3	19	23	31	139	44	51	241	27
Hull	34	12	3	19	23	34	148	48	54	258	27
Widnes	34	11	5	18	24	26	126	30	61	243	27
Leigh	34	10	5	19	27	40	174	41	56	250	25
Runcorn	34	11	2	21	29	31	151	40	55	245	24
Keighley	34	8	5	21	33	21	129	50	73	319	21
Huddersfield	34	10	0	24	17	42	160	52	83	353	20

CHAMPIONSHIP PLAY-OFF at Hanson Lane, Halifax

BRADFORD	1	1	5	SALFORD	0	0	0

SECOND DIVISION

					FOR			AGAINST			
	P.	W.	D.	L.	G.	T.	Pts.	G.	T.	Pts.	Pts.
Wakefield T.	32	27	1	4	70	83	389	9	17	57	55
St. Helens	32	23	3	6	47	78	328	21	21	105	49
Holbeck	32	24	1	7	38	60	256	21	26	120	49
Rochdale H.	32	22	2	8	41	79	319	13	26	104	46
York	32	20	1	11	41	54	244	17	21	97	41
Brighouse R.	32	19	3	10	21	50	192	26	28	136	41
Castleford	32	18	3	11	31	41	185	34	42	194	39
Bramley	32	16	4	12	32	39	181	30	40	180	36
Barrow	32	16	3	13	33	51	219	24	38	162	35
Pontefract	32	14	6	12	27	40	174	21	36	150	34
Dewsbury	32	12	3	17	25	45	185	20	55	205	27
Millom	32	12	2	18	25	45	185	34	47	209	26
Lancaster	32	8	2	22	15	33	129	42	69	291	18
Birkenhead	32	7	0	25	12	17	75	44	82	334	14
South Shields	32	6	1	25	16	36	140	42	84	336	13
Morecambe	32	5	3	24	12	16	72	46	65	287	13
Normanton	32	4	0	28	24	19	105	66	93	411	8

PROMOTION PLAY-OFF at Huddersfield

ST. HELENS	1	2	7	HOLBECK	0	0	0

1904-05:

FIRST DIVISION

	P.	W.	D.	L.	FOR G.	FOR T.	FOR Pts.	AGAINST G.	AGAINST T.	AGAINST Pts.	Pts.
Oldham	34	25	1	8	48	65	291	28	34	158	51
Bradford	34	23	2	9	39	72	294	24	36	156	48
Broughton R.	34	22	2	10	35	75	295	41	31	175	46
Leeds	34	20	4	10	35	54	232	30	30	150	44
Warrington	34	20	2	12	38	48	220	30	30	150	42
Salford	34	19	2	13	45	62	276	36	44	204	40
Wigan	34	18	1	15	34	54	230	36	41	195	37
Hull	34	15	4	15	37	50	224	41	44	214	34
Hunslet	34	16	1	17	60	40	240	39	46	216	33
Halifax	34	15	2	17	39	42	204	25	35	155	32
Leigh	34	14	3	17	21	41	165	34	47	209	31
Hull K.R.	34	15	0	19	43	38	200	35	50	220	30
Swinton	34	13	2	19	22	37	155	38	40	196	28
Wakefield T.	34	13	2	19	44	22	154	35	47	211	28
Batley	34	12	3	19	38	28	160	45	46	228	27
Widnes	34	13	1	20	22	28	128	44	64	280	27
St. Helens	34	9	1	24	33	34	168	51	83	351	19
Runcorn	34	7	1	26	26	27	133	47	69	301	15

SECOND DIVISION

	P.	W.	D.	L.	FOR G.	FOR T.	FOR Pts.	AGAINST G.	AGAINST T.	AGAINST Pts.	Pts.
Dewsbury	26	22	2	2	35	59	247	6	12	48	46
Barrow	26	22	0	4	35	72	286	10	16	68	44
York	26	18	3	5	32	47	205	14	16	76	39
Keighley	26	15	2	9	44	57	259	17	20	94	32
Huddersfield	26	14	2	10	33	55	231	19	35	143	30
Rochdale H.	26	11	4	11	23	36	154	26	31	145	26
Millom	26	12	0	14	23	31	139	25	41	173	24
Pontefract	26	10	1	15	39	26	156	26	41	175	21
Castleford	26	9	3	14	19	22	104	38	41	199	21
Normanton	26	9	1	16	18	23	105	42	48	228	19
Brighouse R.	26	8	1	17	21	23	111	26	39	169	17
Lancaster	26	8	1	17	17	24	106	37	61	257	17
Morecambe	26	7	2	17	14	20	88	40	64	272	16
Bramley	26	5	2	19	16	21	95	43	51	239	12
Birkenhead	4	0	0	4	0	0	0	9	25	93	0

Birkenhead resigned from the League after four games. These are not included in the league table.

1962-63:

FIRST DIVISION

	P.	W.	D.	L.	FOR G.	FOR T.	FOR Pts.	AGAINST G.	AGAINST T.	AGAINST Pts.	Pts.
Swinton	30	22	1	7	87	66	372	57	39	231	45
St. Helens	30	19	1	10	102	107	525	67	42	260	39
Widnes	30	19	1	10	68	63	325	74	51	301	39
Castleford	30	16	3	11	68	78	370	72	59	321	35
Wakefield T.	30	16	1	13	84	88	432	73	71	359	33
Warrington	30	15	2	13	80	77	391	77	61	337	32
Leeds	30	16	0	14	75	61	333	71	74	364	32
Wigan	30	14	2	14	91	98	476	81	77	393	30
Huddersfield	30	14	0	16	80	46	298	55	56	278	28
Hull K.R.	30	13	1	16	85	73	389	93	67	387	27
Featherstone R.	30	12	3	15	91	69	389	82	81	407	27
Workington T.	30	12	3	15	73	88	410	84	91	441	27
Halifax	30	13	1	16	75	68	354	90	79	417	27
Hull	30	10	2	18	71	70	352	99	88	462	22
Oldham	30	9	1	20	66	52	288	84	88	432	19
Bramley	30	9	0	21	73	40	266	110	120	580	18

SECOND DIVISION

	P.	W.	D.	L.	FOR G.	FOR T.	FOR Pts.	AGAINST G.	AGAINST T.	AGAINST Pts.	Pts.
Hunslet	26	22	0	4	89	110	508	50	38	214	44
Keighley	26	21	0	5	102	82	450	47	31	187	42
York	26	16	1	9	86	82	418	51	47	243	33
Blackpool B.	26	15	0	11	58	55	281	56	45	247	30
Rochdale H.	26	14	1	11	57	56	282	57	43	243	29
Barrow	26	14	0	12	82	83	413	68	48	280	28
Leigh	26	14	0	12	77	69	361	63	46	264	28
Batley	26	13	1	12	61	51	275	65	64	322	27
Whitehaven	26	12	2	12	60	66	318	66	58	306	26
Doncaster	26	10	0	16	53	59	283	64	67	329	20
Liverpool C.	26	9	1	16	39	27	159	65	66	328	19
Salford	26	8	1	17	50	57	271	83	92	442	17
Dewsbury	26	8	0	18	55	30	200	66	71	345	16
Bradford N.	26	2	1	23	38	29	163	106	140	632	5

1963-64:

FIRST DIVISION

					FOR			AGAINST			
	P.	W.	D.	L.	G.	T.	Pts.	G.	T.	Pts.	Pts.
Swinton	30	25	0	5	82	79	401	59	28	202	50
Wigan	30	21	2	7	100	110	530	72	50	294	44
St. Helens	30	20	1	9	86	82	418	52	54	266	41
Featherstone R.	30	18	1	11	94	99	485	71	74	364	37
Workington T.	30	18	1	11	74	96	436	70	64	332	37
Castleford	30	18	0	12	74	96	436	67	68	338	36
Wakefield T.	30	16	0	14	91	102	488	72	65	339	32
Halifax	30	15	1	14	70	76	368	83	74	388	31
Hull K.R.	30	15	0	15	89	90	448	70	76	368	30
Warrington	30	15	0	15	58	86	374	73	78	380	30
Hunslet	30	14	0	16	88	65	371	95	99	487	28
Widnes	30	13	0	17	67	68	338	73	80	386	26
Leeds	30	10	0	20	73	59	323	89	105	493	20
Huddersfield	30	10	0	20	66	44	264	76	87	413	20
Keighley	30	5	0	25	68	39	253	103	131	599	10
Hull	30	4	0	26	54	53	267	109	111	551	8

SECOND DIVISION

					FOR			AGAINST			
	P.	W.	D.	L.	G.	T.	Pts.	G.	T.	Pts.	Pts.
Oldham	24	21	1	2	101	102	508	39	30	168	43
Leigh	24	16	2	6	84	81	411	58	36	224	34
Dewsbury	24	15	2	7	55	43	239	47	42	220	32
Barrow	24	14	1	9	57	79	351	56	56	280	29
Bramley	24	14	0	10	66	56	300	65	42	256	28
Blackpool B.	24	12	1	11	52	65	299	60	61	303	25
York	24	12	0	12	58	67	317	56	46	250	24
Rochdale H.	24	8	1	15	43	41	209	53	55	271	17
Liverpool C.	24	8	1	15	43	38	200	48	55	261	17
Batley	24	8	0	16	51	24	174	62	60	304	16
Whitehaven	24	8	0	16	40	31	173	58	75	341	16
Salford	24	8	0	16	49	40	218	79	78	392	16
Doncaster	24	7	1	16	40	34	182	58	65	311	15

*Bradford Northern disbanded after playing 13 matches. They won one and lost 12. For 109, Against 284. These matches were declared null and void.

1973-74:

FIRST DIVISION

					FOR			AGAINST			
	P.	W.	D.	L.	G.	T.	Pts.	G.	T.	Pts.	Pts.
Salford	30	23	1	6	130	124	632	79	47	299	47
St. Helens	30	22	2	6	119	119	595	67	43	263	46
Leeds	30	20	1	9	100	118	554	90	66	378	41
Widnes	30	18	1	11	103	75	431	94	47	329	37
Warrington	30	16	1	13	99	72	414	82	68	368	33
Dewsbury	30	16	1	13	97	65	389	90	98	474	33
Wakefield T.	30	16	0	14	88	98	470	87	79	411	32
Featherstone	30	14	2	14	94	85	443	86	75	397	30
Castleford	30	12	4	14	96	76	420	93	75	411	28
Rochdale H.	30	13	2	15	89	67	379	95	75	415	28
Wigan	30	12	3	15	92	81	427	83	66	364	27
Bramley	30	11	3	16	73	66	344	101	85	457	25
Oldham	30	12	1	17	76	63	341	109	92	494	25
Hull K.R.	30	9	2	19	97	78	428	114	108	552	20
Leigh	30	7	0	23	76	58	326	131	131	655	14
Whitehaven	30	7	0	23	79	50	308	107	140	634	14

SECOND DIVISION

					FOR			AGAINST			
	P.	W.	D.	L.	G.	T.	Pts.	G.	T.	Pts.	Pts.
Bradford N.	26	24	0	2	140	109	607	49	41	221	48
York	26	21	0	5	96	79	429	51	39	219	42
Keighley	26	20	0	6	119	67	439	53	48	250	40
Halifax	26	18	0	8	77	102	460	65	56	298	36
Workington T.	26	17	0	9	89	81	421	77	52	310	34
Hull	26	16	0	10	93	93	465	68	40	256	32
Swinton	26	15	0	11	69	89	405	69	46	276	30
Batley	26	12	0	12	68	50	286	76	53	311	24
Barrow	26	11	0	15	47	40	214	51	63	291	22
Huddersfield	26	9	0	17	69	75	363	89	72	394	18
N. Hunslet	26	7	0	19	61	50	272	89	80	418	14
Blackpool B.	26	7	0	19	58	52	272	111	121	585	14
Doncaster	26	3	0	23	25	36	158	117	150	684	6
Huyton	26	2	0	24	43	32	182	89	94	460	4

1974-75

FIRST DIVISION

					FOR				AGAINST				
	P.	W.	D.	L.	Dr.	Gls.	Trs.	Pts.	Dr.	Gls.	Trs.	Pts.	Pts.
St. Helens	30	26	1	3	-	108	115	561	3	59	36	229	53
Wigan	30	21	0	9	1	102	104	517	4	74	63	341	42
Leeds	30	19	1	10	2	90	133	581	4	80	65	359	39
Featherstone R.	30	19	1	10	4	89	83	431	2	68	67	339	39
Widnes	30	18	1	11	2	67	82	382	4	59	61	305	37
Warrington	30	17	1	12	6	85	84	428	8	84	60	356	35
Bradford N.	30	16	1	13	4	79	77	393	7	81	69	376	33
Castleford	30	14	3	13	2	101	92	480	2	94	79	427	31
Salford	30	14	1	15	-	83	95	451	4	76	65	351	29
Wakefield T.	30	12	5	13	3	97	81	440	1	80	86	419	29
Keighley	30	13	0	17	4	73	50	300	3	80	87	424	26
Dewsbury	30	11	0	19	9	85	57	350	1	89	109	506	22
York	30	10	0	20	5	93	56	359	1	94	103	498	20
Bramley	30	9	0	21	2	69	66	338	4	108	91	493	18
Rochdale H.	30	8	0	22	4	58	33	219	1	90	73	400	16
Halifax	30	5	1	24	1	56	52	269	-	119	146	676	11

SECOND DIVISION

					FOR				AGAINST				
	P.	W.	D.	L.	Dr.	Gls.	Trs.	Pts.	Dr.	Gls.	Trs.	Pts.	Pts.
Huddersfield	26	21	0	5	5	104	92	489	3	48	38	213	42
Hull K.R.	26	20	1	5	2	106	138	628	4	61	41	249	41
Oldham	26	19	0	7	4	84	78	406	1	57	36	223	38
Swinton	26	17	1	8	2	95	69	399	3	55	47	254	35
Workington T.	26	16	0	10	3	88	64	371	1	62	50	275	32
Whitehaven	26	14	1	11	1	58	56	285	3	48	45	234	29
Huyton	26	12	2	12	3	68	54	301	1	52	62	291	26
Hull	26	12	1	13	-	58	76	344	5	80	48	309	25
Barrow	26	12	2	13	5	69	65	338	2	59	65	315	24
Leigh	26	11	1	14	-	73	52	302	7	76	63	340	23
New Hunslet	26	10	2	14	4	67	57	309	1	73	79	384	22
Blackpool B.	26	7	1	18	7	49	52	261	3	84	82	417	15
Batley	26	4	1	21	-	43	37	197	2	106	102	520	9
Doncaster	26	1	1	24	-	30	29	147	-	131	161	745	3

1975-76

FIRST DIVISION

					FOR				AGAINST				
	P.	W.	D.	L.	Dr.	Gls.	Trs.	Pts.	Dr.	Gls.	Trs.	Pts.	Pts.
Salford	30	22	1	7	4	112	109	555	1	74	67	350	45
Featherstone R.	30	21	2	7	3	101	107	526	2	80	62	348	44
Leeds	30	21	0	9	5	112	114	571	5	99	64	395	42
St. Helens	30	19	1	10	2	110	97	513	7	79	50	315	39
Wigan	30	18	3	9	2	109	98	514	5	89	72	399	39
Widnes	30	18	1	11	5	100	81	448	7	73	72	369	37
Wakefield T.	30	17	0	13	2	112	90	496	2	84	80	410	34
Hull K.R.	30	17	0	13	4	89	88	446	3	101	89	472	34
Castleford	30	16	1	13	-	128	111	589	2	90	72	398	33
Warrington	30	15	2	13	2	80	73	381	3	87	93	456	32
Bradford N.	30	13	1	16	1	90	91	454	5	95	85	450	27
Oldham	30	11	1	18	5	81	71	380	1	105	93	490	23
Dewsbury	30	10	1	19	7	65	50	287	2	91	100	484	21
Keighley	30	7	0	23	8	70	42	274	-	93	94	468	14
Huddersfield	30	5	0	25	3	80	69	370	4	136	127	657	10
Swinton	30	3	0	27	-	59	40	238	4	122	111	581	6

SECOND DIVISION

					FOR				AGAINST				
	P.	W.	D.	L.	Dr.	Gls.	Trs.	Pts.	Dr.	Gls.	Trs.	Pts.	Pts.
Barrow	26	20	3	3	3	87	63	366	4	46	39	213	43
Rochdale H.	26	19	3	4	4	86	57	347	1	41	39	200	41
Workington T.	26	18	4	4	5	104	102	519	1	52	41	228	40
Leigh	26	19	1	6	2	112	115	571	3	59	32	217	39
Hull	26	19	1	6	5	94	128	577	2	69	46	278	39
New Hunslet	26	15	1	10	6	88	63	371	6	70	54	308	31
York	26	12	1	13	1	88	90	447	10	90	68	394	25
Bramley	26	11	1	14	1	77	63	344	6	77	70	370	23
Huyton	26	10	0	16	3	55	43	242	2	70	77	373	20
Whitehaven	26	8	2	16	4	45	53	253	3	64	72	347	18
Halifax	26	7	1	18	1	66	63	322	2	88	94	460	15
Batley	26	6	1	19	8	53	38	228	4	94	80	432	13
Blackpool B.	26	6	1	19	6	40	46	224	1	84	97	460	13
Doncaster	26	2	0	24	-	39	39	195	4	130	154	726	4

1976-77

FIRST DIVISION

					FOR				AGAINST				
	P.	W.	D.	L.	Dr.	Gls.	Trs.	Pts.	Dr.	Gls.	Trs.	Pts.	Pts.
Featherstone R.	30	21	2	7	10	114	110	568	4	78	58	334	44
St. Helens	30	19	1	10	7	108	108	547	5	80	60	345	39
Castleford	30	19	1	10	3	111	98	519	5	72	67	350	39
Hull K.R.	30	18	1	11	2	91	104	496	7	99	70	415	37
Warrington	30	18	0	12	11	115	97	532	9	71	85	406	36
Salford	*29	17	1	11	2	111	112	560	8	80	78	402	35
Wigan	30	15	2	13	2	88	95	463	3	91	77	416	32
Bradford N.	30	15	2	13	10	83	104	488	2	102	88	470	32
Leeds	*29	14	2	13	4	80	101	467	10	81	89	439	30
Widnes	30	15	0	15	3	77	82	403	7	85	72	393	30
Wakefield T.	30	13	2	15	4	93	99	487	3	87	101	480	28
Workington T.	30	13	1	16	13	78	61	352	10	72	83	403	27
Rochdale H.	30	11	0	19	8	91	59	367	5	93	86	449	22
Leigh	30	8	1	21	5	69	57	314	6	116	132	634	17
Barrow	30	8	0	22	5	68	68	345	4	114	132	628	16
Oldham	30	7	0	23	2	58	68	322	3	114	145	666	14

**The Salford v. Leeds match was abandoned after a fatal injury to Chris Sanderson (Leeds) and not replayed. Leeds were winning 5-2 after 38 mins. but the match was declared null and void.*

SECOND DIVISION

					FOR				AGAINST				
	P.	W.	D.	L.	Dr.	Gls.	Trs.	Pts.	Dr.	Gls.	Trs.	Pts.	Pts.
Hull	26	22	1	3	7	95	134	599	7	45	47	238	45
Dewsbury	26	19	2	5	14	71	91	429	4	42	37	199	40
Bramley	26	19	0	7	3	88	95	464	11	69	76	377	38
New Hunslet	26	17	3	6	9	81	80	411	8	50	41	231	37
York	26	17	0	9	6	67	94	422	6	60	51	279	34
Keighley	26	16	1	9	2	98	96	486	4	51	43	235	33
Huddersfield	26	13	0	13	4	69	85	397	9	61	66	329	26
Whitehaven	26	11	1	14	5	54	59	290	6	65	70	346	23
Huyton	26	11	0	15	4	56	62	302	8	65	88	402	22
Halifax	26	10	0	16	2	64	57	301	2	74	93	429	20
Swinton	26	8	2	16	4	52	51	261	5	82	79	406	18
Batley	26	7	1	18	6	56	48	262	3	88	94	461	15
Blackpool B.	26	5	1	20	10	44	45	233	5	81	99	464	11
Doncaster	26	1	0	25	2	47	49	243	-	109	162	704	2

1977-78

FIRST DIVISION

					FOR				AGAINST				
	P.	W.	D.	L.	Dr.	Gls.	Trs.	Pts.	Dr.	Gls.	Trs.	Pts.	Pts.
Widnes	30	24	2	4	2	103	135	613	7	51	44	241	50
**Bradford N.	29	21	2	6	4	92	104	500	4	64	53	291	44
St. Helens	30	22	1	7	6	123	142	678	5	74	77	384	45
Hull K.R.	30	16	3	11	5	98	98	495	8	87	79	419	35
Wigan	30	17	1	12	11	84	101	482	8	89	83	435	35
Salford	30	16	0	14	7	89	95	470	8	87	88	446	32
Featherstone R.	29	15	2	12	2	84	91	443	5	81	95	452	32
Leeds	30	15	1	14	8	99	102	512	10	93	88	460	31
Warrington	30	15	0	15	7	121	104	561	13	81	64	367	30
Castleford	30	13	2	15	1	95	108	515	5	112	118	583	28
Workington T.	30	11	4	15	7	96	69	406	9	96	106	519	26
Wakefield T.	30	12	1	17	9	87	70	393	4	82	94	450	25
Hull	30	10	3	17	8	64	74	358	5	83	103	480	23
New Hunslet	30	11	0	19	9	72	55	318	6	97	106	518	22
Bramley	30	5	4	21	4	56	55	281	2	117	124	608	14
Dewsbury	30	2	2	26	9	39	40	207	-	108	121	579	6

**Bradford N. second on percentage as last game was cancelled following Featherstone's strike.

SECOND DIVISION

					FOR				AGAINST				
	P.	W.	D.	L.	Dr.	Gls.	Trs.	Pts.	Dr.	Gls.	Trs.	Pts.	Pts.
Leigh	26	21	0	5	10	114	100	538	5	44	46	231	42
Barrow	26	21	0	5	4	89	113	521	6	45	46	234	42
Rochdale H.	26	21	0	5	2	96	81	437	7	38	39	200	42
Huddersfield	26	18	0	8	3	89	107	502	5	65	63	324	36
York	26	16	2	8	4	88	89	447	9	62	51	286	34
Oldham	26	17	0	9	3	79	86	419	5	70	60	325	34
Keighley	26	11	3	12	5	59	78	357	8	70	63	337	25
Swinton	26	11	1	14	5	68	76	369	2	82	73	385	23
Whitehaven	26	10	2	14	6	53	55	277	10	65	62	326	22
Huyton	26	9	2	15	13	42	51	250	8	67	70	352	20
Doncaster	26	9	0	17	5	67	55	304	6	99	108	528	18
Batley	26	5	1	20	8	42	47	233	7	96	99	496	11
Blackpool B.	26	5	1	20	17	55	45	262	2	86	123	543	11
Halifax	26	2	0	24	1	35	37	182	6	87	117	531	4

1978-79

FIRST DIVISION

					FOR				AGAINST				
	P.	W.	D.	L.	Dr.	Gls.	Trs.	Pts.	Dr.	Gls.	Trs.	Pts.	Pts.
Hull K.R.	30	23	0	7	9	107	131	616	7	65	69	344	46
Warrington	30	22	0	8	14	123	87	521	5	67	67	340	44
Widnes	30	21	2	7	11	92	95	480	3	68	61	322	44
Leeds	30	19	1	10	6	96	119	555	12	77	68	370	39
St. Helens	30	16	2	12	10	92	97	485	13	75	72	379	34
Wigan	30	16	1	13	6	83	104	484	10	73	85	411	33
Castleford	30	16	1	13	4	85	108	498	14	91	91	469	33
Bradford N.	30	16	0	14	3	89	114	523	7	89	77	416	32
Workington T.	30	13	3	14	10	82	68	378	11	71	64	345	29
Wakefield T.	30	13	1	16	10	63	82	382	3	75	101	456	27
Leigh	30	13	1	16	12	80	78	406	7	96	112	535	27
Salford	30	11	2	17	3	76	78	389	6	78	91	435	24
Barrow	30	9	2	19	8	72	72	368	2	96	114	536	20
Featherstone R.	30	8	1	21	3	108	94	501	8	107	109	549	17
Rochdale H.	30	8	0	22	7	64	54	297	4	108	115	565	16
Huddersfield	30	7	1	22	3	55	67	314	7	131	152	725	15

SECOND DIVISION

					FOR				AGAINST				
	P.	W.	D.	L.	Dr.	Gls.	Trs.	Pts.	Dr.	Gls.	Trs.	Pts.	Pts.
Hull	26	26	0	0	1	133	145	702	7	45	26	175	52
New Hunslet	26	21	1	4	15	83	91	454	7	56	33	218	43
York	26	17	1	8	7	85	83	426	6	74	63	343	35
Blackpool B.	26	15	3	8	36	69	49	321	7	56	51	272	33
Halifax	26	15	2	9	8	62	60	312	7	40	37	198	32
Dewsbury	26	15	0	11	4	77	70	368	7	57	57	292	30
Keighley	26	12	2	12	6	75	67	357	14	61	54	298	26
Bramley	26	12	1	13	2	71	77	375	10	61	70	342	25
Oldham	26	10	1	15	7	55	60	297	6	84	87	435	21
Whitehaven	26	8	3	15	5	59	58	297	15	72	83	408	19
Swinton	26	7	2	17	1	63	74	349	13	83	91	452	16
Doncaster	26	7	0	19	4	48	53	259	3	98	116	547	14
Huyton	26	3	3	20	10	49	51	261	8	95	105	513	9
Batley	26	4	1	21	8	42	34	194	4	89	99	479	9

1979-80

FIRST DIVISION

	P.	W.	D.	L.	FOR Dr.	FOR Gls.	FOR Trs.	FOR Pts.	AGAINST Dr.	AGAINST Gls.	AGAINST Trs.	AGAINST Pts.	Pts.
Bradford N.	30	23	0	7	11	79	93	448	11	57	49	272	46
Widnes	30	22	1	7	14	95	114	546	11	63	52	293	45
Hull	30	18	3	9	3	83	95	454	1	65	63	326	39
Salford	30	19	1	10	11	107	90	495	7	71	75	374	39
Leeds	30	19	0	11	6	94	132	590	7	85	71	390	38
Leigh	30	16	1	13	7	93	86	451	10	85	58	354	33
Hull K.R.	30	16	1	13	8	111	103	539	10	87	87	445	33
St. Helens	30	15	2	13	7	93	104	505	15	82	77	410	32
Warrington	30	15	2	13	7	92	57	362	10	76	65	357	32
Wakefield T.	30	14	2	14	9	90	82	435	10	87	95	466	30
Castleford	30	13	2	15	1	96	91	466	9	98	90	475	28
Workington	30	12	2	16	7	85	57	348	11	95	94	483	26
Wigan	30	9	3	18	9	78	67	366	6	101	105	523	21
Hunslet	30	7	1	22	16	75	60	346	5	107	103	528	15
York	30	6	1	23	5	71	76	375	2	120	135	647	13
Blackpool B.	30	5	0	25	10	47	42	230	6	110	129	613	10

SECOND DIVISION

	P.	W.	D.	L.	FOR Dr.	FOR Gls.	FOR Trs.	FOR Pts.	AGAINST Dr.	AGAINST Gls.	AGAINST Trs.	AGAINST Pts.	Pts.
Featherstone R.	26	21	2	3	8	145	142	724	6	59	52	280	44
Halifax	26	19	3	4	14	91	89	463	11	50	34	213	41
Oldham	26	19	3	4	7	103	100	513	9	57	51	276	41
Barrow	26	18	1	7	9	102	123	582	12	59	50	280	37
Whitehaven	26	15	1	10	11	73	80	397	6	51	56	276	31
Dewsbury	26	13	2	11	6	78	82	408	8	70	65	343	28
Rochdale H.	26	9	5	12	8	68	57	315	6	71	75	373	23
Swinton	26	11	1	14	8	70	61	331	5	82	89	436	23
Batley	26	10	2	14	10	48	42	232	3	83	67	370	22
Bramley	26	10	1	15	9	60	67	330	12	77	95	451	21
Keighley	26	10	0	16	5	68	67	342	12	69	82	396	20
Huddersfield	26	10	0	16	2	59	81	363	10	88	79	423	20
Huyton	26	5	0	21	6	40	41	209	3	105	114	555	10
Doncaster	26	1	1	24	3	41	37	196	3	125	160	733	3

1980-81

SLALOM LAGER CHAMPIONSHIP

					FOR				AGAINST				
	P.	W.	D.	L.	Dr.	Gls.	Trs.	Pts.	Dr.	Gls.	Trs.	Pts.	Pts.
Bradford N.	30	20	1	9	15	87	86	447	7	73	64	345	41
Warrington	30	19	1	10	6	108	79	459	10	76	56	330	39
Hull K.R.	30	18	2	10	10	101	99	509	11	95	69	408	38
Wakefield T.	30	18	2	10	13	105	107	544	5	91	89	454	38
Castleford	30	18	2	10	3	101	107	526	6	102	83	459	38
Widnes	30	16	2	12	5	84	85	428	11	72	67	356	34
Hull	30	17	0	13	13	84	87	442	10	88	88	450	34
St. Helens	30	15	1	14	8	92	91	465	14	76	68	370	31
Leigh	30	14	1	15	13	92	73	416	12	81	80	414	29
Leeds	30	14	0	16	5	64	85	388	7	100	87	468	28
Barrow	30	13	0	17	7	76	82	405	12	87	104	498	26
Featherstone R.	30	12	0	18	16	95	87	467	11	93	83	446	24
Halifax	30	11	0	19	18	89	63	385	1	82	95	450	22
Salford	30	10	1	19	7	98	90	473	8	112	117	583	21
Workington T.	30	9	3	18	5	72	62	335	14	103	79	457	21
Oldham	30	7	2	21	3	91	59	362	8	108	113	563	16

SECOND DIVISION

					FOR				AGAINST				
	P.	W.	D.	L.	Dr.	Gls.	Trs.	Pts.	Dr.	Gls.	Trs.	Pts.	Pts.
York	28	23	0	5	7	117	136	649	6	69	61	331	46
Wigan	28	20	3	5	1	103	130	597	7	62	54	293	43
Fulham	28	20	0	8	11	77	94	447	12	48	43	237	40
Whitehaven	28	19	1	8	21	71	82	409	13	45	49	250	39
Huddersfield	28	18	1	9	4	73	93	429	5	58	63	310	37
Swinton	28	17	2	9	3	88	87	440	16	50	62	302	36
Keighley	28	14	1	13	21	92	80	445	11	95	100	501	29
Hunslet	28	13	1	14	3	81	94	447	6	80	88	430	27
Bramley	28	13	1	14	5	79	90	433	6	81	89	431	27
Rochdale H.	28	13	0	15	14	76	80	406	9	77	85	418	26
Batley	28	12	0	16	13	81	51	328	4	82	79	405	24
Dewsbury	28	11	1	16	10	69	66	346	13	72	69	364	23
Doncaster	28	5	0	23	5	58	43	250	4	96	122	562	10
Blackpool B.	28	4	1	23	5	30	49	212	10	83	81	419	9
Huyton	28	2	0	26	0	38	45	211	1	135	175	796	4

1981-82

SLALOM LAGER CHAMPIONSHIP

	P.	W.	D.	L.	FOR Dr.	FOR Gls.	FOR Trs.	FOR Pts.	AGAINST Dr.	AGAINST Gls.	AGAINST Trs.	AGAINST Pts.	Pts.
Leigh	30	24	1	5	17	126	101	572	7	72	64	343	49
Hull	30	23	1	6	7	125	118	611	10	64	45	273	47
Widnes	30	23	1	6	7	98	116	551	7	68	58	317	47
Hull K.R.	30	22	1	7	14	112	109	565	5	79	52	319	45
Bradford N.	30	20	1	9	13	80	84	425	11	69	61	332	41
Leeds	30	17	1	12	3	95	107	514	9	95	73	418	35
St. Helens	30	17	1	12	11	89	92	465	8	85	79	415	35
Warrington	30	14	2	14	4	102	65	403	11	107	81	468	30
Barrow	30	13	0	17	6	84	78	408	11	76	94	445	26
Featherstone R.	30	12	1	17	5	111	85	482	8	106	91	493	25
Wigan	30	12	0	18	6	86	82	424	9	102	74	435	24
Castleford	30	10	1	19	4	109	88	486	10	108	93	505	21
Fulham	30	9	1	20	7	80	66	365	11	114	100	539	19
Wakefield T.	30	9	1	20	14	69	63	341	7	102	105	526	19
York	30	4	2	24	6	75	58	330	2	144	161	773	10
Whitehaven	30	2	3	25	8	45	42	224	6	95	123	565	7

SECOND DIVISION

	P.	W.	D.	L.	FOR Dr.	FOR Gls.	FOR Trs.	FOR Pts.	AGAINST Dr.	AGAINST Gls.	AGAINST Trs.	AGAINST Pts.	Pts.
Oldham	32	30	0	2	2	147	146	734	11	71	41	276	60
Carlisle	32	28	0	4	7	114	138	649	8	66	52	296	56
Workington T.	32	24	0	8	7	163	148	777	11	69	54	311	48
Halifax	32	22	0	10	19	97	101	516	12	68	64	340	44
Salford	32	20	1	11	0	130	132	656	10	78	89	433	41
Hunslet	32	18	1	13	4	102	91	481	11	87	89	452	37
Keighley	32	18	0	14	18	95	102	514	8	86	82	426	36
Cardiff C.	32	17	1	14	7	110	113	566	11	116	102	549	35
Dewsbury	32	16	0	16	21	78	60	357	10	89	92	464	32
Swinton	32	15	0	17	13	102	99	514	10	81	82	418	30
Huddersfield	32	13	1	18	4	63	80	370	11	100	104	523	27
Bramley	32	13	0	19	6	66	81	381	8	104	99	513	26
Rochdale H.	32	10	1	21	7	87	60	361	9	101	91	484	21
Batley	32	8	0	24	12	90	55	357	7	128	111	596	16
Blackpool B.	32	7	0	25	5	54	76	341	7	116	123	608	14
Doncaster	32	5	1	26	17	76	50	319	4	147	165	793	11
Huyton	32	5	0	27	1	62	57	296	1	128	150	707	10

1982-83

SLALOM LAGER CHAMPIONSHIP

					FOR				AGAINST				
	P.	W.	D.	L.	Dr.	Gls.	Trs.	Pts.	Dr.	Gls.	Trs.	Pts.	Pts.
Hull	30	23	1	6	3	97	125	572	5	63	54	293	47
Hull K.R.	30	21	1	8	6	89	104	496	4	67	46	276	43
Wigan	30	20	3	7	5	90	99	482	5	50	55	270	43
St. Helens	30	19	1	10	14	89	108	516	3	79	78	395	39
Widnes	30	18	2	10	3	93	115	534	5	83	62	357	38
Leeds	30	18	2	10	2	86	102	480	7	92	84	443	38
Castleford	30	18	1	11	1	125	126	629	2	93	90	458	37
Oldham	30	15	2	13	3	77	63	346	2	75	56	320	32
Bradford N.	30	14	2	14	8	80	71	381	7	59	63	314	30
Leigh	30	13	3	14	3	103	93	488	7	71	75	374	29
Warrington	30	13	2	15	3	99	74	423	3	82	81	410	28
Featherstone R.	30	10	4	16	2	75	66	350	6	93	85	447	24
Barrow	30	11	1	18	3	89	97	472	1	90	108	505	23
Workington T.	30	6	2	22	0	72	58	318	2	125	148	696	14
Halifax	30	5	1	24	6	55	35	221	4	112	141	651	11
Carlisle	30	2	0	28	2	50	50	252	1	135	160	751	4

SECOND DIVISION

					FOR				AGAINST				
	P.	W.	D.	L.	Dr.	Gls.	Trs.	Pts.	Dr.	Gls.	Trs.	Pts.	Pts.
Fulham	32	27	1	4	4	124	149	699	4	67	52	294	55
Wakefield T.	32	25	2	5	7	115	145	672	3	81	72	381	52
Salford	32	24	0	8	1	131	141	686	4	67	75	363	48
Whitehaven	32	20	3	9	5	78	101	464	10	54	60	298	43
Bramley	32	20	1	11	4	101	118	560	9	69	74	369	41
Hunslet	32	17	5	10	8	109	109	553	5	97	83	448	39
Swinton	32	19	1	12	9	105	110	549	7	81	95	454	39
Cardiff C.	32	17	2	13	10	110	114	572	11	86	87	444	36
Keighley	32	15	5	12	6	94	92	470	12	75	87	423	35
York	32	15	0	17	5	92	109	516	4	86	93	455	30
Blackpool B.	32	13	1	18	4	70	79	381	7	84	86	433	27
Huddersfield	32	13	1	18	1	60	92	397	9	100	105	524	27
Rochdale H.	32	10	5	17	9	65	74	361	2	88	97	469	25
Dewsbury	32	8	1	23	8	58	67	325	7	91	106	507	17
Batley	32	6	1	25	6	73	51	305	6	124	155	719	13
Huyton	32	6	0	26	5	52	47	250	3	117	150	687	12
Doncaster	32	2	1	29	11	73	50	307	0	143	171	799	5

CHAMPIONSHIP PLAY-OFFS

Following the breakaway from the English Rugby Union, 22 clubs formed the Northern Rugby Football League. Each club played 42 matches and Manningham won the first Championship as league leaders in 1895-96.

This format was then abandoned and replaced by the Yorkshire Senior and Lancashire Senior Combination leagues until 1901-02 when 14 clubs broke away to form the Northern Rugby League with Broughton Rangers winning the first Championship.

The following season two divisions were formed with the Division One title going to Halifax (1902-03), Bradford (1903-04), who won a play-off against Salford 5-0 at Halifax after both teams tied with 52 points, and Oldham (1904-05).

In 1905-06 the two divisions were merged with Leigh taking the Championship as league leaders. They won the title on a percentage basis as the 31 clubs did not play the same number of matches. The following season the top four play-off was introduced as a fairer means of deciding the title.

The top club played the fourth-placed, the second meeting the third, with the higher club having home advantage. The final was staged at a neutral venue.

It was not until 1930-31 that all clubs played the same number of league matches, but not all against each other, the top four play-off being a necessity until the reintroduction of two divisions in 1962-63.

This spell of two division football lasted only two seasons and the restoration of the Championship table brought about the introduction of a top-16 play-off, this format continuing until the reappearance of two divisions in 1973-74.

Since then the Championship Trophy has been awarded to the leaders of the First Division, with the Second Division champions receiving a silver bowl.

Slalom Lager launched a three-year sponsorship deal of the Championship and the Premiership in 1980-81 in a £215,000 package, extending the deal for another three years from 1983-84 for £270,000.

CHAMPIONSHIP PLAY-OFF FINALS

Season	*Winners*		*Runners-up*		*Venue*	*Attendance*	*Receipts*
Top Four Play-Offs							
1906-07	Halifax	18	Oldham	3	Huddersfield	13,200	£722
1907-08	Hunslet	7	Oldham	7	Salford	14,000	£690
Replay	Hunslet	12	Oldham	2	Wakefield	14,054	£800
1908-09	Wigan	7	Oldham	3	Salford	12,000	£630
1909-10	Oldham	13	Wigan	7	Broughton	10,850	£520
1910-11	Oldham	20	Wigan	7	Broughton	15,543	£717
1911-12	Huddersfield	13	Wigan	5	Halifax	15,000	£591
1912-13	Huddersfield	29	Wigan	2	Wakefield	17,000	£914
1913-14	Salford	5	Huddersfield	3	Leeds	8,091	£474
1914-15	Huddersfield	35	Leeds	2	Wakefield	14,000	£750
COMPETITION SUSPENDED DURING WAR TIME							
1919-20	Hull	3	Huddersfield	2	Leeds	12,900	£1,615
1920-21	Hull	16	Hull K.R.	14	Leeds	10,000	£1,320
1921-22	Wigan	13	Oldham	2	Broughton	26,000	£1,825
1922-23	Hull K.R.	15	Huddersfield	5	Leeds	14,000	£1,370
1923-24	Batley	13	Wigan	7	Broughton	13,729	£968
1924-25	Hull K.R.	9	Swinton	5	Rochdale	21,580	£1,504
1925-26	Wigan	22	Warrington	10	St. Helens	20,000	£1,100
1926-27	Swinton	13	St. Helens Recs.	8	Warrington	24,432	£1,803
1927-28	Swinton	11	Featherstone R.	0	Oldham	15,451	£1,136
1928-29	Huddersfield	2	Leeds	0	Halifax	25,604	£2,028
1929-30	Huddersfield	2	Leeds	2	Wakefield	30,350	£2,087
Replay	Huddersfield	10	Leeds	0	Halifax	18,563	£1,319
1930-31	Swinton	14	Leeds	7	Wigan	31,000	£2,100
1931-32	St. Helens	9	Huddersfield	5	Wakefield	19,386	£943
1932-33	Salford	15	Swinton	5	Wigan	18,000	£1,053
1933-34	Wigan	15	Salford	3	Warrington	31,564	£2,114
1934-35	Swinton	14	Warrington	3	Wigan	27,700	£1,710
1935-36	Hull	21	Widnes	2	Huddersfield	17,276	£1,208

1936-37	Salford	13	Warrington	11	Wigan	31,500	£2,000
1937-38	Hunslet	8	Leeds	2	Leeds United FC	54,112	£3,572
1938-39	Salford	8	Castleford	6	Man. City FC	69,504	£4,301

WAR-TIME EMERGENCY PLAY-OFFS

For the first two seasons the Yorkshire League and Lancashire League champions met in a two-leg final as follows:

1939-40	*Swinton*	*13*	*Bradford N.*	*21*	*Swinton*	*4,800*	*£237*
	Bradford N.	*16*	*Swinton*	*9*	*Bradford*	*11,721*	*£570*
	Bradford N. won 37-22 on aggregate						
1940-41	*Wigan*	*6*	*Bradford N.*	*17*	*Wigan*	*11,245*	*£640*
	Bradford N.	*28*	*Wigan*	*9*	*Bradford*	*20,205*	*£1,148*
	Bradford N. won 45-15 on aggregate						

For the remainder of the War the top four in the War League played-off as follows:

1941-42	*Dewsbury*	*13*	*Bradford N.*	*0*	*Leeds*	*18,000*	*£1,121*
1942-43	*Dewsbury*	*11*	*Halifax*	*3*	*Dewsbury*	*7,000*	*£400*
	Halifax	*13*	*Dewsbury*	*22*	*Halifax*	*9,700*	*£683*

Dewsbury won 33-16 on aggregate but the Championship was declared null and void because they had played an ineligible player

1943-44	*Wigan*	*13*	*Dewsbury*	*9*	*Wigan*	*14,000*	*£915*
	Dewsbury	*5*	*Wigan*	*12*	*Dewsbury*	*9,000*	*£700*
	Wigan won 25-14 on aggregate						
1944-45	*Halifax*	*9*	*Bradford N.*	*2*	*Halifax*	*9,426*	*£955*
	Bradford N.	*24*	*Halifax*	*11*	*Bradford*	*16,000*	*£1,850*
	Bradford N. won 26-20 on aggregate						

Season	*Winners*		*Runners-up*		*Venue*	*Attendance*	*Receipts*
1945-46	Wigan	13	Huddersfield	4	Man. C. FC	67,136	£8,387
1946-47	Wigan	13	Dewsbury	4	Man. C. FC	40,599	£5,895
1947-48	Warrington	15	Bradford N.	5	Man. C. FC	69,143	£9,792
1948-49	Huddersfield	13	Warrington	12	Man. C. FC	75,194	£11,073
1949-50	Wigan	20	Huddersfield	2	Man. C. FC	65,065	£11,500
1950-51	Workington T.	26	Warrington	11	Man. C. FC	61,618	£10,993
1951-52	Wigan	13	Bradford N.	6	Huddersfield Town FC	48,684	£8,215
1952-53	St. Helens	24	Halifax	14	Man. C. FC	51,083	£11,503
1953-54	Warrington	8	Halifax	7	Man. C. FC	36,519	£9,076
1954-55	Warrington	7	Oldham	3	Man. C. FC	49,434	£11,516
1955-56	Hull	10	Halifax	9	Man. C. FC	36,675	£9,179
1956-57	Oldham	15	Hull	14	Bradford	62,199	£12,054
1957-58	Hull	20	Workington T.	3	Bradford	57,699	£11,149
1958-59	St. Helens	44	Hunslet	22	Bradford	52,560	£10,146
1959-60	Wigan	27	Wakefield T.	3	Bradford	83,190	£14,482
1960-61	Leeds	25	Warrington	10	Bradford	52,177	£10,475
1961-62	Huddersfield	14	Wakefield T.	5	Bradford	37,451	£7,979

TWO DIVISIONS 1962-63 and 1963-64

Top Sixteen Play-Offs

1964-65	Halifax	15	St. Helens	7	Swinton	20,786	£6,141
1965-66	St. Helens	35	Halifax	12	Swinton	30,634	£8,750
1966-67	Wakefield T.	7	St. Helens	7	Leeds	20,161	£6,702
Replay	Wakefield T.	21	St. Helens	9	Swinton	33,537	£9,800
1967-68	Wakefield T.	17	Hull K.R.	10	Leeds	22,586	£7,697
1968-69	Leeds	16	Castleford	14	Bradford	28,442	£10,130
1969-70	St. Helens	24	Leeds	12	Bradford	26,358	£9,791
1970-71	St. Helens	16	Wigan	12	Swinton	21,745	£10,200
1971-72	Leeds	9	St. Helens	5	Swinton	24,055	£9,513
1972-73	Dewsbury	22	Leeds	13	Bradford	18,889	£9,479

CHAMPIONSHIP FINAL . . . . A 10-YEAR REVIEW

1961-62 HUDDERSFIELD 14 Dyson (4g); Breen, Deighton, Booth, Wicks (1t); Davies, Smales (1t); Slevin, Close, Noble, Kilroy, Bowman, Ramsden
WAKEFIELD T. 5 Round; F. Smith, Skene, N. Fox (1t, 1g), Hirst; Poynton, Holliday; Wilkinson, Kosanovic, Firth, Briggs, Vines, Turner
Referee: N. T. Railton (Wigan)

TWO DIVISIONS – NO PLAY-OFFS 1963 and 1964

1964-65 HALIFAX 15 James (3g); Jackson (1t), Burnett (2t), Kellett, Freeman; Robinson, Daley; Roberts, Harrison, Scroby, Fogerty, Dixon, Renilson
ST. HELENS 7 F. Barrow; Harvey, Vollenhoven, Northey, Killeen (1t, 2g); Murphy, Smith; Tembey (Warlow), Dagnall, Watson, French, Mantle, Laughton
Referee: D. S. Brown (Dewsbury)

1965-66 ST. HELENS 35 F. Barrow; A. Barrow (1t), Murphy (1g), Benyon, Killeen (3t, 6g); Harvey; Bishop; Halsall (3t), Sayer, Watson, French, Warlow (Hitchen), Mantle
HALIFAX 12 Cooper (3g); Jones, Burnett, Dixon, Freeman; Robinson, Baker (1t); Roberts, Harrison, Scroby, Ramshaw (Duffy), Fogerty (1t), Renilson
Referee: J. Manley (Warrington)

1966-67 WAKEFIELD T. 7 Cooper; Hirst, Brooke, N. Fox (2g), Coetzer; Poynton, Owen (1t); Bath, Prior, Campbell, Clarkson, Haigh, D. Fox
ST. HELENS 7 F. Barrow; Vollenhoven, A. Barrow, Smith, Killeen (2g); Douglas, Bishop; Warlow, Sayer, Watson (1t), French, Hogan (Robinson), Mantle
Referee: G. Philpott (Leeds)

Replay: WAKEFIELD T. 21 Cooper; Hirst (1t), Brooke (2t), N. Fox (3g), Coetzer; Poynton (1t), Owen (1t); Bath, Prior, Campbell, Clarkson, Haigh, D. Fox
ST. HELENS 9 F. Barrow; Vollenhoven (1t), A. Barrow, Smith, Killeen (2g); Douglas, Bishop (1g); Warlow, Sayer, Watson, French, Hogan, Mantle
Referee: J. Manley (Warrington)

1967-68 WAKEFIELD T. 17 G. Cooper; Coetzer, Brooke, N. Fox (1t, 2g), Batty; Poynton (1g), Owen (1t); Jeanes (1t), Shepherd, D. Fox (1g), Haigh, McLeod, Hawley
HULL K.R. 10 Wainwright; C. Young, Moore (1t), A. Burwell, Longstaff (1t); Millward (2g), C. Cooper; L. Foster, Flanagan, Mennell, Lowe, Major, F. Foster
Referee: D. S. Brown (Preston)

1968-69 LEEDS 16 Risman (4g); Cowan (1t), Hynes, Watson, Atkinson (1t); Shoebottom, Seabourne (Langley); Clark (Hick), Crosby, K. Eyre, Joyce, Ramsey (1g), Batten
CASTLEFORD 14 Edwards; Briggs, Howe, Thomas, Lowndes; Hardisty (1t, 1g), Hepworth; Hartley, Dickinson (1t), J. Ward, Redfearn (3g), Lockwood, Reilly (Fox)
Referee: W. H. Thompson (Huddersfield)

1969-70 ST. HELENS 24 F. Barrow; L. Jones, Benyon, Walsh (1t, 2g), E. Prescott (2t), Myler, Heaton; Halsall, Sayer (1t), Watson, Mantle, E. Chisnall, Coslett (4g)
LEEDS 12 Holmes (3g); Alan Smith (1t), Hynes, Cowan (1t), Atkinson; Shoebottom, Seabourne; J. Burke, Crosby, A. Eyre, Ramsey (Hick), Eccles, Batten
Referee: W. H. Thompson (Huddersfield)

1970-71 ST. HELENS 16 Pimblett; L. Jones, Benyon (1t), Walsh, Blackwood (1t); Whittle, Heaton; J. Stephens, A. Karalius, Rees (Wanbon), Mantle, E. Chisnall, Coslett (5g)
WIGAN 12 Tyrer (1g); Kevin O'Loughlin; Francis, Rowe, Wright; D. Hill, Ayres; Hogan, Clarke, Fletcher, Ashurst (1t, 2g), Robinson (1t) (Cunningham), Laughton
Referee: E. Lawrinson (Warrington)

1971-72 LEEDS 9 Holmes (Hick); Alan Smith, Langley, Dyl, Atkinson (1t); Hardisty, Barham; Clawson (3g), Ward, Fisher (Pickup), Cookson, Eccles, Batten
ST. HELENS 5 Pimblett; L. Jones (Whittle), Benyon, Walsh (1g), Wilson; Kelly, Heaton; Rees, Greenall (1t), J. Stephens, Mantle, E. Chisnall, Coslett
Referee: S. Shepherd (Oldham)

1972-73 DEWSBURY 22 Rushton; Ashcroft, Clark, N. Stephenson (5g, 1t), Day; Agar (1t), A. Bates; Beverley (Taylor), M. Stephenson (2t), Lowe, Grayshon, J. Bates, Whittington
LEEDS 13 Holmes; Alan Smith, Hynes (1g), Dyl (1t), Atkinson; Hardisty, Hepworth; Clawson (1g), Fisher (Ward), Clarkson (Langley), Cookson (1t), Eccles (1t), Haigh
Referee: H. G. Hunt (Prestbury)

LEAGUE LEADERS TROPHY

While the top 16 play-off decided the Championship between 1964 and 1973 it was decided to honour the top club in the league table with a League Leaders Trophy. The winners were:

1964-65 St. Helens
1965-66 St. Helens
1966-67 Leeds
1967-68 Leeds
1968-69 Leeds
1969-70 Leeds
1970-71 Wigan
1971-72 Leeds
1972-73 Warrington

CLUB CHAMPIONSHIP (Merit Table)

With the reintroduction of two divisions, a complicated merit table and Division Two preliminary rounds system produced a 16 club play-off with the Club Championship finalists as follows:

Season	*Winners*		*Runners-up*		*Venue*	*Attendance*	*Receipts*
1973-74	Warrington	13	St. Helens	12	Wigan	18,040	£10,032

This format lasted just one season and was replaced by the Premiership.

CLUB CHAMPIONSHIP FINAL . . . . A REVIEW

1973-74 WARRINGTON 13 Whitehead (2g); M. Philbin (1t), Noonan (1t), Pickup (Lowe), Bevan; Whittle, A. Murphy; D. Chisnall, Ashcroft, Brady (1t), Wanbon (Gaskell), Mather, B. Philbin
ST. HELENS 12 Pimblett; Brown, Wills, Wilson (2t), Mathias; Eckersley, Heaton; Mantle, Liptrot, M. Murphy, E. Chisnall (Warlow), Nicholls, Coslett (3g)
Referee: P. Geraghty (York)

PREMIERSHIP

With the further reintroduction of two divisions in 1973-74, it was declared that the title of Champions would be awarded to the leaders of the First Division.

However, it was also decided to continue the tradition of an end-of-season play-off, the winners to receive the newly instituted Premiership Trophy.

In the first season of the Premiership, 1974-75, the top 12 Division One clubs and the top four from Division Two went into a first round draw, the luck of the draw operating through to the final, played on a neutral venue.

The following season the play-off was reduced to the top eight clubs in the First Division, the ties being decided on a merit basis i.e. 1st v 8th, 2nd v 7th etc. At the semi-final stage the highest placed clubs had the option of when to play at home in the two-legged tie.

In 1978-79 the two-leg system was scrapped and the higher placed clubs had home advantage right through to the neutrally staged final.

*For full details of the Premiership Trophy see the CUPS section.

COUNTY LEAGUE

In the early seasons of the code the Lancashire Senior and Yorkshire Senior Competitions, not to be confused with the later reserve leagues, were major leagues. The winners were:

	Lancashire SC	**Yorkshire SC**
1895-96	Runcorn	Manningham
1896-97	Broughton Rangers	Brighouse Rangers
1897-98	Oldham	Hunslet
1898-99	Broughton Rangers	Batley
1899-00	Runcorn	Bradford
1900-01	Oldham	Bradford
1901-02	Wigan	Leeds

With the introduction of two divisions in 1902-03, the county league competitions were scrapped until they reappeared as the Lancashire League and Yorkshire League in 1907-08. Clubs from the same county played each other home and away to decide the titles. These games were included in the main championship table along with inter-county fixtures. The county leagues continued until 1970, with the exception of war-time interruptions and two seasons when regional leagues with play-offs operated during the 1960s two division era. They were then abolished when a more integrated fixture formula meant clubs did not play all others from the same county, this system later being replaced by the present two division structure.

LANCASHIRE LEAGUE CHAMPIONS

Season	*Winners*
1907-08	Oldham
1908-09	Wigan
1909-10	Oldham
1910-11	Wigan
1911-12	Wigan
1912-13	Wigan
1913-14	Wigan
1914-15	Wigan
1915-18	Competition Suspended during War-time
1918-19	Rochdale H.
1919-20	Widnes
1920-21	Wigan
1921-22	Oldham
1922-23	Wigan
1923-24	Wigan
1924-25	Swinton
1925-26	Wigan
1926-27	St. Helens R.
1927-28	Swinton
1928-29	Swinton
1929-30	St. Helens
1930-31	Swinton
1931-32	St. Helens
1932-33	Salford
1933-34	Salford
1934-35	Salford
1935-36	Liverpool S.
1936-37	Salford
1937-38	Warrington
1938-39	Salford
1939-40	Swinton — War Emergency Leagues
1940-41	Wigan — War Emergency Leagues
1941-45	Competition Suspended during war-time
1945-46	Wigan
1946-47	Wigan
1947-48	Warrington
1948-49	Warrington
1949-50	Wigan
1950-51	Warrington
1951-52	Wigan
1952-53	St. Helens
1953-54	Warrington
1954-55	Warrington
1955-56	Warrington
1956-57	Oldham
1957-58	Oldham
1958-59	Wigan
1959-60	St. Helens
1960-61	Swinton
1961-62	Wigan
1962-64	See Regional
1964-65	St. Helens
1965-66	St. Helens
1966-67	St. Helens

YORKSHIRE LEAGUE CHAMPIONS

Season	*Winners*
1907-08	Hunslet
1908-09	Halifax
1909-10	Wakefield T.
1910-11	Wakefield T.
1911-12	Huddersfield
1912-13	Huddersfield
1913-14	Huddersfield
1914-15	Huddersfield
1915-18	Competition Suspended during War-time
1918-19	Hull
1919-20	Huddersfield
1920-21	Halifax
1921-22	Huddersfield
1922-23	Hull
1923-24	Batley
1924-25	Hull K.R.
1925-26	Hull K.R.
1926-27	Hull
1927-28	Leeds
1928-29	Huddersfield
1929-30	Huddersfield
1930-31	Leeds
1931-32	Hunslet
1932-33	Castleford
1933-34	Leeds
1934-35	Leeds
1935-36	Hull
1936-37	Leeds
1937-38	Leeds
1938-39	Castleford
1939-40	Bradford N. — War Emergency Leagues
1940-41	Bradford N. — War Emergency Leagues
1941-45	Competition Suspended during war-time
1945-46	Wakefield T.
1946-47	Dewsbury
1947-48	Bradford N.
1948-49	Huddersfield
1949-50	Huddersfield
1950-51	Leeds
1951-52	Huddersfield
1952-53	Halifax
1953-54	Halifax
1954-55	Leeds
1955-56	Halifax
1956-57	Leeds
1957-58	Halifax
1958-59	Wakefield T.
1959-60	Wakefield T.
1960-61	Leeds
1961-62	Wakefield T.
1962-64	See Regional
1964-65	Castleford
1965-66	Wakefield T.
1966-67	Leeds

1967-68	Warrington
1968-69	St. Helens
1969-70	Wigan

1967-68	Leeds
1968-69	Leeds
1969-70	Leeds

REGIONAL LEAGUES

DURING the 1962-63 and 1963-64 two divisions campaigns the county leagues were replaced by the Eastern and Western Divisions. Each club played four other clubs home and away. There was then a top four play-off to decide the regional championship. The finals were played at neutral venues as follows:

Eastern Division							
1962-63	Hull K.R.	13	Huddersfield	10	Leeds	6,751	£1,342
1963-64	Halifax	20	Castleford	12	Huddersfield	10,798	£1,791
Western Division							
1962-63	Workington T.	9	Widnes	9	Wigan	13,588	£2,287
Replay	Workington T.	10	Widnes	0	Wigan	7,584	£1,094
1963-64	St. Helens	10	Swinton	7	Wigan	17,363	£3,053

EASTERN DIVISION FINAL . . . . A REVIEW

1962-63 HULL K.R. 13 Kellett (2g); Paul (2t), Major, B. Burwell, Harris (1t); A. Burwell, Bunting; Coverdale, Flanagan, J. Drake, Tyson, Murphy, Bonner
HUDDERSFIELD 10 Dyson (2g); Senior, Booth, Haywood (1t), Stocks; Deighton, Smales (1t); Rowe, Close, Noble, Kilroy, Bowman, Redfearn
Referee: T. W. Watkinson (Manchester)

1963-64 HALIFAX 20 James (4g); Jackson (2t), Burnett, Kellett, Freeman; Robinson (1t), Marchant; Roberts, Shaw, Scott, Dixon (1t), Fogerty, Renilson
CASTLEFORD 12 Edwards; Howe (1t), G. Ward, Small, Gamble; Hardisty, Hepworth: Hirst, C. Dickinson (1t), Clark (3g), Bryant, Walker, Walton
Referee: R. L. Thomas (Oldham)

WESTERN DIVISION FINAL . . . . A REVIEW

1962-63 WORKINGTON T. 9 Lowdon (3g); Glastonbury, O'Neil, Brennan, Pretorious (1t); Archer, Roper: Herbert, Ackerley, W. Martin, Edgar, McLeod, Foster
WIDNES 9 Randall (3g); R. Chisnall, Lowe, Thompson (1t), Heyes; F. Myler, Owen; Hurtsfield, Kemel, E. Bate, R. Bate, Measures, V. Karalius
Referee: M. Coates (Pudsey)

Replay WORKINGTON T. 10 Lowdon (2g); Glastonbury (1t), O'Neil, Brennan, Pretorious (1t); Archer, Roper; Herbert, Ackerley, W. Martin, Edgar, McLeod, Foster
WIDNES 0 Randall; A. Hughes, Lowe, Thompson, Heyes; F. Myler, Owen; Hurstfield, Kemel, E. Bate, R. Bate, Measures, V. Karalius
Referee: M. Coates (Pudsey)

1963-64 ST. HELENS 10 Coslett (2g); Vollenhoven, Williams, Northey (1t), Killeen; Harvey, Murphy; Tembey, Burdell, Owen, French (1t), Warlow, Laughton
SWINTON 7 Gowers; Speed, Fleet, Parkinson, Stopford (1t); Williams, Cartwright; Bate, D. Clarke, Halliwell, Morgan, Rees, Blan (2g)
Referee: E. Clay (Leeds)

●AFTER the breakaway from the English Rugby Union, 22 clubs formed the Northern Union and played each other home and away.

1895-96

		P	W	D	L	F	A	Pts
1	Manningham	42	33	0	9	367	158	66
2	Halifax	42	30	5	7	312	139	65
3	Runcorn	42	24	8	10	314	143	56
4	Oldham	42	27	2	13	374	194	56
5	Brighouse R.	42	22	9	11	247	129	53
6	Tyldesley	42	21	8	13	260	164	50
7	Hunslet	42	24	2	16	279	207	50
8	Hull	42	23	3	16	259	158	49
9	Leigh	42	21	4	17	214	269	46
10	Wigan	42	19	7	16	245	147	45
11	Bradford	42	18	9	15	254	175	45
12	Leeds	42	20	3	19	258	247	43
13	Warrington	42	17	5	20	198	240	39
14	St. Helens*	42	15	8	19	195	230	36
15	Liversedge	42	15	4	23	261	355	34
16	Widnes	42	14	4	24	177	323	32
17	Stockport	42	12	8	22	171	315	32
18	Batley	42	12	7	23	137	298	31
19	Wakefield T.	42	13	4	25	156	318	30
20	Huddersfield	42	10	4	28	194	274	24
21	Broughton R.	42	8	8	26	165	244	24
22	Rochdale H.	42	4	8	30	78	388	16

*Deducted 2 points for playing ineligible player.

●So many clubs had joined the Northern Union that it was decided to abandon the one league system and introduce two county leagues.

1896-97

LANCASHIRE SENIOR COMPETITION

		P	W	D	L	F	A	Pts
1	Broughton R.	26	19	5	2	201	52	43
2	Oldham	26	20	2	4	243	59	42
3	Tyldesley	26	15	2	9	159	80	32
4	Runcorn	26	13	5	8	134	62	31
5	Stockport	26	14	2	10	157	137	30
6	Swinton	26	12	5	9	125	82	29
7	Warrington	26	11	5	10	100	124	27
8	Leigh	26	11	4	11	105	147	26
9	St. Helens	26	10	4	12	122	160	24
10	Widnes	26	10	3	13	113	164	23
11	Wigan	26	8	7	11	73	118	23
12	Rochdale H.	26	8	1	17	121	167	17
13	Salford	26	3	5	18	76	191	11
14	Morecambe	26	3	0	23	52	238	6

CHAMPIONSHIP PLAY-OFF
At Headingley, Leeds

	T	G	P		T	G	P
HUNSLET	1	1	5	BRADFORD	0	1	2

YORKSHIRE SENIOR COMPETITION

		P	W	D	L	F	A	Pts
1	Brighouse R.	30	22	4	4	213	68	48
2	Manningham	30	21	4	5	291	129	46
3	Halifax	30	18	4	8	219	112	40
4	Hunslet	30	16	4	10	211	138	36
5	Hull	30	15	6	9	152	125	36
6	Batley	30	15	5	10	164	126	35
7	Bradford	30	15	3	12	170	157	33
8	Wakefield T.	30	13	4	13	172	154	30
9	Castleford	30	11	6	13	178	161	28
10	Huddersfield	30	10	7	13	142	179	27
11	Liversedge	30	13	0	17	176	233	26
12	Leeds	30	10	4	16	115	123	24
13	Leeds Parish Ch.	30	9	4	17	129	162	22
14	Bramley	30	9	3	18	101	193	21
15	Holbeck	30	7	4	19	86	223	18
16	Heckmondwike	30	3	4	23	72	308	10

1897-98

LANCASHIRE SENIOR COMPETITION

		P	W	D	L	F	A	Pts
1	Oldham	26	23	1	2	295	94	47
2	Swinton	26	20	3	3	321	83	43
3	Widnes	26	19	1	6	251	114	39
4	Salford*	26	16	3	7	275	182	33
5	Broughton R.	26	13	4	9	183	108	30
6	Wigan	26	11	1	14	124	173	23
7	Leigh*	26	11	2	13	176	170	22
8	St. Helens	26	10	2	14	161	192	22
9	Warrington	26	10	2	14	131	178	22
10	Runcorn	26	9	2	15	142	184	20
11	Stockport	26	8	2	16	154	253	18
12	Tyldesley	26	8	1	17	111	281	17
13	Rochdale H.	26	7	0	19	146	247	14
14	Morecambe	26	4	2	20	74	285	10

*Deducted 2 points for fielding an ineligible player.

YORKSHIRE SENIOR COMPETITION

		P	W	D	L	F	A	Pts
1	Hunslet	30	22	4	4	327	117	48
2	Bradford	30	23	2	5	319	139	48
3	Batley	30	17	3	10	234	111	37
4	Halifax	30	16	3	11	193	164	35
5	Manningham	30	15	4	11	276	181	34
6	Castleford	30	16	1	13	256	208	33
7	Wakefield T.	30	16	1	13	248	214	33
8	Leeds P.C.	30	15	1	14	187	213	31
9	Leeds	30	13	4	13	186	171	30
10	Huddersfield	30	12	3	15	208	170	27
11	Hull	30	11	4	15	192	187	26
12	Bramley	30	11	4	15	156	199	26
13	Brighouse R.	30	9	5	16	143	172	23
14	Holbeck	30	11	0	19	171	310	22
15	Heckmondwike	30	9	2	19	148	315	20
16	Liversedge	30	3	1	26	76	449	7

1898-99

LANCASHIRE SENIOR COMPETITION

		P	W	D	L	F	A	Pts
1	Broughton R.	26	21	0	5	277	74	42
2	Oldham	26	20	0	6	385	58	40
3	Salford	26	18	2	6	206	113	38
4	Widnes	26	17	2	7	196	113	36
5	Leigh	26	17	0	9	168	125	34
6	Swinton*	26	16	2	8	228	79	32
7	Runcorn	26	15	2	9	193	113	32
8	St. Helens	26	12	3	11	168	180	27
9	Warrington	26	11	1	14	134	217	23
10	Rochdale H.	26	9	3	14	112	216	21
11	Stockport	26	5	1	20	102	317	11
12	Tyldesley	26	3	5	18	82	240	11
13	Wigan	26	4	2	20	66	238	10
14	Morecambe	26	2	1	23	47	281	5

*Deducted 2 points for a breach of professional rules.

YORKSHIRE SENIOR COMPETITION

		P	W	D	L	F	A	Pts
1	Batley	30	23	2	5	279	75	48
2	Hull	30	23	1	6	429	101	47
3	Bradford	30	21	0	9	330	139	42
4	Leeds P.C.	30	20	2	8	201	114	42
5	Hunslet	30	16	5	9	314	140	37
6	Huddersfield	30	15	3	12	169	147	33
7	Manningham*	30	15	2	13	222	212	30
8	Halifax	30	15	0	15	156	158	30
9	Wakefield T.	30	11	6	13	209	161	28
10	Brighouse R.	30	12	2	16	114	191	26
11	Leeds	30	11	3	16	127	186	25
12	Castleford	30	10	4	16	159	214	24
13	Holbeck	30	10	4	16	134	220	24
14	Bramley	30	7	3	20	62	266	17
15	Liversedge	30	5	3	22	131	439	13
16	Heckmondwike	30	4	4	22	70	343	12

*Deducted 2 points for a breach of professional rules.

1899-1900

LANCASHIRE SENIOR COMPETITION

		P	W	D	L	F	A	Pts
1	Runcorn	26	22	2	2	232	33	46
2	Oldham	26	21	1	4	340	75	43
3	Swinton	26	19	1	6	210	108	39
4	St. Helens	26	16	3	7	207	119	35
5	Widnes	26	12	4	10	174	146	28
6	Warrington	26	12	1	13	174	128	25
7	Broughton R.*	26	13	1	12	132	138	25
8	Salford	26	12	0	14	196	176	24
9	Stockport	26	10	2	14	126	136	22
10	Leigh	26	8	5	13	119	211	21
11	Rochdale H.*	26	9	1	16	90	181	17
12	Millom	26	7	1	18	112	234	15
13	Wigan	26	7	1	18	73	230	15
14	Tyldesley	26	2	1	23	66	336	5

*Two points deducted for a breach of professional rules.

YORKSHIRE SENIOR COMPETITION

		P	W	D	L	F	A	Pts
1	Bradford	30	24	2	4	324	98	50
2	Batley	30	21	6	3	219	72	48
3	Halifax	30	20	3	7	193	120	43
4	Wakefield T.	30	18	5	7	203	120	41
5	Huddersfield	30	17	4	9	181	110	38
6	Hull K.R.*	30	15	4	11	181	129	32
7	Hull	30	15	0	15	249	154	30
8	Hunslet	30	14	2	14	182	168	30
9	Manningham	30	13	3	14	207	203	29
10	Bramley	30	13	0	17	121	190	26
11	Castleford	30	11	3	16	155	199	25
12	Brighouse R.	30	9	3	18	80	231	21
13	Holbeck*	30	8	4	18	138	236	18
14	Leeds P.C.	30	7	3	20	135	207	17
15	Leeds	30	7	3	20	103	225	17
16	Liversedge	30	5	1	24	94	303	11

*Two points deducted for a breach of professional rules.

1900-01

LANCASHIRE SENIOR COMPETITION

		P	W	D	L	F	A	Pts
1	Oldham	26	22	1	3	301	67	45
2	Swinton	26	21	2	3	283	66	44
3	Runcorn	26	20	0	6	240	100	40
4	Broughton R.	26	17	2	7	211	84	36
5	Salford	26	15	0	11	229	149	30
6	Warrington	26	12	3	11	149	126	27
7	Leigh	26	12	2	12	157	143	26
8	Barrow	26	10	2	14	140	169	22
9	Wigan	26	8	3	15	98	227	19
10	Rochdale H.	26	8	2	16	103	257	18
11	Millom	26	8	0	18	85	194	16
12	Stockport	26	6	3	17	102	184	15
13	St. Helens*	26	6	2	18	82	228	12
14	Widnes	26	6	0	20	85	271	12

*Two points deducted for a breach of the professional rules.

YORKSHIRE SENIOR COMPETITION

		P	W	D	L	F	A	Pts
1	Bradford*	30	26	1	3	387	100	51
2	Halifax	30	22	3	5	309	147	47
3	Hunslet	30	20	0	10	252	142	40
4	Batley	30	17	5	8	166	131	39
5	Hull*	30	19	1	10	291	141	37
6	Huddersfield	30	17	1	12	241	130	35
7	Brighouse R.	30	16	0	14	194	162	32
8	Hull K.R.	30	15	2	13	195	169	32
9	Wakefield T.	30	14	3	13	242	148	31
10	Leeds P.C.	30	12	6	12	115	108	30
11	Bramley	30	12	5	13	138	163	29
12	Manningham	30	9	1	20	115	258	19
13	Leeds	30	7	3	20	144	255	17
14	Holbeck*	30	7	3	20	110	263	15
15	Castleford	30	5	4	21	92	331	14
16	Liversedge	30	2	2	26	43	386	6

*Two points deducted for a breach of the professional rules.

● Fourteen clubs resigned from the two county leagues to form a new Northern Rugby League.

1901-02

		P	W	D	L	F	A	Pts
1	Broughton R.	26	21	1	4	285	112	43
2	Salford*	26	15	3	8	235	125	31
3	Runcorn*	26	15	2	9	185	101	30
4	Swinton**	26	16	0	10	226	121	28
5	Halifax	26	12	4	10	142	165	28
6	Bradford*	26	14	1	11	201	157	27
7	Warrington*	26	14	0	12	162	150	26
8	Hull	26	11	2	13	166	193	24
9	Oldham	26	10	2	14	190	169	22
10	Leigh	26	11	0	15	158	162	22
11	Hunslet**	26	13	0	13	164	207	22
12	Batley	26	8	4	14	136	198	20
13	Huddersfield	26	8	2	16	122	262	18
14	Brighouse R.	26	3	1	22	74	324	7

*Two points deducted **four points deducted for breaches of professional rules.

1902-03 to 1904-05 two divisions — see start of this section

W. Wray — an early Hunslet stalwart.

● With the ending of two divisions the clubs again formed one major league. Clubs from the same county all played each other and arranged inter-county fixtures. Not all clubs played the same number of matches and so positions were decided on a percentage basis.

1905-06

		P	W	D	L	F	A	Pts	%
1	Leigh	30	23	2	5	245	130	48	80.00
2	Hunslet	32	25	0	7	370	148	50	78.12
3	Leeds	34	25	2	7	377	123	52	76.47
4	Oldham	40	28	2	10	446	125	58	72.50
5	Keighley	28	19	1	8	255	164	39	69.64
6	Wigan	34	22	1	11	441	167	45	66.17
7	Hull K.R.	36	22	3	11	246	218	47	65.27
8	Broughton R.	34	21	1	12	400	222	43	63.23
9	Halifax	38	20	8	10	261	232	48	63.15
10	Runcorn	30	17	3	10	264	136	37	61.66
11	Huddersfield	30	17	2	11	224	174	36	60.00
12	Bradford	34	19	2	13	371	199	40	58.82
13	Swinton	32	17	3	12	203	168	37	57.81
14	St. Helens	30	16	1	13	244	212	33	55.00
15	Warrington	38	19	3	16	270	184	41	53.94
16	Wakefield T.	32	13	4	15	188	262	30	46.87
17	Hull	36	16	1	19	304	220	33	45.83
18	Salford	34	14	3	17	272	270	31	45.58
19	Pontefract	28	11	1	16	211	196	23	41.07
20	Batley	34	11	5	18	173	215	27	39.70
21	Widnes	28	10	2	16	129	242	22	39.28
22	Dewsbury	36	13	2	21	162	252	28	38.88
23	Bramley	26	9	2	15	126	246	20	38.46
24	York	34	11	2	21	170	249	24	35.29
25	Barrow	32	9	4	19	138	324	22	34.37
26	Normanton	24	4	2	18	50	280	10	20.83
27	Millom	20	3	2	15	77	328	8	20.00
28	Castleford	20	3	2	15	45	325	8	20.00
29	Rochdale H.	32	3	6	23	105	327	12	18.75
30	Morecambe	26	2	4	20	99	282	8	15.38
31	Brighouse R.	26	3	2	21	87	333	8	15.38

● A top four play-off was introduced for the first time to decide the championship. The top club played the fourth, and the second met the third with the higher placed club having ground advantage. The final was at a neutral venue.

1906-07

		P	W	D	L	F	A	Pts	%
1	Halifax	34	27	2	5	649	229	56	82.35
2	Oldham	34	26	1	7	457	227	53	77.94
3	Runcorn	30	23	0	7	546	216	46	76.66
4	Keighley	24	17	1	6	431	231	35	72.91
5	Wigan	34	23	1	10	656	278	47	69.11
6	Leeds	30	19	2	9	424	301	40	66.66
7	Hunslet	32	21	0	11	520	354	42	65.62
8	Warrington	34	21	1	12	554	304	43	63.23
9	Broughton R.	30	17	1	12	496	235	35	58.33
10	Salford	32	18	0	14	462	349	36	56.25
11	Barrow	26	13	1	12	333	356	27	51.92
12	Widnes	20	9	1	10	221	320	19	47.50
13	Hull K.R.	32	15	0	17	390	366	30	46.87
14	Dewsbury	28	12	1	15	393	377	25	44.64
15	Leigh	28	12	1	15	318	311	25	44.64
16	Wakefield T.	28	12	1	15	348	409	25	44.64
17	Swinton	32	14	0	18	308	380	28	43.75
18	Bradford	30	12	2	16	387	367	26	43.33
19	Huddersfield	32	13	0	19	469	477	26	40.62
20	Rochdale H.	26	9	1	16	292	312	19	36.53
21	Batley	24	8	1	15	228	326	17	35.41
22	St. Helens	26	9	0	17	374	353	18	34.61
23	Hull	32	11	0	21	337	515	22	34.37
24	York	24	5	0	19	217	514	10	20.83
25	Bramley	20	1	0	19	85	466	2	5.00
26	Liverpool C.	30	0	0	30	76	1398	0	0.00

Pontefract resigned from the league after 8 matches and their record was expunged from the table. Their record was as follows:

P8 W3 L5 F63 A154 37.50%

CHAMPIONSHIP PLAY-OFF

Semi-finals

Halifax	9	Keighley	4
Oldham	11	Runcorn	3

FINAL

At Fartown, Huddersfield

	T	G	P		T	G	P
HALIFAX	4	3	18	OLDHAM	1	0	3

1907-08

		P	W	D	L	F	A	Pts	%
1	Oldham	32	28	2	2	396	121	58	90.62
2	Hunslet	32	25	1	6	389	248	51	79.68
3	Broughton R.	30	23	1	6	421	191	47	78.33
4	Wigan	32	23	1	8	501	181	47	73.43
5	Halifax	34	22	1	11	483	275	45	66.17
6	Hull K.R.	32	21	0	11	460	307	42	65.62
7	Warrington	30	18	3	9	431	156	39	65.00
8	Wakefield T.	32	20	1	11	422	322	41	64.06
9	Salford	32	19	3	10	344	187	41	64.06
10	Batley	32	20	0	12	360	306	40	62.05
11	Keighley	32	17	1	14	320	356	35	54.68
12	Bradford N.	32	17	0	15	313	350	34	53.12
13	Runcorn	30	15	0	15	255	219	30	50.00
14	Barrow	32	15	0	17	244	272	30	46.87
15	Huddersfield	32	14	1	17	439	330	29	45.31
16	Hull	34	15	0	19	349	323	30	44.11
17	Rochdale H.	30	13	0	17	232	290	26	43.33
18	Dewsbury	32	13	1	18	290	358	27	42.18
19	Leigh	30	11	1	18	279	362	23	38.33
20	Leeds	32	10	1	21	270	397	21	32.81
21	Swinton	30	9	1	20	180	316	19	31.66
22	York	30	9	0	21	284	437	18	30.00
23	Merthyr Tydfil	30	8	1	21	229	400	17	28.33
24	Widnes	30	6	4	20	179	335	16	26.66
25	St. Helens	32	7	3	22	228	500	17	26.56
26	Ebbw Vale	30	6	2	22	153	426	14	23.33
27	Bramley	32	5	1	26	188	674	11	17.18

CHAMPIONSHIP PLAY-OFF

Semi-finals

Hunslet	28	Broughton R.	3
Oldham	12	Wigan	5

FINAL

At Weaste, Salford

	T	G	P		T	G	P
HUNSLET	1	2	7	OLDHAM	1	2	7

FINAL REPLAY

At Belle Vue, Wakefield

	T	G	P		T	G	P
HUNSLET	2	3	12	OLDHAM	0	1	2

1908-09

		P	W	D	L	F	A	Pts	%
1	Wigan	32	28	0	4	706	207	56	87.50
2	Halifax	34	28	1	5	526	174	57	83.82
3	Oldham	32	26	0	6	488	176	52	81.25
4	Batley	32	23	3	6	412	176	49	76.56
5	Huddersfield	34	21	3	10	504	292	45	66.17
6	Wakefield T.	31	20	1	10	471	318	41	66.12
7	Salford	32	20	1	11	455	309	41	64.06
8	Merthyr Tydfil	18	11	1	6	184	156	23	63.88
9	Broughton R.	32	19	1	12	420	330	39	60.93
10	Warrington	32	18	2	12	473	266	38	59.37
11	Runcorn	28	16	1	11	271	191	33	58.92
12	Hunslet	32	18	1	13	361	299	37	57.81
13	Hull	34	19	1	14	487	366	39	57.35
14	Ebbw Vale	24	12	1	11	249	269	25	52.08
15	Leeds	32	15	1	16	398	355	31	48.43
16	Hull K.R.	32	14	1	17	429	423	29	45.31
17	St. Helens	28	11	3	14	312	421	25	44.64
18	York	32	13	1	18	394	510	27	42.18
19	Dewsbury	30	12	1	17	350	324	25	41.66
20	Keighley	30	12	1	17	338	355	25	41.66
21	Leigh	28	11	0	17	214	308	22	39.28
22	Swinton	32	11	1	20	258	440	23	35.93
23	Bradford N.	32	11	0	21	324	451	22	34.37
24	Mid-Rhondda	18	5	1	12	111	214	11	30.55
25	Rochdale H.	30	8	2	20	195	384	18	30.00
26	Barrow	32	9	1	22	245	507	19	29.69
27	Widnes	28	6	3	19	197	359	15	26.78
28	Treherbert	18	4	1	13	81	212	9	25.00
29	Barry	18	3	0	15	76	445	6	16.66
30	Bramley	26	3	0	23	162	582	6	11.53
31	Aberdare	17	1	0	16	134	406	2	5.88

CHAMPIONSHIP PLAY-OFF

Semi-finals

Halifax	3	Oldham	3
Wigan	18	Batley	2

Semi-final Replay

Oldham	8	Halifax	2

FINAL

At Weaste, Salford

	T	G	P		T	G	P
WIGAN	1	2	7	OLDHAM	1	0	3

1909-10

		P	W	D	L	F	A	Pts	%
1	Oldham	34	29	2	3	604	184	60	88.23
2	Salford	31	24	1	6	387	210	49	79.03
3	Wigan	30	23	1	6	545	169	47	78.33
4	Wakefield T.	32	24	0	8	435	242	48	75.00
5	Keighley	28	19	0	9	382	242	38	67.85
6	Leeds	34	21	1	12	451	317	43	63.26
7	Warrington	34	20	2	12	408	252	42	61.76
8	Huddersfield	34	21	0	13	477	301	42	61.76
9	Halifax	34	21	0	13	395	269	42	61.76
10	St. Helens	31	18	2	11	468	367	38	61.29
11	Hull K.R.	35	19	1	15	410	376	39	55.71
12	Leigh	32	15	5	12	218	206	35	54.68
13	Hull	36	19	0	17	456	373	38	52.77
14	Batley	33	16	2	15	313	201	34	51.51
15	Hunslet	32	16	0	16	321	347	32	50.00
16	Runcorn	30	14	1	15	232	317	29	48.33
17	Ebbw Vale	24	9	2	13	156	211	20	41.66
18	Widnes	28	10	3	15	152	244	23	41.07
19	Rochdale H.	32	13	0	19	272	371	26	40.62
20	Dewsbury	30	11	1	18	253	338	23	38.33
21	Swinton	30	10	2	18	203	306	22	36.66
22	Broughton R.	34	10	2	22	295	498	22	32.35
23	Bradford N.	34	9	1	24	176	388	19	27.94
24	York	30	6	1	23	269	473	13	21.66
25	Bramley	29	6	0	23	181	532	12	20.68
26	Barrow	28	5	1	22	146	377	11	19.64
27	Merthyr Tydfil	21	2	1	18	94	354	5	11.90
28	Treherbert	12	0	0	12	55	289	0	0.00

CHAMPIONSHIP PLAY-OFF

Semi-finals

Oldham	12	Wakefield T.	6
Salford	6	Wigan	17

FINAL

At Wheater's Field, Broughton

	T	G	P		T	G	P
OLDHAM	3	2	13	WIGAN	1	2	7

1910-11

		P	W	D	L	F	A	Pts	%
1	Wigan	34	28	1	5	650	205	57	83.82
2	Oldham	34	28	1	5	441	210	57	83.82
3	Wakefield T.	33	24	1	8	493	264	49	74.24
4	Widnes	30	19	3	8	310	137	41	68.33
5	Hull K.R.	33	21	3	9	587	294	45	68.18
6	Hunslet	34	21	0	13	431	389	42	61.76
7	Huddersfield	36	22	0	14	702	293	44	61.11
8	Hull	36	20	3	13	453	347	43	59.72
9	Warrington	31	15	5	11	284	303	35	56.45
10	Dewsbury	30	16	0	14	284	333	32	53.33
11	Swinton	34	18	0	16	333	262	36	52.94
12	Leeds	33	16	2	15	385	340	34	51.51
13	Rochdale H.	34	17	1	16	355	320	35	51.47
14	Halifax	36	18	1	17	371	328	37	51.38
15	Keighley	29	14	1	14	246	447	29	50.00
16	Salford	32	14	2	16	335	337	30	46.87
17	Batley	31	14	1	16	272	223	29	46.77
18	Broughton R.	32	14	1	17	208	338	29	45.31
19	St. Helens	34	14	1	19	377	449	29	42.64
20	Leigh	32	13	0	19	219	355	26	40.63
21	Barrow	32	11	1	20	272	395	23	35.94
22	Runcorn	30	9	3	18	230	331	21	35.00
23	Bradford N.	32	10	1	21	173	390	21	32.81
24	York	30	9	0	21	273	423	18	30.00
25	Ebbw Vale	30	9	0	21	178	297	18	30.00
26	Merthyr Tydfil	18	5	0	13	90	335	10	27.77
27	Coventry	32	6	1	25	288	524	13	20.31
28	Bramley	32	5	1	26	150	521	11	17.18

PLAY-OFF FOR FIRST PLACE

At Belle Vue, Wakefield

Wigan	11	Oldham	3

CHAMPIONSHIP PLAY-OFF

Semi-finals

Oldham	15	Wakefield T.	12
Wigan	16	Widnes	0

FINAL

At Wheater's Field, Broughton

	T	G	P		T	G	P
OLDHAM	4	4	20	WIGAN	1	2	7

1911-12

		P	W	D	L	F	A	Pts	%
1	Huddersfield	36	31	1	4	996	238	63	87.50
2	Wigan	34	27	1	6	483	215	55	80.88
3	Hull K.R.	34	25	0	9	597	294	50	73.52
4	Hunslet	34	24	1	9	554	286	49	72.05
5	Oldham	34	23	1	10	562	299	47	69.11
6	Wakefield T.	34	22	1	11	447	405	45	66.17
7	St. Helens	32	21	0	11	527	283	42	65.62
8	Dewsbury	32	18	1	13	403	341	37	57.81
9	Broughton R.	34	19	1	14	322	254	39	57.35
10	Hull	38	20	3	15	449	335	43	56.57
11	Leeds	34	19	0	15	467	331	38	55.83
12	Widnes	32	16	3	13	301	242	35	54.68
13	Leigh	32	17	1	14	309	296	35	54.68
14	Halifax	34	17	3	14	377	282	37	54.41
15	Batley	32	17	0	15	267	268	34	53.12
16	Rochdale H.	34	16	0	18	335	397	32	47.05
17	York	32	14	1	17	307	418	29	45.31
18	Warrington	32	13	2	17	288	296	28	43.75
19	Barrow	30	12	1	17	263	425	25	41.66
20	Salford	32	11	4	17	269	324	26	40.62
21	Swinton	32	11	3	18	266	356	25	39.06
22	Keighley	28	10	1	17	253	431	21	37.50
23	Coventry	34	6	2	26	208	646	14	20.58
24	Runcorn	28	5	1	22	147	369	11	19.64
25	Ebbw Vale	30	4	3	23	168	520	11	18.33
26	Bradford N.	36	4	0	32	250	657	8	11.11
27	Bramley	30	1	3	26	133	740	5	8.33

CHAMPIONSHIP PLAY-OFF

Semi-finals

Huddersfield	27	Hunslet	3
Wigan	41	Hull K.R.	3

FINAL

At Thrum Hall, Halifax

	T	G	P		T	G	P
HUD'SFIELD	3	2	13	WIGAN	1	1	5

1912-13

		P	W	D	L	F	A	Pts	%
1	Huddersfield	32	28	0	4	732	217	56	87.50
2	Wigan	34	28	0	6	702	249	56	82.35
3	Hull K.R.	32	23	1	8	469	273	47	73.43
4	Dewsbury	34	23	1	10	534	230	47	69.11
5	Hunslet	34	22	2	10	468	252	46	67.66
6	Broughton R.	30	17	4	9	303	173	38	63.33
7	Salford	30	19	0	11	245	182	38	63.33
8	Wakefield T.	33	20	2	11	348	350	42	63.33
9	Batley	32	18	1	13	379	218	37	57.81
10	Leeds	34	19	1	14	497	281	39	57.36
11	Oldham	32	17	2	13	341	273	36	56.24
12	Rochdale H.	34	17	2	15	327	277	36	52.94
13	Hull	34	16	3	15	318	328	35	51.47
14	Widnes	32	15	2	15	333	319	32	50.00
15	Swinton	32	15	1	16	248	256	31	48.44
16	St. Helens	32	14	1	17	370	331	29	45.31
17	Bradford N.	34	14	2	18	253	336	30	44.12
18	Warrington	32	13	2	17	214	278	28	43.75
19	Runcorn	30	11	0	19	209	347	22	36.66
20	York	29	10	0	19	256	465	20	34.48
21	Halifax	32	10	2	20	269	367	22	34.38
22	Barrow	30	9	2	19	235	351	20	33.33
23	Leigh	30	8	0	22	153	321	16	26.67
24	Keighley	28	4	3	21	143	419	11	19.64
25	Bramley	31	4	1	26	172	686	9	14.52
26	Coventry	27	0	1	26	157	896	1	1.85

The Wakefield T. v. Coventry and Bramley v. York games were cancelled by permission of the League committee.

CHAMPIONSHIP PLAY-OFF

Semi-finals

Huddersfield	30	Dewsbury	3
Wigan	16	Hull K.R.	3

FINAL

At Belle Vue, Wakefield

	T	G	P		T	G	P
HUD'SFIELD	7	4	29	WIGAN	0	1	2

1913-14

		P	W	D	L	F	A	Pts	%
1	Huddersfield	34	28	2	4	830	258	58	85.29
2	Salford	32	25	1	6	320	140	51	79.69
3	Wigan	34	25	2	7	676	252	52	76.47
4	Hull	34	24	1	9	507	264	49	72.06
5	Barrow	30	20	0	10	335	256	40	66.66
6	Hull K.R.	34	20	2	12	393	298	42	61.76
7	Rochdale H.	34	18	4	12	356	270	40	58.83
8	Widnes	32	17	1	14	262	241	35	54.69
9	Leeds	34	18	1	15	342	290	37	54.42
10	Hunslet	34	18	1	15	437	397	37	54.42
11	Warrington	34	17	2	15	280	332	36	52.94
12	Dewsbury	36	18	2	16	378	377	38	52.78
13	Swinton	30	15	1	14	243	232	31	51.66
14	Oldham	34	17	0	17	403	265	34	50.00
15	Batley	32	14	3	15	253	276	31	48.43
16	Broughton R.	32	14	0	18	235	264	28	43.75
17	Wakefield T.	34	12	3	19	257	382	27	39.71
18	Halifax	32	12	1	19	359	320	25	39.06
19	St. Helens	32	12	1	19	376	440	25	39.06
20	Leigh	30	10	0	20	165	329	20	33.33
21	Runcorn	30	10	0	20	165	442	20	33.33
22	Keighley	30	9	1	20	159	385	19	31.64
23	Bramley	30	7	0	23	163	464	14	23.33
24	Bradford N.	34	7	1	26	223	492	15	22.06
25	York	34	6	0	28	237	688	12	17.65

CHAMPIONSHIP PLAY-OFF

Semi-finals

Huddersfield	23	Hull	5
Salford	16	Wigan	5

FINAL

At Headingley, Leeds

	T	G	P		T	G	P
SALFORD	1	1	5	HUD'SFIELD	1	0	3

1914-15

		P	W	D	L	F	A	Pts	%
1	Huddersfield	34	28	4	2	888	235	60	88.24
2	Wigan	32	25	1	6	679	206	51	79.69
3	Leeds	34	24	3	7	486	207	51	75.02
4	Rochdale H.	34	24	2	8	306	194	50	73.53
5	Hull	36	24	1	11	705	301	49	68.06
6	Broughton R.	30	18	1	11	308	289	37	61.66
7	St. Helens	32	19	0	13	368	342	38	59.37
8	Halifax	34	18	3	13	342	268	39	57.36
9	Oldham	34	17	4	13	375	301	38	55.89
10	Wakefield T.	32	17	1	14	309	340	35	54.69
11	Hull K.R.	34	17	2	15	374	324	36	52.94
12	Widnes	32	14	3	15	291	292	31	48.44
13	Warrington	32	14	3	15	242	323	31	48.44
14	Batley	34	15	1	18	229	288	31	45.59
15	Leigh	31	14	0	17	252	185	28	45.16
16	Swinton	30	13	1	16	171	240	27	45.00
17	Dewsbury	32	12	2	18	310	353	26	40.62
18	Hunslet	32	12	0	20	298	356	24	37.50
19	Bradford N.	32	11	1	20	249	464	23	35.93
20	Bramley	32	11	1	20	143	474	23	35.93
21	Salford	30	8	4	18	134	313	20	33.33
22	Barrow	32	10	1	21	288	363	21	32.81
23	York	32	9	2	21	261	422	20	31.25
24	Keighley	30	6	2	22	120	542	14	29.37
25	Runcorn	27	0	1	26	84	590	1	1.85

CHAMPIONSHIP PLAY-OFF

Semi-finals

Wigan	4	Leeds	15
Huddersfield	33	Rochdale H.	2

FINAL

At Belle Vue, Wakefield

	T	G	P		T	G	P
HUD'SFIELD	7	7	35	LEEDS	0	1	2

Competitive matches suspended during First World War from 1915-16 to 1917-18

● The ban on competitive football was removed in September 1918, officially organised games commencing in January 1919, on a regional basis.

1918-19

LANCASHIRE LEAGUE

		P	W	D	L	F	A	Pts	%
1	Rochdale H.	13	10	0	3	109	53	20	76.92
2	Leigh	12	8	2	2	99	31	18	75.00
3	Wigan	11	7	1	3	164	87	15	68.18
4	Warrington	17	10	1	6	145	105	21	61.76
5	Barrow	5	3	0	2	52	66	6	60.00
6	Widnes	12	7	0	5	120	83	14	58.33
7	Salford	15	7	0	8	107	95	14	46.66
8	Oldham	14	6	1	7	159	121	13	46.43
9	St. Helens	9	3	0	6	29	109	6	33.33
10	St. Helens Rec.	13	3	2	8	75	134	8	30.77
11	Broughton R.	14	4	0	10	80	144	8	28.70
12	Swinton	15	3	1	11	64	179	7	23.33

YORKSHIRE LEAGUE

		P	W	D	L	F	A	Pts	%
1	Hull	16	13	0	3	392	131	26	81.25
2	Leeds	16	10	1	5	183	112	21	65.62
3	Bramley	14	8	1	5	140	89	17	60.71
4	Halifax	15	8	1	6	187	82	17	56.66
5	Dewsbury	13	5	4	4	150	100	14	53.85
6	Batley	15	7	1	7	77	117	15	50.00
7	Hull K.R.	14	5	2	7	129	139	12	42.85
8	Wakefield T.	14	4	2	8	73	156	10	35.71
9	York	4	1	0	3	18	141	2	25.00
10	Hunslet	13	3	0	10	97	262	6	23.03
11	Bradford N.	10	2	0	8	51	168	4	20.00

1919-20

		P	W	D	L	F	A	Pts	%
1	Huddersfield	34	29	0	5	759	215	58	85.29
2	Hull	34	25	1	8	587	276	51	75.00
3	Leeds	32	23	0	9	445	208	46	71.87
4	Widnes	30	21	1	8	250	115	43	71.67
5	Barrow	32	22	1	9	477	202	45	70.31
6	Halifax	34	23	1	10	390	168	47	69.12
7	Rochdale H.	34	22	1	11	363	203	45	66.18
8	Oldham	34	21	1	12	333	226	43	63.23
9	Dewsbury	32	18	2	12	299	262	38	59.37
10	Warrington	30	15	2	13	236	198	32	53.33
11	St. Helens Rec.	28	13	3	12	329	196	29	51.79
12	Batley	32	15	2	15	223	319	32	50.00
13	Wigan	32	15	1	16	281	266	31	48.44
14	Leigh	28	12	2	14	175	228	26	46.43
15	Salford	32	14	1	17	202	269	29	45.31
16	St. Helens	30	12	2	16	278	285	26	43.33
17	Swinton	30	12	1	17	201	274	25	41.67
18	Wakefield T.	32	11	4	17	229	494	26	40.62
19	Hull K.R.	32	10	2	20	250	325	22	34.37
20	Bramley	30	8	4	18	163	372	20	33.33
21	York	30	8	1	21	213	422	17	28.33
22	Hunslet	34	9	0	25	167	384	18	26.47
23	Broughton R.	32	7	2	23	184	460	16	25.00
24	Bradford N.	32	7	1	24	177	479	15	23.44
25	Keighley	32	6	0	26	106	471	12	18.75

CHAMPIONSHIP PLAY-OFF

Semi-finals

Huddersfield	7	Widnes	5
Hull	11	Leeds	0

FINAL

At Headingley, Leeds

	T	G	P		T	G	P
HULL	1	0	3	HUD'SFIELD	0	1	2

1920-21

		P	W	D	L	F	A	Pts	%
1	Hull K.R.	32	24	1	7	432	233	49	76.56
2	Hull	36	27	0	9	722	267	54	75.00
3	Halifax	38	27	0	11	492	184	54	71.05
4	Wigan	34	23	1	10	435	238	47	69.12
5	Swinton	34	22	1	11	289	250	45	66.18
6	Dewsbury	34	20	3	11	349	233	43	63.23
7	York	30	18	1	11	280	225	37	61.67
8	Leeds	34	20	1	13	380	209	41	60.29
9	Broughton R.	30	16	3	11	283	164	35	58.33
10	Rochdale H.	34	18	2	14	311	301	38	55.88
11	Widnes	30	15	2	13	231	252	32	53.33
12	Barrow	32	17	0	15	328	254	34	53.12
13	Warrington	34	17	2	15	295	289	36	52.94
14	Huddersfield	36	18	2	16	376	283	38	52.78
15	St. Helens Rec.	30	15	1	14	299	201	31	51.67
16	Batley	32	16	1	15	312	225	33	51.56
17	St. Helens	30	14	0	16	254	304	28	46.67
18	Oldham	34	13	3	18	267	254	29	42.65
19	Wakefield T.	34	14	1	19	253	426	29	42.65
20	Leigh	32	10	3	19	173	316	23	35.94
21	Bramley	30	9	0	21	153	371	18	30.00
22	Hunslet	32	8	1	23	190	298	17	26.56
23	Bradford N.	32	6	1	25	177	656	13	20.31
24	Keighley	34	5	0	29	159	655	10	14.71
25	Salford	32	2	2	28	111	463	6	9.37

CHAMPIONSHIP PLAY-OFF

Semi-finals

Hull	27	Halifax	10
Hull K.R.	26	Wigan	4

FINAL

At Headingley, Leeds

	T	G	P		T	G	P
HULL	4	2	16	HULL K.R.	2	4	14

1921-22

		P	W	D	L	F	A	Pts	%
1	Oldham	36	29	1	6	521	201	59	81.94
2	Wigan	32	22	1	9	446	159	45	70.31
3	Hull	38	25	0	13	538	326	50	65.79
4	Huddersfield	36	23	1	12	608	271	47	65.28
5	Leeds	38	24	1	13	583	289	49	64.47
6	Batley	38	23	2	13	381	299	48	63.16
7	Rochdale H.	34	20	2	12	352	225	42	61.76
8	Halifax	36	21	2	13	418	218	44	61.11
9	Leigh	34	19	3	12	295	228	41	60.29
10	York	36	21	1	14	311	231	43	59.72
11	Hull K.R.	38	21	0	17	420	356	42	55.26
12	St. Helens Rec.	36	19	1	16	417	315	39	54.17
13	Dewsbury	36	19	1	16	290	339	39	54.17
14	Barrow	34	18	0	16	311	321	36	52.94
15	Warrington	36	16	1	19	285	418	33	45.83
16	Widnes	32	13	3	16	227	240	29	45.31
17	Wakefield T.	36	16	0	20	335	313	32	44.44
18	Broughton R.	32	13	2	17	284	247	28	43.75
19	Hunslet	36	13	5	18	215	400	31	43.05
20	Swinton	34	14	0	20	248	312	28	41.18
21	Bramley	34	13	2	19	251	496	28	41.18
22	St. Helens	34	12	1	21	255	399	25	36.76
23	Salford	34	9	4	21	164	312	22	32.35
24	Featherstone R	36	10	2	24	280	463	22	30.55
25	Keighley	36	4	1	31	134	581	9	12.50
26	Bradford N.	34	2	1	31	134	744	5	7.35

CHAMPIONSHIP PLAY-OFF

Semi-finals

Oldham	13	Huddersfield	5
Wigan	27	Hull	8

FINAL

At The Cliff, Broughton

	T	G	P		T	G	P
WIGAN	1	5	13	OLDHAM	0	1	2

1922-23

		P	W	D	L	F	A	Pts	%
1	Hull	36	30	0	6	587	304	60	83.33
2	Huddersfield	34	26	0	8	644	279	52	76.47
3	Swinton	36	27	0	9	467	240	54	75.00
4	Hull K.R.	36	26	1	9	597	231	53	73.61
5	Wigan	36	25	2	9	721	262	52	72.22
6	Leigh	32	22	0	10	360	281	44	68.75
7	Oldham	36	24	0	12	389	236	48	66.66
8	Leeds	38	24	2	12	502	297	50	65.78
9	Rochdale H.	36	22	0	14	389	355	44	61.11
10	York	34	17	5	12	254	252	39	57.35
11	St. Helens Rec.	36	19	0	17	319	292	38	52.77
12	Featherstone R	34	17	1	16	413	368	35	51.47
13	Wakefield T.	36	17	2	17	349	306	36	50.00
14	Batley	36	16	2	18	347	372	34	47.22
15	Warrington	36	17	0	19	348	410	34	47.22
16	Barrow	36	16	0	20	339	426	32	44.44
17	Salford	36	14	2	20	263	421	30	41.66
18	Hunslet	38	14	2	22	316	371	30	39.47
19	St. Helens	34	13	0	21	364	427	26	38.23
20	Halifax	38	14	1	23	272	442	29	38.15
21	Dewsbury	36	12	3	21	337	440	27	37.50
22	Widnes	34	11	1	22	195	350	23	33.82
23	Keighley	38	12	1	25	236	449	25	32.89
24	Broughton R.	32	10	1	21	230	319	21	32.81
25	Wigan Highfield	32	7	1	24	208	432	15	23.43
26	Bradford N.	34	6	1	27	180	676	13	19.11
27	Bramley	36	5	2	29	184	572	12	16.66

CHAMPIONSHIP PLAY-OFF

Semi-finals

Huddersfield	16	Swinton	5
Hull	2	Hull K.R.	16

FINAL

At Headingley, Leeds

	T	G	P		T	G	P
HULL K.R.	3	3	15	HUD'SFIELD	1	1	5

1923-24	P	W	D	L	F	A	Pts	%
1 Wigan	38	31	0	7	824	228	62	81.57
2 Batley	36	24	3	9	432	287	51	70.83
3 Oldham	36	23	2	11	579	296	48	66.66
4 Leigh	34	20	3	11	407	250	43	63.23
5 Huddersfield	36	21	1	14	481	352	43	59.72
6 St. Helens Rec.	32	19	0	13	363	255	38	59.37
7 Swinton	34	20	0	14	346	312	40	58.82
8 Rochdale H.	36	19	4	13	318	330	42	58.33
9 York	36	18	5	13	323	258	41	56.94
10 Hunslet	36	18	5	13	328	332	41	56.94
11 Hull K.R.	36	19	2	15	408	377	40	55.55
12 Leeds	38	20	0	18	448	350	40	52.63
13 Halifax	38	20	0	18	360	357	40	52.63
14 Widnes	34	16	3	15	275	245	35	51.47
15 Broughton R.	34	15	4	15	286	251	34	50.00
16 St. Helens	34	16	0	18	332	522	32	47.05
17 Hull	38	17	1	20	439	447	35	46.05
18 Dewsbury	36	15	3	18	279	289	33	45.83
19 Wakefield T.	36	15	2	19	313	358	32	44.44
20 Warrington	36	16	0	20	341	395	32	44.44
21 Barrow	36	15	1	20	366	372	31	43.05
22 Keighley	36	14	1	21	291	427	29	40.27
23 Featherstone R.	36	12	3	21	348	545	27	37.50
24 Wigan Highfield	36	12	0	24	324	428	24	33.33
25 Salford	34	8	1	25	175	466	17	25.00
26 Bradford N.	34	8	0	26	190	524	16	23.52
27 Bramley	34	7	0	27	228	528	14	20.58

1924-25	P	W	D	L	F	A	Pts	%
1 Swinton	36	30	0	6	499	224	60	83.33
2 Hull K.R.	34	25	3	6	492	171	53	77.94
3 Wigan	36	27	1	8	784	258	55	76.38
4 St. Helens Rec.	38	26	3	9	564	267	55	72.36
5 Oldham	34	21	1	12	531	248	43	68.23
6 Leeds	36	21	3	12	341	278	45	62.50
7 Huddersfield	36	21	1	14	458	351	43	59.72
8 Dewsbury	36	20	2	14	310	269	42	58.33
9 Warrington	36	19	2	15	427	386	40	55.55
10 St. Helens	34	17	3	14	332	381	37	54.41
11 Batley	36	19	1	16	441	350	39	54.16
12 Rochdale H.	36	18	2	16	348	329	38	52.72
13 Hunslet	35	18	0	17	402	362	36	51.42
14 Wakefield T.	35	17	1	17	330	314	35	50.00
15 Keighley	36	17	1	18	305	420	35	48.61
16 Barrow	34	16	1	17	288	336	33	48.52
17 Featherstone R.	34	15	0	19	315	337	30	44.11
18 Hull	36	14	3	19	368	422	31	43.05
19 Salford	34	13	3	18	160	399	29	42.64
20 Leigh	34	13	1	20	328	433	27	39.70
21 Halifax	38	14	2	22	317	431	30	39.47
22 Broughton R.	34	12	1	21	244	429	25	36.76
23 York	36	12	1	23	272	351	25	34.72
24 Wigan Highfield	32	10	1	21	224	432	21	32.81
25 Widnes	34	10	1	23	257	462	21	30.83
26 Bradford N.	38	8	4	26	285	584	20	26.31
27 Bramley	36	2	2	32	167	565	6	8.33

1925-26	P	W	D	L	F	A	Pts	%
1 Wigan	38	29	3	6	641	310	61	80.26
2 Warrington	36	27	1	8	472	279	55	76.38
3 Swinton	36	26	2	8	442	223	54	75.00
4 Hull	38	24	3	11	547	329	51	67.10
5 St. Helens Rec.	36	23	2	11	437	278	48	66.66
6 Hull K.R.	34	20	3	11	416	320	43	63.23
7 Oldham	34	19	3	12	431	251	41	60.29
8 Wakefield T.	36	21	1	14	445	317	43	59.72
9 Leeds	36	20	2	14	526	611	42	58.33
10 St. Helens	34	18	2	14	410	282	38	55.88
11 Batley	38	20	2	16	325	296	42	55.26
12 York	36	19	0	17	359	350	38	52.77
13 Halifax	38	19	2	17	364	323	40	52.63
14 Barrow	36	17	3	16	313	303	37	51.38
15 Featherstone R.	32	15	2	15	362	362	32	50.00
16 Dewsbury	36	18	0	18	310	402	36	50.00
17 Widnes	34	15	0	19	339	397	30	44.11
18 Huddersfield	36	14	2	20	365	474	30	41.66
19 Wigan Highfield	32	12	1	19	280	323	25	39.06
20 Hunslet	36	14	0	22	389	435	28	38.88
21 Salford	34	11	4	19	246	393	26	38.23
22 Rochdale H.	36	13	1	22	320	414	27	37.50
23 Bradford N.	38	14	0	24	306	580	28	36.84
24 Leigh	32	8	2	22	270	435	18	28.12
25 Broughton R.	34	9	0	25	316	510	18	26.47
26 Keighley	36	9	1	26	290	577	19	26.38
27 Bramley	34	3	0	31	152	588	6	8.82

1923-24 CHAMPIONSHIP PLAY-OFF

Semi-finals

Batley	38	Oldham	0
Wigan	27	Leigh	0

FINAL

At The Cliff, Broughton

	T	G	P		T	G	P
BATLEY	3	2	13	WIGAN	1	2	7

1924-25 CHAMPIONSHIP PLAY-OFF

Semi-finals

Swinton	20	St. Helens Rec.	2
Hull K.R.	13	Wigan	4

FINAL

At The Athletic Ground, Rochdale

	T	G	P		T	G	P
HULL K.R.	1	3	9	SWINTON	1	1	5

1925-26 CHAMPIONSHIP PLAY-OFF

Semi-finals

Warrington	11	Swinton	8
Wigan	34	Hull	0

FINAL

At Knowsley Road, St. Helens

	T	G	P		T	G	P
WIGAN	6	2	22	WARRINGTON	2	2	10

1926-27

		P	W	D	L	F	A	Pts	%
1	St. Helens Rec.	38	29	3	6	544	235	61	80.26
2	Swinton	38	29	2	7	471	275	60	78.98
3	Wigan	40	29	0	11	691	366	58	72.50
4	St. Helens	34	23	1	10	538	283	47	69.11
5	Hull	38	25	1	12	434	317	51	67.10
6	Hull K.R.	36	21	5	10	456	244	47	65.27
7	Leigh	36	23	1	12	404	331	47	65.27
8	Rochdale H.	36	23	0	13	378	285	46	63.88
9	Leeds	40	23	1	16	582	371	47	58.75
10	Hunslet	42	24	1	17	533	380	49	58.33
11	Featherstone R.	38	21	1	16	504	369	43	56.57
12	Dewsbury	38	20	3	15	344	284	43	56.57
13	Oldham	38	19	4	15	489	346	42	55.26
14	Halifax	40	19	4	17	411	289	42	52.50
15	Wakefield T.	36	17	3	16	386	330	37	51.38
16	Warrington	38	18	1	19	409	524	37	48.68
17	Barrow	38	18	0	20	311	412	36	47.36
18	York	36	16	1	19	368	519	33	45.83
19	Batley	36	14	2	20	317	325	30	41.66
20	Salford	36	14	2	20	306	353	30	41.66
21	Broughton R.	36	14	1	21	369	392	29	40.27
22	Keighley	36	14	1	21	242	469	29	40.27
23	Huddersfield	40	16	0	24	414	562	32	40.00
24	Widnes	34	11	0	23	283	479	22	32.35
25	Wigan Highfield	34	9	1	24	239	383	19	27.94
26	Bramley	36	8	1	27	200	636	17	23.61
27	Pontypridd	32	7	1	24	223	447	15	23.43
28	Bradford N.	36	6	0	30	288	652	12	16.66
29	Castleford	36	5	1	30	274	550	11	15.27

1926-27 CHAMPIONSHIP PLAY-OFF

Semi-finals

St. Helens Rec.	33	St. Helens	0
Swinton	23	Wigan	3

FINAL

At Wilderspool, Warrington

	T	G	P		T	G	P
SWINTON	3	2	13	ST. HELENS REC.	2	1	8

1927-28

		P	W	D	L	F	A	Pts	%
1	Swinton	36	27	3	6	439	189	57	79.16
2	Leeds	42	32	0	10	619	307	64	76.19
3	Featherstone R.	36	25	1	10	387	234	51	70.83
4	Hunslet	40	28	0	12	546	308	56	70.00
5	St. Helens Rec.	36	24	0	12	499	251	48	66.66
6	Oldham	36	23	1	12	422	261	47	65.27
7	Wigan Highfield	32	19	1	12	272	240	39	60.93
8	Wigan	40	24	0	16	601	345	48	60.00
9	Leigh	34	20	0	14	298	236	40	58.82
10	Wakefield T.	40	22	2	16	476	355	46	57.50
11	St. Helens	36	19	1	16	485	336	39	54.17
12	Huddersfield	40	21	1	18	475	341	43	53.75
13	Hull K.R.	38	17	5	16	342	333	39	51.31
14	Halifax	40	19	2	19	341	328	40	50.00
15	Dewsbury	38	17	3	18	334	329	37	48.68
16	Bradford N.	32	13	2	17	204	333	28	43.75
17	Warrington	36	14	2	20	352	483	30	41.66
18	Barrow	34	13	1	20	249	337	27	39.70
19	Batley	38	14	2	22	264	466	30	39.47
20	Hull	38	12	6	20	312	347	30	39.47
21	York	36	13	1	22	233	350	27	37.50
22	Keighley	36	13	1	22	230	415	27	37.50
23	Widnes	32	11	0	21	196	418	22	34.37
24	Rochdale H.	34	11	1	22	192	448	23	33.82
25	Castleford	32	9	3	20	217	389	21	32.81
26	Salford	32	9	1	22	220	434	19	29.68
27	Broughton R.	32	8	0	24	285	450	16	25.00
28	Bramley	32	7	0	25	175	402	14	21.87

Pontypridd resigned from the League in October and their record was expunged from the table. They had played eight matches as follows:
P8 W1 L7 F46 A149 12.50%

1927-28 CHAMPIONSHIP PLAY-OFF

Semi-finals

Leeds	12	Featherstone R.	15
Swinton	12	Hunslet	2

FINAL

At Watersheddings, Oldham

	T	G	P		T	G	P
SWINTON	3	1	11	F'STONE R.	0	0	0

1928-29

		P	W	D	L	F	A	Pts	%
1	Huddersfield	38	26	4	8	476	291	56	73.68
2	Hull K.R.	40	27	3	10	436	239	57	71.25
3	Leeds	38	26	2	10	695	270	54	71.05
4	Salford	34	23	2	9	395	222	48	70.58
5	Wigan	38	26	1	11	636	308	53	69.73
6	Swinton	36	23	2	11	429	249	48	66.66
7	Warrington	36	22	2	12	568	295	46	63.88
8	St. Helens Rec.	38	22	1	15	545	374	45	59.21
9	Oldham	36	18	4	14	439	343	40	55.55
10	St. Helens	38	19	4	15	460	381	42	55.26
11	Hull	40	20	4	16	458	395	44	55.00
12	Leigh	34	17	3	14	285	279	37	54.41
13	Hunslet	38	19	4	15	539	356	42	55.26
14	Wigan Highfield	32	16	1	15	262	333	33	51.56
15	Dewsbury	36	17	2	17	380	387	36	50.00
16	Wakefield T.	40	17	4	19	400	461	38	47.50
17	Halifax	40	18	3	19	379	399	39	48.75
18	Barrow	32	13	2	17	396	387	28	43.75
19	Batley	38	14	2	22	278	442	30	39.47
20	Broughton R.	30	11	1	18	235	401	23	38.33
21	Castleford	34	11	4	19	268	369	26	38.23
22	York	34	12	0	22	259	409	24	35.29
23	Bramley	34	11	2	21	241	437	24	35.29
24	Widnes	34	11	2	21	222	439	24	35.29
25	Featherstone R.	38	10	4	24	277	451	24	31.57
26	Rochdale H.	34	10	0	24	235	434	20	29.41
27	Keighley	34	8	2	24	209	422	18	26.47
28	Bradford N.	38	5	3	30	242	871	13	17.10

Carlisle City resigned from the league in November and their record was expunged from the table. They had played 10 matches as follows:

P10 W1 L9 F59 A166 10%

CHAMPIONSHIP PLAY-OFF

Semi-finals

Huddersfield	13	Salford	5
Hull K.R.	4	Leeds	7

FINAL

At Thrum Hall, Halifax

	T	G	P		T	G	P
HUD'SFIELD	0	1	2	LEEDS	0	0	0

1929-30

		P	W	D	L	F	A	Pts	%
1	St. Helens	40	27	1	12	549	295	55	68.75
2	Huddersfield	38	25	2	11	510	317	52	68.42
3	Salford	36	23	3	10	397	214	49	68.05
4	Leeds	40	25	2	13	672	302	52	65.00
5	Dewsbury	38	23	3	12	415	282	49	64.47
6	Hull K.R.	38	22	4	12	396	290	48	63.15
7	Wigan	38	23	1	14	590	303	47	61.84
8	Warrington	36	21	1	14	483	389	43	59.72
9	Hunslet	38	21	3	14	535	358	45	59.21
10	Oldham	38	20	4	14	393	306	44	57.89
11	Halifax	40	21	1	18	384	348	43	53.75
12	Hull	38	19	2	17	417	399	40	52.63
13	St. Helens Rec.	36	17	3	16	355	414	37	51.38
14	Swinton	36	17	2	17	332	220	36	50.00
15	Widnes	32	15	2	15	309	266	32	50.00
16	Wigan Highfield	32	16	0	16	257	266	32	50.00
17	Wakefield T.	40	19	1	20	399	428	39	48.75
18	Leigh	32	15	0	17	309	296	30	46.87
19	York	36	16	1	19	277	328	33	45.83
20	Keighley	36	14	2	20	244	427	30	41.66
21	Broughton R.	34	14	0	20	271	437	28	41.17
22	Rochdale H.	34	13	2	19	258	442	28	41.17
23	Featherstone R.	36	12	3	21	255	398	27	37.50
24	Bramley	36	10	5	21	199	399	25	34.72
25	Barrow	32	10	2	20	352	388	22	34.37
26	Castleford	36	10	2	24	230	535	22	30.55
27	Batley	36	7	2	27	221	543	16	22.22
28	Bradford N.	38	7	2	29	299	718	16	21.05

CHAMPIONSHIP PLAY-OFF

Semi-finals

Huddersfield	15	Salford	10
St. Helens	6	Leeds	10

FINAL

At Belle Vue, Wakefield

	T	G	P		T	G	P
HUD'SFIELD	0	1	2	LEEDS	0	1	2

FINAL REPLAY

At Thrum Hall, Halifax

	T	G	P		T	G	P
HUD'SFIELD	2	2	10	LEEDS	0	0	0

• With all clubs playing the same number of matches, positions no longer needed to be decided on a percentage basis. All the clubs still did not meet each other and the play-offs continued.

1930-31

		P	W	D	L	F	A	Pts
1	Swinton	38	31	2	5	504	156	64
2	Leeds	38	29	1	8	695	258	59
3	Wigan	38	28	2	8	657	199	58
4	Oldham	38	27	4	7	464	178	58
5	Huddersfield	38	27	2	9	545	272	56
6	Halifax	38	25	3	10	405	283	53
7	St. Helens	38	25	1	12	502	344	51
8	Hunslet	38	24	2	12	573	278	50
9	Salford	38	23	3	12	420	256	49
10	Warrington	38	23	2	13	447	291	48
11	York	38	23	1	14	441	361	47
12	St. Helens Rec.	38	21	2	15	436	243	44
13	Hull K.R.	38	21	0	17	345	399	42
14	Wakefield T.	38	20	0	18	510	438	40
15	Wigan Highfield	38	17	3	18	398	435	37
16	Hull	38	17	2	19	398	428	36
17	Broughton R.	38	15	5	18	376	366	35
18	Dewsbury	38	14	2	22	418	406	30
19	Barrow	38	12	6	20	350	481	30
20	Castleford	38	15	0	23	351	539	30
21	Leigh	38	11	3	24	248	479	25
22	Widnes	38	11	2	25	245	450	24
23	Batley	38	11	1	26	245	505	23
24	Rochdale H.	38	10	2	26	330	557	22
25	Keighley	38	8	0	30	212	705	16
26	Featherstone R.	38	7	1	30	265	536	15
27	Bramley	38	5	3	30	251	636	13
28	Bradford N.	38	4	1	33	227	809	9

CHAMPIONSHIP PLAY-OFF

Semi-finals

Leeds	13	Wigan	0
Swinton	16	Oldham	3

FINAL

At Central Park, Wigan

	T	G	P		T	G	P
SWINTON	2	4	14	LEEDS	1	2	7

1931-32

		P	W	D	L	F	A	Pts
1	Huddersfield	38	30	1	7	636	368	61
2	St. Helens	38	29	2	7	699	279	60
3	Leeds	38	27	1	10	603	307	55
4	Hunslet	38	27	1	10	672	359	55
5	Salford	38	26	2	10	551	211	54
6	Swinton	38	26	1	11	523	253	53
7	Wigan	38	22	2	14	559	361	46
8	Warrington	38	22	2	14	495	412	46
9	York	38	22	2	14	455	382	46
10	Wakefield T.	38	21	3	14	545	388	45
11	Oldham	38	20	2	16	461	437	42
12	Rochdale H.	38	19	2	17	458	458	40
13	St. Helens Rec.	38	18	1	19	523	523	37
14	Hull K.R.	38	18	0	20	409	413	36
15	Dewsbury	38	17	2	19	421	467	36
16	Halifax	38	17	1	20	432	379	35
17	Batley	38	16	1	21	358	433	33
18	Broughton R.	38	16	1	21	351	382	33
19	Featherstone R.	38	15	2	21	374	415	32
20	Widnes	38	14	4	20	363	458	32
21	Hull	38	14	3	21	415	461	31
22	Castleford	38	14	1	23	402	515	29
23	Barrow	38	14	1	23	368	560	29
24	Leigh	38	13	2	23	353	487	28
25	Bramley	38	12	1	25	333	751	25
26	Keighley	38	10	0	28	228	630	20
27	Wigan Highfield	38	6	2	30	350	707	14
28	Bradford N.	38	5	1	32	313	854	11

CHAMPIONSHIP PLAY-OFF

Semi-finals

Huddersfield	12	Hunslet	9
St. Helens	9	Leeds	0

FINAL

At Belle Vue, Wakefield

	T	G	P		T	G	P
ST. HELENS	1	3	9	HUD'SFIELD	1	1	5

1932-33

		P	W	D	L	F	A	Pts
1	Salford	38	31	2	5	751	165	64
2	Swinton	38	26	2	10	412	247	54
3	York	38	24	4	10	571	273	52
4	Wigan	38	25	2	11	717	411	52
5	Warrington	38	26	0	12	625	426	52
6	Barrow	38	24	2	12	508	332	50
7	Hunslet	38	23	0	15	529	365	46
8	Castleford	38	21	4	13	403	326	46
9	Huddersfield	38	21	0	17	504	333	42
10	Leeds	38	20	2	16	544	423	42
11	St. Helens	38	20	2	16	554	494	42
12	Widnes	38	19	2	17	446	406	40
13	Broughton R.	38	18	4	16	289	322	40
14	Oldham	38	19	1	18	438	464	39
15	Rochdale H.	38	19	1	18	497	533	39
16	St. Helens Rec.	38	16	4	18	419	416	36
17	Keighley	38	16	3	19	418	428	35
18	Hull	38	16	2	20	467	460	34
19	Wakefield T.	38	15	4	19	370	483	34
20	Halifax	38	16	1	21	434	392	33
21	Hull K.R.	38	15	0	23	383	490	30
22	Bradford N.	38	14	2	22	377	587	30
23	Leigh	38	15	0	23	364	610	30
24	Dewsbury	38	14	0	24	361	503	28
25	Batley	38	12	1	25	293	450	25
26	Featherstone R.	38	8	2	28	302	594	18
27	Wigan Highfield	38	8	2	28	240	734	18
28	Bramley	38	6	1	31	219	768	13

CHAMPIONSHIP PLAY-OFF

Semi-finals

Salford	14	Wigan	2
Swinton	11	York	4

FINAL

At Central Park, Wigan

	T	G	P		T	G	P
SALFORD	3	3	15	SWINTON	1	1	5

1933-34

		P	W	D	L	F	A	Pts
1	Salford	38	31	1	6	715	281	63
2	Wigan	38	26	0	12	739	334	52
3	Leeds	38	26	0	12	597	376	52
4	Halifax	38	26	0	12	457	340	52
5	York	38	24	1	13	481	370	48
6	Hunslet	38	23	1	14	608	441	47
7	Widnes	38	21	4	13	393	324	46
8	Warrington	38	22	1	15	508	370	45
9	Swinton	38	22	1	15	418	322	45
10	Hull	38	21	3	14	553	438	45
11	Keighley	38	22	1	15	429	367	45
12	Huddersfield	38	20	1	17	500	330	41
13	St. Helens	38	20	0	18	550	500	40
14	London Highfield	38	20	0	18	509	489	40
15	Oldham	38	17	3	18	400	520	37
16	Castleford	38	17	1	20	476	468	35
17	Rochdale H.	38	17	0	21	442	524	34
18	St. Helens Rec.	38	16	1	21	455	477	33
19	Hull K.R.	38	16	1	21	444	482	33
20	Batley	38	16	1	21	390	436	33
21	Leigh	38	15	2	21	479	537	32
22	Wakefield T.	38	15	2	21	332	404	32
23	Broughton R.	38	15	1	22	415	495	31
24	Barrow	38	15	0	23	375	464	30
25	Dewsbury	38	12	1	25	313	587	25
26	Bramley	38	11	1	26	367	790	23
27	Bradford N.	38	8	0	30	337	714	16
28	Featherstone R.	38	4	0	34	232	734	8

CHAMPIONSHIP PLAY-OFF

Semi-finals

Salford	28	Halifax	3
Wigan	14	Leeds	10

FINAL

At Wilderspool, Warrington

	T	G	P		T	G	P
WIGAN	3	3	15	SALFORD	1	0	3

1934-35

		P	W	D	L	F	A	Pts
1	Swinton	38	30	1	7	468	175	61
2	Warrington	38	28	3	7	445	253	59
3	Wigan	38	26	4	8	790	290	56
4	Salford	38	27	1	10	478	272	55
5	Leeds	38	26	2	10	531	321	54
6	Hull	38	25	0	13	562	430	50
7	Huddersfield	38	22	3	13	552	379	47
8	York	38	21	3	14	527	374	45
9	Castleford	38	20	3	15	512	355	43
10	St. Helens Rec.	38	21	1	16	431	404	43
11	Hunslet	38	21	0	17	549	461	42
12	Keighley	38	20	2	16	398	479	42
13	Broughton R.	38	20	1	17	451	357	41
14	Halifax	38	18	4	16	380	314	40
15	Liverpool S.	38	18	2	18	399	287	38
16	Wakefield T.	38	18	1	19	494	331	37
17	Widnes	38	18	0	20	395	339	36
18	Oldham	38	15	4	19	358	447	34
19	Rochdale H.	38	16	1	21	395	521	33
20	Barrow	38	15	1	22	396	460	31
21	St. Helens	38	14	3	21	278	377	31
22	Dewsbury	38	14	2	22	307	501	30
23	Hull K.R.	38	13	1	24	414	514	27
24	Leigh	38	13	0	25	311	589	26
25	Bradford N.	38	11	1	26	321	580	23
26	Batley	38	9	1	28	306	603	19
27	Featherstone R.	38	6	0	32	293	804	12
28	Bramley	38	4	1	33	337	861	9

CHAMPIONSHIP PLAY-OFF

Semi-finals

Swinton	10	Salford	2
Warrington	9	Wigan	0

FINAL

At Central Park, Wigan

	T	G	P		T	G	P
SWINTON	2	4	14	WARRINGTON	1	0	3

1935-36

		P	W	D	L	F	A	Pts
1	Hull	38	30	1	7	607	306	61
2	Liverpool S.	38	27	2	9	426	248	56
3	Widnes	38	25	4	9	433	190	54
4	Wigan	38	25	1	12	543	328	51
5	Salford	38	25	0	13	481	261	50
6	Broughton R.	38	23	3	12	461	315	49
7	York	38	22	4	12	490	309	48
8	Leeds	38	23	2	13	534	385	48
9	Huddersfield	38	23	0	15	580	356	46
10	Barrow	38	21	3	14	436	297	45
11	Warrington	38	21	3	14	414	325	45
12	Castleford	38	22	0	16	503	366	44
13	Halifax	38	20	3	15	410	380	43
14	Swinton	38	19	3	16	432	318	41
15	Oldham	38	20	1	17	377	351	41
16	Hunslet	38	20	1	17	390	405	41
17	Batley	38	19	2	17	408	516	40
18	Keighley	38	18	2	18	320	374	38
19	Bradford N.	38	16	2	20	374	392	34
20	Rochdale H.	38	17	0	21	380	439	34
21	Acton & Willesden	38	13	4	21	382	529	30
22	Wakefield T.	38	13	2	23	348	436	28
23	St. Helens	38	13	1	24	272	399	27
24	Streatham & Mitcham	38	12	2	24	390	520	26
25	Bramley	38	12	2	24	348	644	26
26	St. Helens Rec.	38	11	1	26	261	483	23
27	Leigh	38	10	2	26	224	506	22
28	Hull K.R.	38	9	3	26	306	472	21
29	Dewsbury	38	6	2	30	246	569	14
30	Featherstone R.	38	5	4	29	269	625	14

CHAMPIONSHIP PLAY-OFF

Semi-finals

Hull	13	Wigan	2
Liverpool S.	9	Widnes	10

FINAL

At Fartown, Huddersfield

	T	G	P		T	G	P
HULL	3	6	21	WIDNES	0	1	2

1936-37

		P	W	D	L	F	A	Pts
1	Salford	38	29	3	6	529	196	61
2	Warrington	38	28	3	7	468	189	59
3	Leeds	38	28	1	9	627	262	57
4	Liverpool S.	38	26	3	9	425	226	55
5	Wigan	38	26	0	12	591	335	52
6	Castleford	38	25	2	11	490	325	52
7	Hull	38	24	2	12	535	312	50
8	Wakefield T.	38	23	1	14	442	372	47
9	Barrow	38	20	5	13	481	325	45
10	St. Helens Rec.	38	21	2	15	410	343	44
11	Huddersfield	38	21	1	16	671	405	43
12	Hunslet	38	21	0	17	512	405	42
13	Oldham	38	20	1	17	437	343	41
14	Halifax	38	19	3	16	329	418	41
15	Bradford N.	38	19	2	17	429	360	40
16	Swinton	38	19	2	17	366	312	40
17	Broughton R.	38	18	3	17	363	353	39
18	Keighley	38	19	0	19	395	356	38
19	Hull K.R.	38	17	1	20	414	387	35
20	Widnes	38	17	1	20	270	308	35
21	Rochdale H.	38	15	1	22	311	468	31
22	St. Helens	38	13	4	21	343	431	30
23*	Streatham & Mitcham	38	14	0	24	366	339	28
24	York	38	14	0	24	412	536	28
25	Batley	38	12	2	24	352	590	26
26	Dewsbury	38	12	1	25	295	514	25
27	Bramley	38	10	1	27	323	667	21
28	Leigh	38	5	4	29	237	615	14
29	Newcastle	38	5	1	32	300	890	11
30	Featherstone R.	38	5	0	33	317	858	10

*Streatham & Mitcham disbanded after playing 26 matches. The 12 unplayed matches were recorded as wins for their would-be apponents.

CHAMPIONSHIP PLAY-OFF

Semi-finals

Salford	15	Liverpool S.	7
Warrington	12	Leeds	2

FINAL

At Central Park, Wigan

	T	G	P		T	G	P
SALFORD	1	5	13	WARRINGTON	1	4	11

1937-38

		P	W	D	L	F	A	Pts
1	Hunslet	36	25	3	8	459	301	53
2	Leeds	36	25	2	9	530	227	52
3	Swinton	36	24	2	10	392	198	50
4	Barrow	36	25	0	11	447	260	50
5	Warrinton	36	23	1	12	534	286	47
6	Salford	36	23	1	12	493	293	47
7	Castleford	36	23	1	12	481	320	47
8	Widnes	36	22	2	12	475	210	46
9	Wigan	36	22	1	13	478	329	45
10	Wakefield T.	36	21	3	12	476	346	45
11	Oldham	36	21	2	13	392	276	44
12	Bradford N.	36	20	4	12	439	355	44
13	Hull	36	19	3	14	479	364	41
14	Halifax	36	19	2	15	531	393	40
15	Batley	36	17	2	17	392	367	36
16	Keighley	36	17	2	17	267	318	36
17	Liverpool S.	36	17	1	18	284	324	35
18	York	36	15	5	16	381	492	35
19	Broughton R.	36	16	2	18	394	413	34
20	Dewsbury	36	15	1	20	388	407	31
21	St. Helens	36	14	3	19	370	476	31
22	St. Helens Rec.	36	15	1	20	353	471	31
23	Huddersfield	36	14	1	21	499	502	29
24	Hull K.R.	36	13	1	22	354	476	27
25	Rochdale H.	36	9	1	26	338	567	19
26	Featherstone R.	36	8	2	26	311	606	18
27	Leigh	36	7	3	26	203	597	17
28	Newcastle	36	2	4	30	206	750	8
29	Bramley	36	2	2	32	221	653	6

CHAMPIONSHIP PLAY-OFF

Semi-finals

Hunslet	13	Barrow	7
Leeds	5	Swinton	2

FINAL

At Elland Road, Leeds

	T	G	P		T	G	P
HUNSLET	2	1	8	LEEDS	0	1	2

1938-39

		P	W	D	L	F	A	Pts
1	Salford	40	30	3	7	551	191	63
2	Castleford	40	29	3	8	502	287	61
3	Halifax	40	28	3	9	544	349	59
4	Huddersfield	40	28	2	10	647	345	58
5	Leeds	40	25	4	11	509	291	54
6	Swinton	40	26	1	13	418	286	53
7	Warrington	40	26	0	14	520	329	52
8	Barrow	40	24	3	13	380	287	51
9	Wigan	40	25	0	15	564	365	50
10	Widnes	40	22	3	15	453	274	47
11	Wakefield T.	40	20	5	15	501	320	45
12	Hull	40	21	3	16	460	362	45
13	Keighley	40	21	1	18	361	384	43
14	Oldham	40	20	2	18	405	289	42
15	Hunslet	40	19	4	17	344	390	42
16	Bradford N.	40	19	1	20	493	392	39
17	Hul K.R.	40	18	3	19	441	448	39
18	York	40	18	2	20	485	554	38
19	Liverpool S.	40	18	1	21	291	298	37
20	Broughton R.	40	18	1	21	408	447	37
21	St. Helens	40	17	0	23	387	494	34
22	Featherstone R.	40	13	2	25	292	541	28
23	Batley	40	11	1	28	270	537	23
24	St. Helens Rec.	40	11	0	29	311	504	22
25	Bramley	40	8	5	27	348	627	21
26	Leigh	40	7	3	30	234	667	17
27	Dewsbury	40	5	2	33	252	557	12
28	Rochdale H.	40	4	0	36	261	817	8

CHAMPIONSHIP PLAY-OFF

Semi-finals

Castleford	21	Halifax	4
Salford	15	Huddersfield	0

FINAL

At Maine Road, Manchester

	T	G	P		T	G	P
SALFORD	2	1	8	CASTLEFORD	2	0	6

1939-40 WAR EMERGENCY LEAGUE

YORKSHIRE SECTION

		P	W	D	L	F	A	Pts
1	Bradford	28	21	0	7	574	302	42
2	Huddersfield	28	19	1	8	545	340	39
3	Hull	28	18	0	8	376	265	36
4	Halifax	28	17	0	11	462	339	34
5	Castleford	28	16	1	11	364	300	33
6	Hunslet	28	16	1	11	430	339	33
7	Featherstone R.	28	15	0	13	373	365	30
8	Wakefield T.	28	14	0	14	479	314	28
9	Leeds	28	14	0	14	390	330	28
10	Hull K.R.	27	13	0	14	343	434	26
11	Dewsbury	27	11	2	14	291	406	24
12	York	28	10	3	15	349	467	23
13	Batley	27	8	0	19	255	406	16
14	Keighley	27	6	2	19	221	476	14
15	Bramley	28	4	0	24	248	617	8

LANCASHIRE SECTION

		P	W	D	L	F	A	Pts
1	Swinton	22	17	0	5	378	158	34
2	Salford	22	16	2	4	328	171	34
3	Wigan	22	16	1	5	301	157	33
4	Widnes	22	15	2	5	305	176	32
5	Warrington	22	11	1	10	281	258	23
6	St. Helens	22	11	1	10	288	224	23
7	Barrow	22	10	1	11	303	286	21
8	Oldham	21	8	2	11	241	242	18
9	Rochdale H.	21	8	0	13	197	306	16
10	Leigh	22	6	1	15	188	346	13
11	Liverpool S.	22	3	3	16	154	357	9
12	Broughton R.	22	3	0	19	160	443	6

CHAMPIONSHIP FINAL

First Leg

	T	G	P		T	G	P
SWINTON	3	2	13	BRADFORD N.	5	3	21

Second Leg

	T	G	P		T	G	P
BRADFORD N.	4	2	16	SWINTON	1	3	9

Aggregate: Bradford N. 37 Swinton 22

1940-41 WAR EMERGENCY LEAGUE

YORKSHIRE LEAGUE

		P	W	D	L	F	A	Pts
1	Bradford N.	25	23	1	1	469	126	47
2	Hull	26	20	0	6	341	227	40
3	Huddersfield	25	14	2	9	422	297	30
4	Leeds	25	14	1	10	372	235	29
5	Halifax	22	14	0	8	357	229	28
6	Hunslet	25	14	0	11	328	279	28
7	Featherstone R.	24	14	0	10	255	257	28
8	Wakefield T.	23	12	0	11	237	214	24
9	Castleford	24	11	0	13	224	239	22
10	Dewsbury	23	6	2	15	238	301	14
11	Keighley	26	5	1	20	200	447	11
12	Bramley	21	5	1	15	129	364	11
13	York	23	5	0	18	227	388	10
14	Batley	20	5	0	15	148	344	10

LANCASHIRE SECTION

		P	W	D	L	F	A	Pts
1	Wigan	16	15	1	0	297	71	31
2	Warrington	16	13	0	3	236	42	26
3	St. Helens	14	10	1	3	280	83	21
4	Salford	14	9	0	5	216	95	18
5	Oldham	16	6	1	9	161	205	13
6	Swinton	13	6	0	7	121	132	12
7	Liverpool S.	14	2	1	11	147	270	5
8	Broughton R.	10	0	0	10	71	247	0
9	Leigh	13	0	0	13	62	446	0

CHAMPIONSHIP FINAL

First Leg

	T	G	P		T	G	P
WIGAN	2	0	6	BRADFORD N.	5	1	17

Second Leg

	T	G	P		T	G	P
BRADFORD N.	6	5	28	WIGAN	3	0	9

Aggregate: Bradford N. 45 Wigan 15

1941-42 WAR EMERGENCY LEAGUE

		P	W	D	L	F	A	Pts	%
1	Dewsbury	24	19	1	4	431	172	39	81.25
2	Bradford N.	17	13	1	3	318	130	27	79.41
3	Halifax	17	13	0	4	262	139	26	76.47
4	Hull	18	12	0	6	265	146	24	66.66
5	Hunslet	18	10	0	8	212	177	20	55.55
6	Wigan	20	11	0	9	241	207	22	55.00
7	Oldham	20	11	0	9	209	209	22	55.00
8	Leeds	23	12	1	10	245	213	25	54.34
9	Huddersfield	23	12	0	11	355	276	24	52.17
10	Keighley	23	12	0	11	224	306	24	52.17
11	Wakefield T.	19	9	0	10	195	215	18	47.36
12	Featherstone R.	18	8	0	10	166	181	16	44.44
13	St. Helens	19	8	0	11	217	270	16	42.10
14	Castleford	20	8	0	12	195	253	16	40.00
15	York	22	6	0	16	231	386	12	27.27
16	Batley	18	3	1	14	133	269	7	19.44
17	Bramley	19	0	0	19	104	454	0	0.00

CHAMPIONSHIP PLAY-OFF

Semi-finals

Bradford N.	15	Halifax	8
Dewsbury	32	Hull	18

FINAL

At Headingley, Leeds

	T	G	P		T	G	P
DEWSBURY	3	2	13	BRADFORD N.	0	0	0

1942-43 WAR EMERGENCY LEAGUE

		P	W	D	L	F	A	Pts	%
1	Wigan	16	13	0	3	301	142	26	81.25
2	Dewsbury	16	12	1	3	270	114	25	78.12
3	Bradford N.	19	13	1	5	312	183	27	71.05
4	Halifax	19	13	0	6	297	149	26	68.42
5	Leeds	17	11	1	5	337	145	23	67.64
6	Huddersfield	18	12	0	6	215	189	24	66.66
7	Wakefield T.	19	11	1	7	267	192	23	60.52
8	Featherstone R.	19	10	1	8	179	138	21	55.26
9	Keighley	18	5	2	11	145	235	12	33.33
10	Batley	15	4	0	11	159	294	8	26.66
11	Hull	15	4	0	11	125	295	8	26.66
12	Oldham	19	4	0	15	142	306	8	21.05
13	York	17	3	1	13	109	311	7	20.58
14	St. Helens	15	2	0	13	108	273	4	13.33

CHAMPIONSHIP PLAY-OFF

Qualifying Game

Bradford N.	16	Huddersfield	13

Semi-finals

Dewsbury	3	Bradford N.	8
Wigan	4	Halifax	13

Bradford N. were disqualified for fielding an ineligible player.

FINAL

First Leg

	T	G	P		T	G	P
DEWSBURY	3	1	11	HALIFAX	1	0	3

Second Leg

	T	G	P		T	G	P
HALIFAX	3	2	13	DEWSBURY	6	2	22

Aggregate: Dewsbury 33 Halifax 16

Championship declared null and void because Dewsbury fielded an ineligible player.

1943-44

WAR EMERGENCY LEAGUE

		P	W	D	L	F	A	Pts	%
1	Wakefield T.	22	19	0	3	359	97	38	86.36
2	Wigan	21	17	0	4	302	141	34	80.95
3	Hull	21	15	0	6	236	189	30	71.42
4	Dewsbury	22	15	1	6	304	169	31	70.45
5	Halifax	22	15	0	7	279	166	30	68.18
6	Bradford N.	19	11	1	7	292	125	23	60.52
7	Leeds	21	12	1	8	262	252	25	59.52
8	Hunslet	22	12	0	10	287	245	24	54.54
9	Barrow	22	11	0	11	315	199	22	50.00
10	Keighley	21	9	0	12	151	216	18	42.85
11	Huddersfield	21	7	1	13	223	230	15	35.71
12	Oldham	21	7	0	14	137	371	14	33.33
13	Featherstone R.	22	6	0	16	202	229	12	27.27
14	Batley	21	5	1	15	176	299	11	26.19
15	York	22	5	1	16	196	470	11	25.00
16	St. Helens	20	1	0	19	123	446	2	5.00

CHAMPIONSHIP PLAY-OFF

Semi-finals

Wakefield T.	5	Dewsbury	11
Wigan	27	Hull	10

FINAL

First Leg

	T	G	P		T	G	P
WIGAN	3	2	13	DEWSBURY	1	3	9

Second Leg

	T	G	P		T	G	P
DEWSBURY	1	1	5	WIGAN	2	3	12

Aggregate: Wigan 25 Dewsbury 14

1944-45

WAR EMERGENCY LEAGUE

		P	W	D	L	F	A	Pts	%
1	Bradford N.	20	17	0	3	337	69	34	85.00
2	Halifax	16	13	1	2	288	78	27	84.37
3	Wakefield T.	23	17	0	6	380	203	34	73.91
4	Wigan	24	17	1	6	302	138	35	72.91
5	Barrow	23	15	1	7	219	167	31	67.39
6	Castleford	23	14	2	7	274	139	30	65.21
7	Dewsbury	22	11	1	10	243	215	23	52.27
8	Batley	22	10	2	10	186	239	22	50.00
9	Huddersfield	24	8	6	10	281	252	22	45.83
10	Leeds	23	9	2	12	223	236	20	43.47
11	Hunslet	21	7	2	12	164	245	16	38.09
12	Hull	23	8	1	14	193	281	17	36.95
13	Oldham	23	8	1	14	189	282	17	36.95
14	Featherstone R.	22	8	0	14	153	229	16	36.36
15	Keighley	21	7	0	14	114	283	14	33.33
16	St. Helens	23	4	1	18	177	394	9	19.56
17	York	23	4	1	18	153	426	9	19.56

CHAMPIONSHIP PLAY-OFF

Semi-finals

Bradford N.	18	Wigan	15
Halifax	17	Wakefield T.	11

FINAL

First Leg

	T	G	P		T	G	P
HALIFAX	1	3	9	BRADFORD N.	0	1	2

Second Leg

	T	G	P		T	G	P
BRADFORD N.	6	3	24	HALIFAX	1	4	11

Aggregate: Bradford N. 26 Halifax 20

1945-46

		P	W	D	L	F	A	Pts
1	Wigan	36	29	2	5	783	219	60
2	Huddersfield	36	27	1	8	688	286	55
3	Wakefield T.	36	26	0	10	707	283	52
4	Bradford N.	36	24	3	9	544	288	51
5	Barrow	36	22	4	10	535	363	48
6	Dewsbury	36	23	0	13	396	210	46
7	Hunslet	36	21	4	11	525	306	46
8	Salford	36	23	0	13	415	342	46
9	Batley	36	21	4	11	418	403	46
10	Warrington	36	21	3	12	430	343	45
11	Castleford	36	22	0	14	326	298	44
12	Widnes	36	19	3	14	449	272	41
13	Featherstone R.	36	19	1	16	395	397	39
14	Halifax	36	19	0	17	374	374	38
15	Oldham	36	18	0	18	352	403	36
16	Broughton R.	36	16	3	17	352	399	35
17	Hull	36	16	2	18	482	451	34
18	Hull K.R.	36	15	3	18	375	459	33
19	Workington T.	36	15	0	21	358	421	30
20	St. Helens	36	13	1	22	398	527	27
21	Swinton	36	9	5	22	338	528	23
22	Keighley	36	9	2	25	307	640	20
23	Leeds	36	9	1	26	351	581	19
24	Rochdale H.	36	9	1	26	221	513	19
25	Bramley	36	9	0	27	271	620	18
26	Liverpool S.	36	5	2	29	263	700	12
27	York	36	4	1	31	328	769	9

CHAMPIONSHIP PLAY-OFF

Semi-finals

Wigan	18	Bradford N.	4
Huddersfield	8	Wakefield T.	3

FINAL

At Maine Road, Manchester

	T	G	P		T	G	P
WIGAN	3	2	13	HUD'SFIELD	0	2	4

1946-47

		P	W	D	L	F	A	Pts
1	Wigan	36	29	1	6	567	196	59
2	Dewsbury	36	27	1	8	411	158	55
3	Widnes	36	26	2	8	284	140	54
4	Leeds	36	25	2	9	573	305	52
5	Warrington	36	26	0	10	432	236	52
6	Bradford N.	36	24	3	9	525	300	51
7	Huddersfield	36	24	2	10	572	332	50
8	Oldham	36	22	2	12	376	243	46
9	Leigh	36	21	0	15	319	238	42
10	Wakefield T.	36	20	2	14	399	357	42
11	Workington T.	36	19	2	15	345	270	40
12	Barrow	36	18	4	14	385	371	40
13	Castleford	36	19	1	16	401	354	39
14	Hunslet	36	17	2	17	355	355	36
15	Hull	36	17	0	19	388	370	34
16	Hull K.R.	36	15	3	18	359	455	33
17	Batley	36	15	1	20	398	390	31
18	Belle Vue R.	36	14	3	19	388	375	31
19	St. Helens	36	14	1	21	425	366	29
20	Halifax	36	13	2	21	281	440	28
21	York	36	12	2	22	327	549	26
22	Salford	36	11	2	23	280	401	24
23	Liverpool S.	36	11	1	24	322	497	23
24	Swinton	36	11	1	24	262	466	23
25	Keighley	36	10	1	25	299	509	21
26	Featherstone R.	36	9	1	26	217	477	19
27	Rochdale H.	36	9	0	27	223	430	18
28	Bramley	36	5	0	31	232	706	10

CHAMPIONSHIP PLAY-OFF

Semi-finals

Wigan	21	Leeds	11
Dewsbury	5	Widnes	2

FINAL

At Maine Road, Manchester

	T	G	P		T	G	P
WIGAN	3	2	13	DEWSBURY	0	2	4

1947-48

		P	W	D	L	F	A	Pts
1	Wigan	36	31	1	4	776	258	63
2	Warrington	36	30	1	5	688	232	61
3	Huddersfield	36	26	2	8	669	240	54
4	Bradford N.	36	26	0	10	549	310	52
5	Workington T.	36	22	4	10	426	236	48
6	Hunslet	36	21	4	11	449	239	46
7	Widnes	36	21	1	14	331	228	43
8	St. Helens	36	20	2	14	476	305	42
9	Leeds	36	20	2	14	588	409	42
10	Wakefield T.	36	20	2	14	496	378	42
11	Salford	36	20	1	15	347	443	41
12	Hull	36	19	1	16	454	301	39
13	Castleford	36	19	1	16	456	383	39
14	Leigh	36	18	1	17	374	452	37
15	Dewsbury	36	17	2	17	232	301	36
16	Oldham	36	17	1	18	306	385	35
17	Belle Vue R.	36	17	0	19	333	358	34
18	Halifax	36	16	0	20	309	449	32
19	Swinton	36	15	1	20	316	403	31
20	Keighley	36	15	1	20	295	432	31
21	Barrow	36	14	2	20	336	419	30
22	Rochdale H.	36	11	2	23	231	311	24
23	Bramley	36	12	0	24	330	482	24
24	Batley	36	11	1	24	281	482	23
25	Hull K.R.	36	10	1	25	303	470	21
26	Liverpool S.	36	8	1	27	192	550	17
27	Featherstone R.	36	6	0	30	270	724	12
28	York	36	4	1	31	216	849	9

CHAMPIONSHIP PLAY-OFF

Semi-finals

Wigan	3	Bradford N.	15
Warrington	17	Huddersfield	5

FINAL

At Maine Road, Manchester

	T	G	P		T	G	P
WARRINGTON	3	3	15	BRADFORD N.	1	1	5

1948-49

		P	W	D	L	F	A	Pts
1	Warrington	36	31	0	5	728	247	62
2	Wigan	36	28	1	7	802	285	57
3	Huddersfield	36	27	0	9	626	290	54
4	Barrow	36	25	1	10	459	252	51
5	Widnes	36	24	2	10	358	188	50
6	Batley	36	23	0	13	404	348	46
7	Salford	36	20	5	11	371	267	45
8	Workington T.	36	22	1	13	437	318	45
9	Swinton	36	21	3	12	354	305	45
10	Bradford N.	36	22	0	14	344	298	44
11	St. Helens	36	20	1	15	481	282	41
12	Wakefield T.	36	19	1	16	570	396	39
13	Hull	36	19	0	17	375	416	38
14	Leeds	36	18	1	17	490	478	37
15	Keighley	36	17	3	16	299	336	37
16	Hunslet	36	17	0	19	366	377	34
17	Hull K.R.	36	17	0	19	386	457	34
18	Leigh	36	14	5	17	290	330	33
19	Castleford	36	16	0	20	382	356	32
20	Dewsbury	36	15	1	20	355	346	31
21	Belle Vue R.	36	14	1	21	290	414	29
22	Rochdale H.	36	12	3	21	230	335	27
23	Oldham	36	12	3	21	283	450	27
24	Bramley	36	12	2	22	362	546	26
25	Halifax	36	11	3	22	258	372	25
26	Featherstone R.	36	9	3	24	305	519	21
27	Whitehaven	36	6	2	28	216	597	14
28	York	36	5	2	29	194	597	12
29	Liverpool S.	36	3	2	31	145	758	8

CHAMPIONSHIP PLAY-OFF

Semi-finals

Warrington	23	Barrow	8
Wigan	5	Huddersfield	14

FINAL

At Maine Road, Manchester

	T	G	P		T	G	P
HUD'SFIELD	3	2	13	WARRINGTON	2	3	12

1949-50

		P	W	D	L	F	A	Pts
1	Wigan	36	31	1	4	853	320	63
2	Huddersfield	36	28	1	7	694	362	57
3	Swinton	36	25	4	7	516	261	54
4	Halifax	36	25	0	11	496	251	50
5	Salford	36	24	2	10	427	306	50
6	Leigh	36	24	1	11	459	269	49
7	St. Helens	36	23	2	11	540	260	48
8	Leeds	36	24	0	12	602	365	48
9	Dewsbury	36	23	0	13	468	266	46
10	Workington T.	36	22	1	13	514	319	45
11	Warrington	36	22	0	14	579	367	44
12	Castleford	36	20	0	16	431	386	40
13	Keighley	36	20	0	16	375	390	40
14	Wakefield T.	36	19	0	17	523	447	38
15	Hunslet	36	18	1	17	405	317	37
16	Widnes	36	16	4	16	373	316	36
17	Belle Vue R.	36	16	2	18	388	393	34
18	Oldham	36	15	4	17	395	411	34
19	Hull	36	15	3	18	364	527	33
20	Barrow	36	14	1	21	393	464	29
21	Bradford N.	36	14	1	21	335	413	29
22	Hull K.R.	36	14	1	21	305	474	29
23	Whitehaven	36	11	4	21	262	432	26
24	Batley	36	10	0	26	346	555	20
25	Featherstone R.	36	9	2	25	300	551	20
26	Bramley	36	6	1	29	258	676	13
27	Rochdale H.	36	5	2	29	200	547	12
28	York	36	6	0	30	274	807	12
29	Liverpool S.	36	4	0	32	198	821	8

CHAMPIONSHIP PLAY-OFF

Semi-finals

Huddersfield	9	Swinton	0
Wigan	5	Halifax	5

Replay

Halifax	2	Wigan	18

FINAL

At Maine Road, Manchester

	T	G	P		T	G	P
WIGAN	4	4	20	HUD'SFIELD	0	1	2

1950-51

		P	W	D	L	F	A	Pts
1	Warrington	36	30	0	6	738	250	60
2	Wigan	36	29	1	6	774	288	59
3	Workington T.	36	27	0	9	734	328	54
4	Leigh	36	24	2	10	420	288	50
5	Leeds	36	24	0	12	678	441	48
6	St. Helens	36	22	1	13	527	359	45
7	Hunslet	36	22	1	13	526	361	45
8	Batley	36	21	1	14	391	400	43
9	Huddersfield	36	20	2	14	575	410	42
10	Wakefield T.	36	19	3	14	587	521	41
11	Halifax	36	20	0	16	523	407	40
12	Belle Vue R.	36	19	2	15	427	374	40
13	Dewsbury	36	19	2	15	440	327	40
14	Bradford N.	36	19	0	17	406	404	38
15	Oldham	36	17	2	17	403	347	36
16	Keighley	36	16	3	17	359	442	35
17	Swinton	36	16	1	19	395	435	33
18	Hull	36	15	2	19	351	499	32
19	Salford	36	15	1	20	380	419	31
20	Barrow	36	14	2	20	385	518	30
21	Whitehaven	36	13	3	20	257	411	29
22	Rochdale H.	36	14	1	21	321	534	29
23	Hull K.R.	36	12	2	22	450	699	26
24	Bramley	36	11	3	22	380	530	25
25	Castleford	36	12	1	23	376	548	25
26	Featherstone R.	36	12	1	23	375	562	25
27	Widnes	36	10	1	25	265	382	21
28	York	36	8	1	27	266	706	17
29	Liverpool S.	36	2	1	33	193	712	5

CHAMPIONSHIP PLAY-OFF

Semi-finals

Wigan	5	Workington T.	8
Warrington	15	Leigh	9

FINAL

At Maine Road, Manchester

	T	G	P		T	G	P
WORK'N T.	6	4	26	WARRINGTON	3	1	11

1951-52

		P	W	D	L	F	A	Pts
1	Bradford N.	36	28	1	7	758	326	57
2	Wigan	36	27	1	8	750	296	55
3	Hull	36	26	1	9	552	393	53
4	Huddersfield	36	26	0	10	785	446	52
5	Oldham	36	25	1	10	558	331	51
6	Warrington	36	24	1	11	622	396	49
7	Leigh	36	23	2	11	489	365	48
8	Workington T.	36	23	0	13	540	347	46
9	Hunslet	36	22	1	13	559	404	45
10	Barrow	36	21	2	13	697	345	44
11	Doncaster	36	21	1	14	422	371	43
12	Widnes	36	20	2	14	491	395	42
13	Leeds	36	19	2	15	578	514	40
14	Swinton	36	18	3	15	432	382	39
15	Salford	36	18	2	16	454	386	38
16	Wakefield T.	36	19	0	17	596	518	38
17	Batley	36	18	1	17	440	498	37
18	Dewsbury	36	18	0	18	419	439	36
19	Whitehaven	36	16	4	16	280	356	36
20	St. Helens	36	16	2	18	426	358	34
21	Halifax	36	16	2	18	474	403	34
22	Featherstone R.	36	14	2	20	431	470	30
23	Belle Vue R.	36	12	3	21	351	446	27
24	York	36	12	3	21	363	583	27
25	Hull K.R.	36	10	1	25	416	708	21
26	Rochdale H.	36	10	1	25	328	585	21
27	Bramley	36	10	1	25	300	577	21
28	Castleford	36	8	1	27	370	579	17
29	Keighley	36	8	1	27	351	617	17
30	Cardiff	36	5	0	31	342	1,024	10
31	Liverpool C.	36	4	0	32	199	915	8

CHAMPIONSHIP PLAY-OFF

Semi-finals

Wigan	13	Hull	9
Bradford N.	18	Huddersfield	15

FINAL

At Leeds Road, Huddersfield

	T	G	P		T	G	P
WIGAN	3	2	13	BRADFORD N.	0	3	6

1952-53

		P	W	D	L	F	A	Pts
1	St. Helens	36	32	2	2	769	273	66
2	Halifax	36	29	2	5	620	309	60
3	Bradford N.	36	28	0	8	700	329	56
4	Huddersfield	36	27	2	7	747	366	56
5	Barrow	36	27	1	8	585	322	55
6	Leeds	36	24	0	12	690	452	48
7	Leigh	36	23	2	11	556	377	48
8	Oldham	36	22	2	12	599	280	46
9	Warrington	36	20	1	15	733	486	41
10	Whitehaven	36	19	3	14	465	486	41
11	Wigan	36	19	2	15	673	414	40
12	Hunslet	36	20	0	16	485	358	40
13	Salford	36	20	0	16	508	441	40
14	Swinton	36	18	0	18	441	401	36
15	Hull	36	17	2	17	461	451	36
16	Workington T.	36	16	2	18	453	460	34
17	Keighley	36	16	1	19	465	547	33
18	Wakefield T.	36	16	0	20	410	595	32
19	Dewsbury	36	15	1	20	410	440	31
20	Castleford	36	15	0	21	392	502	30
21	Batley	36	14	2	20	405	579	30
22	Rochdale H.	36	13	3	20	443	536	29
23	Widnes	36	13	2	21	336	478	28
24	Featherstone R.	36	12	1	23	415	535	25
25	York	36	10	0	26	370	496	20
26	Doncaster	36	10	0	26	377	665	20
27	Belle Vue R.	36	10	0	26	301	705	20
28	Hull K.R.	36	9	1	26	337	646	19
29	Bramley	36	6	0	30	293	898	12
30	Liverpool C.	36	4	0	32	225	837	8

CHAMPIONSHIP PLAY-OFF

Semi-finals

Halifax	18	Bradford N.	16
St. Helens	46	Huddersfield	0

FINAL

At Maine Road, Manchester

	T	G	P		T	G	P
ST. HELENS	6	3	24	HALIFAX	2	4	14

1953-54

		P	W	D	L	F	A	Pts
1	Halifax	36	30	2	4	538	219	62
2	Warrington	36	30	1	5	663	311	61
3	St. Helens	36	28	2	6	672	297	58
4	Workington T.	36	29	0	7	604	333	58
5	Hull	36	25	0	11	685	349	50
6	Huddersfield	36	24	0	12	689	417	48
7	Wigan	36	23	1	12	688	392	47
8	Barrow	36	23	0	13	574	377	46
9	Bradford N.	36	22	0	14	628	414	44
10	Leeds	36	22	0	14	766	517	44
11	Wakefield T.	36	19	1	16	671	508	39
12	Oldham	36	17	4	15	504	366	38
13	Leigh	36	19	0	17	547	459	38
14	Featherstone R.	36	18	2	16	478	431	38
15	Hunslet	36	19	0	17	455	451	38
16	Widnes	36	16	3	17	420	431	35
17	York	36	17	0	19	412	401	34
18	Keighley	36	15	3	18	473	533	33
19	Rochdale H.	36	14	3	19	404	457	31
20	Dewsbury	36	14	3	19	432	508	31
21	Whitehaven	36	14	1	21	362	544	29
22	Salford	36	13	2	21	370	438	28
23	Swinton	36	13	1	22	341	513	27
24	Batley	36	13	1	22	367	658	27
25	Bramley	36	11	3	22	437	746	25
26	Castleford	36	11	1	24	437	728	23
27	Belle Vue R.	36	7	2	27	307	714	16
28	Doncaster	36	5	2	29	340	840	12
29	Hull K.R.	36	5	2	29	298	737	12
30	Liverpool C.	36	4	0	32	304	777	8

CHAMPIONSHIP PLAY-OFF

Semi-finals

Halifax	18	Workington T.	7
Warrington	11	St. Helens	0

FINAL

At Maine Road, Manchester

	T	G	P		T	G	P
WARRINGTON	0	4	8	HALIFAX	1	2	7

1954-55

		P	W	D	L	F	A	Pts
1	Warrington	36	29	2	5	718	321	60
2	Oldham	36	29	2	5	633	313	60
3	Leeds	36	26	2	8	667	378	54
4	Halifax	36	26	1	9	579	269	53
5	Wigan	36	26	1	9	643	328	53
6	Leigh	36	25	2	9	738	399	52
7	St. Helens	36	25	1	10	631	337	51
8	Barrow	36	24	0	12	581	386	48
9	Featherstone R.	36	23	1	12	572	424	47
10	Workington T.	36	23	0	13	573	391	46
11	Huddersfield	36	22	0	14	790	483	44
12	Rochdale H.	36	20	3	13	396	346	43
13	York	36	21	0	15	439	374	42
14	Hunslet	36	20	0	16	582	477	40
15	Whitehaven	36	18	3	15	406	424	39
16	Wakefield T.	36	18	0	18	589	577	36
17	Bradford N.	36	17	2	17	476	475	36
18	Keighley	36	18	0	18	433	543	36
19	Hull	36	16	3	17	547	486	35
20	Swinton	36	16	1	19	398	451	33
21	Castleford	36	13	4	19	518	516	30
22	Widnes	36	13	0	23	325	478	26
23	Bramley	36	11	1	24	434	602	23
24	Liverpool C.	36	11	1	24	402	582	23
25	Hull K.R.	36	10	0	26	347	756	20
26	Salford	36	7	3	26	279	527	17
27	Doncaster	36	8	1	27	346	664	17
28	Batley	36	7	0	29	278	677	14
29	Blackpool B.	36	7	0	29	303	759	14
30	Belle Vue R.	36	7	0	29	248	666	14
31	Dewsbury	36	5	0	31	255	717	10

CHAMPIONSHIP PLAY-OFF

Semi-finals

Warrington	17	Halifax	9
Oldham	25	Leeds	6

FINAL

At Maine Road, Manchester

	T	G	P		T	G	P
WARRINGTON	1	2	7	OLDHAM	1	0	3

1955-56

		P	W	D	L	F	A	Pts	%*
1	Warrington	34	27	1	6	712	349	55	80.88
2	Halifax	36	28	2	6	761	306	58	80.55
3	St. Helens	34	27	0	7	766	351	54	79.41
4	Hull	36	25	1	10	720	458	51	70.83
5	Wigan	34	22	2	10	596	402	46	67.64
6	Featherstone R.	36	23	2	11	579	464	48	66.66
7	Barrow	34	21	2	11	676	506	44	64.70
8	Bradford N.	36	22	2	12	622	455	46	63.88
9	Oldham	34	20	0	14	658	455	40	58.82
10	Swinton	34	19	2	13	441	373	40	58.82
11	Leigh	34	19	2	13	588	565	40	58.82
12	Leeds	36	21	0	15	698	564	42	58.33
13	York	36	20	0	16	503	472	40	55.55
14	Huddersfield	36	18	1	17	606	544	37	51.37
15	Workington T.	34	17	0	17	532	520	34	50.00
16	Keighley	36	18	0	18	495	525	36	50.00
17	Wakefield T.	36	17	0	19	581	539	34	47.22
18	Hunslet	36	17	0	19	511	588	34	47.22
19	Bramley	34	16	0	18	535	605	32	47.05
20	Rochdale H.	34	15	0	19	475	514	30	44.11
21	Whitehaven	34	14	1	19	482	499	29	42.64
22	Salford	34	13	1	20	391	575	27	39.70
23	Widnes	34	11	0	23	403	519	22	32.35
24	Hull K.R.	36	11	1	24	365	747	23	31.94
25	Doncaster	34	7	5	22	349	592	19	27.94
26	Blackpool B.	34	9	0	25	449	745	18	26.47
27	Castleford	36	9	0	27	462	751	18	25.00
28	Liverpool C.	34	8	0	26	375	685	16	23.52
29	Dewsbury	34	8	0	26	315	700	16	23.52
30	Batley	34	7	1	26	367	645	15	22.05

*Positions decided on percentage basis after Belle Vue Rangers withdrew shortly before the start of the season.

CHAMPIONSHIP PLAY-OFF

Semi-finals

Halifax	23	St. Helens	8
Warrington	0	Hull	17

FINAL

At Maine Road, Manchester

	T	G	P		T	G	P
HULL	2	2	10	HALIFAX	3	0	9

1956-57

		P	W	D	L	F	A	Pts
1	Oldham	38	33	0	5	893	365	66
2	Hull	38	29	2	7	764	432	60
3	Barrow	38	29	0	9	702	481	58
4	Leeds	38	28	0	10	818	490	56
5	St. Helens	38	25	3	10	902	355	53
6	Wigan	38	26	0	12	750	417	52
7	Hunslet	38	26	0	12	688	417	52
8	Wakefield T.	38	23	1	14	747	545	47
9	Huddersfield	38	23	0	15	667	533	46
10	Warrington	38	21	1	16	571	565	43
11	York	38	21	0	17	641	538	42
12	Halifax	38	21	0	17	559	514	42
13	Salford	38	19	2	17	518	499	40
14	Workington T.	38	20	0	18	494	516	40
15	Featherstone R.	38	19	0	19	612	504	38
16	Rochdale H.	38	19	0	19	510	611	38
17	Leigh	38	18	1	19	684	608	37
18	Whitehaven	38	18	1	19	601	646	37
19	Swinton	38	18	0	20	576	594	36
20	Keighley	38	17	1	20	494	534	35
21	Bradford N.	38	17	0	21	479	672	34
22	Bramley	38	14	2	22	558	632	30
23	Widnes	38	15	0	23	439	526	30
24	Blackpool B.	38	14	0	24	470	875	28
25	Castleford	38	11	2	25	488	739	24
26	Hull K.R.	38	11	2	25	395	672	24
27	Liverpool C.	38	9	1	28	356	854	19
28	Batley	38	8	0	30	399	700	16
29	Dewsbury	38	5	1	32	391	819	11
30	Doncaster	38	3	0	35	321	835	6

CHAMPIONSHIP PLAY-OFF

Semi-finals

Hull	45	Barrow	14
Oldham	22	Leeds	12

FINAL

At Odsal, Bradford

	T	G	P		T	G	P
OLDHAM	3	3	15	HULL	2	4	14

1957-58

		P	W	D	L	F	A	Pts
1	Oldham	38	33	1	4	803	415	67
2	St. Helens	38	32	0	6	842	336	64
3	Workington T.	38	28	2	8	685	356	58
4	Hull	38	27	2	9	920	431	56
5	Wigan	38	27	0	11	815	430	54
6	Halifax	38	25	2	11	819	441	52
7	Leigh	38	24	0	14	625	457	48
8	Featherstone R.	38	23	1	14	606	497	47
9	Wakefield T.	38	22	2	14	729	477	46
10	Widnes	38	23	0	15	608	453	46
11	Hunslet	38	22	1	15	611	569	45
12	York	38	19	4	15	627	489	42
13	Warrington	38	19	1	18	669	529	39
14	Leeds	38	18	1	19	657	662	37
15	Salford	38	18	1	19	471	542	37
16	Hull K.R.	38	17	2	19	477	570	36
17	Whitehaven	38	17	1	20	559	579	35
18	Huddersfield	38	17	1	20	531	675	35
19	Rochdale H.	38	17	1	20	466	642	35
20	Bradford N.	38	16	2	20	574	594	34
21	Barrow	38	16	2	20	579	688	34
22	Keighley	38	15	2	21	576	527	32
23	Bramley	38	14	2	22	477	728	30
24	Swinton	38	13	3	22	506	589	29
25	Blackpool B.	38	12	0	26	488	726	24
26	Batley	38	10	0	28	434	722	20
27	Liverpool C.	38	9	1	28	442	728	19
28	Dewsbury	38	6	4	28	375	944	16
29	Castleford	38	7	1	30	443	893	15
30	Doncaster	38	4	0	34	246	971	8

CHAMPIONSHIP PLAY-OFF

Semi-finals

Oldham	8	Hull	20
St. Helens	13	Workington T.	14

FINAL

At Odsal, Bradford

	T	G	P		T	G	P
HULL	4	4	20	WORK'N T.	1	0	3

1958-59

		P	W	D	L	F	A	Pts
1	St. Helens	38	31	1	6	1,005	450	63
2	Wigan	38	29	0	9	894	491	58
3	Hunslet	38	27	3	8	819	493	57
4	Oldham	38	28	1	9	791	477	57
5	Wakefield T.	38	27	1	10	790	393	55
6	Swinton	38	27	1	10	691	442	55
7	Hull	38	25	1	12	796	413	51
8	Widnes	38	23	0	15	672	474	46
9	Warrington	38	22	0	16	780	585	44
10	Bradford N.	38	20	2	16	593	563	42
11	York	38	20	1	17	621	622	41
12	Halifax	38	19	2	17	695	594	40
13	Featherstone R.	38	18	3	17	597	613	39
14	Leeds	38	19	0	19	608	653	38
15	Keighley	38	18	1	19	560	629	37
16	Leigh	38	18	0	20	585	562	36
17	Barrow	38	18	0	20	573	602	36
18	Hull K.R.	38	18	0	20	542	619	36
19	Huddersfield	38	18	0	20	573	677	36
20	Workington T.	38	16	3	19	499	585	35
21	Whitehaven	38	17	0	21	659	627	34
22	Salford	38	16	1	21	603	680	33
23	Bramley	38	15	1	22	409	579	31
24	Blackpool B.	38	15	0	23	477	753	30
25	Castleford	38	13	0	25	527	732	26
26	Rochdale H.	38	11	1	26	398	649	23
27	Batley	38	10	1	27	433	679	21
28	Liverpool C.	38	8	0	30	476	954	16
29	Dewsbury	38	7	0	31	378	859	14
30	Doncaster	38	5	0	33	329	924	10

CHAMPIONSHIP PLAY-OFF

Semi-finals

St. Helens	42	Oldham	4
Wigan	11	Hunslet	22

FINAL

At Odsal, Bradford

	T	G	P		T	G	P
ST. HELENS	8	10	44	HUNSLET	4	5	22

1959-60

		P	W	D	L	F	A	Pts
1	St. Helens	38	34	1	3	947	343	69
2	Wakefield T.	38	32	0	6	831	348	64
3	Hull	38	28	1	9	758	474	57
4	Wigan	38	27	2	9	828	390	56
5	Featherstone R.	38	27	0	11	730	437	54
6	Whitehaven	38	22	3	13	594	533	47
7	Warrington	38	22	2	14	650	482	46
8	Swinton	38	22	2	14	654	503	46
9	Oldham	38	22	1	15	744	461	45
10	Hunslet	38	21	3	14	595	488	45
11	Leigh	38	20	4	14	600	502	44
12	Huddersfield	38	21	1	16	603	510	43
13	Hull K.R.	38	20	1	17	517	575	41
14	Leeds	38	20	0	18	641	573	40
15	Salford	38	19	2	17	629	583	40
16	Batley	38	18	3	17	476	506	39
17	Widnes	38	18	1	19	598	519	37
18	Castleford	38	18	0	20	561	630	36
19	Workington T.	38	18	0	20	448	530	36
20	Keighley	38	17	1	20	575	659	35
21	York	38	17	0	21	579	698	34
22	Halifax	38	15	2	21	627	561	32
23	Rochdale H.	38	15	0	23	435	519	30
24	Barrow	38	13	1	24	422	562	27
25	Bramley	38	10	2	26	393	673	22
26	Bradford N.	38	9	3	26	450	645	21
27	Liverpool C.	38	9	3	26	383	720	21
28	Blackpool B.	38	9	1	28	400	819	19
29	Dewsbury	38	4	1	33	337	982	9
30	Doncaster	38	2	1	35	284	1,064	5

CHAMPIONSHIP PLAY-OFF

Semi-finals

St. Helens	9	Wigan	19
Wakefield T.	24	Hull	4

FINAL

At Odsal, Bradford

	T	G	P		T	G	P
WIGAN	5	6	27	WAKEFIELD T.	1	0	3

1960-61

		P	W	D	L	F	A	Pts
1	Leeds	36	30	0	6	620	258	60
2	Warrington	36	27	1	8	701	269	55
3	Swinton	36	27	1	8	647	271	55
4	St. Helens	36	27	0	9	773	304	54
5	Wigan	36	26	0	10	689	334	52
6	Leigh	36	26	0	10	588	299	52
7	Wakefield T.	36	26	0	10	576	326	52
8	Oldham	36	25	1	10	667	359	51
9	Featherstone R.	36	23	1	12	520	403	47
10	Workington T.	36	21	0	15	515	468	42
11	Hull	36	20	1	15	606	448	41
12	Hull K.R.	36	19	2	15	472	462	40
13	Halifax	36	19	1	16	500	436	39
14	Huddersfield	36	18	2	16	449	429	38
15	Hunslet	36	18	0	18	442	415	36
16	Whitehaven	36	17	2	17	448	478	36
17	Castleford	36	16	2	18	465	502	34
18	York	36	16	2	18	502	547	34
19	Batley	36	16	1	19	343	415	33
20	Widnes	36	16	0	20	396	514	32
21	Blackpool B.	36	14	3	19	405	443	31
22	Bramley	36	12	1	23	333	517	25
23	Salford	36	11	2	23	341	689	24
24	Bradford N.	36	10	2	24	312	580	22
25	Keighley	36	10	1	25	349	553	21
26	Barrow	36	9	2	25	305	578	20
27	Dewsbury	36	8	3	25	296	573	19
28	Rochdale H.	36	9	0	27	296	733	18
29	Liverpool C.	36	5	1	30	296	768	11
30	Doncaster	36	3	0	33	287	768	6

CHAMPIONSHIP PLAY-OFF

Semi-finals

Leeds	11	St. Helens	4
Warrington	13	Swinton	5

FINAL

At Odsal, Bradford

	T	G	P		T	G	P
LEEDS	5	5	25	WARRINGTON	2	2	10

1961-62

		P	W	D	L	F	A	Pts
1	Wigan	36	32	1	3	885	283	65
2	Wakefield T.	36	32	1	3	822	288	65
3	Featherstone R.	36	28	1	7	621	370	57
4	Huddersfield	36	25	2	9	494	351	52
5	Workington T.	36	25	0	11	658	362	50
6	Widnes	36	25	0	11	508	309	50
7	Leeds	36	25	0	11	593	390	50
8	Hull K.R.	36	24	0	12	513	451	48
9	St. Helens	36	23	0	13	606	302	46
10	Oldham	36	22	1	13	643	344	45
11	Swinton	36	21	1	14	527	326	43
12	Castleford	36	21	0	15	501	369	42
13	Bramley	36	19	4	13	450	393	42
14	Warrington	36	19	2	15	576	435	40
15	Halifax	36	18	3	15	400	334	39
16	Hull	36	18	1	17	573	415	37
17	Leigh	36	17	0	19	388	497	34
18	Barrow	36	14	1	21	423	558	29
19	Keighley	36	13	2	21	365	467	28
20	York	36	12	1	23	462	531	25
21	Salford	36	12	1	23	385	740	25
22	Whitehaven	36	11	2	23	383	539	24
23	Blackpool B.	36	11	1	24	335	600	23
24	Rochdale H.	36	9	4	23	317	595	22
25	Hunslet	36	10	1	25	350	582	21
26	Batley	36	9	2	25	255	538	20
27	Dewsbury	36	8	2	26	260	543	18
28	Doncaster	36	8	1	27	294	668	17
29	Liverpool C.	36	6	0	30	224	753	12
30	Bradford N.	36	5	1	30	288	766	11

CHAMPIONSHIP PLAY-OFF

Semi-finals

Wigan	11	Huddersfield	13
Wakefield T.	13	Featherstone R.	8

FINAL

At Odsal, Bradford

	T	G	P		T	G	P
HUD'SFIELD	2	4	14	WAKEFIELD T.	1	1	5

1962-63 and 1963-64 two divisions — see start of this section.

● With yet another return to one league it was decided to extend the championship play-off to the top 16 clubs.

1964-65

		P	W	D	L	F	A	Pts
1	St. Helens	34	28	0	6	621	226	56
2	Wigan	34	26	0	8	626	260	52
3	Castleford	34	25	1	8	555	294	51
4	Wakefield T.	34	24	2	8	486	228	50
5	Warrington	34	24	1	9	416	292	49
6	Workington T.	34	23	1	10	497	326	47
7	Halifax	34	22	1	11	629	335	45
8	Hull K.R.	34	22	0	12	587	377	44
9	Oldham	34	20	1	13	444	312	41
10	Leeds	34	20	0	14	469	349	40
11	Swinton	34	19	1	14	334	250	39
12	Leigh	34	19	1	14	446	349	39
13	Hull	34	19	0	15	412	381	38
14	Hunslet	34	19	0	15	477	466	38
15	Featherstone R.	34	18	0	16	436	463	36
16	Barrow	34	18	0	16	383	408	36
17	Bradford N.	34	15	1	18	345	347	31
18	Huddersfield	34	15	0	19	368	419	30
19	Widnes	34	14	2	18	348	410	30
20	Whitehaven	34	14	1	19	308	402	29
21	Dewsbury	34	13	2	19	298	407	28
22	Salford	34	11	2	21	307	420	24
23	Liverpool C.	34	10	2	22	248	519	22
24	Bramley	34	10	1	23	309	456	21
25	York	34	10	0	24	347	535	20
26	Batley	34	9	1	24	263	613	19
27	Keighley	34	9	0	25	303	592	18
28	Doncaster	34	9	0	25	296	616	18
29	Rochdale H.	34	7	1	26	293	493	15
30	Blackpool B.	34	6	2	26	248	554	14

CHAMPIONSHIP PLAY-OFF

First Round

Wigan	8	Featherstone R.	15
Castleford	18	Hunslet	7
Halifax	28	Leeds	11
Warrington	10	Leigh	4
Wakefield T.	15	Hull	9
St. Helens	23	Barrow	7
Workington T.	29	Swinton	2
Hull K.R.	26	Oldham	14

Second Round

Wakefield T.	17	Warrington	8
St. Helens	24	Hull K.R.	6
Castleford	11	Workington T.	3
Halifax	31	Featherstone R.	6

Semi-finals

Castleford	18	Halifax	26
St. Helens	10	Wakefield T.	5

FINAL

At Station Road, Swinton

	T	G	P		T	G	P
HALIFAX	3	3	15	ST. HELENS	1	2	7

1965-66

		P	W	D	L	F	A	Pts
1	St. Helens	34	28	1	5	521	275	57
2	Swinton	34	27	1	6	510	283	55
3	Wigan	34	27	0	7	604	302	54
4	Wakefield T.	34	25	2	7	562	239	52
5	Castleford	34	23	3	8	524	233	49
6	Leeds	34	24	0	10	493	295	48
7	Bradford N.	34	21	1	12	375	247	43
8	Workington T.	34	21	1	12	423	306	43
9	Oldham	34	20	3	11	398	347	43
10	Halifax	34	21	0	13	482	318	42
11	Huddersfield	34	20	0	14	420	267	40
12	Hull K.R.	34	20	0	14	496	321	40
13	Hull	34	20	0	14	447	346	40
14	Widnes	34	17	0	17	444	347	34
15	Featherstone R.	34	17	0	17	408	399	34
16	Warrington	34	16	1	17	287	339	33
17	Hunslet	34	15	2	17	378	436	32
18	Salford	34	15	1	18	360	438	31
19	Keighley	34	15	0	19	266	452	30
20	Leigh	34	14	1	19	309	418	29
21	Barrow	34	13	1	20	410	367	27
22	Bramley	34	12	2	20	331	475	26
23	York	34	11	0	23	316	507	22
24	Dewsbury	34	10	1	23	257	424	21
25	Rochdale H.	34	10	0	24	284	387	20
26	Liverpool C.	34	9	2	23	307	494	20
27	Blackpool B.	34	9	1	24	331	549	19
28	Batley	34	6	2	26	196	576	14
29	Doncaster	34	6	0	28	228	586	12
30	Whitehaven	34	4	2	28	191	585	10

CHAMPIONSHIP PLAY-OFF

First Round

Bradford N.	7	Halifax	21
Castleford	10	Hull K.R.	13
Leeds	19	Huddersfield	7
St. Helens	35	Warrington	7
Swinton	43	Featherstone R.	2
Wakefield T.	36	Hull	6
Wigan	27	Widnes	10
Workington T.	6	Oldham	7

Second Round

St. Helens	15	Oldham	10
Swinton	2	Halifax	33
Wakefield T.	9	Hull K.R.	10
Wigan	22	Leeds	5

Semi-finals

St. Helens	14	Hull K.R.	6
Wigan	12	Halifax	25

FINAL

At Station Road, Swinton

	T	G	P		T	G	P
ST. HELENS	7	7	35	HALIFAX	2	3	12

1966-67

		P	W	D	L	F	A	Pts
1	Leeds	34	29	0	5	704	373	58
2	Hull K.R.	34	26	2	6	691	335	54
3	Wakefield T.	34	27	0	7	631	339	54
4	St. Helens	34	22	3	9	551	344	47
5	Bradford N.	34	22	2	10	506	346	46
6	Workington T.	34	22	1	11	517	345	45
7	Swinton	34	20	3	11	472	354	43
8	Castleford	34	21	0	13	560	409	42
9	Hull	34	18	3	13	492	430	39
10	Oldham	34	18	2	14	466	362	38
11	Halifax	34	18	2	14	567	477	38
12	Warrington	34	18	1	15	423	438	37
13	Leigh	34	17	3	14	412	433	37
14	Salford	34	18	1	15	398	424	37
15	Barrow	34	17	2	15	479	407	36
16	Widnes	34	15	5	14	366	412	35
17	Wigan	34	17	0	17	513	456	34
18	Rochdale H.	34	15	4	15	408	395	34
19	Dewsbury	34	15	1	18	374	390	31
20	Featherstone R.	34	12	3	19	401	477	27
21	Huddersfield	34	13	0	21	369	379	26
22	York	34	13	0	21	457	615	26
23	Bramley	34	12	0	22	371	488	24
24	Keighley	34	11	1	22	413	615	23
25	Hunslet	34	9	2	23	402	578	20
26	Blackpool B.	34	9	2	23	333	509	20
27	Whitehaven	34	10	0	24	313	593	20
28	Liverpool C.	34	9	0	25	332	552	18
29	Doncaster	34	8	1	25	361	677	17
30	Batley	34	7	0	27	280	610	14

CHAMPIONSHIP PLAY-OFF

First Round

Bradford N.	12	Warrington	6
Castleford	21	Hull	7
Hull K.R.	17	Barrow	15
Leeds	27	Widnes	18
St. Helens	34	Leigh	12
Swinton	12	Oldham	12
Wakefield T.	48	Salford	8
Workington T.	23	Halifax	14

Replay

Oldham	7	Swinton	15

Second Round

Hull K.R.	36	Swinton	10
Leeds	9	Castleford	13
St. Helens	15	Bradford N.	8
Wakefield T.	22	Workington T.	2

Semi-finals

Hull K.R.	6	Wakefield T.	18
St. Helens	14	Castleford	3

FINAL

At Headingley, Leeds

	T	G	P		T	G	P
WAKEFIELD T.	1	2	7	ST.HELENS	1	2	7

Replay

At Station Road, Swinton

	T	G	P		T	G	P
WAKEFIELD T.	5	3	21	ST. HELENS	1	3	9

1967-68

		P	W	D	L	F	A	Pts
1	Leeds	34	28	0	6	720	271	56
2	Wakefield T.	34	24	1	9	600	295	49
3	Hull K.R.	34	24	1	9	620	348	49
4	St. Helens	34	24	1	9	472	334	49
5	Warrington	34	24	0	10	539	290	48
6	Bradford N.	34	24	0	10	560	309	48
7	Leigh	34	22	1	11	426	254	45
8	Castleford	34	22	1	11	510	344	45
9	Salford	34	22	0	12	470	313	44
10	Workington T.	34	21	1	12	522	355	43
11	Wigan	34	21	0	13	602	350	42
12	Hull	34	21	0	13	530	432	42
13	Halifax	34	19	2	13	441	459	40
14	Swinton	34	18	1	15	485	448	37
15	Huddersfield	34	17	2	15	343	336	36
16	Widnes	34	17	1	16	538	420	35
17	Dewsbury	34	17	0	17	329	426	34
18	Featherstone R.	34	16	0	18	455	437	32
19	Barrow	34	14	0	20	420	485	28
20	Bramley	34	14	0	20	380	498	28
21	Hunslet	34	13	0	21	430	507	26
22	Oldham	34	13	0	21	433	559	26
23	Rochdale H.	34	13	0	21	335	489	26
24	Liverpool C.	34	11	2	21	363	493	24
25	Whitehaven	34	10	1	23	300	577	21
26	York	34	9	1	24	368	687	19
27	Keighley	34	8	0	26	295	475	16
28	Blackpool B.	34	6	1	27	307	634	13
29	Doncaster	34	4	2	28	264	768	10
30	Batley	34	4	1	29	247	711	9

CHAMPIONSHIP PLAY-OFF

First Round

Bradford N.	8	Wigan	28
Castleford	47	Salford	15
Hull K.R.	17	Swinton	2
Leeds	31	Widnes	17
Leigh	43	Workington T.	4
St. Helens	31	Halifax	2
Wakefield T.	20	Huddersfield	11
Warrington	12	Hull	9

Second Round

Hull K.R.	22	Leigh	3
Leeds	7	Wigan	11
St. Helens	20	Warrington	0
Wakefield T.	17	Castleford	14

Semi-finals

Hull K.R.	23	St. Helens	10
Wakefield T.	26	Wigan	9

FINAL

At Headingley, Leeds

	T	G	P		T	G	P
WAKEFIELD T.	3	4	17	HULL K.R.	2	2	10

1968-69

		P	W	D	L	F	A	Pts
1	Leeds	34	29	2	3	775	358	60
2	St. Helens	34	27	2	5	669	262	56
3	Wigan	34	25	2	7	732	368	52
4	Castleford	34	24	2	8	462	255	50
5	Swinton	34	23	0	11	503	412	46
6	Salford	34	19	5	10	573	309	43
7	Featherstone R.	34	21	1	12	523	346	43
8	Workington T.	34	21	0	13	512	379	42
9	Leigh	34	19	4	11	447	371	42
10	Hull K.R.	34	20	0	14	566	445	40
11	York	34	20	0	14	477	440	40
12	Wakefield T.	34	19	1	14	473	375	39
13	Hull	34	18	3	13	494	419	39
14	Widnes	34	19	1	14	506	434	39
15	Keighley	34	18	1	15	380	407	37
16	Oldham	34	18	0	16	479	474	36
17	Warrington	34	17	1	16	561	546	35
18	Halifax	34	16	2	16	468	485	34
19	Bradford N.	34	16	0	18	525	475	32
20	Barrow	34	13	1	20	454	559	27
21	Rochdale H.	34	13	0	21	342	485	26
22	Dewsbury	34	12	1	21	306	430	25
23	Hunslet	34	11	0	23	439	554	22
24	Doncaster	34	11	0	23	279	622	22
25	Huddersfield	34	9	1	24	296	553	19
26	Batley	34	8	1	25	294	577	17
27	Huyton	34	8	0	26	273	657	16
28	Bramley	34	7	0	27	313	575	14
29	Blackpool B.	34	7	0	27	382	752	14
30	Whitehaven	34	6	1	27	360	539	13

CHAMPIONSHIP PLAY-OFF

First Round

Castleford	14	Hull	10
Featherstone R.	16	Hull K.R.	5
Leeds	32	Oldham	12
Salford	13	York	7
St. Helens	25	Keighley	7
Swinton	9	Wakefield T.	5
Wigan	26	Widnes	10
Workington T.	11	Leigh	9

Second Round

Castleford	50	Swinton	8
Leeds	18	Workington T.	10
St. Helens	47	Featherstone R.	4
Wigan	21	Salford	26

Semi-finals

Leeds	22	Salford	12
St. Helens	6	Castleford	18

FINAL

At Odsal, Bradford

	T	G	P		T	G	P
LEEDS	2	5	16	CASTLEFORD	2	4	14

1969-70

		P	W	D	L	F	A	Pts
1	Leeds	34	30	0	4	674	314	60
2	Castleford	34	25	1	8	493	298	51
3	St. Helens	34	23	1	10	702	292	47
4	Wigan	34	23	0	11	698	420	46
5	Hull K.R.	34	22	2	10	566	395	46
6	Salford	34	22	1	11	572	332	45
7	Leigh	34	21	3	10	554	325	45
8	Featherstone R.	34	22	1	11	558	385	45
9	Swinton	34	20	4	10	550	351	44
10	Widnes	34	21	2	11	473	355	44
11	Hull	34	20	2	12	420	357	42
12	Bradford N.	34	19	0	15	511	404	38
13	Whitehaven	34	18	2	14	404	450	38
14	Warrington	34	17	2	15	559	421	36
15	Huddersfield	34	17	1	16	377	395	35
16	Halifax	34	16	0	18	395	454	32
17	Batley	34	15	1	18	388	485	31
18	Bramley	34	14	1	19	374	498	29
19	Barrow	34	14	1	19	379	511	29
20	Rochdale H.	34	13	3	18	334	524	29
21	Wakefield T.	34	13	2	19	521	452	28
22	Dewsbury	34	13	1	20	383	451	27
23	Hunslet	34	13	1	20	391	574	27
24	Workington T.	34	12	2	20	416	483	26
25	Keighley	34	13	0	21	370	555	26
26	York	34	11	1	22	378	502	23
27	Doncaster	34	7	0	27	264	564	14
28	Huyton	34	5	3	26	177	643	13
29	Oldham	34	6	0	28	343	590	12
30	Blackpool B.	34	6	0	28	318	762	12

CHAMPIONSHIP PLAY-OFF

First Round

Leigh	21	Widnes	10
Hull K.R.	26	Bradford N.	13
Leeds	24	Halifax	4
Wigan	20	Whitehaven	20
Featherstone R.	24	Swinton	18
St. Helens	36	Warrington	8
Salford	11	Hull	4
Castleford	17	Huddersfield	7

Replay

Whitehaven	9	Wigan	4

Second Round

Hull K.R.	27	Salford	16
Castleford	15	Featherstone R.	3
Leeds	45	Whitehaven	10
St. Helens	16	Leigh	5

Semi-finals

Leeds	47	Hull K.R.	5
Castleford	9	St. Helens	9

Replay

St. Helens	21	Castleford	12

FINAL

At Odsal, Bradford

	T	G	P		T	G	P
ST. HELENS	4	6	24	LEEDS	2	3	12

1970-71

		P	W	D	L	F	A	Pts
1	Wigan	34	30	0	4	662	308	60
2	St. Helens	34	29	0	5	748	231	58
3	Leeds	34	28	0	6	856	352	56
4	Leigh	34	26	0	8	636	380	52
5	Wakefield T.	34	24	1	9	760	330	49
6	Keighley	34	21	0	13	448	375	42
7	Salford	34	20	1	13	641	432	41
8	Hull	34	20	1	13	610	444	41
9	Workington T.	34	20	1	13	504	467	41
10	Halifax	34	20	0	14	538	497	40
11	Dewsbury	34	17	3	14	474	406	37
12	Castleford	34	18	0	16	467	403	36
13	Hull K.R.	34	18	0	16	447	524	36
14	Batley	34	16	2	16	492	411	34
15	Huddersfield	34	16	2	16	440	434	34
16	Oldham	34	12	7	15	487	434	31
17	Bramley	34	15	1	18	385	528	31
18	Widnes	34	14	2	18	439	422	30
19	York	34	14	1	19	428	451	29
20	Featherstone R.	34	14	1	19	572	635	29
21	Barrow	34	14	0	20	479	483	28
22	Warrington	34	13	2	19	449	657	28
23	Swinton	34	13	0	21	404	505	26
24	Huyton	34	11	2	21	229	508	24
25	Rochdale H.	34	9	3	22	318	533	21
26	Blackpool B.	34	10	1	23	380	647	21
27	Bradford N.	34	8	2	24	339	662	18
28	Doncaster	34	7	3	24	306	695	17
29	Whitehaven	34	8	1	25	298	698	17
30	Hunslet	34	6	1	27	355	739	13

CHAMPIONSHIP PLAY-OFF

First Round

Hull	14	Workington T.	3
Keighley	7	Dewsbury	20
Leeds	28	Batley	0
Leigh	10	Hull K.R.	5
Salford	33	Halifax	3
St. Helens	28	Huddersfield	5
Wakefield T.	10	Castleford	4
Wigan	12	Oldham	7

Second Round

Leeds	37	Salford	22
Leigh	5	Wakefield T.	8
St. Helens	30	Hull	5
Wigan	36	Dewsbury	12

Semi-finals

St. Helens	22	Leeds	7
Wigan	49	Wakefield T.	15

FINAL

At Station Road, Swinton

	T	G	P		T	G	P
ST. HELENS	2	5	16	WIGAN	2	3	12

1971-72

		P	W	D	L	F	A	Pts
1	Leeds	34	28	2	4	750	325	58
2	Bradford N.	34	26	2	6	724	357	54
3	St. Helens	34	26	1	7	661	297	53
4	Wigan	34	25	0	9	702	314	50
5	Salford	34	25	0	9	720	338	50
6	Swinton	34	23	2	9	554	368	48
7	Featherstone R.	34	23	1	10	632	372	47
8	Rochdale H.	34	21	1	12	429	306	43
9	Wakefield T.	34	21	0	13	587	414	42
10	Castleford	34	20	1	13	488	368	41
11	Widnes	34	19	3	12	476	388	41
12	Dewsbury	34	18	2	14	431	352	38
13	Oldham	34	18	1	15	573	480	37
14	Hull K.R.	34	18	0	16	432	498	36
15	Warrington	34	16	3	15	537	397	35
16	Leigh	34	17	0	17	421	407	34
17	Huddersfield	34	17	0	17	394	435	34
18	Barrow	34	16	2	16	375	508	34
19	Hull	34	16	0	18	488	495	32
20	York	34	15	2	17	465	498	32
21	Halifax	34	14	0	20	398	564	28
22	Bramley	34	13	0	21	333	542	26
23	Whitehaven	34	12	0	22	394	523	24
24	Workington	34	11	2	21	303	533	24
25	Blackpool B.	34	11	0	23	351	560	22
26	Keighley	34	8	0	26	330	740	16
27	Huyton	34	7	1	26	277	610	15
28	Batley	34	5	2	27	249	628	12
29	Doncaster	34	5	0	29	234	729	10
30	Hunslet	34	2	0	32	300	662	4

CHAMPIONSHIP PLAY-OFF

First Round

Bradford N.	37	Warrington	0
Featherstone R.	14	Castleford	18
Leeds	40	Leigh	2
Rochdale H.	18	Wakefield T.	13
St. Helens	25	Hull K.R.	5
Salford	23	Dewsbury	7
Swinton	11	Widnes	15
Wigan	18	Oldham	8

Second Round

Bradford N.	22	Castleford	12
Leeds	20	Widnes	9
St. Helens	17	Rochdale H.	5
Wigan	9	Salford	21

Semi-finals

Bradford N.	10	St. Helens	14
Leeds	10	Salford	0

FINAL

At Station Road, Swinton

	T	G	P		T	G	P
LEEDS	1	3	9	ST. HELENS	1	1	5

1972-73

		P	W	D	L	F	A	Pts
1	Warrington	34	27	2	5	816	400	56
2	Featherstone R.	34	27	0	7	768	436	54
3	Leeds	34	26	1	7	810	324	53
4	St. Helens	34	24	2	8	623	298	50
5	Wakefield T.	34	25	0	9	814	398	50
6	Salford	34	25	0	9	723	383	50
7	Castleford	34	25	0	9	704	404	50
8	Dewsbury	34	23	0	11	534	354	46
9	Oldham	34	20	2	12	604	349	42
10	Hull K.R.	34	20	1	13	731	522	41
11	Rochdale H.	34	20	1	13	438	426	41
12	Widnes	34	19	0	15	592	458	38
13	Leigh	34	18	2	14	479	390	38
14	Bramley	34	18	1	15	452	465	37
15	Whitehaven	34	18	1	15	408	512	37
16	Wigan	34	17	1	16	577	491	35
17	York	34	17	1	16	586	575	35
18	Halifax	34	17	0	17	543	562	34
19	Batley	34	15	0	19	537	600	30
20	Keighley	34	15	0	19	451	505	30
21	Swinton	34	14	1	19	441	458	29
22	Workington T.	34	12	1	21	444	464	25
23	Bradford N.	34	12	0	22	582	685	24
24	Huddersfield	34	10	2	22	465	598	22
25	Hull	34	11	0	23	494	693	22
26	Barrow	34	7	0	27	351	775	14
27	Doncaster	34	6	0	28	298	911	12
28	Hunslet	34	5	0	29	371	916	10
29	Blackpool B.	34	4	0	30	324	972	8
30	Huyton	34	3	1	30	243	879	7

CHAMPIONSHIP PLAY-OFF

First Round

Castleford	24	Hull K.R.	12
Dewsbury	29	Oldham	14
Featherstone R.	14	Whitehaven	4
Leeds	45	Bramley	8
St. Helens	29	Leigh	14
Salford	10	Rochdale H.	14
Wakefield T.	33	Widnes	6
Warrington	30	Wigan	15

Second Round

Featherstone R.	7	Dewsbury	26
Leeds	30	Castleford	5
St. Helens	28	Wakefield T.	0
Warrington	16	Rochdale H.	9

Semi-finals

Leeds	7	St. Helens	2
Warrington	7	Dewsbury	12

FINAL

At Odsal, Bradford

	T	G	P		T	G	P
DEWSBURY	4	5	22	LEEDS	3	2	13

● *Two divisions reintroduced. See start of this section.*

A pensive Great Britain coach, Frank Myler.

COACHES

COACHES

This chapter is a unique compilation of first team coaching appointments over the past decade, featuring a club-by-club coaches register, an index of appointments and a detailed dossier of the 1983-84 coaches.

In the last 10 seasons more than 130 different coaches have held first team coaching posts. During that time clubs have made more than 200 first team coaching appointments.

CLUB-BY-CLUB REGISTER

The following is a list of coaches each club has had since the start of the 1974-75 season.

BARROW

Frank Foster	May 73 - Apr. 83
Tommy Dawes	May 83 -

BATLEY

Don Fox	Nov. 72 - Oct. 74
Alan Hepworth	Nov. 74 - Apr. 75
Dave Cox	May 75 - June 75
Trevor Walker	June 75 - June 77
Albert Fearnley	June 77 - Oct. 77
Dave Stockwell	Oct. 77 - June 79
*Tommy Smales	June 79 - Oct. 81
Trevor Lowe	Oct. 81 - May 82
Terry Crook	June 82 -

* *Ex-forward*

BLACKPOOL BOROUGH

Tommy Blakeley	Aug. 74 - Apr. 76
Jim Crellin	May 76 - Mar. 77
Joe Egan Jnr.	Mar. 77 - Oct. 77
Albert Fearnley (Manager)	Nov. 77 - Apr. 79
Bakary Diabira	Nov. 78 - June 79
Graham Rees	June 79 - Mar. 80
Geoff Lyon	July 80 - Aug. 81
Bob Irving	Aug. 81 - Feb. 82
John Mantle	Feb. 82 - Mar. 82
Tommy Dickens	Mar. 82 -

BRADFORD NORTHERN

Ian Brooke	Jan. 73 - Sept. 75
Roy Francis	Oct. 75 - Apr. 77
Peter Fox	Apr. 77 -

BRAMLEY

Arthur Keegan	May 73 - Sept. 76
Peter Fox	Sept. 76 - Apr. 77
*Tommy Smales	May 77 - Dec. 77
Les Pearce	Jan. 78 - Oct. 78
Don Robinson	Oct. 78 - May 79
Dave Stockwell	June 79 - June 80
Keith Hepworth	June 80 - May 82
Maurice Bamford	May 82 - Oct. 83
Peter Jarvis	Oct. 83 -

* *Ex-forward*

CARDIFF CITY

John Mantle	May 81 - Dec. 81
David Watkins	Dec. 81 -

CARLISLE

Allan Agar	May 81 - June 82
Mick Morgan	July 82 - Feb. 83
John Atkinson	Feb. 83 -

CASTLEFORD

Dave Cox	Apr. 74 - Nov. 74
*Malcolm Reilly	Dec. 74 -

* *Shortly after his appointment Reilly returned to Australia to fulfil his contract before resuming at Castleford early the next season.*

DEWSBURY

Maurice Bamford	June 74 - Oct. 74
Alan Hardisty	Oct. 74 - June 75
Dave Cox	June 75 - July 77
Ron Hill	July 77 - Dec. 77
Lewis Jones	Dec. 77 - Apr. 78
Jeff Grayshon	May 78 - Oct. 78
Alan Lockwood	Oct. 78 - Oct. 80
Bernard Watson	Oct. 80 - Oct. 82
Ray Abbey	Nov. 82 - Apr. 83
*Tommy Smales	May 83 - Feb. 84
Jack Addy	Feb. 84 -

* *Ex-forward*

DONCASTER

Ted Strawbridge	Feb. 73 - Apr. 75
Derek Edwards	July 75 - Nov. 76
Don Robson	Nov. 76 - Sept. 77
Trevor Lowe	Sept. 77 - Apr. 79
*Tommy Smales	Feb. 78 - Apr. 79
Billy Yates	Apr. 79 - May 80
Don Vines	Sept. 79 - Jan. 80
Bill Kenny	June 80 - May 81
Alan Rhodes	Aug. 81 - Mar. 83
Clive Sullivan M.B.E.	Mar. 83 - May 84

**Ex-forward, who shared the coaching post with Trevor Lowe for just over a year.*

FEATHERSTONE ROVERS

*Tommy Smales	July 74 - Sept. 74
Keith Goulding	Sept. 74 - Jan. 76
†Tommy Smales	Feb. 76 - May 76
Keith Cotton	June 76 - Dec. 77
Keith Goulding	Dec. 77 - May 78
Terry Clawson	July 78 - Nov. 78
†Tommy Smales	Nov. 78 - Apr. 79
Paul Daley	May 79 - Jan. 81
Vince Farrar	Feb. 81 - Nov. 82
Allan Agar	Dec. 82

**Ex-forward*
†Ex-scrum half

FULHAM

Reg Bowden	July 80 - June 84

HALIFAX

Derek Hallas	Aug. 74 - Oct. 74
Les Pearce	Oct. 74 - Apr. 76
Alan Kellett	May 76 - Apr. 77
Jim Crellin	June 77 - Oct. 77
Harry Fox	Oct. 77 - Feb. 78
Maurice Bamford	Feb. 78 - May 80
Mick Blacker	June 80 - June 82
Ken Roberts	June 82 - Sept. 82
Colin Dixon	Sept. 82 -

HUDDERSFIELD

Brian Smith	Jan. 73 - Mar. 76
Keith Goulding	Mar. 76 - Dec. 76
Bob Tomlinson	Jan. 77 - May 77
Neil Fox	June 77 - Feb. 78
*Roy Francis	-
Keith Goulding	May 78 - July 79
Ian Brooke	July 79 - Mar. 80
Maurice Bamford	May 80 - May 81
Les Sheard	June 81 - Nov. 82
Dave Mortimer	Nov. 82 - Aug. 83
Mel Bedford	Aug. 83 - Nov. 83
Brian Lockwood	Nov. 83 -

**Although Roy Francis was appointed he was unable to take over and Dave Heppleston stood in until the next appointment.*

HULL

David Doyle-Davidson	May 74 - Dec. 77
Arthur Bunting	Jan. 78 -

Ian Brooke, former coach of Huddersfield.

HULL KINGSTON ROVERS

Arthur Bunting	Feb. 72 - Nov. 75
Harry Poole	Dec. 75 - Mar. 77
Roger Millward M.B.E.	Mar. 77 -

Loose forward Harry Poole, 1966 Tour captain and coach at Hull K.R.

HUNSLET

Paul Daley	Apr. 74 - Aug. 78
Bill Ramsey	Aug. 78 - Dec. 79
Drew Broatch	Dec. 79 - Apr. 81
Paul Daley	Apr. 81 -

HUYTON

Terry Gorman	Aug. 74 - May 77
Geoff Fletcher	Aug. 77 -

KEIGHLEY

Alan Kellett	Jan. 73 - May 75
Roy Sabine	Aug. 75 - Oct. 77
Barry Seabourne	Nov. 77 - Mar. 79
Albert Fearnley (Manager)	Apr. 79 - Aug. 79
Alan Kellett	Apr. 79 - Apr. 80
Albert Fearnley	May 80 - Feb. 81
Bakary Diabira	Feb. 81 - Sept. 82
Lee Greenwood	Sept. 82 - Oct. 83
Geoff Peggs	Nov. 83 -

KENT INVICTA

Bill Goodwin	Apr. 83 - Nov. 83
Steve Lane	Nov. 83 - May 84

LEEDS

Roy Francis	June 74 - May 75
Syd Hynes	June 75 - Apr. 81
Robin Dewhurst	June 81 - Oct. 83
Maurice Bamford	Nov. 83 -

LEIGH

Eddie Cheetham	May 74 - Mar. 75
Kevin Ashcroft	June 75 - Jan. 77
Bill Kindon	Jan. 77 - Apr. 77
John Mantle	Apr. 77 - Nov. 78
Tom Grainey	Nov. 78 - Dec. 80
*Alex Murphy	Nov. 80 - June 82
*Colin Clarke	June 82 - Dec. 82
Peter Smethurst	Dec. 82 - Apr. 83
Tommy Bishop	June 83 - June 84

**From Dec. 80 to June 82 Clarke was officially appointed coach and Murphy manager*

MANSFIELD

Mick Blacker	May 84 -

OLDHAM

Jim Challinor	Aug. 74 - Dec. 76
Terry Ramshaw	Jan. 77 - Feb. 77
Dave Cox	July 77 - Dec. 78
Graham Starkey (Mngr)	Jan. 79 - May 81
Bill Francis	June 79 - Dec. 80
Frank Myler	May 81 - Apr. 83
Peter Smethurst	Apr. 83 - Feb. 84
Frank Barrow	Feb. 84 - Feb. 84
Brian Gartland	Mar. 84 - June 84

ROCHDALE HORNETS

Frank Myler	May 71 - Oct. 74
Graham Starkey	Oct. 74 - Nov. 75
Henry Delooze	Nov. 75 - Nov. 76
Kel Coslett	Nov. 76 - Aug. 79
Paul Longstaff	Sept. 79 - May 81
Terry Fogerty	May 81 - Jan. 82
Dick Bonser	Jan. 82 - May 82
Bill Kirkbride	June 82 -

ST. HELENS

Eric Ashton M.B.E.	May 74 - May 80
Kel Coslett	June 80 - May 82
Billy Benyon	May 82 -

SALFORD

Les Bettinson	Dec. 73 - Mar. 77
Colin Dixon	Mar. 77 - Jan. 78
Stan McCormick	Feb. 78 - Mar. 78
Alex Murphy	May 78 - Nov. 80
Kevin Ashcroft	Nov. 80 - Mar. 82
Alec McInnes	Mar. 82 - May 82
Malcolm Aspey	May 82 - Oct. 83
Mike Coulman	Oct. 83 - May 84
Kevin Ashcroft	May 84 -

SHEFFIELD

Alan Rhodes	Apr. 84 -

SWINTON

Austin Rhodes	June 74 - Nov. 75
Bob Fleet	Nov. 75 - Nov. 76
John Stopford	Nov. 76 - Apr. 77
Terry Gorman	June 77 - Nov. 78
Ken Halliwell	Nov. 78 - Dec. 79
Frank Myler	Jan. 80 - May 81
Tom Grainey	May 81 - Oct. 83
Jim Crellin	Nov. 83 -

WAKEFIELD TRINITY

Peter Fox	June 74 - May 76
Geoff Gunney	June 76 - Nov. 76
Brian Lockwood	Nov. 76 - Jan. 78
Ian Brooke	Jan. 78 - Jan. 79
Bill Kirkbride	Jan. 79 - Apr. 80
Ray Batten	Apr. 80 - May 81
Bill Ashurst	June 81 - Apr. 82
Ray Batten	May 82 - July 83
Derek Turner	July 83 - Feb. 84
Bob Haigh	Feb. 84 - May 84
Geoff Wraith	May 84 -

WARRINGTON

Alex Murphy	May 71 - May 78
Billy Benyon	June 78 - Mar. 82
Kevin Ashcroft	Mar. 82 - May 84

WHITEHAVEN

Jeff Bawden	May 72 - May 75
Ike Southward	Aug. 75 - June 76
Bill Smith	Aug. 76 - Oct. 78
Ray Dutton	Oct. 78 - Oct. 79
Phil Kitchin	Oct. 79 - Jan. 82
Arnold Walker	Jan. 82 - May 82
Tommy Dawes	June 82 - May 83
Frank Foster	June 83 -

St. Helens' coach Eric Ashton gives his players a half-time pointer.

WIDNES

Vince Karalius	Jan. 72 - May 75
Frank Myler	May 75 - May 78
Doug Laughton	May 78 - Mar. 83
Harry Dawson / Colin Tyrer	Mar. 83 - May 83
*Vince Karalius / Harry Dawson	May 83 -

**Dawson quit as coach in March 1984 with Karalius continuing as team manager.*

WIGAN

Ted Toohey	May 74 - Jan. 75
Joe Coan	Jan. 75 - Sept. 76
Vince Karalius	Sept. 76 - Sept. 79
Kel Coslett	Oct. 79 - Apr. 80
George Fairbairn	Apr. 80 - May 81
Maurice Bamford	May 81 - May 82
Alex Murphy	June 82 -

WORKINGTON TOWN

Ike Southward	Aug. 73 - June 75
Paul Charlton	June 75 - June 76
Ike Southward	June 76 - Feb. 78
Sol Roper	Feb. 78 - Apr. 80
Keith Irving	Aug. 80 - Oct. 80
Tommy Bishop	Nov. 80 - June 82
Paul Charlton	July 82 - Dec. 82
Dave Cox	Mar. 83 - Mar. 83
Harry Archer/Bill Smith	May 83 -

YORK

Keith Goulding	Nov. 73 - Sept. 74
Gary Cooper	Dec. 74 - Sept. 76
Mal Dixon	Sept. 76 - Dec. 78
Paul Daley	Jan. 79 - May 79
David Doyle-Davidson	July 79 - July 80
Bill Kirkbride	Aug. 80 - Apr. 82
Alan Hardisty	May 82 - Jan. 83
Phil Lowe	Mar. 83 -

A Wembley victory salute for Vince Karalius after the Widnes victory over Warrington in 1975.

REPRESENTATIVE REGISTER

The following is a list of international and county coaches since 1974-75.

GREAT BRITAIN

Jim Challinor	Dec. 71 - Aug. 74
David Watkins	1977 World Championship
Peter Fox	1978 Test series v. Australia
Eric Ashton	1979 tour
Johnny Whiteley	Aug. 80 - Nov. 82
Frank Myler	Dec. 82 -

ENGLAND

Alex Murphy	Jan. 75 - Nov. 75 (Inc. World Championship tour)
Peter Fox	1976-77
Frank Myler	1977-78
Eric Ashton	1978-79 & 1979-80
Johnny Whiteley	1980-81 & 1981-82

WALES

Les Pearce	Jan. 75 - Nov. 75 (Inc. World Championship tour)
David Watkins/Bill Francis	1976-77
Kel Coslett/Bill Francis	1977-78
Kel Coslett	1978-79 to 1981-82
David Watkins	1982-83

GREAT BRITAIN UNDER-24s

Johnny Whiteley	1976-1982
Frank Myler	1983 -

CUMBRIA

Ike Southward	1975-76
Frank Foster	1976-77 & 1977-78
Sol Roper	1978-79
Frank Foster	1979-80
Phil Kitchin	1980-81 to 1981-82
Frank Foster	1982-83

LANCASHIRE

Alex Murphy	1973-74 to 1977-78
Eric Ashton M.B.E.	1978-79 to 1979-80
Tom Grainey	1980-81 to 1981-82
Doug Laughton	1982-83

YORKSHIRE

Johnny Whiteley	1970-71 to 1979-80
Arthur Keegan	1980-81
Johnny Whiteley	1981-82 to 1982-83

OTHER NATIONALITIES

Dave Cox	1974-75 to 1975-76

Johnny Whiteley, former coach of Great Britain, England, Great Britain Under-24s and Yorkshire, discussing tactics with the 1977 Under-24 front row of, left to right, Mick Gibbins, Graham Liptrot and Roy Dickinson.

INDEX OF COACHES

The following is an index of coaches who have held first team coaching posts since the start of the 1974-75 season with the alphabetical listing of clubs they coached in this period.

Ray Abbey (Dewsbury)
Jack Addy (Dewsbury)
Allan Agar (Carlisle, Featherstone R.)
Harry Archer (Workington T.)
Kevin Ashcroft (Leigh, Salford, Warrington)
Eric Ashton M.B.E. (St. Helens)
Bill Ashurst (Wakefield T.)
Mal Aspey (Salford)
John Atkinson (Carlisle)

Maurice Bamford (Bramley, Dewsbury, Halifax, Huddersfield, Leeds, Wigan)
Frank Barrow (Oldham)
Ray Batten (Wakefield T.)
Jeff Bawden (Whitehaven)
Mel Bedford (Huddersfield)
Billy Benyon (St. Helens, Warrington)
Les Bettinson (Salford)
Tommy Bishop (Leigh, Workington T.)
Mick Blacker (Halifax, Mansfield)
Tommy Blakeley (Blackpool B.)
Dick Bonser (Rochdale H.)
Reg Bowden (Fulham)
Drew Broatch (Hunslet)
Ian Brooke (Bradford N., Huddersfield, Wakefield T.)
Arthur Bunting (Hull, Hull K.R.)

Jim Challinor (Oldham)
Paul Charlton (Workington T.)
Eddie Cheetham (Leigh)
Colin Clarke (Leigh)
Terry Clawson (Featherstone R.)
Joe Coan (Wigan)
Gary Cooper (York)
Kel Coslett (Rochdale H., St. Helens, Wigan)
Keith Cotton (Featherstone R.)
Mike Coulman (Salford)
Dave Cox (Batley, Castleford, Dewsbury, Huyton Oldham, Workington T.)
Jim Crellin (Blackpool B., Halifax, Swinton)
Terry Crook (Batley)

Paul Daley (Featherstone R., Hunslet, York)
Tommy Dawes (Barrow, Whitehaven)
Harry Dawson (Widnes)
Henry Delooze (Rochdale H.)
Robin Dewhurst (Leeds)
Bakary Diabira (Blackpool B., Keighley)
Tommy Dickens (Blackpool B.)
Colin Dixon (Halifax, Salford)
Mal Dixon (York)
David Doyle-Davidson (Hull, York)
Ray Dutton (Whitehaven)

Derek Edwards (Doncaster)
Joe Egan Jnr. (Blackpool B.)

George Fairbairn (Wigan)
Vince Farrar (Featherstone R.)
Albert Fearnley (Batley, Blackpool B., Keighley)
Bob Fleet (Swinton)
Geoff Fletcher (Huyton)
Terry Fogerty (Rochdale H.)
Frank Foster (Barrow, Whitehaven)
Don Fox (Batley)
Harry Fox (Halifax)
Neil Fox (Huddersfield)
Peter Fox (Bradford N., Bramley, Wakefield T.)
Bill Francis (Oldham)
Roy Francis (Bradford N., Huddersfield, Leeds)

Peter Fox.

Brian Gartland (Oldham)
Bill Goodwin (Kent Invicta)
Terry Gorman (Huyton, Swinton)
Keith Goulding (Featherstone R., Huddersfield, York)
Tom Grainey (Leigh, Swinton)
Jeff Grayshon (Dewsbury)
Lee Greenwood (Keighley)
Geoff Gunney (Wakefield T.)

Bob Haigh (Wakefield T.)
Derek Hallas (Halifax)
Ken Halliwell (Swinton)
Alan Hardisty (Dewsbury, York)
Alan Hepworth (Batley)
Keith Hepworth (Bramley)
Ron Hill (Dewsbury)
Syd Hynes (Leeds)

1978 Wembley success for Leeds coach Syd Hynes.

Bob Irving (Blackpool B.)
Keith Irving (Workington T.)

Peter Jarvis (Bramley)
Lewis Jones (Dewsbury)

Vince Karalius (Widnes, Wigan)
Arthur Keegan (Bramley)
Alan Kellett (Halifax, Keighley)
Bill Kenny (Doncaster)
Bill Kindon (Leigh)
Phil Kitchin (Whitehaven)

Steve Lane (Kent Invicta)
Doug Laughton (Widnes)
Alan Lockwood (Dewsbury)
Brian Lockwood (Huddersfield, Wakefield T.)
Paul Longstaff (Rochdale H.)
Phil Lowe (York)
Trevor Lowe (Batley, Doncaster)
Geoff Lyon (Blackpool B.)

John Mantle (Blackpool B., Cardiff C., Leigh)
Stan McCormick (Salford)
Alan McInnes (Salford)
Roger Millward M.B.E. (Hull K.R.)
Mick Morgan (Carlisle)
David Mortimer (Huddersfield)
Alex Murphy (Leigh, Salford, Warrington, Wigan)
Frank Myler (Oldham, Rochdale H., Swinton, Widnes)

Les Pearce (Bramley, Halifax)
Geoff Peggs (Keighley)
Harry Poole (Hull K.R.)

John Mantle.

Bill Ramsey (Hunslet)
Terry Ramshaw (Oldham)
Graham Rees (Blackpool B.)
Malcolm Reilly (Castleford)
Alan Rhodes (Doncaster, Sheffield)
Austin Rhodes (Swinton)
Ken Roberts (Halifax)
Don Robinson (Bramley)
Don Robson (Doncaster)
Sol Roper (Workington T.)

Roy Sabine (Keighley)
Barry Seabourne (Keighley)
Les Sheard (Huddersfield)
Tommy Smales [*Scrum-half*] (Featherstone R.)
Tommy Smales [*Forward*] (Batley, Bramley, Dewsbury, Doncaster, Featherstone R.)
Peter Smethurst (Leigh, Oldham)
Bill Smith (Whitehaven, Workington T.)
Brian Smith (Huddersfield)
Ike Southward (Whitehaven, Workington T.)
Graham Starkey (Oldham, Rochdale H.)
Dave Stockwell (Bramley, Batley)
John Stopford (Swinton)
Ted Strawbridge (Doncaster)
Clive Sullivan M.B.E. (Doncaster, Hull)

Bob Tomlinson (Huddersfield)
Ted Toohey (Wigan)
Derek Turner (Wakefield T.)
Colin Tyrer (Widnes)

Don Vines (Doncaster)

Arnold Walker (Whitehaven)
Trevor Walker (Batley)
David Watkins (Cardiff C.)
Bernard Watson (Dewsbury)
Geoff Wraith (Wakefield T.)

Billy Yates (Doncaster)

Arnold Walker.

Peter Smethurst.

David Watkins.

DOSSIER OF 1983-84 COACHES

The following is a dossier of the coaching and playing careers of coaches holding first team posts during 1983-84 up to the end of May. BF — beaten finalist.

JACK ADDY
Dewsbury: Feb. 84 -
Played for: Dewsbury

ALLAN AGAR
Carlisle: May 81 - June 82 (Promotion)
Featherstone R.: Dec. 82 - (RL Cup winners)
Played for: Featherstone R., Dewsbury, New Hunslet, Hull K.R., Wakefield T., Carlisle

HARRY ARCHER
Workington T.: May 83 - (Promotion)
Played for: Workington T.

KEVIN ASHCROFT
Leigh: June 75 - Jan. 77 (Promotion, Floodlit Trophy BF)
Salford: Nov. 80 - Mar. 82
Warrington: Mar. 82 - May 84 (Lancs. Cup winners)
Salford: May 84 -
Played for: Dewsbury, Rochdale H., Leigh, Warrington, Salford

MAL ASPEY
Salford: May 82 - Oct. 83 (Promotion)
Played for: Widnes, Fulham, Wigan, Salford

JOHN ATKINSON
Carlisle: Feb. 83 -
Played for: Leeds, Carlisle

MAURICE BAMFORD
Dewsbury: Aug. - Oct. 74
Halifax: Feb. 78 - May 80 (Yorks. Cup BF, Promotion)
Huddersfield: May 80 - May 81
Wigan: May 81 - May 82
Bramley: May 82 - Oct. 83
Leeds: Nov. 83 - (John Player winners)
Played for: Dewsbury, Hull, Batley (on loan)

FRANK BARROW
Oldham: Feb. 84 - Feb. 84
Played for: St. Helens, Leigh

MEL BEDFORD
Huddersfield: Aug. 83 - Nov. 83
Played for: Batley, Dewsbury

BILLY BENYON
Warrington: June 78 - Mar. 82 (Lancs. Cup winners, John Player winners and BF)
St. Helens: May 82 - (Lancs. Cup BF)
Played for: St. Helens, Warrington

The Halifax bench during the 1980 Challenge Cup semi-final against Hull K.R. at Leeds. Coach Maurice Bamford, second left, is now in charge of Leeds, while assistant coach Jack Addy, third left, is the current coach of Dewsbury.

TOMMY BISHOP
In Australia: Cronulla, Brisbane, Illawarra, N. Sydney 1969-1980
Workington T.: Nov. 80 - June 82 (Promotion)
Leigh: June 83 -
Played for: Blackpool B., Barrow, St. Helens, Cronulla (Aust.)

MICK BLACKER
Halifax: June 80 - June 82 (Promotion)
Mansfield: May 84 -
Played for: Bradford N., Halifax, Warrington

REG BOWDEN
Fulham: July 80 - (Promotion (2))
Played for: Widnes, Fulham

ARTHUR BUNTING
Hull K.R.: Feb. 72 - Nov. 75 (Yorks. Cup BF, Promotion)
Hull: Jan. 78 - (Div. 1 champs, Div. 2 champs, RL Cup winner and BF (2), Yorks. Cup winners (2), John Player winners, Floodlit Trophy winners, Premier BF (3))
Played for: Bramley, Hull K.R.

MIKE COULMAN
Salford: Oct 83 - May 84
Played for: Salford

JIM CRELLIN
Blackpool B.: May 76 - Mar. 77 (John Player BF)
Halifax: June 77 - Oct. 77
Swinton: Nov. 83 -
Played for: Workington T., Oldham, Rochdale H.

TERRY CROOK
Batley: June 82 -
Played for: Wakefield T., Bramley, Batley

PAUL DALEY
New Hunslet: Apr. 74 - Aug. 78 (Promotion)
York: Jan. 79 - May 79 (Promotion)
Featherstone R.: May 79 - Jan. 81 (Promotion)
Hunslet: Apr. 81 - (Promotion)
Played for: Halifax, Bradford N., Hull K.R., Hunslet

TOMMY DAWES
Whitehaven: June 82 - May 83 (Promotion)
Barrow: May 83 - (Lancs. Cup winners, Div. 2 champs)
Played for: Barrow

HARRY DAWSON
Widnes: Mar. 83 - Mar. 84 (Premier winners, Lancs. Cup BF)
Played for: Widnes

Happier times for Widnes coach Harry Dawson, celebrating victory over Hull in the 1983 Slalom Lager Premiership final.

ROBIN DEWHURST
Leeds: June 81 - Oct. 83 (John Player BF)
Played for: Leeds, Bramley, Batley

TOMMY DICKENS
Blackpool B.: Mar. 82 -
Played for: Leigh, Warrington, Widnes

COLIN DIXON
Salford: Mar. 77 - Jan. 78
Halifax: Sept. 82 - (Promotion)
Played for: Halifax, Salford, Hull K.R.

GEOFF FLETCHER
Huyton: Aug. 77 -
Played for: Leigh, Oldham, Wigan, Workington T., Huyton

FRANK FOSTER
Bradford N.: Dec. 69 - Dec. 69
Barrow: May 73 - Apr. 83
(John Player BF, Div. 2 champs + promotion (2))
Whitehaven: June 83 -
Cumbria: 1976-77, 1979-80, 1982-83
Played for: Workington T., Hull K.R., Bradford N., Barrow, Oldham

PETER FOX
Featherstone R.: Jan. 71 - May 74
(RL Cup Winners & BF)
Wakefield T.: June 74 - May 76
(Yorks. Cup BF)
Bramley: Sept. 76 - Apr. 77 (Promotion)
Bradford N.: Apr. 77 - (Div. 1 champs (2), Yorks. Cup winners and BF (2), Premier winners and BF (2), John Player winners)
England: 1977 (2 matches)
Great Britain: 1978 (3 Tests v. Australia)
Played for: Featherstone R., Batley, Hull K.R. Wakefield T.

BRIAN GARTLAND
Oldham: Mar. 84 -
Non-professional player

BILL GOODWIN
Kent Invicta: Apr. 83 - Nov. 83
Played for: Doncaster, Featherstone R., Batley

TOM GRAINEY
Leigh: Nov. 78 - Dec. 80
Swinton: May 81 - Oct. 83
Lancashire: 1980-81, 1981-82
Played for: Leigh

LEE GREENWOOD
Keighley: Sept. 82 - Oct. 83
Played for: Halifax, Bradford N., Keighley

PETER JARVIS
Bramley: Oct. 83 -
Played for: Hunslet, Bramley, Halifax, Huddersfield

VINCE KARALIUS
Widnes: Jan. 72 - May 75
(RL Cup winners, Lancs. Cup winners, John Player BF, Floodlit Trophy winners and BF (2))
Wigan: Sept. 76 - Sept. 79
Widnes (Manager): May 83 - (Lancs. Cup BF., John Player BF, RL Cup winners)
Played for: St. Helens, Widnes

Tommy Grainey, who parted company with Swinton in October 1983, pictured with his Lancashire County team of 1981.

BILL KIRKBRIDE
Wakefield T.: Jan. 79 - Apr. 80 (RL Cup BF)
York: Aug. 80 - Apr. 82 (Div. 2 champs)
Rochdale H.: June 82 -
Played for: Workington T., Halifax, Castleford, Salford, Leigh (on loan), S. Suburbs (Aust.), Wakefield T., York, Rochdale H.

STEVE LANE
Kent Invicta: Nov. 83 - May 84
Played for: Dewsbury, Hull, Tonneins (France), Roanne (France), Hunslet, Whitehaven, Kent Invicta

BRIAN LOCKWOOD
Wakefield T.: Nov. 76 - Jan. 78
Huddersfield: Nov. 83 -
Played for: Castleford, Balmain (Aust.), Canterbury Bankstown (Aust.), Wakefield T., Hull K.R., Widnes, Oldham

PHIL LOWE
York: Mar. 83 -
Played for: Hull K.R., Manly (Aust.)

ROGER MILLWARD M.B.E.
Hull K.R.: Mar. 77 - (Div. 1 champs (2), RL Cup winners and BF, John Player BF, Premier. winners (2), Yorks. Cup BF, Floodlit Trophy winners and BF)
Played for: Castleford, Hull K.R., Cronulla (Aust.)

DAVID MORTIMER
Huddersfield: June 70 - Apr. 71
Swinton: May 71 - Nov. 72 (Lancs. Cup BF)
Huddersfield: Nov. 82 - Aug. 83
Played for: Wakefield T., Doncaster, Dewsbury

Phil Lowe (left) and Brian Lockwood, opponents in the 1981 Wembley final, and now Second Division rivals as coach of York and Huddersfield respectively.

ALEX MURPHY

Leigh:	Nov. 66 - May 71 (RL Cup winners, Lancs. Cup winners and BF, Floodlit Trophy winners and BF)
Warrington:	May 71 - May 78 (League Leaders, Club Merit winners, RL Cup winners and BF, John Player winners (2), Floodlit Trophy BF, Capt. Morgan winners, Premier. BF)
Salford:	May 78 - Nov. 80
Leigh:	Nov. 80 - June 82 (Div. 1 champs, Lancs. Cup winners)
Wigan:	June 82 - (John Player winners, RL Cup BF)
Lancashire:	1973-74 to 1977-78 (Champions (2))
England:	1975 (10 matches including World Championship (European Champions))

Played for: St. Helens, Leigh, Warrington

FRANK MYLER

Rochdale H.:	May 71 - Oct. 74 (John Player BF, Floodlit Trophy BF)
Widnes:	May 75 - May 78 (Div. 1 champs, RL Cup BF (2), Lancs. Cup winners (2), John Player winners and BF, Premier. BF)
Swinton:	Jan. 80 - May 81
Oldham:	May 81 - May 83 (Div. 2 champs)
Great Britain Under-24s:	1983 (3 matches, 3 wins)
England:	1978 (2 matches, 2 wins—European Champions)
Great Britain:	1983-84 (4 matches, 4 wins not including 1984 tour)

Played for: Widnes, St. Helens, Rochdale H.

GEOFF PEGGS

Keighley:	Nov. 83 -

Played for: Bramley, Rochdale H.

The one-and-only Alex Murphy celebrates yet another success, the 1983 John Player Trophy win by Wigan.

MALCOLM REILLY
Castleford: Dec. 74 - (Yorks Cup winners (2) and BF, Floodlit Trophy winners, John Player winners, Premier BF)
Played for: Castleford, Manly (Aust.)

ALAN RHODES
Doncaster: Aug. 81 - Mar. 83
Sheffield: Apr. 84 -
Played for: Featherstone R., York, Castleford, Doncaster

TOMMY SMALES *Ex-forward*
Dewsbury: Oct. 70 - July 74 (RL Champs, Yorks. Cup BF)
Featherstone R.: July 74 - Sept. 74
Bramley: May 77 - Dec. 77
Doncaster (with Trevor Lowe) Feb. 78 - Apr. 79
Batley: June 79 - Oct. 81
Dewsbury: May 83 - Feb. 84
Played for: Wigan, Barrow, Featherstone R.

PETER SMETHURST
Leigh: May 71 - Oct. 71
Leigh: Dec. 82 - Apr. 83
Oldham: Apr. 83 - Feb. 84
Played for: Swinton, Oldham, Salford, Leigh, Wigan

BILL SMITH
Whitehaven: Aug. 76 - Oct. 78
Workington T.: May 83 - (Promotion)
Played for: Workington T.

CLIVE SULLIVAN M.B.E.
Hull: Feb. 73 - Mar. 74
Doncaster: Mar. 83 - May 84
Played for: Hull, Hull K.R., Oldham, Doncaster

DEREK TURNER
Castleford: July 68 - May 69 (RL Champs BF, RL Cup winners, Yorks. Cup BF)
Leeds: June 69 - May 73 (RL Champs and BF (2), League Leaders (2), RL Cup BF (2), Yorks. Cup winners (2), Yorks. League winners, John Player winners, Floodlit Trophy winners)
Wakefield T.: July 83 - Feb. 84
Played for: Hull K.R., Oldham, Wakefield T.

Featherstone Rovers' loose forward in the 1967 Wembley final, Tommy Smales quit as coach of Dewsbury in February 1984.

DAVID WATKINS
Cardiff C.: Dec. 81 -
Wales: 1977, 1982 (1 match each, 1 win)
Great Britain: 1977 World Cup (4 matches, 2 wins)
Played for: Salford, Swinton, Cardiff C.

GEOFF WRAITH
Wakefield T.: May 84 -
Played for: Wakefield T., Brisbane (Aust.), Castleford

Queensland captain Wally Lewis.

QUEENSLAND TOUR

QUEENSLAND TOUR

Australian state champions Queensland made Rugby League history by staging their first-ever tour of Great Britain in October 1983.

The 21-strong squad of Maroons arrived at the end of a season in which they had won the State of Origin series against New South Wales for the third successive time and hammered a virtual Papua New Guinea Test side 106-3.

Heading the Queensland party was the current Australian coach Arthur Beetson and the Kangaroo vice-captain Wally Lewis, liberally tipped to inherit the captaincy from Max Krilich.

It was decided by the Rugby League Management Committee that the match programme should involve club sides rather than representative teams, the final selection being Hull K.R., Wigan and Leeds. Great Britain mentors Dick Gemmell and Frank Myler insisted that the state visit should not be used as a Great Britain tour trial, in any guise, as suggestions were put forward for representative line-ups to be fielded such as a Great Britain XIII, the Under-24s or an East and West of Pennines.

The Queensland trilogy repeated many of the lessons handed out a year earlier by the all-conquering Kangaroos, despite most of the Maroons not having played a first class game for six weeks.

The runaway victories over Wigan and Leeds featured a tally of 98 points with only four in reply, highlighted by 19 Kangaroo-style tries.

Only the opening shock success by Hull Kingston Rovers saved the mini-tour from being another humiliating whitewash. The Robins proved that committed defence could thwart the sharply-honed Australian attack, though the hard-earned victory was diluted by Rovers best men being two Kiwis — Mark Broadhurst and Gordon Smith.

Queensland centre Gene Miles touches down at Headingley, with Shane Bernardin and Bryan Niebling (right) in support.

1983 QUEENSLAND TOUR OF GREAT BRITAIN

Oct. 16th	L	6-8	Hull K.R.
Oct. 23rd	W	40-2	Wigan
Oct. 29th	W	58-2	Leeds

TOUR PARTY

Managers: Kevin Brasch, Dick Turner
Coach: Arthur Beetson
Liaison Officer: Ted Verrenkamp
Physiotherapist: Darryl Gatley

TOUR SUMMARY

				For			Against		
P	W	D	L	T	G	Pts	T	G	Pts
3	2	0	1	20	12	104	1	4	12

	Club	App	Sub	T	G	Pts
BERNARDIN, Shane	Redcliffe	2	—	—	—	—
BRENNAN, Mitch	Redcliffe	3	—	2	—	8
BRIGGINSHAW, Larry	Eastern Suburbs	1	1	—	—	—
DOWLING, Greg	Wynnum-Manly	2	—	1	—	4
FRENCH, Brett	Wynnum-Manly	3	—	2	—	8
FULLERTON-SMITH, Wally	Redcliffe	2	—	1	—	4
HEUGH, Cavill	Eastern Suburbs	1	1	1	—	4
JONES, Gavin	Eastern Suburbs	1	2	—	—	—
KHAN, Paul	Redcliffe	1	—	—	—	—
KILROY, Joe	North	2	1	2	—	8
LEWIS, Wally	Fortitude Valley	3	—	3	1	14
LINDENBERG, Wayne	Eastern Suburbs	1	1	2	—	8
McNALLY, Shane	Easts	2	—	—	11	22
MILES, Gene	Wynnum-Manly	3	—	3	—	12
MURRAY, Mark	Redcliffe	2	—	—	—	—
NIEBLING, Bryan	Fortitude Valley	2	—	—	—	—
PATERSON, Trevor	Eastern Suburbs	1	1	—	—	—
PHELAN, Chris	Parramatta	3	—	1	—	4
SCOTT, Colin	Wynnum-Manly	2	—	2	—	8
STACEY, Steve	Easts	1	—	—	—	—
TESSMAN, Brad	Southern Suburbs	1	—	—	—	—

Gene Miles.

Brad Tessman.

Mark Murray.

Queensland touring team 1983. Back row, left to right: Stacey, Phelan, Scott, Dowling, Miles, Heugh, Brennan, Tessman, Jones. Middle row, left to right: Gatley, Fullerton-Smith, Kilroy, Murray, French, Paterson, McNally, Lindenberg, Brigginshaw, Bernardin. Front row, left to right: Verrenkamp, Niebling, Beetson, Lewis, Turner, Khan, Brasch.

MATCH BY MATCH

16th October

HULL K.R. 8		QUEENSLAND 6
George Fairbairn	1.	Colin Scott
Garry Clark	2.	Steve Stacey (Joe Kilroy)
Mike Smith	3.	Gene Miles
John Dorahy	4.	Brett French
Gary Prohm	5.	Mitch Brennan
Steve Hartley (David Laws)	6.	Wally Lewis
Gordon Smith	7.	Mark Murray (Wayne Lindenberg)
Roy Holdstock (Andy Kelly)	8.	Paul Khan (Trevor Paterson)
David Watkinson (Tracey Lazenby)	9.	Shane Bernardin
Mark Broadhurst	10.	Brad Tessman
Phil Hogan	11.	Bryan Niebling (Gavin Jones)
Chris Burton	12.	Chris Phelan
David Hall	13.	Wally Fullerton-Smith
T: M. Smith		T: Lewis
G: Fairbairn (2)		G: Lewis

Half-time: 4-6
Referee: Robin Whitfield (Widnes)
Attendance: 6,383

Hull K.R. earned all the glory as Queensland lost 8-6 in a bitter, and sometimes savage, opener to the tour. Rovers lost three injured players — Hartley, Watkinson and Holdstock — in the first half hour. Fortunately, it had been agreed to allow four substitutes on the tour.

The visitors introduced an unexpected physical approach and when the Robins retaliated, there mushroomed an unnerving crowd reaction. New Zealand Test star Broadhurst flattened Maroon hooker Bernardin with a powerful punch in the 35th minute . . . and received a long, standing crowd ovation. Referee Robin Whitfield awarded a penalty to Queensland and there followed a spate of sin bin punishments for further offenders.

Three minutes later Niebling was sent off for 10 minutes for fouling wingman Prohm, who had only just resumed following a blow to the neck while on the ground. The home crowd again applauded an offending Rovers player as Great Britain forward Burton was sin binned in the 50th minute.

Eight minutes later Bernardin received the red card and it seemed the temporary dismissals were becoming no more than rests between the rounds. Ironically, his off-the-ball victim was a fellow Australian, Hull K.R.'s new signing Dorahy.

The penalty count was 16-12 in Rovers favour, including seven against Queensland for foul play, the Robins being penalised four times for fouls.

Rovers had lost hooker Watkinson with a badly gashed head and Hartley with a broken wrist before Holdstock's departure with a face cut and a dead leg resulted in full back Fairbairn opening the Robins' account with a 29th minute penalty.

A second Fairbairn penalty left Rovers trailing 4-6 at half-time, Queensland captain Wally Lewis having notched a sixth minute penalty and an opportunist try seven minutes later.

Spurred on by a fanatical crowd, Rovers battled on in a match with only pride at stake and received just reward with the match-clinching try in the 43rd minute. Left winger Brennan made a mess of covering Gordon Smith's kick to the corner and international centre Mike Smith touched down.

Even the highly rated Lewis lost his composure in a nerve-wracking final half hour, missing a close-in penalty attempt in the closing minutes and electing to take tap penalties instead of kicking for goal.

Gordon Smith took Rovers Man of the Match award in what was essentially a team performance. The Robins did not respond to Queensland's request to a re-match before the end of the tour.

23rd October

WIGAN 2		**QUEENSLAND 40**
Colin Whitfield	1.	Joe Kilroy
Ronnie Braithwaite	2.	Brett French
David Stephenson	3.	Gene Miles
Tim Wilby (Jeff Clare)	4.	Wally Lewis
Henderson Gill	5.	Mitch Brennan
David Wood	6.	Wayne Lindenberg
Jimmy Fairhurst	7.	Larry Brigginshaw
Kerry Helmsley	8.	Greg Dowling
Howie Tamati (Shaun Wane)	9.	Shane McNally
Brian Case	10.	Chris Phelan
Danny Campbell (Mick Scott)	11.	Gavin Jones
Graeme West (Brian Dunn)	12.	Cavill Heugh
John Pendlebury	13.	Trevor Paterson
		T: Lindenberg (2), Brennan, Phelan, Miles, French, Kilroy, Heugh
G: Whitfield		G: McNally (4)

Half-time: 2-22
Referee: Ron Campbell (Widnes)
Attendance: 9,749

In the light of the controversial opening encounter at Craven Park, Wigan coach Alex Murphy challenged Queensland to play football in the second match a week later.

His plea backfired as the Maroons ran in eight glorious tries against a Wigan side which had held the Australian touring side 13-9 a year earlier.

Queensland displayed pace, flair and skill in a one-sided contest. Wigan's only contribution to the excitement was a fire at the back of the popular stand!

The damage to the stand was slight, but Wigan's reputation on the field was severely damaged. The Riversiders' claim of re-emergence as a top class side and Murphy's ego were both badly dented as the John Player Trophy holders put up a pathetic defensive display in front of nearly 10,000 fans.

The star of the afternoon was Queensland stand off Lindenberg who flew in for a brace of tries in what turned out to be his last professional match. After an outstanding game, he announced his premature retirement to dedicate himself to religious work.

Lewis, the captain-elect of Australia, provided all the creative skills which he had kept partially hidden on the Kangaroo tour, while full back Kilroy showed athleticism in a fine all-round display crowned with a try.

Only half backs Fairhurst and Wood contributed anything positive for Wigan, who were branded as anonymous, lacking purpose, ideas, leadership or teamwork. Full back Whitfield missed numerous tackles after his third minute goal gave Wigan a 2-0 lead. He had two further chances to hit the target before Kilroy paved the way for Brennan to open the Queensland scoring, after which it was only a matter of how many points would be piled up.

Before the interval the Maroons added tries from Phelan, Miles and French, with three goals from McNally. In an equally rampaging second half, tries came from Kilroy, Heugh and two from Lindenberg, McNally adding a goal.

Wigan could only wish that the hoards of firemen on the ground had used their hoses to dampen the fire of the Queenslanders rather than the over-heated gas cylinders at the rear of the stand!

Full back Joe Kilroy — one of the surprise sensations of the tour — battles with Leeds duo John Holmes (left) and Kevin James.

29th October

LEEDS 2		QUEENSLAND 58
Ian Wilkinson (David Heselwood)	1.	Joe Kilroy
Paul Prendiville	2.	Brett French
David Creasser (Colin Cooper)	3.	Gene Miles
Steve Martin	4.	Mitch Brennan
Andy Smith	5.	Colin Scott
John Holmes	6.	Wally Lewis
Kevin Dick	7.	Mark Murray
Roy Dickinson (Gary Moorby)	8.	Greg Dowling (Gavin Jones)
Russ Sowden	9.	Shane McNally
Keith Rayne	10.	Shane Bernardin (Cavill Heugh)
Kevin Rayne	11.	Chris Phelan (Larry Brigginshaw)
Kevin Squire (Kevin James)	12.	Bryan Niebling
David Heron	13.	Wally Fullerton-Smith
		T: Lewis (2), Scott (2), Miles (2), Dowling, Brennan, Fullerton-Smith French, Kilroy
G: Creasser		G: McNally (7)

Half-time: 2-22
Referee: Billy Thompson (Huddersfield)
Attendance: 5,647

Queensland rounded off their historic tour with a breathtaking 11-try rout to send Leeds to their heaviest home defeat. The four-point tries took the score past the 54-3 defeat inflicted by Bradford Northern in 1945-46.

Maroons captain Lewis used Headingley as a stage for a five-star performance which finally justified his rating as the world's most complete Rugby League player. He scored two tries and laid on the final pass for two more in a display which opened with raw determination and closed bordering on unopposed boredom.

The Leeds players had voiced discontent at the recruitment of overseas players, an influx which was obviously threatening their places. Only Balmain captain Martin was included in the line-up and the British-bred players did their case no good whatsoever by crashing to the Queenslanders only a year after being thrashed by the Kangaroos 31-4.

After the rout, Leeds Football Chairman Harry Jepson announced that the club were in the hunt for the signatures of a handful of the Queensland party, Lewis being the prime target.

As 12 months earlier, the Australian players gave a classic lesson in support play at speed. On the rare occasions that a Leeds player made a break he looked vainly for support. When a Queenslander went away he was spoiled for choice as players lined up to score. And score they did!

The contrast in style was evident not only on attack. The Leeds tackling consisted mainly of pulling and pushing, while the Maroons jack-knifed the man in possession.

The only bright spots for Leeds were a 4-3 pull in the scrums and a 19-11 penalty count from referee Billy Thompson.

As Queensland left British shores lamenting the standard of defences, coupled with attitude and training methods, Great Britain manager Dick Gemmell commented: 'We've learned nothing new, we've seen it all before.' Twelve months earlier, in fact, and the M.M.P. Tour Down Under only seven months away!

Hull's trio of 1984 Great Britain tourists: Garry Schofield (left), Lee Crooks, scoring, and Wayne Proctor.

GREAT BRITAIN TOURS

GREAT BRITAIN TOURS

1984 M.M.P. TOUR

Great Britain bosses Dick Gemmell and Frank Myler launched their preparations for the 1984 tour Down Under 12 months before departure date.

An invited squad of 44 players attended three weekend training camps during the summer of 1983, augmented by weekly personal training schedules. The three-month fitness programme was devised by Rod McKenzie, senior lecturer at Carnegie College in Leeds and newly appointed as the League's official fitness consultant.

The squad system ran until the first month of the season, culminating in a behind-closed-doors practice match at Swinton in early September.

A squad was then named to prepare for the two Under-24 fixtures with France in November and December and another smaller Great Britain party named for the build up to the first Dominion Insurance Test against France in Avignon. Before the return Test at Leeds, Gemmell and Myler named a squad of 42 players to work through until the mid-April tour selection.

The large squad met weekly at Fartown, Huddersfield, amid continual controversy as clubs demanded the release of Great Britain squad players because of matches and training sessions.

The club-and-country row came to a head in the week of the Leeds Test when Widnes ordered their 10 squad players to boycott Great Britain training. Only winger John Basnett turned up for the international session and the British management decided to take a stand and not consider the absentees for Test selection. Thus, only Basnett from the Widnes camp appeared in the second Test, his international debut.

Bradford Northern also objected to players being kept away from Odsal but later gave approval as Great Britain manager Gemmell issued a public warning that players not attending training sessions would be putting their tour places in jeopardy.

The 42-man squad had to be amended repeatedly because of withdrawals through injury and personal reasons.

Within days of being selected for the squad, Hull utility back Steve Evans — a 1979 tourist — withdrew because of his summer wedding plans and the starting of a new business venture. In the week of the second Test at Leeds, Leigh back John Woods — another 1979 tourist — pulled out because of family and business commitments.

Featherstone Rovers back row forward Peter Smith was the next to withdraw. Having battled bravely to overcome a painful back injury, Smith had to rule himself out of the three-month trip because of a shoulder injury. Hull K.R. loose forward David Hall, capped for the first time in the 1984 French Tests, asked not to be considered having taken over a public house, while Widnes forward John Wood declared himself unavailable within a week of Test selection because of family reasons.

Meanwhile, Hull K.R. hooker David Watkinson had broken his leg in the opening minutes of the Test in Avignon, while Trevor Skerrett and Lee Crooks (Hull), plus Tony Myler (Widnes) were all battling to regain fitness after knee operations.

To counterbalance the withdrawals, the British bosses called up Ian Wilkinson (Leeds), Kevin Beardmore (Castleford), Neil Holding and Harry Pinner (St. Helens), and Brian Case (Wigan).

The 30-man touring squad was revealed on April 16th, but not without further amendments. Skipper Trevor Skerrett, having been appointed for the tour leadership in December, lost the battle to prove his fitness, while prop Len Casey, the oldest member of the party at 34, was ruled out because of a six month suspension.

The Humberside duo were replaced by Hull's Wayne Proctor and St. Helens' utility man Chris Arkwright. A week later the Saints' centre or stand off, who had just switched to the back row, attended the official photo call and kitting out session at Leeds on the Tuesday before departure when he could not train because of a swollen knee. The Great Britain management sent Arkwright to a local specialist and withdrew him the following day on the advice that he would not be able to withstand the rigours of a 25-match, three-month tour with twice daily training. Oldham's Terry Flanagan was called up as the replacement.

Gemmell and Myler were joined on the management team by physiotherapist Ronnie Barritt, a 1979 tourist; Rod McKenzie as the first-ever Great Britain fitness director; and the League's Finance Officer Roland Davis as Business Manager.

The 35-strong party left Britain on May 13th, with a scheduled return date of August 10th.

Leigh's Steve Donlan and Wayne Proctor were the only tourists from outside the various training squads.

Garry Schofield became Britain's youngest-ever tourist, the Hull centre celebrating his 19th birthday on July 1st.

The personnel used for the squad preparations was:

1983 SUMMER TRAINING SQUAD

Steve Evans, David Topliss, Lee Crooks, Trevor Skerrett (Hull); Mike Smith, David Watkinson, George Fairbairn, Phil Hogan, Garry Clark (Hull K.R.); Brian Noble, Keith Mumby, Ellery Hanley (Bradford N.); Joe Lydon, Mick Burke, Tony Myler, Andrew Gregory, Mike O'Neill, David Hulme, Keiron O'Loughlin (Widnes); Keith England, Kevin Beardmore, Gary Hyde, Kevin Ward, John Joyner (Castleford); Ray Ashton, Mike Worrall, Andrew Goodway, Terry Flanagan (Oldham); John Fieldhouse, Ronnie Duane (Warrington); Gary Moorby, Neil Holding, Chris Arkwright, Roy Haggerty (St. Helens); Ian Hartley, Howard Burns (Workington T.); John Woods, Des Drummond (Leigh); Peter Smith, David Hobbs (Featherstone R.); David Moll (Keighley); Andrew Smith (Leeds); Graham King (Hunslet); Ron Smith (Salford).

In addition, the following were called up for the practice match at Swinton in September: Mick Crane (Hull), Bob Eccles (Warrington), Wally Jones (Oldham) and Dennis Ramsdale (Wigan).

1984 TRAINING SQUAD

Mick Adams (Widnes), Ray Ashton (Oldham), John Basnett (Widnes), Mick Burke (Widnes), Chris Burton (Hull K.R.), David Cairns (Barrow), Len Casey (Hull K.R.), Garry Clark (Hull K.R.), Lee Crooks (Hull), Andy Dannatt (Hull), Des Drummond (Leigh), Steve Evans (Hull), Ronnie Duane (Warrington), George Fairbairn (Hull K.R.), Terry Flanagan (Oldham), Des Foy (Oldham), Andy Gregory (Widnes), Andy Goodway (Oldham), David Hall (Hull K.R.), Ellery Hanley (Bradford N.), David Hobbs (Featherstone R.), Dick Jasiewicz (Bradford N.), John Joyner (Castleford), Joe Lydon (Widnes), Keith Mumby (Bradford N.), Tony Myler (Widnes), Brian Noble (Bradford N.), Mike O'Neill (Widnes), Steve O'Neill (Widnes), Alan Rathbone (Bradford N.), Keith Rayne (Leeds), Garry Schofield (Hull), Trevor Skerrett (Hull), Mike Smith (Hull K.R.), Peter Smith (Featherstone R.), Kevin Ward (Castleford), David Watkinson (Hull K.R.), Fred Whitfield (Widnes), John Wood (Widnes), John Woods (Leigh), Mick Worrall (Oldham).

Withdrawals: Evans, Hall, P. Smith, Wood and Woods.

Additions: Kevin Beardmore (Castleford), Brian Case (Wigan), Neil Holding (St. Helens), Harry Pinner (St. Helens) and Ian Wilkinson (Leeds).

1984 M.M.P. TOUR SQUAD

Manager: Dick Gemmell
Coach: Frank Myler
Business Manager: Roland Davis
Physiotherapist: Ronnie Barritt
Fitness Director: Rod McKenzie

			INTERNATIONAL APPEARANCES*				
BACKS:	*Club*	*Age*	*G.B.*	*Tourist*	*England*	*U-24s*	*Colts*
Ray Ashton	Oldham	23	—	—	—	3	2
Mick Burke	Widnes	25	3 + 1	—	—	5	—
Garry Clark	Hull K.R.	19	2	—	—	3	1
Steve Donlan	Leigh	29	—	—	—	—	—
Des Drummond	Leigh	26	10	—	4	5	—
Ronnie Duane	Warrington	20	3	—	—	2	2
Des Foy	Oldham	20	2	—	—	2	—
Andy Gregory	Widnes	22	5	—	—	1	—
Ellery Hanley	Bradford N.	23	1 + 1	—	—	2	—
Neil Holding	St. Helens	23	—	—	1	4	1
John Joyner	Castleford	29	14	1979	4	4 + 1	—
Joe Lydon	Widnes	20	3	—	—	3	—
Keith Mumby	Bradford N.	27	4	1979	2	6	—
Tony Myler	Widnes	23	2	—	—	3	2
Garry Schofield	Hull	18	1	—	—	+2	1
Mike Smith	Hull K.R.	26	9 + 1	1979	5	7	—
FORWARDS:	*Club*	*Age*	*G.B.*	*Tourist*	*England*	*U-24s*	*Colts*
Mick Adams	Widnes	32	5 + 1	1979	3 + 2	—	—
Kevin Beardmore	Castleford	23	—	—	—	—	—
Chris Burton	Hull K.R.	27	1	—	—	—	1
Brian Case	Wigan	26	—	—	1	3 + 1	—
Lee Crooks	Hull	20	2 + 1	—	—	1	5
Terry Flanagan	Oldham	23	2	—	—	5	2
Andy Goodway	Oldham	22	3	—	—	2	—
David Hobbs	Featherstone R.	25	2	—	—	2	—
Brian Noble	Bradford N.	23	4	—	—	4	2
Mike O'Neill	Widnes	23	3	—	—	3 + 2	4
Harry Pinner	St. Helens	27	1 + 1	—	3	4 + 4	1
Wayne Proctor	Hull	20	—	—	—	1	3
Keith Rayne	Leeds	27	2	—	2	2	—
Mick Worrall	Oldham	22	1	—	—	3	1

* As at April 1984
+ indicates substitute appearances

● A detailed review of the 1984 M.M.P. tour of Australia, New Zealand and Papua New Guinea will be featured in the 1985-86 *Rothmans Rugby League Yearbook*.

GREAT BRITAIN TOURS . . . A REVIEW

1910 TOUR

IN AUSTRALIA
Played 14 Won 9 Lost 4 Drew 1
For
Tries 76 Goals 56 Points 340
Against
Tries 51 Goals 47 Points 247
Won Test series 2-0

IN NEW ZEALAND
Played 4 Won 4
For
Tries 43 Goals 29 Points 187
Against
Tries 11 Goals 7 Points 47
Won Test series 1-0

TOUR PARTY:

Managers: J. Clifford (Huddersfield) and J.H. Houghton (St. Helens)
Captain: J. Lomas (Salford)

	App	Tries	Gls	Pts
A. Avery (Oldham)	11	7	0	21
J. Bartholomew (Huddersfield)	5	3	1	11
W. Batten (Hunslet)	12	5	1	17
F. Boylen (Hull)	7	1	5	13
E. Curzon (Salford)	6	3	0	9
J. Davies (Huddersfield)	5	1	0	3
F. Farrar (Hunslet)	4	4	1	14
B. Jenkins (Wigan)	11	14	0	42
T. Jenkins (Ebbw Vale)	10	3	4	17
W. Jukes (Hunslet)	12	10	0	30
H. Kershaw (Wakefield T.)	10	5	0	15
J. Leytham (Wigan)	12	12	5	46
J. Lomas (Salford)	13	10	53	136
T. Newbould (Wakefield T.)	7	2	0	6
R. Ramsdale (Wigan)	7	2	0	6
J. Riley (Halifax)	9	11	0	33
G. Ruddick (Broughton R.)	9	2	0	6
J. Sharrock (Wigan)	9	0	3	6
F. Shugars (Warrington)	12	1	0	3
F. Smith (Hunslet)	12	4	0	12
J. Thomas (Wigan)	12	7	12	45
W. Ward (Leeds)	4	1	0	3
F. Webster (Leeds)	14	3	0	9
W. Winstanley (Leigh)	14	5	0	15
F. Young (Leeds)	2	0	0	0

T. Helm (Oldham) did not play on the tour after being injured en route. In the first match against Newcastle guest appearances were made by J. Devereux (Hull), D. Frawley (Warrington, 2 tries), A. Morton (Hull, 1 try), A. Burge and T. Byrne.

1914 TOUR

IN AUSTRALIA
Played 12 Won 9 Lost 3
For
Tries 77 Goals 55 Points 341
Against
Tries 24 Goals 31 Points 134
Won Test series 2-1

IN NEW ZEALAND
Played 6 Won 6
For
Tries 46 Goals 28 Points 194
Against
Tries 12 Goals 13 Points 62
Won Test series 1-0

TOUR PARTY:

Managers: J. Clifford (Huddersfield) and J.H. Houghton (St. Helens)
Captain: H. Wagstaff (Huddersfield)

	App	Tries	Gls	Pts
J. Chilcott (Huddersfield)	11	1	0	3
L. Clampitt (Broughton R.)	11	2	0	6
D. Clark (Huddersfield)	6	1	0	3
A. Coldrick (Wigan)	10	6	0	18
W. Davies (Leeds)	13	13	2	43
A. Francis (Hull)	3	6	0	18
J. Guerin (Hunslet)	8	1	14	31
W. Hall (Oldham)	12	6	0	18
D. Holland (Oldham)	12	7	0	21
J.W. Jarman (Leeds)	9	3	1	11
B. Jenkins (Wigan)	10	8	0	24
A. Johnson (Widnes)	12	7	2	25
F. Longstaff (Huddersfield)	8	2	4	14
S. Moorhouse (Huddersfield)	10	19	0	57
J. O'Garra (Widnes)	8	5	0	15
W. Prosser (Halifax)	8	3	0	9
R. Ramsdale (Wigan)	9	1	0	3
J. Robinson (Rochdale H.)	5	4	3	18
J. Rogers (Huddersfield)	7	2	3	12
W. Roman (Rochdale H.)	7	1	0	3
J. Smales (Hunslet)	7	2	0	6
F. Smith (Hunslet)	12	2	0	6
G. Thomas (Wigan)	6	1	3	9
H. Wagstaff (Huddersfield)	13	11	4	41
F. Williams (Halifax)	7	7	0	21
A. Wood (Oldham)	9	1	47	97

J.B. Houghton, son of the tour manager, made one appearance and scored a try.

1920 TOUR

IN AUSTRALIA
Played 15 Won 12 Lost 3
For
Tries 83 Goals 64 Points 377
Against
Tries 48 Goals 42 Points 228
Lost Test series 2-1

IN NEW ZEALAND
Played 10 Won 9 Lost 1
For
Tries 89 Goals 47 Points 361
Against
Tries 24 Goals 16 Points 104
Won Test series 3-0

TOUR PARTY:

Managers: S. Foster (Halifax) and J. Wilson (Hull K.R.)
Captain: H. Wagstaff (Huddersfield)

	App	Tries	Gls	Pts
J. Bacon (Leeds)	17	23	2	73
J. Bowers (Rochdale H.)	11	4	0	12
J. Cartwright (Leigh)	15	1	0	3
D. Clark (Huddersfield)	12	3	0	9
W. Cunliffe (Warrington)	15	1	0	3
E. Davies (Oldham)	11	13	0	39
J. Doyle (Barrow)	8	8	0	24
F. Gallagher (Dewsbury)	11	3	0	9
B. Gronow (Huddersfield)	16	2	65	136
H. Hilton (Oldham)	19	9	0	27
D. Hurcombe (Wigan)	13	5	1	17
A. Johnson (Widnes)	12	2	0	6
E. Jones (Rochdale H.)	15	3	0	9
R. Lloyd (Halifax)	11	4	0	12
A. Milnes (Halifax)	9	1	0	3
J. Parkin (Wakefield T.)	13	19	1	59
G. Rees (Leeds)	5	0	0	0
W. Reid (Widnes)	10	8	0	24
J. Rogers (Huddersfield)	9	2	3	12
G. Skelhorne (Warrington)	13	4	0	12
J.C. Stacey (Halifax)	11	7	0	21
S. Stockwell (Leeds)	11	15	1	47
W. Stone (Hull)	17	24	1	74
G. Thomas (Huddersfield)	18	1	7	17
H. Wagstaff (Huddersfield)	13	10	0	30
A. Wood (Oldham)	7	0	29	58

J. Wilson (tour manager) made three appearances, scoring one goal.

1924 TOUR

IN AUSTRALIA
Played 18 Won 14 Lost 4
For
Tries 104 Goals 77 Points 466
Against
Tries 56 Goals 45 Points 258
Won Test series 2-1

IN NEW ZEALAND
Played 9 Won 7 Lost 2
For
Tries 64 Goals 40 Points 272
Against
Tries 25 Goals 21 Points 117
Lost Test series 2-1

TOUR PARTY:

Managers: J.H. Dannatt (Hull) and E. Osborne (Warrington)
Captain: J. Parkin (Wakefield T.)

	App	Tries	Gls	Pts
J. Bacon (Leeds)	8	2	0	6
J. Bennett (Rochdale H.)	19	2	0	6
W. Bentham (Broughton R.)	7	7	0	21
H. Bowman (Hull)	14	8	0	24
A. Brough (Oldham)	12	14	1	44
W. Burgess (Barrow)	22	3	1	11
C. Carr (Barrow)	17	9	0	27
W. Cunliffe (Warrington)	17	3	0	9
J. Darwell (Leigh)	15	5	0	15
F. Evans (Swinton)	14	13	0	39
F. Gallagher (Batley)	16	3	0	9
B. Gronow (Huddersfield)	8	1	5	13
T. Howley (Wigan)	21	13	0	39
D. Hurcombe (Wigan)	11	5	0	15
E. Knapman (Oldham)	11	0	1	2
W. Mooney (Leigh)	12	0	1	2
J. Parkin (Wakefield T.)	13	13	6	51
C. Pollard (Wakefield T.)	9	6	1	20
J. Price (Wigan)	9	8	0	24
D. Rees (Halifax)	12	2	0	6
J. Ring (Wigan)	15	23	0	69
S. Rix (Oldham)	17	17	0	51
R. Sloman (Oldham)	3	0	0	0
J. Sullivan (Wigan)	17	0	84	168
J. Thompson (Leeds)	18	6	17	52
S. Whitty (Hull)	14	5	0	15

1928 TOUR

IN AUSTRALIA
Played 16 Won 11 Lost 4 Drew 1
For
Tries 67 Goals 60 Points 321
Against
Tries 43 Goals 45 Points 219
Won Test series 2-1

IN NEW ZEALAND
Played 8 Won 7 Lost 1
For
Tries 55 Goals 36 Points 237
Against
Tries 16 Goals 12 Points 72
Won Test series 2-1

TOUR PARTY:

Managers: G.F. Hutchins (Oldham) and E. Osborne (Warrington)
Captain: J. Parkin (Wakefield T.)

	App	Tries	Gls	Pts
T. Askin (Featherstone R.)	15	9	0	27
N. Bentham (Wigan Highfield)	14	1	0	3
F. Bowen (St. Helens Rec.)	16	2	0	6
H. Bowman (Hull)	14	2	0	6
J. Brough (Leeds)	15	6	0	18
W. Burgess (Barrow)	12	1	1	5
O. Dolan (St. Helens Rec.)	7	0	1	2
A. Ellaby (St. Helens)	14	20	2	64
B. Evans (Swinton)	12	1	0	3
J. Evans (Swinton)	3	1	0	3
L. Fairclough (St. Helens)	12	11	0	33
A. Fildes (St. Helens Rec.)	13	3	0	9
A. Frodsham (St. Helens)	17	15	0	45
W. Gowers (Rochdale H.)	9	0	25	50
T.E. Gwynne (Hull)	11	7	0	21
B. Halfpenny (St. Helens)	10	8	0	24
W. Horton (Wakefield T.)	15	5	0	15
J. Oliver (Batley)	9	4	0	12
J. Parkin (Wakefield T.)	4	2	0	6
W. Rees (Swinton)	19	4	0	12
M. Rosser (Leeds)	9	3	0	9
R. Sloman (Oldham)	12	4	0	12
J. Sullivan (Wigan)	15	3	52	113
J. Thompson (Leeds)	14	4	14	40
W. Williams (Salford)	12	0	1	2
H. Young (Bradford N.)	9	6	0	18

1932 TOUR

IN AUSTRALIA
Played 18 Won 15 Lost 2 Drew 1
For
Tries 105 Goals 84 Points 483
Against
Tries 32 Goals 38 Points 172
Won Test series 2-1

IN NEW ZEALAND
Played 8 Won 8
For
Tries 65 Goals 52 Points 299
Against
Tries 17 Goals 18 Points 87
Won Test series 3-0

TOUR PARTY:

Managers: R.F. Anderton (Warrington) and G.F. Hutchins (Oldham)
Captain: J. Sullivan (Wigan)

	App	Tries	Gls	Pts
L. Adams (Leeds)	9	2	0	6
A. Atkinson (Castleford)	20	14	0	42
S. Brogden (Huddersfield)	15	14	0	42
F. Butters (Swinton)	1	1	0	3
I. Davies (Halifax)	9	7	0	21
W. Dingsdale (Warrington)	5	1	0	3
A. Ellaby (St. Helens)	14	21	0	63
B. Evans (Swinton)	14	2	0	6
J. Feetham (Salford)	10	5	0	15
N. Fender (York)	14	11	0	33
A. Fildes (St. Helens)	19	6	0	18
M. Hodgson (Swinton)	19	2	13	32
W. Horton (Wakefield T.)	14	2	0	6
B. Hudson (Salford)	12	18	0	54
J. Lowe (Leeds)	10	1	0	3
E. Pollard (Wakefield T.)	12	8	0	24
A. Risman (Salford)	17	9	0	27
G. Robinson (Wakefield T.)	7	3	0	9
N. Silcock (Widnes)	11	2	1	8
S. Smith (Leeds)	14	15	0	45
J. Sullivan (Wigan)	21	1	110	223
J. Thompson (Leeds)	15	0	12	24
L. White (Hunslet)	13	3	0	9
W. Williams (Salford)	15	1	0	3
J. Woods (Barrow)	12	18	0	54
J. Wright (Swinton)	16	3	0	9

1936 TOUR

MATCH RESULTS:

IN AUSTRALIA
Played 17 Won 14 Lost 3
For
Tries 79 Goals 82 Points 401
Against
Tries 38 Goals 45 Points 204
Won Test series 2-1

IN NEW ZEALAND
Played 8 Won 8
For
Tries 52 Goals 27 Points 210
Against
Tries 8 Goals 16 Points 56
Won Test series 2-0

TOUR PARTY:

Managers: R.F. Anderton (Warrington) and W. Popplewell (Bramley)
Captain: J. Brough (Leeds)

	App	Tries	Gls	Pts
J. Arkwright (Warrington)	10	6	0	18
T. Armitt (Swinton)	12	0	0	0
A. Atkinson (Castleford)	12	6	5	28
W. Belshaw (Liverpool S.)	17	3	12	33
H. Beverley (Hunslet)	11	5	0	15
S. Brogden (Leeds)	15	12	0	36
J. Brough (Leeds)	14	1	3	9
E.G. Davies (Wigan)	9	3	0	9
A. Edwards (Salford)	16	21	0	63
H. Ellerington (Hull)	11	6	0	18
G. Exley (Wakefield T.)	13	5	0	15
H. Field (York)	15	1	0	3
F. Harris (Leeds)	1	2	0	6
M. Hodgson (Swinton)	18	3	65	139
B. Hudson (Salford)	13	12	0	36
E. Jenkins (Salford)	16	5	2	19
H. Jones (Keighley)	8	1	0	3
T. McCue (Widnes)	9	3	0	9
J. Miller (Warrington)	17	3	0	9
J. Morley (Wigan)	10	6	0	18
A. Risman (Salford)	14	9	22	71
N. Silcock (Widnes)	13	1	0	3
S. Smith (Leeds)	6	9	0	27
L.A. Troup (Barrow)	15	4	0	12
W. Watkins (Salford)	15	4	0	12
H. Woods (Liverpool S.)	15	0	0	0

1946 TOUR

MATCH RESULTS:

IN AUSTRALIA
Played 20 Won 16 Lost 3 Drew 1
For
Tries 146 Goals 100 Points 638
Against
Tries 36 Goals 45 Points 198
Won Test series 2-0 with one drawn

IN NEW ZEALAND
Played 7 Won 5 Lost 2
For
Tries 35 Goals 20 Points 145
Against
Tries 12 Goals 21 Points 78
Lost Test series 1-0

TOUR PARTY:

Managers: W. Popplewell (Bramley) and W.M. Gabbatt (Barrow)
Captain: A. Risman (Salford)

	App	Tries	Gls	Pts
A. Bassett (Halifax)	11	18	0	54
E. Batten (Bradford N.)	13	18	0	54
G. Curran (Salford)	16	2	0	6
W. Davies (Bradford N.)	14	5	0	15
J. Egan (Wigan)	17	6	0	18
T. Foster (Bradford N.)	10	1	0	3
K. Gee (Wigan)	18	1	0	3
W. Horne (Barrow)	14	9	6	39
W.F. Hughes (Workington T.)	13	4	0	12
D. Jenkins (Leeds)	11	1	0	3
A. Johnson (Warrington)	17	15	3	51
J. Jones (Barrow)	11	1	1	5
J. Kitching (Bradford N.)	12	17	0	51
B. Knowelden (Barrow)	13	15	0	45
J. Lewthwaite (Barrow)	15	25	0	75
T. McCue (Widnes)	15	0	0	0
H. Murphy (Wakefield T.)	1	1	0	3
R. Nicholson (Huddersfield)	11	5	0	15
I. Owens (Leeds)	18	11	4	41
D. Phillips (Oldham)	18	3	0	9
A. Risman (Salford)	14	3	31	71
M. Ryan (Wigan)	4	1	0	3
E. Ward (Bradford N.)	16	5	43	101
E.H. Ward (Wigan)	12	5	32	79
F. Whitcombe (Bradford N.)	19	3	0	9
L. White (York)	18	6	0	18

1950 TOUR

IN AUSTRALIA
Played 19 Won 15 Lost 4
For
Tries 133 Goals 102 Points 603
Against
Tries 22 Goals 56 Points 178
Lost Test series 2-1

IN NEW ZEALAND
Played 6 Won 4 Lost 2
For
Tries 37 Goals 25 Points 161
Against
Tries 16 Goals 20 Points 88
Lost Test series 2-0

TOUR PARTY:

Managers: G. Oldroyd (Dewsbury) and T. Spedding (Belle Vue R.)
Captain: E. Ward (Bradford N.)

	App	Tries	Gls	Pts
E. Ashcroft (Wigan)	11	5	0	15
T. Bradshaw (Wigan)	15	1	0	3
J. Cunliffe (Wigan)	17	14	8	58
A. Daniels (Halifax)	5	5	0	15
T. Danby (Salford)	18	34	0	102
J. Egan (Wigan)	15	3	0	9
J. Featherstone (Warrington)	14	10	0	30
K. Gee (Wigan)	14	1	9	21
E. Gwyther (Belle Vue R.)	15	2	0	6
F. Higgins (Widnes)	14	4	0	12
J. Hilton (Wigan)	12	22	0	66
W. Horne (Barrow)	5	2	13	32
J. Ledgard (Leigh)	12	2	37	80
H. Murphy (Wakefield T.)	13	2	1	8
D. Naughton (Widnes)	8	2	0	6
F. Osmond (Swinton)	10	4	0	12
A. Pepperell (Workington T.)	11	7	0	21
D. Phillips (Belle Vue R.)	12	7	0	21
R. Pollard (Dewsbury)	9	5	6	27
G. Ratcliffe (Wigan)	11	6	0	18
M. Ryan (Wigan)	12	4	1	14
R. Ryan (Warrington)	12	5	0	15
H. Street (Dewsbury)	15	2	0	6
K. Traill (Bradford N.)	15	7	0	21
E. Ward (Bradford N.)	15	7	52	125
R. Williams (Leeds)	15	7	0	21

1954 TOUR

IN AUSTRALIA
Played 22 Won 13 Lost 7 Drew 1
One match abandoned. (Scores included in points total)
For
Tries 133 Goals 114 Points 627
Against
Tries 78 Goals 96 Points 426
Lost Test series 2-1

IN NEW ZEALAND
Played 10 Won 8 Lost 2
For
Tries 60 Goals 56 Points 292
Against
Tries 14 Goals 32 Points 106
Won Test series 2-1

TOUR PARTY:

Managers: T. Hesketh (Wigan) and H. Rawson (Hunslet)
Captain: R. Williams (Hunslet)

	App	Tries	Gls	Pts
E. Ashcroft (Wigan)	15	11	0	33
W. Boston (Wigan)	18	36	0	108
J. Bowden (Huddersfield)	20	2	0	6
B. Briggs (Huddersfield)	17	4	0	12
A. Burnell (Hunslet)	17	10	0	30
E. Cahill (Rochdale H.)	8	0	14	28
F. Castle (Barrow)	5	6	0	18
J. Cunliffe (Wigan)	16	7	29	79
D. Greenall (St. Helens)	21	13	0	39
G. Gunney (Hunslet)	18	6	0	18
T. Harris (Hull)	14	3	0	9
G. Helme (Warrington)	16	5	0	15
J. Henderson (Workington T.)	11	1	0	3
P. Jackson (Barrow)	17	7	0	21
B.L. Jones (Leeds)	21	8	127	278
T. McKinney (Salford)	22	2	0	6
T. O'Grady (Oldham)	17	28	0	84
C. Pawsey (Leigh)	15	4	0	12
A. Prescott (St. Helens)	20	1	0	3
R. Price (Warrington)	17	8	0	24
N. Silcock (Wigan)	19	7	0	21
K. Traill (Bradford N.)	18	1	0	3
A. Turnbull (Leeds)	2	2	0	6
D. Valentine (Huddersfield)	19	7	0	21
J. Wilkinson (Halifax)	18	6	0	18
R. Williams (Hunslet)	15	8	0	24

1958 TOUR

IN AUSTRALIA
Played 21 Won 19 Lost 1 Drew 1
For
Tries 184 Goals 129 Points 810
Against
Tries 64 Goals 93 Points 378
Won Test series 2-1

IN NEW ZEALAND
Played 9 Won 8 Lost 1
For
Tries 88 Goals 61 Points 386
Against
Tries 18 Goals 27 Points 108
Drew Test series 1-1

TOUR PARTY:

Managers: B. Manson (Swinton) and T. Mitchell (Workington T.)
Captain: A. Prescott (St. Helens)
Coach: J. Brough (Workington T.)

	App	Tries	Gls	Pts
A. Ackerley (Halifax)	18	1	0	3
H. Archer (Workington T.)	8	0	0	0
E. Ashton (Wigan)	19	30	13	116
D. Bolton (Wigan)	8	6	0	18
F. Carlton (St. Helens)	8	20	0	60
J. Challinor (Warrington)	14	11	0	33
A. Davies (Oldham)	20	13	0	39
B. Edgar (Workington T.)	18	6	0	18
E. Fraser (Warrington)	18	6	110	238
D. Goodwin (Barrow)	16	3	0	9
T. Harris (Hull)	14	7	0	21
R. Huddart (Whitehaven)	24	17	0	51
K. Jackson (Oldham)	5	0	0	0
P. Jackson (Barrow)	16	5	0	15
V. Karalius (St. Helens)	17	3	0	9
M. Martyn (Leigh)	16	23	0	69
B. McTigue (Wigan)	18	3	19	47
G. Moses (St. Helens)	17	5	0	15
A. Murphy (St. Helens)	20	21	3	69
F. Pitchford (Oldham)	12	9	0	27
A. Prescott (St. Helens)	9	0	0	0
I. Southward (Workington T.)	19	25	45	165
M. Sullivan (Wigan)	19	38	0	114
A. Terry (St. Helens)	14	2	0	6
J. Whiteley (Hull)	13	8	0	24
W. Wookey (Workington T.)	10	10	0	30

1962 TOUR

IN AUSTRALIA
Played 21 Won 18 Lost 3
For
Tries 151 Goals 113 Points 679
Against
Tries 61 Goals 60 Points 303
Won Test series 2-1

IN NEW ZEALAND
Played 9 Won 6 Lost 3
For
Tries 73 Goals 50 Points 319
Against
Tries 35 Goals 28 Points 161
Lost Test series 2-0

TOUR PARTY:

Managers: S. Hadfield (Wakefield T.) and A. Walker (Rochdale H.)
Captain: E. Ashton (Wigan)
Coach: C. Hutton (Hull K.R.)

	App	Tries	Gls	Pts
E. Ashton (Wigan)	15	21	14	91
D. Bolton (Wigan)	16	7	0	21
W. Boston (Wigan)	17	22	0	66
F. Carlton (Wigan)	15	17	0	51
G. Cooper (Featherstone R.)	16	13	0	39
B. Edgar (Workington T.)	15	4	0	12
R. Evans (Wigan)	15	0	0	0
E. Fraser (Warrington)	15	2	20	46
N. Fox (Wakefield T.)	21	19	85	227
D. Fox (Featherstone R.)	5	3	0	9
L. Gilfedder (Warrington)	22	11	44	121
N. Herbert (Workington T.)	17	1	0	3
R. Huddart (St. Helens)	23	13	0	39
B. McTigue (Wigan)	15	1	0	3
A. Murphy (St. Helens)	11	9	0	27
K. Noble (Huddersfield)	12	1	0	3
H. Poynton (Wakefield T.)	12	3	0	9
G. Round (Wakefield T.)	20	13	0	39
W. Sayer (Wigan)	16	2	0	6
J. Shaw (Halifax)	17	2	0	6
P. Small (Castleford)	16	17	0	51
M. Sullivan (St. Helens)	19	14	0	42
I. Southward (Workington T.)	12	11	0	33
J. Taylor (Hull K.R.)	12	9	0	27
D. Turner (Wakefield T.)	16	9	0	27
J. Wilkinson (Wakefield T.)	14	0	0	0

Appearances include playing substitutes

1966 TOUR

IN AUSTRALIA
Played 22 Won 13 Lost 9
For
Tries 112 Goals 85 Points 506
Against
Tries 47 Goals 83 Points 307
Lost Test series 2-1

IN NEW ZEALAND
Played 8 Won 8
For
Tries 57 Goals 47 Points 265
Against
Tries 10 Goals 24 Points 78
Won Test series 2-0

TOUR PARTY:

Managers: W. Spaven (Hull K.R.) and J. Errock (Oldham)
Captain: H. Poole (Leeds)

	App	Tries	Gls	Pts
W. Aspinall (Warrington)	20	10	0	30
T. Bishop (St. Helens)	15	3	1	11
I. Brooke (Bradford N.)	18	13	0	39
W. Bryant (Castleford)	17	7	0	21
A. Buckley (Swinton)	18	5	0	15
W. Burgess (Barrow)	17	14	0	42
C. Clarke (Wigan)	16	3	1	11
C. Crewdson (Keighley)	13	0	0	0
C. Dooler (Featherstone R.)	15	5	0	15
B. Edgar (Workington T.)	17	3	0	9
P. Flanagan (Hull K.R.)	16	3	0	9
T. Fogerty (Halifax)	20	5	0	15
K. Gowers (Swinton)	15	0	67	134
A. Hardisty (Castleford)	16	10	0	30
B. Jones (Wakefield T.)	15	24	0	72
A. Keegan (Hull)	15	1	62	127
J. Mantle (St. Helens)	11	3	0	9
F. Myler (Widnes)	16	7	0	21
H. Poole (Leeds)	16	6	0	18
W. Ramsey (Hunslet)	15	5	0	15
K. Roberts (Halifax)	19	4	0	12
D. Robinson (Swinton)	22	4	0	12
G. Shelton (Hunslet)	13	4	0	12
J. Stopford (Swinton)	17	16	1	50
C. Watson (St. Helens)	14	3	0	9
G. Wriglesworth (Leeds)	16	11	0	33

Appearances include playing substitutes

1970 TOUR

IN AUSTRALIA
Played 17 Won 15 Lost 1 Drew 1
For
Tries 104 Goals 92 Points 496
Against
Tries 27 Goals 66 Points 213
Won Test series 2-1

IN NEW ZEALAND
Played 7 Won 7
For
Tries 61 Goals 37 Points 257
Against
Tries 9 Goals 24 Points 75
Won Test series 3-0

TOUR PARTY:

Manager: J. Harding (Leigh)
Captain: F. Myler (St. Helens)
Coach: J. Whiteley (Hull)

	App	Tries	Gls	Pts
J. Atkinson (Leeds)	18	15	0	45
D. Chisnall (Leigh)	14	1	0	3
R. Dutton (Widnes)	9	2	43	92
D. Edwards (Castleford)	6	0	0	0
A. Fisher (Bradford N.)	11	2	0	6
P. Flanagan (Hull K.R.)	14	8	1	26
A. Hardisty (Castleford)	15	12	0	36
D. Hartley (Castleford)	16	2	0	6
K. Hepworth (Castleford)	14	4	0	12
C. Hesketh (Salford)	13	9	0	27
S. Hynes (Leeds)	17	19	9	75
R. Irving (Oldham)	17	6	0	18
D. Laughton (Wigan)	15	9	0	27
P. Lowe (Hull K.R.)	15	11	0	33
R. Millward (Hull K.R.)	16	18	23	100
F. Myler (St. Helens)	15	3	0	9
T. Price (Bradford N.)	9	5	51	117
M. Reilly (Castleford)	13	3	1	11
D. Robinson (Wigan)	6	2	1	8
B. Seabourne (Leeds)	8	2	0	6
M. Shoebottom (Leeds)	13	7	0	21
A. Smith (Leeds)	16	15	0	45
C. Sullivan (Hull)	8	3	0	9
J. Thompson (Featherstone R.)	17	4	0	12
J. Ward (Salford)	8	0	0	0
C. Watson (St. Helens)	13	3	0	9

Appearances include playing substitutes

1974 TOUR

IN AUSTRALIA
Played 20 Won 15 Lost 5
For
Tries 104 Goals 93 Drop goals 2 Points 500
Against
Tries 38 Goals 59 Drop goals 3 Points 235
Lost Test series 2-1

IN NEW ZEALAND
Played 8 Won 6 Lost 2
For
Tries 37 Goals 32 Points 175
Against
Tries 8 Goals 27 Points 78
Won Test series 2-1

TOUR PARTY:

Manager: R. Parker (Blackpool B.)
Captain: C. Hesketh (Salford)
Coach: J. Challinor (St. Helens)

	App	Tries	Gls	Pts
K. Ashcroft (Warrington)	14	2	0	6
J. Atkinson (Leeds)	8	8	0	24
A. Bates (Dewsbury)	17	2	0	6
J. Bates (Dewsbury)	6	0	0	0
J. Bevan (Warrington)	17	15	0	45
J. Bridges (Featherstone R.)	8	0	0	0
J. Butler (Rochdale H.)	18	6	0	18
P. Charlton (Salford)	17	4	0	12
E. Chisnall (St. Helens)	18	3	0	9
T. Clawson (Oldham)	13	0	24	48
C. Dixon (Salford)	19	4	0	12
L. Dyl (Leeds)	17	14	0	42
D. Eckersley (St. Helens)	13	3	12	33
K. Gill (Salford)	16	8	0	24
J. Gray (Wigan)	17	2	53(1)	111
C. Hesketh (Salford)	20	4	0	12
J. Mills (Widnes)	16	2	0	6
R. Millward (Hull K.R.)	12	8	18	60
S. Nash (Featherstone R.)	16	5	1(1)	16
G. Nicholls (St. Helens)	18	4	0	12
S. Norton (Castleford)	17	5	0	15
*W. Ramsey (Bradford N.)	7	2	5	16
D. Redfearn (Bradford N.)	18	18	2	58
*M. Richards (Salford)	10	5	0	15
P. Rose (Hull K.R.)	14	5	0	15
J. Thompson (Featherstone R.)	21	1	0	3
D. Watkins (Salford)	8	2	12	30
D. Willicombe (Wigan)	15	8	0	24

J. Challinor (coach) made one appearance and scored a try. Appearances include playing substitutes.
*Replacements for players injured on tour: Ramsey for J. Bates; Richards for Atkinson. ( ) One point drop goal.

1979 TOUR

IN AUSTRALIA
Played 18 Won 13 Lost 4 Drew 1
For
Tries 66 Goals 73 Drop goals 3 Points 347
Against
Tries 39 Goals 68 Points 253
Lost Test series 3-0

IN NEW ZEALAND
Played 9 Won 8 Lost 1
For
Tries 48 Goals 34 Points 212
Against
Tries 15 Goals 12 Points 69
Won Test series 2-1

TOUR PARTY:

Managers: H. Womersley (Bradford N.) and R. Gemmell (Hull)
Captain: D. Laughton (Widnes)
Coach: E. Ashton MBE (St. Helens)

	App	Tries	Gls	Pts
M. Adams (Widnes)	16	0	9(1)	17
D. Barends (Bradford N.)	16	10	0	30
*J. Burke (Wakefield T.)	9	0	0	0
L. Casey (Bradford N.)	14	4	0	12
S. Evans (Featherstone R.)	19	16	0	48
*G. Fairbairn (Wigan)	10	3	19(1)	46
P. Glynn (St. Helens)	15	6	0	18
J. Grayshon (Bradford N.)	14	2	0	6
P. Hogan (Hull K.R.)	14	5	0	15
J. Holmes (Leeds)	13	1	2	7
E. Hughes (Widnes)	17	8	0	24
M. James (St. Helens)	13	3	0	9
J. Joyner (Castleford)	14	6	0	18
D. Laughton (Widnes)	5	0	0	0
G. Liptrot (St. Helens)	11	1	0	3
B. Lockwood (Hull K.R.)	12	1	0	3
T. Martyn (Warrington)	5	3	0	9
R. Mathias (St. Helens)	17	10	0	30
J. Mills (Widnes)	5	2	0	6
R. Millward (Hull K.R.)	3	0	4	8
K. Mumby (Bradford N.)	13	1	8	19
S. Nash (Salford)	6	2	0	6
G. Nicholls (St. Helens)	13	2	0	6
S. Norton (Hull)	9	0	0	0
A. Redfearn (Bradford N.)	10	1	0	3
T. Skerrett (Wakefield T.)	12	1	0	3
M. Smith (Hull K.R.)	11	4	0	12
G. Stephens (Castleford)	15	6	0	18
C. Stone (Hull)	12	0	0	0
*D. Topliss (Wakefield T.)	7	2	0	6
D. Ward (Leeds)	11	0	0	0
D. Watkinson (Hull K.R.)	12	2	0	6
J. Woods (Leigh)	17	12	68(1)	171

*Replacements for players injured on tour: Burke for Mills; Fairbairn for Martyn; Topliss for Millward
( ) One-point drop goal
Appearances include playing substitutes

TOUR RECORDS

IN AUSTRALIA

Highest score: 101-0 v. South Australia in 1914

Biggest defeat: 42-6 v. New South Wales in 1920 (Also **widest margin**)

Fewest defeats: 1 (and 1 draw) from 21 matches in 1958 and from 17 matches in 1970
Most defeats: 9 from 22 matches in 1966

Biggest attendance: 70,419 v. New South Wales (Sydney) in 1950

IN NEW ZEALAND

Highest score: 81-14 v. Bay of Plenty in 1962

Widest margin win: 72-3 v. Buller in 1928
72-3 v. North Island in 1958

Biggest defeat: 46-13 v. Auckland in 1962 (Also **widest margin**)

Fewest defeats: The tourists have won all their matches in the following years: 1910 (4 matches), 1914 (6), 1932 (8), 1936 (8), 1966 (8), 1970 (7)

Most defeats: 3 from 9 matches in 1962

Biggest attendance: 35,000 v. Auckland in 1920

PLAYERS' FULL TOUR RECORDS

Most appearances: 24 by Dick Huddart in 1958

Most tries: 38 by Mick Sullivan in 1958

Most goals and points: 127g, 278 pts by Lewis Jones in 1954

Most tours: 3 by Jonathan Parkin (1920, 1924, 1928)
Jim Sullivan (1924, 1928, 1932)
Joe Thompson (1924, 1928, 1932)
Augustus Risman (1932, 1936, 1946)
Brian Edgar (1958, 1962, 1966)
Roger Millward (1970, 1974, 1979)

Biggest club representation: 8 by Wigan in 1950 — Ernie Ashcroft, Tommy Bradshaw, Jack Cunliffe, Joe Egan, Ken Gee, Jack Hilton, Gordon Ratcliffe, Martin Ryan

Brothers touring together: Bryn and Jack Evans (1928), Don and Neil Fox (1962), Alan and John Bates (1974)

GREAT BRITAIN APPENDIX

In addition to full tours, Great Britain World Cup parties made occasional appearances in other matches in Australia and New Zealand as follows:

1957:
Australia

Western Australia (Perth)	won	66-5	4,000
Queensland (Brisbane)	won	44-5	4,000
French XIII (Auckland)	won	26-12	10,457

1968:
Australia

Toowoomba (Toowoomba)	won	28-10	2,850
Queensland (Brisbane)	won	33-18	12,384
N. Queensland (Townsville)	won	25-2	7,173
N.W. Queensland (Mount Isa)	won	33-5	2,385

1977:
New Zealand

Northern Maoris (Huntly)	won	18-14	2,800
Auckland (Auckland)	lost	10-14	9,000

Australia

Monaro (Queanbeyan)	lost	12-33	10,000
Queensland (Brisbane)	won	18-13	10,000
N. Queensland (Townsville)	lost	14-17	6,000
New South Wales (Sydney)	lost	5-35	7,244
Southern Div. (Gosford)	won	54-6	6,000

SUMMARY OF AUSTRALIAN TOURS OF BRITAIN

	P	W	D	L	For	Agst
1908-09	45	17	6	22	513	474
Lost Test series 2-0, one drawn						
1911-12	35	28	2	5	619	281
Won Test series 2-0, one drawn						
1921-22	36	27	–	9	763	253
Lost Test series 2-1						
1929-30	35	24	2	9	710	347
Lost Test series 2-1, one drawn						
1933-34	37	27	–	10	754	295
Lost Test series 3-0						
1937-38	25	13	1	11	293	232
Lost Test series 2-1						
1948-49	27	15	–	12	348	275
Lost Test series 3-0						
1952-53	27	23	1	3	816	248
Lost Test series 2-1						
1956-57	19	10	–	9	335	296
Lost Test series 2-1						
1959-60	24	15	–	9	495	390
Lost Test series 2-1						
1963-64	22	16	1	5	379	201
Won Test series 2-1						
1967-68	20	12	1	7	293	196
Won Test series 2-1						
1973-74	16	14	–	2	364	141
Won Test series 2-1						
1978-79	16	13	–	3	375	117
Won Test series 2-1						
1982-83	15	15	–	–	423	80
Won Test series 3-0						

SUMMARY OF NEW ZEALAND TOURS OF BRITAIN

	P	W	D	L	For	Agst
1907-08	35	19	2	14	414	294
Won Test series 2-1						
1926-27	34	17	–	17	562	554
Lost Test series 3-0						
1939	2	2	–	–	41	13
Tour abandoned after the outbreak of the Second World War.						
1947-48	27	16	1	10	391	240
Lost Test series 2-1						
1951-52	28	18	–	10	482	348
Lost Test series 3-0						
1955-56	27	14	2	11	473	433
Lost Test series 2-1						
1961-62	20	8	–	12	320	328
Lost Test series 2-1						
1965-66	23	13	1	9	274	259
Lost Test series 2-0, one drawn						
1971-72	20	10	–	10	319	300
Won Test series 2-1						
1980-81	14	7	1	6	202	143
Drew Test series 1-1, one draw						

Great Britain Touring Party 1984. Back row, left to right: Lydon, Donlan, Case, Burke, Schofield, Goodway, Foy, Crooks, Pinner, Clark, Myler, Mumby. Middle row, left to right: McKenzie (Fitness Director), Hobbs, Rayne, Arkwright (withdrawn), O'Neill, Worrall, Duane, Burton, Proctor, Joyner, Smith, Barritt (Physiotherapist). Front row, left to right: Myler (Coach), Beardmore, Ashton, Drummond, Noble (Captain), Gemmell (Manager), Adams (Vice-captain), Hanley, Gregory, Holding, Davies (Business Manager).

Des Drummond in action in the 1984 French Test in Avignon.

GREAT BRITAIN

GREAT BRITAIN

1984 FRENCH TESTS

With the tour Down Under less than four months away, Great Britain called on 23 players for the two-match Dominion Insurance Test series against France.

Britain answered coach Frank Myler's demands for a tighter defence by 'nilling' the French in both Tests. While they gave nothing away, Great Britain also offered little encouragement on attack in the Avignon and Leeds fixtures, which were both lacking in entertainment value.

The Test double gave Myler his ninth consecutive victory at international level, adding to two 1978 European Championship wins with England, and four Great Britain plus three Under-24 successes since his appointment in 1982. But the latest victories still left Myler and manager Dick Gemmell at the drawing board with the 30-man squad for the forthcoming M.M.P. Tour far from finalised.

Britain fielded eight new caps for the first Test at Avignon. Having lost chief architect Tony Myler with a recurrence of his back injury, utility man Joe Lydon was brought in at stand off. Full back George Fairbairn cried off with an ankle injury to be replaced by Keith Mumby, who was named captain when team-mate Brian Noble was ruled out by suspension on the day of departure.

Noble's hooking deputy David Watkinson lasted less than three minutes, suffering a broken leg, Hull's Lee Crooks taking over to win the scrums 4-3.

It was Crooks who broke the scoreless deadlock in the 61st minute with a penalty, his goalkicks being taken under unusual pressure. Each time Crooks began his run up, there was a sudden crack of musket fire from a group of Frenchmen in historical dress hired for a prematch display.

Four minutes later Great Britain scored their first try through Oldham prop forward Andy Goodway. French loose forward Baloup kicked ahead, the ball slamming into the nearby Goodway who held tight and galloped 35 yards on a curving run to the line.

Debutant Keith Rayne reproduced his Leeds club form to take the Dominion Insurance Man of the Match award. He clinched the prize by making one of Britain's few clear breaks to send Des Foy in for a 76th minute try, Crooks adding the goal.

Crooks missed three other shots at goal after taking over from the injured Lydon at halftime. Lydon had hit a post with his only goalkick, a drop goal attempt also missing the mark.

With the inclusion of seven new caps — Hanley's half-time introduction making eight — Britain failed to find a pattern of play, especially against one of the best-ever French defences.

Of the new boys, loose forward David Hall showed only a few touches of his Hull K.R. ball-playing form, while second row man David Hobbs gave a solid performance, making one of the few breaks of the game. Scrum half David Cairns was industrious, the departure of Watkinson forcing him to take the acting half back role at play-the-balls.

Celebrating becoming the Leigh player to have made most full Great Britain appearances, Des Drummond played with plenty of aggression on the wing but the threequarter was rarely in action on attack.

Although the French provided a stiff defence, their attacking ideas were limited to dashes from full back Wosniack and hooker Bernabe, so the British 25 was rarely under pressure.

Under International Board policy, the neutral referee was Sydney official John Gocher who incurred the wrath of the French, who unsuccessfully demanded a change of match official for the return Test. He had awarded penalties 18-10 to Britain.

Before the Headingley encounter three weeks later, the British management named a 41-man squad for weekly training sessions at

Huddersfield in preparation for the tour. On the eve of selection for the second Test, Widnes ordered their 10 representatives to train at Naughton Park rather than with the Great Britain squad. Only winger John Basnett turned up at Fartown and coach Myler confirmed his 'no train, no play' policy by disregarding the other nine Chemics when naming his Test side the following day.

Basnett became one of four new caps in the Headingley side, along with his centre partner Garry Schofield, the 18-year-old Hull centre, and forwards Kevin Ward (Castleford) and Dick Jasiewicz (Bradford N.).

Entertaining football was again a scarce commodity as five penalty goals from David Hobbs gave Britain an embarrassing victory in front of more than 7,500 fans who crowned the disappointing football fare with chants of 'boring'.

There was little satisfaction to be gained from the win, which was based on the excitable French marring another top class defensive display by giving away penalties through indiscipline.

Britain's experimental side was devoid of ideas on attack and after seven changes from the Avignon encounter, there was again little sign of teamwork.

France, who won the scrums 9-5, conceded a 17-11 penalty count and had two players sent to the sin bin. New captain Baloup was the first to go in the 47th minute for pushing the referee, while winger Bernard followed the same route in the 59th minute for trampling on the head of British skipper Noble, who needed five stitches in the resultant wound.

The Dominion Insurance Man of the Match award went to Frenchman Guy Laforgue for a rousing display in the second row, the only British contenders being Hobbs and the ever-dependable Mumby.

Britain rarely tried to open out play with Noble too often electing to make one-man dashes from the play-the-balls to little effect. In the backs, newcomers Schofield and Basnett showed signs of nerves, while substitute Mike Smith — on for the injured Hanley after 35 minutes — introduced some welcome straight running.

Hall went off after 55 minutes having been Britain's most creative player as he tried to open out play with a variety of passes, but without the desired response.

While few reputations were enhanced, the two-match Test series left question marks against the tour prospects of a handful of candidates.

Five-goal second Test hero David Hobbs.

The Great Britain line-up for the first 1984 Test with France in Avignon. Back row, left to right: Crooks, Hanley, Hobbs, Rayne, Goodway, Duane, Foy, Worrall. Front row, left to right: Hall, Lydon, Cairns, Mumby, Watkinson, Drummond, Clark.

Great Britain centre Des Foy on his touchline route to the clinching try in the first Test in Avignon.

Great Britain debutant scrum half David Cairns tackled in possession in Avignon watched over by, left to right, David Hobbs, Ronnie Duane and Lee Crooks, with Ellery Hanley grounded.

FIRST DOMINION INSURANCE TEST

29th January **Avignon**

GREAT BRITAIN 12		FRANCE 0
Keith Mumby (Bradford N.) Capt.	1	Patrick Wosniack (Villefranche)
Des Drummond (Leigh)	2.	Patrick Solal (Hull)
Ronnie Duane (Warrington)	3.	Didier Bernard (Carcassonne)
Des Foy (Oldham)	4.	Philippe Fourquet (Toulouse)
Garry Clark (Hull K.R.)	5.	Hugues Ratier (Lezignan)
Joe Lydon (Widnes)	6.	Andre Perez (Toulouse)
David Cairns (Barrow)	7.	Christian Scichitano (Carpentras)
Keith Rayne (Leeds)	8.	Max Chantal (Villeneuve) Capt.
David Watkinson (Hull K.R.)	9.	Thierry Bernabe (Le Pontet)
Andy Goodway (Oldham)	10.	Pierre Aillieres (Toulouse)
Mick Worrall (Oldham)	11.	Marc Palanques (Carcassonne)
David Hobbs (Featherstone R.)	12.	Guy Laforgue (Catalan)
David Hall (Hull K.R.)	13.	Dominique Baloup (La Reole)
Ellery Hanley (Bradford N.)	14.	Roger Palisse (St. Esteve)
Lee Crooks (Hull)	15.	Manuel Caravaca (Limoux)

T: Goodway, Foy
G: Crooks (2)
Substitutions:
Crooks for Watkinson (3 min.)
Hanley for Lydon (Half-time)
Manager: Dick Gemmell
Coach: Frank Myler

Substitution:
Caravaca for Palanques (39 min.)
Half-time: 0-0
Referee: John Gocher (Sydney)
Attendance: 4,000

SECOND DOMINION INSURANCE TEST

17th February **Leeds**

GREAT BRITAIN 10		FRANCE 0
Keith Mumby (Bradford N.)	1.	Patrick Wosniack (Villefranche)
Garry Clark (Hull K.R.)	2.	Patrick Solal (Hull)
John Joyner (Castleford)	3.	Roger Palisse (St. Esteve)
Garry Schofield (Hull)	4.	Philippe Fourquet (Toulouse)
John Basnett (Widnes)	5.	Didier Bernard (Carcassonne)
Ellery Hanley (Bradford N.)	6.	Andre Perez (Toulouse)
David Cairns (Barrow)	7.	Christian Scichitano (Carpentras)
Keith Rayne (Leeds)	8.	Max Chantal (Villeneuve)
Brian Noble (Bradford N.) Capt.	9.	Patrick Trinque (St. Esteve)
Kevin Ward (Castleford)	10.	Pierre Aillieres (Toulouse)
Dick Jasiewicz (Bradford N.)	11.	Jean-Louis Meurin (Albi)
David Hobbs (Featherstone R.)	12.	Guy Laforgue (Catalan X111)
David Hall (Hull K.R.)	13.	Dominique Baloup (La Reole) Capt.
Mike Smith (Hull K.R.)	14.	Joel Conduche (Villeneuve)
Peter Smith (Featherstone R.)	15.	Bruno Guasch (Le Pontet)

G: Hobbs (5)
Substitutions:
M. Smith for Hanley (35 min.)
P. Smith for Hall (55 min.)
Manager: Dick Gemmell
Coach: Frank Myler

Substitution:
Guasch for Scichitano (69 min.)
Half-time: 4-0
Referee: John Gocher (Sydney)
Attendance: 7,646

* Although early Tests were played under the titles of Northern Union or England, it is acceptable to regard them as Great Britain.

Great Britain v. Australia

12 Dec. 1908	Great Britain	22	Australia	22	QPR, London	2,000
23 Jan. 1909	Great Britain	15	Australia	5	Newcastle-upon-Tyne	22,000
15 Feb. 1909	Great Britain	6	Australia	5	Birmingham	9,000
18 Jun. 1910	Great Britain	27	Australia	20	Sydney	42,000
†2 Jul. 1910	Great Britain	22	Australia	17	Brisbane	18,000
8 Nov. 1911	Great Britain	10	Australia	19	Newcastle-upon-Tyne	6,500
16 Dec. 1911	Great Britain	11	Australia	11	Edinburgh	6,000
1 Jan. 1912	Great Britain	8	Australia	33	Birmingham	4,000
27 Jun. 1914	Great Britain	23	Australia	5	Sydney	40,000
29 Jun. 1914	Great Britain	7	Australia	12	Sydney	55,000
4 Jul. 1914	Great Britain	14	Australia	6	Sydney	34,420
26 Jun. 1920	Great Britain	4	Australia	8	Brisbane	28,000
3 Jul. 1920	Great Britain	8	Australia	21	Sydney	40,000
10 Jul. 1920	Great Britain	23	Australia	13	Sydney	32,000
1 Oct. 1921	Great Britain	6	Australia	5	Leeds	32,000
5 Nov. 1921	Great Britain	2	Australia	16	Hull	21,504
14 Jan. 1922	Great Britain	6	Australia	0	Salford	21,000
23 Jun. 1924	Great Britain	22	Australia	3	Sydney	50,000
28 Jun. 1924	Great Britain	5	Australia	3	Sydney	33,842
12 Jul. 1924	Great Britain	11	Australia	21	Brisbane	36,000
23 Jun. 1928	Great Britain	15	Australia	12	Brisbane	39,200
14 Jul. 1928	Great Britain	8	Australia	0	Sydney	44,548
21 Jul. 1928	Great Britain	14	Australia	21	Sydney	37,000
5 Oct. 1929	Great Britain	8	Australia	31	Hull K.R.	20,000
9 Nov. 1929	Great Britain	9	Australia	3	Leeds	31,402
4 Jan. 1930	Great Britain	0	Australia	0	Swinton	34,709
15 Jan. 1930	Great Britain	3	Australia	0	Rochdale	16,743
6 Jun. 1932	Great Britain	8	Australia	6	Sydney	70,204
18 Jun. 1932	Great Britain	6	Australia	15	Brisbane	26,500
16 Jul. 1932	Great Britain	18	Australia	13	Sydney	50,053
7 Oct. 1933	Great Britain	4	Australia	0	Belle Vue, Manchester	34,000
11 Nov. 1933	Great Britain	7	Australia	5	Leeds	29,618
16 Dec. 1933	Great Britain	19	Australia	16	Swinton	10,990
29 Jun. 1936	Great Britain	8	Australia	24	Sydney	63,920
4 Jul. 1936	Great Britain	12	Australia	7	Brisbane	29,486
18 Jul. 1936	Great Britain	12	Australia	7	Sydney	53,546
16 Oct. 1937	Great Britain	5	Australia	4	Leeds	31,949
13 Nov. 1937	Great Britain	13	Australia	3	Swinton	31,724
18 Dec. 1937	Great Britain	3	Australia	13	Huddersfield	9,093
17 Jun. 1946	Great Britain	8	Australia	8	Sydney	64,527
6 Jul. 1946	Great Britain	14	Australia	5	Brisbane	40,500

20 Jul. 1946	Great Britain	20	Australia	7	Sydney	35,294
9 Oct. 1948	Great Britain	23	Australia	21	Leeds	36,529
6 Nov. 1948	Great Britain	16	Australia	7	Swinton	36,354
29 Jan. 1949	Great Britain	23	Australia	9	Bradford	42,000
12 Jun. 1950	Great Britain	6	Australia	4	Sydney	47,215
1 Jul. 1950	Great Britain	3	Australia	15	Brisbane	35,000
22 Jul. 1950	Great Britain	2	Australia	5	Sydney	47,178
4 Oct. 1952	Great Britain	19	Australia	6	Leeds	34,505
8 Nov. 1952	Great Britain	21	Australia	5	Swinton	32,421
13 Dec. 1952	Great Britain	7	Australia	27	Bradford	30,509
12 Jun. 1954	Great Britain	12	Australia	37	Sydney	65,884
3 Jul. 1954	Great Britain	38	Australia	21	Brisbane	46,355
17 Jul. 1954	Great Britain	16	Australia	20	Sydney	67,577
17 Nov. 1956	Great Britain	21	Australia	10	Wigan	22,473
1 Dec. 1956	Great Britain	9	Australia	22	Bradford	23,634
15 Dec. 1956	Great Britain	19	Australia	0	Swinton	17,542
14 Jun. 1958	Great Britain	8	Australia	25	Sydney	68,777
5 Jul. 1958	Great Britain	25	Australia	18	Brisbane	32,965
19 Jul. 1958	Great Britain	40	Australia	17	Sydney	68,720
17 Oct. 1959	Great Britain	14	Australia	22	Swinton	35,224
21 Nov. 1959	Great Britain	11	Australia	10	Leeds	30,184
12 Dec. 1959	Great Britain	18	Australia	12	Wigan	26,089
9 Jun. 1962	Great Britain	31	Australia	12	Sydney	70,174
30 Jun. 1962	Great Britain	17	Australia	10	Brisbane	34,766
14 Jul. 1962	Great Britain	17	Australia	18	Sydney	42,104
16 Oct. 1963	Great Britain	2	Australia	28	Wembley	13,946
9 Nov. 1963	Great Britain	12	Australia	50	Swinton	30,833
30 Nov. 1963	Great Britain	16	Australia	5	Leeds	20,497
25 Jun. 1966	Great Britain	17	Australia	13	Sydney	57,962
16 Jul. 1966	Great Britain	4	Australia	6	Brisbane	45,057
23 Jul. 1966	Great Britain	14	Australia	19	Sydney	63,503
21 Oct. 1967	Great Britain	16	Australia	11	Leeds	22,293
3 Nov. 1967	Great Britain	11	Australia	17	White City, London	17,445
9 Dec. 1967	Great Britain	3	Australia	11	Swinton	13,615
6 Jun. 1970	Great Britain	15	Australia	37	Brisbane	42,807
20 Jun. 1970	Great Britain	28	Australia	7	Sydney	60,962
4 Jul. 1970	Great Britain	21	Australia	17	Sydney	61,258
3 Nov. 1973	Great Britain	21	Australia	12	Wembley	9,874
24 Nov. 1973	Great Britain	6	Australia	14	Leeds	16,674
1 Dec. 1973	Great Britain	5	Australia	15	Warrington	10,019
15 Jun. 1974	Great Britain	6	Australia	12	Brisbane	30,280
6 Jul. 1974	Great Britain	16	Australia	11	Sydney	48,006
20 Jul. 1974	Great Britain	18	Australia	22	Sydney	55,505
21 Oct. 1978	Great Britain	9	Australia	15	Wigan	17,644
5 Nov. 1978	Great Britain	18	Australia	14	Bradford	26,447

18 Nov. 1978	Great Britain	6	Australia	23	Leeds	29,627
16 Jun. 1979	Great Britain	0	Australia	35	Brisbane	23,051
30 Jun. 1979	Great Britain	16	Australia	24	Sydney	26,837
14 Jul. 1979	Great Britain	2	Australia	28	Sydney	16,844
30 Oct. 1982	Great Britain	4	Australia	40	Hull City FC	26,771
20 Nov. 1982	Great Britain	6	Australia	27	Wigan	23,216
28 Nov. 1982	Great Britain	8	Australia	32	Leeds	17,318

	Played	Won	Lost	Drawn	Tries	Goals	D/Goal	Pts for
Great Britain	93	49	40	4	233	240	3	1182
Australia	93	40	49	4	255	287	4	1343

† 1910 Tour:

Australian records do not recognise this as a Test match, while most British sources claim this second Test win clinched the series and there was no need for a third Test.

Britain played two matches against Australasian sides which included New Zealanders. These are accepted as Tests by Australia. Both were played at Sydney, the first on July 9 was drawn 13-13, the second on July 13 was won by Australasia 32-15.

GREAT BRITAIN-AUSTRALIA TEST MATCH RECORDS

Britain

Highest score:	40-17 Third Test at Sydney July 19, 1958 (Also widest margin win)
Most tries in a match:	4 by J. Leytham (Wigan) Second Test at Brisbane July 2, 1910
Most goals in a match:	10 by B. L. Jones (Leeds) Second Test at Brisbane July 3, 1954
Most points in a match:	20 by B. L. Jones (as above)
	20 (7g,2t) by R. Millward (Hull KR) Second Test at Sydney June 20, 1970.
Biggest attendance:	42,000 Third Test at Bradford Jan. 29, 1949

Australia

Highest score:	50-12 Second Test at Swinton, Nov 9, 1963 (Also widest margin win)
Most tries in a match:*	3 by J. Devereux, First Test at QPR, London, Dec 12, 1908
	3 by R. Gasnier, First Test at Swinton, Oct 17, 1959
	3 by R. Gasnier, First Test at Wembley, Oct 16, 1963
	3 by K. Irvine, Second Test at Swinton, Nov 9, 1963
	3 by K. Irvine, Third Test at Sydney, July 23, 1966
Most goals in a match:	10 by M. Cronin, First Test at Brisbane, June 16, 1979
Most points in a match:	20 by M. Cronin (as above)
	20 (7g,2t) by G. Langlands at Swinton, Nov 9, 1963
Biggest attendance:	70,204 First Test at Sydney June 6, 1932

*In a World Cup match at Perpignan, France, on October 29, 1972, R. Fulton scored three tries.

Great Britain v. New Zealand

25 Jan. 1908	Great Britain	14	New Zealand	6	Leeds	8,182
8 Feb. 1908	Great Britain	6	New Zealand	18	Stamford Brg, Chelsea	14,000
15 Feb. 1908	Great Britain	5	New Zealand	8	Cheltenham	4,000
30 Jul. 1910	Great Britain	52	New Zealand	20	Auckland	16,000
1 Aug. 1914	Great Britain	16	New Zealand	13	Auckland	15,000
31 Jul. 1920	Great Britain	31	New Zealand	7	Auckland	34,000
7 Aug. 1920	Great Britain	19	New Zealand	3	Christchurch	10,000
14 Aug. 1920	Great Britain	11	New Zealand	10	Wellington	4,000
2 Aug. 1924	Great Britain	8	New Zealand	16	Auckland	22,000
6 Aug. 1924	Great Britain	11	New Zealand	13	Wellington	6,000
9 Aug. 1924	Great Britain	31	New Zealand	18	Dunedin	14,000
2 Oct. 1926	Great Britain	28	New Zealand	20	Wigan	14,500
13 Nov. 1926	Great Britain	21	New Zealand	11	Hull	7,000
15 Jan. 1927	Great Britain	32	New Zealand	17	Leeds	6,000
4 Aug. 1928	Great Britain	13	New Zealand	17	Auckland	28,000
18 Aug. 1928	Great Britain	13	New Zealand	5	Dunedin	12,000
25 Aug. 1928	Great Britain	6	New Zealand	5	Christchurch	21,000
30 Jul. 1932	Great Britain	24	New Zealand	9	Auckland	25,000
13 Aug. 1932	Great Britain	25	New Zealand	14	Christchurch	5,000
20 Aug. 1932	Great Britain	20	New Zealand	18	Auckland	6,500
8 Aug. 1936	Great Britain	10	New Zealand	8	Auckland	25,000
15 Aug. 1936	Great Britain	23	New Zealand	11	Auckland	17,000
10 Aug. 1946	Great Britain	8	New Zealand	13	Auckland	10,000
4 Oct. 1947	Great Britain	11	New Zealand	10	Leeds	28,445
8 Nov. 1947	Great Britain	7	New Zealand	10	Swinton	29,031
20 Dec. 1947	Great Britain	25	New Zealand	9	Bradford	42,680
29 Jul. 1950	Great Britain	10	New Zealand	16	Christchurch	10,000
12 Aug. 1950	Great Britain	13	New Zealand	20	Auckland	20,000
6 Oct. 1951	Great Britain	21	New Zealand	15	Bradford	37,475
10 Nov. 1951	Great Britain	20	New Zealand	19	Swinton	29,938
15 Dec. 1951	Great Britain	16	New Zealand	12	Leeds	18,649
24 Jul. 1954	Great Britain	27	New Zealand	7	Auckland	22,097
31 Jul. 1954	Great Britain	14	New Zealand	20	Greymouth	4,240
14 Aug. 1954	Great Britain	12	New Zealand	6	Auckland	6,186
8 Oct. 1955	Great Britain	25	New Zealand	6	Swinton	21,937
12 Nov. 1955	Great Britain	27	New Zealand	12	Bradford	24,443
17 Dec. 1955	Great Britain	13	New Zealand	28	Leeds	10,438
26 Jul. 1958	Great Britain	10	New Zealand	15	Auckland	25,000
9 Aug. 1958	Great Britain	32	New Zealand	15	Auckland	25,000
30 Sept. 1961	Great Britain	11	New Zealand	29	Leeds	16,540
21 Oct. 1961	Great Britain	23	New Zealand	10	Bradford	19,980
4 Nov. 1961	Great Britain	35	New Zealand	19	Swinton	22,536
28 Jul. 1962	Great Britain	0	New Zealand	19	Auckland	14,976
11 Aug. 1962	Great Britain	8	New Zealand	27	Auckland	16,411

25 Sept. 1965	Great Britain	7	New Zealand	2	Swinton	8,541
23 Oct. 1965	Great Britain	15	New Zealand	9	Bradford	15,740
6 Nov. 1965	Great Britain	9	New Zealand	9	Wigan	7,919
6 Aug. 1966	Great Britain	25	New Zealand	8	Auckland	14,494
20 Aug. 1966	Great Britain	22	New Zealand	14	Auckland	10,657
11 Jul. 1970	Great Britain	19	New Zealand	15	Auckland	15,948
19 Jul. 1970	Great Britain	23	New Zealand	9	Christchurch	8,600
25 Jul. 1970	Great Britain	33	New Zealand	16	Auckland	13,137
25 Sept. 1971	Great Britain	13	New Zealand	18	Salford	3,764
16 Oct. 1971	Great Britain	14	New Zealand	17	Castleford	4,108
6 Nov. 1971	Great Britain	12	New Zealand	3	Leeds	5,479
27 Jul. 1974	Great Britain	8	New Zealand	13	Auckland	10,466
4 Aug. 1974	Great Britain	17	New Zealand	8	Christchurch	6,316
10 Aug. 1974	Great Britain	20	New Zealand	0	Auckland	11,574
21 Jul. 1979	Great Britain	16	New Zealand	8	Auckland	9,000
5 Aug. 1979	Great Britain	22	New Zealand	7	Christchurch	8,500
11 Aug. 1979	Great Britain	11	New Zealand	18	Auckland	7,000
18 Oct. 1980	Great Britain	14	New Zealand	14	Wigan	7,031
2 Nov. 1980	Great Britain	8	New Zealand	12	Bradford	10,946
15 Nov. 1980	Great Britain	10	New Zealand	2	Leeds	8,210

	Played	Won	Lost	Drawn	Tries	Goals	D/Goal	Pts for
Great Britain	64	42	20	2	243	187	2	1105
New Zealand	64	20	42	2	144	187	0	806

GREAT BRITAIN-NEW ZEALAND TEST MATCH RECORDS

Britain

Highest score:	*52-20 First Test at Auckland, July 30 1910 (Also widest margin win)
Most tries in a match:	4 by W. Boston (Wigan) First Test at Auckland, July 24, 1954
Most goals in a match:	*7 by N. Fox (Wakefield T.) Third Test at Swinton Nov 4, 1961
	7 by E. Fraser (Warrington) Second Test at Auckland Aug 9, 1958
Most points in a match:	*15 (6g-1t) by J. Lomas (Salford) First Test at Auckland July 30, 1910
Biggest attendance:	42,680 Third Test at Bradford, Dec 20, 1947

* In a World Cup match at Pau, France, on November 4 1972, Britain won 53-19 with J. Holmes (Leeds) scoring 26 points from 10 goals and two tries.
In a World Cup match at Sydney on June 8, 1968, Bev Risman scored 7 goals.

New Zealand

Highest score:	*29-11 First Test at Leeds, Sept 30, 1961
Widest margin win:	19-0 First Test at Auckland, July 28, 1962
	27-8 Second Test at Auckland, Aug 11, 1962

No player has scored three tries or more in a Test.

Most goals and points:	*7g-14pts by D. White Second Test at Greymouth, July 31, 1954
	J. Fagan, First Test at Headingley, Sep 30, 1961
	E. Wiggs, Second Test at Auckland, Aug 20, 1966
Biggest attendance:	34,000 First Test at Auckland, July 31, 1920

* In a World Cup match at Sydney, Australia, on June 25, 1957, New Zealand won 29-21 with W. Sorenson scoring 7 goals-14 points.

* Results since France were given Test match status.

Great Britain v. France

26 Jan. 1957	Great Britain	45	France	12	Leeds	20,221
3 Mar. 1957	Great Britain	19	France	19	Toulouse	16,000
10 Apr. 1957	Great Britain	29	France	14	St Helens	23,250
3 Nov. 1957	Great Britain	25	France	14	Toulouse	15,000
23 Nov. 1957	Great Britain	44	France	15	Wigan	19,152
2 Mar. 1958	Great Britain	23	France	9	Grenoble	20,000
14 Mar. 1959	Great Britain	50	France	15	Leeds	22,000
5 Apr. 1959	Great Britain	15	France	24	Grenoble	8,500
6 Mar. 1960	Great Britain	18	France	20	Toulouse	
26 Mar. 1960	Great Britain	17	France	17	St Helens	14,000
11 Dec. 1960	Great Britain	21	France	10	Bordeaux	8,000
28 Jan. 1961	Great Britain	27	France	8	St Helens	18,000
17 Feb. 1962	Great Britain	15	France	20	Wigan	17,277
11 Mar. 1962	Great Britain	13	France	23	Perpignan	14,000
2 Dec. 1962	Great Britain	12	France	17	Perpignan	5,000
3 Apr. 1963	Great Britain	42	France	4	Wigan	19,487
8 Mar. 1964	Great Britain	11	France	5	Perpignan	
18 Mar. 1964	Great Britain	39	France	0	Leigh	4,750
6 Dec. 1964	Great Britain	8	France	18	Perpignan	15,000
23 Jan. 1965	Great Britain	17	France	7	Swinton	9,959
16 Jan. 1966	Great Britain	13	France	18	Perpignan	6,000
5 Mar. 1966	Great Britain	4	France	8	Wigan	14,004
22 Jan. 1967	Great Britain	16	France	13	Carcassonne	
4 Mar. 1967	Great Britain	13	France	23	Wigan	7,448
11 Feb. 1968	Great Britain	22	France	13	Paris	8,000
2 Mar. 1968	Great Britain	19	France	8	Bradford	14,196
30 Nov. 1968	Great Britain	34	France	10	St Helens	6,080
2 Feb. 1969	Great Britain	9	France	13	Toulouse	10,000
7 Feb. 1971	Great Britain	8	France	16	Toulouse	14,960
17 Mar. 1971	Great Britain	24	France	2	St Helens	7,783
6 Feb. 1972	Great Britain	10	France	9	Toulouse	11,508
12 Mar. 1972	Great Britain	45	France	10	Bradford	7,313
20 Jan. 1974	Great Britain	24	France	5	Grenoble	5,500

17 Feb. 1974	Great Britain	29	France	0	Wigan	10,105
6 Dec. 1981	Great Britain	37	France	0	Hull	13,173
20 Dec. 1981	Great Britain	2	France	19	Marseilles	6,500
20 Feb. 1983	Great Britain	20	France	5	Carcassonne	3,826
6 Mar. 1983	Great Britain	17	France	5	Hull	6,055
29 Jan. 1984	Great Britain	12	France	0	Avignon	4,000
17 Feb. 1984	Great Britain	10	France	0	Leeds	7,646

	Played	Won	Lost	Drawn	Tries	Goals	D/Goal	Pts for
Great Britain	40	26	12	2	174	167	0	858
France	40	12	26	2	77	107	3	448

GREAT BRITAIN-FRANCE TEST MATCH RECORDS

Britain

Highest score:	50-15 at Leeds, March 14, 1959
Widest margin win:	39-0 at Leigh, March 18, 1964
Most tries in a match:	4 by A. Murphy (St. Helens) at Leeds, March 14, 1959
Most goals in a match:	10 by B. Ganley (Oldham) at Wigan, Nov 23, 1957
Most points in a match:	21 (9g,1t) by N. Fox (Wakefield T) at Wigan, April 3, 1963
	21 (9g,1t) by N. Fox (Wakefield T) at Leigh, March 18, 1964
Biggest attendance:	23,250 at St. Helens, April 10, 1957

France

Highest score:	24-15 at Grenoble, April 5, 1959
Widest margin win:	19-2 at Marseilles, December 20, 1981
Most tries in a match:	No player has scored 3 or more.
Most goals in a match:	7 by P. Lacaze at Wigan, March 4, 1967
Most points in a match:	14 by P. Lacaze (as above).
	14 (4g,2t) by G. Benausse at Wigan, February 17, 1962
*Biggest Attendance:	20,000 at Grenoble, March 2, 1958

*In a World Cup match at Toulouse on November 7, 1954, there were 37,471.

GREAT BRITAIN v. France

Pre-Test status

1952	May	22	Lost	12-22	Paris
1953	May	24	Lost	17-28	Lyons
1954	April	27	Won	17-8	Bradford
1955	Dec.	11	Lost	5-17	Paris
1956	April	11	Won	18-10	Bradford

Other match

1982	July	31	Lost	7-8	Venice

GREAT BRITAIN IN THE WORLD CUP

1954 Winners: Great Britain (Played in France)

					Venue	
30 Oct.	France	22	New Zealand	13	Paris	13,240
31 Oct.	Great Britain	28	Australia	13	Lyons	10,250
7 Nov.	Great Britain	13	France	13	Toulouse	37,471
7 Nov.	Australia	34	New Zealand	15	Marseilles	20,000
11 Nov.	Great Britain	26	New Zealand	6	Bordeaux	14,000
11 Nov.	Australia	5	France	15	Nantes	13,000
Play off						
13 Nov.	Great Britain	16	France	12	Paris	30,368

Final Table

	P.	*W.*	*D.*	*L.*	*For Pts.*	*Against Pts.*	*Pts.*
Great Britain	3	2	1	0	67	32	5
France	3	2	1	0	50	31	5
Australia	3	1	0	2	52	58	2
New Zealand	3	0	0	3	34	82	0

1957 Winners: Australia (Played in Australia)

					Venue	
15 June	Great Britain	23	France	5	Sydney	50,007
15 June	Australia	25	New Zealand	5	Brisbane	29,636
17 June	Great Britain	6	Australia	31	Sydney	57,955
17 June	New Zealand	10	France	14	Brisbane	
22 June	Australia	26	France	9	Sydney	35,158
25 June	Great Britain	21	New Zealand	29	Sydney	14,263

Final Table

	P.	*W.*	*D.*	*L.*	*For Pts.*	*Against Pts.*	*Pts.*
Australia	3	3	0	0	82	20	6
Great Britain	3	1	0	2	50	65	2
New Zealand	3	1	0	2	44	60	2
France	3	1	0	2	28	59	2

1960 Winners: Great Britain (Played in England)

					Venue	
24 Sept.	Great Britain	23	New Zealand	8	Bradford	20,577
24 Sept.	Australia	13	France	12	Wigan	20,278
1 Oct.	Australia	21	New Zealand	15	Leeds	10,773
1 Oct.	Great Britain	33	France	7	Swinton	22,923
8 Oct.	Australia	3	Great Britain	10	Bradford	32,773
8 Oct.	New Zealand	9	France	0	Wigan	2,876

Final Table

	P.	*W.*	*D.*	*L.*	*For Pts.*	*Against Pts.*	*Pts.*
Great Britain	3	3	0	0	66	18	6
Australia	3	2	0	1	37	37	4
New Zealand	3	1	0	2	32	44	2
France	3	0	0	3	19	55	0

1968 Winners: Australia (Played in Australia and New Zealand)

					Venue	
25 May	Australia	25	Great Britain	10	Sydney	62,256
25 May	France	15	New Zealand	10	Auckland	18,000
1 June	Australia	31	New Zealand	12	Brisbane	23,608
2 June	France	7	Great Britain	2	Auckland	15,760
8 June	Australia	37	France	4	Brisbane	32,600
8 June	Great Britain	38	New Zealand	14	Sydney	14,105

Final Table

	P.	*W.*	*D.*	*L.*	*For Pts.*	*Against Pts.*	*Pts.*
Australia	3	3	0	0	93	26	6
France	3	2	0	1	26	49	4
Great Britain	3	1	0	2	50	46	2
New Zealand	3	0	0	3	36	84	0

Play off final

10 Jun.	Australia	20	France	2	Sydney	54,290

1970 Winners: Australia (Played in England)

					Venue	
21 Oct.	Australia	47	New Zealand	11	Wigan	9,586
24 Oct.	Great Britain	11	Australia	4	Leeds	15,084
25 Oct.	New Zealand	16	France	15	Hull	3,824
28 Oct.	Great Britain	6	France	0	Castleford	8,958
31 Oct.	Great Britain	27	New Zealand	17	Swinton	5,609
1 Nov.	France	17	Australia	15	Bradford	6,215

Final Table

	P.	*W.*	*D.*	*L.*	*For Pts.*	*Against Pts.*	*Pts.*
Great Britain	3	3	0	0	44	21	6
Australia	3	1	0	2	66	39	2
France	3	1	0	2	32	37	2
New Zealand	3	1	0	2	44	89	2

Play off Final

7 Nov.	Australia	12	Great Britain	7	Leeds	18,776

1972 Winners: Great Britain (Played in France)

					Venue	
28 Oct.	France	20	New Zealand	9	Marseilles	20,748
29 Oct.	Great Britain	27	Australia	21	Perpignan	6,324
1 Nov.	Australia	9	New Zealand	5	Paris	8,000
1 Nov.	Great Britain	13	France	4	Grenoble	5,321
4 Nov.	Great Britain	53	New Zealand	19	Pau	7,500
5 Nov.	Australia	31	France	9	Toulouse	10,332

Final Table

	P.	*W.*	*D.*	*L.*	*For Pts.*	*Against Pts.*	*Pts.*
Great Britain	3	3	0	0	93	44	6
Australia	3	2	0	1	61	41	4
France	3	1	0	2	33	53	2
New Zealand	3	0	0	3	33	82	0

Play off Final

11 Nov.	Great Britain	10	Australia	10	Lyon	4,231

No further score after extra-time so Great Britain took championship because they had scored the greater number of points in the qualifying League table.

1977 Winners: Australia (Played in Australia and New Zealand)

					Venue	
29 May	Australia	27	New Zealand	12	Auckland	
5 June	Great Britain	23	France	4	Auckland	10,000
11 June	Australia	21	France	9	Sydney	
12 June	Great Britain	30	New Zealand	12	Christchurch	7,000
18 June	Australia	19	Great Britain	5	Brisbane	27,000
19 June	New Zealand	28	France	20	Auckland	

Final Table

	P.	*W.*	*D.*	*L.*	*For Pts.*	*Against Pts.*	*Pts.*
Australia	3	3	0	0	67	26	6
Great Britain	3	2	0	1	58	35	4
New Zealand	3	1	0	2	52	77	2
France	3	0	0	3	33	72	0

Play off Final

25 June	Australia	13	Great Britain	12	Sydney	24,400

* For details of the 1975 World Championship see ENGLAND AND WALES section.

Great Britain 1972 World Cup squad members, left to right: Mick Stephenson, Steve Nash, Brian Lockwood, Bob Irving and David Redfearn.

Great Britain trio, from left to right, Dave Valentine, Jim Featherstone and Dai Bevan cover Australia's Tom Ryan in the 1952 third Test at Bradford.

GREAT BRITAIN REPRESENTATION CLUB BY CLUB

Only six current clubs have not had a player selected for Great Britain in Test or World Cup matches — Blackpool Borough, Bramley and Doncaster, plus newcomers Cardiff City, Carlisle and Kent Invicta. Of the extinct clubs only Broughton Rangers (later Belle Vue Rangers), Merthyr Tydfil, St. Helens Recs and Runcorn had players selected for Britain.

Wigan hold the record for most players selected with a remarkable number of 61. Of those players, seven once lined up in a Test together — another record. They were backs Martin Ryan, Gordon Ratcliffe, Ernie Ashcroft, Jack Hilton and Tommy Bradshaw; plus forwards Ken Gee and Joe Egan. Hilton scored both Britain's tries in the 6-4 victory over Australia at Sydney on 12 June, 1950.

Mick Sullivan gained Test honours with four clubs — Huddersfield (16), Wigan (19), St. Helens (10) and York (1). Billy Boston gained the most Test honours with a single club, making all 31 of his appearances for Britain while with Wigan.

The following is a club by club register of Great Britain players. The figure in brackets after a player's name is the number of Great Britain appearances he made while serving the club under whose entry he is listed, and the number after the + sign indicates playing substitute. This is followed by the time span between his first and last British cap while at that club.

BARROW (19 players)
W. Burgess (16) 1924-29
W. Burgess (13) 1962-68
D. Cairns (2) 1984
C. Camilleri (2) 1980
C. Carr (7) 1924-26
F. Castle (4) 1952-54
R. Francis (1) 1947
H. Gifford (2) 1908
D. Goodwin (5) 1957-58
J. Grundy (12) 1955-57
P. Hogan (4+1) 1977-78
W. Horne (8) 1946-52
P. Jackson (27) 1954-58
J. Jones (1) 1946
B. Knowelden (1) 1946
E. Szymala (1+1) 1981
E. Toohey (3) 1952
L. A. Troup (2) 1936
J. Woods (1) 1933

BATLEY (3 players)
N. Field (1) 1963
F. Gallagher (8) 1924-26
J. Oliver (4) 1928

BRADFORD NORTHERN (26 players)
D. Barends (2) 1979
E. Batten (4) 1946-47
I. Brooke (5) 1966
L. Casey (5) 1979
W. T. H. Davies (3) 1946-47
A. Fisher (8) 1970-78
T. Foster (3) 1946-48
J. Grayshon (11) 1979-82
E. Hanley (1+1) 1984
R. Jasiewicz (1) 1984
J. Kitching (1) 1946
A. Mann (2) 1908
K. Mumby (4) 1982-84
B. Noble (4) 1982-84
T. Price (1) 1970
J. Rae (1) 1965
W. Ramsey (+1) 1974
A. Rathbone (2+1) 1982-83
A. Redfearn (1) 1979
D. Redfearn (6+1) 1972-74
T. Smales (3) 1965
H. Smith (2) 1926
J. Thompson (1) 1978
K. Traill (8) 1950-54
E. Ward (20) 1946-52
F. Whitcombe (2) 1946

BROUGHTON/BELLE VUE RANGERS (8 players)
W. Bentham (2) 1924
L. Clampitt (3) 1907-14
E. Gwyther (6) 1947-51
A. Hogg (1) 1907
S. McCormick (2) 1948
D. Phillips (1) 1950
J. Price (2) 1921
J. Ruddick (3) 1907-10

CASTLEFORD (19 players)
A. Atkinson (11) 1929-36
W. Bryant (4+1) 1964-67
A. Croston (1) 1937
B. Cunniffe (1) 1937
W. J. Davies (1) 1933
D. Edwards (3+2) 1968-71
A. Hardisty (12) 1964-70
D. Hartley (9) 1968-70
K. Hepworth (11) 1967-70
J. Joyner (14) 1978-84
B. Lockwood (7) 1972-74
R. Millward (1) 1966
S. Norton (2+1) 1974
M. Reilly (9) 1970
P. Small (1) 1962
G. Stephens (5) 1979
D. Walton (1) 1965
J. Ward (3) 1963-64
K. Ward (1) 1984

DEWSBURY (6 players)
A. Bates (2+2) 1974
F. Gallagher (4) 1920-21
J. Ledgard (2) 1947
R. Pollard (1) 1950
M. Stephenson (5+1) 1971-72
H. Street (4) 1950

FEATHERSTONE ROVERS (12 players)
T. Askin (6) 1928
K. Bridges (3) 1974
T. Clawson (2) 1962
M. Dixon (2) 1962-64
S. Evans (5+3) 1979-80
D. Fox (1) 1963
D. Hobbs (2) 1984
G. Jordan (2) 1964-67
A. Morgan (4) 1968
S. Nash (16) 1971-74
P. Smith (1+5) 1977-84
J. Thompson (19+1) 1970-77

FULHAM (1 player)
J. Dalgreen (1) 1982

HALIFAX (27 players)
A. Ackerley (2) 1952-58
A. Bassett (2) 1946
J. Beames (2) 1921
N. Bentham (2) 1929
H. Beverley (2) 1937
O. Burgham (1) 1911
A. Daniels (3) 1952-55
W. T. Davies (1) 1911
C. Dixon (1) 1968
P. Eccles (1) 1907
T. Fogerty (1+1) 1966
A. Halmshaw (1) 1971
R. Lloyd (1) 1920
A. Milnes (2) 1920
S. Prosser (1) 1914
D. Rees (1) 1926
C. Renilson (7+1) 1965-68
J. Riley (1) 1910
K. Roberts (10) 1963-66
A. Robinson (3) 1907-08
D. Schofield (1) 1955
J. Shaw (5) 1960-62
J. C. Stacey (1) 1920
J. Thorley (4) 1954
J. Wilkinson (6) 1954-55
F. Williams (2) 1914
D. Willicombe (1) 1974

HUDDERSFIELD (24 players)
J. Bowden (3) 1954
K. Bowman (3) 1962-63
B. Briggs (1) 1954
S. Brogden (9) 1929-33
J. Chilcott (3) 1914
D. Clark (11) 1911-20
D. Close (1) 1967
R. Cracknell (2) 1951
J. Davies (2) 1911
F. Dyson (1) 1959
B. Gronow (7) 1911-20
F. Longstaff (2) 1914
K. Loxton (1) 1971
S. Moorhouse (2) 1914
R. Nicholson (3) 1946-48
J. Rogers (7) 1914-21
K. Senior (2) 1965-67
T. Smales (5) 1962-64
M. Sullivan (16) 1954-57
G. Thomas (8) 1920-21
D. Valentine (15) 1948-54
R. Valentine (1) 1967
H. Wagstaff (12) 1911-21
H. Young (1) 1929

HULL (27 players)
W. Batten (1) 1921
H. Bowman (8) 1924-29
F. Boylen (1) 1908
R. Coverdale (4) 1954
M. Crane (1) 1982
L. Crooks (2+1) 1982-84
J. Drake (1) 1960
W. Drake (1) 1962
S. Evans (2) 1982
V. Farrar (1) 1978
R. Gemmell (2) 1968-69
T. E. Gwynne (3) 1928-29
T. Harris (25) 1954-60
M. Harrison (7) 1967-73
W. Holder (1) 1907
A. Keegan (9) 1966-69
E. Morgan (2) 1921
S. Norton (9) 1978-82
P. Rose (1) 1982
G. Schofield (1) 1984
T. Skerrett (6) 1980-82
W. Stone (8) 1920-21
C. Sullivan (17) 1967-73
H. Taylor (3) 1907
R. Taylor (2) 1921-26
D. Topliss (1) 1982
J. Whiteley (15) 1957-62

Terry Hollindrake, Keighley's only Great Britain international.

HULL KINGSTON ROVERS (23 players)
C. Burton (1) 1982
A. Burwell (7+1) 1967-69
L. Casey (7+2) 1977-83
G. Clark (2) 1984
A. Dockar (1) 1947
G. Fairbairn (3) 1981-82
J. Feetham (1) 1929
P. Flanagan (14) 1962-70
F. Foster (1) 1967
D. Hall (2) 1984
S. Hartley (3) 1980-81
P. Hogan (2+2) 1979
R. Holdstock (2) 1980
W. Holliday (8+1) 1964-67
B. Lockwood (1+1) 1978-79
P. Lowe (12) 1970-78
R. Millward (27+1) 1967-78
H. Poole (1) 1964
P. Rose (1+3) 1974-78
M. Smith (9+1) 1979-84
B. Tyson (3) 1963-67
D. Watkinson (3+1) 1979-84
C. Young (5) 1967-68

HUNSLET (23 players)
W. Batten (9) 1907-11
H. Beverley (4) 1936-37
A. Burnell (3) 1951-54
H. Crowther (1) 1929
J. Evans (4) 1951-52
K. Eyre (1) 1965
B. Gabbitas (1) 1959
G. Gunney (11) 1954-65
D. Hartley (2) 1964
J. Higson (2) 1908
D. Jenkins (1) 1929
A. Jenkinson (2) 1911
W. Jukes (6) 1908-10
B. Prior (1) 1966
W. Ramsey (7) 1965-66
B. Shaw (5) 1956-60
G. Shelton (7) 1964-66
F. Smith (9) 1910-14
S. Smith (4) 1954
C. Thompson (2) 1951
L. White (7) 1932-33
R. Williams (3) 1954
H. Wilson (3) 1907

HUYTON/LIVERPOOL/WIGAN HIGHFIELD (4 players)
R. Ashby (1) 1964
W. Belshaw (6) 1936-37
N. Bentham (6) 1928
H. Woods (5) 1936

KEIGHLEY (1 player)
T. Hollindrake (1) 1955

LEEDS (55 players)
L. Adams (1) 1932
J. Atkinson (26) 1968-80
J. Bacon (11) 1920-26
R. Batten (3) 1969-73
J. Birch (1) 1907
S. Brogden (7) 1936-37
J. Brough (5) 1928-36
G. Brown (6) 1954-55
M. Clark (5) 1968
T. Clawson (3) 1972
W. A. Davies (2) 1914
K. Dick (2) 1980
L. Dyl (11) 1974-82
A. Fisher (3) 1970-71
R. Gemmell (1) 1964
R. Haigh (3+1) 1970-71
D. Hallas (2) 1961
F. Harrison (3) 1911
D. Heron (1+1) 1982
J. Holmes (14+6) 1971-82
S. Hynes (12+1) 1970-73
J. W. Jarman (2) 1914
D. Jeanes (3) 1972
D. Jenkins (1) 1947
B. L. Jones (15) 1954-57
K. Jubb (2) 1937
J. Lowe (1) 1932
I. Owens (4) 1946
S. Pitchford (4) 1977
H. Poole (2) 1966
D. Prosser (1) 1937
Keith Rayne (2) 1984
B. Risman (5) 1968
D. Robinson (5) 1956-60
D. Rose (4) 1954
B. Seabourne (1) 1970
B. Shaw (1) 1961
M. Shoebottom (10+2) 1968-71
B. Simms (1) 1962
A. Smith (10) 1970-73
S. Smith (10) 1929-33
J. Stevenson (15) 1955-58
S. Stockwell (3) 1920-21
A. Terry (1) 1962
A. Thomas (4) 1926-29
P. Thomas (1) 1907
J. Thompson (12) 1924-32
A. Turnbull (1) 1951
D. Ward (12) 1977-82
W. Ward (1) 1910
F. Webster (3) 1910
R. Williams (9) 1948-51
H. Woods (1) 1937
G. Wriglesworth (5) 1965-66
F. Young (1) 1908

LEIGH (17 players)
K. Ashcroft (5) 1968-70
J. Cartwright (7) 1920-21
D. Chisnall (2) 1970
J. Darwell (5) 1924
D. Drummond (10) 1980-84
P. Foster (3) 1955
F. Kitchen (2) 1954
J. Ledgard (9) 1948-54
G. Lewis (1) 1965
M. Martyn (2) 1958-59
W. Mooney (2) 1924
S. Owen (1) 1958
C. Pawsey (7) 1952-54
W. Robinson (2) 1963
Joe Walsh (1) 1971
W. Winstanley (2) 1910
J. Woods (7+3) 1979-83

MERTHYR TYDFIL (1 player)
D. Jones (2) 1907

OLDHAM (38 players)
A. Avery (4) 1910-11
C. Bott (1) 1966
A. Brough (2) 1924
T. Clawson (9) 1973-74
A. Davies (20) 1955-60
E. Davies (3) 1920
T. Flanagan (2) 1983
D. Foy (1) 1984
B. Ganley (3) 1957-58
A. Goodway (3) 1983-84
W. Hall (4) 1914
H. Hilton (7) 1920-21
D. Holland (4) 1914
R. Irving (8+3) 1967-72
K. Jackson (2) 1957
E. Knapman (1) 1924
S. Little (10) 1956-58
T. Llewellyn (2) 1907
J. Lomas (2) 1911
W. Longworth (3) 1908
L. McIntyre (1) 1963
T. O'Grady (5) 1954
J. Oster (1) 1929
D. Parker (2) 1964
D. Phillips (3) 1946
F. Pitchford (2) 1958-62
T. Rees (1) 1929
S. Rix (9) 1924-26
R. Sloman (5) 1928
A. Smith (6) 1907-08
I. Southward (7) 1959-62
L. Thomas (1) 1947
D. Turner (11) 1956-58
G. Tyson (4) 1907-08
T. White (1) 1907
C. Winsdale (1) 1959
A. Wood (4) 1911-14
M. Worrall (1) 1984

ROCHDALE HORNETS (8 players)
J. Baxter (1) 1907
J. Bennett (6) 1924
J. Bowers (1) 1920
T. Fogerty (1) 1974
E. Jones (4) 1920
M. Price (2) 1967
J. Robinson (2) 1914
T. Woods (2) 1911

RUNCORN (2 players)
J. Jolley (3) 1907
R. Padbury (1) 1908

ST. HELENS (38 players)
L. Aston (3) 1947
W. Benyon (5+1) 1971-72
T. Bishop (15) 1966-69
F. Carlton (1) 1958
E. Chisnall (4) 1974
E. Cunningham (1) 1978
R. Dagnall (4) 1961-65
D. Eckersley (2+2) 1973-74
A. Ellaby (13) 1928-33
L. Fairclough (6) 1926-29
A. Fildes (4) 1932
A. Frodsham (3) 1928-29
P. Gorley (2+1) 1980-81
D. Greenall (6) 1951-54
M. Hicks (1) 1965
R. Huddart (12) 1959-63
L. Jones (1) 1971
A. Karalius (4+1) 1971-72
V. Karalius (10) 1958-61
K. Kelly (2) 1972
J. Mantle (13) 1966-73
S. McCormick (1) 1948
T. McKinney (1) 1957
R. Mathias (1) 1979
G. Moses (9) 1955-57
A. Murphy (26) 1958-66
F. Myler (9) 1970
G. Nicholls (22) 1973-79
H. Pinner (1+1) 1980
A. Prescott (28) 1951-58
A. Rhodes (4) 1957-61
J. Stott (1) 1947
M. Sullivan (10) 1961-62
J. Tembey (2) 1963-64
A. Terry (10) 1958-61
John Walsh (4+1) 1972
J. Warlow (3+1) 1964-68
C. Watson (29+1) 1963-71

ST. HELENS RECS (5 players)
F. Bowen (3) 1928
A. Fildes (11) 1926-29
J. Greenall (1) 1921
J. Owen (1) 1921
J. Wallace (1) 1926

Alan Davies (Oldham).

SALFORD (27 players)
W. Burgess (1) 1969
P. Charlton (17+1) 1970-74
M. Coulman (2+1) 1971
G. Curran (6) 1946-48
E. Curzon (1) 1910
T. Danby (3) 1950
C. Dixon (11+2) 1969-74
A. Edwards (7) 1936-37
J. Feetham (7) 1932-33
K. Fielding (3) 1974-77
K. Gill (5+2) 1974-77
J. Gore (1) 1926
C. Hesketh (21+2) 1970-74
B. Hudson (8) 1932-37
E. Jenkins (9) 1933-37
J. Lomas (5) 1908-10
T. McKinney (7) 1951-54
A. Middleton (1) 1929
S. Nash (8) 1977-82
M. Richards (2) 1974
A. Risman (17) 1932-46
J. Spencer (1) 1907
J. Ward (1) 1970
S. Warwick (2) 1907
D. Watkins (2+4) 1971-74
W. Watkins (7) 1933-37
W. Williams (2) 1929-32

SWINTON (15 players)
T. Armitt (8) 1933-37
A. Buckley (7) 1963-66
F. Butters (2) 1929
W. Davies (1) 1968
B. Evans (10) 1926-33
F. Evans (4) 1924
J. Evans (3) 1926
K. Gowers (14) 1962-66
H. Halsall (1) 1929
M. Hodgson (16) 1929-37
R. Morgan (2) 1963
W. Rees (11) 1926-29
D. Robinson (12) 1965-67
J. Stopford (12) 1961-66
J. Wright (1) 1932

WAKEFIELD TRINITY (22 players)
I. Brooke (8) 1967-68
N. Fox (29) 1959-69
R. Haigh (2) 1968-70
W. Horton (14) 1928-33
D. Jeanes (5) 1971-72
B. Jones (3) 1964-66
H. Kershaw (2) 1910
F. Mortimer (2) 1956
H. Murphy (1) 1950
H. Newbould (1) 1910
J. Parkin (17) 1920-29
C. Pollard (1) 1924
E. Pollard (2) 1932
H. Poynton (3) 1962
D. Robinson (5) 1954-55
G. Round (8) 1959-62
T. Skerrett (4) 1979
S. Smith (1) 1929
D. Topliss (3) 1973-79
D. Turner (13) 1959-62
D. Vines (3) 1959
J. Wilkinson (7) 1959-62

WARRINGTON (38 players)
J. Arkwright (6) 1936-37
K. Ashcroft (+1) 1974
W. Aspinall (1) 1966
W. Belshaw (2) 1937
N. Bentham (2) 1929
J. Bevan (6) 1974-78
T. Blinkhorn (1) 1929
E. Brooks (3) 1908
J. Challinor (3) 1958-60
N. Courtney (+1) 1982
W. Cunliffe (11) 1920-26
G. Dickenson (1) 1908
W. Dingsdale (3) 1929-33
R. Duane (3) 1983-84
R. Eccles (1) 1982
J. Featherstone (6) 1948-52
E. Fraser (16) 1958-61
L. Gilfedder (5) 1962-63
R. Greenough (1) 1960
G. Helme (12) 1948-54
K. Holden (1) 1963
A. Johnson (6) 1946-47
K. Kelly (2) 1980-82
T. McKinney (3) 1955
J. Miller (6) 1933-36
A. Murphy (1) 1971
A. Naughton (2) 1954
T. O'Grady (1) 1961
H. Palin (2) 1947
K. Parr (1) 1968
A. Pimblett (3) 1948
R. Price (9) 1954-57
R. Ryan (5) 1950-52
R. Ryder (1) 1952
F. Shugars (1) 1910
G. Skelhorne (7) 1920-21
G. Thomas (1) 1907
D. Whitehead (3) 1971

WIGAN (61 players)
R. Ashby (1) 1965
E. Ashcroft (11) 1947-54
E. Ashton (26) 1957-63
W. Ashurst (3) 1971-72
F. Barton (1) 1951
J. Barton (2) 1960-61
J. Bennett (1) 1926
D. Bevan (1) 1952
W. Blan (3) 1951
D. Bolton (23) 1957-63
W. Boston (31) 1954-63
T. Bradshaw (6) 1947-50
F. Carlton (1) 1962
W. Cherrington (1) 1960
C. Clarke (7) 1965-73
A. Coldrick (4) 1914
F. Collier (1) 1963
J. Cunliffe (4) 1950-54
J. Egan (14) 1946-50
R. Evans (4) 1961-62
G. Fairbairn (14) 1977-80
T. Fogerty (1) 1967
W. Francis (4) 1967-77
D. Gardiner (1) 1965
K. Gee (17) 1946-51
H. Gill (3) 1981-82
J. Gray (5+3) 1974
C. Hill (1) 1966
D. Hill (1) 1971
J. Hilton (4) 1950
T. Howley (6) 1924
W. Hudson (1) 1948
D. Hurcombe (8) 1920-24
B. Jenkins (12) 1907-14
K. Jones (2) 1970
R. Kinnear (1) 1929
D. Laughton (11) 1970-71
J. Lawrenson (3) 1948
J. Leytham (5) 1907-10
B. McTigue (25) 1958-63
J. Miller (1) 1911
J. Morley (2) 1936-37
J. Price (4) 1924
R. Ramsdale (8) 1910-14
G. Ratcliffe (3) 1947-50
J. Ring (2) 1924-26
D. Robinson (1) 1970
M. Ryan (4) 1947-50
W. Sayer (7) 1961-63
J. Sharrock (4) 1910-11
N. Silcock (3) 1954
R. Silcock (1) 1908
D. Stephenson (2) 1982
J. Sullivan (25) 1924-33
M. Sullivan (19) 1957-60
G. Thomas (1) 1914
J. Thomas (8) 1907-11
Ed. Ward (3) 1946-47
L. White (2) 1947
D. Willicombe (2) 1974
W. Winstanley (3) 1911

WHITEHAVEN (4 players)
W. Holliday (1) 1964
R. Huddart (4) 1958
P. Kitchin (1) 1965
A. Walker (1) 1980

WIDNES (31 players)
M. Adams (5+1) 1979-80
J. Basnett (1) 1984
K. Bentley (1) 1980
M. Burke (3+1) 1980-83
F. Collier (1) 1964
R. Dutton (6) 1970
K. Elwell (3) 1977-80
R. French (4) 1968
L. Gorley (4+1) 1980-82
A. Gregory (5) 1981-83
I. Hare (1) 1967
F. Higgins (6) 1950-51
H. Higgins (2) 1937
E. Hughes (8) 1978-82
A. Johnson (4) 1914-20
G. Kemel (2) 1965
V. Karalius (2) 1963
D. Laughton (4) 1973-79
J. Lydon (3) 1983-84
T. McCue (6) 1936-46
J. Measures (2) 1963
J. Mills (6) 1974-79
A. Myler (2) 1983
F. Myler (14+1) 1960-67
G. Nicholls (7) 1971-72
D. O'Neill (2+1) 1971-72
M. O'Neill (3) 1982-83
G. Shaw (1) 1980
N. Silcock (12) 1932-37
J. Warlow (3) 1971
S. Wright (7) 1977-78

WORKINGTON TOWN (9 players)
E. Bowman (4) 1977
P. Charlton (1) 1965
B. Edgar (11) 1958-66
N. Herbert (6) 1961-62
W. Martin (1) 1962
V. McKeating (2) 1951
A. Pepperell (2) 1950-51
I. Southward (4) 1958
G. Wilson (3) 1951

YORK (7 players)
E. Dawson (1) 1956
H. Field (3) 1936
G. Smith (3) 1963-64
J. Stevenson (4) 1959-60
M. Sullivan (1) 1963
B. Watts (5) 1954-55
L. White (4) 1946

GREAT BRITAIN TEAMS 1908-1984

The following is a compendium of Great Britain Test and World Cup teams.

Early records do not always make clear the positions in which players appeared. This was particularly true of pack formations and half back pairings.

In cases of doubt a player is listed in what appeared to be his most regular position.

Initials are included where more than one celebrated player shared a surname in the same era. Teams against France are included from 1957, the year in which the European encounters gained Test status.

Only playing substitutes are included on the teamsheet.

Key: (WC): World Cup t: try g: goal

1908 New Zealand

Leeds: 25 Jan

Won 14-6

Taylor, H (Hull)
Hogg (Broughton)
Llewellyn (Oldham) 1t
Jenkins, B (Wigan)
Leytham (Wigan) 1t
Jolley (Runcorn) 1g
Thomas, J (Wigan)
Ruddick (Broughton)
Jones, D (Merthyr)
Smith, A (Oldham)
Robinson, A (Halifax) 2t
Wilson, H (Hunslet)
Warwick (Salford)

1908 New Zealand

Chelsea: 8 Feb

Lost 6-18

Taylor, H (Hull)
Eccles (Halifax) 1t
Llewellyn (Oldham)
Jenkins, B (Wigan)
Leytham (Wigan) 1t
Jolley (Runcorn)
Baxter (Rochdale)
Ruddick (Broughton)
Jones, D (Merthyr)
Smith, A (Oldham)
Thomas, G (Warrington)
Wilson, H (Hunslet)
Warwick (Salford)

1908 New Zealand

Cheltenham: 15 Feb

Lost 5-8

Taylor, H (Hull)
Tyson, G (Oldham)
Thomas, P (Leeds)
Jenkins, B (Wigan)
Batten, W (Hunslet)
Jolley (Runcorn) 1t
White, T (Oldham) 1g
Spencer (Salford)
Holder (Hull)
Birch (Leeds)
Clampitt (Broughton)
Wilson, H (Hunslet)
Smith, A (Oldham)

1908 Australia

QPR, London: 12 Dec

Drew 22-22

Gifford (Barrow)
Tyson, G (Oldham) 1t
Dickenson (Warrington)
Jenkins, B (Wigan)
Batten, W (Hunslet) 2t
Brooks (Warrington) 1t, 2g
Thomas, J (Wigan) 1t
Jukes (Hunslet)
Higson (Hunslet)
Mann (Bradford)
Longworth (Oldham)
Smith, A (Oldham)
Robinson, A (Halifax) 1t

1909 Australia

Newcastle: 23 Jan

Won 15-5

Gifford (Barrow)
Tyson, G (Oldham) 1t
Lomas (Salford) 1t,3g
Jenkins, B (Wigan)
Batten, W (Hunslet)
Brooks (Warrington)
Thomas, J (Wigan) 1t
Jukes (Hunslet)
Higson (Hunslet)
Silcock, R (Wigan)
Longworth (Oldham)
Smith, A (Oldham)
Robinson, A (Halifax)

1909 Australia

Birmingham: 15 Feb

Won 6-5

Young, F (Leeds)
Tyson, G (Oldham) 1t
Lomas (Salford)
Jenkins, B (Wigan)
Batten, W (Hunslet)
Brooks (Warrington)
Thomas, J (Wigan) 1t
Jukes (Hunslet)
Padbury (Runcorn)
Mann (Bradford)
Longworth (Oldham)
Smith, A (Oldham)
Boylen (Hull)

1910 Australia

Sydney: 18 June

Won 27-20

Sharrock (Wigan)
Leytham (Wigan) 2t,1g
Lomas (Salford) 1g
Jenkins, B (Wigan)
Batten, W (Hunslet) 1t
Thomas, J (Wigan) 1t,1g
Newbould (Wakefield)
Webster (Leeds)
Ward, W (Leeds)
Curzon (Salford)
Jukes (Hunslet) 3t
Ramsdale (Wigan)
Avery (Oldham)

1910 Australia

Brisbane: 2 July

Won 22-17

Sharrock (Wigan)
Leytham (Wigan) 4t
Lomas (Salford) 2g
Riley (Halifax)
Batten, W (Hunslet)
Thomas, J (Wigan) 1t
Smith, F (Hunslet)
Webster (Leeds)
Winstanley (Leigh)
Kershaw (Wakefield) 1t
Jukes (Hunslet)
Ramsdale (Wigan)
Ruddick (Broughton)

1910 New Zealand

Auckland: 30 July

Won 52-20

Sharrock (Wigan) 1g
Leytham (Wigan) 2t
Lomas (Salford) 1t,6g
Jenkins, B (Wigan) 2t
Batten, W (Hunslet)
Thomas, J (Wigan) 1t,1g
Smith, F (Hunslet) 1t
Webster (Leeds)
Winstanley (Leigh)
Kershaw (Wakefield) 2t
Jukes (Hunslet)
Shugars (Warrington)
Avery (Oldham) 3t

1911 Australia

Newcastle-upon-Tyne: 8 Nov

Lost 10-19

Sharrock (Wigan)
Miller, J (Wigan)
Wagstaff (Huddersfield)
Jenkins, B (Wigan)
Davies, W.T (Halifax) 2t
Smith, F (Hunslet)
Thomas, J (Wigan) 2g
Burgham (Halifax)
Winstanley (Wigan)
Gronow (Huddersfield)
Clampitt (Broughton)
Harrison, F (Leeds)
Avery (Oldham)

1911 Australia

Edinburgh: 16 Dec

Drew 11-11

Wood (Oldham) 1g
Jenkinson (Hunslet)
Wagstaff (Huddersfield) 2t
Lomas (Oldham) 1t
Batten, W (Hunslet)
Smith, F (Hunslet)
Davies, J (Huddersfield)
Ramsdale (Wigan)
Winstanley (Wigan)
Gronow (Huddersfield)
Clark, D (Huddersfield)
Woods, T (Rochdale)
Harrison, F (Leeds)

1912 Australia

Birmingham: 1 Jan

Lost 8-33

Wood (Oldham) 1g
Jenkinson (Hunslet)
Jenkins, B (Wigan)
Lomas (Oldham) 1t
Batten, W (Hunslet)
Smith, F (Hunslet)
Davies, J (Huddersfield)
Ramsdale (Wigan)
Winstanley (Wigan)
Avery (Oldham)
Clark, D (Huddersfield) 1t
Woods, T (Rochdale)
Harrison, F (Leeds)

1914 Australia

Sydney: 27 June

Won 23-5

Jarman (Leeds)
Robinson, J (Rochdale) 1t,2g
Jenkins, B (Wigan)
Wagstaff (Huddersfield)
Moorhouse (Huddersfield) 2t
Hall (Oldham)
Smith, F (Hunslet)
Ramsdale (Wigan)
Longstaff (Huddersfield) 2g
Chilcott (Huddersfield)
Clark, D (Huddersfield) 1t
Coldrick (Wigan)
Holland (Oldham) 1t

1914 Australia

Sydney: 29 June

Lost 7-12

Thomas, G (Wigan)
Robinson, J (Rochdale)
Hall (Oldham)
Wagstaff (Huddersfield)
Williams, F (Halifax)
Rogers (Huddersfield) 2g
Smith, F (Hunslet)
Ramsdale (Wigan)
Jarman (Leeds)
Chilcott (Huddersfield)
Clark, D (Huddersfield)
Coldrick (Wigan) 1t
Holland (Oldham)

1914 Australia

Sydney: 4 July

Won 14-6

Wood (Oldham) 4g
Davies, W.A (Leeds) 1t
Hall (Oldham)
Wagstaff (Huddersfield)
Williams, F (Halifax)
Prosser, S (Halifax)
Smith, F (Hunslet)
Ramsdale (Wigan)
Johnson, A (Widnes) 1t
Chilcott (Huddersfield)
Clark, D (Huddersfield)
Coldrick (Wigan)
Holland (Oldham)

1914 New Zealand
Auckland: 1 Aug
Won 16-13
Wood (Oldham) 2g
Davies, W.A (Leeds) 1t
Jenkins, B (Wigan)
Wagstaff (Huddersfield)
Moorhouse (Huddersfield) 2t
Hall (Oldham)
Smith, F (Hunslet)
Ramsdale (Wigan)
Johnson, A (Widnes) 1t
Clampitt (Broughton)
Longstaff (Huddersfield)
Coldrick (Wigan)
Holland (Oldham)

1920 Australia
Brisbane: 26 June
Lost 4-8
Thomas, G (Huddersfield)
Stone (Hull)
Hurcombe (Wigan)
Wagstaff (Huddersfield)
Bacon (Leeds)
Parkin (Wakefield)
Rogers (Huddersfield)
Gronow (Huddersfield) 2g
Johnson, A (Widnes)
Clark, D (Huddersfield)
Hilton, H (Oldham)
Milnes (Halifax)
Gallagher (Dewsbury)

1920 Australia
Sydney: 3 July
Lost 8-21
Thomas, G (Huddersfield)
Stone (Hull)
Hurcombe (Wigan)
Wagstaff (Huddersfield)
Bacon (Leeds)
Lloyd (Halifax)
Rogers (Huddersfield)
Gronow (Huddersfield) 1g
Johnson, A (Widnes) 1t
Clark, D (Huddersfield)
Hilton, H (Oldham)
Milnes (Halifax)
Gallagher (Dewsbury) 1t

1920 Australia
Sydney: 10 July
Won 23-13
Thomas, G (Huddersfield)
Rogers (Huddersfield) 3g
Stone (Hull) 2t
Bacon (Leeds) 1t
Stockwell (Leeds) 1g
Jones, E (Rochdale)
Parkin (Wakefield)
Cunliffe, W (Warrington)
Cartwright (Leigh)
Skelhorne (Warrington)
Hilton, H (Oldham) 2t
Clark, D (Huddersfield)
Gallagher (Dewsbury)

1920 New Zealand
Auckland: 31 July
Won 31-7
Thomas, G (Huddersfield)
Stone (Hull) 3t
Hurcombe (Wigan)
Davies, E (Oldham)
Bacon (Leeds) 1t
Jones, E (Rochdale)
Parkin (Wakefield) 3t
Cunliffe, W (Warrington)
Cartwright (Leigh)
Skelhorne (Warrington)
Hilton, H (Oldham)
Gronow (Huddersfield) 5g
Clark, D (Huddersfield)

1920 New Zealand
Christchurch: 7 Aug
Won 19-3
Stacey (Halifax)
Stone (Hull) 2t
Wagstaff (Huddersfield)
Davies, E (Oldham)
Bacon (Leeds) 1t
Jones, E (Rochdale)
Parkin (Wakefield) 1t
Cunliffe, W (Warrington)
Cartwright (Leigh)
Skelhorne (Warrington)
Hilton, H (Oldham) 1t
Gronow (Huddersfield) 2g
Clark, D (Huddersfield)

1920 New Zealand
Wellington: 14 Aug
Won 11-10
Thomas, G (Huddersfield)
Stone (Hull)
Wagstaff (Huddersfield)
Davies, E (Oldham)
Bacon (Leeds) 1t
Jones, E (Rochdale)
Parkin (Wakefield)
Bowers (Rochdale) 1t
Cartwright (Leigh)
Skelhorne (Warrington)
Hilton, H (Oldham)
Gronow (Huddersfield) 1g
Clark, D (Huddersfield) 1t

1921 Australia
Leeds: 1 Oct
Won 6-5
Thomas, G (Huddersfield)
Stone (Hull) 1t
Wagstaff (Huddersfield)
Bacon (Leeds)
Stockwell (Leeds) 1t
Parkin (Wakefield)
Rogers (Huddersfield)
Cunliffe, W (Warrington)
Cartwright (Leigh)
Skelhorne (Warrington)
Morgan, E (Hull)
Beames (Halifax)
Price, J (Broughton)

1921 Australia
Hull: 5 Nov
Lost 2-16
Thomas, G (Huddersfield)
Stone (Hull)
Batten, W (Hull)
Bacon (Leeds)
Stockwell (Leeds)
Parkin (Wakefield)
Rogers (Huddersfield) 1g
Cunliffe, W (Warrington)
Cartwright (Leigh)
Skelhorne (Warrington)
Morgan, E (Hull)
Beames (Halifax)
Price, J (Broughton)

1922 Australia

Salford: 14 Jan

Won: 6-0

Thomas, G (Huddersfield)
Hurcombe (Wigan)
Wagstaff (Huddersfield)
Bacon (Leeds)
Owen, J. (St. Helens Rec)
Greenhall, J (St. Helens Rec)
Rogers (Huddersfield)
Cunliffe, W (Warrington)
Cartwright (Leigh)
Skelhorne (Warrington)
Taylor (Hull)
Hilton, H (Oldham) 1t
Gallagher (Dewsbury) 1t

1924 Australia

Sydney: 23 June

Won: 22-3

Sullivan, J (Wigan) 5g
Rix (Oldham) 1t
Howley (Wigan)
Ring (Wigan)
Carr (Barrow)
Hurcombe (Wigan)
Parkin (Wakefield) 2t
Cunliffe, W (Warrington)
Bennett (Rochdale)
Burgess, W (Barrow)
Price, J (Wigan) 1t
Darwell (Leigh)
Gallagher (Batley)

1924 Australia

Sydney: 28 June

Won 5-3

Sullivan, J (Wigan) 1g
Rix (Oldham)
Carr (Barrow)
Howley (Wigan)
Evans, F (Swinton)
Gallagher (Batley)
Parkin (Wakefield) 1t
Cunliffe, W (Warrington)
Bennett (Rochdale)
Burgess, W (Barrow)
Brough, A (Oldham)
Darwell (Leigh)
Thompson, J (Leeds)

1924 Australia

Brisbane: 12 July

Lost 11-21

Sullivan, J (Wigan) 1g
Rix (Oldham)
Bacon (Leeds)
Howley (Wigan)
Evans, F (Swinton) 2t
Parkin (Wakefield) 1t
Hurcombe (Wigan)
Cunliffe, W (Warrington)
Bennett (Rochdale)
Burgess, W (Barrow)
Price, J (Wigan)
Darwell (Leigh)
Gallagher (Batley)

1924 New Zealand

Auckland: 2 Aug

Lost 8-16

Knapman (Oldham)
Bentham, W (Broughton) 1t
Rix (Oldham)
Howley (Wigan)
Evans, F (Swinton)
Mooney (Leigh)
Gallagher (Batley)
Cunliffe, W (Warrington)
Bennett (Rochdale)
Burgess, W (Barrow)
Price, J (Wigan)
Darwell (Leigh)
Thompson, J (Leeds) 1t,1g

1924 New Zealand

Wellington: 6 Aug

Lost 11-13

Pollard, C (Wakefield)
Bentham, W (Broughton)
Rix (Oldham) 1t
Howley (Wigan) 1t
Carr (Barrow) 1t
Mooney (Leigh)
Hurcombe (Wigan)
Burgess, W (Barrow)
Bennett (Rochdale)
Bowman, H (Hull)
Thompson, J (Leeds) 1g
Darwell (Leigh)
Gallagher (Batley)

1924 New Zealand

Dunedin: 9 Aug

Won 31-18

Sullivan, J (Wigan) 5g
Howley (Wigan) 1t
Carr (Barrow) 1t
Rix (Oldham)
Evans, F (Swinton) 1t
Hurcombe (Wigan) 1t
Parkin, J (Wakefield)
Burgess, W (Barrow)
Bennett (Rochdale)
Bowman, H (Hull)
Price, J (Wigan) 1t
Brough, A (Oldham) 2t
Gallagher (Batley)

1926 New Zealand

Wigan: 2 Oct

Won 28-20

Sullivan, J (Wigan) 5g
Ring (Wigan)
Evans, J (Swinton) 1t
Carr (Barrow) 1t
Rix (Oldham) 1t
Parkin (Wakefield)
Rees, W (Swinton)
Burgess, W (Barrow)
Bennett (Wigan)
Cunliffe, W (Warrington)
Taylor (Hull) 2t
Rees, D (Halifax)
Gallagher (Batley) 1t

1926 New Zealand

Hull: 13 Nov

Won 21-11

Sullivan, J (Wigan) 3g
Wallace (St. Helens Rec) 1t
Evans, J (Swinton)
Carr (Barrow)
Rix (Oldham)
Parkin (Wakefield)
Fairclough (St. Helens) 1t
Burgess, W (Barrow)
Smith, H (Bradford)
Bowman, H (Hull)
Thomas, A (Leeds) 2t
Fildes (St. Helens Rec) 1t
Gallagher (Batley)

1927 New Zealand
Leeds: 15 Jan
Won 32-17
Sullivan, J (Wigan) 4g
Rix (Oldham)
Evans, J (Swinton) 1t
Carr (Barrow) 3t
Bacon (Leeds) 2t
Evans, B (Swinton)
Rees, W (Swinton) 1t
Burgess, W (Barrow)
Smith, H (Bradford)
Bowman, H (Hull) 1t
Thomas, A (Leeds)
Fildes (St. Helens Rec)
Gore (Salford)

1928 Australia
Brisbane: 23 June
Won 15-12
Sullivan, J (Wigan) 3g
Askin (Featherstone)
Oliver (Batley)
Brough, J (Leeds)
Ellaby (St. Helens) 1t
Fairclough (St. Helens) 1t
Rees, W (Swinton)
Burgess, W (Barrow)
Bentham, N (Wigan High)
Bowman, H (Hull)
Sloman (Oldham)
Fildes (St. Helens Rec)
Horton (Wakefield) 1t

1928 Australia
Sydney: 14 July
Won 8-0
Sullivan, J (Wigan) 1g
Askin (Featherstone)
Oliver (Batley)
Brough, J (Leeds)
Ellaby (St. Helens) 1t
Rees, W (Swinton)
Parkin (Wakefield) 1t
Burgess, W (Barrow)
Bentham, N (Wigan High)
Thompson, J (Leeds)
Sloman (Oldham)
Fildes (St. Helens Rec)
Horton (Wakefield)

1928 Australia
Sydney: 21 July
Lost 14-21
Sullivan, J (Wigan) 4g
Ellaby (St. Helens)
Oliver (Batley)
Askin (Featherstone)
Gwynne (Hull)
Fairclough (St. Helens) 2t
Rees, W (Swinton)
Burgess, W (Barrow)
Bentham, N (Wigan High)
Bowman, H (Hull)
Sloman (Oldham)
Fildes (St. Helens Rec)
Horton (Wakefield)

1928 New Zealand
Auckland: 4 Aug
Lost 13-17
Sullivan, J (Wigan) 2g
Ellaby (St. Helens) 1t
Oliver (Batley) 1t
Brough, J (Leeds)
Askin (Featherstone)
Fairclough (St. Helens) 1t
Rees, W (Swinton)
Burgess, W (Barrow)
Bentham, N (Wigan High)
Bowen (St. Helens Rec)
Sloman (Oldham)
Fildes (St. Helens Rec)
Horton (Wakefield)

1928 New Zealand
Dunedin: 18 Aug
Won 13-5
Sullivan, J (Wigan) 2g
Ellaby (St. Helens) 1t
Askin (Featherstone)
Brough, J (Leeds)
Frodsham (St. Helens)
Evans, B (Swinton)
Rees, W (Swinton) 1t
Burgess, W (Barrow)
Bentham, N (Wigan High)
Bowen (St. Helens Rec) 1t
Sloman (Oldham)
Fildes (St. Helens Rec)
Horton (Wakefield)

1928 New Zealand
Christchurch: 25 Aug
Won 6-5
Sullivan, J (Wigan)
Gwynne (Hull)
Fairclough (St. Helens) 1t
Askin (Featherstone) 1t
Frodsham (St. Helens)
Parkin (Wakefield)
Rees, W (Swinton)
Thompson, J (Leeds)
Bentham, N (Wigan High)
Bowman, H (Hull)
Bowen (St. Helens Rec)
Fildes (St. Helens Rec)
Horton (Wakefield)

1929 Australia
Hull KR: 5 Oct
Lost 8-31
Rees, T (Oldham)
Gwynne (Hull)
Kinnear (Wigan)
Dingsdale (Warrington)
Frodsham (St. Helens)
Fairclough (St. Helens)
Rees, W (Swinton)
Thompson, J (Leeds) 1g
Bentham, N (Halifax)
Bowman, H (Hull)
Middleton (Salford) 1t
Horton (Wakefield)
Feetham (Hull KR) 1t

1929 Australia
Leeds: 9 Nov
Won 9-3
Sullivan, J (Wigan) 3g
Ellaby (St. Helens)
Atkinson, A (Castleford) 1t
Dingsdale (Warrington)
Smith, S (Wakefield)
Parkin (Wakefield)
Rees, W (Swinton)
Burgess, W (Barrow)
Bentham, N (Halifax)
Jenkins, D (Hunslet)
Hodgson (Swinton)
Fildes (St. Helens Rec)
Butters (Swinton)

1930 Australia

Swinton: 4 Jan

Drew: 0-0

Sullivan, J (Wigan)
Ellaby (St. Helens)
Atkinson, A (Castleford)
Halsall (Swinton)
Smith, S (Leeds)
Parkin (Wakefield)
Oster (Oldham)
Burgess, W (Barrow)
Bentham, N (Warrington)
Thomas, A (Leeds)
Hodgson (Swinton)
Fildes (St. Helens Rec)
Butters (Swinton)

1930 Australia

Rochdale: 15 Jan

Won 3-0

Sullivan, J (Wigan)
Blinkhorn (Warrington)
Atkinson, A (Castleford)
Brogden (Huddersfield)
Smith, S (Leeds) 1t
Evans, B (Swinton)
Rees, W (Swinton)
Williams, W (Salford)
Bentham, N (Warrington)
Thomas, A (Leeds)
Crowther (Hunslet)
Fildes (St. Helens Rec)
Young, H (Huddersfield)

1932 Australia

Sydney: 6 June

Won 8-6

Sullivan, J (Wigan) 1g
Ellaby (St. Helens) 1t
Atkinson, A (Castleford) 1t
Brogden (Huddersfield)
Smith, S (Leeds)
Pollard, E (Wakefield)
Evans, B (Swinton)
Thompson, J (Leeds)
White, L (Hunslet)
Silcock, N (Widnes)
Hodgson (Swinton)
Horton (Wakefield)
Feetham (Salford)

1932 Australia

Brisbane: 18 June

Lost 6-15

Sullivan, J (Wigan)
Ellaby (St. Helens)
Atkinson, A (Castleford)
Brogden (Huddersfield)
Smith, S (Leeds) 1t
Pollard, E (Wakefield) 1t
Adams, L (Leeds)
Thompson, J (Leeds)
White, L (Hunslet)
Silcock, N (Widnes)
Hodgson (Swinton)
Horton (Wakefield)
Feetham (Salford)

1932 Australia

Sydney: 16 July

Won 18-13

Sullivan, J (Wigan) 3g
Ellaby (St. Helens)
Atkinson, A (Castleford)
Brogden (Huddersfield) 1t
Smith, S (Leeds) 3t
Risman, A (Salford)
Evans, B (Swinton)
Thompson, J (Leeds)
White, L (Hunslet)
Williams, W (Salford)
Hodgson (Swinton)
Fildes (St. Helens)
Horton (Wakefield)

1932 New Zealand

Auckland: 30 July

Won 24-9

Sullivan, J (Wigan) 3g
Ellaby (St. Helens) 2t
Atkinson, A (Castleford) 2t
Risman, A (Salford)
Smith, S (Leeds) 1t
Brogden (Huddersfield)
Evans, B (Swinton)
Thompson, J (Leeds)
Lowe, J (Leeds)
Silcock, N (Widnes) 1t
Hodgson (Swinton)
Fildes (St. Helens)
Feetham (Salford)

1932 New Zealand

Christchurch: 13 Aug

Won 25-14

Sullivan, J (Wigan) 5g
Ellaby (St. Helens)
Atkinson, A (Castleford) 2t
Risman, A (Salford)
Smith, S (Leeds) 1t
Brogden (Huddersfield) 1t
Evans, B (Swinton)
Thompson, J (Leeds)
White, L (Hunslet)
Silcock, N (Widnes)
Hodgson (Swinton)
Fildes (St. Helens)
Horton (Wakefield) 1t

1932 New Zealand

Auckland: 20 Aug

Won 20-18

Sullivan, J (Wigan) 4g
Hudson, B (Salford) 2t
Atkinson, A (Castleford)
Risman, A (Salford)
Smith, S (Leeds) 1t
Brogden (Huddersfield)
Evans, B (Swinton)
Thompson, J (Leeds)
White, L (Hunslet)
Wright, J (Swinton)
Hodgson (Swinton)
Fildes (St. Helens) 1t
Feetham (Salford)

1933 Australia

Belle Vue (Manchester): 7 Oct

Won 4-0

Sullivan, J (Wigan) 2g
Ellaby (St. Helens)
Risman, A (Salford)
Brogden (Huddersfield)
Smith, S (Leeds)
Davies, W.J (Castleford)
Evans, B (Swinton)
Miller, J (Warrington)
White, L (Hunslet)
Silcock, N (Widnes)
Hodgson (Swinton)
Horton (Wakefield)
Feetham (Salford)

1933 Australia
Leeds: 11 Nov
Won 7-5
Sullivan, J (Wigan) 2g
Hudson, B (Salford)
Risman, A (Salford)
Dingsdale (Warrington)
Woods, J (Barrow) 1t
Brogden (Huddersfield)
Evans, B (Swinton)
Miller, J (Warrington)
White, L (Hunslet)
Silcock, N (Widnes)
Hodgson (Swinton)
Horton (Wakefield)
Feetham (Salford)

1933 Australia
Swinton: 16 Dec
Won 19-16
Sullivan, J (Wigan) 5g
Hudson, B (Salford) 1t
Atkinson, A (Castleford)
Risman, A (Salford)
Smith, S (Leeds) 1t
Watkins, W (Salford)
Jenkins, E (Salford)
Miller, J (Warrington)
Armitt (Swinton)
Silcock, N (Widnes)
Hodgson (Swinton)
Horton (Wakefield)
Feetham (Salford) 1t

1936 Australia
Sydney: 29 June
Lost 8-24
Belshaw (Liverpool S)
Morley (Wigan)
Atkinson, A (Castleford)
Brogden (Leeds)
Edwards, A (Salford)
Jenkins, E (Salford)
McCue (Widnes)
Miller, J (Warrington)
Field, H (York)
Silcock, N (Widnes)
Hodgson (Swinton) 1g
Woods, H (Liverpool S)
Beverley (Hunslet) 2t

1936 Australia
Brisbane: 4 July
Won 12-7
Brough, J (Leeds)
Edwards, A (Salford) 2t
Risman, A (Salford) 2g
Belshaw (Liverpool S)
Brogden (Leeds)
Jenkins, E (Salford)
Watkins, W (Salford)
Silcock, N (Widnes)
Armitt (Swinton)
Woods, H (Liverpool S)
Hodgson (Swinton) 1g
Arkwright (Warrington)
Beverley (Hunslet)

1936 Australia
Sydney: 18 July
Won 12-7
Belshaw (Liverpool S)
Edwards, A (Salford)
Risman, A (Salford)
Brogden (Leeds) 1t
Hudson, B (Salford) 1t
Jenkins, E (Salford)
Watkins, W (Salford)
Silcock, N (Widnes)
Armitt (Swinton)
Woods, H (Liverpool S)
Hodgson (Swinton) 3g
Arkwright (Warrington)
Beverley (Hunslet)

1936 New Zealand
Auckland: 8 Aug
Won 10-8
Belshaw (Liverpool S)
Edwards, A (Salford) 1t
Risman, A (Salford)
Brogden (Leeds)
Hudson, B (Salford)
Jenkins, E (Salford) 1t
Watkins, W (Salford)
Miller, J (Warrington)
Armitt (Swinton)
Field, H (York)
Hodgson (Swinton) 2g
Woods, H (Liverpool S)
Troup (Barrow)

1936 New Zealand
Auckland: 15 Aug
Won 23-11
Belshaw (Liverpool S)
Edwards, A (Salford) 1t
Risman, A (Salford) 4g
Brogden (Leeds)
Hudson, B (Salford) 1t
Jenkins, E (Salford)
Watkins, W (Salford)
Miller, J (Warrington) 1t
Armitt (Swinton)
Field, H (York)
Arkwright (Warrington) 2t
Woods, H (Liverpool S)
Troup (Barrow)

1937 Australia
Leeds: 16 Oct
Won 5-4
Belshaw (Liverpool S)
Cunniffe (Castleford)
Croston (Castleford)
Risman, A (Salford)
Morley (Wigan)
Jenkins, E (Salford) 1t
McCue (Widnes)
Silcock, N (Widnes)
Armitt (Swinton)
Woods, H (Leeds)
Hodgson (Swinton) 1g
Arkwright (Warrington)
Beverley (Hunslet)

1937 Australia
Swinton: 13 Nov
Won 13-3
Belshaw (Warrington)
Hudson, B (Salford) 1t
Brogden (Leeds)
Risman, A (Salford) 2g
Edwards, A (Salford) 2t
Jenkins, E (Salford)
Watkins, W (Salford)
Silcock, N (Widnes)
Armitt (Swinton)
Higgins, H (Widnes)
Jubb (Leeds)
Arkwright (Warrington)
Beverley (Halifax)

1937 Australia

Huddersfield: 18 Dec

Lost 3-13

Belshaw (Warrington)
Hudson, B (Salford) 1t
Brogden (Leeds)
Risman, A (Salford)
Edwards, A (Salford)
Jenkins, E (Salford)
Watkins, W (Salford)
Prosser, D (Leeds)
Armitt (Swinton)
Higgins, H (Widnes)
Jubb (Leeds)
Arkwright (Warrington)
Beverley (Halifax)

1946 Australia

Sydney: 17 June

Drew 8-8

Risman, A (Salford) 1g
Batten, E (Bradford)
Ward, E (Bradford)
Kitching (Bradford)
Johnson, A (Warrington)
Horne (Barrow) 1t
McCue (Widnes)
Gee (Wigan)
Egan (Wigan)
Whitcombe (Bradford) 1t
White, L (York)
Phillips (Oldham)
Owens (Leeds)

1946 Australia

Brisbane: 6 July

Won 14-5

Ward, E (Bradford) 1g
Bassett (Halifax) 3t
Risman, A (Salford)
Ward, Ed (Wigan) 1g
Johnson, A (Warrington) 1t
Horne (Barrow)
McCue (Widnes)
Gee (Wigan)
Egan (Wigan)
Whitcombe (Bradford)
White, L (York)
Phillips (Oldham)
Owens (Leeds)

1946 Australia

Sydney: 20 July

Won 20-7

Ward, E (Bradford)
Bassett (Halifax) 2t
Risman, A (Salford) 3g
Ward, Ed (Wigan) 1g
Batten, E (Bradford)
Horne (Barrow)
McCue (Widnes)
Gee (Wigan)
Egan (Wigan)
Curran (Salford) 1t
White, L (York)
Phillips (Oldham)
Owens (Leeds) 1t

1946 New Zealand

Auckland: 10 Aug

Lost 8-13

Jones, J (Barrow)
Batten, E (Bradford) 1t
Ward, E (Bradford) 1t,1g
Knowelden (Barrow)
Johnson, A (Warrington)
Davies, W.T.H (Bradford)
McCue (Widnes)
Gee (Wigan)
Curran (Salford)
Nicholson (Huddersfield)
White, L (York)
Foster, T (Bradford)
Owens (Leeds)

1947 New Zealand

Leeds: 4 Oct

Won 11-10

Ledgard (Dewsbury)
Ratcliffe (Wigan)
Ward, Ed (Wigan) 1g
Stott (St. Helens)
Johnson, A (Warrington) 1t
Davies, W.T.H (Bradford)
Bradshaw (Wigan)
Gee (Wigan)
Egan (Wigan)
Gwyther (Belle Vue) 1t
Thomas, L (Oldham)
Aston (St. Helens) 1t
Dockar (Hull KR)

1947 New Zealand

Swinton: 8 Nov

Lost 7-10

Ledgard (Dewsbury) 2g
Batten, E (Bradford)
Ward, E (Bradford)
Ashcroft, E (Wigan)
Johnson, A (Warrington)
Davies, W.T.H (Bradford)
Jenkins, D (Leeds) 1t
Gee (Wigan)
Egan (Wigan)
Gwyther (Belle Vue)
White, L (Wigan)
Aston (St. Helens)
Palin (Warrington)

1947 New Zealand

Bradford: 20 Dec

Won 25-9

Ryan, M (Wigan)
Francis, R (Barrow) 2t
Ward, E (Bradford) 4g
Ashcroft, E (Wigan)
Johnson, A (Warrington)
Horne, W (Barrow) 1g
Bradshaw (Wigan)
Gee (Wigan) 1t
Egan (Wigan)
Curran (Salford)
White, L (Wigan)
Aston (St. Helens)
Palin (Warrington) 2t

1948 Australia

Leeds: 9 Oct

Won 23-21

Ledgard (Leigh)
Lawrenson (Wigan)
Pimblett (Warrington) 2t
Ward, E (Bradford) 1g
McCormick (BVR) 2t
Horne (Barrow)
Helme (Warrington)
Gee (Wigan)
Egan (Wigan)
Curran (Salford)
Foster, T (Bradford) 2t
Nicholson (Huddersfield)
Valentine, D (Huddersfield) 1t

1948 Australia
Swinton: 6 Nov
Won 16-7
Ryan, M (Wigan)
Lawrenson (Wigan) 2t
Pimblett (Warrington) 2t
Ward, E (Bradford) 2g
McCormick (BVR)
Williams, R (Leeds)
Helme (Warrington)
Gee (Wigan)
Egan (Wigan)
Curran (Salford)
Foster, T (Bradford)
Nicholson (Huddersfield)
Valentine, D (Huddersfield)

1949 Australia
Bradford: 29 Jan
Won 23-9
Ryan, M (Wigan)
Lawrenson (Wigan)
Pimblett (Warrington)
Ward, E (Bradford) 4g,1t
McCormick (St. Helens) 1t
Williams, R (Leeds) 1t
Helme (Warrington)
Gee (Wigan)
Egan (Wigan)
Curran (Salford) 2t
Hudson, W (Wigan)
Featherstone (Warrington)
Valentine, D (Huddersfield)

1950 Australia
Sydney: 12 June
Won 6-4
Ryan, M (Wigan)
Ratcliffe (Wigan)
Ward, E (Bradford)
Ashcroft, E (Wigan)
Hilton, J (Wigan) 2t
Williams, R (Leeds)
Bradshaw (Wigan)
Gee (Wigan)
Egan (Wigan)
Gwyther (BVR)
Ryan, R (Warrington)
Higgins, F (Widnes)
Street (Dewsbury)

1950 Australia
Brisbane: 1 July
Lost 3-15
Ledgard (Leigh)
Ratcliffe (Wigan)
Ward, E (Bradford)
Ashcroft, E (Wigan)
Danby (Salford) 1t
Williams, R (Leeds)
Bradshaw (Wigan)
Gee (Wigan)
Egan (Wigan)
Gwyther (BVR)
Murphy, H (Wakefield)
Higgins, F (Widnes)
Street (Dewsbury)

1950 Australia
Sydney: 22 July
Lost 2-5
Ledgard (Leigh)
Danby (Salford)
Ward, E (Bradford) 1g
Ashcroft, E (Wigan)
Hilton, J (Wigan)
Cunliffe, J (Wigan)
Bradshaw (Wigan)
Gee (Wigan)
Egan (Wigan)
Gwyther (BVR)
Phillips (BVR)
Higgins, F (Widnes)
Street (Dewsbury)

1950 New Zealand
Christchurch: 29 July
Lost 10-16
Ledgard (Leigh)
Pollard, R (Dewsbury) 1t
Ward, E (Bradford) 2g
Ashcroft, E (Wigan)
Hilton, J (Wigan)
Williams, R (Leeds) 1t
Pepperell, A (Workington)
Gee (Wigan)
Egan (Wigan)
Featherstone (Warrington)
Ryan, R (Warrington)
Higgins, F (Widnes)
Traill (Bradford)

1950 New Zealand
Auckland: 12 Aug
Lost 13-20
Cunliffe, J (Wigan)
Danby (Salford)
Ward, E (Bradford) 2g,1t
Street (Dewsbury)
Hilton, J (Wigan)
Williams, R (Leeds)
Bradshaw (Wigan)
Gee (Wigan)
Egan (Wigan)
Featherstone (Warrington) 1t
Ryan, R (Warrington) 1t
Higgins, F (Widnes)
Traill (Bradford)

1951 New Zealand
Bradford: 6 Oct
Won 21-15
Cunliffe, J (Wigan)
Cracknell (Huddersfield) 1t
Ward, E (Bradford)
Greenall, D (St. Helens) 1t
Wilson, G (Workington) 3t
Williams, R (Leeds)
Burnell (Hunslet)
Gee (Wigan) 3g
McKeating (Workington)
Gwyther (BVR)
Ryan, R (Warrington)
Thompson, C (Hunslet)
Blan (Wigan)

1951 New Zealand
Swinton: 10 Nov
Won 20-19
Ledgard (Leigh) 4g
Cracknell (Huddersfield) 1t
Ward, E (Bradford)
Greenall, D (St. Helens)
Wilson, G (Workington) 1t
Williams, R (Leeds)
Burnell (Hunslet)
Gee (Wigan)
McKeating (Workington) 1t
Prescott (St. Helens)
Blan (Wigan)
Thompson, C (Hunslet)
Traill (Bradford) 1t

1951 New Zealand
Leeds: 15 Dec
Won 16-12

Evans (Hunslet)
Turnbull (Leeds) 2t
Ward, E (Bradford) 2g
Greenall, D (St. Helens)
Wilson, G (Workington) 1t
Williams, R (Leeds)
Pepperell, A (Workington)
Prescott, A (St. Helens)
McKinney (Salford)
Barton, F (Wigan)
Higgins, F (Widnes)
Blan (Wigan) 1t
Valentine, D (Huddersfield)

1952 Australia
Leeds: 4 Oct
Won 19-6

Evans (Hunslet)
Daniels (Halifax) 1t
Ward, E (Bradford)
Ryder (Warrington) 1t
Castle (Barrow) 1t
Horne (Barrow) 5g
Toohey (Barrow)
Prescott, A (St. Helens)
Ackerley (Halifax)
Featherstone (Warrington)
Ryan, R (Warrington)
Pawsey (Leigh)
Traill (Bradford)

1952 Australia
Swinton: 8 Nov
Won 21-5

Evans (Hunslet)
Daniels (Halifax)
Ward, E (Bradford) 1t,2g
Greenall, D (St. Helens) 2t
Castle (Barrow) 2t
Horne (Barrow) 1g
Toohey (Barrow)
Prescott, A (St. Helens)
McKinney (Salford)
Featherstone (Warrington)
Valentine, D (Huddersfield)
Pawsey (Leigh)
Traill (Bradford)

1952 Australia
Bradford: 13 Dec
Lost 7-27

Evans (Hunslet) 2g
Bevan, D (Wigan)
Ward, E (Bradford)
Greenall, D (St. Helens)
Castle (Barrow)
Horne (Barrow) 1t
Toohey (Barrow)
Prescott, A (St. Helens)
McKinney (Salford)
Featherstone (Warrington)
Valentine, D (Huddersfield)
Pawsey (Leigh)
Traill (Bradford)

1954 Australia
Sydney: 12 June
Lost 12-37

Cunliffe, J (Wigan)
Jones, B.L (Leeds) 3g
Jackson, P (Barrow) 1t
Ashcroft, E (Wigan)
Castle (Barrow)
Price, R (Warrington)
Helme (Warrington)
Prescott, A (St. Helens)
McKinney (Salford)
Wilkinson (Halifax)
Silcock, N (Wigan) 1t
Valentine, D (Huddersfield)
Traill (Bradford)

1954 Australia
Brisbane: 3 July
Won 38-21

Jones, B.L (Leeds) 10g
Boston (Wigan) 2t
Jackson, P (Barrow) 1t
Ashcroft, E (Wigan)
O'Grady (Oldham)
Williams, R (Hunslet) 1t
Helme (Warrington) 1t
Prescott, A (St. Helens)
McKinney (Salford)
Bowden (Huddersfield)
Silcock, N (Wigan)
Pawsey (Leigh) 1t
Valentine, D (Huddersfield)

1954 Australia
Sydney: 17 July
Lost 16-20

Jones, B.L (Leeds) 2g
Boston (Wigan)
Jackson, P (Barrow)
Ashcroft, E (Wigan) 1t
O'Grady (Oldham)
Williams, R (Hunslet) 2t
Helme (Warrington)
Prescott, A (St. Helens)
McKinney (Salford)
Bowden (Huddersfield)
Silcock, N (Wigan)
Pawsey (Leigh)
Valentine, D (Huddersfield) 1t

1954 New Zealand
Auckland: 24 July
Won 27-7

Jones, B.L (Leeds) 3g
Boston (Wigan) 4t
Jackson, P (Barrow)
Ashcroft, E (Wigan) 2t
O'Grady (Oldham)
Price, R (Warrington)
Helme (Warrington)
Prescott, A (St. Helens)
Harris (Hull) 1t
Wilkinson (Halifax)
Gunney (Hunslet)
Pawsey (Leigh)
Valentine, D (Huddersfield)

1954 New Zealand
Greymouth: 31 July
Lost 14-20

Jones, B.L (Leeds) 4g
Boston (Wigan)
Jackson, P (Barrow)
Greenall, D (St. Helens)
O'Grady (Oldham) 1t
Williams, R (Hunslet)
Helme (Warrington)
Prescott, A (St. Helens)
Harris (Hull)
Wilkinson (Halifax) 1t
Gunney (Hunslet)
Briggs (Huddersfield)
Valentine, D (Huddersfield)

1954 New Zealand
Auckland: 14 Aug
Won 12-6
Jones, B.L (Leeds) 3g
Boston (Wigan)
Jackson, P (Barrow)
Ashcroft, E (Wigan)
O'Grady (Oldham) 1t
Price (Warrington) 1t
Burnell (Hunslet)
Prescott (St. Helens)
McKinney (Salford)
Bowden (Huddersfield)
Gunney (Hunslet)
Pawsey (Leigh)
Traill (Bradford)

1954 Australia (WC)
Lyons: 31 Oct
Won 28-13
Ledgard (Leigh) 5g
Rose, D (Leeds) 1t
Jackson, P (Barrow) 2t
Sullivan, M (Huddersfield)
Kitchen (Leigh) 1t
Brown (Leeds) 2t
Helme (Warrington)
Thorley (Halifax)
Smith, S (Hunslet)
Coverdale (Hull)
Watts (York)
Robinson, D (Wakefield)
Valentine, D (Huddersfield)

1954 France (WC)
Toulouse: 7 Nov
Drew 13-13
Ledgard (Leigh) 2g
Rose, D (Leeds) 1t
Jackson, P (Barrow)
Naughton, A (Warrington)
Sullivan, M (Huddersfield)
Brown (Leeds) 1t
Helme (Warrington) 1t
Thorley (Halifax)
Smith, S (Hunslet)
Coverdale (Hull)
Watts (York)
Robinson, D (Wakefield)
Valentine, D (Huddersfield)

1954 New Zealand (WC)
Bordeaux: 11 Nov
Won 26-6
Ledgard (Leigh) 4g,1t
Rose, D (Leeds) 1t
Jackson, P (Barrow) 1t
Sullivan (Huddersfield)
Kitchen (Leigh) 2t
Brown (Leeds) 1t
Helme (Warrington)
Thorley (Halifax)
Smith, S (Hunslet)
Coverdale (Hull)
Watts (York)
Robinson, D (Wakefield)
Valentine, D (Huddersfield)

1954 France (WC)
Paris: 13 Nov
Won 16-12
Ledgard (Leigh) 2g
Rose, D (Leeds) 1t
Jackson, P (Barrow)
Naughton, A (Warrington)
Sullivan, M (Huddersfield)
Brown (Leeds) 2t
Helme (Warrington) 1t
Thorley (Halifax)
Smith, S (Hunslet)
Coverdale (Hull)
Watts (York)
Robinson, D (Wakefield)
Valentine, D (Huddersfield)

1955 New Zealand
Swinton: 8 Oct
Won 25-6
Moses (St. Helens)
Boston (Wigan) 1t
Jackson, P (Barrow)
Jones, B.L (Leeds) 5g
Sullivan, M (Huddersfield) 2t
Price (Warrington)
Stevenson (Leeds)
Prescott, A (St. Helens)
McKinney (Warrington)
Wilkinson (Halifax) 1t
Grundy (Barrow) 1t
Robinson, D (Wakefield)
Foster, P (Leigh)

1955 New Zealand
Bradford: 12 Nov
Won 27-12
Moses (St. Helens)
Daniels (Halifax)
Jackson, P (Barrow)
Jones, B.L (Leeds) 3g
Sullivan, M (Huddersfield) 3t
Brown (Leeds)
Stevenson (Leeds) 1t
Prescott, A (St. Helens) 1t
McKinney (Warrington)
Wilkinson (Halifax) 1t
Grundy (Barrow)
Watts (York) 1t
Foster, P (Leigh)

1955 New Zealand
Leeds: 17 Dec
Lost 13-28
Jones, B.L (Leeds) 2g,1t
Hollindrake (Keighley)
Jackson, P (Barrow)
Davies, A (Oldham)
Sullivan, M (Huddersfield) 1t
Brown (Leeds) 1t
Stevenson (Leeds)
Prescott, A (St. Helens)
McKinney (Warrington)
Wilkinson (Halifax)
Grundy (Barrow)
Schofield (Halifax)
Foster, P (Leigh)

1956 Australia
Wigan: 17 Nov
Won 21-10
Mortimer (Wakefield) 3g
Boston (Wigan) 2t
Jackson, P (Barrow)
Davies, A (Oldham) 1t
Sullivan, M (Huddersfield) 1t
Price (Warrington)
Stevenson (Leeds)
Prescott, A (St. Helens)
Harris (Hull)
Shaw, B (Hunslet)
Grundy (Barrow) 1t
Robinson, D (Leeds)
Dawson (York)

1956 Australia
Bradford: 1 Dec
Lost 9-22
Mortimer (Wakefield) 3g
Boston (Wigan)
Jackson, P (Barrow)
Davies, A (Oldham)
Sullivan, M (Huddersfield)
Price (Warrington)
Stevenson (Leeds) 1t
Prescott, A (St. Helens)
Harris (Hull)
Shaw, B (Hunslet)
Grundy (Barrow)
Robinson, D (Leeds)
Turner (Oldham)

1956 Australia
Swinton: 15 Dec
Won 19-0
Moses (St. Helens)
Boston (Wigan) 1t
Jackson, P (Barrow)
Davies, A (Oldham) 2g
Sullivan, M (Huddersfield) 1t
Price (Warrington)
Stevenson (Leeds)
Prescott, A (St. Helens)
Harris (Hull)
Little (Oldham) 1t
Grundy (Barrow)
Gunney (Hunslet) 1t
Turner (Oldham) 1t

1957 France
Leeds: 26 Jan
Won 45-12
Moses (St. Helens)
Boston (Wigan) 1t
Jackson, P (Barrow)
Jones, B.L (Leeds) 9g,1t
Sullivan, M (Huddersfield) 1t
Bolton (Wigan) 1t
Stevenson (Leeds)
Prescott, A (St. Helens) 1t
Harris (Hull)
Little (Oldham) 1t
Grundy (Barrow)
Gunney (Hunslet) 1t
Turner (Oldham) 2t

1957 France
Toulouse: 3 Mar
Drew 19-19
Moses (St. Helens)
Boston (Wigan) 1t
Jackson, P (Barrow)
Jones, B.L (Leeds) 1t,5g
Sullivan, M (Huddersfield)
Price (Warrington)
Stevenson (Leeds)
Prescott, A (St. Helens) 1t
Harris (Hull)
Little (Oldham)
Grundy (Barrow)
Gunney (Hunslet)
Turner (Oldham)

1957 France
St. Helens: 10 Apr
Won 29-14
Moses (St. Helens) 1t
Boston (Wigan)
Jackson, P (Barrow)
Jones, B.L (Leeds) 1t,7g
Sullivan, M (Huddersfield) 2t
Price (Warrington) 1t
Stevenson (Leeds)
Prescott, A (St. Helens)
Harris (Hull)
Little (Oldham)
Grundy (Barrow)
Gunney (Hunslet)
Turner (Oldham)

1957 France (WC)
Sydney: 15 June
Won 23-5
Moses (St. Helens)
Boston (Wigan) 1t
Jackson, P (Barrow) 1t
Davies, A (Oldham)
Sullivan, M (Huddersfield) 2t
Jones, B.L (Leeds) 4g
Stevenson (Leeds) 1t
Prescott, A (St. Helens)
Harris (Hull)
Little (Oldham)
Grundy (Barrow)
Gunney (Hunslet)
Turner (Oldham)

1957 Australia (WC)
Sydney: 17 June
Lost 6-31
Moses (St. Helens)
Boston (Wigan)
Ashton (Wigan)
Davies, A (Oldham)
Sullivan, M (Huddersfield)
Jones, B.L (Leeds) 3g
Stevenson (Leeds)
Prescott, A (St. Helens)
Harris (Hull)
Little (Oldham)
Grundy (Barrow)
Whiteley (Hull)
Turner (Oldham)

1957 New Zealand (WC)
Sydney: 25 June
Lost 21-29
Moses (St. Helens)
Ashton (Wigan)
Jackson, P (Barrow) 1t
Jones, B.L (Leeds) 1t,3g
Sullivan, M (Huddersfield) 1t
Rhodes (St. Helens)
Stevenson (Leeds)
Prescott, A (St. Helens)
McKinney (St. Helens)
Little (Oldham) 1t
Grundy (Barrow) 1t
Gunney (Hunslet)
Turner (Oldham)

1957 France
Toulouse: 3 Nov
Won 25-14
Ganley (Oldham) 5g,1t
Boston (Wigan)
Jackson, P (Barrow)
Davies, A (Oldham) 1t
Sullivan, M (Wigan) 2t
Bolton (Wigan)
Stevenson (Leeds)
Prescott, A (St. Helens)
Harris (Hull)
Jackson, K (Oldham)
Little (Oldham)
Goodwin (Barrow)
Turner (Oldham) 1t

1957 France
Wigan: 23 Nov
Won 44-15
Ganley (Oldham) 10g
Boston (Wigan) 1t
Jackson, P (Barrow)
Davies, A (Oldham) 1t
Sullivan, M (Wigan) 1t
Bolton (Wigan) 3t
Stevenson (Leeds) 1t
Prescott, A (St. Helens)
Harris (Hull)
Jackson, K (Oldham)
Little (Oldham)
Goodwin (Barrow)
Turner (Oldham) 1t

1958 France
Grenoble: 2 March
Won 23-9
Ganley (Oldham) 4g
Boston (Wigan) 1t
Jackson, P (Barrow)
Davies, A (Oldham)
Sullivan, M (Wigan) 1t
Bolton (Wigan)
Stevenson (Leeds) 1t
Prescott, A (St. Helens) 1t
Harris (Hull)
Owen, S (Leigh)
Little (Oldham)
Goodwin (Barrow)
Turner (Oldham) 1t

1958 Australia
Sydney: 14 June
Lost 8-25
Fraser (Warrington)
Southward (Workington) 1t,1g
Jackson, P (Barrow)
Davies, A (Oldham)
Sullivan, M (Wigan)
Bolton (Wigan) 1t
Murphy, A (St. Helens)
Prescott, A (St. Helens)
Harris (Hull)
Terry (St. Helens)
Edgar (Workington)
Martyn, M (Leigh)
Whiteley (Hull)

1958 Australia
Brisbane: 5 July
Won 25-18
Fraser (Warrington) 5g
Southward (Workington) 2t
Ashton (Wigan)
Challinor (Warrington) 1t
Sullivan, M (Wigan) 1t
Bolton (Wigan)
Murphy, A (St. Helens) 1t
Prescott, A (St. Helens)
Harris (Hull)
McTigue (Wigan)
Huddart (Whitehaven)
Whiteley (Hull)
Karalius, V (St. Helens)

1958 Australia
Sydney: 19 July
Won 40-17
Fraser (Warrington) 8g
Southward (Workington) 1t
Ashton (Wigan)
Davies, A (Oldham) 1t
Sullivan, M (Wigan) 3t
Jackson, P (Barrow)
Murphy, A (St. Helens) 1t
Terry (St. Helens) 1t
Harris (Hull)
McTigue (Wigan)
Huddart (Whitehaven)
Whiteley (Hull) 1t
Karalius, V (St. Helens)

1958 New Zealand
Auckland: 26 July
Lost 10-15
Fraser (Warrington) 2g
Carlton (St. Helens)
Ashton (Wigan)
Davies, A (Oldham)
Sullivan, M (Wigan) 1t
Jackson, P (Barrow) 1t
Pitchford, F (Oldham)
McTigue (Wigan)
Ackerley (Halifax)
Goodwin (Barrow)
Huddart (Whitehaven)
Whiteley (Hull)
Karalius, V (St. Helens)

1958 New Zealand
Auckland: 9 Aug
Won 32-15
Fraser (Warrington) 7g
Southward (Workington)
Ashton (Wigan) 2t
Challinor (Warrington)
Sullivan, M (Wigan) 3t
Davies, A (Oldham)
Murphy, A (St. Helens) 1t
Edgar (Workington)
Harris (Hull)
McTigue (Wigan)
Huddart (Whitehaven)
Goodwin (Barrow)
Karalius, V (St. Helens)

1959 France
Leeds: 14 March
Won 50-15
Fraser (Warrington) 7g
Southward (Oldham)
Ashton (Wigan) 1t
Davies, A (Oldham) 1t
Sullivan, M (Wigan) 3t
Bolton (Wigan) 1t
Murphy, A (St. Helens) 4t
Terry (St. Helens)
Harris (Hull) 1t
McTigue (Wigan)
Vines (Wakefield) 1t
Whiteley (Hull)
Karalius, V (St. Helens)

1959 France
Grenoble: 5 April
Lost 15-24
Fraser (Warrington) 3g
Southward (Oldham)
Davies, A (Oldham)
Fox, N (Wakefield) 2t
Sullivan, M (Wigan)
Gabbitas (Hunslet)
Murphy, A (St. Helens)
Terry (St. Helens)
Harris (Hull)
McTigue (Wigan) 1t
Vines (Wakefield)
Winslade (Oldham)
Whiteley (Hull)

1959 Australia
Swinton: 17 Oct
Lost 14-22
Fraser (Warrington) 4g
Boston (Wigan) 1t
Ashton (Wigan)
Davies, A (Oldham)
Sullivan, M (Wigan)
Bolton (Wigan)
Murphy, A (St. Helens)
Terry (St. Helens)
Harris (Hull)
McTigue (Wigan)
Huddart (St. Helens)
Martyn, M (Leigh)
Turner (Wakefield) 1t

1959 Australia
Leeds: 21 Nov
Won 11-10
Dyson (Huddersfield)
Southward (Oldham)
Ashton (Wigan)
Fox, N (Wakefield) 1t,1g
Sullivan, M (Wigan)
Bolton (Wigan)
Stevenson (York)
Terry (St. Helens)
Harris (Hull)
Robinson, D (Leeds) 1t
McTigue (Wigan)
Vines (Wakefield)
Whiteley (Hull) 1t

1959 Australia
Wigan: 12 Dec
Won 18-12
Round (Wakefield)
Southward (Oldham) 1t
Ashton (Wigan)
Fox, N (Wakefield) 1t,6g
Sullivan, M (Wigan)
Bolton (Wigan)
Stevenson (York)
Terry (St. Helens)
Harris (Hull)
Robinson, D (Leeds)
McTigue (Wigan)
Wilkinson (Wakefield)
Whiteley (Hull)

1960 France
Toulouse: 6 March
Lost 18-20
Fraser (Warrington)
Southward (Oldham)
Ashton (Wigan) 1t
Fox, N (Wakefield) 3g,2t
Sullivan, M (Wigan) 1t
Bolton (Wigan)
Stevenson (York)
Wilkinson (Wakefield)
Harris (Hull)
Drake, J (Hull)
McTigue (Wigan)
Cherrington (Wigan)
Turner (Wakefield)

1960 France
St. Helens: 26 March
Drew 17-17
Fraser (Warrington)
Southward (Oldham)
Ashton (Wigan)
Fox, N (Wakefield) 4g,1t
Sullivan, M (Wigan) 1t
Bolton (Wigan) 1t
Stevenson (York)
Wilkinson (Wakefield)
Harris (Hull)
Robinson, D (Leeds)
McTigue (Wigan)
Whiteley (Hull)
Turner (Wakefield)

1960 New Zealand (WC)
Bradford: 24 Sep
Won 23-8
Fraser (Warrington) 4g
Greenough (Warrington)
Ashton (Wigan) 1t
Davies, A (Oldham) 1t
Sullivan, M (Wigan)
Myler (Widnes) 1t
Murphy, A (St. Helens) 1t
Wilkinson (Wakefield)
Harris (Hull)
McTigue (Wigan) 1t
Whiteley (Hull)
Karalius, V (St. Helens)
Turner (Wakefield)

1960 France (WC)
Swinton: 1 Oct
Won 33-7
Fraser (Warrington) 6g
Challinor (Warrington)
Rhodes (St. Helens) 2t
Davies, A (Oldham) 2t
Sullivan, M (Wigan) 1t
Myler (Widnes) 1t
Murphy, A (St. Helens)
Wilkinson (Wakefield) 1t
Shaw, J (Halifax)
McTigue (Wigan)
Shaw, B (Hunslet)
Karalius, V (St. Helens)
Whiteley (Hull)

1960 Australia (WC)
Bradford: 8 Oct
Won 10-3
Rhodes (St. Helens) 2g
Boston (Wigan) 1t
Ashton (Wigan)
Davies, A (Oldham)
Sullivan, M (Wigan) 1t
Myler (Widnes)
Murphy, A (St. Helens)
Wilkinson (Wakefield)
Shaw, J (Halifax)
McTigue (Wigan)
Shaw, B (Hunslet)
Turner (Wakefield)
Karalius, V (St. Helens)

1960 France
Bordeaux: 11 Dec
Won 21-10
Fraser (Warrington) 1g
Boston (Wigan)
Fox, N (Wakefield) 2t,2g
Davies, A (Oldham)
Sullivan, M (Wigan)
Myler (Widnes) 1t
Murphy, A (St. Helens) 1t
Terry (St. Helens)
Shaw, J (Halifax) 1t
Barton, J (Wigan)
Karalius, V (St. Helens)
Shaw, B (Hunslet)
Turner (Wakefield)

1961 France
St. Helens: 28 Jan
Won 27-8
Fraser (Warrington) 6g
Boston (Wigan) 1t
Sullivan, M (St. Helens)
Hallas (Leeds)
Stopford (Swinton) 1t
Myler (Widnes)
Murphy, A (St. Helens) 2t
Terry (St. Helens)
Shaw, J (Halifax)
McTigue (Wigan)
Shaw, B (Leeds) 1t
Turner (Wakefield)
Karalius, V (St. Helens)

1961 New Zealand
Leeds: 30 Sep
Lost 11-29
Rhodes (St. Helens) 1g
Boston (Wigan) 2t
Ashton (Wigan)
Hallas (Leeds)
O'Grady (Warrington)
Bolton (Wigan)
Murphy, A (St. Helens) 1t
Barton, J (Wigan)
Sayer (Wigan)
McTigue (Wigan)
Huddart (St. Helens)
Edgar (Workington)
Turner (Wakefield)

1961 New Zealand
Bradford: 21 Oct
Won 23-10
Fraser (Warrington)
Boston (Wigan)
Ashton (Wigan) 1t
Fox, N (Wakefield) 4g
Sullivan, M (St. Helens) 2t
Bolton (Wigan) 1t
Murphy, A (St. Helens)
Terry (St. Helens)
Dagnall (St. Helens)
McTigue (Wigan)
Huddart (St. Helens)
Whiteley (Hull)
Evans, R (Wigan) 1t

1961 New Zealand
Swinton: 4 Nov
Won 35-19
Fraser (Warrington) 1t
Boston (Wigan)
Ashton (Wigan) 1t
Fox, N (Wakefield) 7g
Sullivan, M (St. Helens) 2t
Bolton (Wigan)
Murphy, A (St. Helens) 1t
Herbert (Workington) 1t
Dagnall (St. Helens) 1t
McTigue (Wigan)
Huddart (St. Helens)
Whiteley (Hull)
Evans, R (Wigan)

1962 France
Wigan: 17 Feb
Lost 15-20
Round (Wakefield)
Boston (Wigan)
Ashton (Wigan) 1t
Fox, N (Wakefield) 3g
Sullivan, M (St. Helens) 1t
Bolton (Wigan)
Murphy, A (St. Helens)
Terry (Leeds)
Simms (Leeds)
Dixon, M (Featherstone)
Huddart (St. Helens) 1t
Clawson (Featherstone)
Whiteley (Hull)

1962 France
Perpignan: 11 March
Lost 13-23
Round (Wakefield)
Boston (Wigan)
Ashton (Wigan) 1t
Fox, N (Wakefield) 2g
Sullivan, M (St. Helens) 1t
Bolton (Wigan)
Pitchford, F (Oldham)
Herbert (Workington) 1t
Sayer (Wigan)
McTigue (Wigan)
Huddart (St. Helens)
Clawson (Featherstone)
Evans, R (Wigan)

1962 Australia
Sydney: 9 June
Won 31-12
Round (Wakefield)
Boston (Wigan) 1t
Ashton (Wigan) 2t
Fox, N (Wakefield) 5g
Sullivan, M (St. Helens) 2t
Bolton (Wigan)
Murphy, A (St. Helens)
Herbert (Workington)
Sayer (Wigan)
McTigue (Wigan)
Huddart (St. Helens) 1t
Edgar (Workington)
Turner (Wakefield) 1t

1962 Australia
Brisbane: 30 June
Won 17-10
Round (Wakefield)
Boston (Wigan) 2t
Ashton (Wigan) 1g
Fox, N (Wakefield) 3g
Sullivan, M (St. Helens)
Poynton (Wakefield)
Murphy, A (St. Helens) 1t
Herbert (Workington)
Sayer (Wigan)
McTigue (Wigan)
Huddart (St. Helens)
Edgar (Workington)
Gilfedder (Warrington)

1962 Australia
Sydney: 14 July
Lost 17-18
Round (Wakefield)
Boston (Wigan)
Ashton (Wigan) 1t
Fox, N (Wakefield) 4g,1t
Sullivan, M (St. Helens)
Poynton (Wakefield)
Murphy, A (St. Helens) 1t
Herbert (Workington)
Sayer (Wigan)
McTigue (Wigan)
Huddart (St. Helens)
Edgar (Workington)
Turner (Wakefield)

1962 New Zealand
Auckland: 28 July
Lost 0-19
Round (Wakefield)
Southward (Workington)
Gilfedder (Warrington)
Fox, N (Wakefield)
Carlton (Wigan)
Bolton (Wigan)
Sullivan (St. Helens)
Herbert (Workington)
Sayer (Wigan)
McTigue (Wigan)
Huddart (St. Helens)
Evans, R (Wigan)
Turner (Wakefield)

1962 New Zealand
Auckland: 11 Aug
Lost 8-27
Round (Wakefield)
Boston (Wigan)
Gilfedder (Warrington) 1g
Fox, N (Wakefield) 1t
Small (Castleford) 1t
Bolton (Wigan)
Poynton (Wakefield)
Wilkinson (Wakefield)
Shaw, J (Halifax)
McTigue (Wigan)
Huddart (St. Helens)
Edgar (Workington)
Turner (Wakefield)

1962 France
Perpignan: 2 Dec
Lost 12-17
Gowers (Swinton)
Burgess, W (Barrow)
Ashton (Wigan) 1t
Fox, N (Wakefield) 3g,1t
Sullivan, M (St. Helens)
Myler (Widnes)
Smales (Huddersfield)
Drake, W (Hull)
Flanagan (Hull KR)
Martin (Workington)
Gilfedder (Warrington)
Bowman, K (Huddersfield)
Turner (Wakefield)

1963 France
Wigan: 3 April
Won 42-4
Gowers (Swinton)
Boston (Wigan) 1t
Ashton (Wigan) 1t
Fox, N (Wakefield) 9g,1t
Stopford (Swinton) 2t
Bolton (Wigan) 1t
Smales (Huddersfield) 2t
Robinson, W (Leigh)
Flanagan (Hull KR)
McTigue (Wigan)
Morgan, R (Swinton)
Bowman, K (Huddersfield)
Gilfedder (Warrington)

1963 Australia
Wembley: 16 Oct
Lost 2-28
Gowers (Swinton)
Burgess, W (Barrow)
Ashton (Wigan)
Fox, N (Wakefield) 1g
Field, N (Batley)
Bolton (Wigan)
Murphy, A (St. Helens)
Tembey (St. Helens)
Sayer (Wigan)
Tyson, B (Hull KR)
Measures (Widnes)
Bowman, K (Huddersfield)
Karalius, V (Widnes)

1963 Australia
Swinton: 9 Nov
Lost 12-50
Gowers (Swinton)
Sullivan, M (York)
Ashton (Wigan)
Fox, N (Wakefield) 3g
Stopford (Swinton) 1t
Myler (Widnes)
Murphy, A (St. Helens)
Robinson, W (Leigh)
McIntyre (Oldham)
Watson (St. Helens)
Measures (Widnes) 1t
Morgan, R (Swinton)
Karalius, V (Widnes)

1963 Australia
Leeds: 30 Nov
Won 16-5
Gowers (Swinton)
Smith, G (York) 1t
Holden (Warrington)
Buckley (Swinton)
Stopford (Swinton) 1t
Bolton (Wigan)
Smales (Huddersfield)
Collier (Wigan)
Ward, J (Castleford) 1t
Watson (St. Helens)
Huddart (St. Helens)
Roberts (Halifax)
Fox, D (Featherstone) 1t,2g

1964 France
Perpignan: 8 March
Won 11-5
Gowers (Swinton) 1g
Smith, G (York)
Shelton (Hunslet) 2t
Buckley (Swinton) 1t
Stopford (Swinton)
Hardisty (Castleford)
Smales (Huddersfield)
Hartley, D (Hunslet)
Ward, J (Castleford)
Collier (Widnes)
Bryant (Castleford)
Roberts (Halifax)
Parker (Oldham)

1964 France
Leigh: 18 March
Won 39-0
Ashby (Liverpool C)
Smith, G (York) 1t
Shelton (Hunslet)
Fox, N (Wakefield) 9g,1t
Jordan (Featherstone) 1t
Hardisty (Castleford) 2t
Smales (Huddersfield)
Hartley, D (Hunslet)
Ward, J (Castleford)
Dixon, M (Featherstone) 1t
Bryant (Castleford)
Roberts (Halifax)
Parker (Oldham) 1t

1964 France
Perpignan: 6 Dec
Lost 8-18
Gowers (Swinton) 1g
Jones, B (Wakefield) 1t
Myler (Widnes)
Gemmell (Leeds)
Stopford (Swinton)
Hardisty (Castleford) 1t
Murphy, A (St. Helens)
Tembey (St. Helens)
Dagnall (St. Helens)
Warlow (St. Helens)
Holliday (Whitehaven)
Gunney (Hunslet)
Poole (Hull KR)

1965 France
Swinton: 23 Jan
Won 17-7
Ashby (Wigan)
Jones, B (Wakefield) 1t
Myler (Widnes)
Fox, N (Wakefield) 7g
Stopford (Swinton)
Hardisty (Castleford)
Murphy, A (St. Helens)
Roberts (Halifax)
Dagnall (St. Helens)
Tyson, B (Hull KR)
Holliday (Hull KR)
Gunney (Hunslet)
Walton (Castleford)

1965 New Zealand
Swinton: 25 Sep
Won 7-2
Gowers (Swinton)
Wriglesworth (Leeds)
Myler (Widnes)
Shelton (Hunslet)
Senior (Huddersfield)
Kitchin (Whitehaven)
Smales (Bradford)
Gardiner (Wigan)
Kemel (Widnes)
Roberts (Halifax)
Holliday (Hull KR) 2g
Hicks (St. Helens)
Renilson (Halifax) 1t

1965 New Zealand
Bradford: 23 Oct
Won 15-9
Charlton (Workington)
Burgess, W (Barrow) 1t
Shelton (Hunslet) 1t
Buckley (Swinton)
Stopford (Swinton) 1t
Hardisty (Castleford)
Smales (Bradford)
Roberts (Halifax)
Kemel (Widnes)
Edgar (Workington)
Holliday (Hull KR) 3g
Ramsey (Hunslet)
Rae (Bradford)

1965 New Zealand
Wigan: 6 Nov
Drew 9-9
Gowers (Swinton) 3g
Burgess, W (Barrow) 1t
Shelton (Hunslet)
Lewis (Leigh)
Stopford (Swinton)
Murphy, A (St. Helens)
Smales (Bradford)
Roberts (Halifax)
Clarke (Wigan)
Eyre, K (Hunslet)
Holliday (Hull KR)
Ramsey (Hunslet)
Robinson, D (Swinton)

1966 France
Perpignan: 16 Jan
Lost 13-18
Gowers (Swinton)
Jones, B (Wakefield) 1t
Shelton (Hunslet)
Fox, N (Wakefield) 2g
Stopford (Swinton) 1t
Hill, C (Wigan)
Murphy, A (St. Helens) 1t
Roberts (Halifax)
Clarke (Wigan)
Watson (St. Helens)
Holliday (Hull KR)
Mantle (St. Helens)
Robinson, D (Swinton)

1966 France
Wigan: 5 March
Lost 4-8
Gowers (Swinton) 2g
Burgess, W (Barrow)
Shelton (Hunslet)
Buckley (Swinton)
Stopford (Swinton)
Millward (Castleford)
Murphy, A (St. Helens)
Bott (Oldham)
Prior (Hunslet)
Watson (St. Helens)
Ramsey (Hunslet)
Mantle (St. Helens)
Robinson, D (Swinton)
Sub: Holliday (Hull KR)

1966 Australia
Sydney: 25 June
Won 17-13
Keegan (Hull) 3g
Burgess, W (Barrow) 1t
Brooke (Bradford)
Buckley (Swinton)
Stopford (Swinton)
Hardisty (Castleford) 1t
Bishop (St. Helens) 1g
Edgar (Workington)
Flanagan (Hull KR)
Watson (St. Helens) 1t
Bryant (Castleford)
Mantle (St. Helens)
Robinson, D (Swinton)

1966 Australia
Brisbane: 16 July
Lost 4-6
Keegan (Hull) 2g
Burgess, W (Barrow)
Brooke (Bradford)
Myler (Widnes)
Wriglesworth (Leeds)
Hardisty (Castleford)
Bishop (St. Helens)
Edgar (Workington)
Flanagan (Hull KR)
Watson (St. Helens)
Ramsey (Hunslet)
Mantle (St. Helens)
Robinson, D (Swinton)

1966 Australia
Sydney: 23 July
Lost 14-19
Gowers (Swinton) 4g
Burgess, W (Barrow)
Brooke (Bradford)
Buckley (Swinton)
Wriglesworth (Leeds)
Hardisty (Castleford) 2t
Bishop (St. Helens)
Edgar (Workington)
Flanagan (Hull KR)
Watson (St. Helens)
Ramsey (Hunslet)
Mantle (St. Helens)
Robinson, D (Swinton)
Sub: Bryant (Castleford)

1966 New Zealand
Auckland: 6 Aug
Won 25-8
Gowers (Swinton) 5g
Burgess, W (Barrow) 1t
Brooke (Bradford) 1t
Buckley (Swinton)
Wriglesworth (Leeds)
Hardisty (Castleford)
Bishop (St. Helens)
Roberts (Halifax)
Clarke (Wigan) 1t
Watson (St. Helens) 1t
Ramsey (Hunslet)
Poole (Leeds)
Robinson, D (Swinton)
Sub: Myler (Widnes) 1t

1966 New Zealand
Auckland: 20 Aug
Won 22-14
Gowers (Swinton) 5g
Burgess, W (Barrow) 1t
Brooke (Bradford) 2t
Myler (Widnes)
Wriglesworth (Leeds)
Aspinall (Warrington) 1t
Bishop (St. Helens)
Roberts (Halifax)
Flanagan (Hull KR)
Watson (St. Helens)
Ramsey (Hunslet)
Poole (Leeds)
Robinson, D (Swinton)
Sub: Fogerty (Halifax)

1967 France
Carcassonne: 22 Jan
Won 16-13
Keegan (Hull)
Hare (Widnes)
Myler (Widnes)
Fox, N (Wakefield) 2g
Sullivan, C (Hull) 2t
Hardisty (Castleford) 2t
Hepworth (Castleford)
Harrison, M (Hull)
Clarke (Wigan)
Tyson, B (Hull KR)
Irving (Oldham)
Fogerty (Wigan)
Robinson, D (Swinton)

1967 France
Wigan: 4 March
Lost 13-23
Keegan (Hull) 1t
Burgess, W (Barrow)
Myler (Widnes)
Fox, N (Wakefield) 2g
Senior (Huddersfield)
Hardisty (Castleford) 1t
Hepworth (Castleford)
Harrison, M (Hull)
Close (Huddersfield)
Watson (St. Helens)
Irving (Oldham)
Bryant (Castleford)
Robinson, D (Swinton) 1t

1967 Australia
Leeds: 21 Oct
Won 16-11
Keegan (Hull)
Young, C (Hull KR) 1t
Brooke (Wakefield)
Price, M (Rochdale)
Burgess (Barrow)
Millward (Hull KR) 3g,1t
Bishop (St. Helens) 1g
Holliday (Hull KR) 1g
Flanagan (Hull KR)
Watson (St. Helens)
Irving (Oldham)
Mantle (St. Helens)
Robinson, D (Swinton)

1967 Australia
White City (London): 3 Nov
Lost 11-17
Keegan (Hull)
Young, C (Hull KR)
Brooke (Wakefield)
Fox, N (Wakefield) 3g
Francis, W (Wigan)
Millward (Hull KR)
Bishop (St. Helens) 1t,1g
Holliday (Hull KR)
Flanagan (Hull KR)
Watson (St. Helens)
Irving (Oldham)
Mantle (St. Helens)
Foster, F (Hull KR)

1967 Australia
Swinton: 9 Dec
Lost 3-11
Keegan (Hull)
Young, C (Hull KR)
Brooke (Wakefield)
Price, M (Rochdale) 1t
Jordan (Featherstone)
Millward (Hull KR)
Bishop (St. Helens)
Holliday (Hull KR)
Flanagan (Hull KR)
Watson (St. Helens)
Irving (Oldham)
Valentine, R (Huddersfield)
Robinson, D (Swinton)
Sub: Burwell (Hull KR)
Renilson (Halifax)

1968 France
Paris: 11 Feb
Won 22-13
Risman, B (Leeds) 5g,2t
Young, C (Hull KR)
Brooke (Wakefield)
Fox, N (Wakefield)
Burwell (Hull KR) 1t
Millward (Hull KR) 1t
Bishop (St. Helens)
Clark, M (Leeds)
Flanagan (Hull KR)
Watson (St. Helens)
French (Widnes)
Morgan, A (Featherstone)
Renilson (Halifax)
Sub: Edwards, D (Castleford)

1968 France
Bradford: 2 March
Won 19-8
Risman, B (Leeds) 2g
Young, C (Hull KR) 1t
Brooke (Wakefield)
Fox, N (Wakefield)
Burwell (Hull KR) 2t
Millward (Hull KR) 1t
Bishop (St. Helens)
Clark, M (Leeds)
Flanagan (Hull KR)
Watson (St. Helens)
French (Widnes)
Morgan, A (Featherstone) 1t
Renilson (Halifax)

1968 Australia (WC)
Sydney: 25 May
Lost 10-25
Risman, B (Leeds) 2g
Brooke (Wakefield) 1t
Burwell (Hull KR)
Shoebottom (Leeds)
Sullivan, C (Hull) 1t
Millward (Hull KR)
Bishop (St. Helens)
Clark, M (Leeds)
Ashcroft, K (Leigh)
Watson (St. Helens)
French (Widnes)
Haigh (Wakefield)
Renilson (Halifax)

1968 France (WC)
Auckland: 2 June
Lost 2-7
Risman, B (Leeds) 1g
Sullivan, C (Hull)
Brooke (Wakefield)
Burwell (Hull KR)
Atkinson, J (Leeds)
Millward (Hull KR)
Bishop (St. Helens)
Clark, M (Leeds)
Flanagan (Hull KR)
Watson (St. Helens)
Morgan, A (Featherstone)
Haigh (Wakefield)
Renilson (Halifax)
Sub: Warlow (St. Helens)

1968 New Zealand (WC)
Sydney: 8 June
Won 38-14
Risman, B (Leeds) 7g
Sullivan, C (Hull) 3t
Brooke (Wakefield) 1t
Burwell (Hull KR) 2t
Atkinson, J (Leeds)
Millward (Hull KR)
Bishop (St. Helens)
Clark, M (Leeds)
Flanagan (Hull KR)
Warlow (St. Helens)
French (Widnes)
Morgan, A (Featherstone) 1t
Renilson (Halifax)
Sub: Shoebottom (Leeds) 1t
Watson (St. Helens)

1968 France
St. Helens: 30 Nov
Won 34-10
Keegan (Hull)
Burgess, W (Barrow) 3t
Fox, N (Wakefield) 5g
Gemmell (Hull) 2t
Burwell (Hull KR) 1t
Davies, W (Swinton)
Bishop (St. Helens)
Hartley, D (Castleford)
Ashcroft, K (Leigh) 1t
Warlow (St. Helens)
Dixon, C (Halifax) 1t
Parr (Warrington)
Renilson (Halifax)

1969 France
Toulouse: 2 Feb
Lost 9-13
Keegan (Hull)
Burgess, W (Salford)
Fox, N (Wakefield) 3g
Gemmell (Hull)
Burwell (Hull KR)
Shoebottom (Leeds)
Bishop (St. Helens)
Hartley, D (Castleford)
Ashcroft, K (Leigh)
Watson (St. Helens)
Dixon, C (Salford) 1t
Mantle (St. Helens)
Batten, R (Leeds)

1970 Australia
Brisbane: 6 June
Lost 15-37
Price, T (Bradford) 3g
Sullivan, C (Hull)
Myler (St. Helens)
Shoebottom (Leeds)
Atkinson, J (Leeds)
Hardisty (Castleford)
Hepworth (Castleford)
Chisnall, D (Leigh)
Flanagan (Hull KR) 1t
Watson (St. Helens) 1t
Laughton (Wigan) 1t
Robinson, D (Wigan)
Reilly (Castleford)
Sub: Irving (Oldham)

1970 Australia
Sydney: 20 June
Won 28-7
Edwards, D (Castleford)
Smith, A (Leeds)
Hynes (Leeds) 1g
Myler (St. Helens)
Atkinson, J (Leeds) 1t
Millward (Hull KR) 7g,2t
Hepworth (Castleford)
Hartley, D (Castleford)
Fisher (Bradford) 1t
Watson (St. Helens)
Laughton (Wigan)
Thompson, J (Featherstone)
Reilly (Castleford)
Sub: Shoebottom (Leeds)

1970 Australia
Sydney: 4 July
Won 21-17
Shoebottom (Leeds)
Smith, A (Leeds)
Hynes (Leeds) 1t
Myler (St. Helens)
Atkinson, J (Leeds) 2t
Millward (Hull KR) 3g,1t
Hepworth (Castleford)
Hartley, D (Castleford) 1t
Fisher (Bradford)
Watson (St. Helens)
Laughton (Wigan)
Thompson, J (Featherstone)
Reilly (Castleford)

1970 New Zealand
Auckland: 11 July
Won 19-15
Shoebottom (Leeds)
Smith, A (Leeds)
Hynes (Leeds) 2g,1t
Myler (St. Helens)
Atkinson, J (Leeds) 1t
Millward (Hull KR) 1t
Seabourne (Leeds)
Hartley, D (Castleford)
Fisher (Bradford)
Watson (St. Helens)
Laughton (Wigan) 2t
Thompson, J (Featherstone)
Reilly (Castleford)

1970 New Zealand
Christchurch: 19 July
Won 23-9
Dutton (Widnes) 4g
Smith, A (Leeds)
Hynes (Leeds)
Myler (St. Helens) 1t
Atkinson, J (Leeds)
Millward (Hull KR) 2t
Hepworth (Castleford)
Hartley, D (Castleford)
Fisher (Bradford)
Watson (St. Helens)
Laughton (Wigan) 1t
Thompson, J (Featherstone)
Reilly (Castleford) 1t

1970 New Zealand
Auckland: 25 July
Won 33-16
Dutton (Widnes) 5g
Smith, A (Leeds) 1t
Hesketh (Salford) 1t
Myler (St. Helens)
Atkinson, J (Leeds)
Millward (Hull KR) 1g
Hepworth (Castleford) 1t
Watson (St. Helens) 1t
Fisher (Bradford)
Ward, J (Salford)
Irving (Oldham)
Lowe, P (Hull KR) 2t
Reilly (Castleford)
Sub: Hynes (Leeds) 1t

1970 Australia (WC)
Leeds: 24 Oct
Won 11-4
Dutton (Widnes) 3g
Smith, A (Leeds)
Hynes (Leeds) 1t,1g
Myler (St. Helens)
Atkinson, J (Leeds)
Shoebottom (Leeds)
Hepworth (Castleford)
Hartley, D (Castleford)
Fisher (Bradford)
Watson (St. Helens)
Laughton (Wigan)
Thompson, J (Featherstone)
Reilly (Castleford)

1970 France (WC)
Castleford: 28 Oct
Won 6-0
Dutton (Widnes) 3g
Jones, K (Wigan)
Hynes (Leeds)
Myler (St. Helens)
Atkinson, J (Leeds)
Shoebottom (Leeds)
Hepworth (Castleford)
Hartley, D (Castleford)
Ashcroft, K (Leigh)
Watson (St. Helens)
Laughton (Wigan)
Thompson, J (Featherstone)
Reilly (Castleford)

1970 New Zealand (WC)
Swinton: 31 Oct
Won 27-17
Dutton (Widnes) 6g
Jones, K (Wigan)
Hynes (Leeds) 1t
Hesketh (Salford) 1t
Atkinson, J (Leeds) 1t
Shoebottom (Leeds)
Hepworth (Castleford)
Chisnall, D (Leigh)
Ashcroft, K (Leigh)
Watson (St. Helens) 1t
Haigh (Leeds)
Thompson, J (Featherstone)
Laughton (Wigan) 1t
Sub: Charlton (Salford)

1970 Australia (WC)
Leeds: 7 Nov
Lost 7-12
Dutton (Widnes) 1g
Smith, A (Leeds)
Hynes (Leeds) 1g
Myler (St. Helens)
Atkinson, J (Leeds) 1t
Shoebottom (Leeds)
Hepworth (Castleford)
Hartley, D (Castleford)
Fisher (Leeds)
Watson (St. Helens)
Laughton (Wigan)
Thompson, J (Featherstone)
Reilly (Castleford)
Sub: Hesketh (Salford)
Haigh (Leeds)

1971 France
Toulouse: 7 Feb
Lost 8-16
Whitehead (Warrington) 1g
Smith, A (Leeds) 1t
Hynes (Leeds)
Benyon (St. Helens)
Atkinson, J (Leeds)
Hill, D (Wigan)
Shoebottom (Leeds)
Jeanes (Wakefield) 1t
Fisher (Leeds)
Warlow (Widnes)
Mantle (St. Helens)
Haigh (Leeds)
Laughton (Wigan)
Sub: Hesketh (Salford)
Thompson, J (Featherstone)

1971 France
St. Helens: 17 March
Won 24-2
Whitehead (Warrington) 1t,3g
Smith, A (Leeds) 1t
Hesketh (Salford)
Benyon (St. Helens) 1t
Atkinson, J (Leeds)
Millward (Hull KR) 2t
Nash (Featherstone)
Warlow (Widnes)
Fisher (Leeds)
Watson (St. Helens)
Mantle (St. Helens)
Thompson, J (Featherstone) 1t
Laughton (Wigan)
Sub: Watkins, D (Salford)
Coulman (Salford)

1971 New Zealand
Salford: 25 Sep
Lost 13-18
Whitehead (Warrington) 2g
Jones, L (St. Helens)
Benyon (St. Helens) 1t
Hesketh (Salford) 1t
Sullivan, C (Hull)
Millward (Hull KR)
Nash (Featherstone)
Warlow (Widnes)
Karalius, A (St. Helens)
Jeanes (Wakefield)
Ashurst (Wigan) 1t
Coulman (Salford)
Mantle (St. Helens)
Sub: Edwards, D (Castleford)

1971 New Zealand
Castleford: 16 Oct
Lost 14-17
Edwards, D (Castleford)
Sullivan, C (Hull) 1t
Watkins, D (Salford) 1g
Hesketh (Salford)
Walsh, Joe (Leigh) 1t
Millward (Hull KR) 1t
Murphy, A (Warrington)
Harrison, M (Hull)
Karalius, A (St. Helens)
Coulman (Salford) 1t
Dixon, C (Salford)
Mantle (St. Helens)
Haigh (Leeds)
Sub: Benyon (St. Helens)
Stephenson, M (Dewsbury)

1971 New Zealand
Leeds: 6 Nov
Won 12-3
Edwards, D (Castleford)
Sullivan, C (Hull)
Hesketh (Salford)
Holmes (Leeds) 2g,2dg
Atkinson, J (Leeds) 2t
Millward (Hull KR)
Loxton (Huddersfield)
Harrison, M (Hull)
Karalius, A (St. Helens)
Jeanes (Wakefield)
Irving (Oldham)
Nicholls (Widnes)
Halmshaw (Halifax)
Sub: O'Neill, D (Widnes)

1972 France
Toulouse: 6 Feb
Won 10-9
Charlton (Salford)
Sullivan, C (Hull) 1t
Holmes (Leeds) 2g
Benyon (St. Helens) 1t
Atkinson, J (Leeds)
Kelly (St. Helens)
Nash (Featherstone)
Harrison, M (Hull)
Karalius, A (St. Helens)
Jeanes (Wakefield)
Ashurst (Wigan)
Lowe, P (Hull KR)
Nicholls (Widnes)

1972 France
Bradford: 12 March
Won 45-10
Charlton (Salford) 1t
Sullivan, C (Hull) 1t
Holmes (Leeds) 1t,6g
Benyon (St. Helens) 1t
Atkinson, J (Leeds) 1t
Kelly (St. Helens)
Nash (Featherstone)
Harrison, M (Hull)
Stephenson, M (Dewsbury) 1t
Jeanes (Wakefield) 1t
Ashurst (Wigan) 2t
Lowe, P (Hull KR) 1t
Nicholls (Widnes)
Sub: Walsh, John (St. Helens) 1t
Irving (Oldham)

1972 Australia (WC)
Perpignan: 29 Oct
Won 27-21
Charlton (Salford)
Sullivan, C (Hull) 1t
Hesketh (Salford)
Walsh, John (St. Helens)
Atkinson, J (Leeds) 1t
O'Neill, D (Widnes) 1t
Nash (Featherstone)
Clawson (Leeds) 6g
Stephenson, M (Dewsbury) 1t
Jeanes (Leeds)
Lockwood (Castleford)
Lowe, P (Hull KR) 1t
Nicholls (Widnes)
Sub: Holmes (Leeds)

1972 France (WC)
Grenoble: 1 Nov
Won 13-4
Charlton (Salford)
Sullivan, C (Hull) 1t
Hesketh (Salford)
Walsh, John (St. Helens)
Atkinson, J (Leeds)
O'Neill, D (Widnes)
Nash (Featherstone)
Clawson (Leeds) 2g
Stephenson, M (Dewsbury)
Lockwood, B (Castleford)
Dixon, C (Salford)
Lowe, P (Hull KR) 2t
Nicholls (Widnes)

1972 New Zealand (WC)
Pau: 4 Nov
Won 53-19
Charlton (Salford) 1t
Sullivan, C (Hull) 1t
Hesketh (Salford) 1t
Walsh, John (St. Helens)
Atkinson, J (Leeds) 2t
Holmes (Leeds) 10g,2t
Nash (Featherstone) 1t
Jeanes (Leeds) 1t
Stephenson, M (Dewsbury) 1t
Lockwood (Castleford)
Irving (Oldham)
Lowe, P (Hull KR)
Nicholls (Widnes) 1t
Sub: Redfearn, D (Bradford)
Karalius, A (St. Helens)

1972 Australia (WC)
Lyon: 11 Nov
Drew 10-10
Charlton (Salford)
Sullivan, C (Hull) 1t
Hesketh (Salford)
Walsh, John (St. Helens)
Atkinson, J (Leeds)
Holmes (Leeds)
Nash (Featherstone)
Clawson (Leeds) 2g
Stephenson, M (Dewsbury) 1t
Jeanes (Leeds)
Lockwood, B (Castleford)
Lowe, P (Hull KR)
Nicholls (Widnes)
Sub: Irving (Oldham)

1973 Australia
Wembley: 3 Nov
Won 21-12
Charlton (Salford)
Sullivan (Hull)
Hynes (Leeds)
Hesketh (Salford)
Atkinson, J (Leeds)
Topliss (Wakefield)
Nash (Featherstone) 1dg
Clawson (Oldham) 4g
Clarke (Wigan) 1t
Lockwood (Castleford) 1t
Nicholls (St. Helens)
Lowe, P (Hull KR) 2t
Batten (Leeds)

1973 Australia
Leeds: 24 Nov
Lost 6-14
Charlton (Salford)
Sullivan (Hull)
Hynes (Leeds)
Hesketh (Salford)
Atkinson, J (Leeds)
Topliss (Wakefield)
Nash (Featherstone)
Clawson (Oldham) 3g
Clarke (Wigan)
Lockwood (Castleford)
Mantle (St. Helens)
Lowe, P (Hull KR)
Batten, R (Leeds)
Sub: Eckersley (St. Helens)
Dixon, C (Salford)

1973 Australia
Warrington: 1 Dec
Lost 5-15
Charlton (Salford)
Smith, A (Leeds)
Hynes (Leeds)
Hesketh (Salford)
Sullivan, C (Hull)
Eckersley (St. Helens)
Millward (Hull KR) 1t,1g
Clawson (Oldham)
Clarke (Wigan)
Harrison, M (Hull)
Nicholls (St. Helens)
Lowe, P (Hull KR)
Laughton (Widnes)
Sub: Watkins, D (Salford)
Dixon, C (Salford)

1974 France
Grenoble: 20 Jan
Won 24-5
Charlton (Salford)
Fielding (Salford) 3t
Willicombe (Halifax) 1t
Hesketh (Salford)
Redfearn, D (Bradford)
Gill, K (Salford) 1t
Bates, A (Dewsbury)
Clawson (Oldham) 3g
Bridges (Featherstone)
Lockwood (Castleford)
Dixon, C (Salford)
Nicholls (St. Helens)
Laughton (Widnes) 1t
Sub: Watkins, D (Salford)
Gray (Wigan)

1974 France
Wigan: 17 Feb
Won 29-0
Charlton (Salford) 2t
Fielding (Salford)
Willicombe (Wigan) 1t
Hesketh (Salford)
Redfearn, D (Bradford) 2t
Gill, K (Salford)
Bates, A (Dewsbury)
Clawson (Oldham) 2g
Bridges (Featherstone)
Fogerty (Rochdale)
Dixon, C (Salford)
Nicholls (St. Helens)
Laughton (Widnes) 1t
Sub: Watkins, D (Salford) 1g
Gray (Wigan) 1t,1g

1974 Australia
Brisbane: 15 June
Lost 6-12
Charlton (Salford)
Redfearn, D (Bradford)
Watkins, D (Salford) 1g
Hesketh (Salford)
Bevan, J (Warrington)
Millward (Hull KR)
Nash (Featherstone)
Clawson (Oldham) 2g
Bridges (Featherstone)
Mills (Widnes)
Dixon, C (Salford)
Thompson, J (Featherstone)
Nicholls (St. Helens)
Sub: Eckersley (St. Helens)
Gray (Wigan)

1974 Australia
Sydney: 6 July
Won 16-11
Charlton (Salford)
Dyl (Leeds)
Eckersley (St. Helens)
Hesketh (Salford)
Millward (Hull KR)
Gill, K (Salford) 1t
Nash (Featherstone)
Mills (Widnes)
Gray (Wigan) 3g,1dg
Thompson, J (Featherstone)
Dixon, C (Salford) 1t
Chisnall, E (St. Helens) 1t
Nicholls (St. Helens)
Sub: Norton (Castleford)

1974 Australia
Sydney: 20 July
Lost 18-22
Charlton (Salford)
Richards (Salford) 1t
Dyl (Leeds) 1t
Hesketh (Salford)
Bevan, J (Warrington)
Gill, K (Salford)
Nash (Featherstone)
Clawson (Oldham)
Gray (Wigan) 6g
Thompson, J (Featherstone)
Dixon, C (Salford)
Chisnall, E (St. Helens)
Nicholls (St. Helens)
Sub: Millward (Hull KR)
Rose, P (Hull KR)

1974 New Zealand
Auckland: 27 July
Lost 8-13
Charlton (Salford)
Redfearn, D (Bradford)
Dyl (Leeds)
Hesketh (Salford)
Bevan, J (Warrington) 1t
Gill, K (Salford)
Nash (Featherstone) 1t
Clawson (Oldham) 1g
Gray (Wigan)
Thompson, J (Featherstone)
Dixon, C (Salford)
Norton (Castleford)
Nicholls (St. Helens)
Sub: Ashcroft (Warrington)

1974 New Zealand
Christchurch: 4 Aug
Won 17-8
Charlton (Salford)
Redfearn, D (Bradford) 1t
Dyl (Leeds) 1t
Dixon, C (Salford)
Richards (Salford)
Hesketh (Salford) 1t
Nash (Featherstone)
Mills (Widnes)
Gray (Wigan) 4g
Thompson, J (Featherstone)
Chisnall, E (St. Helens)
Norton (Castleford)
Nicholls (St. Helens)
Sub: Bates, A (Dewsbury)

1974 New Zealand
Auckland: 10 Aug
Won 20-0
Charlton (Salford)
Redfearn, D (Bradford)
Willicombe (Wigan)
Dyl (Leeds) 1t
Bevan, J (Warrington) 2t
Hesketh (Salford) 1t
Nash (Featherstone)
Clawson (Oldham)
Gray (Wigan) 4g
Thompson, J (Featherstone)
Chisnall, E (St. Helens)
Dixon, C (Salford)
Nicholls (St. Helens)
Sub: Bates, A (Dewsbury)
Ramsey (Bradford)

1977 France (WC)
Auckland: 5 June
Won 23-4
Fairbairn (Wigan) 7g
Fielding (Salford)
Holmes (Leeds)
Dyl (Leeds) 1t
Wright, S (Widnes) 1t
Millward (Hull KR) 1t
Nash (Salford)
Thompson, J (Featherstone)
Ward, D (Leeds)
Pitchford, S (Leeds)
Bowman, E (Workington)
Nicholls (St. Helens)
Hogan (Barrow)
Sub: Gill, K (Salford)
Casey (Hull KR)

1977 New Zealand (WC)
Christchurch: 12 June
Won 30-12
Fairbairn (Wigan) 6g
Wright, S (Widnes) 2t
Holmes (Leeds)
Dyl (Leeds)
Francis, W (Wigan)
Millward (Hull KR) 1t
Nash (Salford)
Thompson, J (Featherstone)
Ward, D (Leeds)
Pitchford, S (Leeds)
Bowman, E (Workington) 1t
Nicholls (St. Helens) 1t
Hogan (Barrow) 1t
Sub: Casey (Hull KR)

1977 Australia (WC)
Brisbane: 18 June
Lost 5-19
Fairbairn (Wigan) 1g
Wright, S (Widnes)
Francis, W (Wigan)
Dyl (Leeds)
Fielding (Salford)
Millward (Hull KR) 1t
Nash (Salford)
Thompson, J (Featherstone)
Ward, D (Leeds)
Pitchford, S (Leeds)
Bowman, E (Workington)
Nicholls (St. Helens)
Hogan (Barrow)
Sub: Holmes (Leeds)
Smith, P (Featherstone)

1977 Australia (WC)
Sydney: 25 June
Lost 12-13
Fairbairn (Wigan) 3g
Wright, S (Widnes)
Holmes (Leeds)
Dyl (Leeds)
Francis, W (Wigan)
Millward (Hull KR)
Nash (Salford)
Thompson, J (Featherstone)
Elwell (Widnes)
Pitchford, S (Leeds) 1t
Bowman, E (Workington)
Casey (Hull KR)
Hogan (Barrow)
Sub: Gill, K (Salford) 1t
Smith, P (Featherstone)

1978 Australia
Wigan: 21 Oct
Lost 9-15
Fairbairn (Wigan) 3g
Wright, S (Widnes)
Hughes (Widnes)
Cunningham (St. Helens)
Bevan, J (Warrington) 1t
Millward (Hull KR)
Nash (Salford)
Thompson, J (Bradford)
Ward, D (Leeds)
Rose, P (Hull KR)
Nicholls (St. Helens)
Casey (Hull KR)
Norton (Hull)
Sub: Holmes (Leeds)
Hogan (Barrow)

1978 Australia
Bradford: 5 Nov
Won 18-14
Fairbairn (Wigan) 6g
Wright, S (Widnes) 2t
Joyner (Castleford)
Dyl (Leeds)
Atkinson, J (Leeds)
Millward (Hull KR)
Nash (Salford)
Mills (Widnes)
Fisher (Bradford)
Lockwood (Hull KR)
Nicholls (St. Helens)
Lowe, P (Hull KR)
Norton (Hull)
Sub: Holmes (Leeds)
Rose, P (Hull KR)

1978 Australia
Leeds: 18 Nov
Lost 6-23
Fairbairn (Wigan)
Wright, S (Widnes)
Joyner (Castleford)
Bevan, J (Warrington) 1t
Atkinson, J (Leeds)
Millward (Hull KR) 1t
Nash (Salford)
Mills (Widnes)
Fisher (Bradford)
Farrar (Hull)
Nicholls (St. Helens)
Lowe, P (Hull KR)
Norton (Hull)
Sub: Holmes (Leeds)
Rose, P (Hull KR)

1979 Australia
Brisbane: 16 June
Lost 0-35
Woods, J (Leigh)
Barends (Bradford)
Joyner (Castleford)
Hughes (Widnes)
Mathias (St. Helens)
Holmes (Leeds)
Stephens (Castleford)
Mills (Widnes)
Ward, D (Leeds)
Skerrett (Wakefield)
Nicholls (St. Helens)
Laughton (Widnes)
Norton (Hull)
Sub: Evans, S (Featherstone)
Hogan (Hull KR)

1979 Australia
Sydney: 30 June
Lost 16-24
Fairbairn (Wigan)
Barends (Bradford)
Joyner (Castleford) 1t
Woods, J (Leigh) 5g
Hughes (Widnes) 1t
Holmes (Leeds)
Stephens (Castleford)
Nicholls (St. Helens)
Ward, D (Leeds)
Skerrett (Wakefield)
Casey (Bradford)
Grayshon (Bradford)
Adams, M (Widnes)
Sub: Evans, S (Featherstone)
Watkinson (Hull KR)

1979 Australia
Sydney: 14 July
Lost 2-28
Fairbairn (Wigan) 1g
Evans, S (Featherstone)
Joyner (Castleford)
Woods, J (Leigh)
Hughes (Widnes)
Topliss (Wakefield)
Redfearn, A (Bradford)
Nicholls (St. Helens)
Ward, D (Leeds)
Casey (Bradford)
Hogan (Hull KR)
Grayshon (Bradford)
Norton (Hull)
Sub: Holmes (Leeds)
Adams, M (Widnes)

1979 New Zealand
Auckland: 21 July
Won 16-8
Fairbairn (Wigan) 1t,2g
Evans, S (Featherstone) 1t
Joyner (Castleford)
Smith, M (Hull KR) 1t
Hughes (Widnes) 1t
Holmes (Leeds)
Stephens (Castleford)
Casey (Bradford)
Ward, D (Leeds)
Nicholls (St. Helens)
Hogan (Hull KR)
Grayshon (Bradford)
Adams, M (Widnes)
Sub: Lockwood (Hull KR)

1979 New Zealand
Christchurch: 5 Aug
Won 22-7
Fairbairn (Wigan) 5g
Evans, S (Featherstone) 1t
Joyner (Castleford)
Smith, M (Hull KR)
Hughes (Widnes) 1t
Holmes (Leeds)
Stephens (Castleford)
Nicholls (St. Helens)
Ward, D (Leeds)
Skerrett (Wakefield)
Casey (Bradford) 1t
Grayshon (Bradford) 1t
Adams, M (Widnes)

1979 New Zealand
Auckland: 11 Aug
Lost 11-18
Fairbairn (Wigan) 1g
Evans, S (Featherstone)
Joyner (Castleford)
Smith, M (Hull KR) 1t
Hughes (Widnes) 1t
Holmes (Leeds)
Stephens (Castleford) 1t
Skerrett (Wakefield)
Ward, D (Leeds)
Nicholls (St. Helens)
Casey (Bradford)
Grayshon (Bradford)
Adams, M (Widnes)
Sub: Woods, J (Leigh)
Hogan (Hull KR)

1980 New Zealand
Wigan: 18 Oct
Drew 14-14
Fairbairn (Wigan) 4g
Camilleri (Barrow) 1t
Joyner (Castleford)
Smith, M (Hull KR) 1t
Bentley (Widnes)
Hartley, S (Hull KR)
Dick (Leeds)
Holdstock (Hull KR)
Watkinson (Hull KR)
Skerrett (Hull)
Gorley, L (Widnes)
Grayshon (Bradford)
Casey (Hull KR)
Sub: Pinner (St. Helens)

1980 New Zealand
Bradford: 2 Nov
Lost 8-12
Fairbairn (Wigan) 4g
Drummond (Leigh)
Joyner (Castleford)
Smith, M (Hull KR)
Camilleri (Barrow)
Kelly (Warrington)
Dick (Leeds)
Holdstock (Hull KR)
Elwell (Widnes)
Shaw, G (Widnes)
Casey (Hull KR)
Grayshon (Bradford)
Pinner (St. Helens)
Sub: Evans, S (Featherstone)
Gorley, L (Widnes)

1980 New Zealand
Leeds: 15 Nov
Won 10-2
Burke (Widnes) 2g
Drummond (Leigh) 2t
Joyner (Castleford)
Evans, S (Featherstone)
Atkinson, J (Leeds)
Woods, J (Leigh)
Walker (Whitehaven)
Skerrett (Hull)
Elwell (Widnes)
Casey (Hull KR)
Gorley, P (St. Helens)
Adams, M (Widnes)
Norton (Hull)

1981 France
Hull: 6 Dec
Won 37-0
Fairbairn (Hull KR) 1g
Drummond (Leigh) 2t
Smith, M (Hull KR)
Woods, J (Leigh) 1t, 7g
Gill (Wigan) 3t
Hartley (Hull KR) 1t
Gregory (Widnes)
Grayshon (Bradford N)
Ward, D (Leeds)
Skerrett (Hull)
Gorley, L (Widnes)
Gorley, P (St. Helens)
Norton (Hull)
Sub: Burke (Widnes)
Szymala (Barrow)

1981 France
Marseilles: 20 Dec
Lost 2-19
Burke (Widnes)
Drummond (Leigh)
Smith, M (Hull KR)
Woods, J (Leigh) 1g
Gill (Wigan)
Hartley (Hull KR)
Gregory (Widnes)
Grayshon (Bradford N)
Watkinson (Hull KR)
Skerrett (Hull)
Gorley, L (Widnes)
Szymala (Barrow)
Norton (Hull)
Sub: Gorley, P (St. Helens)

1982 Australia
Hull City FC: 30 Oct
Lost 4-40
Fairbairn (Hull KR)
Drummond (Leigh)
Hughes (Widnes)
Dyl (Leeds)
Evans, S (Hull)
Woods, J (Leigh)
Nash (Salford)
Grayshon (Bradford N)
Ward, D (Leeds)
Skerrett (Hull)
Gorley, L (Widnes)
Crooks (Hull) 2g
Norton (Hull)
Sub: D. Heron (Leeds)

1982 Australia
Wigan: 20 Nov
Lost 6-27
Mumby (Bradford N) 3g
Drummond (Leigh)
Smith, M (Hull KR)
Stephenson, D (Wigan)
Gill (Wigan)
Holmes (Leeds)
Kelly, K (Warrington)
Grayshon (Bradford N)
Dalgreen (Fulham)
Skerrett (Hull)
Eccles (Warrington)
Burton (Hull KR)
Heron, D (Leeds)
Subs: Woods, J (Leigh)
Rathbone (Bradford N)

1982 Australia
Leeds: 28 Nov
Lost 8-32
Fairbairn (Hull KR)
Drummond (Leigh)
Stephenson, D. (Wigan)
Smith, M (Hull KR)
Evans (Hull) 1t
Topliss (Hull)
Gregory (Widnes)
O'Neill, M (Widnes)
Noble (Bradford N)
Rose (Hull)
Smith, P (Featherstone R)
Crooks (Hull) 2g, 1dg
Crane (Hull)
Sub: Courtney (Warrington)

1983 France
Carcassone: 20 Feb
Won 20-5
Burke (Widnes) 1g
Drummond (Leigh)
Joyner (Castleford) 1t
Duane, R (Warrington)
Lydon (Widnes) 1t, 3g
Myler, A (Widnes)
Gregory (Widnes)
O'Neill, M (Widnes)
Noble (Bradford N) lt
Goodway (Oldham) 1t
Casey (Hull KR)
Rathbone (Bradford N)
Flanagan (Oldham)
Subs: Woods, J (Leigh)
Smith, P (Featherstone R)

1983 France
Hull: 6 March
Won 17-5
Mumby (Bradford N) 4g
Drummond (Leigh)
Joyner (Castleford)
Duane, R (Warrington) 1t
Lydon (Widnes)
Myler, A (Widnes)
Gregory (Widnes) 1t
O'Neill, M (Widnes)
Noble (Bradford N)
Goodway (Oldham)
Casey (Hull KR)
Rathbone (Bradford N)
Flanagan (Oldham)
Sub: Smith, P (Featherstone R) 1t

1984 France
Avignon: 29 Jan
Won 12-0
Mumby (Bradford N)
Drummond (Leigh)
Duane, R (Warrington)
Foy, D (Oldham) 1t
Clark (Hull KR)
Lydon (Widnes)
Cairns (Barrow)
Rayne, Keith (Leeds)
Watkinson (Hull KR)
Goodway (Oldham) 1t
Worrall, M (Oldham)
Hobbs, D (Featherstone R)
Hall (Hull KR)
Subs: Hanley (Bradford N)
Crooks (Hull) 2g

1984 France
Leeds: 17 Feb
Won 10-0
Mumby (Bradford N)
Clark (Hull KR)
Joyner (Castleford)
Schofield (Hull)
Basnett (Widnes)
Hanley (Bradford N)
Cairns (Barrow)
Rayne, Keith (Leeds)
Noble (Bradford N)
Ward, K (Castleford)
Jasiewicz (Bradford N)
Hobbs, D (Featherstone R) 5g
Hall (Hull KR)
Subs: Smith, M (Hull KR)
Smith, P (Featherstone R)

RECORD TEAM CHANGES

The record number of team changes made by the Great Britain selectors is 10. This has happened on three occasions — all against Australia — and in the first two cases resulted in unexpected victories.

In 1929, Britain crashed 31-8 to Australia in the first Test at Hull KR and retained only three players for the second Test at Leeds where they won 9-3.

After their biggest ever defeat of 50-12 in the 1963 second Test at Swinton, Britain dropped nine players and were forced to make another change when Vince Karalius was injured and replaced by Don Fox. Britain stopped Australia making a clean sweep of the series by winning 16-5 at Leeds in the last Test.

Following the 40-4 first Test defeat at Hull City's soccer ground in 1982, the selectors again made 10 changes, not including substitutes. The changes made little difference this time as Britain went down 27-6 in the second Test at Wigan.

Britain have never fielded the same team for three or more successive Tests.

Great Britain prop forward Andy Goodway collared by French winger Patrick Solal in the 1984 Test in Avignon.

GREAT BRITAIN REGISTER

The following is a record of the 523 players who have appeared for Great Britain in 222 Test and World Cup matches.

It does not include matches against France before 1957, the year they were given official Test match status.

Figures in brackets are the total of appearances, with the plus sign indicating substitute appearances, e.g. (7+3).

For matches against touring teams, the year given is for the first half of the season.

World Cup matches are in bold letters. Substitute appearances are in lower case letters.

A - Australia, F - France, NZ - New Zealand.

GREAT BRITAIN RECORDS

MOST APPEARANCES:

46	Mick Sullivan*
31	Billy Boston
29+1	Cliff Watson
29	George Nicholls
29	Neil Fox
28+1	Roger Millward
28	Alan Prescott
27	Phil Jackson
27	Alex Murphy
26	Eric Ashton
26	John Atkinson
25	Brian McTigue
25	Jim Sullivan
25	Tommy Harris

Eric Ashton.

* Mick Sullivan's record number of appearances included a record run of 36 successive matches. In addition he played in two matches against France before they were given Test status.

MOST TRIES:

40, Mick Sullivan (Also scored two against France before they were given Test status)

MOST GOALS AND POINTS:

93 goals, (14 tries), 228 points, Neil Fox

LONGEST TEST CAREERS:

14 years	—	Gus Risman	1932 to 1946 (17 appearances)
13 years 9 months	—	Billy Batten	1908 to 1921 (10 appearances)
13 years 6 months	—	Alex Murphy	1958 to 1971 (27 appearances)
12 years 9 months	—	Roger Millward	1966 to 1978 (28+1 appearances)
12 years 6 months	—	John Atkinson	1968 to 1980 (26 appearances)
12 years 6 months	—	Terry Clawson	1962 to 1974 (14 appearances)

YOUNGEST TEST PLAYER

Roger Millward (born 16 September, 1947) was not quite 18 years 6 months old when he made his debut for Britain against France at Wigan on 15 March, 1966. Five months earlier he was a non-playing substitute for the second Test against New Zealand.

ACKERLEY, A (2) Halifax: 1952 A; 1958 NZ
ADAMS, L (1) Leeds: 1932 A
ADAMS, M (5+1) Widnes: 1979 Aa, NZ3; 1980 NZ
ARKWRIGHT, J (6) Warrington: 1936 A2, NZ; 1937 A3
ARMITT, T (8) Swinton: 1933 A; 1936 A2, NZ2; 1937 A3
ASHBY, R (2) Liverpool: 1964 F; Wigan: 1965 F
ASHCROFT, E (11) Wigan: 1947 NZ2; 1950 A3, NZ; 1954 A3, NZ2
ASHCROFT, K (5+1) Leigh: **1968 A**; 1968 F; 1969 F; **1970 F,NZ**; Warrington: 1974 nz
ASHTON, E (26) Wigan: **1957 A,NZ**; 1958 A2,NZ2; 1959 F, A3; 1960 F2; **1960 NZ,A**; 1961 NZ3; 1962 F3,A3; 1963 F,A2
ASHURST, W (3) Wigan: 1971 NZ; 1972 F2
ASKIN, T (6) Featherstone R: 1928 A3,NZ3
ASPINALL, W (1) Warrington: 1966 NZ
ASTON, L (3) St. Helens: 1947 NZ3
ATKINSON, A (11) Castleford: 1929 A3; 1932 A3,NZ3; 1933 A; 1936 A
ATKINSON, J (26) Leeds: **1968 F,NZ**; 1970 A3,NZ3; **1970 A2,F,NZ**; 1971 F2,NZ; 1972 F2; **1972 A2,F,NZ**; 1973 A2; 1978 A2; 1980 NZ
AVERY, A (4) Oldham: 1910 A,NZ; 1911 A2

BACON, J (11) Leeds: 1920 A3,NZ3; 1921 A3; 1924 A; 1926 NZ
BARENDS, D (2) Bradford N: 1979 A2
BARTON, F (1) Wigan: 1951 NZ
BARTON, J. (2) Wigan: 1960 F; 1961 NZ
BASNETT, J. (1) Widnes: 1984 F
BASSETT, A (2) Halifax: 1946 A2
BATES, A (2+2) Dewsbury: 1974 F2,nz2
BATTEN, E (4) Bradford N: 1946 A2,NZ; 1947 NZ
BATTEN, R. (3) Leeds: 1969 F; 1973 A2
BATTEN, W (10) Hunslet: 1907 NZ; 1908 A3; 1910 A2,NZ; 1911 A2; Hull: 1921 A
BAXTER, J (1) Rochdale H: 1907 NZ
BEAMES, J (2) Halifax: 1921 A2
BELSHAW, W (8) Liverpool S: 1936 A3,NZ2; 1937 A; Warrington: A2
BENNETT, J (7) Rochdale H: 1924 A3,NZ3; Wigan: 1926 NZ
BENTHAM, N (10) Wigan H: 1928 A3,NZ3; Halifax: 1929 A2; Warrington: 1929(cont) A2
BENTHAM, W (2) Broughton R: 1924 NZ2
BENTLEY, K (1) Widnes: 1980 NZ
BENYON, W (5+1) St. Helens: 1971 F2,NZ,nz; 1972 F2
BEVAN, D (1) Wigan: 1952 A
BEVAN, J (6) Warrington: 1974 A2,NZ2; 1978 A2
BEVERLEY, H (6) Hunslet: 1936 A3; 1937 A; Halifax: A2
BIRCH, J (1) Leeds: 1907 NZ
BISHOP, T (15) St. Helens: 1966 A3,NZ2; 1967 A3; 1968 F3; **1968 A,F,NZ**; 1969 F
BLAN, W (3) Wigan: 1951 NZ3
BLINKHORN, T (1) Warrington: 1929 A
BOLTON, D (23) Wigan: 1957 F3; 1958 F,A2; 1959 F,A3; 1960 F2; 1961 NZ3; 1962 F2,A,NZ2; 1963 F,A2
BOSTON, W (31) Wigan: 1954 A2,NZ3; 1955 NZ; 1956 A3; 1957 F5; **1957 F,A**; 1958 F; 1959 A; 1960 F; **1960 A**; 1961 F,NZ3; 1962 F2,A3,NZ; 1963 F
BOTT, C (1) Oldham: 1966 F
BOWDEN, J (3) Huddersfield: 1954 A2,NZ
BOWEN, F (3) St. Helens Rec: 1928 NZ3
BOWERS, J (1) Rochdale H: 1920 NZ
BOWMAN, E (4) Workington T: **1977 F, NZ, A2**
BOWMAN, H (8) Hull: 1924 NZ2; 1926 NZ2; 1928 A2,NZ; 1929 A
BOWMAN, K (3) Huddersfield: 1962 F; 1963 F,A
BOYLEN, F (1) Hull: 1908 A
BRADSHAW, T (6) Wigan: 1947 NZ2; 1950 A3,NZ
BRIDGES, K (3) Featherstone R: 1974 F2,A
BRIGGS, B (1) Huddersfield: 1954 NZ
BROGDEN, S (16) Huddersfield: 1929 A; 1932 A3,NZ3; 1933 A2; Leeds: 1936 A3,NZ2; 1937 A2
BROOKE, I (13) Bradford N: 1966 A3,NZ2; Wakefield: 1967 A3; 1968 F2; **1968 A,F,NZ**
BROOKS, E (3) Warrington: 1908 A3
BROUGH, A (2) Oldham: 1924 A,NZ
BROUGH, J (5) Leeds: 1928 A2,NZ2; 1936A

BROWN, G (6) Leeds: **1954 F2,NZ,A**; 1955 NZ2
BRYANT, W (4+1) Castleford: 1964 F2; 1966 Aa; 1967 F
BUCKLEY, A (7) Swinton: 1963 A; 1964 F; 1965 NZ; 1966 F,A2,NZ
BURGESS, W (16) Barrow: 1924 A3,NZ3; 1926 NZ3; 1928 A3,NZ2; 1929 A2
BURGESS, W (14) Barrow: 1962 F; 1963 A; 1965 NZ2; 1966 F,A3,NZ2; 1967 F,A; 1968 F; Salford: 1969 F
BURGHAM, O (1) Halifax: 1911 A
BURKE, M (3+1) Widnes: 1980 NZ; 1981 fF; 1983 F
BURNELL, A (3) Hunslet: 1951 NZ2; 1954 NZ
BURTON, C (1) Hull KR: 1982 A
BURWELL, A (7+1) Hull KR: 1967 a; 1968 F3; **1968 A,F,NZ**; 1969 F
BUTTERS, F (2) Swinton: 1929 A2

CAIRNS, D (2) Barrow: 1984 F2
CAMILLERI, C (2) Barrow: 1980 NZ2
CARLTON, F (2) St. Helens: 1958 NZ; Wigan: 1962 NZ
CARR, C (7) Barrow: 1924 A2,NZ2; 1926 NZ3
CARTWRIGHT, J (7) Leigh: 1920 A,NZ3; 1921 A3
CASEY, L (12+2) Hull KR: **1977 f,nz,A**; 1978 A; Bradford N: 1979 A2,NZ3; Hull KR: 1980 NZ3; 1983 F2
CASTLE, F (4) Barrow: 1952 A3; 1954 A
CHALLINOR, J (3) Warrington: 1958 A,NZ; **1960 F**
CHARLTON, P (18+1) Workington T: 1965 NZ; Salford: **1970 nz**; 1972 F2; **1972 A2,F,NZ**; 1973 A3; 1974 F2,A3,NZ3
CHERRINGTON, N (1) Wigan: 1960 F
CHILCOTT, J (3) Huddersfield: 1914 A3
CHISNALL, D (2) Leigh: 1970 A; **1970 NZ**
CHISNALL, E (4) St. Helens: 1974 A2,NZ2
CLAMPITT, L (3) Broughton R: 1907 NZ; 1911 A; 1914 NZ
CLARK, D (11) Huddersfield: 1911 A2; 1914 A3; 1920 A3,NZ3
CLARK, G (2) Hull KR: 1984 F2
CLARK, M (5) Leeds: 1968 F2; **1968 A,F,NZ**
CLARKE, C (7) Wigan: 1965 NZ; 1966 F,NZ; 1967 F; 1973 A3
CLAWSON, T (14) Featherstone R: 1962 F2; Leeds: **1972 A2,F**; Oldham: 1973 A3; 1974 F2,A2,NZ2
CLOSE, D (1) Huddersfield: 1967 F
COLDRICK, A (4) Wigan: 1914 A3,NZ
COLLIER, F (2) Wigan: 1963 A; Widnes: 1964 F
COULMAN, M (2+1) Salford: 1971 f,NZ2
COURTNEY, N (+1) Warrington: 1982 a
COVERDALE, R (4) Hull: **1954 F2,NZ,A**
CRACKNELL, R (2) Huddersfield: 1951 NZ2
CRANE, M (1) Hull: 1982 A
CROOKS, L (2+1) Hull: 1982 A2; 1984 f
CROSTON, A (1) Castleford: 1937 A
CROWTHER, H (1) Hunslet: 1929 A
CUNNIFFE, B (1) Castleford: 1937 A
CUNNINGHAM, E (1) St. Helens: 1978 A
CUNLIFFE, J (4) Wigan: 1950 A,NZ; 1951 NZ; 1954 A
CUNLIFFE, W (11) Warrington: 1920 A,NZ2; 1921 A3; 1924 A3,NZ; 1926 NZ
CURRAN, G (6) Salford: 1946 A,NZ; 1947 NZ; 1948 A3
CURZON, E (1) Salford: 1910 A

DAGNALL, R (4) St.Helens: 1961 NZ2; 1964 F; 1965 F
DALGREEN, J (1) Fulham: 1982 A
DANBY, T (3) Salford: 1950 A2,NZ
DANIELS, A (3) Halifax: 1952 A2; 1955 NZ
DARWELL, J (5) Leigh: 1924 A3,NZ2
DAVIES, A (20) Oldham: 1955 NZ; 1956 A3; **1957 F,A**; 1957 F2; 1958 F,A2,NZ2; 1959 F2,A; **1960 NZ,F,A**; 1960 F
DAVIES, E (3) Oldham: 1920 NZ3
DAVIES, J (2) Huddersfield: 1911 A2
DAVIES, W.A (2) Leeds: 1914 A,NZ
DAVIES, W.J (1) Castleford: 1933 A
DAVIES, W.T (1) Halifax: 1911 A
DAVIES, W.T.H (3) Bradford N: 1946 NZ; 1947 NZ2
DAVIES, W (1) Swinton: 1968 F
DAWSON, E (1) York: 1956 A
DICK, K (2) Leeds: 1980 NZ2
DICKENSON, G (1) Warrington: 1908 A
DINGSDALE, W (3) Warrington: 1929 A2; 1933 A
DIXON, C (12+2) Halifax: 1968 F; Salford: 1969 F; 1971 NZ; **1972 F**; 1973 a2; 1974 F2,A3,NZ3
DIXON, M (2) Featherstone R: 1962 F; 1964 F
DOCKAR, A (1) Hull KR: 1947 NZ
DRAKE, J (1) Hull: 1960 F
DRAKE, W (1) Hull: 1962 F
DRUMMOND, D (10) Leigh: 1980 NZ2; 1981 F2; 1982 A3; 1983 F2; 1984 F
DUANE, R (3) Warrington: 1983 F2; 1984 F
DUTTON, R (6) Widnes: 1970 NZ2; **1970 A2,F,NZ**
DYSON, F (1) Huddersfield: 1959 A
DYL, L (11) Leeds: 1974 A2,NZ3; **1977 F,NZ,A2**; 1978 A; 1982 A

ECCLES, P (1) Halifax: 1907 NZ
ECCLES, R (1) Warrington: 1982 A
ECKERSLEY, D (2+2) St.Helens: 1973 Aa; 1974 Aa
EDGAR, B (11) Workington T: 1958 A,NZ; 1961 NZ; 1962 A3,NZ; 1965 NZ; 1966 A3
EDWARDS, A (7) Salford: 1936 A3,NZ2; 1937 A2
EDWARDS, D (3+2) Castleford: 1968 f; 1970 A; 1971 NZ2nz
EGAN, J (14) Wigan: 1946 A3; 1947 NZ3; 1948 A3; 1950 A3,NZ2
ELLABY, A (13) St.Helens: 1928 A3,NZ2; 1929 A2; 1932 A3,NZ2; 1933 A
ELWELL, K (3) Widnes: **1977 A;** 1980 NZ2
EVANS, B (10) Swinton: 1926 NZ; 1928 NZ; 1929 A; 1932 A2,NZ3; 1933 A2
EVANS, F (4) Swinton: 1924 A2,NZ2
EVANS, J (4) Hunslet: 1951 NZ; 1952 A3

EVANS, J (3) Swinton: 1926 NZ3
EVANS, R (4) Wigan: 1961 NZ2; 1962 F,NZ
EVANS, S (7+3) Featherstone R: 1979 Aa2,NZ3, 1980 NZnz; Hull: 1982 A2
EYRE, K (1) Hunslet: 1965 NZ

FAIRBAIRN, G (17) Wigan: **1977 F,NZ,A2**; 1978 A3; 1979 A2,NZ3; 1980 NZ2; Hull KR: 1981 F; 1982 A2
FAIRCLOUGH, L (6) St.Helens: 1926 NZ; 1928 A2,NZ2; 1929 A
FARRAR, V (1) Hull: 1978 A
FEATHERSTONE, J (6) Warrington: 1948 A; 1950 NZ2; 1952 A3
FEETHAM, J (8) Hull KR: 1929 A;
Salford: 1932 A2,NZ2; 1933 A3
FIELD, H (3) York: 1936 A,NZ2
FIELD, N (1) Batley: 1963 A
FIELDING, K (3) Salford: 1974 F2; **1977 F**
FILDES, A (15) St.Helens Recs: 1926 NZ2; 1928 A3,NZ3; 1929 A3; St.Helens: 1932 A,NZ3
FISHER, A (11) Bradford N: 1970 A2,NZ3; **1970 A**; Leeds: **A;** 1971 F2; Bradford N: 1978 A2
FLANAGAN, P (14) Hull KR: 1962 F; 1963 F; 1966 A3,NZ; 1967 A3; 1968 F2; **1968 F,NZ**; 1970 A
FLANAGAN, T (2) Oldham: 1983 F2
FOGERTY, T (2+1) Halifax: 1966 nz; Wigan: 1967 F; Rochdale H: 1974 F
FOSTER, F (1) Hull KR: 1967 A
FOSTER, P (3) Leigh: 1955 NZ3
FOSTER, T (3) Bradford N: 1946 NZ; 1948 A2
FOX, D (1) Featherstone R: 1963 A
FOX, N (29) Wakefield T: 1959 F,A2; 1960 F3; 1961 NZ2; 1962 F3,A3,NZ2; 1963 A2,F; 1964 F; 1965 F; 1966 F; 1967 F2,A; 1968 F3; 1969 F
FOY, D (1) Oldham: 1984 F
FRANCIS, R (1) Barrow: 1947 NZ
FRANCIS, W (4) Wigan: 1967 A; **1977 NZ,A2**
FRASER, E (16) Warrington: 1958 A3,NZ2; 1959 F2,A; 1960 F3; **1960 F,NZ**; 1961 F,NZ2
FRENCH, R (4) Widnes: 1968 F2; **1968 A,NZ**
FRODSHAM, A (3) St.Helens: 1928 NZ2; 1929 A

GABBITAS, B (1) Hunslet: 1959 F
GALLAGHER, F (12) Dewsbury: 1920 A3; 1921 A; Batley: 1924 A3,NZ3; 1926 NZ2
GANLEY, B (3) Oldham: 1957 F2; 1958 F
GARDINER, D (1) Wigan: 1965 NZ
GEE, K (17) Wigan: 1946 A3,NZ; 1947 NZ3; 1948 A3; 1950 A3,NZ2; 1951 NZ2
GEMMELL, R (3) Leeds: 1964 F; Hull: 1968 F; 1969 F
GIFFORD, H (2) Barrow: 1908 A2
GILFEDDER, L (5) Warrington: 1962 A,NZ2,F; 1963 F
GILL, H (3) Wigan: 1981 F2; 1982 A
GILL, K (5+2) Salford: 1974 F2,A2,NZ; **1977 f,a**
GOODWAY, A (3) Oldham: 1983 F2; 1984 F
GOODWIN, D (5) Barrow: 1957 F2; 1958 F,NZ2
GORE, J (1) Salford: 1926 NZ
GORLEY, L (4+1) Widnes: 1980 NZnz; 1981 F2; 1982 A
GORLEY, P (2+1) St.Helens: 1980 NZ; 1981 Ff
GOWERS, K (14) Swinton: 1962 F; 1963 F,A3; 1964 F2; 1965 NZ2; 1966 F2,A,NZ2
GRAY, J (5+3) Wigan: 1974 f2,A2a,NZ3
GRAYSHON, J (11) Bradford N: 1979 A2,NZ3; 1980 NZ2; 1981 F2; 1982 A2
GREENALL, D (6) St.Helens: 1951 NZ3; 1952 A2; 1954 NZ
GREENALL, J (1) St.Helens Rec: 1921 A
GREENOUGH, R (1) Warrington: **1960 NZ**
GREGORY, A (5) Widnes: 1981 F2; 1982 A; 1983 F2
GRONOW, B (7) Huddersfield: 1911 A2, 1920 A2, NZ3
GRUNDY, J (12) Barrow: 1955 NZ3; 1956 A3; 1957 F3; **1957 F,A,NZ**
GUNNEY, G (11) Hunslet: 1954 NZ3; 1956 A; 1957 F3; **1957 F,NZ**; 1964 F; 1965 F
GWYNNE, T E (3) Hull: 1928 A,NZ; 1929 A
GWYTHER, E (6) Belle Vue R: 1947 NZ2; 1950 A3; 1951 NZ

HAIGH, R (5+1) Wakefield T: **1968 A,F**; Leeds: **1970 NZ,a**; 1971 F,NZ
HALL, D (2) Hull KR: 1984 F2
HALL, W (4) Oldham: 1914 A3,NZ
HALLAS, D (2) Leeds: 1961 F,NZ
HALMSHAW, A (1) Halifax: 1971 NZ
HALSALL, H (1) Swinton: 1929 A
HANLEY, E (1+1) Bradford N: 1984 fF

Jeff Grayshon.

HARDISTY, A (12) Castleford: 1964 F3; 1965 F,NZ; 1966 A3,NZ; 1967 F2; 1970 A
HARE, I (1) Widnes: 1967 F
HARRIS, T (25) Hull: 1954 NZ2; 1956 A3; 1957 F5; **1957 F,A**; 1958 A3,NZ,F; 1959 F2,A3; 1960 F2; **1960 NZ**
HARRISON, F (3) Leeds: 1911 A3
HARRISON, M (7) Hull: 1967 F2; 1971 NZ2; 1972 F2; 1973 A
HARTLEY, D (11) Hunslet: 1964 F2; Castleford: 1968 F; 1969 F; 1970 A2,NZ2; **1970 A2,F**
HARTLEY, S (3) Hull KR: 1980 NZ; 1981 F2
HELME, G (12) Warrington: 1948 A3; 1954 A3,NZ2; **1954 F2,A,NZ**
HEPWORTH, K (11) Castleford: 1967 F2; 1970 A3,NZ2; **1970 A2,F,NZ**
HERBERT, N (6) Workington T: 1961 NZ; 1962 F,A3,NZ
HERON, D (1+1) Leeds: 1982 aA
HESKETH, C (21+2) Salford: 1970 NZ; **1970 NZ,a**; 1971 Ff,NZ3; **1972 A2,F,NZ**; 1973 A3; 1974 F2,A3,NZ3
HICKS, M (1) St.Helens: 1965 NZ
HIGGINS, F (6) Widnes: 1950 A3,NZ2; 1951 NZ
HIGGINS, H (2) Widnes: 1937 A2
HIGSON, J (2) Hunslet: 1908 A2
HILL, C (1) Wigan: 1966 F
HILL, D (1) Wigan: 1971 F
HILTON, H (7) Oldham: 1920 A3,NZ3; 1921 A
HILTON, J (4) Wigan: 1950 A2,NZ2
HOBBS, D (2) Featherstone R: 1984 F2
HODGSON, M (16) Swinton: 1929 A2; 1932 A3,NZ3; 1933 A3; 1936 A3,NZ; 1937 A
HOGAN, P (6+3) Barrow: **1977 F,NZ,A2**; 1978 a; Hull KR: 1979 Aa,NZ,nz
HOGG, A (1) Broughton R: 1907 NZ
HOLDEN, K (1) Warrington: 1963 A
HOLDER, W (1) Hull: 1907 NZ
HOLDSTOCK, R (2) Hull KR: 1980 NZ2
HOLLAND, D (4) Oldham: 1914 A3,NZ
HOLLIDAY, W (9+1) Whitehaven: 1964 F; Hull KR: 1965 F,NZ3; 1966 Ff; 1967 A3
HOLLINDRAKE, T (1) Keighley: 1955 NZ
HOLMES, J (14+6) Leeds: 1971 NZ; 1972 F2; **1972 Aa,NZ**; **1977 F,NZ,Aa**; 1978 a3; 1979 A2a,NZ3; 1982 A
HORNE, W (8) Barrow: 1946 A3; 1947 NZ; 1948 A; 1952 A3
HORTON, W (14) Wakefield T: 1928 A3,NZ3; 1929 A; 1932 A3,NZ; 1933 A3
HOWLEY, T (6) Wigan: 1924 A3,NZ3
HUDDART, R (16) Whitehaven: 1958 A2,NZ2; St.Helens: 1959 A; 1961 NZ3; 1962 F2,A3,NZ2; 1963 A
HUDSON, B (8) Salford: 1932 NZ; 1933 A2; 1936 A,NZ2; 1937 A2
HUDSON, W (1) Wigan: 1948 A
HUGHES, E (8) Widnes: 1978 A; 1979 A3,NZ3; 1982 A
HURCOMBE, D (8) Wigan: 1920 A2,NZ; 1921 A; 1924 A2,NZ2
HYNES, S (12+1) Leeds: 1970 A2,NZ2nz; **1970 A2,F,NZ**; 1971 F; 1973 A3

IRVING, R (8+3) Oldham: 1967 F2,A3; 1970 a,NZ; 1971 NZ; 1972 f; **1972 NZ,a**

JACKSON, K (2) Oldham: 1957 F2
JACKSON, P (27) Barrow: 1954 A3,NZ3; **1954 F2,A,NZ**; 1955 NZ3; 1956 A3; **1957 F,NZ**; 1957 F5; 1958 F,A2,NZ
JARMAN, J.W. (2) Leeds: 1914 A2
JASIEWICZ, R (1) Bradford N: 1984 F
JEANES, D (8) Wakefield T: 1971 F,NZ2; 1972 F2; Leeds: **1972 A2,NZ**
JENKINS, B (12) Wigan: 1907 NZ3; 1908 A3; 1910 A,NZ; 1911 A2, 1914 A,NZ
JENKINS, D (1) Hunslet: 1929 A
JENKINS, D (1) Leeds: 1947 NZ
JENKINS, E (9) Salford: 1933 A; 1936 A3,NZ2; 1937 A3
JENKINSON, A (2) Hunslet: 1911 A2
JOHNSON, A (4) Widnes: 1914 A,NZ; 1920 A2
JOHNSON, A (6) Warrington: 1946 A2,NZ; 1947 NZ3
JOLLEY, J (3) Runcorn: 1907 NZ3
JONES, B (3) Wakefield T: 1964 F; 1965 F; 1966 F
JONES, B.L (15) Leeds: 1954 A3,NZ3; 1955 NZ3; 1957 F3; **1957 F,A,NZ**
JONES, D (2) Merthyr: 1907 NZ2
JONES, E (4) Rochdale H: 1920 A,NZ3
JONES, J (1) Barrow: 1946 NZ
JONES, K (2) Wigan: **1970 F,NZ**
JONES, L (1) St.Helens: 1971 NZ
JORDAN, G (2) Featherstone R: 1964 F; 1967 A
JOYNER, J (14) Castleford: 1978 A2; 1979 A3,NZ3; 1980 NZ3; 1983 F2; 1984 F
JUBB, K (2) Leeds: 1937 A2
JUKES, W (6) Hunslet: 1908 A3; 1910 A2,NZ

KARALIUS, A (4+1) St.Helens: 1971 NZ3; 1972 F; **1972 nz**
KARALIUS, V (12) St.Helens: 1958 A2,NZ2; 1959 F; **1960 NZ,F,A**; 1960 F; 1961 F; Widnes: 1963 A2
KEEGAN, A (9) Hull: 1966 A2; 1967 F2,A3; 1968 F; 1969 F
KELLY, K (4) St.Helens: 1972 F2; Warrington: 1980 NZ; 1982 A
KEMEL, G (2) Wic' es: 1965 NZ2
KERSHAW, H (2) Wakefield T: 1910 A,NZ
KINNEAR, R (1) Wigan: 1929 A
KITCHEN, F (2) Leigh: **1954 A,NZ**
KITCHIN, P (1) Whitehaven: 1965 NZ
KITCHING, J (1) Bradford N: 1946 A
KNAPMAN, E (1) Oldham: 1924 NZ
KNOWELDEN, B (1) Barrow: 1946 NZ

LAUGHTON, D (15) Wigan: 1970 A3,NZ2; **1970 A2,F,NZ**; 1971 F2; Widnes: 1973 A; 1974 F2; 1979 A
LAWRENSON, J (3) Wigan: 1948 A3
LEDGARD, J (11) Dewsbury: 1947 NZ2; Leigh: 1948 A; 1950 A2,NZ; 1951 NZ; **1954 F2,A,NZ**
LEWIS, G (1) Leigh: 1965 NZ
LEYTHAM, J (5) Wigan: 1907 NZ2; 1910 A2,NZ
LITTLE, S (10) Oldham: 1956 A; 1957 F5; **1957 F,A,NZ**; 1958 F
LLEWELLYN, T (2) Oldham: 1907 NZ2
LLOYD, R (1) Halifax: 1920 A
LOCKWOOD, B (8+1) Castleford: **1972 A2,F,NZ**; 1973 A2; 1974 F; Hull KR: 1978 A; 1979 nz
LOMAS, J (7) Salford: 1908 A2; 1910 A2,NZ; Oldham: 1911 A2
LONGSTAFF, F (2) Huddersfield: 1914 A,NZ
LONGWORTH, W (3) Oldham: 1908 A3
LOWE, J (1) Leeds: 1932 NZ
LOWE, P (12) Hull KR: 1970 NZ; 1972 F2; **1972 A2,F,NZ**; 1973 A3, 1978 A2
LOXTON, K (1) Huddersfield: 1971 NZ
LYDON, J (3) Widnes: 1983 F2; 1984 F

MANN, A (2) Bradford N: 1908 A2
MANTLE, J (13) St.Helens: 1966 F2,A3; 1967 A2; 1969 F; 1971 F2,NZ2; 1973 A
MARTIN, W (1) Workington T: 1962 F
MARTYN, M (2) Leigh: 1958 A; 1959 A
McCORMICK, S (3) Belle Vue R: 1948 A2; St.Helens: A
McCUE, T (6) Widnes: 1936 A; 1937 A; 1946 A3,NZ
McINTYRE, L (1) Oldham: 1963 A
McKEATING, V (2) Workington T: 1951 NZ2
McKINNEY, T (11) Salford: 1951 NZ; 1952 A2; 1954 A3,NZ; Warrington: 1955 NZ3; St.Helens: **1957 NZ**
McTIGUE, B (25) Wigan: 1958 A2,NZ2; 1959 F2,A3; 1960 F2; **1960 NZ,F,A**; 1961 F,NZ3; 1962 F,A3,NZ2; 1963 F
MATHIAS, R (1) St.Helens: 1979 A
MEASURES, J (2) Widnes: 1963 A2
MIDDLETON, A (1) Salford: 1929 A
MILLER, J (1) Wigan: 1911 A
MILLER, J (6) Warrington: 1933 A3; 1936 A,NZ2
MILLS, J (6) Widnes: 1974 A2,NZ; 1978 A2; 1979 A
MILLWARD, R (28+1) Castleford: 1966 F; Hull KR: 1967 A3; 1968 F2; **1968 A,F,NZ**; 1970 A2,NZ3; 1971 F,NZ3; 1973 A; 1974 A2a; **1977 F,NZ,A2**; 1978 A3
MILNES, A (2) Halifax: 1920 A2
MOONEY, W (2) Leigh: 1924 NZ2
MOORHOUSE, S (2) Huddersfield: 1914 A,NZ
MORGAN, A (4) Featherstone R: 1968 F2; **1968 F,NZ**
MORGAN, E (2) Hull: 1921 A2
MORGAN, R (2) Swinton: 1963 F,A
MORLEY, J (2) Wigan: 1936 A; 1937 A
MORTIMER, F (2) Wakefield T: 1956 A2
MOSES, G (9) St.Helens: 1955 NZ2; 1956 A; 1957 F3; **1957 F,A,NZ**
MUMBY, K (4) Bradford N: 1982 A; 1983 F; 1984 F2
MURPHY, A (27) St.Helens: 1958 A3,NZ; 1959 F2,A; **1960 NZ,F,A**; 1960 F; 1961 F,NZ3; 1962 F,A3; 1963 A2; 1964 F; 1965 F,NZ; 1966 F2; Warrington: 1971 NZ
MURPHY, H (1) Wakefield T: 1950 A
MYLER, A (2) Widnes: 1983 F2
MYLER, F (23+1) Widnes: **1960 NZ,F,A**; 1960 F; 1961 F; 1962 F; 1963 A; 1964 F; 1965 F,NZ; 1966 A,NZnz; 1967 F2; St.Helens: 1970 A3,NZ3; **1970 A2,F**

NASH, S (24) Featherstone R: 1971 F,NZ; 1972 F2; **1972 A2,F,NZ**; 1973 A2; 1974 A3,NZ3; Salford: **1977 F,NZ,A2**; 1978 A3; 1982 A
NAUGHTON, A (2) Warrington: **1954 F2**
NEWBOULD, H (1) Wakefield T: 1910 A
NICHOLLS, G (29) Widnes: 1971 NZ; 1972 F2; **1972 A2,F,NZ**; St.Helens: 1973 A2; 1974 F2,A3,NZ3; **1977 F,NZ,A**; 1978 A3; 1979 A3,NZ3
NICHOLSON, R (3) Huddersfield: 1946 NZ; 1948 A2
NOBLE, B (4) Bradford N: 1982 A; 1983 F2; 1984 F
NORTON, S (11+1) Castleford: 1974 a,NZ2; Hull: 1978 A3; 1979 A2; 1980 NZ; 1981 F2; 1982 A

O'GRADY, T (6) Oldham: 1954 A2,NZ3; Warrington: 1961 NZ
OLIVER, J (4) Batley: 1928 A3,NZ
O'NEILL, D (2+1) Widnes: 1971 nz; **1972 A,F**
O'NEILL, M (3) Widnes: 1982 A; 1983 F2
OSTER, J (1) Oldham: 1929 A
OWEN, J (1) St.Helens Recs: 1921 A
OWEN, S (1) Leigh: 1958 F
OWENS, I (4) Leeds: 1946 A3,NZ

PADBURY, R (1) Runcorn: 1908 A
PALIN, H (2) Warrington: 1947 NZ2
PARKER, D (2) Oldham: 1964 F2
PARKIN, J (17) Wakefield T: 1920 A2,NZ3; 1921 A2; 1924 A3,NZ; 1926 NZ2; 1928 A,NZ; 1929 A2
PARR, K (1) Warrington: 1968 F
PAWSEY, C (7) Leigh: 1952 A3; 1954 A2,NZ2
PEPPERELL, A (2) Workington T: 1950 NZ; 1951 NZ
PHILLIPS, D (4) Oldham: 1946 A3, Belle Vue R: 1950 A
PIMBLETT, A (3) Warrington: 1948 A3
PINNER, H (1+1) St.Helens: 1980 nzNZ
PITCHFORD, F (2) Oldham: 1958 NZ; 1962 F
PITCHFORD, S (4) Leeds: **1977 F,NZ,A2**
POLLARD, C (1) Wakefield T: 1924 NZ
POLLARD, E (2) Wakefield T: 1932 A2
POLLARD, R (1) Dewsbury: 1950 NZ
POOLE, H (3) Hull KR: 1964 F; Leeds: 1966 NZ2
POYNTON, H (3) Wakefield T: 1962 A2,NZ

PRESCOTT, A (28) St.Helens: 1951 NZ2; 1952 A3; 1954 A3,NZ3; 1955 NZ3; 1956 A3; 1957 F5; **1957 F,A,NZ**; 1958 F,A2
PRICE, J (6) Broughton R: 1921 A2; Wigan: 1924 A2,NZ2
PRICE, M (2) Rochdale H: 1967 A2
PRICE, R (9) Warrington: 1954 A,NZ2; 1955 NZ; 1956 A3; 1957 F2
PRICE, T (1) Bradford N: 1970 A
PRIOR, B (1) Hunslet: 1966 F
PROSSER, D (1) Leeds: 1937 A
PROSSER, S (1) Halifax: 1914 A

RAE, J (1) Bradford N: 1965 NZ
RAMSDALE, R (8) Wigan: 1910 A2; 1911 A2; 1914 A3,NZ
RAMSEY, W (7+1) Hunslet: 1965 NZ2; 1966 F,A2,NZ2; Bradford N; 1974 nz
RATCLIFFE, G (3) Wigan: 1947 NZ; 1950 A2
RATHBONE, A (2+1) Bradford N: 1982 a; 1983 F2
RAYNE, KEITH (2) Leeds: 1984 F2
REDFEARN, A (1) Bradford N: 1979 A
REDFEARN, D (6+1) Bradford N: **1972 nz**; 1974 F2,A,NZ3
REES, D (1) Halifax: 1926 NZ
REES, T (1) Oldham: 1929 A
REES, W (11) Swinton: 1926 NZ2; 1928 A3,NZ3; 1929 A3
REILLY, M (9) Castleford: 1970 A3,NZ3; **1970 A2,F**
RENILSON, C (7+1) Halifax: 1965 NZ; 1967 a; 1968 F3; **1968 A,F,NZ**
RHODES, A (4) St.Helens: **1957 NZ**; **1960 F,A**; 1961 NZ
RICHARDS, M (2) Salford: 1974 A,NZ
RILEY, J (1) Halifax: 1910 A
RING, J (2) Wigan: 1924 A; 1926 NZ
RISMAN, A (17) Salford: 1932 A,NZ3; 1933 A3; 1936 A2,NZ2; 1937 A3; 1946 A3
RISMAN, B (5) Leeds: 1968 F2; **1968 A,F,NZ**
RIX, S (9) Oldham: 1924 A3,NZ3; 1926 NZ3
ROBERTS, K (10) Halifax: 1963 A; 1964 F2; 1965 F,NZ3; 1966 F,NZ2
ROBINSON, A (3) Halifax: 1907 NZ; 1908 A2
ROBINSON, Dave (13) Swinton: 1965 NZ; 1966 F2,A3,NZ2; 1967 F2,A2; Wigan: 1970 A
ROBINSON, Don (10) Wakefield T: **1954 F2,NZ,A**; 1955 NZ; Leeds: 1956 A2; 1959 A2; 1960 F
ROBINSON, J (2) Rochdale H: 1914 A2
ROBINSON, W (2) Leigh: 1963 F,A
ROGERS, J (7) Huddersfield: 1914 A; 1920 A3; 1921 A3
ROSE, D (4) Leeds: **1954 F2,A,NZ**
ROSE, P (2+3) Hull KR: 1974 a; 1978 Aa2; Hull: 1982 A
ROUND, G (8) Wakefield T: 1959 A; 1962 F2,A3,NZ2
RUDDICK, J (3) Broughton R: 1907 NZ2; 1910 A
RYAN, M (4) Wigan: 1947 NZ; 1948 A2; 1950 A
RYAN, R (5) Warrington: 1950 A,NZ2; 1951 NZ; 1952 A
RYDER, R (1) Warrington: 1952 A
SAYER, W (7) Wigan: 1961 NZ; 1962 F,A3,NZ; 1963 A
SCHOFIELD, D (1) Halifax: 1955 NZ
SCHOFIELD, G (1) Hull: 1984 F
SEABOURNE, B (1) Leeds: 1970 NZ
SENIOR, K (2) Huddersfield: 1965 NZ; 1967 F
SHARROCK, J (4) Wigan: 1910 A2,NZ; 1911 A
SHAW, B (6) Hunslet: 1956 A2; **1960 F,A**; 1960 F; Leeds: 1961 F
SHAW, G (1) Widnes: 1980 NZ
SHAW, J (5) Halifax: **1960 F,A**; 1960 F; 1961 F; 1962 NZ
SHELTON, G (7) Hunslet: 1964 F2; 1965 NZ3; 1966 F2
SHOEBOTTOM, M (10+2) Leeds: **1968 A,nz**; 1969 F; 1970 A2a,NZ; **1970 A2,F,NZ**; 1971 F
SHUGARS, F (1) Warrington: 1910 NZ
SILCOCK, N (12) Widnes: 1932 A2,NZ2; 1933 A3; 1936 A3; 1937 A2
SILCOCK, N (3) Wigan: 1954 A3
SILCOCK, R (1) Wigan: 1908 A
SIMMS, B (1) Leeds: 1962 F
SKELHORNE, G (7) Warrington: 1920 A,NZ3; 1921 A3
SKERRETT, T (10) Wakefield T: 1979 A2,NZ2; Hull: 1980 NZ2; 1981 F2; 1982 A2
SLOMAN, R (5) Oldham: 1928 A3,NZ2
SMALES, T (8) Huddersfield: 1962 F; 1963 F,A; 1964 F2; Bradford N: 1965 NZ3
SMALL, P (1) Castleford: 1962 NZ
SMITH, A (6) Oldham: 1907 NZ3; 1908 A3
SMITH, A (10) Leeds: 1970 A2,NZ3; **1970 A2**; 1971 F2; 1973 A
SMITH, F (9) Hunslet: 1910 A,NZ; 1911 A3; 1914 A3,NZ
SMITH, G (3) York: 1963 A; 1964 F2
SMITH, H (2) Bradford N: 1926 NZ2
SMITH, M (9+1) Hull KR: 1979 NZ3; 1980 NZ2; 1981 F2; 1982 A2; 1984 f
SMITH, P (1+5) Featherstone R: **1977 a2;**1982 A; 1983 f2; 1984 f
SMITH, S (11) Wakefield T: 1929 A; Leeds: A2; 1932 A3,NZ3; 1933 A2
SMITH, S (4) Hunslet: **1954 A,NZ,F2**
SOUTHWARD, I (11) Workington T: 1958 A3,NZ; Oldham: 1959 F2,A2; 1960 F2; 1962 NZ
SPENCER, J (1) Salford: 1907 NZ
STACEY, J.C (1) Halifax: 1920 NZ
STEPHENS, G (5) Castleford: 1979 A2,NZ3
STEPHENSON, D (2) Wigan: 1982 A2
STEPHENSON, M (5+1) Dewsbury: 1971 nz; 1972 F; **1972 A2,F,NZ**
STEVENSON, J (19) Leeds: 1955 NZ3; 1956 A3; 1957 F5; **1957 F,A,NZ**; 1958 F; York: 1959 A2; 1960 F2
STOCKWELL, S (3) Leeds: 1920 A; 1921 A2
STONE, W (8) Hull: 1920 A3,NZ3; 1921 A2
STOPFORD, J (12) Swinton: 1961 F; 1963 F,A2; 1964 F2; 1965 F,NZ2; 1966 F2,A
STOTT, J (1) St.Helens: 1947 NZ
STREET, H (4) Dewsbury: 1950 A3,NZ
SULLIVAN, C (17) Hull: 1967 F; **1968 A,F,NZ**; 1970 A; 1971 NZ3; 1972 F2; **1972 A2,F,NZ**; 1973 A3

SULLIVAN, J (25) Wigan: 1924 A3,NZ; 1926 NZ3; 1928 A3,NZ3; 1929 A3; 1932 A3,NZ3; 1933 A3
SULLIVAN, M (46) Huddersfield: **1954 F2,NZ,A**; 1955 NZ3; 1956 A3; 1957 F3; **1957 F,A,NZ**; Wigan: 1957 F2; 1958 F,A3,NZ2; 1959 F2,A3; 1960 F3; **1960 F,NZ,A**; St.Helens: 1961 F,NZ2; 1962 F3,A3,NZ; York: 1963 A
SZYMALA, E (1+1) Barrow: 1981 fF

TAYLOR, H (3) Hull: 1907 NZ3
TAYLOR, R (2) Hull: 1921 A; 1926 NZ
TEMBEY, J (2) St.Helens: 1963 A; 1964 F
TERRY, A (11) St.Helens: 1958 A2; 1959 F2,A3; 1960 F; 1961 F,NZ; Leeds: 1962 F
THOMAS, A (4) Leeds: 1926 NZ2; 1929 A2
THOMAS, G (1) Warrington: 1907 NZ
THOMAS, G (9) Wigan: 1914 A; Huddersfield: 1920 A3,NZ2; 1921 A3
THOMAS, J (8) Wigan: 1907 NZ; 1908 A3; 1910 A2,NZ; 1911 A
THOMAS, L (1) Oldham: 1947 NZ
THOMAS, P (1) Leeds: 1907 NZ
THOMPSON, C (2) Hunslet: 1951 NZ2
THOMPSON, J (12) Leeds: 1924 A,NZ2; 1928 A,NZ; 1929 A; 1932 A3,NZ3
THOMPSON, J (20+1) Featherstone R: 1970 A2,NZ2; **1970 A2,F,NZ**; 1971 Ff; 1974 A3,NZ3; **1977 F,NZ,A2**; Bradford N: 1978 A
THORLEY, J (4) Halifax: **1954 F2,NZ,A**
TOOHEY, E (3) Barrow: 1952 A3
TOPLISS, D (4) Wakefield T: 1973 A2; 1979 A; Hull: 1982 A
TRAILL, K (8) Bradford N: 1950 NZ2; 1951 NZ; 1952 A3; 1954 A,NZ
TROUP, L A (2) Barrow: 1936 NZ2
TURNBULL, A (1) Leeds: 1951 NZ
TURNER, D (24) Oldham: 1956 A2; 1957 F5; **1957 F,A,NZ**; 1958 F; Wakefield: 1959 A; 1960 F3; **1960 NZ,A**; 1961 F,NZ; 1962 A2,NZ2,F
TYSON, B (3) Hull KR: 1963 A; 1965 F; 1967 F
TYSON, G (4) Oldham: 1907 NZ; 1908 A3

VALENTINE, D (15) Huddersfield: 1948 A3; 1951 NZ; 1952 A2; 1954 A3,NZ2; **1954 F2,NZ,A**
VALENTINE, R (1) Huddersfield: 1967 A
VINES, D (3) Wakefield T: 1959 F2,A

WAGSTAFF, H (12) Huddersfield: 1911 A2; 1914 A3,NZ; 1920 A2,NZ2; 1921 A2
WALLACE, J (1) St.Helens Recs: 1926 NZ
WALKER, A (1) Whitehaven: 1980 NZ
WALSH, Joe (1) Leigh: 1971 NZ
WALSH, John (4+1) St.Helens: 1972 f; **1972 A2,F,NZ**
WALTON, D (1) Castleford: 1965 F
WARD, D (12) Leeds: **1977 F,NZ,A**; 1978 A; 1979 A3,NZ3; 1981 F; 1982 A
WARD, Edward (3) Wigan: 1946 A2; 1947 NZ
WARD, Ernest (20) Bradford N: 1946 A3,NZ; 1947 NZ2; 1948 A3; 1950 A3,NZ2; 1951 NZ3; 1952 A3
WARD, J (4) Castleford: 1963 A; 1964 F2; Salford: 1970 NZ
WARD, K (1) Castleford: 1984 F
WARD, W (1) Leeds: 1910 A
WARLOW, J (6+1) St.Helens: 1964 F; **1968 f,NZ**; 1968 F; Widnes: 1971 F2,NZ
WARWICK, S (2) Salford: 1907 NZ2
WATKINS, D (2+4) Salford: 1971 f,NZ; 1973 a; 1974 f2,A
WATKINS, W (7) Salford: 1933 A; 1936 A2,NZ2; 1937 A2
WATKINSON, D (3+1) Hull KR: 1979 a; 1980 NZ; 1981 F; 1984 F
WATSON, C (29+1) St.Helens: 1963 A2; 1966 F2,A3,NZ2; 1967 F,A3; 1968 F2; **1968 A,F,nz**; 1969 F; 1970 A3,NZ3; **1970 A2,F,NZ**; 1971 F
WATTS, B (5) York: **1954 F2,NZ,A**; 1955 NZ
WEBSTER, F (3) Leeds: 1910 A2,NZ
WHITCOMBE, F (2) Bradford N: 1946 A2
WHITE, L (7) Hunslet: 1932 A3,NZ2; 1933 A2
WHITE, L (6) York: 1946 A3,NZ; Wigan: 1947 NZ2
WHITE, T (1) Oldham: 1907 NZ
WHITEHEAD, D (3) Warrington: 1971 F2,NZ
WHITELEY, J (15) Hull: **1957 A**; 1958 A3,NZ; 1959 F2,A2; 1960 F; **1960 NZ,F**; 1961 NZ2; 1962 F
WILKINSON, J (13) Halifax: 1954 A,NZ2; 1955 NZ3; Wakefield T: 1959 A; 1960 F2; **1960 NZ,F,A**; 1962 NZ
WILLIAMS, F (2) Halifax: 1914 A2
WILLIAMS, R (12) Leeds: 1948 A2; 1950 A2,NZ2; 1951 NZ3; Hunslet: 1954 A2,NZ
WILLIAMS, W (2) Salford: 1929 A; 1932 A
WILLICOMBE, D (3) Halifax: 1974 F; Wigan: F,NZ
WILSON, G (3) Workington T: 1951 NZ3
WILSON, H (3) Hunslet: 1907 NZ3
WINSLADE, C (1) Oldham: 1959 F
WINSTANLEY, W (5) Leigh: 1910 A,NZ; Wigan: 1911 A3
WOOD, A (4) Oldham: 1911 A2; 1914 A,NZ
WOODS, H (6) Liverpool S: 1936 A3,NZ2; Leeds: 1937 A
WOODS, J (1) Barrow: 1933 A
WOODS, J (7+3) Leigh: 1979 A3,nz; 1980 NZ; 1981 F2; 1982 Aa; 1983 f
WOODS, T (2) Rochdale H: 1911 A2
WORRALL, M (1) Oldham: 1984 F
WRIGHT, J (1) Swinton: 1932 NZ
WRIGHT, S (7) Widnes: **1977 F,NZ,A2**; 1978 A3
WRIGLESWORTH, G (5) Leeds: 1965 NZ; 1966 A2,NZ2

YOUNG, C (5) Hull KR: 1967 A3; 1968 F2
YOUNG, F (1) Leeds: 1908 A
YOUNG, H (1) Huddersfield: 1929 A

GREAT BRITAIN WORLD CUP SQUADS

Captains in bold

1954 IN FRANCE

D. Valentine (Huddersfield)
W. Banks (Huddersfield)
H. Bradshaw (Huddersfield)
G. Brown (Leeds)
R. Coverdale (Hull)
G. Helme (Warrington)
P. Jackson (Barrow)
F. Kitchen (Leigh)
J. Ledgard (Leigh)
A. Naughton (Warrington)
D. Robinson (Wakefield T)
D. Rose (Leeds)
R. Rylance (Huddersfield)
S. Smith (Hunslet)
M. Sullivan (Huddersfield)
J. Thorley (Halifax)
B. Watts (York)
J. Whiteley (Hull)

Manager: G. Shaw (Castleford)

1957 IN AUSTRALIA

A. Prescott (St. Helens)
E. Ashton (Wigan)
W. Boston (Wigan)
A. Davies (Oldham)
J. Grundy (Barrow)
G. Gunney (Hunslet)
T. Harris (Hull)
P. Jackson (Barrow)
L. Jones (Leeds)
S. Little (Oldham)
T. McKinney (St. Helens)
G. Moses (St. Helens)
R. Price (Warrington)
A. Rhodes (St. Helens)
J. Stevenson (Leeds)
M. Sullivan (Huddersfield)
D. Turner (Oldham)
J. Whiteley (Hull)

Managers: W. Fallowfield (RL secretary) and H. Rawson (Hunslet)

1960 IN ENGLAND

E. Ashton (Wigan)
W. Boston (Wigan)
J. Challinor (Warrington)
A. Davies (Oldham)
E. Fraser (Warrington)
R. Greenough (Warrington)
T. Harris (Hull)
V. Karalius (St. Helens)
B. McTigue (Wigan)
A. Murphy (St. Helens)
F. Myler (Widnes)
A. Rhodes (St. Helens)
B. Shaw (Hunslet)
J. Shaw (Halifax)
M. Sullivan (Wigan)
D. Turner (Wakefield T)
J. Whiteley (Hull)
J. Wilkinson (Wakefield T)

Manager: W. Fallowfield (RL secretary)

1968 IN AUSTRALIA AND NEW ZEALAND

B. Risman (Leeds)
J. Atkinson (Leeds)
K. Ashcroft (Leigh)
T. Bishop (St. Helens)
I. Brooke (Wakefield T)
A. Burwell (Hull KR)
M. Clark (Leeds)
D. Edwards (Castleford)
P. Flanagan (Hull KR)
R. French (Widnes)
R. Haigh (Wakefield T)
R. Millward (Hull KR)
A. Morgan (Featherstone R)
C. Renilson (Halifax)
M. Shoebottom (Leeds)
C. Sullivan (Hull)
R. Warlow (St. Helens)
C. Watson (St. Helens)
C. Young (Hull KR)

Manager: W. Fallowfield (RL Secretary)

Coach: C. Hutton (Hull KR)

1970 IN ENGLAND

F. Myler (St. Helens)
K. Ashcroft (Leigh)
J. Atkinson (Leeds)
P. Charlton (Salford)
D. Chisnall (Leigh)
R. Dutton (Widnes)
A. Fisher (Bradford N & Leeds)
R. Haigh (Leeds)
D. Hartley (Castleford)
C. Hesketh (Salford)
K. Hepworth (Castleford)
S. Hynes (Leeds)
K. Jones (Wigan)
D. Laughton (Wigan)
M. Reilly (Castleford)
M. Shoebottom (Leeds)
A. Smith (Leeds)
J. Thompson (Featherstone R)
C. Watson (St. Helens)

Manager: J. Harding (Leigh)

Coach: J. Whiteley (Hull KR)

1972 IN FRANCE

C. Sullivan (Hull)
J. Atkinson (Leeds)
P. Charlton (Salford)
T. Clawson (Leeds)
C. Dixon (Salford)
C. Hesketh (Salford)
J. Holmes (Leeds)
R. Irving (Oldham)
D. Jeanes (Leeds)
A. Karalius (St. Helens)
B. Lockwood (Castleford)
P. Lowe (Hull KR)
S. Nash (Featherstone R)
G. Nicholls (Widnes)
D. O'Neill (Widnes)
D. Redfearn (Bradford N)
M. Stephenson (Dewsbury)
D. Topliss (Wakefield T)
John Walsh (St. Helens)

Manager: W. Spaven (Hull KR)

Coach: J. Challinor (St. Helens)

1977 IN AUSTRALIA AND NEW ZEALAND

R. Millward (Hull KR)
E. Bowman (Workington T)
L. Casey (Hull KR)
L. Dyl (Leeds)
K. Elwell (Widnes)
G. Fairbairn (Wigan)
K. Fielding (Salford)
W. Francis (Wigan)
K. Gill (Salford)
A. Hodkinson (Rochdale H)
P. Hogan (Barrow)
J. Holmes (Leeds)
S. Lloyd (Castleford)
S. Nash (Salford)
G. Nicholls (St. Helens)
S. Pitchford (Leeds)
P. Smith (Featherstone R)
J. Thompson (Featherstone R)
D. Ward (Leeds)
S. Wright (Widnes)

Manager: R. Parker (Blackpool B)

Coach: D. Watkins (Salford)

*For details of the 1975 World Championship Squads see ENGLAND AND WALES section.

Under-24s centre Ellery Hanley in action at Oldham.

UNDER-24s

UNDER-24s

Three weeks after scraping home amid controversy on French soil, Great Britain Under-24s celebrated the return of five shooting stars to outgun France completely by 48-1.

The inclusion of captain Brian Noble, Ellery Hanley, Tony Myler, Andy Goodway and Lee Crooks for the return encounter inspired Britain to an eight-try record-breaking rout at Oldham.

Less than a month earlier in Villeneuve, success had been less convincing. Coach Frank Myler and manager Dick Gemmell announced a 21-man squad for training and before naming the team had lost the injured Myler, the suspended Goodway and Roy Haggerty plus Andy Gregory who was getting married the same day as the match. The final line-up was sent reeling only a couple of days before departure with the withdrawal of Hanley, Crooks and skipper Noble through injury.

In an 11th hour reshuffle, Wakefield Trinity hooker Colin Maskill was called up for his debut along with teenage Hull second row man Wayne Proctor, while Neil Holding stepped up from the bench to take the stand off role. Substitute jerseys were given to newcomers Garry Schofield and Keith England.

Fielding a total of seven new caps, Great Britain had only one short training session together before taking part in one of the most entertaining and fairest Anglo-French encounters.

Britain opened the scoring after nine minutes with an opportunist try by debutant hooker Maskill, Joe Lydon adding the goal. Four minutes later quick French passing sent loose forward Bret past Oldham centre Des Foy, Rocci's drop goal in the 22nd minute bringing the score to 6-5 in the visitors' favour.

Scrum half Ray Ashton scored the first of an impressive hat-trick of tries in the 26th minute. Packmen Mick Worrall, Brian Dunn, Mike O'Neill and Proctor all handled smartly before centre Ronnie Duane's one-handed inside pass sent Ashton scampering 20 yards to the line, for Lydon to add the goal.

Shortly afterwards England replaced the injured Proctor and while Dunn was receiving treatment the tormenting Rocci was put through by his half back partner Dauphin for a 37th minute touchdown, the stand off adding the goal. On the stroke of half-time British captain Terry Flanagan combined with Worrall to open the way for their clubmate Ashton to record his second try, Lydon again adding the goal to give Britain an 18-11 interval lead.

The second half signalled the start of an even greater effort by a French side being spurred on by the skill of Rocci and Bret and the strength of Rabot and Saumitou. Rocci sent centre Fourquet over for a 47th minute try, adding the goal himself, to bring the home side within a point.

Even a typically forceful try by Duane in the 57th minute did not halt France's purposeful drive and Rocci's penalty six minutes later was added to by a second try for Fourquet — intercepting Holding's pass — to give France a 23-22 lead with only 12 minutes left.

As the game threatened to slip away from Britain, it was Holding who made amends. Taking Worrall's inside pass, the St. Helens half back sidestepped three defenders and fed the ever-supporting Ashton who collected his hat-trick and the Man of the Match award. Lydon added the goal to complete the scoring.

Before the match-winning try, Britain became confused regarding the use of substitutes, taking advantage of the domestic four substitutions rule rather than the international two replacements only. Proctor returned to the field for the injured O'Neill only to be ordered off after more than 10 minutes following belated protests from the French officials. The confusion was added to by Proctor leaving the field, only for the displaced Holding — and not O'Neill — to go back on. Although the controversy was judged not to have affected the run of play, France later lodged an objection with the International Board secretary.

For the return match at the Watersheddings, Britain made those five vital changes, including Hull forward Crooks, already capped at Test and Colts levels, making his Under-24 debut. Coach Frank Myler celebrated his 46th birthday in the best possible fashion as Britain won their 13th successive encounter against France since Under-24 football was reintroduced in 1976.

Myler's nephew, stand off Tony, led the way with a hat-trick of tries in a Dominion Insurance Man of the Match performance. All eight tries were scored by the backs. Full back Lydon had a field day with his eight goals and 20 points — he also scored a try — both records for an Under-24 match.

Myler opened the scoring after only three minutes. From the first scrum, the Widnes half back did the run-round with centre Hanley to push off a would-be tackler and stride over the line after a 25-yard diagonal run. He also opened the second half scoring, tantalising the French with a dummy and weaving round two defenders. His hat-trick came in the 67th minute from a clever kick by loose forward Flanagan.

The Oldham crowd took Hanley to their hearts before he went off with a hip injury in the 38th minute. Receiving the ball 75 yards out, there seemed no danger until he pushed and shoved his way through two tackles to stumble into the clear for a run to the line with two men encouragingly always in support.

But the biggest Watersheddings cheer was reserved for home centre Des Foy who also raced 75 yards for a fleet-footed try. Hanley's replacement, Hull's 18-year-old Schofield, took his time to settle but went on to score a fine try.

Britain's midfield supremacy was so well established that there was little need for the wingers to become involved, St. Helens flanker Barry Ledger taking his only opportunity to touch down after forceful running by Oldham duo Foy and Ashton.

The final try came, appropriately, from the faultless Lydon. The Widnes utility man crowned an afternoon of immaculate fielding, touch kicking, running and eight-out-of-eight marksmanship, with a 40-yard run to the line.

Noble led the Under-24s for the first time and took three scrums against the head despite being beaten overall 11-8. French referee François Desplats gave an 11-6 penalty count in favour of his countrymen in a game which once again was refreshingly free from incident.

In the pack, Crooks grafted throughout, while Goodway — starved of match practice through suspension — ran stronger as the game went on in the unaccustomed role of number eight. Substitute John Fieldhouse, a 56th minute replacement for the injured Dunn, was taken off with knee ligament trouble.

Despite the record scoreline, British management found a great deal of delight in restricting France to a Rocci drop goal early in a vastly entertaining game.

Try scorer Colin Maskill.

11th November **Villeneuve**

GREAT BRITAIN 28		FRANCE 23
Joe Lydon (Widnes)	1.	Patrick Wosniack (Villefranche)
Garry Clark (Hull K.R.)	2.	Hugues Ratier (Lezignan)
Ronnie Duane (Warrington)	3.	Philippe Fourquet (Toulouse)
Des Foy (Oldham)	4.	Roger Palisse (St. Esteve)
Barry Ledger (St. Helens)	5.	Paul Jean (Limoux)
Neil Holding (St. Helens)	6.	Patrick Rocci (Le Pontet)
Ray Ashton (Oldham)	7.	Serge Dauphin (Cavaillon)
Mike O'Neill (Widnes)	8.	Jean Luc Rabot (Villeneuve)
Colin Maskill (Wakefield T.)	9.	Thierry Bernabe (Le Pontet)
Brian Dunn (Wigan)	10.	Serge Titeux (Le Pontet)
Mick Worrall (Oldham)	11.	Jean Saumitou (Villeneuve)
Wayne Proctor (Hull)	12.	Pierre Montgaillard (XIII Catalan)
Terry Flanagan (Oldham) Capt.	13.	Serge Bret (St. Esteve)
Garry Schofield (Hull)	14.	Gilles Dumas (St. Gaudens)
Keith England (Castleford)	15.	Thierry Butignol (A.S. Carcassonne)

T: Ashton (3), Maskill, Duane
G: Lydon (4)
Substitutions:
England for Proctor (29 min.)
Schofield for Holding (73 min.)
Half-time: 18-11
Manager: Dick Gemmell
Coach: Frank Myler
Referee: Fred Lindop (Wakefield)

T: Fourquet (2), Bret, Rocci
G: Rocci (3, 1dg)
Substitutions:
Butignol for Bret (63 min.)
Dumas for Dauphin (75 min.)
Attendance: 2,000

Ronnie Duane.

Keith England.

Wayne Proctor.

4th December **Oldham**

GREAT BRITAIN 48		FRANCE 1
Joe Lydon (Widnes)	1.	Patrick Wosniack (Villefranche)
Garry Clark (Hull K.R.)	2.	Hugues Ratier (Lezignan)
Ellery Hanley (Bradford N.)	3.	Philippe Fourquet (Toulouse) Capt.
Des Foy (Oldham)	4.	Roger Palisse (St. Esteve)
Barry Ledger (St. Helens)	5.	Paul Jean (Limoux)
Tony Myler (Widnes)	6.	Patrick Rocci (Le Pontet)
Ray Ashton (Oldham)	7.	Gilles Dumas (St. Gaudens)
Andy Goodway (Oldham)	8.	Jean Luc Rabot (Villeneuve)
Brian Noble (Bradford N.) Capt.	9.	Thierry Barnabe (Le Pontet)
Lee Crooks (Hull)	10.	Serge Titeux (Le Pontet)
Mick Worrall (Oldham)	11.	Mare Palanque (A.S. Carcassonne)
Brian Dunn (Wigan)	12.	Pierre Montgaillard (XIII Catalan)
Terry Flanagan (Oldham)	13.	Thierry Butignol (A.S. Carcassonne)
Garry Schofield (Hull)	14.	Serge Dauphin (Cavaillon)
John Fieldhouse (Warrington)	15.	Frank Romano (Carpentras)

T: Myler (3), Hanley, Foy, Ledger, Schofield, Lydon
G: Lydon (8)
Substitutions:
Schofield for Hanley (38 min.)
Fieldhouse for Dunn (56 min.)
Manager: Dick Gemmell
Coach: Frank Myler
Referee: François Desplats (Toulouse)

G. Rocci (dg)
Substitutions:
Dauphin for Rocci (46 min.)
Romano for Montgaillard (49 min.)
Half-time: 18-1
Attendance: 4,287

Terry Flanagan.

Andy Goodway.

Brian Noble.

UNDER-24s RESULTS

3 Apr. 1965	Great Britain	17	France	9	Toulouse
20 Oct. 1965	Great Britain	12	France	5	Oldham
26 Nov. 1966	Great Britain	4	France	7	Bayonne
17 Apr. 1969	Great Britain	42	France	2	Castleford
14 Nov. 1976	Great Britain	19	France	2	Hull K.R.
5 Dec. 1976	Great Britain	11	France	9	Albi
12 Nov. 1977	Great Britain	27	France	9	Hull
18 Dec. 1977	Great Britain	8	France	4	Tonneins
4 Oct. 1978	Great Britain	8	Australia	30	Hull K.R.
14 Jan. 1979	Great Britain	15	France	3	Limoux
24 Nov. 1979	Great Britain	14	France	2	Leigh
13 Jan. 1980	Great Britain	11	France	7	Carcassonne
5 Nov. 1980	Great Britain	14	New Zealand	18	Fulham
10 Jan. 1981	Great Britain	9	France	2	Villeneuve
16 Jan. 1982	Great Britain	19	France	16	Leeds
21 Feb. 1982	Great Britain	24	France	12	Tonneins
16 Jan. 1983	Great Britain	19	France	5	Carpentras
11 Nov. 1983	Great Britain	28	France	23	Villeneuve
4 Dec. 1983	Great Britain	48	France	1	Oldham

Hat-trick hero Tony Myler, Man of the Match at Oldham.

Great Britain Under-24's since reintroduction in 1976

14th November 1976 Craven Park, Hull
GREAT BRITAIN 19 FRANCE 2

1. Keith Mumby (Bradford N.)
2. Peter Muscroft (New Hunslet)
3. Peter Roe (Bradford N.)
4. Mike Smith (Hull K.R.)
5. David Smith (Leeds)
6. Bruce Burton (Castleford) Capt.
7. Jimmy Nulty (Wigan)
8. Roy Dickinson (Leeds)
9. Eddie Szymala (Barrow)
10. John Wood (Widnes)
11. Jimmy Crampton (Hull)
12. Sammy Turnbull (Salford)
13. Harry Pinner (St. Helens)
14. David Hall (Hull K.R.)
15. David Ward (Leeds)

T: Nulty, D. Smith, Turnbull
G: Mumby (5)
Substitutions:
Hall for D. Smith (77 min.)
Ward for Dickinson (75 min.)
Manager: Harry Womersley
Coach: Johnny Whiteley
Referee: Mick Naughton (Widnes)
Attendance: 6,086

5th December 1976 Albi
GREAT BRITAIN 11 FRANCE 9

1. Keith Mumby (Bradford N.)
2. Peter Muscroft (New Hunslet)
3. Peter Roe (Bradford N.)
4. Mike Smith (Hull K.R.)
5. David Smith (Leeds)
6. Bruce Burton (Castleford) Capt.
7. Jimmy Nulty (Wigan)
8. Roy Dickinson (Leeds)
9. Eddie Szymala (Barrow)
10. John Wood (Widnes)
11. Jimmy Crampton (Hull)
12. Sammy Turnbull (Salford)
13. Harry Pinner (St. Helens)
14. John Joyner (Castleford)
15. David Ward (Leeds)

T: Roe, D. Smith
G: Mumby (2), Pinner (dg)
Substitutions:
Joyner for Muscroft (69 min.)
Ward for Wood (3 min.)
Manager: Harry Womersley
Coach: Johnny Whiteley
Referee: Francois Auriolle (France)
Attendance: 1,800

12th November 1977 Boulevard, Hull
GREAT BRITAIN 27 FRANCE 9

1. Keith Mumby (Bradford N.)
2. Peter Roe (Bradford N.)
3. John Gilbert (Featherstone R.)
4. John Joyner (Castleford)
5. Steve Fenton (Castleford)
6. John Woods (Leigh)
7. Mick Shepherd (Huddersfield)
8. Roy Dickinson (Leeds)
9. Graham Liptrot (St. Helens)
10. Mick Gibbins (Featherstone R.)
11. Trevor Skerrett (Wakefield T.)
12. Jimmy Crampton (Hull) Capt.
13. Keith Bell (Featherstone R.)
14. Mike Smith (Hull K.R.)
15. Harry Pinner (St. Helens)

T: Fenton, Woods, Crampton, Gilbert, Pinner
G: Woods (6)
Substitutions:
Pinner for Skerrett (65 min.)
Manager: Bill Oxley
Coach: Johnny Whiteley
Referee: Joe Jackson (Pudsey)
Attendance: 2,000

18th December 1977 Tonneins
GREAT BRITAIN 8 FRANCE 4

1. Keith Mumby (Bradford N.)
2. Peter Roe (Bradford N.)
3. Mike Smith (Hull K.R.)
4. John Joyner (Castleford)
5. Steve Fenton (Castleford)
6. John Woods (Leigh)
7. Mick Shepherd (Huddersfield)
8. Roy Dickinson (Leeds)
9. Graham Liptrot (St. Helens)
10. Alf Wilkinson (Leigh)
11. Mick Gibbins (Featherstone R.)
12. Jimmy Crampton (Hull) Capt.
13. Keith Bell (Featherstone R.)
14. John Gilbert (Featherstone R.)
15. Harry Pinner (St. Helens)

T: Woods, Bell
G: Woods
Substitutions:
Pinner for Gibbins (55 min.)
Manager: Bill Oxley
Coach: Johnny Whiteley
Referee: M. Sagot (France)
Attendance: 3,500

4th October 1978 Craven Park, Hull

GREAT BRITAIN 8 AUSTRALIA 30

1. Keith Mumby (Bradford N.)
2. Peter Muscroft (New Hunslet)
3. Mike Smith (Hull K.R.)
4. John Joyner (Castleford)
5. Jim Hornby (Wigan)
6. John Woods (Leigh)
7. Dale Fennell (Featherstone R.)
8. Roy Dickinson (Leeds)
9. Graham Liptrot (St. Helens)
10. Roy Holdstock (Hull K.R.)
11. Bob Eccles (Warrington)
12. Peter Smith (Featherstone R.)
13. Phil Hogan (Barrow) Capt.
14. Steve Evans (Featherstone R.)
15. Harry Pinner (St. Helens)

G: Mumby (4)
Substitution:
Pinner for P. Smith (54 min.)

Manager: Frank Dyson
Coach: Johnny Whiteley
Referee: Fred Lindop (Wakefield)
Attendance: 6,418

14th January 1979 Limoux

GREAT BRITAIN 15 FRANCE 3

1. John Woods (Leigh)
2. Terry Richardson (Castleford)
3. John Joyner (Castleford)
4. Mike Smith (Hull K.R.)
5. Jim Hornby (Wigan)
6. Barry Banks (York)
7. Neil Holding (St. Helens)
8. Steve O'Neill (Wigan)
9. Graham Liptrot (St. Helens)
10. Brian Case (Warrington)
11. Ian Potter (Warrington)
12. Ian Hartley (Workington T.)
13. Phil Hogan (Hull K.R.) Capt.
14. John Gilbert (Featherstone R.)
15. Harry Pinner (St. Helens)

T: Holding, Joyner
G: Woods (4), Holding (dg)
Substitutions:
Gilbert for Richardson (79 min.)
Pinner for Case (73 min.)
Manager: Frank Dyson
Coach: Johnny Whiteley
Referee: Billy Thompson (Huddersfield)
Attendance: 2,950

24th November 1979 Leigh

GREAT BRITAIN 14 FRANCE 2

1. Mick Burke (Widnes)
2. Des Drummond (Leigh)
3. David Stephenson (Salford)
4. Mike Smith (Hull K.R.)
5. Steve Fenton (Castleford)
6. John Woods (Leigh) Capt.
7. David Cairns (Barrow)
8. Roy Holdstock (Hull K.R.)
9. Malcolm Smith (Wigan)
10. Bob Eccles (Warrington)
11. Malcolm Swann (Leigh)
12. Keith Rayne (Wakefield T.)
13. Harry Pinner (St. Helens)
14. Ian Rudd (Workington T.)
15. Alan Rathbone (Leigh)

T: Fenton, Drummond
G: Burke (4)
Substitutions:
Rudd for Smith (66 min.)
Rathbone for Rayne (66 min.)
Manager: Bill Oxley
Coach: Johnny Whiteley
Referee: Francois Auriolle (France)
Attendance: 4,077

13th January 1980 Carcassonne

GREAT BRITAIN 11 FRANCE 7

1. Mick Burke (Widnes)
2. Des Drummond (Leigh)
3. David Stephenson (Salford)
4. Mike Smith (Hull K.R.)
5. Steve Fenton (Castleford)
6. Ian Rudd (Workington T.)
7. Neil Holding (St. Helens)
8. Roy Holdstock (Hull K.R.)
9. Paul O'Neill (Salford)
10. Keith Rayne (Wakefield T.)
11. Kevin Ward (Castleford)
12. Kevin James (Bramley)
13. Harry Pinner (St. Helens) Capt.
14. Steve Dennison (Hull)
15. Alan Rathbone (Leigh)

T: Drummond, Stephenson, Fenton
G: Burke

Manager: Bill Oxley
Coach: Johnny Whiteley
Referee: Fred Lindop (Wakefield)
Attendance: 3,460

Wigan's Brian Dunn off-loads to Joe Lydon, with Des Foy in support in the return match at Oldham.

5th November 1980 Fulham

GREAT BRITAIN 14 NEW ZEALAND 18

1. Mick Burke (Widnes)
2. Rick Thackray (Warrington)
3. David Stephenson (Salford)
4. Gary Hyde (Castleford)
5. Steve Fenton (Castleford)
6. Steve Evans (Featherstone R.) Capt.
7. Neil Holding (St. Helens)
8. Gary Van Bellen (Bradford N.)
9. Paul O'Neill (Salford)
10. Brian Case (Warrington)
11. Kevin Ward (Castleford)
12. Vince Fox (Whitehaven)
13. Terry Flanagan (Oldham)
14. Keith Bentley (Widnes)
15. Mike O'Neill (Widnes)

T: Evans, Holding
G: Burke (4)
Substitutions:
Bentley for Thackray (64 min.)
O'Neill for Van Bellen (68 min.)
Manager: Colin Hutton
Coach: Johnny Whiteley
Referee: Stan Wall (Leigh)
Attendance: 2,395

10th January 1981 Villeneuve

GREAT BRITAIN 9 FRANCE 2

1. Keith Mumby (Bradford N.)
2. Des Drummond (Leigh)
3. John Gilbert (Featherstone R.)
4. Colin Whitfield (Salford)
5. Steve Fenton (Castleford)
6. Steve Evans (Featherstone R.) Capt.
7. Paul Harkin (Hull K.R.)
8. Steve O'Neill (Wigan)
9. Paul O'Neill (Salford)
10. Brian Case (Warrington)
11. Ian Potter (Warrington)
12. Kevin Ward (Castleford)
13. Terry Flanagan (Oldham)
14. Kevin Dick (Leeds)
15. Mike O'Neill (Widnes)

T: Drummond
G: Whitfield (3)
Manager: Colin Hutton
Coach: Johnny Whiteley
Referee: Stan Wall (Leigh)
Attendance: 1,345

16th January 1982 Leeds

GREAT BRITAIN 19 FRANCE 16

1. Mick Burke (Widnes)
2. Des Drummond (Leigh)
3. David Stephenson (Salford)
4. Chris Arkwright (St. Helens)
5. Henderson Gill (Wigan)
6. Ellery Hanley (Bradford N.)
7. Andrew Gregory (Widnes)
8. Mike O'Neill (Widnes)
9. Brian Noble (Bradford N.)
10. Barry Johnson (Castleford) Capt.
11. David Hobbs (Featherstone R.)
12. Ian Potter (Leigh)
13. Andrew Timson (Castleford)
14. John Myler (Widnes)
15. Brian Case (Warrington)

T: Drummond, Stephenson, Timson
G: Burke (3), Hobbs (2)
Substitutions:
Myler for Burke (Half-time)
Case for Hanley (Half-time)
Manager: Colin Hutton
Coach: Johnny Whiteley
Referee: Marcel Alba (Perpignan)
Attendance: 1,151

21st February 1982 Tonneins

GREAT BRITAIN 24 FRANCE 12

1. John Myler (Widnes)
2. Des Drummond (Leigh)
3. David Stephenson (Wigan)
4. Steve Evans (Hull) Capt.
5. Phil Ford (Warrington)
6. Tony Myler (Widnes)
7. David Cairns (Barrow)
8. Gary Van Bellen (Bradford N.)
9. Brian Noble (Bradford N.)
10. Barry Johnson (Castleford)
11. David Hobbs (Featherstone R.)
12. Ian Potter (Leigh)
13. Andrew Timson (Castleford)
14. Gary Hyde (Castleford)
15. Mike O'Neill (Widnes)

T: Drummond (3), Evans
G: Hobbs (5), J. Myler
Substitutions:
Hyde for Stephenson (Half-time)
O'Neill for Johnson (68 min.)
Manager: Colin Hutton
Coach: Johnny Whiteley
Referee: Gerry Kershaw (York)
Attendance: 3,780

16th January 1983 Carpentras

GREAT BRITAIN 19 FRANCE 5

1. Mick Burke (Widnes)
2. Garry Clark (Hull K.R.)
3. Ronnie Duane (Warrington)
4. Joe Lydon (Widnes)
5. David Moll (Keighley)
6. Tony Myler (Widnes)
7. Ray Ashton (Oldham)
8. Mike O'Neill (Widnes)
9. Brian Noble (Bradford N.)
10. Andy Goodway (Oldham)
11. Mick Worrall (Oldham)
12. John Fieldhouse (Warrington)
13. Terry Flanagan (Oldham) Capt.
14. David Hulme (Widnes)
15. Ron Smith (Salford)

T: Clark (3), Fieldhouse, Duane
G: Burke (2)
Substitution:
Smith for Fieldhouse (59 min.)
Manager: Dick Gemmell
Coach: Frank Myler
Referee: John Holdsworth (Leeds)
Attendance: 1,500

Under-24s full back Joe Lydon under pressure from French hooker Thierry Barnabe.

GREAT BRITAIN UNDER-24s REGISTER
Since reintroduction in 1976

The following is a register of appearances for Great Britain Under-24s since this classification of match was reintroduced in 1976.

Figures in brackets are the total appearances, with the plus sign indicating substitute appearances, e.g. (7+3).

Away matches are in bold letters. Substitute appearances are in lower case letters.

A - Australia, F - France, NZ - New Zealand.

ARKWRIGHT, C. (1) St. Helens: 1982 F
ASHTON, R. (3) Oldham: 1983 **F, F,** F

BANKS, B. (1) York: 1979 **F**
BELL, K. (2) Featherstone R.: 1977 F, **F**
BENTLEY, K. (+1) Widnes: 1980 nz
BURKE, M. (5) Widnes: 1979 F; 1980 **F**, NZ; 1982 F; 1983 **F**
BURTON, B. (2) Castleford: 1976 F, **F**

CAIRNS, D. (2) Barrow: 1979 F; 1982 **F**
CASE, B. (3+1) Warrington: 1979 **F**; 1980 NZ: 1981 **F**; 1982 f
CLARK, G. (3) Hull K.R.: 1983 **F, F,** F
CRAMPTON, J. (4) Hull: 1976 F, **F**; 1977 F, **F**
CROOKS, L. (1) Hull: 1983 F

DICKINSON, R. (5) Leeds: 1976 F, **F**; 1977 F, **F**; 1978 A
DRUMMOND, D. (5) Leigh: 1979 F; 1980 **F**; 1981 **F**; 1982 F, **F**
DUANE, R. (2) Warrington: 1983 **F, F**
DUNN, B. (2) Wigan: 1983 **F**, F

ECCLES, R. (2) Warrington: 1978 A; 1979 F
ENGLAND, K. (+1) Castleford: 1983 **f**
EVANS, S. (3) Featherstone R.: 1980 NZ; 1981 **F**; Hull: 1982 **F**

FENNELL, D. (1) Featherstone R.: 1978 A
FENTON, S. (6) Castleford: 1977 F, **F**; 1979 F; 1980 **F**, NZ; 1981 **F**
FIELDHOUSE, J. (1+1) Warrington: 1983 **F**, f
FLANAGAN, T. (5) Oldham: 1980 NZ; 1981 **F**; 1983 **F**, **F**, F
FORD, Phil (1) Warrington: 1982 **F**
FOX, V. (1) Whitehaven: 1980 NZ
FOY, D. (2) Oldham: 1983 **F**, F

GIBBINS, M. (2) Featherstone R.: 1977 F, **F**
GILBERT, J. (2+1) Featherstone R.: 1977 F; 1977 **f**; 1981 **F**
GILL, H. (1) Wigan: 1982 F
GOODWAY, A. (2) Oldham: 1983 **F**, F
GREGORY, A. (1) Widnes: 1982 F

HALL, D. (+1) Hull K.R.: 1976 f
HANLEY, E. (2) Bradford N.: 1982 F; 1983 F
HARKIN, P. (1) Hull K.R.: 1981 **F**
HARTLEY, I. (1) Workington T.: 1979 **F**
HOBBS, D. (2) Featherstone R.: 1982 F, **F**
HOGAN, P. (2) Barrow: 1978 A; Hull K.R.: 1979 **F**
HOLDING, N. (4) St. Helens: 1979 **F**; 1980 **F**, NZ; 1983 **F**
HOLDSTOCK, R. (3) Hull K.R.: 1978 A; 1979 F; 1980 **F**
HORNBY, J. (2) Wigan: 1978 A; 1979 **F**
HYDE, G. (1+1) Castleford: 1980 NZ; 1982 **f**

JAMES, K. (1) Bramley: 1980 **F**
JOHNSON, B. (2) Castleford: 1982 F, **F**
JOYNER, J. (4+1) Castleford: 1976 **f**; 1977 F, **F**; 1978 A; 1979 **F**

LEDGER, B. (2) St. Helens: 1983 **F**, F
LIPTROT, G. (4) St. Helens: 1977 F, **F**; 1978 A; 1979 **F**
LYDON, J. (3) Widnes: 1983 **F**, **F**, F

MASKILL, C. (1) Wakefield T.: 1983 **F**
MOLL, D. (1) Keighley: 1983 **F**
MUMBY, K. (6) Bradford N.: 1976 F, **F**; 1977 F, **F**; 1978 A; 1981 **F**
MUSCROFT, P. (3) New Hunslet: 1976 F, **F**; 1978 A
MYLER, A. (3) Widnes: 1982 **F**; 1983 **F**, F
MYLER, J. (1+1) Widnes: 1982 f; **F**

NOBLE, B. (4) Bradford N.: 1982 F, **F**; 1983 **F**, F
NULTY, J. (2) Wigan: 1976 F, **F**

O'NEILL, M. (3+2) Widnes: 1980 nz; 1982 F, **f**; 1983 **F**, **F**
O'NEILL, P. (3) Salford: 1980 **F**, NZ; 1981 **F**
O'NEILL, S. (2) Wigan: 1979 **F**; 1981 **F**

PINNER, H. (4+4) St. Helens: 1976 F, **F**; 1977 f, **f**; 1978 a; 1979 **f**, F, 1980 **F**
POTTER, I. (4) Warrington: 1979 **F**; 1981 **F**; Leigh: 1982 F, **F**
PROCTOR, W. (1) Hull: 1983 **F**

RATHBONE, A. (+1) Leigh: 1979 f
RAYNE, Keith (2) Wakefield T.: 1979 F; 1980 **F**
RICHARDSON, T. (1) Castleford: 1979 **F**
ROE, P. (4) Bradford N.: 1976 F, **F**; 1977 F, **F**
RUDD, I. (1+1) Workington T.: 1979 f; 1980 **F**

SCHOFIELD, G. (+2) Hull: 1983 **f**, f
SHEPHERD, M. (2) Huddersfield: 1977 F, **F**
SKERRETT, T. (1) Wakefield T.: 1977 F
SMITH, D. (2) Leeds: 1976 F, **F**
SMITH, Malcolm (1) Wigan: 1979 F
SMITH, Mike (7) Hull K.R.: 1976 F, **F**; 1977 **F**; 1978 A; 1979 **F**, F; 1980 **F**
SMITH, P. (1) Featherstone R.: 1978 A
SMITH, R. (+1) Salford: 1983 **f**
STEPHENSON, D. (5) Salford: 1979 F; 1980 **F**, NZ; 1982 F; Wigan: 1982 **F**
SWANN, M. (1) Leigh: 1979 F
SYZMALA, E. (2) Barrow: 1976 F, **F**

THACKRAY, R. (1) Warrington: 1980 NZ
TIMSON, A. (2) Castleford: 1982 F, **F**
TURNBULL, S. (2) Salford: 1976 F, **F**

VAN BELLEN, G. (2) Bradford N.: 1980 NZ; 1982 **F**

WARD, D. (+2) Leeds: 1976 f, **f**
WARD, K. (3) Castleford: 1980 **F**, NZ; 1981 **F**
WHITFIELD, C. (1) Salford: 1981 **F**
WILKINSON, A. (1) Leigh: 1977 **F**
WOOD, J. (2) Widnes: 1977 F, **F**
WOODS, J. (5) Leigh: 1977 F, **F**; 1978 A; 1979 **F**, F
WORRALL, M. (3) Oldham: 1983 **F**, **F**, F

International prop Roy Holdstock, star of Hull K.R.'s title success in the Yorkshire Senior Competition play-off final at Castleford.

A-TEAMS

A-TEAMS

LANCASHIRE COMBINATION

FINAL TABLE 1983-84

	P.	W.	D.	L.	For	Agt.	Pts.
Warrington	16	13	1	2	452	201	27
Wigan	16	11	0	5	335	320	22
St. Helens	16	8	2	6	272	278	18
Widnes	16	8	1	7	300	267	17
Oldham	16	8	1	7	293	294	17
Barrow	16	7	0	9	316	309	14
Swinton	16	6	1	9	269	259	13
Leigh	16	5	0	11	247	367	10
Salford	16	3	0	13	222	411	6

YORKSHIRE SENIOR COMPETITION

FINAL TABLE 1983-84

					FOR				AGAINST				
	P.	W.	D.	L.	Dr.	Gls.	Trs.	Pts.	Dr.	Gls.	Trs.	Pts.	Pts.
Castleford	22	19	0	3	0	101	119	678	2	42	39	242	38
Hull K.R.	21	17	0	4	1	91	124	679	2	33	34	204	34
Leeds	22	16	1	5	1	89	140	739	3	39	53	293	33
Hull	22	15	0	7	2	82	106	590	3	50	60	343	30
Featherstone R.	22	12	2	8	5	55	66	379	5	53	68	383	26
Bradford N.	21	10	2	9	2	55	67	380	4	56	62	364	22
Halifax	22	9	2	11	3	46	63	347	2	80	104	578	20
Dewsbury	22	8	1	13	5	57	63	371	4	70	79	460	17
Hunslet	21	8	1	12	3	58	76	423	3	83	91	533	17
Batley	22	5	1	16	13	46	34	241	3	71	106	569	11
York	22	3	1	18	2	33	40	228	7	79	108	597	7
Keighley	21	2	1	18	4	45	42	262	3	102	136	751	5

LANCASHIRE COMBINATION

1983-84 RESULTS

Home. / Away.	Barrow	Leigh	Oldham	St. Helens	Salford	Swinton	Warrington	Widnes	Wigan
Barrow	—	28-26	18-24	19-4	33-6	14-13	0-25	22-19	12-14
Leigh	20-16	—	25-18	6-20	14-18	16-23	8-30	20-12	23-18
Oldham	20-16	16-12	—	19-2	30-24	12-12	30-12	18-6	18-32
St. Helens	48-26	14-12	26-8	—	24-10	24-18	24-24	18-16	8-14
Salford	6-28	28-35	24-18	12-15	—	14-17	8-46	10-4	8-12
Swinton	0-10	38-6	5-12	14-10	38-18	—	6-13	18-14	16-32
Warrington	36-28	24-4	20-12	42-12	36-8	28-14	—	38-6	28-14
Widnes	24-20	26-10	28-12	16-16	44-10	16-10	19-10	—	38-28
Wigan	24-23	38-10	32-30	22-19	20-18	20-17	8-40	7-12	—

YORKSHIRE SENIOR COMPETITION

1983-84 RESULTS

Home. / Away.	Batley	Bradford N.	Castleford	Dewsbury	Featherstone R.	Halifax	Hull	Hull K.R.	Hunslet	Keighley	Leeds	York
Batley	—	15-16	12-34	12-6	19-20	16-16	4-62	10-6	14-28	36-8	4-42	4-7
Bradford N.	18-20	—	6-20	30-2	14-8	32-4	14-60	10-12	—	23-6	4-30	36-10
Castleford	56-0	38-20	—	40-5	36-4	42-6	42-10	16-12	30-24	30-4	20-10	46-12
Dewsbury	40-6	12-34	2-40	—	30-6	32-18	15-22	10-18	22-13	25-16	10-16	26-8
Featherstone R.	12-8	18-18	10-4	20-10	—	14-21	23-20	14-20	22-21	34-0	21-16	36-10
Halifax	16-3	0-18	8-38	28-18	32-32	—	8-26	10-4	6-28	46-15	10-52	16-2
Hull	70-10	27-22	10-12	46-14	18-4	30-14	—	12-4	36-18	64-14	19-22	34-6
Hull K.R.	70-6	50-10	38-2	24-0	14-0	70-10	23-10	—	52-16	—	22-18	54-10
Hunslet	26-8	28-12	11-34	22-22	12-25	22-30	0-42	8-50	—	46-28	42-22	14-1
Keighley	20-30	6-10	4-66	12-28	18-37	8-12	20-44	16-52	11-4	—	8-70	20-12
Leeds	28-2	26-26	30-12	19-18	34-4	56-9	44-4	4-26	48-12	62-8	—	54-0
York	18-4	16-7	4-20	10-14	8-15	20-27	10-28	10-54	18-28	20-20	14-36	—

LANCASHIRE COUNTY CHALLENGE SHIELD 1983-84

*Two-legged ties

PRELIMINARY ROUND

Barrow	22	Salford	22
	18		44

FIRST ROUND

Oldham	8	Swinton	0
	26		16
Salford	12	Widnes	16
	0		38
Warrington	18	St. Helens	9
	9		14
Wigan	28	Leigh	12
	12		34

SEMI-FINALS

Leigh	14	Warrington	26
	2		28
Oldham	14	Widnes	8
	14		8

FINAL

Oldham	13	Warrington	23
	18		20
Aggregate:			
Oldham	31	Warrington	43

YORKSHIRE SENIOR COMPETITION CHALLENGE CUP 1983-84

FIRST ROUND

Dewsbury	6	Castleford	42
Halifax	20	Hull K.R.	12
Hull	30	Bradford N.	16
Hunslet	35	York	10

Byes: Batley, Featherstone R., Keighley, Leeds

SECOND ROUND

Featherstone R.	25	Castleford	22
Halifax	19	Hull	21
Hunslet	20	Batley	12
Keighley	12	Leeds	24

SEMI-FINALS

Featherstone R.	18	Hunslet	29
Hull	30	Leeds	14

FINAL

Hull	28	Hunslet	10

YORKSHIRE SENIOR COMPETITION TOP FOUR PLAY-OFF 1983-84

Castleford (1st)	22	Hull (4th)	8
Hull K.R. (2nd)	68	Leeds (3rd)	6

FINAL

Castleford	16	Hull K.R.	20

Wigan second row man Shaun Wane on duty for Great Britain Colts against France at Arles.

COLTS

COLTS

COLTS LEAGUE

FINAL TABLE 1983-84

					FOR				AGAINST				
	P.	W.	D.	L.	Dr.	Gls.	Trs.	Pts.	Dr.	Gls.	Trs.	Pts.	Pts.
Castleford	24	23	0	1	0	141	184	1018	6	33	32	200	46
Leeds	25	20	0	5	6	101	156	832	4	45	44	270	40
Hull	23	19	0	4	4	82	98	560	4	57	51	322	38
Bradford N.	24	15	1	8	7	95	152	805	4	62	52	336	31
Hull K.R.	24	14	2	8	4	91	122	674	0	48	44	272	30
Hunslet	23	15	0	8	2	73	104	564	4	55	62	362	30
Huddersfield	24	15	0	9	1	68	120	617	2	55	81	436	30
Wigan	24	14	1	9	1	102	143	777	7	81	59	405	29
Leigh	22	12	1	9	6	96	93	570	5	51	82	435	25
Wakefield T.	22	11	0	11	4	60	114	580	3	65	66	397	22
Oldham	23	11	0	12	1	80	84	497	5	69	78	455	22
Barrow	25	11	0	14	13	76	85	505	0	80	104	576	22
St. Helens	23	9	0	14	4	67	73	430	5	98	113	653	18
Halifax	25	8	0	17	2	60	60	362	7	99	133	737	16
Bramley	18	7	1	10	1	36	59	309	4	46	60	336	15
York	25	3	0	22	1	30	30	181	1	106	188	965	6
Salford	23	3	0	20	2	39	24	176	3	110	186	967	6
Rochdale H.	25	1	0	24	5	22	16	113	1	115	204	1047	2
Cardiff C.	6	0	0	6	1	3	4	23	0	47	82	422	0

Powerhouse Hull Colts product Andy Dannatt in action for Great Britain in Arles.

COLTS LEAGUE

1983-84 RESULTS

Home. / Away.	Barrow	Bradford N.	Bramley	Cardiff C.	Castleford	Halifax	Huddersfield	Hull	Hull K.R.	Hunslet	Leeds	Leigh	Oldham	Rochdale H.	St. Helens	Salford	Wakefield T.	Wigan	York
Barrow	—	6-36	15-0	—	—	42-14	22-36	3-14	—	4-10	—	—	8-16	34-4	16-28	42-8	48-12	6-44	40-2
Bradford N.	—	—	56-0	—	17-42	—	—	13-14	6-6	12-14	12-16	29-2	40-16	48-4	28-27	—	—	42-2	78-0
Bramley	14-31	—	—	—	—	12-20	2-20	—	—	—	18-29	14-14	12-13	32-16	—	36-6	8-48	—	16-2
Cardiff C.	—	—	—	—	6-82	—	—	—	—	—	0-62	—	6-48	—	—	—	—	—	—
Castleford	62-15	12-16	—	—	—	52-6	—	18-12	30-10	22-4	32-12	72-8	32-8	—	68-2	—	—	26-22	78-0
Halifax	10-13	6-54	16-18	—	—	—	17-21	—	—	14-30	8-22	—	28-16	24-11	26-27	22-0	4-66	—	18-8
Huddersfield	46-6	6-64	22-20	54-4	14-42	52-6	—	18-20	—	—	0-44	—	—	52-0	—	34-2	8-6	—	88-0
Hull	18-20	4-38	—	—	2-16	40-8	—	—	32-24	28-0	19-16	32-14	—	—	18-4	48-10	—	32-8	—
Hull K.R.	34-8	16-14	—	—	12-22	54-4	46-8	8-14	—	26-0	38-0	22-10	66-16	—	30-0	—	34-8	22-22	56-0
Hunslet	—	—	—	72-6	4-22	—	44-0	32-14	10-2	—	9-15	—	—	54-0	14-20	—	—	14-12	48-13
Leeds	38-15	24-6	—	—	—	—	—	14-22	24-6	38-6	—	36-4	—	62-0	30-0	66-0	48-0	14-16	60-4
Leigh	54-6	44-15	—	—	8-20	73-10	—	20-26	22-15	23-27	9-37	—	29-0	—	26-12	—	16-10	18-4	—
Oldham	44-12	—	24-7	—	—	30-6	6-18	8-20	—	12-18	8-34	—	—	22-8	—	56-14	—	12-34	40-0
Rochdale H.	0-23	—	4-30	—	3-62	8-32	0-50	0-42	2-62	—	—	2-30	4-44	—	0-60	16-18	1-50	—	0-26
St. Helens	—	18-51	—	—	8-48	—	21-10	—	12-24	14-24	14-66	12-26	34-28	—	—	64-3	9-8	6-50	—
Salford	10-54	0-70	0-34	—	0-88	0-21	4-14	—	4-50	0-94	—	8-50	—	16-18	—	—	—	33-24	22-10
Wakefield T.	30-5	19-44	—	—	—	36-6	20-6	14-20	—	13-16	—	—	25-18	74-2	—	—	—	—	44-2
Wigan	—	34-16	—	104-1	6-24	32-8	30-12	24-29	12-11	36-20	24-25	—	—	76-4	39-12	—	56-12	—	—
York	8-39	—	0-36	—	—	20-28	10-28	12-58	—	—	—	8-54	0-12	24-6	4-8	16-10	8-36	6-62	—

COLTS CHALLENGE CUP 1984

PRELIMINARY ROUND

Bradford N.	50	York	4

FIRST ROUND

Hull	32	Hunslet	0
Halifax	6	Bradford N.	36
Huddersfield	18	Barrow	6
Leigh	17	Hull K.R.	2
Rochdale H.	14	Oldham	12
St. Helens	50	Salford	2
Wakefield T.	10	Castleford	24
Wigan	20	Leeds	21

SECOND ROUND

Castleford	68	St. Helens	2
Huddersfield	12	Bradford N.	30
Hull	22	Leeds	16
Rochdale H.	0	Leigh	68

SEMI-FINALS

Bradford N.	13	Hull	14
Leigh	24	Castleford	32

FINAL at Hull K.R.

Castleford	24	Hull	11

COLTS CHALLENGE CUP ROLL OF HONOUR

1976:
Wigan 24 Hull K.R. 12
at Wigan

1977:
Hull K.R. 15 St. Helens 13
at Leeds

1978:
Castleford 19 Wakefield T. 10
at Leeds

1979:
Hull 17 Widnes 17
at Bradford
Replay:
Hull 22 Widnes 14
at Wakefield

1980:
Leeds 25 Widnes 14
at Wigan

1981:
Hull 32 Castleford 17
at Leeds

1982:
Hull 19 Hull K.R. 16
at Leeds

1983:
Hunslet 11 Hull K.R. 3
at Hull K.R.

1984:
Castleford 24 Hull 11
at Hull K.R.

The Jim Challinor Memorial Trophy for the Man-of-the-Match in the Final:

1977: Steve Crooks (Hull K.R.)
1978: Paul Bastow (Castleford)
1979: Gary Peacham (Hull)
1980: Ian Mackintosh (Leeds)
1981: Lee Crooks (Hull)
1982: Tracey Lazenby (Hull K.R.)
1983: Andrew Tosney (Hunslet)
1984: Dean Mountain (Castleford)

COLTS PREMIERSHIP 1984

FIRST ROUND

Bradford N. (4)	31	Hull K.R. (5)	12
Castleford (1)	20	Wigan (8)	38
Hull (3)	50	Hunslet (6)	12
Leeds (2)	38	Huddersfield (7)	10

* Positions in brackets denote league position

SEMI-FINALS

Hull	16	Bradford N.	6
Leeds	28	Wigan	10

FINAL at Leeds

Hull	8	Leeds	24

Hull loose forward Gary Divorty, captain of Great Britain Colts at Wigan.

COLTS PREMIERSHIP ROLL OF HONOUR

1976:
Hull K.R. 26 Wakefield T. 12
at Swinton

1977:
Bradford N. 29 Hull K.R. 15
at Swinton

1978:
Wakefield T. 23 Hull K.R. 20
at Swinton

1979:
Hull 17 Hull K.R. 9
at Huddersfield

1980:
Oldham 21 Leeds 13
at Swinton

1981:
Hull K.R. 27 Hull 21
at Leeds

1982:
Hull 19 Hull K.R. 11
at Leeds

1983:
Hull 34 Leigh 5
at Leeds

1984:
Leeds 24 Hull 8
at Leeds

The Dave Valentine Memorial Trophy for the Man-of-the-Match in the Final:

1977: Paul Harkin (Bradford N.)
1978: David Wandless (Wakefield T.)
1979: Kevin Hickman (Hull K.R.)
1980: Andrew Mackintosh (Leeds)
1981: Malcolm Beall (Hull K.R.)
1982: Shaun Patrick (Hull)
1983: Andrew Kamis (Hull)
1984: Paul Medley (Leeds)

COLTS INTERNATIONALS

28th January, 1984 **Arles**

GREAT BRITAIN 24		**FRANCE 10**
Steve Rea (Barrow)	1.	Vincent Baloup (La Reole)
Norman Francis (Leeds)	2.	Didier Couston (Carpentras)
Garry Schofield (Hull) Capt.	3.	Claude Gilbert (XIII Catalan)
Shaun Allen (St. Helens)	4.	Patrick Alberola (Lezignan)
Richard Francis (Bradford N.)	5.	Gerard Nicolas (Toulouse)
David Creasser (Leeds)	6.	Didier Lacourt (Toulouse)
Darren Beazant (Leigh)	7.	Patrick Entat (Avignon)
Andrew Dannatt (Leigh)	8.	Jean Marie Frileux (Carcassonne)
Paul Groves (Salford)	9.	Marc Guach (Pia-Le Barcares)
Adrian Crawford (Bradford N.)	10.	Phillippe Gil (Carcassonne)
Shaun Wane (Wigan)	11.	Franck Romano (Carpentras)
John Westhead (Leigh)	12.	Daniel Bonnet (Limoux)
Gary Divorty (Hull)	13.	Phillipe Bosch (Villefranche)
Keith Holden (Wigan)	14.	Dominique Espugna (Lezignan)
Ian Fletcher (Castleford)	15.	Thierry Brenctz (Albi)
Jeff Clare (Wigan)	16.	Arman Mimouni (Pia-Le Barcares)
T: Schofield (2), Allen, Francis		T: Lacourt
G: Creasser (2), Divorty (2)		G: Lacourt (3)
Substitutions:		Substitutions:
Fletcher for Crawford (57 min.)		Mimouni for Frileux (60 min.)
Holden for Beazant (67 min.)		Brenctz for Romano (72 min.)
Clare for Allen (72 min.)		Espugna for Gilbert (74 min.)
Manager: Harry Jepson		Half-time: 6-8
Coach: Geoff Lyon		Referee: M. R. Whitfield (Widnes)
		Attendance: 1,800

18th February, 1984 **Wigan**

GREAT BRITAIN 22		**FRANCE 26**
Steve Rea (Barrow)	1.	Didier Lacourt (Toulouse)
Ian Thomas (Huddersfield)	2.	Jean Esponella (Pia)
Jeff Clare (Wigan)	3.	Vincent Baloup (La Reole)
Steve Parrish (Bradford N.)	4.	Neol Sautrice (Pia)
Les Quirk (Barrow)	5.	Didier Couston (Toulouse)
Mike Ford (Wigan)	6.	Dominique Espugna (Lezignan)
Darren Beazant (Leigh)	7.	Patrick Entat (Avignon)
Andrew Dannatt (Hull)	8.	Jean Marie Frileux (Carcassonne)
Paul Groves (Salford)	9.	Phillipe Duclaux (Avignon)
Adrian Crawford (Bradford N.)	10.	Thierry Brenctz (Albi)
Ian Fletcher (Castleford)	11.	Daniel Bonnet (Limoux)
John Westhead (Leigh)	12.	Phillipe Bosch (Villefranche) Capt.
Gary Divorty (Hull) Capt.	13.	Didier Casaillere (Pia)
Keith Holden (Wigan)	14.	Didier Buttignol (Carcassonne)
Paul Hardman (Leigh)	15.	Emmanuel Joets (Le Pontet)
Shaun Fairhurst (Leigh)	16.	Jacques Bouscayrol (Villefranche)
T: Quirk (2), Thomas, Beazant		T: Baloup, Espugna, Entat, Bonnet, Couston
G: Clare (3)		G: Lacourt (3)
Substitutions:		Substitutions:
Holden for Beazant (65 min.)		Buttignol for Sautrice (58 min.)
Hardman for Crawford (65 min.)		
Fairhurst for Quirk (73 min.)		Half-time: 16-12
Manager: Harry Jepson		Referee: Francois Desplats (Toulouse)
Coach: Geoff Lyon		Attendance: 1,200

COLTS INTERNATIONAL RESULTS

1975-76:
France 39 Great Britain 5 .... Cannes
Great Britain 31 France 12 .... Salford

1976-77:
France 15 Great Britain 19 .... Avignon
Great Britain 6 France 2 .... Wigan

1977-78:
Great Britain 8 France 7 .... Widnes
France 24 Great Britain 13 .... Perpignan

1978-79:
Great Britain 17 France 7 .... Craven Park, Hull
France 22 Great Britain 5 .... Perpignan

1979-80:
France 11 Great Britain 29 .... Perpignan
Great Britain 31 France 2 .... Oldham

1980-81:
Great Britain 5 France 5 .... Leeds
France 25 Great Britain 12 .... Cavaillon

1981-82:
Great Britain 8 France 10 .... Hull
France 4 Great Britain 15 .... Limoux

1982-3:
France 12 Great Britain 12 .... Apt
Great Britain 24 France 10 .... Leigh

1982 Tour:
Australia 20 Great Britain 15 .... Brisbane

1983-84:
France 10 Great Britain 24 .... Arles
Great Britain 22 France 26 .... Wigan

Great Britain Colts v France at Wigan. Back row, left to right: Alan Hindle (Assistant Manager), Clare (Wigan), Dannatt (Hull), Westhead (Leigh), Parrish (Bradford N.), Fairhurst (Leigh), Hardman (Leigh). Middle row, left to right: Ford (Wigan), Thomas (Huddersfield), Harry Jepson (Manager), Divorty (Hull, Capt), Geoff Lyon (Coach), Rea (Barrow), Quirk (Barrow), Ivor Edwards (Management Committee). Front row, left to right: Alan Bass (Physiotherapist), Crawford (Bradford N.), Groves (Salford), Beazant (Leigh), Holden (Wigan), Fletcher (Castleford).

GREAT BRITAIN COLTS TEAMS

Cannes, 7.3.76:
Midgley (Wakefield T.), Morgan (Wakefield T.), Noble (Wakefield T.), Woods (Leigh), Peters (Leeds), Slater (Bradford N.), Crossley (Wakefield T.), Gaskell (Wigan), Brierley (Rochdale H.), Woods (Hull K.R.), Harrison (Leeds), Davidson (Hull K.R.), Bailey (Castleford). Subs: Burke (Leigh), Derbyshire (Wigan), Gittens (Leigh).
T: Woods. G: Noble.
Salford, 28.3.76:
Oulton (Castleford), Morgan (Wakefield T.), Davies (Wigan), Driver (Leeds), Newall (Bradford N.), Walsh (Wigan), Dick (Leeds), Roberts (Bradford N.), Miller (Leeds), Budby (Leeds), Dootson (Wigan), Burton (Leeds), Pinner (St. Helens). Subs: Slater (Bradford N.), Fletcher (Warrington), Birts (Bradford N.).
T: Dick (2), Oulton (2), Davies, Miller, Walsh.
G: Dick (5).

Avignon, 6.3.77:
Irvine (St. Helens), Whitfield (Bradford N.), Wilby (Leeds), Endersby (Wakefield T.), Naravu (Rochdale H.), Slater (Bradford N.), Harkin (Bradford N.), Edmonds (Hull K.R.), Whitehouse (Leeds), Nulty (St. Helens), Douglas (Hull K.R.), Oldham (Salford), Heron (Leeds). Subs: Saxon (St. Helens), Crooks (Hull K.R.), Parkes (St. Helens).
T: Douglas, Naravu, Whitfield. G: Endersby (2).

Wigan, 26.3.77:
Irvine (St. Helens), Whitfield (Bradford N.), Wilby (Leeds), Endersby (Wakefield T.), Parkes (St. Helens), Slater (Bradford N.), Harkin (Bradford N.), Edmonds (Hull K.R.), Whitehouse (Leeds), Nulty (St. Helens), Douglas (Hull K.R.), Oldham (Salford), Heron (Leeds). Subs: Saxon (St. Helens), Crooks (Hull K.R.), Roberts (Bradford N.).
G: Endersby (3).

Widnes, 15.1.78:
Bailey (Salford), Jackson (St. Helens), Worgan (Leigh), Arkwright (St. Helens), Barron (Leeds), Morgan (Widnes), Winterbottom (Leeds), Woods (Hull K.R.), Whitehouse (Leeds), Baybutt (St. Helens), Norton (Castleford), Smith (St. Helens), Williams (Salford), Subs: Douglas (Hull K.R.), Pitts (Bradford N.), Reed (Wakefield T.).
T: Baybutt, Smith. G: Winterbottom.

Perpignan, 25.2.78:
Bailey (Salford), Reed (Castleford), Arkwright (St. Helens), Worgan (Leigh), Martin (Wakefield T.), Moran (Widnes), Winterbottom (Leeds), Roberts (Bradford N.), Whitehouse (Leeds), Baybutt (St. Helens), Johnson (Bradford N.), Garside (Rochdale H.), Slatter (Wakefield T.), Subs: Okulicz (Bradford N.), Rathbone (Leigh), Pitts (Bradford N.).
T: Arkwright, Baybutt, Slatter. G: Bailey (2)

Hull, 3.2.79:
Bailey (Salford), Whitfield (Hull K.R.), Bentley (Widnes), Hyde (Castleford), Gill (Bradford N.), Holding (St. Helens), Simpson (St. Helens), Beaumont (Hull), Kiss (Wigan), Connaughton (Wigan), O'Neill (Widnes), Haggerty (St. Helens), Jones (Salford). Subs: Beardmore (Castleford), Finnegan (Widnes), Stockley (Wigan).
T: Bentley, Holding, Jones. G: Holding (4).
Perpignan, 25.3.79:
Bailey (Salford), Whitfield (Hull K.R.), Bentley (Widnes), Hyde (Castleford), Gill (Bradford N.), Tinker (Wakefield T.), Simpson (St. Helens), Beaumont (Hull), O'Neill P. (Salford), Kiss (Wigan), O'Neill M. (Widnes), Haggerty (St. Helens), Finnegan (Widnes), Subs: Beardmore (Castleford), Garside (Rochdale H.), Stockley (Wigan).
T: O'Neill. G: Bailey.

Perpignan, 26.1.80:
Whitfield (Salford), Meadows (St. Helens), Myler (Widnes), Dennison (Hull), Nicholson (Hunslet), Mackintosh (Leeds), Ashton (Oldham), Beaumont (Hull), Noble (Bradford N.), O'Neill (Widnes), James (Castleford), Heron (Leeds), Flanagan (Oldham), Subs: Kirwan (Oldham), Timson (Castleford), Smith (Widnes).
T: Smith (2), Whitfield, Myler, Noble, Flanagan
G: Dennison (4), Whitfield, Ashton (dg)

Oldham, 15.3.80:
Whitfield (Salford), Meadows (St. Helens), Myler (Widnes), Dennison (Hull), Nicholson (Hunslet), Mackintosh (Leeds), Ashton (Oldham), O'Neill (Widnes), Noble (Bradford N.), Smith (Widnes), James (Castleford), Heron (Leeds), Flanagan (Oldham). Subs: Kirwan (Oldham), Timson (Castleford), Rose (Wakefield T.).
T: Meadows (2), Myler, O'Neill, James, Whitfield, Kirwan. G: Dennison (5).

Leeds, 31.1.81:
Alstead (Leigh), Cooper (Leeds), O'Rourke (Oldham), Morrell (Wakefield T.), Dobb (Oldham), Seabrook (Oldham), Birkby (Castleford), Leigh (Salford), Whittle (St. Helens), Ema (Hull K.R.), Platt (Oldham), Crooks (Hull), Hirst (Hunslet), Subs: Fletcher (Salford), Worrall (Oldham), Campbell (Leeds).
T: Seabrook. G: Platt.

Cavaillon, 21.2.81:
Alstead (Leigh), Dobb (Oldham), O'Rourke (Oldham), Cooper (Leeds), Scruton (Hull), Seabrook (Oldham), Fletcher (Salford), Waite (Castleford), Whittle (St. Helens), Gratton (Rochdale H.), Lowndes (Oldham), Crooks (Hull), Platt (Oldham), Subs: Birkby (Castleford), Suddaby (Hull), Campbell (Leeds).
T: Alstead, Fletcher. G: Platt (3).

Hull, 6.12.81:
Whelan (Castleford), Jones (Wakefield T.), Marchant (Castleford), Wardle (Hull K.R.), Lazenby (Hull K.R.), Conway (Leeds), Johnson (Leigh), Sykes (Leeds), O'Toole (Featherstone R.), Crooks (Hull), Platt (Oldham), Proctor (Hull), Fleming (Bradford N.). Subs: Howard (St. Helens), Beall (Hull K.R.), England (Castleford).
T: Proctor, O'Toole. G: Crooks.

Limoux 21.2.82.
Mellor (Swinton), Jones (Wakefield T.), Duane (Warrington), Wood (Wigan), Dobb (Oldham), Wardle (Hull K.R.), Hulme (Widnes), Crooks (Hull), Swaine (Oldham), Lowndes (Oldham), Platt (Oldham), England (Castleford), Wane (Wigan). Subs: Marchant (Castleford), Sykes (Leeds), Conway (Leeds).
T: Mellor G: Mellor (4), Crooks (1, 2dg.).

Brisbane 27.6.82
Mellor (Swinton), Marchant (Castleford), Lazenby (Hull K.R.), Cullen (Warrington), Clark (Hull K.R.), Hulme (Widnes), Conway (Leeds), Lowndes (Oldham), Horton (Castleford), England (Castleford), Beall (Hull K.R.), Duane (Warrington). Subs: Atherton (Leigh), O'Toole (Featherstone R.).
T: Hulme, England, O'Toole. G: Mellor (2), O'Toole.

Apt 15.1.83
Conway (Leeds), Atkinson (Oldham), Banks (Featherstone R.), Atherton (Leigh), Maher (Oldham), Jones (Castleford), Walsh (Hull K.R.), Hartley (Castleford), Hughes (Leigh), Forber (St. Helens), Proctor (Hull), England (Castleford), Bell (Hull). Subs: Horton (Castleford), Williams (Wakefield T.), Platt (St. Helens).
T: England (2). G: Bell (3).

Leigh 5.3.83
Atherton (Leigh), Thornton (Hull K.R.), Eden (Wakefield T.), Atkinson (Oldham), Ingham (Leeds), Jones (Castleford), Conway (Leeds), Crooks (Hull), Hughes (Leigh), England (Castleford), Proctor (Hull), Platt (St. Helens), Williams (Wakefield T.). Subs: Tosney (Hunslet), Beall (Hull K.R.), Dannatt (Hull).
T: Eden, Jones, Atkinson, Atherton, England, Ingham.
G: Crooks (3).

GREAT BRITAIN COLTS 1982 TOUR OF PAPUA NEW GUINEA AND AUSTRALIA

MATCH RESULTS

In Papua New Guinea

Highland Zone	lost	10-15	at Mount Hagen
Papua New Guinea	drew	14-14	at Lae
In Australia			
Toowoomba	won	29-20	at Toowoomba
Queensland	lost	3-4	at Pizzey Park, Gold Coast
Balmain	drew	9-9	at Leichardt Oval
New South Wales	lost	2-17	at Sydney Cricket Ground
Australia	lost	15-20	at Lang Park, Brisbane

SUMMARY

Played 7	Won 1	Drew 2	Lost 4
For	Tries 16	Goals 17	Points 82
Against	Tries 17	Goals 24	Points 99

TOUR PARTY

Managers: Harry Jepson (Leeds)
Alan Hindle (Rochdale H.)
Coach: Geoff Lyon
Physiotherapist: Alan Bass (Bramley)
Captain: Lee Crooks (Hull)

	App	T	G	Pts
Wayne Atherton (Leigh)	2+2	1	0	3
Malcolm Beall (Hull K.R.)	4	0	0	0
Garry Clark (Hull K.R.)	5	2	0	6
Mark Conway (Leeds)	5+1	0	0	0
Lee Crooks (Hull)	3	0	8	16
Paul Cullen (Warrington)	6+1	0	0	0
Stephen Dobb (Oldham)	4	1	0	3
Ronnie Duane (Warrington)	5	1	0	3
Keith England (Castleford)	6	1	0	3
Mark Fleming (Bradford N.)	2+2	1	0	3
Stewart Horton (Castleford)	5	0	0	0
David Hulme (Widnes)	4	3	0	9
David Jones (Wakefield T.)	4	0	0	0
Tracey Lazenby (Hull K.R.)	6	1	0	3
Paul Lowndes (Oldham)	5+1	1	0	3
Tony Marchant (Castleford)	3+1	1	0	3
Paul Mellor (Swinton)	6	1	4	11
Tony O'Toole (Featherstone R.)	2+1	1	4	11
Alan Platt (Oldham)	5	1	1	5
Andrew Sykes (Leeds)	4+1	0	0	0
Shaun Wane (Wigan)	3+1	0	0	0
Stuart Wardle (Hull K.R.)	2+3	0	0	0

+ indicates playing substitute

COLTS COUNTY MATCH

26th November, 1983 **York**

YORKSHIRE 14		**LANCASHIRE 28**
Steve Parrish (Bradford N.)	1.	Steve Rea (Barrow)
Richard Francis (Bradford N.)	2.	Paul Roberts (Wigan)
Garry Schofield (Hull)	3.	Shaun Fairhurst (Leigh)
Ian Thomas (Huddersfield)	4.	Shaun Allen (St. Helens)
Norman Francis (Leeds)	5.	Leslie Quirk (Barrow)
Stephen Hullock (Hunslet)	6.	Michael Ford (Wigan)
Tony Collinson (Hull) Capt.	7.	Darren Beazant (Leigh)
Andrew Bateman (Hunslet)	8.	Ian Sherratt (Bradford N.)
Ian Fletcher (Castleford)	9.	Paul Groves (Salford)
Brendon Hill (Leeds)	10.	Adrian Crawford (Bradford N.)
Andy Dannatt (Hull)	11.	John Mayo (Wigan)
Martin Ketteridge (Castleford)	12.	Christopher Wilson (Wigan)
Gary Divorty (Hull)	13.	Paul Hardman (Leigh)
John Magyar (Castleford)	14.	Clifford Berry (Wigan)
Neil Puckering (Hull)	15.	Gary Hughes (Leigh)

T: Francis, Thomas, Schofield
G: Parrish
Substitutions:
Puckering for Fletcher (45 min.)
Magyar for Hullock (63 min.)
Half-time 14-16
Coach: Barry Seabourne (Leeds)

T: Rea, Fairhurst, Sherratt, Wilson, Quirk
G: Fairhurst (4)

Coach: Brian Gartland (Oldham)
Referee: Stan Wall (Leigh)

COLTS COUNTY CHAMPIONSHIP

21.2.76	Yorkshire	21	Lancashire	15	Huddersfield
6.2.77	Lancashire	14	Yorkshire	31	Salford
26.11.77	Yorkshire	13	Lancashire	22	Wakefield
13.12.78	Lancashire	29	Yorkshire	9	St. Helens
16.11.79	Yorkshire	23	Lancashire	15	Bramley
19.11.80	Lancashire	24	Yorkshire	5	Leigh
28.10.81	Yorkshire	16	Lancashire	7	Hull
27.11.82	Lancashire	18	Yorkshire	21	Barrow
22.4.83	Yorkshire	30	Lancashire	7	Bramley
26.11.83	Yorkshire	14	Lancashire	28	York

Kiwi forward Mark Broadhurst, a 1983-84 signing by Hull K.R. from Australian club Illawara Steelers.

TRANSFERS

TRANSFERS

Hull Kingston Rovers staggered the Rugby world in early June 1981 by paying a world record £72,500 for George Fairbairn, Wigan's Test full back. Then in February 1982, neighbours Hull paid Featherstone Rovers £70,000 for Steve Evans.

The reaction was much the same in 1901 when Salford bought Jim Lomas from Bramley for £100 and in 1913 when Hull doubled the then record transfer fee to £600 to sign Billy Batten from Hunslet.

The first £1,000 transfer came in 1921 when Harold Buck joined Leeds from Hunslet, although there were reports at the time that another player was involved in the deal to make up the four-figure transfer. Other claims for the first £1,000 transfer are attached to Stan Brogden's move from Bradford Northern to Huddersfield in 1929.

The following list gives an indication of how transfer fees have grown this century:

Season	*Player*	*Position*	*From*	*To*	*Fee*
1901-02	Jim Lomas	Centre	Bramley	Salford	£100
1910-11	Jim Lomas	Centre	Salford	Oldham	£300
1912-13	Billy Batten	Centre	Hunslet	Hull	£600
1921-22	Harold Buck	Wing	Hunslet	Leeds	£1,000
1929-30	Stanley Smith	Wing	Wakefield T.	Leeds	£1,075
1933-34	Stanley Brogden	Wing/centre	Huddersfield	Leeds	£1,200
1937-38	Billy Belshaw	Full back	Liverpool S.	Warrington	£1,450
1946-47	Bill Davies	Full back/centre	Huddersfield	Dewsbury	£1,650
1947-48	Bill Hudson	Forward	Batley	Wigan	£2,000
1947-48	Jim Ledgard	Full back	Dewsbury	Leigh	£2,650
1948-49	Ike Owens	Forward	Leeds	Castleford	£2,750
1948-49	Ike Owens	Forward	Castleford	Huddersfield	£2,750
1948-49	Stan McCormick	Wing	Belle Vue R.	St. Helens	£4,000
1949-50	Albert Naughton	Centre	Widnes	Warrington	£4,600
1950-51	Bruce Ryan	Wing	Hull	Leeds	£4,750
1950-51	Joe Egan	Hooker	Wigan	Leigh	£5,000
1950-51	Harry Street	Forward	Dewsbury	Wigan	£5,000
1957-58	Mick Sullivan	Wing	Huddersfield	Wigan	£9,500
1958-59	Ike Southward	Wing	Workington T.	Oldham	£10,650
1960-61	Mick Sullivan	Wing	Wigan	St. Helens	£11,000
1960-61	Ike Southward	Wing	Oldham	Workington T.	£11,002 10s
1968-69	Colin Dixon	Forward	Halifax	Salford	£12,000
1969-70	Paul Charlton	Full back	Workington	Salford	£12,500
1972-73	Eric Prescott	Forward	St. Helens	Salford	£13,500
1975-76	Steve Nash	Half back	Featherstone	Salford	£15,000
1977-78	Bill Ashurst	Forward	Wigan	Wakefield T.	£18,000
1978-79	Clive Pickerill	Half back	Castleford	Hull	£20,000
1978-79	Phil Hogan	Forward	Barrow	Hull K.R.	£35,000
1979-80	Len Casey	Forward	Bradford N.	Hull K.R.	£38,000
1980-81	Trevor Skerrett	Forward	Wakefield T.	Hull	£40,000
1980-81	George Fairbairn	Full back	Wigan	Hull K.R.	£72,500

1983-84 TRANSFER REVIEW

Fewer major transfer deals, but freer movement of players through the loan scheme; almost a total lack of Rugby Union converts, but record fees paid to amateur Rugby League recruits; and a big influx of Australian and New Zealand players. These were the facts that reflected the changing pattern of player recruitment during 1983-84.

Only two years after a season in which there were eight £30,000 signings, including the world record £72,500 pay out when George Fairbairn left Wigan for Hull K.R., few major transfers hit the headlines last season.

With the recession continuing to have its effect on sport in general, there were no straight cash transfers of more than £30,000. Part-exchange became a popular method of bargaining and John Wood was twice involved in the biggest deals. The former Great Britain Under-24 forward moved from Fulham to Salford in a £45,000 exchange deal in June 1983. Fulham received centre Trevor Stockley, rated about £35,000, plus £10,000 cash. Six months later Wood returned to his first club, Widnes, who handed over £30,000 plus Eric Prescott and John Taylor. The deal was again reckoned to be about £45,000.

Another indication of the fall in transfer fees was that Wigan signed Ian Potter from Leigh for just over £20,000. Less than three years earlier, the former England forward had moved from Warrington to Leigh for a then record fee for a forward of £50,000.

There were 99 transfers of players between clubs, plus 149 loan movements which included the return of players to their original club. These figures were similar to the previous season. Apart from newcomers Kent Invicta who had to recruit an entire squad, the most signings were made by Carlisle with 25, including five on loan. Cardiff City made the fewest signings with just four.

In a revolutionary move to help their transfer-listed players find new clubs, Hull introduced a new rent-a-player scheme. Realising that few clubs could now afford to risk paying out all but the smallest of transfer fees, Hull offered to allow some of their players to leave on a one-year contract for 20 per cent of their listed fee.

At the end of the contracts, clubs had the option of returning the players, retaining them on rent, or buying them outright. The most notable transaction involved Paul Prendiville, who was listed at £15,000 and went to Leeds where he helped them win the John Player Special Trophy. The Welsh international winger then returned to Hull at the end of the season having played in 26 matches for Leeds.

The flow of Rugby Union converts has been reduced to a trickle. From more than 20 a season a few years ago they dropped to 12 in 1982-83 and were down to just four last season ... none of them of major importance.

In contrast, fees for top amateur Rugby League recruits reached record heights. The biggest fee created the most publicised amateur signing of all time when Wigan signed half back Shaun Edwards on his 17th birthday in front of the nationwide BBC TV Breakfast Time cameras. The former England RL & RU schoolboy international's contract involved a reputed £35,000.

The total of 145 amateur signings, including Colts, was about the same as the previous season.

Among all the comings and goings of last season the biggest impact was made by the many Australians who took advantage of the lifting of restrictions on Anglo-Aussie transfers. A total of 31 Australians — and 16 New Zealanders — were brought over to enliven the English game.

They varied greatly in standard and stayed for varying lengths of time, but the biggest coup was pulled off by Wakefield Trinity. With the help of sponsors, struggling Trinity paid Wally Lewis, Australia's Test stand off and captain-elect, £1,000-a-game for a 10-match spell.

Hull also signed Test scrum half Peter Sterling for a brief spell in which he played eight matches.

Other Australian Test players to join English clubs were John Dorahy (Hull K.R.) and Steve Martin (Leeds), while Allan McMahon (Featherstone Rovers) was a 1978 tourist.

Kerry Hemsley played 12 times for Wigan before returning to Australia in mid-season. The Balmain prop was then flown back just for the Wembley final against Widnes.

Among the lesser known Australians to make big impressions were Mark Cannon (Wigan), Brett Atkins and Steve Robinson (Castleford), Mark Laurie and Terry Webb (Leeds).

The trend of New Zealand players joining British clubs continued. There were eight in 1981-82 and 18 in 1982-83. Another 16 were recruited last season, including Test players Fred Ah Kuoi (Hull), Mark Broadhurst (Hull K.R.), Howie Tamati (Wigan), Nick Wright (Oldham), Dean Bell (Leeds) and Shane Varley (Leigh). Bell and Varley had previously been at Carlisle and Workington Town respectively.

Bradford Northern created a piece of international history when they signed Phil Ralda, the first Papua New Guinea player to play in England. The Test forward made only two first team appearances before returning home.

The following is a list of the 71 overseas players who were registered with British clubs last season, * denoting Test player.

Leigh's New Zealander Jeff Clarke, grounded by Leeds' loose forward Terry Webb, a Queenslander.

AUSTRALIA (34)

Atkins, Brett	(Castleford)
Brennan, Peter	(Halifax)
Burns, Alan	(Wakefield T.)
Cannon, Mark	(Wigan)
Cole, Peter	(Wigan, Blackpool B.)
*Dorahy, John	(Hull K.R.)
Elvin, Wayne	(Wigan)
Gaynor, Bruce	(Wigan, Blackpool B.)
Gerard, Greg	(Wakefield T., Huddersfield)
Gill, Lyndsay	(Wakefield T.)
Graham, David	(Barrow, Whitehaven)
Hambly, Gary	(York)
Hemsley, Kerry	(Wigan)
Jackson, Robert	(Fulham)
Laurie, Mark	(Leeds)
Laurie, Richard	(Leeds)
Lewis, Scott	(Wakefield T.)
*Lewis, Wally	(Wakefield T.)
Lulham, Rick	(Leeds)
McArthur, Peter	(Barrow)
McMahon, Allan	(Featherstone R.)
*Martin, Steve	(Leeds)
O'Beirne, Mark	(Bramley)
Penola, Colin	(Kent Invicta)
Pierce, Daryl	(Swinton)
Roach, Stephen	(Bramley)
Robinson, Steve	(Castleford)
Schofield, Craig	(Barrow)
Simpson, Mark	(Hull K.R.)
*Sterling, Peter	(Hull)
Waugh, Brad	(Wakefield T.)
Webb, Terry	(Leeds)
Weston, Mark	(Barrow)
Worne, Glen	(Wakefield T.)

NEW ZEALAND (34)

*Ah Kuoi, Fred	(Hull)
*Bell, Dean	(Leeds)
*Bell, Ian	(Carlisle)
*Broadhurst, Mark	(Hull K.R.)
Brown, Peter	(Hunslet)
Campbell, Danny	(Wigan)
Clark, Trevor	(Leeds)
Clarke, Jeff	(Leigh)
Coyle, Craig	(Oldham)
Elia, Mark	(Kent Invicta)
Freeman, Gary	(Kent Invicta, Castleford)
*Friend, Clayton	(Carlisle)
Harding, Dave	(Kent Invicta)
*Kemble, Gary	(Hull)
*Leuluai, James	(Hull)
McEwan, Ashley	(Oldham)
Muller, Rob	(Warrington)
Murray, Thomas	(Bradford N.)
Noel, Tony	(Kent Invicta)
*O'Hara, Dane	(Hull)
O'Shea, Terry	(Kent Invicta)
Pirihi, Terence	(Warrington)
Poasa, Pat	(Warrington)
Poutama, Wayne	(Warrington)
*Prohm, Gary	(Hull K.R.)
Punter, Michael	(Huddersfield)
Sinclair, Alan	(Oldham)
*Smith, Gordon	(Hull K.R.)
*Tamati, Howie	(Wigan)
*Tamati, Kevin	(Widnes)
Townsend, Glen	(Hunslet)
*Varley, Shane	(Leigh)
*West, Graeme	(Wigan)
*Wright, Nick	(Oldham)

FRANCE (1)

*Solal, Patrick	(Hull)

MOROCCO (1)

M'Barki, Hussein	(Fulham)

PAPUA NEW GUINEA (1)

*Ralda, Philip	(Bradford N.)

New Zealand Test hooker Howie Tamati in action for Wigan at Wembley.

The transfer traffic in the opposite direction was very much lighter. By the end of May, only eight British players had signed for clubs Down Under, the only notable short-term transfers being Hull K.R.'s Andy Kelly and Wakefield Trinity's Great Britain Under-24 hooker Colin Maskill. The nine players were:

Andy Kelly	(Hull K.R.)	to	Illawara Steelers (Aus)
Colin Maskill	(Wakefield T.)	to	Valleys, Brisbane (Aus)
Maurice Lucas	(Carlisle)	to	Wellington (NZ)
Karl Portz	(Carlisle)	to	Wellington (NZ)
Peter Lister	(Bramley)	to	Pont Chevalier (NZ)
Karl Harrison	(Bramley)	to	Pont Chevalier (NZ)
Neil Kelly	(Dewsbury)	to	Pont Chevalier (NZ)
Dane Carter	(Barrow)	to	Cooma (NZ)

Most Moves

Geoff Clarkson made yet another move during the season — extending his record number of transfers to 12 — when he left Leigh for Featherstone Rovers on October 27, 1983. He has played for 10 different English clubs and had a brief spell in Australia.

Clarkson, born on August 12, 1943, was the only 40-year-old playing regular first team rugby last season. He turned professional with Wakefield Trinity in 1966 after gaining Yorkshire County forward honours with Wakefield Rugby Union Club.

Clarkson's club career in England is as follows:

1966 — Wakefield T.
1968 — Bradford N.
1970 — Leigh
1971 — Warrington
1972 — Leeds
1975 — York
1976 — Bramley
1978 — Wakefield T. and Hull K.R.
1980 — Bradford N. and Oldham
1981 — Leigh
1983 — Featherstone R.

1983-84 Signings

The following is a register of signings by clubs between June 1983 and May 1984 inclusive. The right hand column lists the club from which the player was recruited (ARL -Amateur Rugby League, RU - Rugby Union).

Although this is a register of signings, it is possible to trace a club's transfers by scrutinising the right hand column.

*Indicates where clubs have agreed to a player being signed "on loan", a temporary transfer, the Rugby Football League prohibiting a subsequent transfer within 28 days. Where a player on loan has not been retained, his return to his original club is also marked *.

BARROW

Date Signed	Player	Club From
1.6.83	*French, Nigel	Cardiff
1.7.83	*Garside, Brett	Rochdale H.
5.8.83	Campbell, Ian	Barrow Colts
5.8.83	Johnson, Robert	Barrow Colts
5.8.83	O'Brien, David	Barrow Colts
5.8.83	Rea, Steven	Holker Pioneers ARL
20.9.83	Clough, David	Dalton ARL
22.10.83	Graham, David	Wagga, Aus.
22.10.83	McArthur, Peter	Wagga, Aus.
5.1.84	*Gee, Peter	Whitehaven
10.1.84	*James, Kevin	Leeds
27.3.84	Irving, Paul	Ulverston ARL

BATLEY

Date Signed	Player	Club From
11.8.83	Hepinstall, Michael	Redhill ARL
11.8.83	Stainburn, John	Batley Boys ARL
11.8.83	Barnett, Paul	Batley Boys ARL
11.8.83	Speight, Stanley	Batley Boys ARL
1.9.83	Cousins, Kevin	Bramley
18.11.83	Reed, Stephen	Featherstone R
19.1.84	Swale, Graham	Bramley
8.3.84	Reeder, Ian	George Hotel ARL
8.3.84	McLeary, Jack	Grasshoughton ARL

BLACKPOOL BOROUGH

Date Signed	Player	Club From
11.8.83	Hunter, Michael	Wigan St. Patrick's ARL
11.8.83	Runciman, Andrew	Blackpool Stanley ARL
11.8.83	O'Hara, Michael	Blackpool ARL
11.8.83	Briscoe, Carl	Wigan ARL
12.8.83	McLoughlin, Brendan	Wigan
18.8.83	Cowburn, Martin	Rose Bridge ARL
15.9.83	Turley, Norman	Rochdale H.
17.9.83	Waddell, Hugh	Burton-on-Trent RU
20.10.83	Price, Billy	Rochdale H.
22.12.83	Cole, Peter	Wigan
22.12.83	Gaynor, Bruce	Wigan
17.2.84	*Glover, John	Whitehaven

BRADFORD NORTHERN

Date Signed	Player	Club From
22.7.83	Francis, Richard	Hunslet Parkside ARL
23.8.83	Moore, Garry	Hunslet Parkside ARL
15.9.83	Bardgett, Paul	Halifax ARL
23.9.83	Ralda, Phillip	PNG
21.10.83	Murray, Tom	Takahiwai, NZ
11.11.83	Preece, Christopher	Salford Colts
19.1.84	*Pullen, Stephen	Keighley
31.1.84	Richards, John	Pointer Panthers ARL
3.4.84	*Meehan, Gary	Kent Invicta
24.4.84	*Parrott, Chris	Bramley

BRAMLEY

Date Signed	Player	Club From
4.8.83	Hindley, Alan	Leigh East ARL
4.8.83	Hickinson, Paul	Bramley ARL
4.8.83	Hough, Michael	—
4.8.83	Sharp, John	—
9.8.83	Boyes, Jeffrey	Hunslet Parkside ARL
9.8.83	Hindley, Steven	Swinton ARL
9.8.83	Stafford, Marvin	—
18.8.83	Okulicz, Edward	Park ARL
17.9.83	*Paterson, John	Dewsbury
17.9.83	Kelly, Hayden	Hunselt
23.1.84	Whittaker, Stephen	Pudsey ARL
21.1.84	Jarvis, Peter	Belle Isle ARL
25.2.84	*Pickerill, Neil	Featherstone R.
1.3.84	*Piwinski, Urek	York
25.3.84	Roach, Stephen	La Reole, Aus.
25.3.84	O'Beirne, Mark	La Reole, Aus.
4.4.84	*Parrott, Chris	Bradford N.
8.4.84	*Brannan, Alistair	Kent Invicta
12.4.84	Nelson, David	Leeds

CARDIFF CITY

Date Signed	Player	Club From
26.8.83	Camilleri, Chris	Widnes
15.9.83	*Walters, Graham	Wakefield T.
19.9.83	*Evans, Alan	Barrow
9.12.83	Marshall, Michael	York

CARLISLE

Date Signed	Player	Club From
4.8.83	Peacham, Gary	Hull
16.8.83	Portz, Karl	Hull
17.8.83	Miller, Sean	Leeds
17.8.83	Gaitley, Bob	Hull
19.8.83	Sutton, Michael	Hull
19.8.83	Hobson, Ian	Huddersfield
19.8.83	Brierley, Steven	Platform One ARL
19.8.83	Robinson, Bryan	Castleford Colts
19.8.83	Tissiman, Les	—
2.9.83	Binder, Tony	Leeds
26.9.83	*Boyd, Denis	Leigh
4.10.83	Todd, Allen	Whitehaven ARL
4.10.83	*Starbuck, Paul	Bradford N.
14.10.83	Langton, Stephen	—
22.3.84	*Armitage, Des	Leeds
22.3.84	*Hardy, Alan	Castleford
24.3.84	Pearson, Alan	Whitehaven ARL
24.3.84	McDonald, Iain	Sheffield Poly ARL
8.4.84	Doyle, Mark	Union ARL
8.4.84	Scott, Tony	Horse & Farrier ARL
8.4.84	Wilson, Alan	Union ARL
8.4.84	Jones, Harold	Union ARL
8.4.84	*Gaitley, Bob	Keighley
19.4.84	Smith, David	Workington T.

CASTLEFORD

Date Signed	Player	Club From
15.6.83	Ketteridge, Martin	Moorends ARL
17.6.83	Greatbatch, Neil	Lock Lane ARL
7.11.83	Moore, Gary	Wakefield Trinity
14.11.83	*Birkby, Ian	Oldham
18.11.83	Freeman, Gary	Kent Invicta
14.1.84	Robinson, Stephen	Penrith, Aus.
17.1.84	Atkins, Brett	Manly, Aus.
3.5.84	*Kellett, Neil	Kent Invicta
3.5.84	*Richardson, Terry	Kent Invicta

Australian forward Brett Atkins, left, a Castleford recruit.

DEWSBURY

Date Signed	Player	Club From
17.9.83	Clayton, Peter	Bramley
18.10.83	*Paterson, John	Bramley
27.10.83	Brewer, Daniel	Knottingley ARL
18.11.83	Thorton, Graham	Huddersfield
21.11.83	*Pickerill, Neil	Featherstone Rovers
29.11.83	Greenwood, Ian	Ossett Trinity ARL
13.1.84	*Thorton, Malcolm	Huddersfield
13.1.84	Diskin, Tony	Dewsbury Celtic ARL
20.1.84	*Buckton, John	Doncaster
10.2.84	Snee, Michael	Halifax ARL
2.5.84	*Brannan, Alistair	Bramley
12.5.84	*Paterson, John	Doncaster

DONCASTER

Date Signed	Player	Club From
18.8.83	Atherton, Clive	Rossington Hornets ARL
18.8.83	Deighton, Kevin R	BP Hull ARL
18.8.83	Marshall, Alf	Schooner ARL
18.8.83	Tyers, Andrew	Rotherham ARL
18.8.83	Wilkinson, Terry	—
7.9.83	*Leighton, Steve	Hull K.R.
7.9.83	*McHugh, Gary	Hull K.R.
18.10.83	Douglas, Graham	Hull K.R.
19.12.83	*Portz, James	Hull
19.12.83	*Chester, Robin	Hull
6.1.84	*Paterson, John	Dewsbury
30.3.84	*Wileman, Ron	Hull

FEATHERSTONE ROVERS

Date Signed	Player	Club From
28.6.83	*Vickers, Dave	Carlisle
28.6.83	*Griffiths, Alan	Carlisle
7.8.83	Fox, Deryck	St. John Fisher ARL
16.8.83	Spurr, Bob	Castleford
16.8.83	Bardgett, Joe	Carlisle
31.8.83	Clarkson, Peter	Wakefield T.
17.9.83	Barends, David	Bradford N.
26.10.83	*Stone, Charlie	Hull
27.10.83	Clarkson, Geoff	Leigh
17.11.83	*Pickerill, Neil	Keighley
17.12.83	McMahon, Allan	Canberra District, Aus.
5.1.84	*Pickerill, Neil	Dewsbury
1.3.84	*Lund, Steve	Bramley
1.3.84	*Slater, Ian	Huddersfield
21.3.84	Hopkins, Calvin	Lock Lane ARL

FULHAM

Date Signed	Player	Club From
8.6.83	Stockley, Trevor	Salford
29.7.83	O'Donovan, John	Rochdale H.
5.8.83	Walters, Gordon	Wests & St. Livrade
17.8.83	Dearden, Alan	—
1.1.84	Jackson, Robert	Penrith, Aus.
20.1.84	*Butler, John	St. Helens
11.3.84	*Tabern, Ray	Leigh

HALIFAX

Date Signed	Player	Club From
5.7.83	Thorpe, Andrew	Halifax Colts
7.7.83	Cerchione, Mario	Halifax Colts
21.8.83	Laws, Stephen	Halifax ARL
20.9.83	Roberts, Ken	Swinton
11.1.84	Hall, Stephen	Moldgreen ARL
11.1.84	Rushforth, Paul	Kippax ARL
13.1.84	South, Keith	—
13.1.84	Batchelor, Timothy	—
9.2.84	Carroll, John	Leeds
1.3.84	McCallion, Seamus	—

Australian John Dorahy, Hull K.R. utility star and 1984 winner of the Harry Sunderland Trophy.

HUDDERSFIELD

Date Signed	Player	Club From
5.5.83	Thomas, Ian	Huddersfield Sups. ARL
24.5.83	*Walsh, David	Salford
4.1.83	*Cooper, Stephen	Doncaster
15.2.83	*Johnson, Tony	Hunslet
21.8.83	Bostock, Michael	Huddersfield Colts
21.8.83	Morris, Roger	Huddersfield Colts
26.8.83	Fitzpatrick, Denis	Belle Vue ARL
22.9.83	Doughty, Greg	Huddersfield Colts
4.11.83	*Thornton, Malcolm	Dewsbury
1.12.83	*Price, Ray	Hull K.R.
25.12.83	Hirt, Robert	Huddersfield ARL
25.12.83	*Johnson, Phil	Featherstone R.
25.12.83	*Rowe, Danny	Hunslet
17.1.84	Thornton, Graham	Dewsbury
20.1.84	*Lockwood, Brian	Widnes
23.2.84	*Paterson, John	Doncaster
24.2.84	Gerard, Gregory	Wakefield T.

HULL

Date Signed	Player	Club From
30.4.83	Puckering, Neil	Hull Colts
21.6.83	*Norfolk, Clive	York
1.7.83	Schofield, Garry	Hunslet Parkside ARL
1.7.83	Divorty, Gary	Heworth ARL
23.9.83	Ah Kuoi, Fred	North Sydney, Aus.
23.9.83	Sterling, Peter	Parramatta, Aus.
10.11.83	*Wilby, Tim	Wigan
8.3.84	Sharp, Jon	Travellers Saints ARL
20.3.84	Tomlinson, Alan	Hull ARL
31.5.84	*Stone, Charlie	Featherstone R.
31.5.84	*Prendiville, Paul	Leeds
31.5.84	*Portz, James	Doncaster
31.5.84	*Wileman, Ron	Doncaster
31.5.84	*Chester, Robin	Doncaster
31.5.84	*Day, Terry	Warrington

HULL KINGSTON ROVERS

Date Signed	Player	Club From
4.8.83	Broadhurst, Mark	Illawarra, Aus.
3.10.83	Dorahy, John	Illawarra, Aus.
13.10.83	Millington, John	Kent Invicta
14.5.84	*McHugh, Gary	Doncaster
14.5.84	*Leighton, Steve	Doncaster
14.5.84	*Proctor, Rob	Keighley
14.5.84	*Muscroft, Peter	Featherstone R.
14.5.84	Marchant, Bill	—

HUNSLET

Date Signed	Player	Club From
1.7.83	Bateman, Andrew	Hunslet Parkside ARL
1.7.83	Rayner, Neil	Hunslet Parkside ARL
6.7.83	*Hendry, Paul	Wakefield T.
14.7.83	Sanderson, Phil	Bradford N.
28.8.83	Sampson, Ian	Bramley
24.9.83	Gray, Neil	Featherstone R.
29.9.83	Saunders, Lee	Hunslet Boys ARL
10.10.83	Townsend, Glen	Mt. Albert, NZ
10.10.83	Brown, Peter	Landerers, NZ
18.11.83	Kay, Andrew	Woolpack ARL
5.1.84	*Johnson, Tony	Huddersfield
6.3.84	*White, Brendan	York
5.4.84	Marson, Andrew	Hunslet Colts
17.4.84	*Coombes, Michael	Oldham

HUYTON

Date Signed	Player	Club From
12.8.83	Garvey, John	Ruskin Park ARL
12.8.83	Shaw, Mark	Widnes Tigers ARL
24.8.83	Morris, David	Simms Cross ARL
27.8.83	Jackson, Antony	—
20.9.83	*Bruen, Bob	Rochdale H.
29.9.83	Bailey, Graham	Blackpool B.
5.10.83	Wood, Peter	Widnes
19.1.84	Peters, Tony	Swinton
25.1.84	Simm, Stephen	Huyton ARL
16.3.84	Crompton, David	Rose Bridge ARL

KEIGHLEY

Date Signed	Player	Club From
15.8.83	*Pickerill, Neil	Featherstone R.
23.8.83	Brearley, Graham	Leeds
28.8.83	Kirk, Stephen	Hunslet
28.8.83	Watts, Gary	Hunslet ARL
19.9.83	*Nicholson, Steve	Wigan
3.11.83	Allan, Mick	Hunslet
3.11.83	Kitchingman, Phil	Hunslet
3.11.83	Lunn, Martyn	Hunslet
27.11.83	*Gaitley, Bob	Carlisle
27.11.83	Ferres, Stephen	Carlisle
8.12.83	*Proctor, Rob	Hull K.R.
15.12.83	*Pullen, Stephen	Bradford N.
27.12.83	*Beale, Graham	Wigan
2.2.84	*Starbuck, Paul	Carlisle

KENT INVICTA

Date Signed	Player	Club From
5.6.83	Mordell, Bob	Oldham
7.6.83	Penola, Colin	—
10.6.83	Tuffs, Neil	Fulham
26.6.83	Woolford, Neil	Jubilee ARL
28.6.83	Elia, Mark	—
7.7.83	Lane, Steve	Whitehaven
17.7.83	French, Nigel	Barrow
20.7.83	Mattison, Neil	Wheldale ARL
27.7.83	Millington, Wayne	Peckham ARL
28.7.83	Hopkins, Lynn	Workington T.
1.8.83	Briscoe, Phillip	Peckham ARL
2.8.83	Cooper, Tony	Swinton
5.8.83	Van Bellen, Ian	Halifax
15.8.83	McCallion, Seamus	Mold Green ARL
15.8.83	Feighan, Frank	Peckham ARL
16.8.83	*Bishop, Gary	Oldham
16.8.83	Millington, John	Hull K.R.
17.8.83	*Alexander, Adrian	Oldham
18.8.83	Brannan, Alistair	Dewsbury
8.9.83	Norton, David	Northcote Tigers, NZ
8.9.83	Freeman, Gary	Northcote Tigers, NZ
16.9.83	O'Shea, Terry	Te Atatu, NZ
7.10.83	Bishop, Neil	Leigh ARL
27.10.83	Noel, Tony	—
27.10.83	Harding, David	Northcote, NZ
12.11.83	Hetherington, Gary	—
11.12.83	Walters, Gordon	Western Suburbs, Aus.
5.1.84	*Richardson, Terry	Castleford
5.1.84	*Kellett, Neil	Castleford
19.1.84	*Meehan, Gary	Bradford N.
22.1.84	*Gilmore, John	Rochdale H.
22.3.84	*Ferres, Steve	Carlisle
7.4.84	*Heron, Wayne	Leeds
7.4.84	*Rose, Stephen	Bramley
10.4.84	*Webb, Andrew	Blackpool B.
10.4.84	*Clarkson, Peter	Featherstone R.
16.4.84	*Freeman, Gary	Castleford
16.4.84	*James, Kevin	Oldham

LEEDS

Date Signed	Player	Club From
5.6.83	Creasser, David	Hunslet Parkside ARL
22.6.83	Bell, Dean	NZ
17.8.83	Turner, Philip	Leeds Colts
1.9.83	Martin, Steve	Balmain, Aus.
1.9.83	Webb, Terry	Redcliffe, Aus.
6.10.83	Moorby, Gary	St. Helens
10.10.83	*James, Kevin	Barrow
22.10.83	*Prendiville, Paul	Hull
28.10.83	Owen, Philip	Milford ARL
22.11.83	Laurie, Richard	Wauchope, Aus.
22.11.83	Lulham, Rickie	Wauchope Aus.
23.11.83	Laurie, Mark	Parramatta, Aus.
25.11.83	Clark, Trevor	Melville, NZ
29.11.83	Francis, Norman	Leeds Colts
30.12.83	Wilson, Paul	Stanningley ARL
25.2.84	Gunn, Richard	Travellers Saints ARL
15.5.84	*Heron, Wayne	Kent Invicta
15.5.84	*Armitage, Des	Carlisle

New Zealand Test threequarter Dean Bell, left, formerly with Carlisle and a 1983-84 signing by Leeds.

LEIGH

Date Signed	Player	Club From
5.6.83	*Bilsbury, Terry	Oldham
5.6.83	Alstead, Peter	Salford
20.6.83	*Platt, Billy	Rochdale H.
19.7.83	Burke, Paul	Leigh Colts
2.8.83	Hughes, Gary	Leigh Colts
16.8.83	*Boyd, Denis	Carlisle
9.9.83	Varley, Shane	Northcote, NZ
29.9.83	Clarke, Jeff	NZ
29.9.83	*Bishop, Neil	Huyton
14.11.83	*Alexander, Adrian	Oldham
7.12.83	*Butler, John	St. Helens
19.12.83	Fairhurst, Shaun	Leigh Colts
22.12.83	Cottrell, Tony	Leigh Miners Wel. ARL
22.12.83	Proudlove, John	St. Helens
28.12.83	Waller, Tony	Warrington
22.1.84	*Laird, Gary	Blackpool B.
22.2.84	Hardman, Paul	Leigh Colts
8.3.84	*Herdman, Martin	Fulham
22.3.84	Gormally, Joe	Leigh Colts

OLDHAM

Date Signed	Player	Club From
13.6.83	*Kirwan, Paddy	Leigh
7.7.83	Morris, Philip	Lock Lane ARL
18.7.83	Garnett, Paul D	Waterhead ARL
29.7.83	Hornby, Jim	Wigan
12.8.83	*Birkby, Ian	Castleford
14.8.83	Naidole, Tom	Wigan
12.9.83	Sanderson, Ian	Firsways ARL
21.9.83	Marsden, Tony	Shaw ARL
22.9.83	Coyle, Craig	Te Atatu, NZ
27.9.83	Sherman, Paul	Birchfield RU
1.11.83	Patterson, Stephen	Oldham St. Annes ARL
10.11.83	Wright, Nick	Manukau, NZ
10.11.83	Chisnall, Chris	Thatto Heath ARL
16.11.83	*Alexander, Adrian	Kent Invicta
24.11.83	Birkby, Ian	Castleford
22.1.84	*James, Kevin	Barrow
22.1.84	*Bishop, Gary	Kent Invicta
29.3.84	*Burgess, Mark	Hunslet
1.4.84	*Bardgett, Joe	Featherstone R.

ROCHDALE HORNETS

Date Signed	Player	Club From
2.8.83	Stapleton, John	Milnrow ARL
9.8.83	Hughes, Brian	York
9.8.83	Brown, Graham	York
18.8.83	*Platt, Billy	Leigh
18.8.83	Keaveney, Alan	Leigh ARL
18.8.83	Morris, Geoff	Castleford
18.8.83	Claughton, George	Castleford
23.8.83	Simpkin, Kevin	Castleford
31.8.83	Turner, Steven	Swinton
31.8.83	*Glover, John	Whitehaven
8.9.83	*Garside, Brett	Barrow
22.9.83	Birdsall, Charlie	Carlisle
20.10.83	Ubermanowicz, Tony	Mayfield ARL
26.10.83	Hartley, Neil	Mayfield ARL
24.11.83	*Munro, Geoff	Oldham

ST. HELENS

Date Signed	Player	Club From
10.6.83	*Brownbill, Paul	Salford
1.7.83	Allen, Shaun	St. Helens Colts
5.7.83	Rule, Steve	Salford
1.8.83	Loughlin, Paul	St. Helens Colts
7.10.83	Burke, Tony	Leeds
17.1.84	*Butler, John	Leigh
21.1.84	*Ganley, Chris	Fulham
22.2.84	Proudlove, John	Leigh
20.4.84	Dwyer, Bernard	Hare and Hounds ARL

SALFORD

Date Signed	Player	Club From
8.6.83	Wood, John	Fulham
1.7.83	Glynn, Peter	St. Helens
11.7.83	Ruddy, David	Orrell RU
14.8.83	Telford, Neil	Wigan St. Patricks ARL
15.8.83	Gill, Michael	Oldham, St. Annes ARL
23.9.83	Bentley, Keith	Barrow
29.9.83	*Boyd, Denis	Carlisle
6.10.83	Lamb, Nigel	Irlam Hornets ARL
1.12.83	Hughes, Barry	Langworthy ARL
10.1.84	*Cooke, Tony	Warrington
22.1.84	Taylor, John	Widnes
22.1.84	Prescott, Eric	Widnes
7.2.84	Marsh, Ian	Wigan St. Patrick ARL
2.3.84	*Brownbill, Paul	St. Helens
2.3.84	*Gee, Peter	Barrow

SWINTON

Date Signed	Player	Club From
1.8.83	*Rowley, Alan	Workington T.
16.8.83	Melling, Alexander	St. Annes ARL
16.8.83	Twist, Robert	Leigh Colts
31.8.83	Bate, Derek	Leigh Miners Wel. ARL
5.9.83	Arrowsmith, Gary	Simms Cross ARL
9.9.83	*Gittins, Tommy	Warrington
18.10.83	Whittle, Stephen	Oldham St. Annes ARL
15.11.83	Snape, Steven	Folly Lane ARL
15.11.83	Cunliffe, Geoff	Wigan
29.11.83	Viller, Mark	Salford Juniors ARL
11.1.84	Cookes, Michael	Rochdale H.
15.4.84	Tomlinson, Steve	Leigh

WAKEFIELD TRINITY

Date Signed	Player	Club From
30.8.83	Stringer, Chris	—
30.8.83	Haigh, Bob	—
21.10.83	Burns, Allan	North Sydney, Aus.
21.10.83	Wane, Glenn	North Sydney, Aus.
8.11.83	Hendry, Paul	Hunslet
10.11.83	Kelly, Richard	Wakefield T. Colts
25.11.83	Waugh, Bradley James	Penrith, Aus.
3.12.83	Lewis, Wally	Fortitude Valley, Aus.
3.12.83	Lewis, Scott	Fortitude Valley, Aus.
29.12.83	Bell, Nigel	Eastmoor ARL
10.1.84	Gerard, Greg	Manley & Mt. Prit. Aus.
14.1.84	Gill, Lindsay	Western Suburbs. Aus.
13.3.84	Oglethorpe, George	—
16.3.84	*McDermott, Paul	York

WARRINGTON

Date Signed	Player	Club From
7.8.83	Roberts, Mark	St. Annes, Oldham ARL
23.8.83	Campbell, Roy	Irlam Hornets ARL
1.9.83	Yates, Mal	Salford
13.9.83	Kerr, John	Boilermakers ARL
19.9.83	*Day, Terry	Hull
5.10.83	Peters, Barry	Blackbrook ARL
9.11.83	Pirihi, Terence	Portland, NZ
14.11.83	Gittins, Tommy	Swinton
30.11.83	Poasa, Pat	West End, NZ
10.2.84	*Cooke, Tony	Salford
31.5.84	*Waller, Tony	Leigh

WHITEHAVEN

Date Signed	Player	Club From
27.8.83	Kirkby, Steve	Barrow
1.9.83	Tomlinson, Brian	Kells ARL
30.9.83	*Thompson, Ian	Workington T.
8.10.83	*McCarron, Alf	Workington T.
22.10.83	Pattinson, Stephen	Barrow
22.10.83	*Gee, Peter	Barrow
9.11.83	Dalton, Matthew	Hensingham ARL
18.11.83	Wright, David	Frizington ARL
23.11.83	*Taylor, Michael	Workington T.
24.11.83	Mason, Mel	Barrow
1.12.83	Graham, David	Barrow
1.12.83	McArthur, Peter	Barrow
15.2.84	*Glover, John	Rochdale H.
29.3.84	*Hoare, Sean	Fulham
14.5.84	*Glover, John	Blackpool B.
14.5.84	*Cottier, Gordon	Workington T.

WIDNES

Date Signed	Player	Club From
13.7.83	Currier, Andrew	Halton Hornets ARL
13.7.83	Quinn, Kevin	Halton ARL
13.7.83	Gladwin, Michael	Port Sunlight ARL
13.7.83	Hulme, Paul	Halton Hornets ARL
15.8.83	Garritty, Tony	Cardiff C.
10.9.83	Lyon, David	Wigan St. Patricks ARL
20.12.83	Wood, Peter	Huyton
22.1.84	Platt, Duncan	—
22.1.84	Wood, John	Salford
27.1.84	Blackwood, Bob	Salford
14.3.84	Ruane, David,	Widnes Tigers ARL

WIGAN

Date Signed	Player	Club From
19.4.83	*Stephens, Gary	Warrington
4.6.83	Owen, Gary	Wigan St. Patricks ARL
13.6.83	*Nicholson, Steve	Bramley
25.6.83	*Nanyn, Michael	Blackpool B.
27.6.83	Holden, Keith	Wigan St. Patricks ARL
9.8.83	Ford, Michael	Oldham St. Annes ARL
23.9.83	*Beale, Graham	Keighley
24.9.83	*Wilby, Tim	Hull
6.10.83	Tamati. Howie	Waitara, NZ
8.10.83	Hemsley, Kerry	Balmain, Aus.
17.10.83	Edwards, Shaun	Wigan St. Patricks ARL
27.10.83	Hampson, Steve	Vulcan RU
11.11.83	Elvin, Wayne	Campbell Tn. City, Aus.
11.11.83	Gaynor, Bruce	Campbell Tn. City, Aus.
11.11.83	Cole, Peter	Campbell Tn. City, Aus.
10.12.83	Cannon, Mark	St. George, Sydney, Aus.
22.1.84	*Courtney, Neil	Warrington
17.2.84	Potter, Ian	Leigh

WORKINGTON TOWN

Date Signed	Player	Club From
7.9.83	*Taylor, Michael	Whitehaven
24.11.83	*Thompson, Ian	Whitehaven
24.11.83	*McCarron, Alfred	Whitehaven
30.11.83	*Cooke, Tony	Warrington
4.1.84	Hopkins, Lynn	Kent Invicta
5.3.84	*Henney, Harold	Salford
9.4.84	*Cottier, Gordon	Whitehaven

YORK

Date Signed	Player	Club From
9.5.83	*Marshall, Michael	Cardiff C.
30.5.83	*White, Brendan	Hull K.R.
18.6.83	*Hughes, Brian	Rochdale H.
4.8.83	Morrell, Wayne	Wakefield T.
12.10.83	Brettell, Kevin	NDLB ARL
5.11.83	Hambley, Gary	South Sydney, Aus.
9.11.83	Pitts, Graham	Civil Service ARL
9.11.83	Palfrey, Michael	Civil Service ARL
10.11.83	Kain, John	Castleford
12.11.83	*Harrison, Chris	Wakefield Trinity
22.12.83	*Nuttall, Steve	Hull K.R.
27.1.84	*Brown, Graham	Rochdale H.
6.4.84	*Piwinski, Urek	Bramley

Greenalls Man of Steel 1984 Joe Lydon receives the award from the legendary Brian Bevan.

AWARDS

AWARDS

THE MAN OF STEEL AWARDS

Launched in the 1976-77 season, the Rugby Football League's official awards are presented to the Man of Steel, the personality judged to have made the most impact on the season; the First and Second Division Players of the Year, decided by a ballot of the players; the Young Player of the Year, under-21 at the start of the season; the Coach of the Year and Referee of the Year.

Having been sponsored by Trumanns Steel for the first seven years, the 1983-84 awards were taken over by Greenall Whitley who presented a record £5,750 in prizes in front of a capacity audience at the Variety Centre, Salford.

Greenalls Man of Steel

Great Britain and Widnes utility back JOE LYDON completed a double inside five days by adding the Greenalls Man of Steel title to the Lance Todd Trophy, awarded as Man of the Match in the Widnes defeat of Wigan in the State Express Challenge Cup final at Wembley.

The Man of Steel title — Lydon's third Greenalls award of the evening — carried a record prize of £1,500 and an inscribed silver champagne goblet worth £300.

The utility star crowned a memorable season in which he had added to his Great Britain and Under-24 caps, created a new Under-24 scoring record, earned second place in the try scoring chart, won the Lance Todd Trophy and been selected for the Great Britain tour Down Under.

Lydon, who celebrated his 20th birthday in November, became the youngest Man of Steel and the first to collect three awards in the same season.

Greenalls First Division Player of the Year

JOE LYDON collected twice as many votes as his nearest rival in the ballot of fellow Slalom Lager Championship players, votes for which were cast in January and April.

The Lance Todd Trophy winner with two spectacular tries at Wembley, Lydon played every back position bar scrum half during the 1983-84 Widnes campaign.

He amassed a total of 244 points from 28 tries and 66 goals. His versatility was further proved by selection for the Under-24s at full back and at stand off for Great Britain in Avignon, his third cap at both levels.

Greenalls Second Division Player of the Year

Barrow scrum half DAVID CAIRNS topped the Second Division players' poll at the end of a season in which he had made his Great Britain debut.

The title helped soften the blow of not being selected for the Great Britain tour Down Under, having played in the French Tests in Avignon and Leeds.

Cairns was a mainstay of the Cumbrians' Second Division Championship success, losing only two of their 34 fixtures, running up a record points total. The 25-year-old scored 16 tries and five drop goals for Barrow, who pulled off one of the shocks of the season by beating Widnes in the Burtonwood Brewery Lancashire Cup. Cairns won the Man of the Match award in Barrow's first county cup triumph for 29 years.

Greenalls Referee of the Year

Huddersfield official BILLY THOMPSON celebrated his farewell season by lifting his third Referee of the Year title.

Four days earlier Thompson had taken charge of the Widnes-Wigan Challenge Cup final, his third Wembley, a fitting climax to his retirement season at the age of 50 after 18 years at top level.

Referee of the Year in 1977 and 1978, and a nominee on three other occasions, Thompson was appointed to the 1983-84 Philips Video Yorkshire Cup final, the John Player Special Trophy and the State Express Challenge Cup final to bring his career tally of cup finals to 26, augmented by 18 internationals and three World Cups and two Championship finals.

Greenalls Young Player of the Year

At 20 years 6 months, Widnes prodigy JOE LYDON collected the Young Player of the Year title to add to his First Division accolade.

The design student celebrated his 20th birthday by setting a new Great Britain Under-24 record with a 20-point haul against France at Oldham, scoring eight goals from eight attempts and adding a spectacular 60-yard try. The second youngest winner of the Lance Todd Trophy and second top try scorer during the season, he added to his tally of Great Britain caps by playing stand off in Avignon and crowned a memorable season by making the round-the world trip to Australasia for his first Great Britain tour.

Greenalls Coach of the Year

TOMMY DAWES celebrated his first season in charge of Barrow by taking the coaching title. A year after guiding Whitehaven to promotion, the former Barrow full back led the Craven Park club to the Second Division Championship title in record-breaking style.

Losing only two of their 34 fixtures, Barrow piled up a record 1,230 points from 41 cup and league matches, featuring a remarkable 209 tries. The tally included a league record for either division of 1,126 points and 196 tries.

Barrow crowned their league success by pulling off the cup shock of the season. The Shipbuilders lifted the Lancashire Cup for the first time in 29 years by beating four First Division sides in Whitehaven at home, Salford and Warrington away and Widnes in the final at Wigan.

**Each of the last five category winners received a cheque for £500 and an inscribed silver wine goblet worth £250.

Barrow coach Tommy Dawes with the Lancashire Cup.

THE MAN OF STEEL AWARDS ROLL OF HONOUR

	Man of Steel	1st Division Player	2nd Division Player	Young Player	Coach	Referee
1977	David Ward (Leeds)	Mal Reilly (Castleford)	Ged Marsh (Blackpool B.)	David Ward (Leeds)	Eric Ashton MBE (St. Helens)	Billy Thompson (Huddersfield)
1978	George Nicholls (St. Helens)	George Nicholls (St. Helens)	John Woods (Leigh)	John Woods (Leigh)	Frank Myler (Widnes)	Billy Thompson (Huddersfield)
1979	Doug Laughton (Widnes)	Mick Adams (Widnes)	Steve Norton (Hull)	Steve Evans (Featherstone R.)	Doug Laughton (Widnes)	Mick Naughton (Widnes)
1980	George Fairbairn (Wigan)	Mick Adams (Widnes)	Steve Quinn (Featherstone R.)	Roy Holdstock (Hull K.R.)	Peter Fox (Bradford N.)	Fred Lindop (Wakefield)
1981	Ken Kelly (Warrington)	Ken Kelly (Warrington)	John Crossley (York)	Des Drummond (Leigh)	Billy Benyon (Warrington)	John Holdsworth (Leeds)
1982	Mick Morgan (Carlisle)	Steve Norton (Hull)	Mick Morgan (Carlisle)	Des Drummond (Leigh)	Arthur Bunting (Hull)	Fred Lindop (Wakefield)
1983	Allan Agar (Featherstone R.)	Keith Mumby (Bradford N.)	Steve Nash (Salford)	Brian Noble (Bradford N.)	Arthur Bunting (Hull)	Robin Whitfield (Widnes)
1984	Joe Lydon (Widnes)	Joe Lydon (Widnes)	David Cairns (Barrow)	Joe Lydon (Widnes)	Tommy Dawes (Barrow)	Billy Thompson (Huddersfield)

NOMINEES:

1977 *1st Division Player:* Bruce Burton (Castleford), Vince Farrar (Featherstone R.). *2nd Division Player:* Jeff Grayshon (Dewsbury), Keith Hepworth (Hull). *Young Player:* Jimmy Crampton (Hull), Harry Pinner (St. Helens). *Coach:* Keith Cotton (Featherstone R.), Mal Reilly (Castleford). *Referee:* John Jackson (Pudsey), Mick Naughton (Widnes).

1978 *1st Division Player:* Roger Millward (Hull K.R.), Harry Pinner (St. Helens). *2nd Division Player:* Phil Hogan (Barrow), Mick Morgan (York). *Young Player:* Neil Hague (Leeds), Keith Mumby (Bradford N.). *Coach:* Eric Ashton MBE (St. Helens), John Mantle (Leigh). *Referee:* Ron Campbell (Widnes), Fred Lindop (Wakefield).

1979 *1st Division Player:* Brian Lockwood (Hull K.R.), Tommy Martyn (Warrington). *2nd Division Player:* Barry Banks (York), John Wolford (Dewsbury). *Young Player:* Mick Burke (Widnes), John Woods (Leigh). *Coach:* Billy Benyon (Warrington), Arthur Bunting (Hull). *Referee:* Fred Lindop (Wakefield), Billy Thompson (Huddersfield).

1980 *1st Division Player:* Len Casey (Hull K.R.), George Fairbairn (Wigan). *2nd Division Player:* Mick Blacker (Halifax), John Wolford (Dewsbury). *Young Player:* Steve Hubbard (Hull K.R.), Harry Pinner (St. Helens), *Coach:* Maurice Bamford (Halifax), Arthur Bunting (Hull). *Referee:* Ron Campbell (Widnes), Billy Thompson (Huddersfield).

1981 *1st Division Player:* Mick Adams (Widnes), Tommy Martyn (Warrington). *2nd Division Player:* Arnie Walker (Whitehaven), Danny Wilson (Swinton). *Young Player:* Paul Harkin (Hull K.R.), Keith Mumby (Bradford N.). *Coach:* Reg Bowden (Fulham), Peter Fox (Bradford N.). *Referee:* Ron Campbell (Widnes), Fred Lindop (Wakefield).

1982 *1st Division Player:* Jeff Grayshon (Bradford N.), Andy Gregory (Widnes). *2nd Division Player:* Denis Boyd (Carlisle), Alan Fairhurst (Swinton). *Young Player:* Lee Crooks (Hull), Andy Gregory (Widnes). *Coach:* Doug Laughton (Widnes), Alex Murphy/Colin Clarke (Leigh). *Referee:* Gerry Kershaw (York), Billy Thompson (Huddersfield).

1983 *1st Division Player:* Bob Eccles (Warrington), David Topliss (Hull). *2nd Division Player:* Tommy David (Cardiff C.), Mike Lampkowski (Wakefield T.). *Young Player:* Ronnie Duane (Warrington), Andy Goodway (Oldham). *Coach:* Alex Murphy (Wigan), Frank Myler (Oldham). *Referee:* John Holdsworth (Leeds), Fred Lindop (Wakefield).

1984 *1st Division Player:* Garry Schofield (Hull), John Woods (Leigh). *2nd Division Player:* Lynn Hopkins (Workington T.), John Wolford (Hunslet). *Young Player:* Gary Divorty (Hull), Garry Schofield (Hull). *Coach:* Arthur Bunting (Hull), Roger Millward MBE (Hull K.R.) *Referee:* Derek Fox (Wakefield), Fred Lindop (Wakefield).

GREENALL WHITLEY — SUNDAY PEOPLE AWARDS

Sponsored by brewers Greenall Whitley and promoted by the Sunday People newspaper, the scheme featured eight Men of the Month awards. In the 1983-84 season, the monthly winners each received tankards and £150. The traditional Personality of the Year award was suspended because of Greenhall Whitley's takeover of the Man of Steel awards.

The Greenall Whitley-Sunday People Awards Roll of Honour

	1977-78	1978-79	1979-80	1980-81	1981-82	1982-83	1983-84
PERSONALITY OF THE YEAR							
	Reg Bowden (Widnes)	Doug Laughton (Widnes)	George Fairbairn (Wigan)	Reg Bowden (Fulham)	Des Drummond (Leigh)	David Topliss (Hull)	—
MEN OF THE MONTH							
Sept	John Woods (Leigh)	Jim Mills (Widnes)	Ian Ball (Barrow)	Paul Harkin (Hull K.R.)	Des Drummond (Leigh)	David Heron (Leeds)	Ellery Hanley (Bradford N.)
Oct.	Green Vigo (Wigan)	Brian Lockwood (Hull K.R.)	Ken Gill (Salford)	Gary Hyde (Castleford)	Andy Gregory (Widnes)	Mal Meninga (Australia)	Gordon Smith (Hull K.R.)
Nov.	Peter Fox (Bradford N.)	Doug Laughton (Widnes)	Steve Quinn (Featherstone R.)	Ken Kelly (Warrington)	Steve Norton (Hull)	Frank Stanton (Australia)	John Basnett (Widnes)
Dec.	Mick Adams (Widnes)	Neil Holding (St. Helens)	George Fairbairn (Wigan)	Billy Benyon (Warrington)	Jeff Grayshon (Bradford N.)	Bob Eccles (Warrington)	Joe Lydon (Widnes)
Jan.	Bill Ashurst (Wigan)	Charlie Stone (Hull)	Mick Adams (Widnes)	Brian Case (Warrington)	Mick Morgan (Carlisle)	Alex Murphy (Wigan)	Maurice Bamford (Leeds)
Feb.	Not awarded — Bad weather	Geoff Wraith (Castleford)	Roy Holdstock (Hull K.R.)	Allan Agar (Wakefield T.)	Des Drummond (Leigh)	Neil Holding (St. Helens)	Bob Beardmore (Castleford)
Mar.	Eddie Cunningham (St. Helens)	Steve Evans (Featherstone R.)	Steve Norton (Hull)	Mick Adams (Widnes)	Lynn Hopkins (Workington T.)	Terry Hudson (Featherstone R.)	Neil Holding (St. Helens)
Apr.	John Holmes (Leeds)	Ken Kelly (Warrington)	Geoff Munro (Oldham)	Keith Mumby (Bradford N.)	John Woods (Leigh)	David Topliss (Hull)	Garry Schofield (Hull)
May.	Geoff Pimblett (St. Helens)	John Sanderson (Leeds)	Mal Aspey (Widnes)	Steve Norton (Hull)	Mick Adams (Widnes)	Allan Agar (Featherstone R.)	—
SPECIAL AWARDS							
	Keith Fielding (Superstars) Colin Welland (BBC Documentary)			Roger Millward (Hull K.R. on retirement as a player)			

GREENALL WHITLEY-SUNDAY PEOPLE TOP SCORERS AWARDS

Launched in the 1976-77 season, this scheme was designed to reward the top try and goal scorers.

Sponsored by brewers Greenall Whitley and promoted by the Sunday People newspaper, the awards were worth £25 a try and £5 a goal in the 1983-84 season.

Hull's 18-year-old centre Garry Schofield — the youngest player to top the try scoring chart — received £950 for his 38 tries. Warrington utility back Steve Hesford shared the goalkicking prize with Castleford scrum half Bob Beardmore, each kicking 142 goals. They shared £710.

For the second time the sponsors offered a bonus of £5,000 for the first player to score 50 tries in the season, the prize remaining unclaimed.

Greenall Whitley - Sunday People Top Scorers Awards Roll of Honour

Top Tries

1976-77	**1977-78**	**1978-79**	**1979-80**	**1980-81**	**1981-82**	**1982-83**	**1983-84**
Stuart Wright (Widnes): 31	Stuart Wright (Widnes): 33	Steve Hartley (Hull K.R.): 35	Keith Fielding (Salford): 30 Steve Hubbard (Hull K.R.): 30	John Crossley (York): 35	John Jones (Work'ton T.): 31	Bob Eccles (Warrington): 37	Garry Schofield (Hull): 38

1976-77	1977-78	1978-79	1979-80	1980-81	1981-82	1982-83	1983-84
Sammy Lloyd (Castle'd): 163	Geoff Pimblett (St. Helens): 178	Sammy Lloyd (Hull): 172	Steve Quinn (F'stone R.): 163	Steve Hesford (Warrington): 147	Lynn Hopkins (Work'ton T.): 190	Steve Diamond (Fulham): 136	Bob Beardmore (Castleford: 142) Steve Hesford (Warrington): 142

DAILY MIRROR — LADA CARS AWARDS

Introduced in the 1979-80 season, the scheme acknowledges the adjudged Team of the Month in both Division One and Two.

A panel of judges representing the Daily Mirror, Lada Cars and the Rugby League selected the two monthly winners who each received a cheque for £200 and a framed citation.

Promoted by the Daily Mirror, the awards were sponsored for the first four seasons by Shopacheck before Lada Cars took over in the 1983-84 season. Lada Cars introduced the first-ever £1,000 Team of the Year title.

The Daily Mirror-Lada Cars Awards Roll of Honour

	1979-80 First Division	**1980-81 First Division**	**1981-82 First Division**	**1982-83 First Division**	**1983-84 First Division**
Aug./Sept.	Salford	Hull K.R.	Leigh	Leeds	Bradford N.
Oct.	Leigh	Castleford	Widnes	Hull	Hull K.R.
Nov.	Leeds	Featherstone R.	Hull K.R.	Castleford	Widnes
Dec.	Hull	Warrington	Hull*	Wigan	Leeds
Jan.	Bradford N.	Halifax		Wigan	Hull
Feb.	Widnes	Wakefield T.	Leigh	Castleford	Castleford
Mar.	Hull	Widnes	Bradford N.	Hull	Wigan
Apr./May	Leigh	Bradford N.	Hull	Widnes	St. Helens

	Second Division	**Second Division**	**Second Division**	**Second Division**	**Second Division**
Aug./Sept.	Halifax	Huddersfield	Oldham	Fulham	Barrow
Oct.	Batley	Fulham	Swinton	Huyton	Halifax
Nov.	Featherstone R.	Wigan	Carlisle	Wakefield T.	Swinton
Dec.	Oldham	Blackpool B.	Carlisle*	Salford	Batley
Jan.	Whitehaven	Keighley		Whitehaven	Barrow
Feb.	Halifax	York	Huyton	Hunslet	Hunslet
Mar.	Barrow	Whitehaven	Oldham	Fulham	Huddersfield
Apr./May	Swinton	Batley	Oldham	Cardiff C.	Blackpool B

*A double-money award to cover both months, badly hit by adverse weather.

Team of the Year

1983-84: Widnes

SLALOM LAGER PRESS PHOTOGRAPHER OF THE YEAR

In 1982 a new award was introduced by Slalom Lager, sponsors of the Championship and Premiership, to recognise achievement in the field of press photography.

In association with Pentax Cameras, Slalom Lager invited portfolios from photographers submitting work for publication in national, daily and weekly newspapers, plus periodicals.

The 1984 winner received a trophy and £1,000 worth of Pentax camera equipment; second placed £250 worth; and third placed £100 worth.

Judging was performed by a team from Slalom Lager, Rugby League HQ and Pentax, headed by Mr. Jack Hickes, a former leading national sports photographer.

1982

1st GERALD WEBSTER, Rugby Leaguer.
2nd TIM CLAYTON, Yorkshire Evening Post.
3rd EDDIE FULLER, Warrington Guardian.

1983

1st TIM CLAYTON, Yorkshire Evening Post
2nd JOHN LEATHERBARROW, Lancashire Evening Post and Chronicle
3rd DENNIS BRADBURY, Rugby Leaguer

1984

1st GARY LONGBOTTOM, Yorkshire Post.
2nd ANDREW VARLEY, Freelance
3rd JOHN VARLEY, Feelance

The Slalom Lager press photograph of the year, by Gary Longbottom of the Yorkshire Post.

DAILY EXPRESS — HEPWORTH TAILORING AWARDS

Launched in the 1978-79 season, the scheme is a joint promotion, the awards being decided by a ballot of Daily Express readers.

In the 1983-84 season, the Player of the Year received a cheque for £500, a £500 tailoring voucher and a silver salver. Periodic awards were presented during the season, each worth £100 together with a £100 tailoring voucher.

The Daily Express-Hepworth Tailoring Roll of Honour

PLAYER OF THE YEAR

1978-79	**1979-80**	**1980-81**	**1981-82**	**1982-83**	**1983-84**
Doug Laughton (Widnes)	Steve Norton (Hull)	Mick Adams (Widnes)	George Fairbairn (Hull K.R.)	David Topliss (Hull)	Garry Schofield (Hull)

PERIODIC AWARDS

1978-79	**1979-80**	**1980-81**	**1981-82**	**1982-83**	
Keith Smith (Wakefield T.)	John Woods (Leigh)	Steve Quinn (Featherstone R.)	Des Drummond (Leigh)	Trevor Skerrett (Hull)	Bob Beardmore (Castleford)
Neil Holding (St. Helens)	Alan Smith (Leeds)	Fred Ah Koui (New Zealand)	Jeff Grayshon (Bradford N.)	Lee Crooks (Hull)	Ian Ball (Barrow)
Reg Bowden (Widnes)	Steve Quinn (Featherstone R.)	Des Drummond (Leigh)	Steve Norton (Hull)	Mal Meninga (Australia)	Mick Burke (Widnes)
Roger Millward (Hull K.R.)	Harry Pinner (St. Helens)	Ken Kelly (Warrington)	George Fairbairn (Hull K.R.)	Garry Clark (Hull K.R.)	Brian Noble (Bradford N.)
Doug Laughton (Widnes)	George Fairbairn (Wigan)	Tommy Martyn (Warrington)	Trevor Skerrett (Hull)	Terry Flanagan (Oldham)	Keith Rayne (Leeds)
Sammy Lloyd (Hull)	Alan Redfearn (Bradford N.)	Steve Hesford (Warrington)	Des Drummond (Leigh)	Brian Noble (Bradford N.)	Ken Kelly (Warrington)
		Mick Adams (Widnes)		Terry Hudson (Featherstone R.)	Garry Schofield (Hull)

Daily Express-Hepworth Tailoring Player of the Year Garry Schofield in action for Great Britain Colts.

PROFESSIONAL PLAYERS ASSOCIATION PLAYER OF THE YEAR

Introduced in 1982-83, the title is determined by a ballot of members of the P.P.A. The award is the Telvista Television Trophy and the 1983-84 prize money was £1,000.

The 1984 winner was Featherstone Rovers' scrum half Deryck Fox in his first season as a professional, having signed for the Colliers after the BARLA Under-18 Tour of New Zealand during the summer of 1983.

The other nominees for the award were: Bob Beardmore (Castleford), David Cairns (Barrow), Keith Mumby (Bradford N.), Harry Pinner (St. Helens), Keith Rayne (Leeds), Garry Schofield (Hull) and John Wolford (Hunslet).

Roll of Honour

1982-83 Keith Mumby (Bradford N.)
1983-84 Deryck Fox (Featherstone R.)

SLALOM LAGER-DAILY STAR STARMEN AWARDS

Introduced in 1982-83, the £1,000 scheme is sponsored by Slalom Lager and promoted by the Daily Star. The Man of the Match for each team in every Slalom Lager Championship and Second Division game is awarded a rating out of 10. The top pollster in the Championship received £650 and a trophy, with £350 and a trophy being presented to the top Second Division player. The inaugural winners were Harry Pinner (St. Helens) and Graham Beale (Keighley), the 1983-84 table toppers being John Woods (Leigh) and John Wolford (Hunslet). The final tables were:

SLALOM LAGER CHAMPIONSHIP

1.	John Woods (Leigh)	129
2.	Ken Kelly (Warrington)	89
3.	Bob Beardmore (Castleford)	82
4.	Deryck Fox (Featherstone R.)	77
5.	Reg Bowden (Fulham)	53
6.	James Leuluai (Hull)	47
7.	Harry Pinner (St. Helens)	47
8.	Steve Diamond (Fulham)	46
9.	Gary Prohm (Hull K.R.)	41
10.	Colin Hall (Whitehaven)	36

SECOND DIVISION

1.	John Wolford (Hunslet)	89
2.	Norman Turley (Blackpool B.)	77
3.	Danny Wilson (Swinton)	77
4.	David Cairns (Barrow)	68
5.	Carl Gibson (Batley)	61
6.	Andy Gascoigne (Bramley)	58
7.	Steve Lane (Kent Invicta)	57
8.	Tommy David (Cardiff C.)	56
9.	Billy Platt (Rochdale H.)	55
10.	John Stapleton (Rochdale H.)	54

Referee of the Year 1984 Billy Thompson who marked his retirement with a Wembley farewell.

REFEREES

REFEREES

SENIOR REFEREES

Allatt, Kevin	Southport
Beaumont, Mick	Huddersfield
Berry, Geoff	Batley
Campbell, Ron	Widnes
Carter, Dave	Widnes
Croft, Jeff	Leeds
Fox, Derek	Wakefield
Haigh, Stephen	Ossett
Hodgson, Cliff	Maryport
Holdsworth, John	Kippax
Kendrew, John	Castleford
Kershaw, Gerry	Easingwold
Lindop, Fred	Wakefield
McDonald, John	Wigan
Mean, John	Leyland
Robinson, Frank	Leeds
Smith, Jim	Halifax
Spencer, Ken	Warrington
Tickle, Frank	St. Helens
Volante, Paul	Batley
Walker, Bernard	Barrow
Wall, Stan	Leigh
Whitfield, Robin	Widnes

REFEREES HONOURS 1983-84

State Express Challenge Cup final:
Billy Thompson

John Player Special Trophy final:
Billy Thompson

Slalom Lager Premiership final:
Ron Campbell

Burtonwood Brewery Lancashire Cup final:
Kevin Allatt

Philips Video Yorkshire Cup final:
Billy Thompson

France v Great Britain Under-24s:
Fred Lindop

France v Great Britain Colts:
Robin Whitfield

REFEREES ROLL OF HONOUR

KEVIN ALLATT
Date of birth: 29.12.42
Grade Two: 1970-71
Grade One: 1972-73
Lancashire Cup 1983-84

MICK BEAUMONT
Date of birth: 27.6.40
Grade Two: 1973-74
Grade One: 1977-78
Lancashire v Cumbria 1979-80

GEOFF BERRY
Date of birth: 26.4.54
Grade Two: 1981-82

RON CAMPBELL
Date of birth: 8.3.36
Grade Two: 1973-74
Grade One: 1974-75
Wales v France 1977-78, 1980-81
Wales v Australia 1978-79
Great Britain v Australia, 1st Test 1978-79
Wales v England 1978-79
England v Wales 1979-80
Lancashire v Yorkshire 1975-76
Yorkshire Cup 1980-81
John Player Trophy 1982-83
Premiership Trophy 1983-84

DAVE CARTER
Date of birth: 29.11.55
Graded: 1984-85

JEFF CROFT
Date of birth: 3.3.45
Graded: 1984-85

DEREK FOX
Date of birth: 2.1.39
Grade Two: 1977-78
Grade One: 1980-81
Lancashire v Cumbria 1981-82

STEPHEN HAIGH
Date of birth: 5.4.45
Grade Two: 1980-81

CLIFF HODGSON
Date of birth: 18.10.40
Grade Two: 1978-79

JOHN HOLDSWORTH
Date of birth: 25.1.47
Grade Two: 1979-80
Grade One: 1980-81
Premiership Trophy 1980-81
Wales v England 1980-81
Cumbria v Yorkshire 1981-82
Lancashire Cup 1982-83
France v Great Britain Under-24s 1982-83

JOHN KENDREW
Date of birth: 22.4.50
Grade Two: 1982-83

GERRY KERSHAW
Date of birth: 24.10.43
Grade Two: 1969-70
Grade One: 1970-71
Challenge Cup 1980-81
Lancashire Cup 1980-81
Floodlit Trophy 1973-74
John Player Trophy 1973-74
Wales v England 1981-82
Wales v Australia 1982-83
France v Great Britain Under-24s 1981-82
Lancashire v Yorkshire 1971-72
Lancashire v Cumbria 1972-73
Cumbria v Other Nationalities 1974-75
Cumbria v Lancashire 1978-79, 1980-81

Widnes man in the middle Robin Whitfield in charge of the France v Great Britain Colts international at Arles.

FRED LINDOP
Date of birth: 20.7.38
Grade Two: 1966-67
Grade One: 1967-68
Great Britain v New Zealand (2nd Test) 1980-81
Great Britain v Australia, 3 Tests 1967-68
France v Great Britain 1968-69
1970 World Cup:
Great Britain v Australia
Great Britain v France
Great Britain v New Zealand
Great Britain v Australia (Final)
Wales v France 1974-75
1975 World Championship:
France v Wales
New Zealand v Australia (at Auckland)
Wales v France
Wales v England 1977-78
Great Britain Under-24s v Australia 1978-79
France v Great Britain Under-24s 1979-80, 1983-84
Australia v New Zealand (2) 1982
Premiership Trophy 1976-77, 1982-83
Challenge Cup 1969-70, 1979-80, 1981-82 (+replay)
Floodlit Trophy 1967-68, 1972-73
John Player Trophy 1974-75, 1978-79, 1981-82
Lancashire Cup 1967-68, 1974-75
Capt. Morgan Trophy 1973-74
Cumbria v Lancashire 1973-74
Lancashire v Other Nationalities 1974-75
Lancashire v Yorkshire 1981-82

JOHN McDONALD
Date of birth: 7.10.37
Grade Two: 1974-75
Grade One: 1975-76
Floodlit Trophy 1978-79
Yorkshire v Cumbria 1978-79, 1981-82
France v Great Britain Colts 1982-83

JOHN MEAN
Date of birth: 12.11.39
Grade Two: 1975-76

FRANK ROBINSON
Date of birth: 12.10.41
Grade Two: 1980-81

JIM SMITH
Date of birth: 2.3.44
Grade Two: 1977-78

KEN SPENCER
Date of birth: 29.8.47
Grade Two: 1974-75

FRANK TICKLE
Date of birth: 26.10.45
Graded: 1984-85

PAUL VOLANTE
Date of birth: 30.6.52
Grade Two: 1983-84

BERNARD WALKER
Date of birth: 27.10.41
Grade Two: 1982-83

STAN WALL
Date of birth: 17.1.35
Grade Two: 1972-73
Grade One: 1974-75
England v Wales 1974-75
Great Britain Under-24s v New Zealand 1980-81
France v Great Britain Under-24s 1980-81
Premiership Trophy 1981-82
Yorkshire Cup 1982-83
Yorkshire v Other Nationalities 1975-76
Cumbria v Yorkshire 1979-80

ROBIN WHITFIELD
Date of birth: 26.11.43
Grade Two: 1979-80
Grade One: 1980-81
Challenge Cup 1982-83
Yorkshire Cup 1981-82
France v Australia (2) 1982-83
New Zealand v Australia 1983
Yorkshire v Lancashire 1981-82

POT POURRI

THE INTERNATIONAL LAWS OF THE GAME and NOTES ON THE LAWS

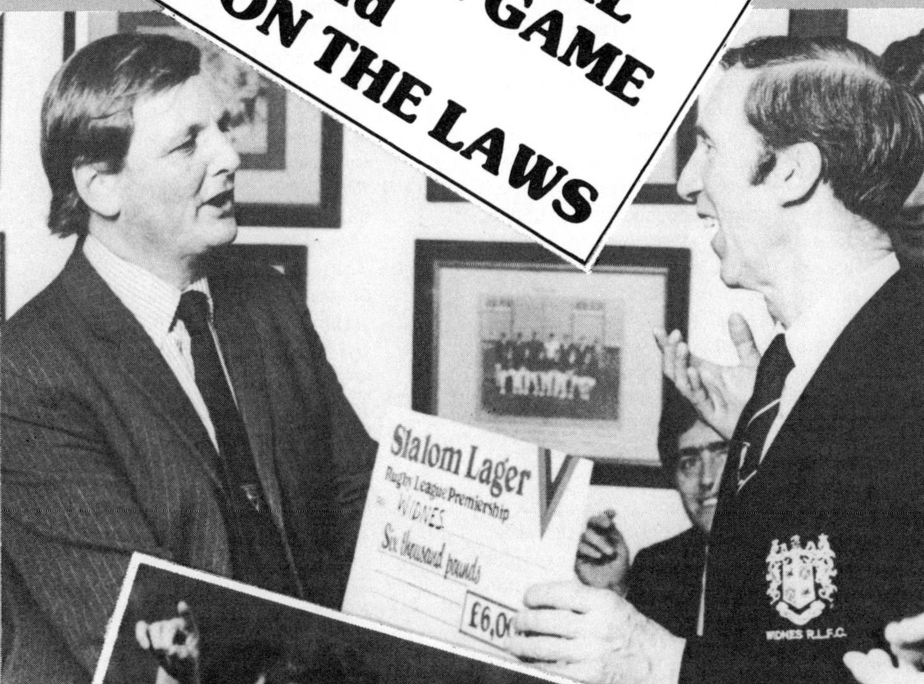

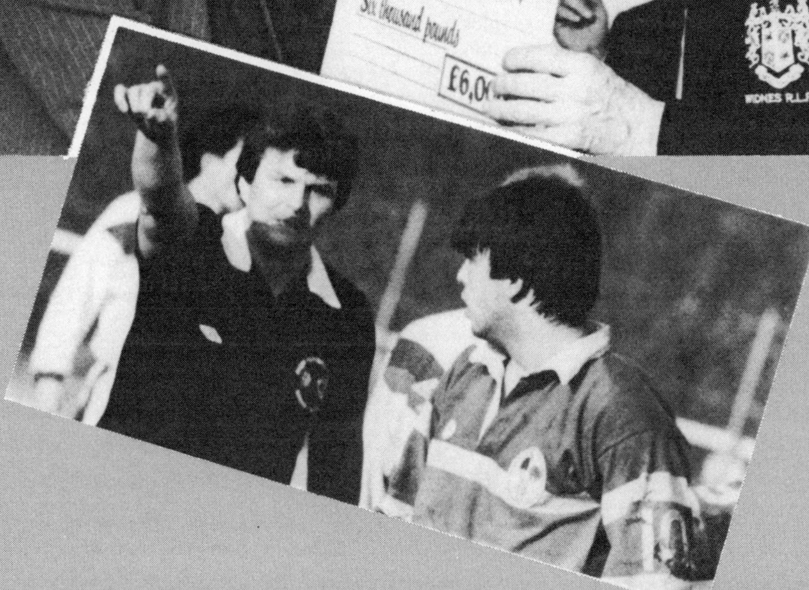

POT POURRI

RULES OF THE GAME . . . A REVIEW

When the Northern Union was formed following the split with the English Rugby Union in 1895, it was decided to retain the R.U. laws of the game. The first changes were made after only two months and within a few years a new code of rugby was emerging as more alterations followed in the quest to make it a more entertaining spectacle.

Rugby League is the result of those changes. Early pleas to 'stop tinkering with the rules' went unheeded. In many instances, particularly concerning scrummaging and the play-the-ball, rules that were abolished were later reinstated.

It was also the case that each country played under varying rules. It was not until season 1981-82 that agreement was reached on international uniformity.

Following an International Board meeting in 1982, several revolutionary changes were made, including the introduction of the four-point try and the hand over of the ball instead of a scrum after a sixth successive tackle. These changes, introduced into Britain at the start of the 1983-84 season, were major developments in the evolution of the game. It is now very different from that played only 20 years ago.

The following is a list of some of the significant changes in the rules since 1895. Only the major changes in the scrummaging and play-the-ball rules are listed as explanatory notes are featured at the end.

1895-96 Penalty for deliberate knock-on. Ball to be put in scrum on the referee's side. *These changes, made in December, were the first break with Rugby Union rules.*

1897-98 Line out abolished and replaced by punt from touch.
All goals to be worth two points. *Previously – four points for a drop goal or a goal from a mark; three for a penalty; two for a conversion.*

1899-1900 Scrum ordered if a tackled player cannot release the ball.
Kick off at halfway after a try. *Previously game restarted on defending team's 25-yard line.*

1901-02 Punt from touch replaced by 10-yard scrum when ball was carried into touch.
Knock-on ruled only if ball touched ground.

1902-03 Punt from touch abolished completely and replaced by 10-yard scrum.
Touch-finding rule introduced, ball having to bounce before entering touch, otherwise scrum took place where kick was made.

1903-04 Kick off or drop out straight into touch followed by scrum at halfway or on 25-yard line.

1906-07 Thirteen-a-side introduced.
Six-man scrum instead of eight.
Scrum after tackle abolished, reverting to tackled player placing the ball on the ground in front of him.

1907-08 Tackled player allowed to regain feet and put down ball in front of him when it could be played with the foot by either side. *This was the forerunner of today's play-the-ball.*

1911-12 All matches to last 80 minutes. *Previously they could be of 70 minutes if both teams agreed.*
Numbering of jerseys compulsory.

1922-23 Goal from a mark abolished. *A mark was made by a player fielding the ball from the opposition and claiming a free kick.*

1950-51 Tap penalty allowed with the offending side having to retire 10 yards. *Previously the offending side did not have to retire from the spot where the penalty was given and the kicker, when not going for goal, usually kicked to touch where a scrum was formed.*

1958-59 Play-the-ball acting half-back conceded a scrum if tackled in possession.

1960-61 Tap penalty abolished, with scrum to follow penalty kick to touch.

1964-65 Substitutes introduced, on the basis of two allowed for injured players, but only up to the start of the second half.
The mark abolished.

1965-66 Substitutes allowed for any reason before and during the half-time interval.

1966-67 Tap penalty reintroduced, this time with the extra advantage of being taken after a kick to touch.
Four-tackle rule introduced for BBC2 Floodlit Trophy matches starting in October, then for all matches from December. A scrum followed if a team was tackled four times in succession.

1967-68 After an unsuccessful drop goal attempt which went dead, play restarted with a 25-yard tap kick by the defending team instead of a drop out. This was later extended to a tap restart for all kicks the attacking side put dead.
Penalty try to be followed by resultant kick at goal from in front of posts.

1969-70 Substitutes to be allowed at any time.

1970-71 Substitution extended to allow a replaced player to go back as a substitute.

1972-73 Six-tackle rule introduced.
Time-keepers with hooters introduced.

1973-74 Penalty awarded for offence committed during the scoring of a try. Kick to be in front of posts after customary goal attempt. *Became known as the seven-point try, later eight-point when try became four points.*

1974-75 Drop goal reduced to one point. *Had recently been used in international matches.*

1975-76 Injured players treated on field while play in progress.
Ten-yard extra penalty for dissent made law. *Previously referees had used the extra penalty at their own discretion.*

1976-77 Differential penalty introduced for technical scrum offences. Tap kick must be taken, not kick for goal or touch.

1979-80 Defending team to drop out from own 25-yard line after an unsuccessful penalty kick had gone dead.

1981-82 Differential scrum penalty extended to offer choice of tap or kick to touch, followed by tap. Kick for goal still not permitted.

1982-83 Sin bin introduced on January 1. *Had previously been used in international matches.*

1983-84 The introduction of seven new or amended laws of the game commissioned by the Rugby League International Board. Their meeting in November 1982 approved the new rules which were introduced by each member country at the start of the next season.

1. Four-point try. *Previously a try was worth three points.*
2. The sixth tackle: When the team in possession tackled for a sixth consecutive time, without the opposition having touched the ball, the tackled player had to release the ball immediately and place it on the ground at the point where he was tackled. Play resumed by the nearest opposing player playing the ball, but this play-the-ball not counting towards their permitted six tackles. *Previously a scrum would have been formed.*
3. Head and ball: At a scrum, the non-offending side had both the loose head and the feed. In the case of a mutual infringement, the attacking side had the head and ball. When the ball was kicked into touch, having bounced within the field of play, the non-kicking side had both head and ball. *Previously the allocation of the loose head and the scrum feed varied according to in which half of the field the scrum was being formed.*
4. The scrum feed: The ball put into the scrum from the referee's side by the ball being rolled along the ground. Must be put into the centre of the tunnel, the player feeding the scrum

holding the ball horizontally, point to point, propelling it from a position between his knees and ankles. *Previously the feed was from below the waist in a downward direction.*

5. Scrum formation: When a scrum was formed, never more than seven players outside the pack. Thus, when a team was at full strength, the loose forward remained in the scrum. A forward could detach himself from the scrum only if the back division was depleted by dismissal or injury. *Previously the loose forward was allowed to detach himself from the scrum at any time.*
6. The kick off: When the ball was kicked off and bounced over the dead-ball line or into touch-in-goal, without being touched by a defending player, play resumed by a drop-out from beneath the posts. If the ball was kicked directly out of play, play resumed by a penalty kick from the centre spot. *Previously play would have been resumed in the first instance by a tap from the 25-yard line.*
7. Offside at play-the-ball: At the play-the-ball, both sides remain in an onside position until the ball has come clear of the tackled player and the player marking him. *Previously players could move up once the ball had touched the ground.*

Scrums

The introduction of the hand over rule last season resulted in yet another reduction in the number of scrums per match. The average of about 25 per match the previous season fell to 15, with sometimes as few as five or six.

Eighty years ago – when a scrum followed every tackle – there were well over 100 per match. They were still averaging more than 70 in the 1940s, despite the unlimited play-the-ball rule.

It was the introduction of the tap penalty that began their reduction and they were down to an average of about 15 in the mid-1960s, just before the four-tackle rule shot them back to around the 30-mark.

Scrummaging has long been described as a blot on the game and the changes made in efforts to improve them are too numerous to mention. They included many variations of who should have the loose head advantage; whether the defending or attacking side should put in the ball; when the hooker should be allowed to strike for the ball and with which foot.

Last season's new rules ensured almost certain possession for the non-offending side, being awarded head and ball advantage.

Play-the-ball

Soon after the breakaway from the English Rugby Union, an improvement on the R.U. method of playing the ball after a tackle was sought.

The R.U. rucking and mauling was considered unsatisfactory and in 1907 the tackled player was allowed to regain his feet before placing the ball when it could be played by either side.

That, basically, was the start of today's play-the-ball. It was never considered satisfactory and down the years has undergone many changes. Originally intended to give both teams an equal chance of gaining possession, failure to stick to the letter of the law resulted in one team being able to retain possession through an unlimited number of play-the-balls.

With the early failure to break the monopoly of possession, efforts were concentrated on how far the teams should be kept apart. The rule makers then appeared to go round in circles. The distance players were supposed to retire from the play-the-ball varied between one and five yards, as well as a period when all players were allowed to stand in line with the acting half-backs.

The introduction of the limited tackles rule switched the emphasis to what was the most satisfactory number of successive play-the-balls one side should be allowed. It changed from four to the present six, which seems to be settled as a fair compromise.

DISCIPLINARY RECORDS

This new sub-section is a first-ever compilation of sendings off and disciplinary verdicts for first team players.

Fulham hooker John Dalgreen, who had a sine die ban reduced to an eight-match suspension on appeal because of a legal technicality.

The following information is based on the workings of the League's Disciplinary Committee which meets monthly during a season.

DISMISSALS .... A five-year review

The following is a review of the number of first team players sent off in each season since 1979-80.

— indicates where a club was not in existence.

	1983-84	1982-83	1981-82	1980-81	1979-80
Barrow	2	2	2	2	2
Batley	3	4	3	2	1
Blackpool B.	3	3	2	1	3
Bradford N.	3	3	11	6	3
Bramley	3	2	0	2	0
Cardiff C.	6	2	7	—	—
Carlisle	8	4	3	—	—
Castleford	5	4	7	4	2
Dewsbury	2	5	10	3	6
Doncaster	10	2	4	2	4
Featherstone R.	1	1	9	2	4
Fulham	6	8	3	3	—
Halifax	3	4	3	3	1
Huddersfield	4	2	3	3	3
Hull	3	4	3	4	4
Hull K.R.	5	4	13	5	3
Hunslet	3	1	4	0	4
Huyton	5	3	3	2	4
Keighley	0	3	3	5	2
Kent Invicta	3	—	—	—	—
Leeds	0	3	5	5	4
Leigh	3	2	6	3	5
Oldham	5	3	8	4	3
Rochdale H.	9	1	7	1	1
St. Helens	3	3	1	2	0
Salford	5	6	3	1	2
Swinton	0	4	1	2	1
Wakefield T.	5	2	6	2	3
Warrington	6	5	10	6	7
Whitehaven	6	2	4	3	3
Widnes	7	4	3	6	5
Wigan	2	3	5	7	5
Workington T.	4	3	3	2	0
York	4	2	3	3	1
Totals	137	104	158	96	86

DISCIPLINARY ANALYSIS 1983-84

The following is a club by club disciplinary record for last season, showing the players sent off in first team matches and the findings of the League's Disciplinary Committee.

The committee's verdict is featured in the brackets after the player's name, each number indicating the match ban imposed. SOS stands for sending off sufficient and NG for not guilty. A suspension reduced on appeal is shown as follows, 6 to 4.

The sin bin suspensions were imposed under the totting-up system where two points were issued for a 10-minute temporary dismissal and one point for a five-minute period off the field. A one-match ban was imposed when the running total reached six points.

*The following sin bin column indicates in brackets the number of one-match bans imposed under the totting-up system. It does not include a record of players' sin bin dismissals which have not reached the six-point total. Midway through the season, the senior referees decided that the sin bin would be operated only for technical offences and verbal abuse of match officials.

Club	**Total sent off**	**Dismissed Player**	**Sin Bins***
Barrow	2	Hodkinson (SOS, 4)	Szymala (1, 1)
Batley	3	Cousins (1), Douglas (3), Winterbottom (SOS)	Winterbottom (1)
Blackpool B.	3	Davis (SOS), Turley (SOS, 2)	
Bradford N.	3	Noble (2 to 1), Rathbone (2, 6)	
Bramley	3	Pickerill (2), Fletcher (1), Brannan (4)	
Cardiff C.	6	Woods (2, 12), Pritchard (6), A. Barwood (4), Ringer (4), Fenwick (2)	Woods (1), Barwood (1)
Carlisle	8	Sutton (2), Hobson (1, 2), Crowther (3), Gaitley (NG), Youngman (2), Armitage (2), Birts (2)	Sutton (1), Robinson (1)
Castleford	5	Hyde (2), James (3), Connell (3), Beardmore (1 to NG), Timson (6)	Timson (1), England (1), Hardy (1)
Dewsbury	2	Wood (4), Catling (4)	
Doncaster	10	Ellis (4, SOS, 4), Noble (SOS, 4), Douglas (2, 4), Buckton (2), Wileman (6, 10)	
Featherstone R.	1	Clarkson (2)	
Fulham	6	Dalgreen (*Sine die* to 8), Allen (1), Hull (6), Doherty (2), Gourley (2), Kinsey (4)	Doherty (1)
Halifax	3	Bond (1), Goodwin (4), Carroll (2)	Whitehouse (1)

Club	Total sent off	Dismissed Player	Sin Bins*
Huddersfield	4	Dixon (2), Rose (6, 8), Knight (3)	J. Johnson (1)
Hull	3	Rose (6), Wileman (6), Skerrett (1)	
Hull K.R.	5	Burton (1), Holdstock* (2), Watson (4), Casey* (2, 6)	
Hunslet	3	Tate (4 to 2), Roe (2), Lean (1)	Smith (1)
Huyton	5	McCabe (2, 6), Secombe (4), Bishop (4), Fletcher (1)	Blackburn (1)
Keighley	0		
Kent Invicta	3	Mordell (1, 3), W. Millington (1)	G. Bishop (1)
Leeds	0		Dickinson (1)
Leigh	3	Pyke (SOS), Bishop (3), Drummond (5 to 4)	Clarke (1)
Oldham	5	Taylor (4), Goodway* (6, SOS), Foy (SOS), Wright (4)	Parrish (1), Goodway (1), Sinclair (1), McCurrie (1)
Rochdale H.	9	Birdsall (1, 3), Deakin (1, 4), Standidge (NG, 3, 6), Duffy (2), Langan (6)	
St. Helens	3	Peters (4, NG), Haggerty (6)	Arkwright (1)
Salford	5	Blackwood (SOS), Bloor (4), Smith (3), Major (2), Prescott (6)	Smith (1)
Swinton	0		Brown (1)
Wakefield T.	5	Cocks (3), Lewis (2), Gill (2, 2), Swann (4)	Pickerill (1), Box (1)
Warrington	6	Ford (4), Forster (6), Chisnall (4), Yates (1), Webb (2), Eccles (3)	Kelly (1)
Whitehaven	6	Stoddart (8), Phythian (3), Hall (4), Banks (1), Hartley (2), Fraser (4)	Fraser (1), Banks (1)
Widnes	7	S. O'Neill* (SOS, 2), Tamati (1, 3), Prescott (2, 6), Gorley (6 to 4)	S. O'Neill (1), Hughes (1)
Wigan	2	Kiss (4), Stephens (SOS)	
Workington T.	4	Beck (1), W. Pattinson (NG, NG), Todd (2)	
York	4	Hooper (2), Hughes (4), Tansley (1), Price (1)	

* The following match suspensions were also meted out by the Disciplinary Committee for offences for which the player was not sent off.

Len Casey	A six-month ban for pushing a touch judge, the ban to run concurrent with an already imposed eight-match suspension on appeal.
Andy Goodway	A two-match ban for making an obscene gesture to the crowd.
Roy Holdstock	A six-match ban brought into force from a suspended sentence.
Steve O'Neill	A two-match ban for making an obscene gesture to the crowd.

SPONSORSHIP

This new sub-section is a first-ever record of the sponsorship programme under the control of the Rugby Football League.

Sponsorship has developed into a major subject in the last decade and is now one of Rugby League's biggest sources of income.

In addition to the League's sponsorship programme, the individual clubs also enter deals for sponsorship of jerseys, kit, matches, man of the match and match ball.

SPONSORSHIP PROGRAMME 1983-84

The following is a compendium of sponsorship activities controlled by the Rugby Football League for the season 1983-84.

Competitions:		
State Express Challenge Cup	£120,000	
Slalom Lager Championship and Premiership	£ 85,000	
John Player Special Trophy	£ 60,000	
M.M.P. Tour	£100,000	
Dominion Insurance Tests	£ 5,000	
		£370,000
Awards:		
Greenalls Man of Steel Awards	£ 7,650	
Daily Mirror/Lada Cars Teams of the Month and Year	£ 5,000	
Greenall Whitley/Sunday People Men of the Month and Top Scorers	£ 4,000	
(Greenall Whitley/Sunday People 50 Tries in a Season Challenge)	(£ 5,000)	
Daily Express/Hepworth Tailoring Men of the Month and Personality of the Year	£ 2,000	
Slalom Lager/Pentax Camera Photographer of the Year	£ 1,350	
Daily Star/Slalom Lager Star Men	£ 1,000	
		£ 21,000
Miscellaneous:		£ 31,000
	GRAND TOTAL	£422,000

COMPETITION SPONSORSHIP

The following is a review of sponsorship of the game's major competitions.

STATE EXPRESS CHALLENGE CUP

	Prel.	1st	2nd	3rd	S.F.	R.U.	Winners	Development Fund	Total
	£	£	£	£	£	£	£	£	£
1979	—	750	1,160	2,000	3,555	6,555	12,555	4,500	60,000
1980	—	750	1,160	2,000	3,555	6,555	12,555	19,500	75,000
1981	—	750	1,160	2,000	3,555	6,555	12,555	29,500	85,000
1982	1,000	1,000	1,400	2,400	4,325	8,000	14,555	30,000	100,000
1983	1,000	1,000	1,400	2,400	4,325	8,000	14,555	40,000	110,000
1984	1,000	1,000	1,400	2,400	4,325	8,000	14,555	48,000	120,000

SLALOM LAGER

	Championship winners	Second Division winners	Premiership winners	Development Fund	Total
	£	£	£	£	£
1980-81	6,000	3,000	4,000	42,000	65,000
1981-82	10,000	6,000	6,000	48,000	70,000
1982-83	12,000	7,000	7,000	54,000	80,000
1983-84	12,000	7,000	7,000	59,000	85,000

JOHN PLAYER SPECIAL TROPHY

	Prel.	1st	2nd	3rd	S.F.	R.U.	Winners	Development Fund	Total
	£	£	£	£	£	£	£	£	£
1971-72	—	—	—	—	1,000	2,500	5,000	—	11,500
1972-73	—	150	300	450	1,000	2,500	5,000	—	18,100
1973-74	—	150	300	450	1,000	2,500	5,000	—	18,100
1974-75	—	150	300	450	1,000	2,500	5,000	—	18,100
1975-76	—	300	450	600	1,500	3,000	6,000	—	22,800
1976-77	—	400	550	700	1,500	3,000	6,000	—	25,600
1977-78	—	450	600	750	1,750	3,500	8,000	—	30,000
1978-79	—	550	700	900	1,750	3,500	8,000	—	33,000
1979-80	—	600	800	1,000	2,000	4,000	8,500	—	36,500
1980-81	—	600	800	1,000	2,000	4,000	8,500	3,500	40,000
1981-82	700	700	900	1,175	2,500	4,500	9,000	7,000	50,000
1982-83	700	700	900	1,175	2,500	5,000	10,000	10,500	55,000
1983-84	700	700	900	1,175	2,500	5,000	10,000	14,100	60,000

BURTONWOOD BREWERY LANCASHIRE CUP

	Winners £	Total £
1976	1,000	4,000
1977	1,500	5,000
1978	1,800	5,500
1979	1,900	6,000
1980	2,530	10,000
1981	2,700	11,000
1982	3,000	11,500
1983	3,200	12,500

YORKSHIRE CUP

	Sponsor	Winners £	Total £
1972	Esso	800	4,000
1973	Esso	1,500	6,000
1974	Esso	1,400	6,000
1975	Esso	1,200	6,000
1976	Esso	1,200	6,000
1977	Esso	1,600	8,000
1978	Esso	2,000	9,000
1979	Esso	2,000	9,500
1980	Websters Brewery	2,750	13,000
1981	Websters Brewery	3,000	14,000
1982	Websters Brewery	2,500	15,000
1983	Philips Video	2,500	15,000

INTERNATIONAL

Great Britain v Australia Tests 1978
Forward Chemicals: £17,500

Great Britain v Australia Tests 1982
Dominion Insurance: £40,000

Great Britain v France Tests 1983
Dominion Insurance: 5,000

Great Britain v France Tests 1984
Dominion Insurance: £5,000

Great Britain Tour 1984
Modern Maintenance Products: £100,000

ATTENDANCES

CLUB ATTENDANCE REVIEW

The following is a review of clubs' home attendances for League matches from 1976-84.

The main figure is the individual club's average gate for League games during that season. The figure in brackets indicates an upward or downward trend compared with the previous season.

Also indicated is the division the club competed in that season, i.e.
1 — First Division, 2 — Second Division.

Club	76-77	77-78	78-79	79-80	80-81	81-82	82-83	83-84
Barrow	1 2599 (+220)	2 2432 (−167)	1 2988 (+556)	2 3143 (+155)	1 4065 (+922)	1 4162 (+97)	1 3852 (−310)	2 3218 (−450)
Batley	2 917 (+238)	2 859 (−58)	2 915 (+56)	2 1330 (+415)	2 1329 (−1)	2 1052 (−277)	2 916 (−136)	2 864 (−52)
Blackpool B.	2 393 (+75)	2 658 (+265)	2 1237 (+579)	1 1576 (+339)	2 684 (−892)	2 768 (+84)	2 679 (−89)	2 625 (−54)
Bradford N.	1 4669 (+160)	1 7236 (+2567)	1 5651 (−1585)	1 6236 (+585)	1 6105 (−131)	1 5816 (−289)	1 4920 (−896)	1 5316 (+386)
Bramley	2 1709 (+630)	1 2062 (+353)	2 1208 (−854)	2 1204 (−4)	2 1050 (−154)	2 928 (−122)	2 809 (−119)	2 759 (−50)
Castleford	1 3756 (+1075)	1 3847 (+91)	1 3672 (−175)	1 3714 (+42)	1 4612 (+898)	1 3791 (−821)	1 3548 (−243)	1 4288 (+740)
Cardiff C.	—	—	—	—	—	2 2008 —	2 854 (−1154)	2 581 (−273)
Carlisle	—	—	—	—	—	2 2950 —	1 1924 (−1026)	2 752 (−1172)
Dewsbury	2 1960 (−436)	1 2160 (+200)	2 1474 (−686)	2 1552 (+78)	2 1377 (−175)	2 1048 (−329)	2 779 (−269)	2 706 (−73)
Doncaster	2 488 (+119)	2 811 (+323)	2 619 (−192)	2 428 (−191)	2 628 (+200)	2 556 (−72)	2 441 (−115)	2 255 (−186)
Featherstone R.	1 3307 (+434)	1 3558 (+251)	1 2661 (−897)	2 2301 (−360)	1 3007 (+706)	1 2806 (−201)	1 2647 (−159)	1 3032 (+385)
Fulham	—	—	—	—	2 6096 —	1 4321 (−1775)	2 2688 (−1633)	1 2238 (−450)
Halifax	2 1429 (+50)	2 1339 (−90)	2 2314 (+975)	2 2969 (+655)	1 4090 (+1121)	2 2818 (−1272)	1 2270 (−548)	2 1254 (−1016)
Huddersfield	2 1520 (−557)	2 2136 (+616)	1 2533 (+397)	2 1654 (−879)	2 1769 (+115)	2 1185 (−584)	2 776 (−409)	2 699 (−77)
Hull	2 3860 (+903)	1 5112 (+1252)	2 6853 (+1741)	1 10021 (+3168)	1 11711 (+1690)	1 13190 (+1479)	1 11525 (−1665)	1 10679 (−846)
Hull K. R.	1 4718 (+670)	1 5352 (+634)	1 5945 (+593)	1 6953 (+1008)	1 8904 (+1951)	1 8723 (−181)	1 7379 (−1344)	1 6966 (−413)
Hunslet	2 1208 (+55)	1 2095 (+887)	2 1469 (−626)	1 1718 (+249)	2 921 (−797)	2 744 (−177)	2 1195 (+451)	2 1338 (+143)

Club	76-77	77-78	78-79	79-80	80-81	81-82	82-83	83-84
Huyton	2 326 (+6)	2 335 (+9)	2 599 (+264)	2 238 (−161)	2 270 (+32)	2 385 (+115)	2 224 (−161)	2 172 (−52)
Keighley	2 1848 (−350)	2 1985 (+137)	2 1594 (−391)	2 1593 (−1)	2 1612 (+19)	2 1576 (−36)	2 1085 (−491)	2 734 (−351)
Kent Invicta	—	—	—	—	—	—	—	2 731 —
Leeds	1 4508 (+162)	1 5539 (+1031)	1 5161 (−378)	1 6681 (+1520)	1 5934 (−747)	1 5599 (−335)	1 5893 (+294)	1 6542 (+649)
Leigh	1 3269 (+1449)	2 3427 (+158)	1 3319 (−108)	1 4418 (+1099)	1 4498 (+80)	1 5939 (+1441)	1 4617 (−1322)	1 4434 (−183)
Oldham	1 2051 (−275)	2 1785 (−266)	2 1207 (−578)	2 2367 (+1160)	1 3220 (+853)	1 2395 (−825)	1 3721 (+1326)	1 4138 (+417)
Rochdale H.	1 1848 (+439)	2 1976 (+128)	1 1689 (−287)	2 1210 (−479)	2 1149 (−61)	2 888 (−261)	2 619 (−269)	2 538 (−81)
St. Helens	1 4736 (−29)	1 5510 (+774)	1 5658 (+148)	1 5577 (−81)	1 4934 (−643)	1 4862 (−72)	1 4543 (−319)	1 4656 (+113)
Salford	1 5457 (+144)	1 4133 (−1324)	1 4100 (−33)	1 4846 (+746)	1 3458 (−1388)	2 2404 (−1054)	2 1928 (−476)	1 2399 (+471)
Swinton	2 1215 (−1473)	2 1480 (+265)	2 1331 (−149)	2 1509 (+178)	2 1935 (+426)	2 1567 (−368)	2 1314 (−253)	2 1077 (−237)
Wakefield T.	1 2931 (−431)	1 3808 (+877)	1 4068 (+265)	1 4559 (+491)	1 4814 (+255)	1 3716 (−1098)	2 2344 (−1372)	1 3483 (+1139)
Warrington	1 4465 (−246)	1 4203 (−262)	1 5194 (+991)	1 5122 (−72)	1 4917 (−205)	1 3838 (−1079)	1 3824 (−14)	1 4059 (+235)
Whitehaven	2 615 (−79)	2 889 (+274)	2 1364 (+475)	2 1761 (+397)	2 2733 (+972)	1 2710 (−23)	2 1742 (−968)	1 1639 (−103)
Widnes	1 6129 (+270)	1 7488 (+1359)	1 6751 (−737)	1 6143 (−608)	1 5306 (−837)	1 5485 (+179)	1 4703 (−782)	1 4687 (−16)
Wigan	1 4699 (+766)	1 5544 (+845)	1 4505 (−1039)	1 4665 (+160)	2 4693 (+28)	1 5497 (+804)	1 7426 (+1929)	1 7479 (+53)
Workington T.	1 2056 (+1155)	1 2722 (+666)	1 2155 (−567)	1 1834 (−321)	1 2188 (+354)	2 1969 (−219)	1 1470 (−499)	2 934 (−536)
York	2 3475 (+1097)	2 3188 (−287)	2 3265 (+77)	1 3934 (+669)	2 3827 (−107)	1 3677 (−150)	2 1685 (−1992)	2 1215 (−470)

COMPETITION ATTENDANCE REVIEW

		76-77	77-78	78-79	79-80	80-81	81-82	82-83	83-84
FIRST DIVISION	Total	918,967	1,051,985	990,728	1,169,956	1,226,428	1,264,520	1,113,915	1,140,548
	Average	3,825	4,402	4,128	4,875	5,110	5,268	4,641	4,752
SECOND DIVISION	Total	272,454	302,902	330,830	302,345	420,994	403,652	321,226	279,673
	Average	1,497	1,664	1,817	1,661	2,005	1,484	1,181	914
LEAGUE AGGREGATE (1st & 2nd Div)	Total	1,190,498	1,354,887	1,321,558	1,472,301	1,647,422	1,668,172	1,435,141	1,420,221
	Average	2,821	3,218	3,123	3,489	3,661	3,258	2,803	2,601
CHALLENGE CUP	Average	9,923	9,910	9,257	10,370	9,993	11,388	8,355	8,399
JOHN PLAYER TROPHY	Average	3,743	4,704	4,427	4,314	5,362	5,590	4,219	3,893
PREMIERSHIP	Average	6,271	8,647	8,502	7,343	11,689	9,454	10,099	8,136
10,000+ATTENDANCES (Number of)		13	18	12	20	36	36	37	26

20,000-plus crowds 1974-84

All matches except the Rugby League Challenge Cup final at Wembley

21,178	Wigan v. Warrington	RL Cup Round 3	Wigan	10 Mar. 1974
21,878	Wigan v. Warrington	RL Cup Round 2	Wigan	23 Feb. 1975
20,386	Wigan v. St. Helens	RL Cup Round 2	Wigan	27 Feb. 1977
26,447	Britain v. Australia	Second Test	Bradford	5 Nov. 1978
29,627	Britain v. Australia	Third Test	Leeds	18 Nov. 1978
20,775	Bradford N. v. Hull	RL Cup Round 3	Bradford	9 Mar. 1980
29,448	Hull v. Hull K.R.	Premiership final	Leeds	16 May 1981
25,245	Hull v. Hull K.R.	John Player final	Leeds	23 Jan. 1982
21,207	Hull v. Castleford	RL Cup semi-final	Leeds	27 Mar. 1982
41,171	Hull v. Widnes	RL Cup final replay	Leeds U. FC	19 May 1982
26,771	Britain v. Australia	First Test	Hull C. FC	30 Oct. 1982
23,216	Britain v. Australia	Second Test	Wigan	20 Nov. 1982
26,031	Hull v. Castleford	RL Cup semi-final	Leeds U. FC	2 Apr. 1983
20,569	Hull v. Hull K.R.	Division One	Hull	8 Apr. 1983
20,077	St. Helens v. Wigan	RL Cup Round 3	St. Helens	11 Mar. 1984

ANALYSIS — 1983-84 SEASON

FIRST DIVISION

Total attendance 1,140,548
Average 4,752

Compared with the previous season, the average gate for the 1983-84 Slalom Lager Championship season rose to an average of 4,752, an annual increase of 2.4 per cent.

For the fifth successive season, Hull, Championship title runners-up, topped the gates table with an average League attendance of 10,679.

Ten of the 16 Championship sides recorded increases in attendances. Promoted Wakefield Trinity registered the biggest increase with an extra 1,139 spectators per home match despite a poor playing record which ended with relegation.

The 240 Championship matches during 1983-84 were watched by an extra 26,633 fans, compared with the previous season's total of 1,113,915.

SECOND DIVISION

Total attendance 279,673
Average 914

Compared with the 1982-83 average of 1,181, Second Division gates decreased by 14 per cent. For the second successive season, only Hunslet recorded an increase in annual attendances, taking them to second in the attendance table behind Champions Barrow.

LEAGUE CHAMPIONSHIP

Aggregate 1,420,221
Average 2,601

Compared with the 1982-83 figures of 1,435,141 fans attracting an average gate of 2,803, the 546 games in 1983-84 were 7 per cent down.

STATE EXPRESS CHALLENGE CUP

A total of 293,994 spectators watched the 1984 Challenge Cup campaign, an average of 8,399. Compared with the 1983 tournament, with an average attendance of 8,355, the 1984 increase was 0.5 per cent.

JOHN PLAYER SPECIAL TROPHY

The 1983-84 competition attracted 125,532 fans, an average of 3,922. Compared with the 1982-83 campaign, with an average of 4,219, there was a decrease of 7 per cent.

SLALOM LAGER PREMIERSHIP

An average of 8,136 watched the seven 1984 Premiership matches, a decrease of 19 per cent compared with the 1983 average of 10,099. The seven 1984 ties attracted a total attendance of 56,957.

PHILIPS VIDEO YORKSHIRE CUP

The 1983 Yorkshire Cup campaign attracted a total of 62,689 spectators, an average gate of 4,179. Compared with the 1982 figures of 57,291 and 3,819 respectively, this was an increase of 9.4 per cent.

BURTONWOOD BREWERY LANCASHIRE CUP

The 1983 Lancashire Cup tournament attracted a total of 49,200, an average attendance of 3,280. Compared with the 1982 figures of 65,487 and 4,092 respectively, there was an annual decrease of 19.8 per cent.

FIVE-FIGURE CROWDS

There were 26 gates topping the 10,000 mark during the 1983-84 season. Following tradition, the season's top attendance was at Wembley for the Widnes – Wigan State Express Challenge Cup Final which attracted 80,116.

As in recent years, Hull dominated the five-figure gate table. The Boulevard staged 11 Slalom Lager Championship matches with five-figure gates, plus two in the Slalom Lager Premiership. Hull were also involved in three other five-figure gates away from home. The five-figure matches were divided into the following competitions:

League	15
Challenge Cup	6
Premiership	3
Yorkshire Cup	2

FIRST DIVISION

	1983-84 Average	Annual Difference
Hull	10679	(− 846)
Wigan	7479	(+ 53)
Hull K.R.	6966	(− 413)
Leeds	6542	(+ 649)
Bradford N.	5316	(+ 386)
Widnes	4687	(− 16)
St. Helens	4656	(+ 113)
Leigh	4434	(− 183)
Castleford	4288	(+ 740)
Oldham	4138	(+ 417)
Warrington	4059	(+ 235)
*Wakefield T.	3483	(+1139)
Featherstone R.	3032	(+ 385)
*Salford	2399	(+ 471)
*Fulham	2238	(− 450)
*Whitehaven	1639	(− 103)

*Denotes promoted 1982-83

SECOND DIVISION

	1983-84 Average	Annual Difference
*Barrow	3218	(− 450)
Hunslet	1338	(+ 143)
*Halifax	1254	(−1016)
York	1215	(− 470)
Swinton	1077	(− 237)
*Workington T.	934	(− 536)
Batley	864	(− 52)
Bramley	759	(− 50)
*Carlisle	752	(−1172)
Keighley	734	(− 351)
Kent Invicta	731	—
Dewsbury	706	(− 73)
Huddersfield	699	(− 77)
Blackpool B.	625	(− 54)
Cardiff C.	581	(− 273)
Rochdale H.	538	(− 81)
Doncaster	255	(− 186)
Huyton	172	(− 52)

*Denotes relegated 1982-83

EXTINCT CLUBS

The last five years have been the most expansive for the game in this country since the early part of the century. The introduction of Mansfield and Sheffield this season, coming after the recent admission of Fulham, Cardiff City, Carlisle and Kent Invicta brought the total of senior clubs to 36 ... the largest League membership since 1902-03.

In that first ever period of two divisions, 36 clubs were split equally into two leagues. Since then the lowest number of clubs in peacetime was 25 between 1914 and 1922.

Of the 22 clubs who formed the first Northern Rugby Football League following the split with the English Rugby Union in 1895, seven are no longer in existence. Nearly 30 more have come and gone.

In recording the number of extinct clubs, some distinction must be made between the early fatalities in the code's formative years and the many expansion attempts that followed.

Some of the early victims were clubs leaving the English Rugby Union and not strong enough to compete in the new major leagues, but continued at a lower level.

After 1895-96 the major leagues were the Lancashire and Yorkshire Senior Competitions until there was another change in 1901-02. Then there was a total of 41 senior clubs ... 14 in the NRL, 13 in the LSC and 14 in the YSC.

The following season, 1902-03, staged the first era of two divisions and it is from then that a more meaningful appraisal can be made of the clubs who have dropped out.

Clubs who departed before that eventful season were two founder members in **Tyldesley** and **Liversedge,** plus **Leeds Parish Church, Heckmondwike, Altrincham, Radcliffe, Goole** and **Sowerby Bridge.**

Wales was an immediate target for expansion and in 1908-09 there were six clubs in the Northern Rugby League ... Merthyr Tydfil, Ebbw Vale, Mid-Rhondda, Treherbert, Barry and Aberdare. By 1912 there was none.

Attention was focussed on London in the 1930s with Acton and Willesden, and Streatham and Mitcham, having brief existences. Mention must also be made of London Highfield, who began as Wigan Highfield and progressed through a change of Liverpool titles to the present day Huyton.

Wigan Highfield entered the League in 1922 and had one season as London Highfield in 1933-34. This venture was promoted by a group of London businessmen with home games played at White City under floodlights on a Saturday night. It was a fair success to begin with, but flopped when crowds dwindled during the winter. For 'home' matches the team caught a Friday evening train from Wigan and returned on Saturday night. The following season the club became Liverpool Stanley.

THE SURVIVORS

Changes of title, or the death of one club to be immediately replaced by another, can also cause confusion. Bradford Northern and Hunslet are two other clubs who have survived changes. See the CLUBS section for details.

Castleford had a senior club between 1896 and 1906, but the present club did not enter the League until 1926-27. Other clubs who have survived since becoming members after 1901-02 are:

Featherstone Rovers (1921-22), Huyton (1922-23), Workington Town (1945-46), Whitehaven (1948-49), Doncaster (1951-52), Blackpool Borough (1954-55), Fulham (1980-81), Cardiff City and Carlisle (1981-82), Kent Invicta (1983-84), plus this season's newcomers Mansfield and Sheffield.

FORMER CLUBS

The following is a list of clubs who have dropped out of the League since 1902-03. County references are the old boundaries.

First season	Club	Last season
1895-1896	Manningham *(Yorkshire)*	1902-1903
	Stockport *(Cheshire)*	1902-1903
	Brighouse Rangers *(Yorkshire)*	1905-1906
	Runcorn *(Cheshire)*	1914-1915
	Broughton Rangers *(Lancashire)* Changed to Belle Vue Rangers in 1946-1947	1954-1955
1896-1897	*Morecambe *(Lancashire)*	1905-1906
	Holbeck *(Yorkshire)*	1903-1904
1899-1900	Millom *(Cumberland)*	1905-1906
1901-1902	Birkenhead Wanderers *(Cheshire)*	1904-1905
	Lancaster *(Lancashire)*	1904-1905
	Normanton *(Yorkshire)*	1905-1906
1902-1903	South Shields *(Durham)*	1903-1904
1903-1904	Pontefract *(Yorkshire)*	1906-1907
1906-1907	Liverpool City *(Lancashire)*	1906-1907
1907-1908	Merthyr Tydfil *(Wales)*	1910-1911
	Ebbw Vale *(Wales)*	1911-1912
1908-1909	Aberdare *(Wales)*	1908-1909
	Barry *(Wales)*	1908-1909
	Mid-Rhondda *(Wales)*	1908-1909
	Treherbert *(Wales)*	1909-1910
1910-1911	Coventry *(Warwickshire)*	1912-1913
1918-1919	St. Helens Recreation *(Lancashire)*	1938-1939
1926-1927	Pontypridd *(Wales)*	1927-1928
1928-1929	Carlisle City *(Cumberland)*	1928-1929
1935-1936	Acton and Willesden *(London)*	1935-1936
	Streatham and Mitcham *(London)*	1936-1937
1936-1937	Newcastle *(Northumberland)*	1937-1938
1951-1952	Cardiff *(Wales)*	1951-1952

*Dropped out of League for two seasons 1899-1901

FIXTURES

SLALOM LAGER CHAMPIONSHIP

SUNDAY, 2nd SEPTEMBER, 1984

Barrow	v.	Halifax	2.30
Bradford N.	v.	Hull K.R.	3.30
Castleford	v.	Wigan	3.30
Hull	v.	Workington T.	3.00
Leigh	v.	Leeds	3.30
Oldham	v.	Hunslet	3.00
St. Helens	v.	Featherstone R.	3.00
Warrington	v.	Widnes	3.00

FRIDAY, 7th SEPTEMBER, 1984

Wigan	v.	Bradford N.	7.30

SUNDAY, 9th SEPTEMBER, 1984

Featherstone R.	v.	Warrington	3.00
Halifax	v.	Castleford	3.30
Hull K.R.	v.	Leigh	3.00
Hunslet	v.	Barrow	3.30
Leeds	v.	St. Helens	3.00
Widnes	v.	Hull	3.00
Workington T.	v.	Oldham	2.30

WEDNESDAY, 12th SEPTEMBER, 1984

Bradford N.	v.	Featherstone R.	7.30
Leigh	v.	Hunslet	7.30
Oldham	v.	Widnes	7.30

SUNDAY, 16th SEPTEMBER, 1984

COUNTY CUP COMPETITIONS — FIRST ROUND

WEDNESDAY, 19th SEPTEMBER, 1984

Featherstone R.	v.	Leeds	7.30
Widnes	v.	Leigh	7.30

SUNDAY, 23rd SEPTEMBER, 1984

Barrow	v.	Featherstone R.	2.30
Bradford N.	v.	Castleford	3.30
Halifax	v.	Workington T.	3.00
Hull K.R.	v.	St. Helens	3.00
Hunslet	v.	Widnes	3.30
Leeds	v.	Oldham	3.00
Leigh	v.	Wigan	3.30
Warrington	v.	Hull	3.00

SUNDAY, 30th SEPTEMBER, 1984

Bradford N.	v.	St. Helens	3.30
Castleford	v.	Warrington	3.30
Halifax	v.	Hunslet	3.00
Hull	v.	Barrow	3.00
Oldham	v.	Leigh	3.00
Widnes	v.	Featherstone R.	3.00
Wigan	v.	Leeds	3.00
Workington T.	v.	Hull K.R.	2.30

SUNDAY, 7th OCTOBER, 1984

Barrow	v.	Oldham	2.30
Bradford N.	v.	Hunslet	3.30
Featherstone R.	v.	Wigan	3.30
Hull K.R.	v.	Hull	3.00
Leeds	v.	Widnes	3.00
Leigh	v.	Workington T.	3.30
St. Helens	v.	Castleford	3.00
Warrington	v.	Halifax	3.00

SUNDAY, 14th OCTOBER, 1984

Castleford	v.	Featherstone R.	3.30
Halifax	v.	Leigh	3.00
Hull	v.	Leeds	3.00
Hunslet	v.	St. Helens	3.30
Oldham	v.	Warrington	3.00
Widnes	v.	Hull K.R.	3.00
Wigan	v.	Barrow	3.00
Workington T.	v.	Bradford N.	2.30

WEDNESDAY, 17th OCTOBER, 1984

St. Helens	v.	Halifax	7.30

SUNDAY, 21st OCTOBER, 1984

Barrow	v.	Castleford	2.30
Bradford N.	v.	Widnes	3.30
Featherstone R.	v.	Halifax	3.30
Hull K.R.	v.	Wigan	3.00
Hunslet	v.	Leeds	3.30
Leigh	v.	Hull	3.30
St. Helens	v.	Oldham	3.00
Warrington	v.	Workington T.	3.00

SATURDAY, 27th OCTOBER, 1984

PHILIPS VIDEO YORKSHIRE CUP FINAL

SUNDAY, 28th OCTOBER, 1984

BURTONWOOD BREWERY LANCASHIRE CUP FINAL

Castleford	v.	Leigh	3.30
Halifax	v.	Hull K.R.	3.00
Hull	v.	Bradford N.	3.00
Leeds	v.	Barrow	3.00
Oldham	v.	Featherstone R.	3.00
Workington T.	v.	Hunslet	2.30

SUNDAY, 4th NOVEMBER, 1984

Barrow	v.	Leigh	2.30
Bradford N.	v.	Oldham	3.30
Featherstone R.	v.	Workington T.	3.30
Hull K.R.	v.	Leeds	3.00
Hunslet	v.	Hull	3.30
Warrington	v.	St. Helens	3.00
Widnes	v.	Castleford	3.00
Wigan	v.	Halifax	3.00

SUNDAY, 11th NOVEMBER, 1984

Castleford	v.	Hunslet	3.30
Halifax	v.	Widnes	3.00
Hull	v.	Warrington	3.00
Leeds	v.	Featherstone R.	3.00
Leigh	v.	Bradford N.	3.30
Oldham	v.	Hull K.R.	3.00
St. Helens	v.	Barrow	3.00
Workington T.	v.	Wigan	2.30

SATURDAY/SUNDAY, 17th/18th NOVEMBER, 1984

JOHN PLAYER SPECIAL TROPHY — FIRST ROUND

SUNDAY, 25th NOVEMBER, 1984

Barrow	v.	Leeds	2.30
Featherstone R.	v.	Leigh	3.30
Hull K.R.	v.	Castleford	3.00
Hunslet	v.	Halifax	3.30
St. Helens	v.	Bradford N.	3.00
Warrington	v.	Oldham	3.00
Widnes	v.	Workington T.	3.00
Wigan	v.	Hull	3.00

SATURDAY/SUNDAY, 1st/2nd DECEMBER, 1984
JOHN PLAYER SPECIAL TROPHY — SECOND ROUND

SUNDAY, 9th DECEMBER, 1984

Castleford	v.	Widnes	3.30
Hull	v.	Halifax	3.00
Hunslet	v.	Bradford N.	3.30
Leigh	v.	Hull K.R.	3.30
Oldham	v.	Barrow	3.00
St. Helens	v.	Leeds	3.00
Warrington	v.	Wigan	3.00
Workington T.	v.	Featherstone R.	2.30

SUNDAY, 16th DECEMBER, 1984

Barrow	v.	Warrington	2.30
Bradford N.	v.	Workington T.	3.30
Featherstone R.	v.	Castleford	3.30
Halifax	v.	St. Helens	3.00
Hull K.R.	v.	Oldham	3.00
Leeds	v.	Hull	3.00
Widnes	v.	Hunslet	3.00
Wigan	v.	Leigh	3.00

SUNDAY, 23rd DECEMBER, 1984

Bradford N.	v.	Halifax	3.30
Castleford	v.	Barrow	3.30
Hull	v.	St. Helens	3.00
Hunslet	v.	Wigan	3.30
Oldham	v.	Leeds	3.00
Warrington	v.	Hull K.R.	3.00
Workington T.	v.	Widnes	2.30

BOXING DAY, WEDNESDAY, 26th DECEMBER, 1984

Barrow	v.	Workington T.	2.30
Featherstone R.	v.	Hull	3.30
Halifax	v.	Bradford N.	3.00
Hunslet	v.	Hull K.R.	3.30
Leeds	v.	Castleford	3.00
Leigh	v.	Warrington	3.30
St. Helens	v.	Wigan	3.00
Widnes	v.	Oldham	3.00

SUNDAY, 30th DECEMBER, 1984

Hull	v.	Featherstone R.	3.00

NEW YEAR'S DAY, TUESDAY, 1st JANUARY, 1985

Castleford	v.	Bradford N.	3.30
Hull K.R.	v.	Hunslet	3.00
Leeds	v.	Leigh	3.00
Oldham	v.	Halifax	3.00
Widnes	v.	St. Helens	3.00
Wigan	v.	Warrington	3.00

SUNDAY, 6th JANUARY, 1985

Bradford N.	v.	Barrow	3.30
Featherstone R.	v.	Oldham	3.30
Halifax	v.	Wigan	3.00
Hull	v.	Hunslet	3.00
Leigh	v.	Widnes	3.30
St. Helens	v.	Hull K.R.	3.00
Warrington	v.	Leeds	3.00
Workington T.	v.	Castleford	2.30

SUNDAY, 13th JANUARY, 1985

Barrow	v.	St. Helens	2.30
Castleford	v.	Hull	3.30
Hull K.R.	v.	Warrington	3.00
Hunslet	v.	Leigh	3.30
Leeds	v.	Workington T.	3.00
Oldham	v.	Bradford N.	3.00
Widnes	v.	Halifax	3.00
Wigan	v.	Featherstone R.	3.00

SUNDAY, 20th JANUARY, 1985

Bradford N.	v.	Wigan	3.30
Featherstone R.	v.	Hull K.R.	3.30
Halifax	v.	Leeds	3.00
Hull	v.	Widnes	3.00
Leigh	v.	Barrow	3.30
Oldham	v.	Castleford	3.00
St. Helens	v.	Workington T.	3.00
Warrington	v.	Hunslet	3.00

SUNDAY, 27th JANUARY, 1985

Barrow	v.	Hunslet	2.30
Bradford N.	v.	Hull	3.30
Castleford	v.	St. Helens	3.30
Halifax	v.	Featherstone R.	3.00
Hull K.R.	v.	Widnes	3.00
Leeds	v.	Warrington	3.00
Wigan	v.	Oldham	3.00
Workington T.	v.	Leigh	2.30

SUNDAY, 3rd FEBRUARY, 1985

Featherstone R.	v.	Barrow	3.30
Hull K.R.	v.	Halifax	3.00
Hunslet	v.	Workington T.	3.30
Oldham	v.	Hull	3.00
St. Helens	v.	Leigh	3.00
Warrington	v.	Bradford N.	3.00
Widnes	v.	Leeds	3.00
Wigan	v.	Castleford	3.00

SATURDAY/SUNDAY, 9th/10th FEBRUARY, 1985
CHALLENGE CUP — FIRST ROUND

SUNDAY, 17th FEBRUARY, 1985

Castleford	v.	Workington T.	3.30
Halifax	v.	Barrow	3.00
Hull	v.	Wigan	3.00
Leeds	v.	Hull K.R.	3.00
Leigh	v.	Oldham	3.30
St. Helens	v.	Hunslet	3.00
Warrington	v.	Featherstone R.	3.00
Widnes	v.	Bradford N.	3.00

SATURDAY/SUNDAY, 23rd/24th FEBRUARY, 1985
CHALLENGE CUP — SECOND ROUND

SUNDAY, 3rd MARCH, 1985

Barrow	v.	Widnes	2.30
Bradford N.	v.	Warrington	3.30
Featherstone R.	v.	St. Helens	3.30
Hull	v.	Leigh	3.00
Hunslet	v.	Castleford	3.30
Wigan	v.	Hull K.R.	3.00
Workington T.	v.	Halifax	2.30

SUNDAY, 10th MARCH, 1985

Castleford	v.	Leeds	3.30
Hull K.R.	v.	Featherstone R.	3.00
Oldham	v.	St. Helens	3.00
Warrington	v.	Barrow	3.00
Widnes	v.	Wigan	3.00
Workington T.	v.	Hull	2.30

FRIDAY, 15th MARCH, 1985

Leigh	v.	Featherstone R.	7.30

SUNDAY, 17th MARCH, 1985

Barrow	v.	Bradford N.	2.30
Castleford	v.	Hull K.R.	3.30
Halifax	v.	Warrington	3.00
Hull	v.	Oldham	3.00
Leeds	v.	Hunslet	3.00
Wigan	v.	Workington T.	3.00

SUNDAY, 24th MARCH, 1985

Barrow	v.	Wigan	2.30
Featherstone R.	v.	Widnes	3.30
Hull K.R.	v.	Bradford N.	3.00
Hunslet	v.	Oldham	3.30
Leigh	v.	Halifax	3.30
St. Helens	v.	Hull	3.00
Warrington	v.	Castleford	3.00
Workington T.	v.	Leeds	2.30

SUNDAY, 31st MARCH, 1985

Bradford N.	v.	Leigh	3.30
Featherstone R.	v.	Hunslet	3.30
Halifax	v.	Hull	3.00
Hull K.R.	v.	Barrow	3.00
Leeds	v.	Wigan	3.00
Oldham	v.	Workington T.	3.00
St. Helens	v.	Warrington	3.00

GOOD FRIDAY, 5th APRIL, 1985

Halifax	v.	Oldham	7.00
Hull	v.	Hull K.R.	3.00
Leeds	v.	Bradford N.	7.30
Leigh	v.	Castleford	7.30
Widnes	v.	Warrington	3.00
Wigan	v.	St. Helens	3.00
Workington T.	v.	Barrow	2.30

EASTER SUNDAY, 7th APRIL, 1985

Barrow	v.	Hull	2.30

EASTER MONDAY, 8th APRIL, 1985

Castleford	v.	Halifax	3.30
Hull K.R.	v.	Workington T.	3.00
Hunslet	v.	Featherstone R.	3.30
Oldham	v.	Wigan	3.00
St. Helens	v.	Widnes	3.00
Warrington	v.	Leigh	3.00

EASTER TUESDAY, 9th APRIL, 1985

Bradford N.	v.	Leeds	7.30

SUNDAY, 14th APRIL, 1985

Featherstone R.	v.	Bradford N.	3.30
Hull	v.	Castleford	3.00
Leeds	v.	Halifax	3.00
Leigh	v.	St. Helens	3.30
Widnes	v.	Barrow	3.00
Wigan	v.	Hunslet	3.00
Workington T.	v.	Warrington	2.30

SUNDAY, 21st APRIL, 1985

Barrow	v.	Hull K.R.	2.30
Castleford	v.	Oldham	3.30
Hunslet	v.	Warrington	3.30
Wigan	v.	Widnes	3.00
Workington T.	v.	St. Helens	2.30

SECOND DIVISION

SUNDAY, 2nd SEPTEMBER, 1984

Bramley	v.	Batley
Carlisle	v.	Doncaster
Dewsbury	v.	Huddersfield
Fulham	v.	Bridgend
Runcorn H.	v.	Mansfield M.
Sheffield E.	v.	Rochdale H.
Swinton	v.	Blackpool B.
Wakefield T.	v.	Keighley
Whitehaven	v.	Salford
York	v.	Southend I.

SUNDAY, 9th SEPTEMBER, 1984

Batley	v.	Runcorn H.
Blackpool B.	v.	York
Bridgend	v.	Swinton
Doncaster	v.	Dewsbury
Huddersfield	v.	Whitehaven
Keighley	v.	Carlisle
Mansfield M.	v.	Wakefield T.
Salford	v.	Rochdale H.
Sheffield E.	v.	Fulham
Southend I.	v.	Bramley

SUNDAY, 16th SEPTEMBER, 1984

COUNTY CUP COMPETITIONS — FIRST ROUND

WEDNESDAY, 19th SEPTEMBER, 1984

Runcorn H.	v.	Sheffield E.

SUNDAY, 23rd SEPTEMBER, 1984

Batley	v.	York
Blackpool B.	v.	Huddersfield
Bridgend	v.	Dewsbury
Keighley	v.	Doncaster
Mansfield M.	v.	Carlisle
Rochdale H.	v.	Runcorn H.
Sheffield E.	v.	Salford
Southend I.	v.	Wakefield T.
Swinton	v.	Fulham
Whitehaven	v.	Bramley

SUNDAY, 30th SEPTEMBER, 1984

Bramley	v.	Mansfield M.
Carlisle	v.	Blackpool B.
Dewsbury	v.	Keighley
Doncaster	v.	Sheffield E.
Fulham	v.	Runcorn H.
Huddersfield	v.	Southend I.
Rochdale H.	v.	Swinton
Salford	v.	Bridgend
Wakefield T.	v.	Batley
York	v.	Whitehaven

SUNDAY, 7th OCTOBER, 1984

Batley	v.	Sheffield E.
Bridgend	v.	Rochdale H.
Carlisle	v.	Fulham
Huddersfield	v.	York
Keighley	v.	Bramley
Mansfield M.	v.	Doncaster
Runcorn H.	v.	Salford
Southend I.	v.	Dewsbury
Swinton	v.	Wakefield T.
Whitehaven	v.	Blackpool B.

SUNDAY, 14th OCTOBER, 1984

Blackpool B.	v.	Bridgend
Bramley	v.	Southend I.
Dewsbury	v.	Mansfield M.
Doncaster	v.	Batley
Rochdale H.	v.	Keighley
Salford	v.	Carlisle
Sheffield E.	v.	Runcorn H.
Wakefield T.	v.	Whitehaven
York	v.	Swinton

SUNDAY, 21st OCTOBER, 1984

Blackpool B.	v.	Sheffield E.
Bramley	v.	Salford
Bridgend	v.	Mansfield M.
Carlisle	v.	Rochdale H.
Dewsbury	v.	York
Doncaster	v.	Huddersfield
Keighley	v.	Wakefield T.
Runcorn	v.	Batley
Swinton	v.	Southend I.
Whitehaven	v.	Fulham

SUNDAY, 28th OCTOBER, 1984

Batley	v.	Carlisle
Fulham	v.	Blackpool B.
Huddersfield	v.	Swinton
Mansfield M.	v.	Runcorn H.
Rochdale H.	v.	Dewsbury
Salford	v.	Whitehaven
Sheffield E.	v.	Bridgend
Southend I.	v.	Keighley
Wakefield T.	v.	Doncaster
York	v.	Bramley

SUNDAY, 4th NOVEMBER, 1984

Blackpool B.	v.	Southend I.
Bramley	v.	Doncaster
Bridgend	v.	Salford

Dewsbury	v.	Wakefield T.
Fulham	v.	York
Keighley	v.	Mansfield M.
Rochdale H.	v.	Batley
Runcorn H.	v.	Carlisle
Swinton	v.	Sheffield E.
Whitehaven	v.	Huddersfield

SUNDAY, 11th NOVEMBER, 1984

Batley	v.	Southend I.
Bridgend	v.	Whitehaven
Carlisle	v.	Swinton
Doncaster	v.	Rochdale H.
Huddersfield	v.	Blackpool B.
Keighley	v.	Runcorn H.
Mansfield M.	v.	Bramley
Salford	v.	Fulham
Sheffield E.	v.	Dewsbury
Wakefield T.	v.	York

SATURDAY/SUNDAY, 17th/18th NOVEMBER, 1984

JOHN PLAYER SPECIAL TROPHY — FIRST ROUND

SUNDAY, 25th NOVEMBER, 1984

Blackpool B.	v.	Carlisle
Bramley	v.	Keighley
Dewsbury	v.	Doncaster
Fulham	v.	Wakefield T.
Rochdale H.	v.	Salford
Runcorn H.	v.	Bridgend
Swinton	v.	Huddersfield
Southend I.	v.	Mansfield M.
Whitehaven	v.	Sheffield E.
York	v.	Batley

SATURDAY/SUNDAY, 1st/2nd DECEMBER, 1984

JOHN PLAYER SPECIAL TROPHY — SECOND ROUND

SUNDAY, 9th DECEMBER, 1984

Batley	v.	Rochdale H.
Blackpool B.	v.	Whitehaven
Bramley	v.	Fulham
Doncaster	v.	Southend I.
Keighley	v.	Sheffield E.
Mansfield M.	v.	York
Runcorn H.	v.	Dewsbury
Salford	v.	Huddersfield
Wakefield T.	v.	Swinton
Bridgend	v.	Carlisle

SUNDAY, 16th DECEMBER, 1984

Carlisle	v.	Runcorn H.
Dewsbury	v.	Bramley
Fulham	v.	Salford
Huddersfield	v.	Batley
Rochdale H.	v.	Doncaster
Sheffield E.	v.	Blackpool B.
Swinton	v.	Bridgend
Whitehaven	v.	Wakefield T.
York	v.	Mansfield M.

SUNDAY, 23rd DECEMBER, 1984

Batley	v.	Mansfield M.
Bramley	v.	Whitehaven
Bridgend	v.	Blackpool B.
Doncaster	v.	Carlisle
Keighley	v.	Rochdale H.
Runcorn H.	v.	Fulham
Salford	v.	Sheffield E.
Southend I.	v.	Swinton
Wakefield T.	v.	Huddersfield
York	v.	Dewsbury

BOXING DAY, WEDNESDAY, 26th DECEMBER, 1984

Batley	v.	Dewsbury
Blackpool B.	v.	Rochdale H.
Doncaster	v.	York
Huddersfield	v.	Keighley
Mansfield M.	v.	Sheffield E.
Swinton	v.	Salford
Wakefield T.	v.	Bramley
Whitehaven	v.	Carlisle

SUNDAY, 30th DECEMBER, 1984

Dewsbury	v.	Batley

NEW YEAR'S DAY, TUESDAY, 1st JANUARY, 1985

Bramley	v.	Wakefield T.
Keighley	v.	Huddersfield
Salford	v.	Blackpool B.
Swinton	v.	Runcorn H.
Southend I.	v.	Fulham

SUNDAY, 6th JANUARY, 1985

Batley	v.	Wakefield T.
Blackpool B.	v.	Swinton
Carlisle	v.	Bridgend
Fulham	v.	Bramley
Huddersfield	v.	Mansfield M.
Keighley	v.	Southend I.
Rochdale H.	v.	Whitehaven
Sheffield E.	v.	Doncaster
York	v.	Salford

SUNDAY, 13th JANUARY, 1985

Bridgend	v.	Sheffield E.
Dewsbury	v.	Carlisle
Doncaster	v.	Keighley
Mansfield M.	v.	Batley
Rochdale H.	v.	Fulham
Runcorn H.	v.	Blackpool B.
Swinton	v.	Bramley
Southend I.	v.	Huddersfield
Wakefield T.	v.	Salford
Whitehaven	v.	York

SUNDAY, 20th JANUARY, 1985

Batley	v.	Bridgend
Bramley	v.	Dewsbury
Carlisle	v.	Mansfield M.
Doncaster	v.	Runcorn H.
Fulham	v.	Swinton
Huddersfield	v.	Wakefield T.
Salford	v.	Southend I.
Sheffield E.	v.	Keighley

SUNDAY, 27th JANUARY, 1985

Carlisle	v.	Salford
Dewsbury	v.	Bridgend
Keighley	v.	Batley
Runcorn H.	v.	Doncaster
Sheffield E.	v.	Whitehaven
Southend I.	v.	Blackpool B.
Swinton	v.	Rochdale H.
Wakefield T.	v.	Mansfield M.
York	v.	Huddersfield

SUNDAY, 3rd FEBRUARY, 1985

Blackpool B.	v.	Runcorn H.
Batley	v.	Bramley
Bridgend	v.	Keighley
Doncaster	v.	Wakefield T.
Huddersfield	v.	Fulham
Mansfield M.	v.	Dewsbury
Rochdale H.	v.	Sheffield E.
Salford	v.	York
Whitehaven	v.	Southend I.

SATURDAY/SUNDAY, 9th/10th FEBRUARY, 1985

CHALLENGE CUP — FIRST ROUND

SUNDAY, 17th FEBRUARY, 1985

Batley	v.	Keighley
Fulham	v.	Carlisle